The Sun, Moon and Venus

A Simple Guide on

How to Get the Most Out of Your Man

By Kimberly Zapf

"Kimmie"

This book is dedicated to the many women to whom I have been blessed to offer my advice on their relationships.

FOREWORD

After reading *The Sun, Moon and Venus: A Simple Guide on How to Get the Most Out of Your Man*, I feel as though this book was written just for me. If you are like me, you may have always had a casual interest in astrology and have picked up sun sign books to read from time to time. However, none have ever been comprehensive, yet simply written to promote understanding. I have found that astrology books are too technical, too long and boring, or they simply describe the character traits associated with the sun signs, leaving the reader wondering, "So what?"

Kimmie has successfully answered the "so what" in writing for the general public who are not in the profession, but have an interest in finding answers and solutions to relationship problems. She has shared her own formula for love; whereby, she uses the Sun and Moon combined with Venus aspects to create lasting relationships. She has included material and explanations that enable the individual to look up their own time and place of birth and very easily find the locations of the heavenly bodies that pertain to them. She has given the definitions to the technical terms used in the book, making no presumption as to the level of knowledge the reader may have in astrology.

Anyone who knows Kimmie personally will attest to the fact that she has dedicated her life to helping everyone she meets, to find love, balance and peace of mind in their lives. She describes herself as a spiritual coach and that is exactly the way her clients, friends and associates see her. Even though she steers away from the title "psychic", she is well-known in her community for her near 100% accuracy in her readings. In *The Sun, Moon and Venus: A Simple Guide on How to Get the Most Out of Your Man*, she draws upon her

God-given gifts of spirituality, intuition and clairaudience. She combines these traits with the insight she has gleaned from twenty years of experience in counseling to formulate solid advice for lasting relationships.

The world in its current precarious situation is in dire need of the *knowledge* that will bring peace; and *all* people desire peace. The light of this precious knowledge is in all people and we must constantly look *inward* for the answers. Relationships are inherent in the universe and all of the world's religions, as well as the most primitive of tribal societies, teach "*Love* your fellow man." Clearly we know that *love* is the way to peace.

Sandra Williams

Author of *Light in the Closet*

TABLE OF CONTENTS

INTRODUCTION

For many years, people have come to me seeking advice on relationships. I have always looked to their Sun, Moon and Venus to help them figure out what their partner is thinking and to help them attain a better relationship.

The Sun is an important aspect because it expresses *individuality;* it is the *"I"* of who your partner is. Knowing this, you can play to his strengths and keep him interested in you!

The Moon is the *internal* reflection of what is happening in one's life, its role is to allow one to process life emotionally. If you can figure out how a man *feels*, you can get into his emotions. This is an important aspect for you to know in order to obtain closeness *emotionally.*

Venus is an important aspect, as it tells us what a guy wants *romantically* in a woman. If you know his Venus, chances are you will be able to do the right things to get him to commit to you long-term.

This guidebook to love is divided into four major sections: the Sun, Moon, Venus and an Ephemeris. The Ephemeris, at the back of the book, will aid even a beginner in locating these aspects at the time and place of their partner's birth.

In each of the Sun sections, I have included supplemental information such as the Sun signs of the opposite sex that are most and least compatible with that particular sign. These are followed by a comprehensive description of the male personality; what he looks for in a woman and advice on how to best seduce him and keep him interested in you. After the descriptive portion is a list of the ruling elements in this man's life, including such things as his spirit type, his life's objectives, ego trait, dominant season, colors, day, metal and stones; as well as, the ruling part of his anatomy and the foods best for him.

Finally, just for interest, at the end of each Sun, Moon and Venus section, you will find a list of some famous and some infamous people of each respective sign.

It has been stated that astrology is one of the world's most ancient studies and has been represented by the astrological symbols that are the same today, from caves, tombs and pyramids. Not only is astrology a universal language, but a universal language connecting all races and all nations throughout centuries of the past.

Actually, the story of man's quest for an understanding of the heavens begins long before the time records were written. There exists very little doubt that astrology is the father of all science. It is perfectly logical to assume that astrologers were the first wise men in even the most primitive of civilizations.

When the sun goes into total or partial eclipse, animals become anxious, restless and unsettled; they seem very tuned in that something may be happening. We often hear crickets making different sounds when different weather patterns are taking place.

The sun is a powerful energy and provides us with this during daylight and is the brightest of all stars that shine from the heavens. At night, you notice that the sky is very different. The sun is not visible, yet you can see the sky illuminating at night. You see bright specks of light shining in the sky. If you look at them they seem to appear in the same places night after night.

At night, another beautiful sight that appears regularly in the sky is the moon. Similar to the sun, it starts its journey from one side of the earth and ends up on the other. Although it does not keep us warm, it does provide us light at night and seems to have a peculiar effect on the bodies of water which surround us. It also has an effect on our emotions.

Those who counsel through astrology find that the most common request for guidance is in the area of relationships and sex. By taking a close look at the aspects in a person's relationship we can often determine what they might do to make it better. Through astrological comparison it can be determined if two people can have a relationship together, as well as identify the areas in which they will most likely get along and those areas in which they are most likely to experience disagreement. Sexual potential, attitude, feelings and natural traumas they will undoubtedly experience can be guided through astrology. A failing marriage can be patched up. Remedies and cures to all the ills of love can be at your fingertips. Difficult times can be anticipated and avoided. A potentially permanent relationship break can be changed into a temporary break.

Your own intuition is the key to love success. Forget rules and follow those inner dictates of your heart. Romance appears when you forget about marriage or commitments and focus on friendships. Don't be discouraged in relationships because of early rejections. Success comes through friendships; financial inquiries turn into romantic escapades, etc. Don't be afraid to show enthusiasm in new loves, as they may misinterpret your calmness as lack of interest.

Many people have asked me to write a book on how to get a man and keep him. Use this book to help you get the man you want, keep his attention and get the commitment you want from him. However, something I always stress to my clients, *"Be careful what you wish for, you may get it!"*

Kimberly Zapf
"Kimmie"
www.innerviews.us
www.litetheway.com

CHAPTER ONE

SUN SIGNS

Our "Sun Sign" means the zodiac sign in which the sun was present at the moment of our birth, in our place of birth. It represents what we *want* to be, not necessarily who we are. It can be best described as our Ego self. It represents characteristics of our personality. By knowing a man's Sun sign, you can discover how to deal with his Ego self.

THE RAM

March 21 – April 19

THE ARIES MAN

> *Most Compatible: Libra, Leo & Sagittarius*
>
> *Least Compatible: Cancer (too moody)*

> **Fire Sign:** This man is primarily energetic, enthusiastic and impulsive (fiery).   Aries

This guy likes to be in charge, but he also needs a lot of confirmation with just enough balance. The Aries man doesn't want you to tell him how great he is all the time; he wants approval *periodically*.

He is usually attracted to computers and sports and he likes to use his hands.

Remember, he's the *"baby"* of the zodiac which means he likes to be first.

His personality has energy, a bit of ego and he is a flirt.

He will look you straight in the eye and not be afraid to tell you what he feels. You're his friend, aren't you? You like him, don't you? If your answer is no, he won't show it outwardly, but be sure he will be crying on the inside. He can't stand it if you don't like him. He'll never show his emotions on the surface if he can help it. If you see him openly weeping, you can be certain that he's been cut to the very soul in some way. Aries would rather be caught dead than be caught weak and some of them literally risk the former, to avoid the latter.

When you want to get something done, the best way to accomplish this is to barter. The Aries man will respond better when you do something for him first; then he feels the need to outdo you.

If you keep him happy *intimately*, you will have his undivided attention. Problems can arise when you get frustrated because you feel that sex is all he thinks about. Where imbalance comes into play in a relationship with Aries, is when the partner starts to feel overwhelmed with being an "object of desire" and not an emotional partner. It is important to not let the relationship start off all physical. Balance it from the beginning and things will go smoothly in the long term.

Aries likes you to rub his ears. This will calm him down.

Don't worry about having to get too close to his family members, as he would rather you put *him* first at all times.

If you are with an Aries man who has a child with someone else, you may run into problems. He has a lot of issues with letting go of the mother of his children…unless, of course, you have a child with him. It's all about *competition* in this relationship.

Seduce Aries by surprising him with a most adventurous and physical workout. For him, *sex* is a physical workout, too.

These guys *do* get married, but the easiest way to get them is to *be* what they are looking for. If you fit the plan, you'll know soon enough – a rush from this guy is hard to miss. If you have to *show* him that you're the right one, do a little challenging – he has trouble turning down a dare. Let's face it…he's a Fire sign and can be ignited.

Keep in mind that his pushy, dashing, confident ways need the fuel of constant encouragement. Here's the secret elixir that gets Aries to the altar…Are you ready? *Common sense!* He won't tell you, but he seeks a stable and sensible mate. Are you the one?

**Physical, Psychological and Personality Characteristics
of Aries   March 21 – April 19**

1st Sign of Zodiac

Characteristics: Personality, the self, beginning, physical health,
early life and physical appearance.

Spirit: Adventurous and courageous

Objectives: To plan and rule

Ego: Dominating and challenging

Ruling Planet: Mars

Empowerment Colors: Reds and scarlet

Moderating Colors: Indigo

Best Day: Tuesday

Modality: Cardinal (outgoing, initiatory and active)

Element: Fire

Season: Spring

Metal: Iron

Stone: Amethyst and diamond

Anatomy: Head and face

Foods: Beef, tomato, zucchini, apple and red pepper

Some Famous People with Sun in Aries

Alec Baldwin, Jackie Chan, Russell Crowe, Robert Downey Jr., Conan O'Brien, William Shatner, Vincent Van Gogh and Christopher Walken.

THE BULL

April 20 – May 20

THE TAURUS MAN

Most Compatible: Virgo & Scorpio

Least Compatible: Sagittarius (not dependable enough)

Earth Sign: This man is primarily materialistic and practical (earthly).   Taurus

This fixed sign can be very stubborn and solid, yet very gentle and capable of considerable patience. Therefore, he will shy away from a woman who is pushy. He likes to take things one at a time and skipping over things will only confuse him. Take the remote away from him when he's watching the Home Shopping Channel. He loves gadgets!

When he hits the pillow at night, he is out like a light. Don't put too much into wanting to pillow talk. My advice is to talk to him *before* bed. You can share intimacy with him, but he is not one to talk afterward.

He loves his hair stroked and if you listen to him talk about work, he will keep talking. This is his favorite subject.

Make sure that if you are on a trip, you plan your bathroom stops. He has a weak bladder.

He tends to be a workaholic and you have to be supportive of the fact that he makes it important. As long as you don't put down his work, you will be in good shape.

Be cautious not to hurt him emotionally. He is good at holding onto hurts. Choose your words wisely with him. He won't throw old hurts at you, he will just hold onto them deeply.

Want to get his attention? When he hugs you, rub the middle of his back. That will send shivers up his spine and make him think about the last time you connected.

Seducing a Taurus man is very simple: take care of your appearance and figure. The way you dress, your perfume…it really matters, as Taurus is a very physical sign.

He's *not* a dreamer. A male Taurus is very realistic – *annoyingly* realistic. Avoid chaos and dreaming.

Don't tell him that you don't handle money very well. He likes a woman who is smart with money. He will automatically get turned off if you don't spend your money wisely.

Surprise him with some gourmet food and try to be a good cook. *Eating should always be part of your strategy to seduce a Taurus!* Tell him that after dinner…you want *him* as dessert! Ask him to give you a massage.

**Physical, Psychological and Personality Characteristics
of Taurus   April 20 – May 20**

2nd Sign of Zodiac

Characteristics: Finances, personal material resources, assets,
    expenditure and attitudes towards money.

Spirit: Conservation, methodical and enjoys comfort

Objectives: To accumulate money

Ego: Affectionate, stubborn and competent

Personality: Indolent and conservative

Ruling Planet: Venus

Empowerment Colors: Pale blue and green

Moderating Colors: Yellow

Best Day: Friday

Modality: Fixed (stable, resolute and determined)

Element: Earth

Season: Spring

Metal: Copper

Stone: Emerald

Anatomy: Neck and throat

Foods: Pork, bacon, celery, carrots, cantaloupe, peaches and french
    fries

Some Famous People with Sun in Taurus

George Clooney, Adolf Hitler and George Lucas.

THE TWINS

May 21 – June 21

THE GEMINI MAN

> *Most Compatible: Sagittarius, Libra & Aquarius*
>
> *Least Compatible: Virgo (strict and hard to satisfy)*

Air Sign: Primarily communicative, oriented on the mental plane and
social (airy).   Gemini

The Gemini man can be tricky. He often shifts from one mood to
another with his highly Mercurial personality. When dealing with
him, get to know both sides of him. That will make it easier to know
which person you are dealing with.

This man loves to pursue his woman. The worst thing you can do is
to chase him. He'll run away if you don't give him space. Starting
the relationship off as a challenge is always good in this instance.

He's like a little boy with a new race car; he wants to see how fast he
can make it go and then he gets bored with it once he's done. Always
be ready to have a new topic of what is happening in the world. If
you shift topics as much as he shifts, he will stay captivated. If you
can provide him with the right amount of balance, he will stay
interested in you.

He loves it when he is the center of attention. Avoid being jealous
and possessive. Remember, balance is important between both
personalities with a Gemini man. Know how to shift back and forth
with him. You can flirt with him by giving him the eye...look at
him...and then turn your attention somewhere else. It will drive him
crazy!

Physical, Psychological and Personality Characteristics of Gemini   **May 21 – June 21**

3rd Sign of Zodiac

Characteristics: Communication, intellect and mental, short journeys, brothers and sisters, neighbors, relatives and attitude.

Spirit: To investigate

Objectives: To advance by communications

Ego: Curious and imaginative

Personality: Talkative and restless

Ruling Planet: Mercury

Empowerment Colors: Blue, slate and violet

Moderating Colors: Orange and browns

Best Day: Wednesday

Modality: Mutable (adaptable and versatile)

Element: Air

Season: Spring

Metal: Mercury

Stone: Agate

Anatomy: Hands, arms and lungs

Foods: Pineapple, lemons, broccoli, cauliflower and eggs

Some Famous People with Sun in Gemini

Mel Blanc, Drew Carey, John Goodman, Lenny Kravitz and Prince William.

THE CRAB

June 22 – July 22

THE CANCER MAN

> *Most Compatible: Capricorn, Scorpio & Pisces*
>
> *Least Compatible: Aries (insensitive and arrogant)*

Water Sign: Primarily responsive, emotional and sensitive (watery).

Cancer

This can be the most difficult sign in the zodiac for a man to be. The Cancer man is moody and highly sensitive.

When you are talking to a Cancer man, choose your words wisely. One slip of the wrong words can send him into his shell. Don't criticize him too much and never ever neglect him.

He gets hurt easily and holds onto hurts. He is very insecure; and if he can feel secure with you, you have it made. He is very sensitive and doesn't always appreciate it when you are blunt with him. His reaction to hurt will depend upon how thick a shell he has developed. He may react by withdrawing or retreating. He avoids direct confrontation as a rule.

His memory is good and he will bring up things from the past and remember them word-for-word. *Think first* about everything you say to this man. He will have everything you said memorized and it won't be fun if you can't back up the reason for your words.

He is quick and clever, but has so much emotion that he will hit you like a hurricane if you are not ready. After he hits you, you will find yourself standing alone wondering what happened and how to get

18

back into his emotions. Watch out. Once you have hurt him, he won't easily let you back into his life.

If you want to get close to a Cancer man, get close to his mother or be *like* a mother. Don't suffocate him, just do things that are motherly, like taking care of him when he is sick, bringing him soup, rubbing his back and telling him how good he is.

He loves food, especially chocolate! Being a good cook won't hurt.

Want to get his attention? Listen to him and do it in a fashion that makes him feel like you *care* about how he feels. He craves this balance.

Keep your home neat. He may not be this way, but he will feel comfortable with a woman who is. He loves his home. Surroundings are important to him.

If you want to seduce a Cancer, make it cozy. Dance cheek to cheek. Buy a romantic video to watch at home.

**Physical, Psychological and Personality Characteristics
of Cancer   June 22 – July 22**

4th Sign of Zodiac

Characteristics: Home, family life, domestic affairs, mother or
father, early childhood, conditioning, your roots, the end of life
and real estate.

Spirit: To win wealth and honors

Ego: Family oriented, unassuming and quiet

Personality: Sensitive and moody

Ruling Planet: Moon

Empowerment Colors: White and silver

Moderating Colors: Violet

Best Day: Monday

Modality: Cardinal (outgoing, initiatory and active)

Element: Water

Season: Summer

Metal: Silver

Stone: Pearl and opal

Anatomy: Breasts and stomach

Foods: Dairy products, pears, coconut, papaya, green beans and
chocolate

Some Famous People with Sun in Cancer

Kevin Bacon, Mel Brooks, George W. Bush, Bill Cosby, Tom Cruise, William Dafoe, Harrison Ford, Tom Hanks, Richard Lewis, Tobey Maguire, Carlos Santana, Fred Savage, Sylvester Stallone, Montel Williams and Robin Williams.

THE LION

July 23 – August 22

THE LEO MAN

> *Most Compatible: Aquarius, Aries & Sagittarius*
>
> *Least Compatible: Scorpio (scheming) & Taurus (stubborn)*

Fire Sign: This man is primarily energetic, enthusiastic and impulsive (fiery).   Leo

---

A Leo man is the leader. He is an achiever and likes to feel in charge. He doesn't want to be chased. Always give him compliments like: "Oh honey, you make me feel safe." If you can give him *sincere* admiration and applause, then you will have a good chance of winning his affections.

He has a love of luxury and lavish good living and an aversion to the ordinary and routine. Consequently, he would be inclined to seek out new stimulating situations and sources of excitement.

On the negative side, he has an overabundance of pride, arrogance, haughtiness and a tendency toward snobbish superiority. These characteristics have to be watched for, controlled and balanced.

He is very stubborn in upholding traditional beliefs.

He likes it when you are independent but also have a bit of dependence on him emotionally.

He can be very stubborn and headstrong about certain issues. Be careful not to push his buttons and set him off emotionally. You might not like what you hear.

The worst thing you can do to a Leo is accuse him of bad intentions. Displaying behavior that makes him think you don't appreciate him runs a close second.

This happy, proud man becomes mighty hurt when you don't see him for his noble intentions.

Loyal and sometimes rather traditional, Leos are, after all, a *fixed* sign. He will hold onto situations and people for a very long time before he gives up.

He may do a lot of bragging about himself, some of which is exaggerated. Don't laugh at him, or you will turn him off.

Don't show a jealous bone. Be enthusiastic and optimistic.

He will tell you frankly when a habit of yours bothers him, get used to it. He isn't trying to hurt you; he just thinks he knows better.

Don't challenge his dominance, or you'll have a wounded lion on your hands.

Seduce Leo by adoring him. Flattery *can* do the trick. You will not seduce a Leo when you can't adore him.

A Leo wants to be in the spotlight. Give him your approval. Make him feel like he's the expert in everything that he does. Give him a massage, do his hair and bathe him. He loves to be doted upon.

Physical, Psychological and Personality Characteristics of Leo   July 23 – August 22

5th Sign of Zodiac

Characteristics: Children, creativity, love affairs, speculation and pleasurable emotions.

Spirit: To rule

Ego: Egotistical, optimistic and brave

Personality: Generous, dramatic and arrogant

Ruling Planet: Sun

Empowerment Colors: Gold, orange and yellow-browns

Moderating Colors: Purple

Best Day: Sunday

Modality: Fixed (stable, resolute and determined)

Season: Summer

Metal: Gold

Stone: Ruby

Anatomy: The heart

Foods: Chicken, peas, beans, garlic, onion and oranges

Some Famous People with Sun in Leo

Ben Affleck, J. C. Chasez, David Duchovny, Jonathon Frakes and Peter O'Toole.

VIRGO

THE VIRGIN

August 23 – September 22

THE VIRGO MAN

> *Most Compatible: Pisces, Capricorn & Taurus*
>
> *Least Compatible: Sagittarius (unreliable)*

Earth Sign: This man is primarily practical and materialistic
(earthly).   Virgo

The Virgo man is a problem solver. Make him feel needed. If you make him feel like he is taking care of things, he will feel attracted to you. Find out what he is good at and ask him to help you. Tell him how much he is appreciated.

He may appear cold and immune to your emotions or tears, but inside he's genuinely concerned and trying to analyze what your problem is so that he can help you. He cares, but he shows it differently than most people.

He may try to tell you how to act and behave. Make sure you remain your own person. He isn't trying to control you; he is just setting standards.

He sometimes will test you if he feels you don't care about him, provoking oppositions. You have to make sure he knows where you stand on issues.

He likes to play the caretaker role, so make sure you make him feel that you are counting on him.

Don't put him in a corner. He needs space to think things through; and when he is ready, he will come to you openly.

If you push him, he will find your weaknesses and may point them out to you. Avoid the needless arguments.

If you want to seduce a Virgo, never criticize his hypochondriac and critical nature. Never try to feed him something he doesn't like...he is touchy about his health and what he eats.

Present a close-to-flawless exterior and interior. The perfectionist side of your Virgo will be drawn to the perfection that they see in you. Be patient and accepting of his attention to detail...benefit from your patience...your Virgo love will take a diligent and practical approach to making your life better. Show him how impressed you are by his constant efforts to improve your surroundings. He will work even harder to provide you with a picture-perfect home.

Be a friend and an intellectual companion, as well as a lover. He usually possesses sharp wit and powerful analytical abilities. He needs a partner who can appreciate and cultivate these qualities.

Run your fingers from his temple to his neck, look at him straight in the eyes and he will become captivated by you!

Physical, Psychological and Personality Characteristics of Virgo   August 23 – September 22

6ᵗʰ Sign of Zodiac

Characteristics: Working conditions, environment, competence, skills and general health.

Spirit: To follow opportunity and serve

Ego: Analytical, critical and detail oriented

Personality: Fault finding, cold, timid and self-possessed

Ruling Planet: Mercury

Empowerment Colors: Violets, blue and soft browns

Moderating Colors: Turquoise

Best Day: Wednesday

Modality: Mutable (adaptable and versatile)

Element: Earth

Season: Summer

Metal: Mercury

Stone: Sapphire

Anatomy: Intestines and the nervous system

Foods: Spinach, seeds, parsley, yogurt and popcorn

Some Famous People with Sun in Virgo

Richard Gere, Stephen King, D. H. Lawrence, Keanu Reeves and Charlie Sheen.

THE SCALES
September 23 – October 22

THE LIBRA MAN

> *Most Compatible: Aries, Aquarius & Gemini*
>
> *Least Compatible: Pisces (too much emotion), Taurus (boring),
> Capricorn (too nit picky)*

Air Sign: This man is primarily oriented on the mental plane, communicative and social (airy).   Libra

---

This guy will irritate you if you are the type of person who wants an answer *now*. He doesn't like to hurt people's feelings, so he may *agree* with you for the moment and *not do* what you are asking him to. It can be frustrating because you are feeling like you never get a straight answer from him.

You may feel like you are waiting for something constantly while he procrastinates. My advice: If he has agreed to something, don't wait for him to set the pace. Go ahead and do it yourself!

Learn to read between the lines.

He likes outer appearances which he judges by eye appeal. Make yourself appealing to the eye…clothes, hair, etc.

He likes to give advice and help others with solutions to their problems which he rationalizes in his mind. Ask him for advice and you will get his attention.

Hint: Do you want to do something with him or go somewhere? Make it *his* idea.

Keep your house and yourself tidy. He gets confused when things are scattered. That is because his thoughts are like this.

Don't get frustrated if he puts his friends first. He likes to feel important. If you feel like you are competing with these people, you probably are. Get used to sharing him. It's part of being with a Libra. Sorry, but that's the sad truth.

Throw out junk, he hates clutter.

Leave him little notes and tell him how much he means to you. He loves it when you stroke the outside of his hands. It turns him on!

Physical, Psychological and Personality Characteristics of Libra   September 23 – October 22

7th Sign of Zodiac

Characteristics: Partnerships, marriage, open conflicts, unions, contracts, lawsuits, dealings with others and the public in general.

Spirit: To operate judiciously

Ego: Strategist, peace seeking, cultural and humane

Personality: Friendly and tactful

Ruling Planet: Venus

Empowerment Colors: Yellow and green

Moderating Colors: Blue

Best Day: Friday

Modality: Cardinal (outgoing, initiatory and active)

Element: Air

Season: Fall

Metal: Copper

Stone: Diamond, quartz and marble

Anatomy: Kidneys

Foods: Whole grains, breads, pasta, lettuce and strawberries

Some Famous People with Sun in Libra

Matt Damon, Eminem, F. Scott Fitzgerald, John Lennon, Christopher Reeve and Bruce Springsteen.

SCORPIO

THE SCORPION / EAGLE

October 23 – November 21

THE SCORPIO MAN

> *Most Compatible: Taurus, Pisces & Cancer*
>
> *Least Compatible: Aquarius (detached and impersonal)*

Water Sign: This man is primarily responsive, emotional and sensitive (watery).   Scorpio

If you like a guy who holds in his emotions, then this is the guy for you. He is very secretive and will reveal things to you slowly.

This is a good person to start out as a friend. Don't let him know you are interested. Let *him* figure you out at the beginning and you will win his heart.

He is passionate about everything that he believes in. He is a philosopher by heart. He has courage and inner strength.

Sex is important to him, so don't ignore this part of the relationship. He has a problem with jealousy sometimes and he really does have to work on it. He will require proof before actually accusing, but sometimes he will go with his instinct. Since he is so intuitive, stay true or get out, because your secret will not stay secret for long.

It's important to cater to the *little* needs that he has, but to be stubborn on the big issues in *your* life. That will keep his attention.

He needs to feel like you appreciate his intellect. Comments like "You are so smart" and "Tell me more" will captivate him!

Don't lie to him or hide things from him. He has a tongue that bites when he is mad. Be prepared if you have angered him. Keep balance by making him feel important with his opinions.

He loves it when you rub his thighs. Kissing is important too!

Physical, Psychological and Personality Characteristics of Scorpio October 23 – November 21

8th Sign of Zodiac

Characteristics: Death, inheritances, the occult, transformation of all kinds, regeneration, sexuality, taxes, death and psychic ability.

Spirit: To penetrate the secrets of nature

Ego: Shrewd, perceptive, strong willed and passionate

Personality: Secretive, vengeful and ardent

Ruling Planet: Pluto and Mars

Empowerment Colors: Scarlet, magenta and purple

Moderating Colors: Green

Best Day: Tuesday

Modality: Fixed (stable, resolute and determined)

Element: Water

Season: Fall

Metal: Steel and iron

Stone: Topaz and opal

Anatomy: Genital, bladder and bowels

Foods: Shellfish, winter squash and watermelon

Some Famous People with Sun in Scorpio

John Cleese, Danny DeVito, Richard Dreyfuss, Bill Gates, John Gotti, Harry Hamlin, Ethan Hawke, Rock Hudson, Pablo Picasso, Prince Charles and Puff Daddy.

SAGITTARIUS

THE ARCHER
November 22 – December 21

THE SAGITTARIUS MAN

> *Most Compatible: Gemini, Aries & Leo*
>
> *Least Compatible: Pisces (too introverted)*

Fire Sign: This man is primarily energetic, enthusiastic and impulsive (fiery).   Sagittarius

---

This guy can move forward full force and then back away so quickly that you wonder if he remembered anything he told you, so don't let it happen.

Slow things down at the beginning of the relationship. Only give him bits and pieces. Put yourself in the driver's seat and he will be challenged. This guy loves challenge in order to stay interested.

He's good at jumping the gun, which causes him to do things half-baked and he sometimes can be a "big thinker" with little that manifests. However, if he can learn to slow down enough to think things through, he can be very successful.

He is good at attracting attention.

Sagittarius can be our greatest teacher. Helping him and getting him to recognize his ideas and slowly put them out there can help him to be successful.

Say to him, "Wait a minute, that's a great idea! However, let's look at how it can work." It will drive him crazy that he has to wait, but keep him around because he can't stand not knowing what comes next.

He is prone to putting his foot in his mouth. Re-interpret what he says to you, the way he should have said it. If you get your feelings hurt easy, this is not the sign for you.

He likes sports and the outdoors, so learn to like these things because he'll expect you to tag along.

Whatever you do, don't ridicule his ideas. He won't like that.

If you like to do things at the last minute, then this is the guy for you. He is great at last-minute plans.

He may have had issues with his father...maybe a separation or a death. Often he is close to his mom. Make sure his mother likes you!

When you're alone with him, talk to him and massage him. He will be drawn to the intellectual and physical stimulation.

Physical, Psychological and Personality Characteristics of Sagittarius November 22 – December 21

9th Sign of Zodiac

Characteristics: Philosophy, religion, law, long journeys, higher education, publishing, foreign travel and interests, ambitions, in-laws and relatives of the marriage partner, dreams, visions, psychic experiences, intuition and spiritual tendencies.

Spirit: Meeting competition

Ego: Independent, studious, intuitive and free-thinking

Personality: Restless, enterprising and over-confident

Ruling Planet: Jupiter

Empowerment Colors: Blue, violet and purple

Moderating Colors: Scarlet

Best Day: Thursday

Modality: Mutable (adaptable and versatile)

Element: Fire

Season: Fall

Metal: Tin

Stone: Topaz

Anatomy: Hips, thighs and muscles

Foods: Lamb, veal, asparagus, cucumber and soybeans

Some Famous People with Sun in Sagittarius

Ludwig von Beethoven, Billy Bragg, Benjamin Bratt, Harry Chapin, Dick Clark, Walt Disney, Brendan Frasier, Ozzy Osbourne, Brad Pitt, Steven Spielberg and Ben Stiller.

CAPRICORN

THE GOAT

December 22 – January 19

THE CAPRICORN MAN

> *Most Compatible: Cancer, Taurus & Virgo*
>
> *Least Compatible: Aries (arrogant, insensitive and erratic)*

Earth Sign: This man is primarily materialistic and practical (earthly). Capricorn

---

If you like a guy who is practical, routine, organized and a penny pincher, then a Capricorn is for you. Show him that you are good with money and keep a tidy house and he will fall for you.

He loves family; however, if he has had problems with the family who raised him, he may be detached from tradition. Find out ahead of time what his background is. He will share if you ask him and find it easier to "convert" if you care.

He will always show action more than words. If he buys you something or does something for you, that means he cares.

He likes you to be hard to get, so make him work for your attention.

Many Capricorns over-analyze things, so watch what you say.

This is a tough sign to get rid of if you aren't interested in him anymore. He will rationalize *why* you let him go.

The more you tweak his curiosity of why you are interested in him, the easier it is to keep his attention.

You don't have to flatter him; he won't care about that. He would rather try and figure you out.

Don't be erratic. If you always like change, then forget it. He won't be open to it. Capricorns are very set in their ways.

He will either have beautiful white, strong teeth, or he'll have constant problems with decay and continual visits to the dentist – one or the other.

Generally speaking, if he avoids the lingering illnesses caused by depression, his tenacity for life is remarkable. But it's no fun for him to be the last leaf on the tree when he's suffering from arthritis and rheumatism. He must seek the sunlight and laugh at the rain to stay healthy.

There is also a tendency to pessimism, melancholy and even unhappiness, which he may be unable to keep to himself, especially if he fails personally. In the extreme, this trait can make him a very depressed individual; unbalanced happiness alternating with the most wretched kind of misery which is so subconsciously buried that he should seek help if such emotions become frequent.

To seduce him, blindfold him and take him to a hotel suite. He'll like the mystery and love that you spent your money on him.

Physical, Psychological and Personality Characteristics of

Capricorn   **December 22 – January 19**

10th Sign of Zodiac

Characteristics: Career, professional, status, mother or father, worldly ambitions, public life and people in power.

Spirit: To persevere and attain goals

Ego: Methodical, cautious, practical and ambitious

Personality: Pessimistic, miserly and ruthless

Empowerment Colors: Dark brown, gray and black

Moderating Colors: Magenta

Ruling Planet: Saturn

Best Day: Saturday

Foods: Nuts, avocado, cabbage, kale and brussels sprouts

Modality: Cardinal (outgoing, active and initiatory)

Element: Earth

Season: Winter

Metal: Lead

Stone: Amber and onyx

Anatomy: The knees, bones and skeleton

Some Famous People with Sun in Capricorn

David Bowie, Nicolas Cage, Jim Carrey, Mel Gibson, Howard Stern and Tiger Woods.

THE WATER BEARER
January 20 – February 18

THE AQUARIUS MAN

Most Compatible: Leo, Gemini & Libra

Least Compatible: Taurus (too boring)

> **Air Sign:** This man is primarily communicative, oriented on the mental plane and social (airy).
>
> Aquarius

This is a sign that can be very unpredictable. Because of this, I would suggest combining both Sun and Moon signs with Aquarius.

Some Aquarians are very sensitive and some are very detached. Nevertheless, he likes to feel like he makes a difference in your life.

He is a constant dreamer…always looking to the future.

He never has one best friend in his life but is surrounded by many.

Be very open-minded with him, because he likes to change his opinion constantly…sometimes going with what's *"in"*. If you don't like change, then forget it. This is not the sign for you.

He needs freedom to explore new things. He is analytical in his mind, but spiritual in his heart.

He will fight for truth and humanity. Sometimes being the underdog will draw him to you because he feels like you are a *"cause"*. He will commit to you once he feels parallel to you.

Give this relationship time to develop. Don't reveal too much of yourself at once. Act like a friend at first, then the emotional ties will form.

If you are feeling sad, he will work hard to bring you up. Give him something to work for. Always stay mysterious.

Don't be clingy or needy. Hold your ground, but show a need for his help. "Help" is the key word.

He is one who is willing to break through the barriers, test the system and challenge the things that are simply out-of-date. That's not likely to change, not even after he's a part of the establishment that he used to criticize. He's the one to whom you share some of those innovative ideas and humanitarian hopes.

Once he trusts you, you are in. He will be open to you. Don't ridicule his ideas. If you do this, he will detach from you and not trust that you are open to his ideas.

He wants to feel like he makes a difference. Be careful not to make him feel useless.

He loves his ankles rubbed. Sex isn't as important as getting into his mind...so tie the two together!

Physical, Psychological and Personality Characteristics

of Aquarius   **January 20 – February 18**

11th Sign of Zodiac

Characteristics: Friends, groups, associations, hopes, wishes and
   goals.

Spirit: To spread philosophical thought

Ego: Aesthetic, altruistic, revolutionary and unconventional

Personality: Stubborn, independent and eccentric

Ruling Planet: Uranus

Empowerment Colors: Blues and purple

Moderating Colors: Red

Best Day: Saturday

Foods: Potatoes, turnips, beets, cranberries and eggplant

Modality: Fixed (stable, resolute and determined)

Element: Air

Season: Winter

Metal: Uranium

Stone: Amethyst

Color: Sky blue

Anatomy: Ankles, shins and circulation

Some Famous People with Sun in Aquarius

Richard Dean Anderson, Nick Carter, Wolfgang Amadeus Mozart, Jack Nicklaus, Tom Selleck, Jerry Springer and Justin Timberlake.

THE FISH

February 19 to March 20

THE PISCES MAN

Most Compatible: Virgo, Cancer & Scorpio

Least Compatible: Gemini (too nervous and high strung)

> **Water Sign:** This man is primarily responsive, emotional and sensitive (watery).
>
> Pisces

He is sensitive, intuitive and loves the unknown, mysterious type of woman. He will talk to you for hours if you show him this side of yourself.

He sometimes procrastinates, so you have to remind him of things to get him going.

He loves romance and if you feed his stomach and create an ambiance of romance, he will love that.

Cuddling is important to him. He loves it when you stroke his hair.

Don't put down his family members, or he will get instantly turned off.

He loves beauty, so fix yourself up. However, don't show off too much in public or he might get jealous.

He can detach his emotions easily if he senses he might get hurt, so watch your words. They could end up being your worst enemy!

He wants to know if he is good at intimacy, so be sure to let him know. However, remember that if you give him a mile, he'll take it…so be careful of your suggestions.

Don't overburden him with other people's issues or issues at work, as he would rather you talk about what's going on with yourself.

He needs his space; give it to him so he can recharge.

He likes to be the center of attention when you are socializing. Let him know how good he is at drawing the attention of others. This will surely attract him to you.

When being intimate, tell him he's the best lover you've ever had. He won't waste a minute "wanting" to prove it to you over and over again!

Physical, Psychological and Personality Characteristics
of Pisces   February 19 – March 20

12th Sign of Zodiac

Characteristics: Personal unconscious, institutions, confinement, that which we haven't integrated into ourselves, karma, secret enemies, self-undoing, exile, limitations and unexpected troubles.

Spirit: Search for security

Ego: Unrealistic, compassionate, perceptive and theatrical

Personality: Shy, timid, romantic and sociable

Ruling Planet: Neptune

Empowerment Colors: Lavender, mauve and white

Moderating Colors: Lemon

Best Day: Friday

Foods: Fish (vertebrate), grapes, dates, figs and caviar

Modality: Mutable (adaptable and versatile)

Element: Water

Season: Winter

Metal: Tin

Stone: Jade and coral

Color: Sea green

Anatomy: Feet and veins

Some Famous People with Sun in Pisces

Billy Crystal, Albert Einstein, George Harrison, Kato Kaelin, Freddie Prinze Jr., Michelangelo, Dr. Seuss and Bruce Willis.

CHAPTER TWO

MOON SIGNS

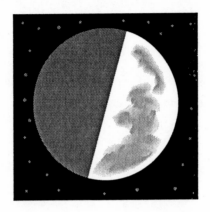

Our Moon Sign represents our "emotional" self. This is the primal subconscious self. This is an important aspect for you to know to obtain closeness emotionally. By knowing a man's Moon Sign, you can get in touch with his emotional side.

MOON in ARIES: This guy has fiery responses. He is quick to react and likes to be in control.

He has a need for independence and action. He likes to feel he is the one who motivated you in some way. One way to catch his attention is to make sure he knows how he helped you to accomplish something in your life. An example would be telling him that he turned you on to something new such as a sport, a hobby, or even an emotion will make him feel connected to you, because he was responsible for it.

He feels safe when there is something going on at all times. Guys with an Aries moon tend to be attracted to "crisis". Therefore, he will be more attracted to a woman who may have something critical going on in her life.

There is a lack of patience in this relationship and he might have that "I gotta know *now!*" attitude. This can get on your nerves. The catch here is that you can capture his attention more by *keeping* him in that "gotta know" mode. It will add fire to the relationship.

He is easily frustrated or irritated with others. His patience is low so if he snaps at you, don't take it personally. He doesn't often think when he speaks. His intention isn't usually to hurt your feelings. His tongue can be fueled faster than his mind. The positive side to this is that he is very expressive and can be generous with compliments. I call this the Moon sign that has bipolar traits. One moment he can be Mr. Happy and the next Mr. Angry. If you don't like to be with a guy whose moods change frequently, then this is not the guy for you.

He loves to be the protector in the relationship and doesn't depend on his partner emotionally…unless, of course, he can't figure you out. Then he will spend lots of time on you.

If you would like to help him de-stress, do something physical with him like jogging or kickboxing. Another suggestion is to hop into bed and keep him happy. He loves physical stimulation!

To turn him on, turn the lights out and let his imagination "wonder" what you might kiss next.

Some Famous People with Moon in Aries

Kevin Spacey, Luciano Pavarotti, Andy Warhol, John Voight, Bill Gates and Alan Alda.

MOON in TAURUS: This man nurtures others with his solid, stable presence. He readily cares for loved ones monetarily or with gifts, either purchased or of his own creation.

He likes things that are warm and he likes clothing that is soft to the touch, as he often has sensitive skin.

He can be very stubborn and reluctant to change his ways. Trying to get him to do new things may be difficult.

If you want to save money, then turn off the home shopping channel. He likes gadgets. To excite him, buy the latest back massager and use it on him!

The first love of his life was his mother. Chances are she spoiled him. If mom was absent, then it may have been a grandmother or other female figure. Because of this, he wants to be nurtured and has a need to feel safe with a woman. Take heed in the word "safe". The minute you rock his foundation and take away his safety, he will disappear faster than you can blink.

To help him feel safe with you, make sure you have a place, preferably your home, where he can go and feel comfortable. He feels safest when surrounded by things that he can touch, see and feel. Finding out what colors he likes, music and textures (i.e. silk or cotton bed sheets) is important. If you create an aura of comfort around him, he will always find his way to your home in times of need. If he doesn't feel comfortable with the surroundings, he will retreat back to what makes him comfortable, i.e., his mother's home!

Some Famous People with Moon in Taurus

Robert Downey Jr., Brendan Frasier, Mick Jagger and Elton John.

MOON in GEMINI: This man nurtures his mate with friendship, witty exchanges and playful excursions.

He can be moody and often shifts into new things quicker than you can change your underwear.

He likes to talk and is in his mind a lot. He zips around in his mind so fast, that sometimes he makes things up and you might wonder where he is coming from.

He over-rationalizes things and can get himself in trouble by coming to the wrong conclusion. Mental stimulation is important and a must for any relationship to have a chance of becoming permanent. These guys don't like to be tied down too tightly.

It's important for a Gemini Moon guy to have a buddy to talk with, to get his thoughts out of trouble.

Being around friends, family and in the public is important to him. Don't chain him up, or he will break loose.

Never be the same with him. Offer him different emotions and personalities. This will keep him around because he will want to figure you out.

Keep him curious, as this man has a strong need for mental stimulation. He can tend to be a talker. If you like talking on the telephone, this guy is for you. He will call you whenever something interesting has popped into his mind. If he is interested in you, plan on getting lots of phone calls. The minute this drops off should signal to you that something is wrong with the relationship. He feels safe when you talk to him and share information with him...things like what is going on in the world and who is dating who. These guys love gossip. The worst thing to do to a guy with the Moon in Gemini is to cut him off when he is talking. This will make him feel like you don't care what he has to share with you. Don't be impatient with him, or he will detach from you faster than you can blink an eye.

Don't get upset with him if he compares you to previous partners. Chances are he has already eliminated them as "number one" if he is comparing you to people in his past. Listen intently to "why" he likes your traits better, instead of getting angry at him for bringing up the past. He may ask you questions so that he can size you up and quiz you on how things felt to you in your past relationships. A good answer would be "they did this, but I like the way you handle yourself better..."

Some Famous People with Moon in Gemini

Mel Blanc, Jim Carrey and John Goodman.

MOON in CANCER: This guy is *ruled* by the Moon, so this makes him a very lunar individual. He is likely to have a round face.

His moods will reflect the different phases of the moon. He can be extremely crabby or happy. He has a paranoid personality which can sometimes create problems in relationships.

He is very sensitive. Be careful not to make him feel like he is trouble to you. He will disappear if he feels he is causing you trouble.

He nurtures with great care. He is in tune with females and can be very "mothering". However, he needs to be mothered in return. He loves his home and can tend to be a homebody.

He feels safest when he is being nurtured and emotionally cared for. When he was young, his mother may have made him feel guilty if he didn't put her first. He probably shifts his moods to please a woman because of this and then gets angry after doing it several times, because of the control you have over him. My advice: Don't make him feel guilty. Work hard on allowing him to bring out his "true" feelings.

Some Famous People with Moon in Cancer

Boris Becker, Clint Eastwood, Harrison Ford, Woody Guthrie, Julio Iglesias, Kurt Kobain, Mike Myers, Sean Penn, Keanu Reeves, Kurt Russell, Adam Sandler and Robin Williams.

MOON in LEO: This guy expects loyalty and needs to feel appreciated.

Don't ignore him, or he will get insecure; unless, of course, he is ignoring you; then ignoring him will get his attention. It's a double-edged sword.

He can be enticed by a woman who is the boss at work – or perhaps by a *bossy* woman.

He likes it if you get attention from others, but don't act like you notice the attention you are getting.

One of the characteristics of the Moon in Leo is self-confidence. He is instinctively intuitive and creative. He has so much life force and moral courage that many weaker people gain material and/or spiritual support from him – and he is often admired for these particular qualities.

If you have children you are in luck! He loves children. His temperament is essentially aggressive, but this is softened by the affectionate side of his nature. He needs to guard against being a bit overbearing in manner.

He needs to be the initiator. Let him be in charge or think he's in charge. He'll feel more comfortable with you.

Once his emotions have been aroused, he remains loyal and steadfast in his dealings. Loyalty is, in fact, the keynote of his emotional life. He is an honorable partner in long-term relationships.

As a parent, he will want the best for his children. He will want to organize their lives for them. He will be ambitious for them to succeed and do well in school. He can come on too strong and be terribly disappointed if his children do not live up to his expectations. He sees their success as *his* success, their failure as *his* failure. He needs to guard against having too high of expectations and to curb a tendency to be in control.

Guys with Moon in Leo are emotionally generous and loving. Under stress, they can become arrogant. Be careful not to put him down when he gets this way. Adding fuel to the fire will just make things worse!

Some Famous People with Moon in Leo

Tom Cruise, Jonathon Frakes, Peter O'Toole, Tom Selleck and Martin Sheen.

MOON in VIRGO: I call this aspect, the anal retentive one.

He is very meticulous and can over-analyze everything, sometimes making you feel like you do not do things well enough. It is very important to know that he is like this before you get yourself entrenched in this relationship. Just let him speak and "blow off" feeling this way. He not only puts this on you but himself also. It is tough to be with a guy with this aspect.

He can be very hurtful with his words. You have to have "thick skin".

He can be very loving and like to touch you when you are intimate. He is a leader, not a pushover. Let him be your problem solver and he'll be hooked on you.

I would suggest talking to him about things *after* intimacy. This is the time he will be most open for conversation.

He likes to feel like he is helping you in order to feel better about himself. He prefers to be a teacher behind the scenes feeling useful if you succeed, because you listened to him.

He may ask you "trick" questions in order to obtain understanding of how you feel about him. If he does this, answer him bluntly. He will spend more time analyzing your words than feeling them.

He isn't finding fault in you because he doesn't care about you. He does it because he cares. If he doesn't offer you suggestions, then you can be sure that he isn't interested.

These guys can be passive, reactive, receptive, introverted and enduring. They attract experiences and "take advantage of opportunities" rather than creating circumstances independently. They prefer to wait and see what happens in a situation than to act forcefully in it. If you aren't a patient person this guy may irritate you. On the other hand, he may be good for you and help you learn patience.

He has a strong personal code of conduct and has high standards in regards toward his loyalty with friends and loved ones. He has the ability to think through the scenarios in a logical order, rather than firefighting when trouble hits. He can be a list maker and if planning a vacation with this guy, he will make sure you have a wonderful time. He loves to plan and loves helping.

Some Famous People with Moon in Virgo

Gene Simmons, John F. Kennedy, Chris Rock, Bill Cosby, Jean-Claude Van Damme, William Dafoe, Sammy Davis Jr. and Richard Burton.

MOON in LIBRA: A man with a Libra moon doesn't like conflict. He probably has a dimple, too. He is attracted to more of a feminine woman.

He doesn't like women who are confrontational. He would rather not get into deep emotional conversations. He likes to be in a one-on-one relationship without all the emotions. If you do want to talk to him about something emotional, wait until after the two of you have shared a passionate moment or after you have spent time with his friends who adore you. Yes, you can earn brownie points by being adored by his friends. He likes the attention you get from others as long as you belong to him.

He falls in love easily and not always with the right person. He tends to fall in love early and frequently. However, because he needs to be surrounded by harmony; the moment discord is present he will move on to the next person. Don't do things that you can't live up to or he will walk away because the relationship wasn't what he expected.

A totally serene relationship is what he seeks; yet when achieved, it is boring to him – so you need to shake things up a little now and then.

Wear soft colors; he loves that. He also loves to have his neck kissed.

Some Famous People with Moon in Libra

Alec Baldwin, George Bush Jr., Nicolas Cage, Walt Disney, D.H. Lawrence, Christian Slater and Bruce Springsteen.

MOON in SCORPIO: Can you say "paranoid" and "moody"? A Scorpio moon is very psychic but sometimes gets the energy in the world mixed up with his personal life. He can assume that the worst is happening when often it is not. You must be able to handle pessimism if you are with this guy.

While he can be moody, he is very emotional and loving. This is a great person to share your dreams with and not be afraid to bring out your "weird" ideas.

He can be a friend and a lover. When intimate, he is very loving and affectionate.

Because he can love so deeply he can become very possessive of his partner. This can be both a physical as well as a psychological sense. He may express this in minor ways, such as little comments about what you are wearing or who you are acquainted with. Little digs can hurt, but they will assure you that he is interested in you. Although he is possessive, he also likes his freedom. If he feels like his freedom is threatened he will get jittery and retreat, sometimes disappearing for days. Don't crowd him. He needs enough space to feel comfort in the relationship.

It is important to him to show your loyalty. He likes an intense and passionate woman.

He also can be enticed by mystery. The more you challenge his will power, the more attention you will get.

Because he is moody, he may seem psychologically imbalanced. Get used to it, because each day will be a different drama.

If he was subjected to emotional manipulation or deprivation in childhood, he is not going to reveal his vulnerability by openly expressing his feelings or needs. If he is raised in a non-threatening environment, he will probably emerge as a mild-mannered, easy-to-get-along-with adult.

This guy is very passionate. Emotional depth is important to him. He loves it when a woman is in trouble and he can save her. Sticking up for the underdog is important to him. He isn't afraid to say what he feels if it means saving a female from distress. The only problem is that he keeps his own emotions snuggled tightly in and often puts others needs first. This can cause a problem when he has done this for too long and then he breaks down because he was holding his emotions in and begins to feel resentment. The way you can recognize ahead of time if he is having a problem, is if he becomes quiet and retreats. He will begin to give short replies to your questions and seem detached from his surroundings. To avoid this, be aware of his emotions and make time for his needs as well.

If you are looking for a relationship that is less than boring, then this is the one for you! Rub his shoulders, he loves that.

Some Famous People with Moon in Scorpio

Ben Affleck, Bjork, Eminem, Harry Hamlin, David Schwimmer and Steven Spielberg.

MOON in SAGITTARIUS: This guy can be passive aggressive. One minute, he will be sweeping you off your feet and the next, he will be detached. Don't give him too much in the beginning. He would rather work at it.

He wants to turn his feelings into physical experiences. He does not initially view his desires from the standpoint of practicality, emotional commitment, or as lessons to be learned.

If you want to get an answer from him, ask the question while driving in the car. He thinks best while he is moving.

He may have an addiction to sugar. This could create mood swings. To turn him on, ask him to pull over on a trip and make kissing stops! He loves adventure.

He may lack sensitivity to other people's feelings. This man is so gung-ho about doing his own thing that he doesn't readily slow down to consider how you might feel about his actions. You first have to get his attention.

He feels more complete when he can investigate you. He would rather be given *little* clues about how you tick, than everything all at once.

Some Famous People with Moon in Sagittarius

Ludwig von Beethoven, Dick Clark, Charles Dickens, Richard Gere, Stephen King, Lenny Kravitz, Wolfgang Amadeus Mozart, Arnold Palmer, Charlie Sheen, Justin Timberlake, Vincent Van Gogh and Tiger Woods.

MOON in CAPRICORN: This guy is hard on himself. He over-rationalizes everything. If he suddenly goes away, it might be because he feels like he messed up. Rather than deal with it and face the repercussions, he'd rather chalk it up to experience.

He expects his partner to be helpful in the struggle for success and achievement. Though never openly demonstrative, he is dependable and loyal. He is very solid and committed when it comes to romantic attachments and marriage. When it comes to commitment, he is the old-fashioned type. He wants one person as long as he feels that person is being true to him or satisfies his financial outlook.

He may have had issues with his father being absent. His mother may have been too busy. He is very sensitive. If you are the type of person who doesn't mind reassuring another person of how worthy they are, then this is the relationship for you.

He may pinch pennies, too. If you are financially stable, you will win brownie points with him.

Emotional detachment is common with this Moon sign.

He is dependable, but boring at times. If you want to get an answer from him, ask him after the bills are paid for the month. He will pay more attention to you.

Anything vague or unspecified in a relationship, whether business or personal, makes him feel insecure. He must know where he stands. Everything must be proper and legal.

When it comes to romance and marriage, it may take him longer to find someone he can love as well as trust.

He would rather you compliment him than rub his back.

Some Famous People with Moon in Capricorn

Matt Damon, Adolf Hitler, James Earl Jones, David Letterman, Ozzy Osbourne and Brad Pitt.

MOON in AQUARIUS: This guy is honest to a fault. He can't stand it if you have lied to him.

It will make him feel good if he feels like you are a cause for him. He likes to save people.

If you are totally independent, he may get bored with you. Make sure you always have a question he can answer without appearing too needy. Chances are he grew up fast in his childhood.

He can throw himself into his work and often forget about balancing his time. If you want his attention, appeal to his mind. He likes work because it challenges his intellect. Making a relationship work for him would be good.

He has difficulty focusing attention on just one person. As far as he's concerned, "the more, the merrier".

Despite whatever eccentricity shows up in his personality, he is emotionally stable. Something in his emotional makeup gives him remarkable ability to calm those who are mentally disturbed or hysterical. Overall, he has a good heart.

If you want to ask him an important question, do it in a conversation in which he feels he is going to take the lead.

He likes his lower back rubbed.

Friendship is very important to him. He has lots of acquaintances. Be prepared to be busy meeting them all. You will find that he is friendly with all of them but close with few of them.

Some Famous People with Moon in Aquarius

J. C. Chasez, George Clooney, Russell Crowe, David Duchovny, John Lennon, George Lucas, Tobey Maguire, Conan O'Brien and Christopher Walken.

MOON in PISCES: This is an ultra-sensitive guy. He probably has beautiful eyes and can give you a look to make your heart melt.

Chances are when he was growing up he tried to "please" a parent and always felt like he fell short of this. He can be insecure and if he feels like he might be hurt, he will shut his feelings off suddenly.

His excess emotions imply the almost certain potential for waging lifelong battles against overindulgences of every kind. As a defense mechanism to protect his inner vulnerability, he may turn into a bully...out to get others, before others get him.

He can be extremely sensitive and easily hurt. Instead of telling you this, he will retreat in silence. He may begin to act and feel like a martyr and you may sometimes push this attitude a little too far. His real fear is rejection. Rejection can make it hard for him to express his true feelings. Strong feelings can sometimes cloud what is really going on inside of him. If he starts to retreat, you can be sure you have hurt him deeply. Give him the space he needs and then offer him a time to discuss his emotions after he has pouted for a few days. Pushing him to talk right away will only cause anger on both sides.

If you want to keep his attention, make him work hard for it. He somehow *needs* to feel insecure in a relationship to keep it interesting.

Don't be afraid to be open with him. Leave a bit of the puzzle out so he can work to make you happy.

He is more attracted to a woman who is curvy than bony.

Run your fingers through his hair; he loves that!

Some Famous People with Moon in Pisces

Michael Bolton, Robert Browning, Carson Daly, Robert DeNiro, Morgan Freeman, Michael Jackson, Martin Luther King, Kevin Kline, Ricky Martin, Michelangelo, Edgar Allen Poe, Elvis Presley, Jason Priestly, Prince, Judge Reinhold, Gene Rodenberry, Charles Schulz, Martin Scorcese, Jerry Seinfeld and Ben Stiller.

CHAPTER THREE

VENUS SIGNS

Venus represents the role we take in relationships and career. Love, getting to know another person, career, mating, socialization and relationship are found in Venus. We act like this sign when we are involved in personal relationships and making choices in our career. Knowing a man's Venus allows you to tap into the part of him that reacts to relationships and career, giving you a better understanding of how to interact with him.

VENUS in ARIES

Venus in Aries' normal softness is touched by an aggressive urge. He goes right after his mate.

He expects spontaneity and likes a good sense of humor. He can be very sensitive if you don't like his humor. He likes to act childlike and is fun-loving. He is attracted to a woman who is energetic and always on the go. He gets turned off by a stuffy woman. He would rather have one who acts younger, giggles and likes to play.

He is addicted to conquest. In order to keep the relationship fresh, you must provide him with constant stimulation. Be very direct and open with him. He thrives on competition. Don't let him start feeling like things are the same, or he will get bored and move on. The word here is "COMPETE". Make him feel like he needs to compete for your attention.

He can be impatient and careless sometimes. He often skips over details making you feel that he didn't put much into the time you spend together. Not surprisingly, early marriages are common with Venus in Aries because he didn't take time to get to know if his partner's wants are the same as his.

He can hurt your feelings by not thinking when he says things. My advice to you: If you are sensitive and don't like big egos, this won't work for you.

Some Famous People with Venus in Aries

George Clooney, Robert Downey Jr., Vince Vaughn, Shaquille O'Neal, Harry Houdini and Jack Nicholson.

VENUS in TAURUS

This guy always seems to attract a female whom he adores, but who often puts him through misery. He can be very possessive and is threatened by a woman who is scattered and moves too fast. Be careful not to push him into making decisions...he likes to feel in control of things. Want to get something out of him? Make it his idea. This guy has a natural affinity for being in control.

His greatest conflict is staying in an unhappy relationship. Don't ever make things too easy for him. He unconsciously likes the challenge. He can get comfortable and settled and can offer you unswerving loyalty.

He needs to be touched. Affection must be given and received physically...his most important need is for touch. Massage is good for him on a regular basis so he can get filled up with strokes – physical ones. He is very sensual and requires you to show him "physically" that you care. Touching him to reassure him is a positive thing. If you are not the type of person who likes to touch, hug or express yourself in a physical way, then this guy is not for you.

To please him, let him know how much value he is in your life. Buy some soft cotton bed sheets. He loves comfort.

Some Famous People with Venus in Taurus

George Lucas, Prince William, Warren Beatty and Charlie Chaplin.

VENUS in GEMINI

He is always inside his mind. If you can make him think and spark his curiosity, you will have him hooked.

He sometimes gets bored, so always leave him wondering where you stand. It's ok to let him know you care, but leave a little so he can figure things out.

He likes a voice that doesn't remind him of someone who was negative in his past. He is very audio-oriented.

This person wants to talk about love or better yet, be listened to. Listen to him and he will be hooked on you. He is playful and can be a big tease. He can rope you in emotionally and pull back. When he pulls back, don't be insecure. Just smile and say "whatever". This is a sure way to get him to come back around.

He hates to be bogged down in a relationship. It's important that he can come and go as he pleases. Support his need for variety and compliment him on his intelligence. Remind him how much fun it is to be with him. If you dislike fickle guys, then forget it. He is as fickle as they come!

Some Famous People with Venus in Gemini
Al Pacino, John F. Kennedy, Russell Crowe and John Goodman.

VENUS in CANCER

This guy loves the home. He wants a woman who is mothering. Nurture a Venus in Cancer by cooking, playing house, fluffing up his pillow, feeding him and taking care of him when he isn't feeling well...all of those soft fuzzy things Mom did for you when you were a kid. If you don't like to be at home, then this guy might bore you. Home is very important to him and so are children. He is ultra-sensitive and often holds on to memories of the past.

He likes predictability. He is moody and when hurt, he can shut his feelings off quickly. He is overly concerned of being abandoned. Make sure you let him know you will be there for him.

He likes a woman who comes across as sweet. He would rather have a woman who is more mother-like than tomboyish. He is often attracted to a more traditional woman who dresses simple. A flashy woman will turn him off. He will be attracted to a woman he can guide, so when you first meet him, let him feel like he is the teacher and you are the student.

Here's some advice: Don't bring up old relationships. He will compare himself to them. He can be very insecure.

Love him unconditionally and feed his emotions with "comfort"!

Some Famous People with Venus in Cancer

Ben Affleck, William Dafoe, Danny Glover, Lenny Kravitz, Keanu Reeves, Martin Sheen, Christian Slater and Robert Plant.

VENUS in LEO

This guy loves to play! If you have children already, this is a good stepfather. He likes to tease and can be downright silly.

He needs admiration and he loves it if you tell him how fun he is.

He likes a partner who gets attention. He is attracted to a woman with the "Wow! factor". He loves an outgoing woman. You need to be confident. He is attracted to a woman who wears jewelry and bright colors. He doesn't want you to be stronger than him. He just wants to know that you can handle him.

If your guy has Venus in Leo, create an energy around you that says "I *know* I am special!" He can be jealous, but this turns him on.

He has a tendency to feel sorry for himself. If you see him sulking cheer him up by giving him a hug or a smile. He doesn't want to talk about it. He would rather you display physical affection.

He loves to be the center of attention and is constantly looking for attention from others. This doesn't mean he is unfaithful, just that he likes to flirt. Don't be jealous or he will turn away from you.

When this guy is in love, he is sincere and whole-hearted. He's one of the most romantic lovers. He will display affection openly if he is interested in you.

Some Famous People with Venus in Leo

George W. Bush, Tom Cruise, Tobey Maguire and George Bernard Shaw.

VENUS in VIRGO

This guy is the *bachelor* of the zodiac. He gets so stuck on finding the perfect partner that he can be highly critical and make you feel insecure. Know this is just his way. In reality, he feels this way about himself.

Often afraid of commitment, this guy is looking for someone who is secure in herself. He wants someone who takes care of herself emotionally and physically. If you want to keep him interested, make him feel like he helps you.

Find out what he is good at and ask him for help. Don't ever get good at it either, or he won't feel useful.

Some Famous People with Venus in Virgo

J.C. Chasez, John Lennon, Robert de Niro, Mick Jagger, Patrick Swayze, Brian Adams and Kevin Spacey.

VENUS in LIBRA

This guy can often put your feelings first and not think of his own needs. Then he gets angry at you, for not putting his needs first.

Often aloof; he can appear to be daydreaming when you talk to him. He loves beauty and probably is very attractive himself. Chances are he has a dimple.

This guy wants to charm you but needs to be secretly charmed himself. Do it by dropping little comments. Don't chase him. If you do, he will run the other way.

He needs to have a somewhat fairytale in his head about you to stay interested. Dress in soft colors. He is attracted to femininity. He will judge you for good manners and your charm. Polish up your language. He doesn't want a woman who uses coarse words.

Some Famous People with Venus in Libra

F. Scott Fitzgerald, Richard Gere, Stephen King and
D. H. Lawrence.

VENUS in SCORPIO

He likes a woman who is sensual and mysterious. When you first meet him, give him a quick smile and walk away. Always keep him guessing what comes next.

This guy is deep, but he can also be very strange when it comes to expectations. He puts sex high on his list. If you want him to feel like he fits in, let him know how good he is at making love to you. He is going for the woman who reaches inside his soul and grabs it.

However, he needs you to be strong when it comes to your emotions. Don't spend too much time crying because you will scare him.

He often has a hard time letting go of past relationships. Venus in Scorpio often stays with a person who captivates him. Don't be surprised if he eventually ends up with his high school sweetheart or someone who reminds him of her.

Some Famous People with Venus in Scorpio
Matt Damon, Bill Gates, Puff Daddy, Jean-Claude Van Damme, Ray Charles, David Schwimmer and Steven Spielberg.

VENUS in SAGITTARIUS

This man needs a partnership that is fun but challenging. He is attracted to confusion, so don't let him ever figure you out, or he will be bored. This is an aspect that sometimes can be unfaithful, as he is automatically turned off by a woman who is dull or overly emotional.

When the going gets tough in his relationship, he will have an overwhelming need to run away. Let him go. If you do, he will be back. He usually needs breathing space for a short amount of time. It's important for him to get out and experience something new before he comes back.

He needs someone who has depth when communicating. He is attracted to women who are teachers, but not know-it-alls. Remember, his honesty can be brutally frank and can easily hurt feelings on occasion. He isn't doing this to hurt you; he just doesn't always think before he speaks.

Keeping the partnership full of life and a sense of humor would be an asset by this Venus placement. Tease him and hide. Let him find you and you will keep him interested.

Some Famous People with Venus in Sagittarius
Kevin Costner, Eddie Van Halen, Jimmy Page, Eddie Vedder and Mark Twain.

VENUS in CAPRICORN

This guy is lucky when it comes to money. Chances are that he might claim to be broke, but his pocketbook is loaded.

If you aren't ambitious, he will eventually ditch you for someone who is. He will see you as a cause, conquer you and then move on. Don't start the relationship out this way and you won't have a problem.

He takes love seriously and if you begin the relationship with strength, he will commit to you forever. However, if you let him down, things may never be the same.

The partnership can be looked upon as a potential "business venture". He is likely to marry someone that he can see as a business partner. He is goal oriented and can often make you feel like his job comes before you. Get used to it, because it probably does.

He wants you to feel like he is responsible and can take care of you. The problem is that if you let him do this 100%, later in the relationship, he will resent you. It is important to maintain a 60-40% responsibility in order to keep the relationship balanced.

Pleasing him involves showing him that you are practical and realistic. He wants to impress you with the things he does.

Some Famous People with Venus in Capricorn

Ludwig von Beethoven, Benjamin Bratt, Jim Carrey, Brad Pitt, Howard Stern, Ben Stiller and Justin Timberlake.

VENUS in AQUARIUS

This guy needs someone who is who she *says* she is. Don't lie to him or he will be gone quicker than you can blink an eye. When you begin the relationship, stress how important honesty is to you.

He doesn't like stereotypical partners. Be different and let him know that you appreciate his individuality.

Start this relationship out with friendship. He is often very open and doesn't like to let his partner get too attached to him. If you can't give him space, then this relationship is doomed.

He is open-minded and wants you to be this way, too. Don't be afraid to try new things. He wants you to acknowledge and appreciate that he doesn't follow the same path as others, in matters of the heart. He wants to know he is superior to other guys. Letting him know how intelligent he is will only earn you brownie points!

Some Famous People with Venus in Aquarius

Richard Dean Anderson, Alec Baldwin, Billy Bragg, Nicolas Cage, Walt Disney, Mel Gibson, Elton John, Ricky Martin, Freddie Prinze Jr. and Wolfgang Amadeus Mozart.

VENUS in PISCES

This man looks for unconditional love. If you hurt him, he can be very unforgiving and downright spiteful.

He can be self-sacrificing when it comes to his family and friends. Don't be jealous of this. This is something you have to accept. It comes with the territory.

He is attracted to creative women like artists and poets, or to women who are psychics or empaths.

He likes a woman whom he can save. It turns him on. Let him feel like he is taking you from a distressful situation into a better one. When you first meet, tell him what a good listener he is and how much of a difference he makes in your life because he listens and cares about your feelings. These guys like to feel they are "emotionally" saving you.

Extraordinarily romantic and visual, he loves to take baths, light candles and make you feel special. However, he sees things through rose-colored glasses and this can create problems.

You can begin the relationship as his ideal partner; and if you don't live up to those expectations, he will detach from you faster than you can say *"I"!*

He may waste time looking for the ideal partner and never find her. Be loving, kind and spiritual and this guy will be hooked.

Some Famous People with Venus in Pisces

Nick Carter, George Harrison, Tom Selleck, John Travolta and Vincent Van Gogh.

ACKNOWLEDGMENTS

I would like to thank Sandra Williams for her friendship and dedication. If it wasn't for her, this book would not be possible. She is a beautiful soul who gave to me unconditionally of her time and effort in putting this book together.

I would also like to thank my Great Grandmother (God rest her soul) for opening me up as a child to spiritual faith. I also thank my family for being patient with me while I spent countless hours writing this.

My appreciation is extended to Kevin Cubberly for his many hours of hard work in obtaining some of the materials and assistance in putting them together.

My deepest gratitude is sent to the thousands of clients who have asked me about their own relationships and gave me the knowledge and understanding to write this book.

Last and not least, I am thankful to be able to give advice on two radio programs in the Toledo, Ohio area. These programs are; "*Inner Views*", with my radio partner Steve Marshall on Star 105.5 FM and with "*Train in the Morning*", on Tower 98.3 FM. Reaching out and helping those in need is truly my purpose. These shows allow me to do this.

EPHEMERIS

The Ephemeris in the following pages will assist you in finding a person's signs. The "TIME" column represents *Greenwich Mean Time (GMT or UTC)*. To use these tables, it is first necessary to convert a birth time to *Greenwich Mean Time*. Use the small table below to determine the number of hours to add to the birth time depending on the time zone the person was born in. For example, if you were born in *Eastern Standard Time* (EST) at 11:45 a.m. you would add 5 hours to get 4:45 p.m. *Greenwich Mean Time*. Remember to take *Daylight Savings Time* into consideration. *Daylight Savings Time* changed slightly in 1986 from the last Sunday in April to the first Sunday in April. The last Sunday in October was not changed in 1986.

Time Zone	Standard Time	Daylight Savings Time
Eastern (EST/EDT)	+5 hours	+4 hours
Central (CST/CDT)	+6 hours	+5 hours
Mountain (MST/MDT)	+7 hours	+6 hours
Pacific (PST/PDT)	+8 hours	+7 hours
Alaska (AST/ADT)	+9 hours	+8 hours
Hawaii (HST/HDT)	+11 hours	+10 hours

*For easy reference in the United States, refer to the map on the page following these instructions.

Keep in mind that other factors, such as location (i.e., Indiana and Arizona) and *War Time* could also affect the conversion to

Greenwich Mean Time. If there is any doubt about what clock changes might have been in effect on the date of birth, consult your local authority or an Atlas.

Now that you have determined the *Greenwich Mean Time* or GMT of the person's birth, you are almost ready to go to the Ephemeris tables!

Here is the key for finding your partner's aspect:

ARI	Aries	LIB	Libra
TAU	Taurus	SCO	Scorpio
GEM	Gemini	SAG	Sagittarius
CAN	Cancer	CAP	Capricorn
LEO	Leo	AQU	Aquarius
VIR	Virgo	PIS	Pisces

When using the Ephemeris look for the year, month, day and time for the moment of one's birth. Here's an example:

A man born was born in Michigan on Sunday, April 23, 1967, at 4:00 p.m. Eastern Standard Time; so his GMT is 9:00 p.m. The SUN table will indicate that from the 20th of April until the 21st of May 1967, the *Sun was in Taurus.* The MOON table will indicate that from 8:34 a.m. on the 22nd of April until 6:00 a.m. on the 24th of April 1967, the *Moon was in Libra.* Finally, the VENUS table will indicate that from the 14th of April until the 10th of May 1967, *Venus was in Gemini.*

The Mathematical tables for looking up the sign positions of the Sun, Moon and Venus are accurate to within 3 hours of the cut-off dates indicated, depending on the exact time and place of birth. The sun changes approximately every 30 days around the 21st of the month. But the date varies from sign to sign and from year to year.

If the person were born on the cusp, either the first or last day of a sign, you should read both sign descriptions. For total accuracy in determining the sign positions you can contact **Lite the Way** at (734) 854-1514 or visit *www.litetheway.com* and order a natal chart.

Congratulations! You have identified the important aspects in analyzing relationships...his Sun, Moon and Venus!!!

TIME ZONES OF THE USA

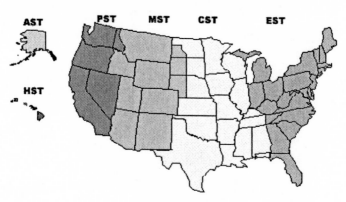

AST PST MST CST EST

HST

Ephemeris

Sun

Date	Sun	Date	Sun	Date	Sun	Date	Sun
Jan. 1, 1920	C A P	Feb. 19, 1923	P I S	Apr. 20, 1926	T A U	Jun. 21, 1929	C A N
Jan. 21, 1920	A Q U	Mar. 21, 1923	A R I	May. 21, 1926	G E M	Jul. 23, 1929	L E O
Feb. 19, 1920	P I S	Apr. 21, 1923	T A U	Jun. 22, 1926	C A N	Aug. 23, 1929	V I R
Mar. 20, 1920	A R I	May. 22, 1923	G E M	Jul. 23, 1926	L E O	Sep. 23, 1929	L I B
Apr. 20, 1920	T A U	Jun. 22, 1923	C A N	Aug. 23, 1926	V I R	Oct. 23, 1929	S C O
May. 21, 1920	G E M	Jul. 23, 1923	L E O	Sep. 23, 1926	L I B	Nov. 22, 1929	S A G
Jun. 21, 1920	C A N	Aug. 24, 1923	V I R	Oct. 24, 1926	S C O	Dec. 22, 1929	C A P
Jul. 23, 1920	L E O	Sep. 24, 1923	L I B	Nov. 23, 1926	S A G	Jan. 20, 1930	A Q U
Aug. 23, 1920	V I R	Oct. 24, 1923	S C O	Dec. 22, 1926	C A P	Feb. 19, 1930	P I S
Sep. 23, 1920	L I B	Nov. 23, 1923	S A G	Jan. 21, 1927	A Q U	Mar. 21, 1930	A R I
Oct. 23, 1920	S C O	Dec. 22, 1923	C A P	Feb. 19, 1927	P I S	Apr. 20, 1930	T A U
Nov. 22, 1920	S A G	Jan. 21, 1924	A Q U	Mar. 21, 1927	A R I	May. 21, 1930	G E M
Dec. 22, 1920	C A P	Feb. 19, 1924	P I S	Apr. 21, 1927	T A U	Jun. 22, 1930	C A N
Jan. 20, 1921	A Q U	Mar. 20, 1924	A R I	May. 22, 1927	G E M	Jul. 23, 1930	L E O
Feb. 19, 1921	P I S	Apr. 20, 1924	T A U	Jun. 22, 1927	C A N	Aug. 23, 1930	V I R
Mar. 21, 1921	A R I	May. 21, 1924	G E M	Jul. 23, 1927	L E O	Sep. 23, 1930	L I B
Apr. 20, 1921	T A U	Jun. 21, 1924	C A N	Aug. 24, 1927	V I R	Oct. 24, 1930	S C O
May. 21, 1921	G E M	Jul. 23, 1924	L E O	Sep. 24, 1927	L I B	Nov. 23, 1930	S A G
Jun. 21, 1921	C A N	Aug. 23, 1924	V I R	Oct. 24, 1927	S C O	Dec. 22, 1930	C A P
Jul. 23, 1921	L E O	Sep. 23, 1924	L I B	Nov. 23, 1927	S A G	Jan. 21, 1931	A Q U
Aug. 23, 1921	V I R	Oct. 23, 1924	S C O	Dec. 22, 1927	C A P	Feb. 19, 1931	P I S
Sep. 23, 1921	L I B	Nov. 22, 1924	S A G	Jan. 21, 1928	A Q U	Mar. 21, 1931	A R I
Oct. 23, 1921	S C O	Dec. 22, 1924	C A P	Feb. 19, 1928	P I S	Apr. 21, 1931	T A U
Nov. 22, 1921	S A G	Jan. 20, 1925	A Q U	Mar. 20, 1928	A R I	May. 22, 1931	G E M
Dec. 22, 1921	C A P	Feb. 19, 1925	P I S	Apr. 20, 1928	T A U	Jun. 22, 1931	C A N
Jan. 20, 1922	A Q U	Mar. 21, 1925	A R I	May. 21, 1928	G E M	Jul. 23, 1931	L E O
Feb. 19, 1922	P I S	Apr. 20, 1925	T A U	Jun. 21, 1928	C A N	Aug. 24, 1931	V I R
Mar. 21, 1922	A R I	May. 21, 1925	G E M	Jul. 23, 1928	L E O	Sep. 24, 1931	L I B
Apr. 20, 1922	T A U	Jun. 21, 1925	C A N	Aug. 23, 1928	V I R	Oct. 24, 1931	S C O
May. 21, 1922	G E M	Jul. 23, 1925	L E O	Sep. 23, 1928	L I B	Nov. 23, 1931	S A G
Jun. 22, 1922	C A N	Aug. 23, 1925	V I R	Oct. 23, 1928	S C O	Dec. 22, 1931	C A P
Jul. 23, 1922	L E O	Sep. 23, 1925	L I B	Nov. 22, 1928	S A G	Jan. 21, 1932	A Q U
Aug. 23, 1922	V I R	Oct. 23, 1925	S C O	Dec. 22, 1928	C A P	Feb. 19, 1932	P I S
Sep. 23, 1922	L I B	Nov. 22, 1925	S A G	Jan. 20, 1929	A Q U	Mar. 20, 1932	A R I
Oct. 24, 1922	S C O	Dec. 22, 1925	C A P	Feb. 19, 1929	P I S	Apr. 20, 1932	T A U
Nov. 23, 1922	S A G	Jan. 20, 1926	A Q U	Mar. 21, 1929	A R I	May. 21, 1932	G E M
Dec. 22, 1922	C A P	Feb. 19, 1926	P I S	Apr. 20, 1929	T A U	Jun. 21, 1932	C A N
Jan. 21, 1923	A Q U	Mar. 21, 1926	A R I	May. 21, 1929	G E M	Jul. 23, 1932	L E O

Date	Sun	Date	Sun	Date	Sun	Date	Sun
Aug. 23, 1932	V I R	Jul. 23, 1938	L E O	May. 21, 1944	G E M	Apr. 20, 1950	T A U
Sep. 23, 1932	L I B	Aug. 23, 1938	V I R	Jun. 21, 1944	C A N	May. 21, 1950	G E M
Oct. 23, 1932	S C O	Sep. 23, 1938	L I B	Jul. 22, 1944	L E O	Jun. 21, 1950	C A N
Nov. 22, 1932	S A G	Oct. 24, 1938	S C O	Aug. 23, 1944	V I R	Jul. 23, 1950	L E O
Dec. 22, 1932	C A P	Nov. 22, 1938	S A G	Sep. 23, 1944	L I B	Aug. 23, 1950	V I R
Jan. 20, 1933	A Q U	Dec. 22, 1938	C A P	Oct. 23, 1944	S C O	Sep. 23, 1950	L I B
Feb. 19, 1933	P I S	Jan. 20, 1939	A Q U	Nov. 22, 1944	S A G	Oct. 23, 1950	S C O
Mar. 21, 1933	A R I	Feb. 19, 1939	P I S	Dec. 21, 1944	C A P	Nov. 22, 1950	S A G
Apr. 20, 1933	T A U	Mar. 21, 1939	A R I	Jan. 20, 1945	A Q U	Dec. 22, 1950	C A P
May. 21, 1933	G E M	Apr. 20, 1939	T A U	Feb. 19, 1945	P I S	Jan. 20, 1951	A Q U
Jun. 21, 1933	C A N	May. 21, 1939	G E M	Mar. 20, 1945	A R I	Feb. 19, 1951	P I S
Jul. 23, 1933	L E O	Jun. 22, 1939	C A N	Apr. 20, 1945	T A U	Mar. 21, 1951	A R I
Aug. 23, 1933	V I R	Jul. 23, 1939	L E O	May. 21, 1945	G E M	Apr. 20, 1951	T A U
Sep. 23, 1933	L I B	Aug. 24, 1939	V I R	Jun. 21, 1945	C A N	May. 21, 1951	G E M
Oct. 23, 1933	S C O	Sep. 23, 1939	L I B	Jul. 23, 1945	L E O	Jun. 22, 1951	C A N
Nov. 22, 1933	S A G	Oct. 24, 1939	S C O	Aug. 23, 1945	V I R	Jul. 23, 1951	L E O
Dec. 22, 1933	C A P	Nov. 23, 1939	S A G	Sep. 23, 1945	L I B	Aug. 23, 1951	V I R
Jan. 20, 1934	A Q U	Dec. 22, 1939	C A P	Oct. 23, 1945	S C O	Sep. 23, 1951	L I B
Feb. 19, 1934	P I S	Jan. 1, 1940	C A P	Nov. 22, 1945	S A G	Oct. 24, 1951	S C O
Mar. 21, 1934	A R I	Jan. 21, 1940	A Q U	Dec. 22, 1945	C A P	Nov. 23, 1951	S A G
Apr. 20, 1934	T A U	Feb. 19, 1940	P I S	Jan. 20, 1946	A Q U	Dec. 22, 1951	C A P
May. 21, 1934	G E M	Mar. 20, 1940	A R I	Feb. 19, 1946	P I S	Jan. 21, 1952	A Q U
Jun. 22, 1934	C A N	Apr. 20, 1940	T A U	Mar. 21, 1946	A R I	Feb. 19, 1952	P I S
Jul. 23, 1934	L E O	May. 21, 1940	G E M	Apr. 20, 1946	T A U	Mar. 20, 1952	A R I
Aug. 23, 1934	V I R	Jun. 21, 1940	C A N	May. 21, 1946	G E M	Apr. 20, 1952	T A U
Sep. 23, 1934	L I B	Jul. 23, 1940	L E O	Jun. 22, 1946	C A N	May. 21, 1952	G E M
Oct. 24, 1934	S C O	Aug. 23, 1940	V I R	Jul. 23, 1946	L E O	Jun. 21, 1952	C A N
Nov. 22, 1934	S A G	Sep. 23, 1940	L I B	Aug. 23, 1946	V I R	Jul. 22, 1952	L E O
Dec. 22, 1934	C A P	Oct. 23, 1940	S C O	Sep. 23, 1946	L I B	Aug. 23, 1952	V I R
Jan. 20, 1935	A Q U	Nov. 22, 1940	S A G	Oct. 24, 1946	S C O	Sep. 23, 1952	L I B
Feb. 19, 1935	P I S	Dec. 21, 1940	C A P	Nov. 22, 1946	S A G	Oct. 23, 1952	S C O
Mar. 21, 1935	A R I	Jan. 20, 1941	A Q U	Dec. 22, 1946	C A P	Nov. 22, 1952	S A G
Apr. 21, 1935	T A U	Feb. 19, 1941	P I S	Jan. 20, 1947	A Q U	Dec. 21, 1952	C A P
May. 22, 1935	G E M	Mar. 21, 1941	A R I	Feb. 19, 1947	P I S	Jan. 20, 1953	A Q U
Jun. 22, 1935	C A N	Apr. 20, 1941	T A U	Mar. 21, 1947	A R I	Feb. 18, 1953	P I S
Jul. 23, 1935	L E O	May. 21, 1941	G E M	Apr. 20, 1947	T A U	Mar. 20, 1953	A R I
Aug. 24, 1935	V I R	Jun. 21, 1941	C A N	May. 21, 1947	G E M	Apr. 20, 1953	T A U
Sep. 23, 1935	L I B	Jul. 23, 1941	L E O	Jun. 22, 1947	C A N	May. 21, 1953	G E M
Oct. 24, 1935	S C O	Aug. 23, 1941	V I R	Jul. 23, 1947	L E O	Jun. 21, 1953	C A N
Nov. 23, 1935	S A G	Sep. 23, 1941	L I B	Aug. 24, 1947	V I R	Jul. 23, 1953	L E O
Dec. 22, 1935	C A P	Oct. 23, 1941	S C O	Sep. 23, 1947	L I B	Aug. 23, 1953	V I R
Jan. 21, 1936	A Q U	Nov. 22, 1941	S A G	Oct. 24, 1947	S C O	Sep. 23, 1953	L I B
Feb. 19, 1936	P I S	Dec. 22, 1941	C A P	Nov. 23, 1947	S A G	Oct. 23, 1953	S C O
Mar. 20, 1936	A R I	Jan. 20, 1942	A Q U	Dec. 22, 1947	C A P	Nov. 22, 1953	S A G
Apr. 20, 1936	T A U	Feb. 19, 1942	P I S	Jan. 21, 1948	A Q U	Dec. 22, 1953	C A P
May. 21, 1936	G E M	Mar. 21, 1942	A R I	Feb. 19, 1948	P I S	Jan. 20, 1954	A Q U
Jun. 21, 1936	C A N	Apr. 20, 1942	T A U	Mar. 20, 1948	A R I	Feb. 19, 1954	P I S
Jul. 23, 1936	L E O	May. 21, 1942	G E M	Apr. 20, 1948	T A U	Mar. 21, 1954	A R I
Aug. 23, 1936	V I R	Jun. 22, 1942	C A N	May. 21, 1948	G E M	Apr. 20, 1954	T A U
Sep. 23, 1936	L I B	Jul. 23, 1942	L E O	Jun. 21, 1948	C A N	May. 21, 1954	G E M
Oct. 23, 1936	S C O	Aug. 23, 1942	V I R	Jul. 22, 1948	L E O	Jun. 21, 1954	C A N
Nov. 22, 1936	S A G	Sep. 23, 1942	L I B	Aug. 23, 1948	V I R	Jul. 23, 1954	L E O
Dec. 22, 1936	C A P	Oct. 24, 1942	S C O	Sep. 23, 1948	L I B	Aug. 23, 1954	V I R
Jan. 20, 1937	A Q U	Nov. 22, 1942	S A G	Oct. 23, 1948	S C O	Sep. 23, 1954	L I B
Feb. 19, 1937	P I S	Dec. 22, 1942	C A P	Nov. 22, 1948	S A G	Oct. 23, 1954	S C O
Mar. 21, 1937	A R I	Jan. 20, 1943	A Q U	Dec. 21, 1948	C A P	Nov. 22, 1954	S A G
Apr. 20, 1937	T A U	Feb. 19, 1943	P I S	Jan. 20, 1949	A Q U	Dec. 22, 1954	C A P
May. 21, 1937	G E M	Mar. 21, 1943	A R I	Feb. 18, 1949	P I S	Jan. 20, 1955	A Q U
Jun. 21, 1937	C A N	Apr. 20, 1943	T A U	Mar. 20, 1949	A R I	Feb. 19, 1955	P I S
Jul. 23, 1937	L E O	May. 21, 1943	G E M	Apr. 20, 1949	T A U	Mar. 21, 1955	A R I
Aug. 23, 1937	V I R	Jun. 22, 1943	C A N	May. 21, 1949	G E M	Apr. 20, 1955	T A U
Sep. 23, 1937	L I B	Jul. 23, 1943	L E O	Jun. 21, 1949	C A N	May. 21, 1955	G E M
Oct. 23, 1937	S C O	Aug. 24, 1943	V I R	Jul. 23, 1949	L E O	Jun. 22, 1955	C A N
Nov. 22, 1937	S A G	Sep. 23, 1943	L I B	Aug. 23, 1949	V I R	Jul. 23, 1955	L E O
Dec. 22, 1937	C A P	Oct. 24, 1943	S C O	Sep. 23, 1949	L I B	Aug. 23, 1955	V I R
Jan. 20, 1938	A Q U	Nov. 23, 1943	S A G	Oct. 23, 1949	S C O	Sep. 23, 1955	L I B
Feb. 19, 1938	P I S	Dec. 22, 1943	C A P	Nov. 22, 1949	S A G	Oct. 24, 1955	S C O
Mar. 21, 1938	A R I	Jan. 21, 1944	A Q U	Dec. 22, 1949	C A P	Nov. 23, 1955	S A G
Apr. 20, 1938	T A U	Feb. 19, 1944	P I S	Jan. 20, 1950	A Q U	Dec. 22, 1955	C A P
May. 21, 1938	G E M	Mar. 20, 1944	A R I	Feb. 19, 1950	P I S	Jan. 21, 1956	A Q U
Jun. 22, 1938	C A N	Apr. 20, 1944	T A U	Mar. 21, 1950	A R I	Feb. 19, 1956	P I S

Date	Sun	Date	Sun	Date	Sun	Date	Sun
Mar. 20, 1956	A R I	Feb. 19, 1962	P I S	Jan. 20, 1968	A Q U	Dec. 22, 1973	C A P
Apr. 20, 1956	T A U	Mar. 21, 1962	A R I	Feb. 19, 1968	P I S	Jan. 20, 1974	A Q U
May. 21, 1956	G E M	Apr. 20, 1962	T A U	Mar. 20, 1968	A R I	Feb. 19, 1974	P I S
Jun. 21, 1956	C A N	May. 21, 1962	G E M	Apr. 20, 1968	T A U	Mar. 21, 1974	A R I
Jul. 22, 1956	L E O	Jun. 21, 1962	C A N	May. 21, 1968	G E M	Apr. 20, 1974	T A U
Aug. 23, 1956	V I R	Jul. 23, 1962	L E O	Jun. 21, 1968	C A N	May. 21, 1974	G E M
Sep. 23, 1956	L I B	Aug. 23, 1962	V I R	Jul. 22, 1968	L E O	Jun. 21, 1974	C A N
Oct. 23, 1956	S C O	Sep. 23, 1962	L I B	Aug. 23, 1968	V I R	Jul. 23, 1974	L E O
Nov. 22, 1956	S A G	Oct. 23, 1962	S C O	Sep. 22, 1968	L I B	Aug. 23, 1974	V I R
Dec. 21, 1956	C A P	Nov. 22, 1962	S A G	Oct. 23, 1968	S C O	Sep. 23, 1974	L I B
Jan. 20, 1957	A Q U	Dec. 22, 1962	C A P	Nov. 22, 1968	S A G	Oct. 23, 1974	S C O
Feb. 18, 1957	P I S	Jan. 20, 1963	A Q U	Dec. 21, 1968	C A P	Nov. 22, 1974	S A G
Mar. 20, 1957	A R I	Feb. 19, 1963	P I S	Jan. 20, 1969	A Q U	Dec. 22, 1974	C A P
Apr. 20, 1957	T A U	Mar. 21, 1963	A R I	Feb. 18, 1969	P I S	Jan. 20, 1975	A Q U
May. 21, 1957	G E M	Apr. 20, 1963	T A U	Mar. 20, 1969	A R I	Feb. 19, 1975	P I S
Jun. 21, 1957	C A N	May. 21, 1963	G E M	Apr. 20, 1969	T A U	Mar. 21, 1975	A R I
Jul. 23, 1957	L E O	Jun. 22, 1963	C A N	May. 21, 1969	G E M	Apr. 20, 1975	T A U
Aug. 23, 1957	V I R	Jul. 23, 1963	L E O	Jun. 21, 1969	C A N	May. 21, 1975	G E M
Sep. 23, 1957	L I B	Aug. 23, 1963	V I R	Jul. 23, 1969	L E O	Jun. 22, 1975	C A N
Oct. 23, 1957	S C O	Sep. 23, 1963	L I B	Aug. 23, 1969	V I R	Jul. 23, 1975	L E O
Nov. 22, 1957	S A G	Oct. 24, 1963	S C O	Sep. 23, 1969	L I B	Aug. 23, 1975	V I R
Dec. 22, 1957	C A P	Nov. 23, 1963	S A G	Oct. 23, 1969	S C O	Sep. 23, 1975	L I B
Jan. 20, 1958	A Q U	Dec. 22, 1963	C A P	Nov. 22, 1969	S A G	Oct. 24, 1975	S C O
Feb. 19, 1958	P I S	Jan. 21, 1964	A Q U	Dec. 22, 1969	C A P	Nov. 22, 1975	S A G
Mar. 21, 1958	A R I	Feb. 19, 1964	P I S	Jan. 20, 1970	A Q U	Dec. 22, 1975	C A P
Apr. 20, 1958	T A U	Mar. 20, 1964	A R I	Feb. 19, 1970	P I S	Jan. 20, 1976	A Q U
May. 21, 1958	G E M	Apr. 20, 1964	T A U	Mar. 21, 1970	A R I	Feb. 19, 1976	P I S
Jun. 21, 1958	C A N	May. 21, 1964	G E M	Apr. 20, 1970	T A U	Mar. 20, 1976	A R I
Jul. 23, 1958	L E O	Jun. 21, 1964	C A N	May. 21, 1970	G E M	Apr. 19, 1976	T A U
Aug. 23, 1958	V I R	Jul. 22, 1964	L E O	Jun. 21, 1970	C A N	May. 20, 1976	G E M
Sep. 23, 1958	L I B	Aug. 23, 1964	V I R	Jul. 23, 1970	L E O	Jun. 21, 1976	C A N
Oct. 23, 1958	S C O	Sep. 23, 1964	L I B	Aug. 23, 1970	V I R	Jul. 22, 1976	L E O
Nov. 22, 1958	S A G	Oct. 23, 1964	S C O	Sep. 23, 1970	L I B	Aug. 23, 1976	V I R
Dec. 22, 1958	C A P	Nov. 22, 1964	S A G	Oct. 23, 1970	S C O	Sep. 22, 1976	L I B
Jan. 20, 1959	A Q U	Dec. 21, 1964	C A P	Nov. 22, 1970	S A G	Oct. 23, 1976	S C O
Feb. 19, 1959	P I S	Jan. 20, 1965	A Q U	Dec. 22, 1970	C A P	Nov. 22, 1976	S A G
Mar. 21, 1959	A R I	Feb. 18, 1965	P I S	Jan. 20, 1971	A Q U	Dec. 21, 1976	C A P
Apr. 20, 1959	T A U	Mar. 20, 1965	A R I	Feb. 19, 1971	P I S	Jan. 20, 1977	A Q U
May. 21, 1959	G E M	Apr. 20, 1965	T A U	Mar. 21, 1971	A R I	Feb. 18, 1977	P I S
Jun. 22, 1959	C A N	May. 21, 1965	G E M	Apr. 20, 1971	T A U	Mar. 20, 1977	A R I
Jul. 23, 1959	L E O	Jun. 21, 1965	C A N	May. 21, 1971	G E M	Apr. 20, 1977	T A U
Aug. 23, 1959	V I R	Jul. 23, 1965	L E O	Jun. 22, 1971	C A N	May. 21, 1977	G E M
Sep. 23, 1959	L I B	Aug. 23, 1965	V I R	Jul. 23, 1971	L E O	Jun. 21, 1977	C A N
Oct. 24, 1959	S C O	Sep. 23, 1965	L I B	Aug. 23, 1971	V I R	Jul. 22, 1977	L E O
Nov. 23, 1959	S A G	Oct. 23, 1965	S C O	Sep. 23, 1971	L I B	Aug. 23, 1977	V I R
Dec. 22, 1959	C A P	Nov. 22, 1965	S A G	Oct. 24, 1971	S C O	Sep. 23, 1977	L I B
Jan. 21, 1960	A Q U	Dec. 22, 1965	C A P	Nov. 22, 1971	S A G	Oct. 23, 1977	S C O
Feb. 19, 1960	P I S	Jan. 20, 1966	A Q U	Dec. 22, 1971	C A P	Nov. 22, 1977	S A G
Mar. 20, 1960	A R I	Feb. 19, 1966	P I S	Jan. 20, 1972	A Q U	Dec. 21, 1977	C A P
Apr. 20, 1960	T A U	Mar. 21, 1966	A R I	Feb. 19, 1972	P I S	Jan. 20, 1978	A Q U
May. 21, 1960	G E M	Apr. 20, 1966	T A U	Mar. 20, 1972	A R I	Feb. 19, 1978	P I S
Jun. 21, 1960	C A N	May. 21, 1966	G E M	Apr. 19, 1972	T A U	Mar. 20, 1978	A R I
Jul. 22, 1960	L E O	Jun. 21, 1966	C A N	May. 20, 1972	G E M	Apr. 20, 1978	T A U
Aug. 23, 1960	V I R	Jul. 23, 1966	L E O	Jun. 21, 1972	C A N	May. 21, 1978	G E M
Sep. 23, 1960	L I B	Aug. 23, 1966	V I R	Jul. 22, 1972	L E O	Jun. 21, 1978	C A N
Oct. 23, 1960	S C O	Sep. 23, 1966	L I B	Aug. 23, 1972	V I R	Jul. 23, 1978	L E O
Nov. 22, 1960	S A G	Oct. 23, 1966	S C O	Sep. 22, 1972	L I B	Aug. 23, 1978	V I R
Dec. 21, 1960	C A P	Nov. 22, 1966	S A G	Oct. 23, 1972	S C O	Sep. 23, 1978	L I B
Jan. 20, 1961	A Q U	Dec. 22, 1966	C A P	Nov. 22, 1972	S A G	Oct. 23, 1978	S C O
Feb. 18, 1961	P I S	Jan. 20, 1967	A Q U	Dec. 21, 1972	C A P	Nov. 22, 1978	S A G
Mar. 20, 1961	A R I	Feb. 19, 1967	P I S	Jan. 20, 1973	A Q U	Dec. 22, 1978	C A P
Apr. 20, 1961	T A U	Mar. 21, 1967	A R I	Feb. 18, 1973	P I S	Jan. 20, 1979	A Q U
May. 21, 1961	G E M	Apr. 20, 1967	T A U	Mar. 20, 1973	A R I	Feb. 19, 1979	P I S
Jun. 21, 1961	C A N	May. 21, 1967	G E M	Apr. 20, 1973	T A U	Mar. 21, 1979	A R I
Jul. 23, 1961	L E O	Jun. 22, 1967	C A N	May. 21, 1973	G E M	Apr. 20, 1979	T A U
Aug. 23, 1961	V I R	Jul. 23, 1967	L E O	Jun. 21, 1973	C A N	May. 21, 1979	G E M
Sep. 23, 1961	L I B	Aug. 23, 1967	V I R	Jul. 22, 1973	L E O	Jun. 21, 1979	C A N
Oct. 23, 1961	S C O	Sep. 23, 1967	L I B	Aug. 23, 1973	V I R	Jul. 23, 1979	L E O
Nov. 22, 1961	S A G	Oct. 24, 1967	S C O	Sep. 23, 1973	L I B	Aug. 23, 1979	V I R
Dec. 22, 1961	C A P	Nov. 23, 1967	S A G	Oct. 23, 1973	S C O	Sep. 23, 1979	L I B
Jan. 20, 1962	A Q U	Dec. 22, 1967	C A P	Nov. 22, 1973	S A G	Oct. 24, 1979	S C O

Date	Sun	Date	Sun	Date	Sun	Date	Sun
Nov. 22, 1979	S A G	Oct. 23, 1985	S C O	Sep. 23, 1991	L I B	Aug. 23, 1997	V I R
Dec. 22, 1979	C A P	Nov. 22, 1985	S A G	Oct. 23, 1991	S C O	Sep. 22, 1997	L I B
Jan. 20, 1980	A Q U	Dec. 21, 1985	C A P	Nov. 22, 1991	S A G	Oct. 23, 1997	S C O
Feb. 19, 1980	P I S	Jan. 20, 1986	A Q U	Dec. 22, 1991	C A P	Nov. 22, 1997	S A G
Mar. 20, 1980	A R I	Feb. 18, 1986	P I S	Jan. 20, 1992	A Q U	Dec. 21, 1997	C A P
Apr. 19, 1980	T A U	Mar. 20, 1986	A R I	Feb. 19, 1992	P I S	Jan. 20, 1998	A Q U
May. 20, 1980	G E M	Apr. 20, 1986	T A U	Mar. 20, 1992	A R I	Feb. 18, 1998	P I S
Jun. 21, 1980	C A N	May. 21, 1986	G E M	Apr. 19, 1992	T A U	Mar. 20, 1998	A R I
Jul. 22, 1980	L E O	Jun. 21, 1986	C A N	May. 20, 1992	G E M	Apr. 20, 1998	T A U
Aug. 22, 1980	V I R	Jul. 23, 1986	L E O	Jun. 21, 1992	C A N	May. 21, 1998	G E M
Sep. 22, 1980	L I B	Aug. 23, 1986	V I R	Jul. 22, 1992	L E O	Jun. 21, 1998	C A N
Oct. 23, 1980	S C O	Sep. 23, 1986	L I B	Aug. 22, 1992	V I R	Jul. 23, 1998	L E O
Nov. 22, 1980	S A G	Oct. 23, 1986	S C O	Sep. 22, 1992	L I B	Aug. 23, 1998	V I R
Dec. 21, 1980	C A P	Nov. 22, 1986	S A G	Oct. 23, 1992	S C O	Sep. 23, 1998	L I B
Jan. 20, 1981	A Q U	Dec. 22, 1986	C A P	Nov. 22, 1992	S A G	Oct. 23, 1998	S C O
Feb. 18, 1981	P I S	Jan. 20, 1987	A Q U	Dec. 21, 1992	C A P	Nov. 22, 1998	S A G
Mar. 20, 1981	A R I	Feb. 19, 1987	P I S	Jan. 20, 1993	A Q U	Dec. 22, 1998	C A P
Apr. 20, 1981	T A U	Mar. 21, 1987	A R I	Feb. 18, 1993	P I S	Jan. 20, 1999	A Q U
May. 21, 1981	G E M	Apr. 20, 1987	T A U	Mar. 20, 1993	A R I	Feb. 19, 1999	P I S
Jun. 21, 1981	C A N	May. 21, 1987	G E M	Apr. 20, 1993	T A U	Mar. 21, 1999	A R I
Jul. 22, 1981	L E O	Jun. 21, 1987	C A N	May. 21, 1993	G E M	Apr. 20, 1999	T A U
Aug. 23, 1981	V I R	Jul. 23, 1987	L E O	Jun. 21, 1993	C A N	May. 21, 1999	G E M
Sep. 23, 1981	L I B	Aug. 23, 1987	V I R	Jul. 22, 1993	L E O	Jun. 21, 1999	C A N
Oct. 23, 1981	S C O	Sep. 23, 1987	L I B	Aug. 23, 1993	V I R	Jul. 23, 1999	L E O
Nov. 22, 1981	S A G	Oct. 23, 1987	S C O	Sep. 23, 1993	L I B	Aug. 23, 1999	V I R
Dec. 21, 1981	C A P	Nov. 22, 1987	S A G	Oct. 23, 1993	S C O	Sep. 23, 1999	L I B
Jan. 20, 1982	A Q U	Dec. 22, 1987	C A P	Nov. 22, 1993	S A G	Oct. 23, 1999	S C O
Feb. 18, 1982	P I S	Jan. 20, 1988	A Q U	Dec. 21, 1993	C A P	Nov. 22, 1999	S A G
Mar. 20, 1982	A R I	Feb. 19, 1988	P I S	Jan. 20, 1994	A Q U	Dec. 22, 1999	C A P
Apr. 20, 1982	T A U	Mar. 20, 1988	A R I	Feb. 18, 1994	P I S	Jan. 20, 2000	A Q U
May. 21, 1982	G E M	Apr. 19, 1988	T A U	Mar. 20, 1994	A R I	Feb. 19, 2000	P I S
Jun. 21, 1982	C A N	May. 20, 1988	G E M	Apr. 20, 1994	T A U	Mar. 20, 2000	A R I
Jul. 23, 1982	L E O	Jun. 21, 1988	C A N	May. 21, 1994	G E M	Apr. 19, 2000	T A U
Aug. 23, 1982	V I R	Jul. 22, 1988	L E O	Jun. 21, 1994	C A N	May. 20, 2000	G E M
Sep. 23, 1982	L I B	Aug. 22, 1988	V I R	Jul. 23, 1994	L E O	Jun. 21, 2000	C A N
Oct. 23, 1982	S C O	Sep. 22, 1988	L I B	Aug. 23, 1994	V I R	Jul. 22, 2000	L E O
Nov. 22, 1982	S A G	Oct. 23, 1988	S C O	Sep. 23, 1994	L I B	Aug. 22, 2000	V I R
Dec. 22, 1982	C A P	Nov. 22, 1988	S A G	Oct. 23, 1994	S C O	Sep. 22, 2000	L I B
Jan. 20, 1983	A Q U	Dec. 21, 1988	C A P	Nov. 22, 1994	S A G	Oct. 23, 2000	S C O
Feb. 19, 1983	P I S	Jan. 20, 1989	A Q U	Dec. 22, 1994	C A P	Nov. 22, 2000	S A G
Mar. 21, 1983	A R I	Feb. 18, 1989	P I S	Jan. 20, 1995	A Q U	Dec. 21, 2000	C A P
Apr. 20, 1983	T A U	Mar. 20, 1989	A R I	Feb. 19, 1995	P I S	Jan. 20, 2001	A Q U
May. 21, 1983	G E M	Apr. 20, 1989	T A U	Mar. 21, 1995	A R I	Feb. 18, 2001	P I S
Jun. 21, 1983	C A N	May. 21, 1989	G E M	Apr. 20, 1995	T A U	Mar. 20, 2001	A R I
Jul. 23, 1983	L E O	Jun. 21, 1989	C A N	May. 21, 1995	G E M	Apr. 20, 2001	T A U
Aug. 23, 1983	V I R	Jul. 22, 1989	L E O	Jun. 21, 1995	C A N	May. 20, 2001	G E M
Sep. 23, 1983	L I B	Aug. 23, 1989	V I R	Jul. 23, 1995	L E O	Jun. 21, 2001	C A N
Oct. 23, 1983	S C O	Sep. 23, 1989	L I B	Aug. 23, 1995	V I R	Jul. 22, 2001	L E O
Nov. 22, 1983	S A G	Oct. 23, 1989	S C O	Sep. 23, 1995	L I B	Aug. 23, 2001	V I R
Dec. 22, 1983	C A P	Nov. 22, 1989	S A G	Oct. 23, 1995	S C O	Sep. 22, 2001	L I B
Jan. 20, 1984	A Q U	Dec. 21, 1989	C A P	Nov. 22, 1995	S A G	Oct. 23, 2001	S C O
Feb. 19, 1984	P I S	Jan. 20, 1990	A Q U	Dec. 22, 1995	C A P	Nov. 22, 2001	S A G
Mar. 20, 1984	A R I	Feb. 18, 1990	P I S	Jan. 20, 1996	A Q U	Dec. 21, 2001	C A P
Apr. 19, 1984	T A U	Mar. 20, 1990	A R I	Feb. 19, 1996	P I S	Jan. 20, 2002	A Q U
May. 20, 1984	G E M	Apr. 20, 1990	T A U	Mar. 20, 1996	A R I	Feb. 18, 2002	P I S
Jun. 21, 1984	C A N	May. 21, 1990	G E M	Apr. 19, 1996	T A U	Mar. 20, 2002	A R I
Jul. 22, 1984	L E O	Jun. 21, 1990	C A N	May. 20, 1996	G E M	Apr. 20, 2002	T A U
Aug. 22, 1984	V I R	Jul. 23, 1990	L E O	Jun. 21, 1996	C A N	May. 21, 2002	G E M
Sep. 22, 1984	L I B	Aug. 23, 1990	V I R	Jul. 22, 1996	L E O	Jun. 21, 2002	C A N
Oct. 23, 1984	S C O	Sep. 23, 1990	L I B	Aug. 22, 1996	V I R	Jul. 23, 2002	L E O
Nov. 22, 1984	S A G	Oct. 23, 1990	S C O	Sep. 22, 1996	L I B	Aug. 23, 2002	V I R
Dec. 21, 1984	C A P	Nov. 22, 1990	S A G	Oct. 23, 1996	S C O	Sep. 23, 2002	L I B
Jan. 20, 1985	A Q U	Dec. 22, 1990	C A P	Nov. 22, 1996	S A G	Oct. 23, 2002	S C O
Feb. 18, 1985	P I S	Jan. 20, 1991	A Q U	Dec. 21, 1996	C A P	Nov. 22, 2002	S A G
Mar. 20, 1985	A R I	Feb. 19, 1991	P I S	Jan. 20, 1997	A Q U	Dec. 22, 2002	C A P
Apr. 20, 1985	T A U	Mar. 21, 1991	A R I	Feb. 18, 1997	P I S	Jan. 20, 2003	A Q U
May. 21, 1985	G E M	Apr. 20, 1991	T A U	Mar. 20, 1997	A R I	Feb. 19, 2003	P I S
Jun. 21, 1985	C A N	May. 21, 1991	G E M	Apr. 20, 1997	T A U	Mar. 21, 2003	A R I
Jul. 22, 1985	L E O	Jun. 21, 1991	C A N	May. 21, 1997	G E M	Apr. 20, 2003	T A U
Aug. 23, 1985	V I R	Jul. 23, 1991	L E O	Jun. 21, 1997	C A N	May. 21, 2003	G E M
Sep. 23, 1985	L I B	Aug. 23, 1991	V I R	Jul. 22, 1997	L E O	Jun. 21, 2003	C A N

113

Date	Sun	Date	Sun	Date	Sun	Date	Sun
Jul. 23, 2003	LEO	Mar. 20, 2009	ARI	Nov. 22, 2014	SAG	Jul. 22, 2020	LEO
Aug. 23, 2003	VIR	Apr. 19, 2009	TAU	Dec. 21, 2014	CAP	Aug. 22, 2020	VIR
Sep. 23, 2003	LIB	May. 20, 2009	GEM	Jan. 20, 2015	AQU	Sep. 22, 2020	LIB
Oct. 23, 2003	SCO	Jun. 21, 2009	CAN	Feb. 18, 2015	PIS	Oct. 22, 2020	SCO
Nov. 22, 2003	SAG	Jul. 22, 2009	LEO	Mar. 20, 2015	ARI	Nov. 21, 2020	SAG
Dec. 22, 2003	CAP	Aug. 22, 2009	VIR	Apr. 20, 2015	TAU	Dec. 21, 2020	CAP
Jan. 20, 2004	AQU	Sep. 22, 2009	LIB	May. 21, 2015	GEM	Jan. 19, 2021	AQU
Feb. 19, 2004	PIS	Oct. 23, 2009	SCO	Jun. 21, 2015	CAN	Feb. 18, 2021	PIS
Mar. 20, 2004	ARI	Nov. 22, 2009	SAG	Jul. 23, 2015	LEO	Mar. 20, 2021	ARI
Apr. 19, 2004	TAU	Dec. 21, 2009	CAP	Aug. 23, 2015	VIR	Apr. 19, 2021	TAU
May. 20, 2004	GEM	Jan. 20, 2010	AQU	Sep. 23, 2015	LIB	May. 20, 2021	GEM
Jun. 21, 2004	CAN	Feb. 18, 2010	PIS	Oct. 23, 2015	SCO	Jun. 21, 2021	CAN
Jul. 22, 2004	LEO	Mar. 20, 2010	ARI	Nov. 22, 2015	SAG	Jul. 22, 2021	LEO
Aug. 22, 2004	VIR	Apr. 20, 2010	TAU	Dec. 22, 2015	CAP	Aug. 22, 2021	VIR
Sep. 22, 2004	LIB	May. 21, 2010	GEM	Jan. 20, 2016	AQU	Sep. 22, 2021	LIB
Oct. 23, 2004	SCO	Jun. 21, 2010	CAN	Feb. 19, 2016	PIS	Oct. 23, 2021	SCO
Nov. 21, 2004	SAG	Jul. 22, 2010	LEO	Mar. 20, 2016	ARI	Nov. 22, 2021	SAG
Dec. 21, 2004	CAP	Aug. 23, 2010	VIR	Apr. 19, 2016	TAU	Dec. 21, 2021	CAP
Jan. 19, 2005	AQU	Sep. 23, 2010	LIB	May. 20, 2016	GEM	Jan. 20, 2022	AQU
Feb. 18, 2005	PIS	Oct. 23, 2010	SCO	Jun. 20, 2016	CAN	Feb. 18, 2022	PIS
Mar. 20, 2005	ARI	Nov. 22, 2010	SAG	Jul. 22, 2016	LEO	Mar. 20, 2022	ARI
Apr. 19, 2005	TAU	Dec. 21, 2010	CAP	Aug. 22, 2016	VIR	Apr. 20, 2022	TAU
May. 20, 2005	GEM	Jan. 20, 2011	AQU	Sep. 22, 2016	LIB	May. 21, 2022	GEM
Jun. 21, 2005	CAN	Feb. 19, 2011	PIS	Oct. 22, 2016	SCO	Jun. 21, 2022	CAN
Jul. 22, 2005	LEO	Mar. 20, 2011	ARI	Nov. 21, 2016	SAG	Jul. 22, 2022	LEO
Aug. 23, 2005	VIR	Apr. 20, 2011	TAU	Dec. 21, 2016	CAP	Aug. 23, 2022	VIR
Sep. 22, 2005	LIB	May. 21, 2011	GEM	Jan. 19, 2017	AQU	Sep. 23, 2022	LIB
Oct. 23, 2005	SCO	Jun. 21, 2011	CAN	Feb. 18, 2017	PIS	Oct. 23, 2022	SCO
Nov. 22, 2005	SAG	Jul. 23, 2011	LEO	Mar. 20, 2017	ARI	Nov. 22, 2022	SAG
Dec. 21, 2005	CAP	Aug. 23, 2011	VIR	Apr. 19, 2017	TAU	Dec. 21, 2022	CAP
Jan. 20, 2006	AQU	Sep. 23, 2011	LIB	May. 20, 2017	GEM	Jan. 20, 2023	AQU
Feb. 18, 2006	PIS	Oct. 23, 2011	SCO	Jun. 21, 2017	CAN	Feb. 18, 2023	PIS
Mar. 20, 2006	ARI	Nov. 22, 2011	SAG	Jul. 22, 2017	LEO	Mar. 20, 2023	ARI
Apr. 20, 2006	TAU	Dec. 22, 2011	CAP	Aug. 22, 2017	VIR	Apr. 20, 2023	TAU
May. 21, 2006	GEM	Jan. 20, 2012	AQU	Sep. 22, 2017	LIB	May. 21, 2023	GEM
Jun. 21, 2006	CAN	Feb. 19, 2012	PIS	Oct. 23, 2017	SCO	Jun. 21, 2023	CAN
Jul. 22, 2006	LEO	Mar. 20, 2012	ARI	Nov. 22, 2017	SAG	Jul. 23, 2023	LEO
Aug. 23, 2006	VIR	Apr. 19, 2012	TAU	Dec. 21, 2017	CAP	Aug. 23, 2023	VIR
Sep. 23, 2006	LIB	May. 20, 2012	GEM	Jan. 20, 2018	AQU	Sep. 23, 2023	LIB
Oct. 23, 2006	SCO	Jun. 20, 2012	CAN	Feb. 18, 2018	PIS	Oct. 23, 2023	SCO
Nov. 22, 2006	SAG	Jul. 22, 2012	LEO	Mar. 20, 2018	ARI	Nov. 22, 2023	SAG
Dec. 22, 2006	CAP	Aug. 22, 2012	VIR	Apr. 20, 2018	TAU	Dec. 22, 2023	CAP
Jan. 20, 2007	AQU	Sep. 22, 2012	LIB	May. 21, 2018	GEM	Jan. 20, 2024	AQU
Feb. 19, 2007	PIS	Oct. 23, 2012	SCO	Jun. 21, 2018	CAN	Feb. 19, 2024	PIS
Mar. 21, 2007	ARI	Nov. 21, 2012	SAG	Jul. 22, 2018	LEO	Mar. 20, 2024	ARI
Apr. 20, 2007	TAU	Dec. 21, 2012	CAP	Aug. 23, 2018	VIR	Apr. 19, 2024	TAU
May. 21, 2007	GEM	Jan. 19, 2013	AQU	Sep. 23, 2018	LIB	May. 20, 2024	GEM
Jun. 21, 2007	CAN	Feb. 18, 2013	PIS	Oct. 23, 2018	SCO	Jun. 20, 2024	CAN
Jul. 23, 2007	LEO	Mar. 20, 2013	ARI	Nov. 22, 2018	SAG	Jul. 22, 2024	LEO
Aug. 23, 2007	VIR	Apr. 19, 2013	TAU	Dec. 21, 2018	CAP	Aug. 22, 2024	VIR
Sep. 23, 2007	LIB	May. 20, 2013	GEM	Jan. 20, 2019	AQU	Sep. 22, 2024	LIB
Oct. 23, 2007	SCO	Jun. 21, 2013	CAN	Feb. 18, 2019	PIS	Oct. 22, 2024	SCO
Nov. 22, 2007	SAG	Jul. 22, 2013	LEO	Mar. 20, 2019	ARI	Nov. 21, 2024	SAG
Dec. 22, 2007	CAP	Aug. 22, 2013	VIR	Apr. 20, 2019	TAU	Dec. 21, 2024	CAP
Jan. 20, 2008	AQU	Sep. 22, 2013	LIB	May. 21, 2019	GEM	Jan. 19, 2025	AQU
Feb. 19, 2008	PIS	Oct. 23, 2013	SCO	Jun. 21, 2019	CAN	Feb. 18, 2025	PIS
Mar. 20, 2008	ARI	Nov. 22, 2013	SAG	Jul. 23, 2019	LEO	Mar. 20, 2025	ARI
Apr. 19, 2008	TAU	Dec. 21, 2013	CAP	Aug. 23, 2019	VIR	Apr. 19, 2025	TAU
May. 20, 2008	GEM	Jan. 20, 2014	AQU	Sep. 23, 2019	LIB	May. 20, 2025	GEM
Jun. 21, 2008	CAN	Feb. 18, 2014	PIS	Oct. 23, 2019	SCO	Jun. 21, 2025	CAN
Jul. 22, 2008	LEO	Mar. 20, 2014	ARI	Nov. 22, 2019	SAG	Jul. 22, 2025	LEO
Aug. 22, 2008	VIR	Apr. 20, 2014	TAU	Dec. 22, 2019	CAP	Aug. 22, 2025	VIR
Sep. 22, 2008	LIB	May. 21, 2014	GEM	Jan. 20, 2020	AQU	Sep. 22, 2025	LIB
Oct. 23, 2008	SCO	Jun. 21, 2014	CAN	Feb. 19, 2020	PIS	Oct. 23, 2025	SCO
Nov. 21, 2008	SAG	Jul. 22, 2014	LEO	Mar. 20, 2020	ARI	Nov. 22, 2025	SAG
Dec. 21, 2008	CAP	Aug. 23, 2014	VIR	Apr. 19, 2020	TAU	Dec. 21, 2025	CAP
Jan. 19, 2009	AQU	Sep. 23, 2014	LIB	May. 20, 2020	GEM		
Feb. 18, 2009	PIS	Oct. 23, 2014	SCO	Jun. 20, 2020	CAN		

Moon

Date	Time	Moon	Date	Time	Moon	Date	Time	Moon
Jan. 2, 1920	12:00 AM	G E M	Jun. 5, 1920	10:00 PM	A Q U	Nov. 9, 1920	8:00 AM	S C O
Jan. 4, 1920	10:24 PM	C A N	Jun. 8, 1920	7:23 AM	P I S	Nov. 11, 1920	2:46 PM	S A G
Jan. 6, 1920	10:24 PM	L E O	Jun. 10, 1920	4:37 PM	A R I	Nov. 14, 1920	4:00 AM	C A P
Jan. 9, 1920	1:43 AM	V I R	Jun. 12, 1920	8:34 PM	T A U	Nov. 16, 1920	4:00 PM	A Q U
Jan. 11, 1920	7:23 AM	L I B	Jun. 14, 1920	12:00 AM	G E M	Nov. 19, 1920	4:00 AM	P I S
Jan. 13, 1920	6:00 PM	S C O	Jun. 16, 1920	10:24 PM	C A N	Nov. 21, 1920	12:55 PM	A R I
Jan. 16, 1920	6:00 AM	S A G	Jun. 18, 1920	10:24 PM	L E O	Nov. 23, 1920	8:18 PM	T A U
Jan. 18, 1920	8:00 PM	C A P	Jun. 20, 1920	10:24 PM	V I R	Nov. 25, 1920	10:17 PM	G E M
Jan. 21, 1920	5:32 AM	A Q U	Jun. 23, 1920	5:32 AM	L I B	Nov. 27, 1920	8:48 PM	C A N
Jan. 23, 1920	2:46 PM	P I S	Jun. 25, 1920	12:55 PM	S C O	Nov. 29, 1920	8:48 PM	L E O
Jan. 25, 1920	10:09 PM	A R I	Jun. 28, 1920	2:00 AM	S A G	Dec. 1, 1920	12:00 AM	V I R
Jan. 28, 1920	3:26 AM	T A U	Jun. 30, 1920	2:00 PM	C A P	Dec. 4, 1920	5:32 AM	L I B
Jan. 30, 1920	6:51 AM	G E M	Jul. 3, 1920	4:00 AM	A Q U	Dec. 6, 1920	12:55 PM	S C O
Feb. 1, 1920	8:00 AM	C A N	Jul. 5, 1920	12:55 PM	P I S	Dec. 8, 1920	12:00 AM	S A G
Feb. 3, 1920	9:36 AM	L E O	Jul. 10, 1920	5:09 AM	T A U	Dec. 11, 1920	10:00 AM	C A P
Feb. 5, 1920	12:00 PM	V I R	Jul. 12, 1920	8:34 AM	G E M	Dec. 13, 1920	12:00 AM	A Q U
Feb. 7, 1920	6:28 PM	L I B	Jul. 14, 1920	9:36 AM	C A N	Dec. 16, 1920	12:00 PM	P I S
Feb. 10, 1920	1:51 AM	S C O	Jul. 16, 1920	8:00 AM	L E O	Dec. 18, 1920	12:00 AM	A R I
Feb. 12, 1920	2:00 PM	S A G	Jul. 18, 1920	8:00 AM	V I R	Dec. 21, 1920	5:32 AM	T A U
Feb. 15, 1920	4:22 AM	C A P	Jul. 20, 1920	12:00 PM	L I B	Dec. 23, 1920	8:34 AM	G E M
Feb. 17, 1920	12:55 PM	A Q U	Jul. 22, 1920	8:18 PM	S C O	Dec. 25, 1920	8:00 AM	C A N
Feb. 19, 1920	10:09 PM	P I S	Jul. 25, 1920	8:00 AM	S A G	Dec. 27, 1920	6:00 AM	L E O
Feb. 22, 1920	5:32 AM	A R I	Jul. 27, 1920	12:00 AM	C A P	Dec. 29, 1920	8:34 AM	V I R
Feb. 24, 1920	8:34 AM	T A U	Jul. 30, 1920	10:00 AM	A Q U	Dec. 31, 1920	10:17 AM	L I B
Feb. 26, 1920	12:00 PM	G E M	Aug. 1, 1920	6:28 PM	P I S	Jan. 2, 1921	6:28 PM	S C O
Feb. 28, 1920	3:26 PM	C A N	Aug. 4, 1920	6:00 AM	A R I	Jan. 5, 1921	3:42 AM	S A G
Mar. 1, 1920	6:51 PM	L E O	Aug. 6, 1920	12:55 PM	T A U	Jan. 7, 1921	7:38 PM	C A P
Mar. 3, 1920	10:17 PM	V I R	Aug. 8, 1920	3:26 PM	G E M	Jan. 10, 1921	6:00 AM	A Q U
Mar. 6, 1920	3:42 AM	L I B	Aug. 10, 1920	6:51 PM	C A N	Jan. 12, 1921	6:00 PM	P I S
Mar. 8, 1920	12:00 PM	S C O	Aug. 12, 1920	5:36 PM	L E O	Jan. 15, 1921	6:00 AM	A R I
Mar. 10, 1920	10:00 PM	S A G	Aug. 14, 1920	7:12 PM	V I R	Jan. 17, 1921	12:55 PM	T A U
Mar. 13, 1920	1:05 PM	C A P	Aug. 16, 1920	10:17 PM	L I B	Jan. 19, 1921	8:18 PM	G E M
Mar. 15, 1920	12:00 AM	A Q U	Aug. 19, 1920	5:32 AM	S C O	Jan. 21, 1921	7:12 PM	C A N
Mar. 18, 1920	7:23 AM	P I S	Aug. 21, 1920	4:00 AM	S A G	Jan. 23, 1921	7:12 PM	L E O
Mar. 20, 1920	12:00 AM	A R I	Aug. 24, 1920	4:00 AM	C A P	Jan. 25, 1921	4:30 PM	V I R
Mar. 22, 1920	3:26 PM	T A U	Aug. 26, 1920	4:00 AM	A Q U	Jan. 27, 1921	8:34 PM	L I B
Mar. 24, 1920	6:51 PM	G E M	Aug. 29, 1920	4:00 AM	P I S	Jan. 30, 1921	1:51 AM	S C O
Mar. 26, 1920	7:12 PM	C A N	Aug. 31, 1920	11:05 AM	A R I	Feb. 1, 1921	12:00 PM	S A G
Mar. 28, 1920	12:00 AM	L E O	Sep. 2, 1920	6:28 PM	T A U	Feb. 6, 1921	12:00 PM	A Q U
Mar. 31, 1920	5:32 AM	V I R	Sep. 4, 1920	12:00 AM	G E M	Feb. 8, 1921	12:00 AM	P I S
Apr. 2, 1920	11:05 AM	L I B	Sep. 7, 1920	1:43 AM	C A N	Feb. 11, 1921	12:00 PM	A R I
Apr. 4, 1920	6:28 PM	S C O	Sep. 9, 1920	3:26 AM	L E O	Feb. 13, 1921	10:00 PM	T A U
Apr. 7, 1920	6:00 AM	S A G	Sep. 11, 1920	5:09 AM	V I R	Feb. 16, 1921	1:43 AM	G E M
Apr. 9, 1920	9:49 PM	C A P	Sep. 13, 1920	8:34 AM	L I B	Feb. 18, 1921	5:09 AM	C A N
Apr. 12, 1920	8:00 AM	A Q U	Sep. 15, 1920	2:46 PM	S C O	Feb. 20, 1921	4:48 AM	L E O
Apr. 14, 1920	4:37 PM	P I S	Sep. 17, 1920	10:09 PM	S A G	Feb. 22, 1921	4:48 AM	V I R
Apr. 16, 1920	12:00 AM	A R I	Sep. 20, 1920	12:00 PM	C A P	Feb. 24, 1921	6:51 AM	L I B
Apr. 19, 1920	1:43 AM	T A U	Sep. 22, 1920	12:00 AM	A Q U	Feb. 26, 1921	10:17 AM	S C O
Apr. 21, 1920	1:36 AM	G E M	Sep. 25, 1920	12:00 PM	P I S	Feb. 28, 1921	6:28 PM	S A G
Apr. 23, 1920	3:12 AM	C A N	Sep. 27, 1920	6:28 PM	A R I	Mar. 3, 1921	6:00 AM	C A P
Apr. 25, 1920	4:48 AM	L E O	Sep. 29, 1920	10:17 PM	T A U	Mar. 5, 1921	6:00 PM	A Q U
Apr. 27, 1920	11:05 AM	V I R	Oct. 2, 1920	3:26 AM	G E M	Mar. 8, 1921	6:00 AM	P I S
Apr. 29, 1920	4:37 PM	L I B	Oct. 4, 1920	6:51 AM	C A N	Mar. 10, 1921	6:00 PM	A R I
May. 2, 1920	1:51 AM	S C O	Oct. 6, 1920	8:00 AM	L E O	Mar. 13, 1921	1:51 AM	T A U
May. 4, 1920	2:00 PM	S A G	Oct. 8, 1920	12:00 PM	V I R	Mar. 15, 1921	6:51 AM	G E M
May. 7, 1920	2:00 AM	C A P	Oct. 10, 1920	3:26 PM	L I B	Mar. 17, 1921	12:00 PM	C A N
May. 9, 1920	5:27 PM	A Q U	Oct. 12, 1920	12:00 AM	S C O	Mar. 19, 1921	12:48 PM	L E O
May. 12, 1920	2:00 AM	P I S	Oct. 15, 1920	7:23 AM	S A G	Mar. 21, 1921	2:24 PM	V I R
May. 14, 1920	9:14 AM	A R I	Oct. 17, 1920	8:00 AM	C A P	Mar. 23, 1921	5:09 PM	L I B
May. 16, 1920	12:00 AM	T A U	Oct. 20, 1920	8:00 AM	A Q U	Mar. 25, 1921	8:34 PM	S C O
May. 18, 1920	1:43 AM	G E M	Oct. 22, 1920	8:00 PM	P I S	Mar. 28, 1921	3:42 AM	S A G
May. 20, 1920	11:12 AM	C A N	Oct. 25, 1920	3:42 AM	A R I	Mar. 30, 1921	2:00 PM	C A P
May. 22, 1920	1:43 AM	L E O	Oct. 27, 1920	8:34 AM	T A U	Apr. 2, 1921	2:00 AM	A Q U
May. 24, 1920	3:26 PM	V I R	Oct. 29, 1920	12:00 AM	G E M	Apr. 4, 1921	2:00 PM	P I S
May. 26, 1920	8:34 PM	L I B	Oct. 31, 1920	1:43 PM	C A N	Apr. 9, 1921	7:23 AM	T A U
May. 29, 1920	7:23 PM	S C O	Nov. 2, 1920	3:26 PM	L E O	Apr. 11, 1921	12:00 PM	G E M
May. 31, 1920	8:00 PM	S A G	Nov. 4, 1920	5:09 PM	V I R	Apr. 13, 1921	5:09 PM	C A N
Jun. 3, 1920	8:00 AM	C A P	Nov. 6, 1920	10:17 PM	L I B	Apr. 15, 1921	8:34 PM	L E O

115

Date	Time	Moon	Date	Time	Moon	Date	Time	Moon
Apr. 17, 1921	10:17 PM	V I R	Sep. 30, 1921	12:00 AM	L I B	Mar. 12, 1922	1:36 AM	V I R
Apr. 20, 1921	1:43 AM	L I B	Oct. 3, 1921	1:36 AM	SCO	Mar. 15, 1922	12:00 AM	L I B
Apr. 22, 1921	5:09 AM	SCO	Oct. 5, 1921	6:51 AM	SAG	Mar. 16, 1922	1:43 AM	SCO
Apr. 24, 1921	12:55 PM	SAG	Oct. 7, 1921	2:46 PM	CAP	Mar. 18, 1922	5:32 AM	SAG
Apr. 26, 1921	8:18 PM	CAP	Oct. 10, 1921	4:00 AM	AQU	Mar. 20, 1922	11:05 AM	CAP
Apr. 29, 1921	10:00 AM	AQU	Oct. 12, 1921	4:00 PM	P I S	Mar. 22, 1922	8:18 PM	AQU
May. 1, 1921	10:00 PM	P I S	Oct. 15, 1921	4:00 AM	A R I	Mar. 25, 1922	10:00 AM	P I S
May. 4, 1921	10:00 AM	A R I	Oct. 17, 1921	2:00 PM	T A U	Mar. 27, 1922	12:00 AM	A R I
May. 6, 1921	4:37 PM	T A U	Oct. 19, 1921	8:18 PM	GEM	Mar. 30, 1922	12:00 PM	T A U
May. 8, 1921	8:34 PM	GEM	Oct. 22, 1921	1:51 AM	CAN	Apr. 1, 1922	8:18 PM	GEM
May. 10, 1921	12:00 AM	CAN	Oct. 24, 1921	5:09 AM	LEO	Apr. 4, 1922	5:32 AM	CAN
May. 13, 1921	1:43 AM	LEO	Oct. 26, 1921	6:24 AM	V I R	Apr. 6, 1922	8:34 AM	LEO
May. 15, 1921	3:26 AM	V I R	Oct. 28, 1921	10:17 AM	L I B	Apr. 8, 1922	12:00 PM	V I R
May. 17, 1921	6:51 AM	L I B	Oct. 30, 1921	12:00 PM	SCO	Apr. 10, 1922	11:12 AM	L I B
May. 19, 1921	12:00 PM	SCO	Nov. 1, 1921	6:28 PM	SAG	Apr. 12, 1922	11:12 AM	SCO
May. 21, 1921	8:18 PM	SAG	Nov. 3, 1921	12:00 AM	CAP	Apr. 14, 1922	12:48 PM	SAG
May. 24, 1921	5:32 AM	CAP	Nov. 6, 1921	12:00 PM	AQU	Apr. 16, 1922	8:18 PM	CAP
May. 26, 1921	6:00 PM	AQU	Nov. 8, 1921	12:00 AM	P I S	Apr. 19, 1922	6:00 AM	AQU
May. 29, 1921	6:00 AM	P I S	Nov. 11, 1921	12:00 PM	A R I	Apr. 21, 1922	6:00 PM	P I S
May. 31, 1921	6:00 PM	A R I	Nov. 13, 1921	8:18 PM	T A U	Apr. 24, 1922	6:00 AM	A R I
Jun. 3, 1921	1:51 AM	T A U	Nov. 16, 1921	3:42 AM	GEM	Apr. 26, 1922	6:00 PM	T A U
Jun. 5, 1921	6:51 AM	GEM	Nov. 18, 1921	6:51 AM	CAN	Apr. 29, 1922	4:00 AM	GEM
Jun. 7, 1921	8:34 AM	CAN	Nov. 20, 1921	10:17 AM	LEO	May. 1, 1922	11:05 AM	CAN
Jun. 9, 1921	8:00 AM	LEO	Nov. 22, 1921	1:43 PM	V I R	May. 3, 1922	4:37 PM	LEO
Jun. 11, 1921	10:17 AM	V I R	Nov. 24, 1921	5:09 PM	L I B	May. 5, 1922	6:51 PM	V I R
Jun. 13, 1921	12:00 PM	L I B	Nov. 26, 1921	8:34 PM	SCO	May. 7, 1922	7:12 PM	L I B
Jun. 15, 1921	5:09 PM	SCO	Nov. 29, 1921	1:51 AM	SAG	May. 9, 1922	8:48 PM	SCO
Jun. 18, 1921	4:00 AM	SAG	Dec. 1, 1921	9:14 AM	CAP	May. 11, 1922	10:24 PM	SAG
Jun. 20, 1921	2:00 PM	CAP	Dec. 3, 1921	8:00 PM	AQU	May. 14, 1922	5:32 AM	CAP
Jun. 23, 1921	2:00 AM	AQU	Dec. 6, 1921	8:00 AM	P I S	May. 16, 1922	12:55 PM	AQU
Jun. 25, 1921	2:00 PM	P I S	Dec. 8, 1921	8:00 PM	A R I	May. 19, 1922	2:00 AM	P I S
Jun. 28, 1921	2:00 AM	A R I	Dec. 11, 1921	8:00 AM	T A U	May. 21, 1922	2:00 PM	A R I
Jun. 30, 1921	11:05 AM	T A U	Dec. 13, 1921	12:00 PM	GEM	May. 24, 1922	2:00 AM	T A U
Jul. 2, 1921	3:26 PM	GEM	Dec. 15, 1921	5:09 PM	CAN	May. 26, 1922	12:00 PM	GEM
Jul. 4, 1921	6:51 PM	CAN	Dec. 17, 1921	6:51 PM	LEO	May. 28, 1922	3:26 PM	CAN
Jul. 6, 1921	5:36 PM	LEO	Dec. 19, 1921	5:36 PM	V I R	May. 30, 1922	8:34 PM	LEO
Jul. 8, 1921	5:36 PM	V I R	Dec. 21, 1921	10:17 PM	L I B	Jun. 1, 1922	12:00 AM	V I R
Jul. 10, 1921	5:36 PM	L I B	Dec. 24, 1921	1:43 AM	SCO	Jun. 4, 1922	3:26 AM	L I B
Jul. 15, 1921	10:00 AM	SAG	Dec. 26, 1921	9:14 AM	SAG	Jun. 6, 1922	5:09 AM	SCO
Jul. 17, 1921	8:00 PM	CAP	Dec. 28, 1921	4:37 PM	CAP	Jun. 8, 1922	8:34 AM	SAG
Jul. 20, 1921	8:00 AM	AQU	Dec. 31, 1921	4:00 AM	AQU	Jun. 10, 1922	1:43 PM	CAP
Jul. 22, 1921	8:00 PM	P I S	Jan. 2, 1922	4:00 PM	P I S	Jun. 12, 1922	10:09 PM	AQU
Jul. 25, 1921	8:00 AM	A R I	Jan. 5, 1922	4:00 AM	A R I	Jun. 15, 1922	10:00 AM	P I S
Jul. 27, 1921	8:00 PM	T A U	Jan. 7, 1922	4:00 PM	T A U	Jun. 17, 1922	10:00 PM	A R I
Jul. 30, 1921	1:51 AM	GEM	Jan. 9, 1922	12:00 AM	GEM	Jun. 20, 1922	10:00 AM	T A U
Aug. 1, 1921	5:09 AM	CAN	Jan. 12, 1922	3:26 AM	CAN	Jun. 22, 1922	6:28 PM	GEM
Aug. 3, 1921	4:48 AM	LEO	Jan. 14, 1922	3:12 AM	LEO	Jun. 27, 1922	3:26 AM	LEO
Aug. 5, 1921	3:12 AM	V I R	Jan. 16, 1922	3:12 AM	V I R	Jun. 29, 1922	4:48 AM	V I R
Aug. 7, 1921	3:12 AM	L I B	Jan. 18, 1922	5:09 AM	L I B	Jul. 1, 1922	8:34 AM	L I B
Aug. 9, 1921	6:51 AM	SCO	Jan. 20, 1922	6:51 AM	SCO	Jul. 3, 1922	12:00 PM	SCO
Aug. 11, 1921	2:46 PM	SAG	Jan. 22, 1922	2:46 PM	SAG	Jul. 5, 1922	3:26 PM	SAG
Aug. 14, 1921	2:00 AM	CAP	Jan. 24, 1922	10:09 PM	CAP	Jul. 7, 1922	10:09 PM	CAP
Aug. 16, 1921	2:00 PM	AQU	Jan. 27, 1922	10:00 AM	AQU	Jul. 10, 1922	5:32 AM	AQU
Aug. 19, 1921	2:00 AM	P I S	Jan. 29, 1922	10:00 PM	P I S	Jul. 12, 1922	6:00 PM	P I S
Aug. 21, 1921	2:00 PM	A R I	Feb. 1, 1922	1:05 PM	A R I	Jul. 15, 1922	6:00 AM	A R I
Aug. 24, 1921	2:00 AM	T A U	Feb. 3, 1922	12:00 AM	T A U	Jul. 17, 1922	6:00 PM	T A U
Aug. 26, 1921	9:14 AM	GEM	Feb. 6, 1922	10:00 AM	GEM	Jul. 20, 1922	3:42 AM	GEM
Aug. 28, 1921	1:43 PM	CAN	Feb. 8, 1922	2:46 PM	CAN	Jul. 22, 1922	11:05 AM	CAN
Aug. 30, 1921	2:24 PM	LEO	Feb. 10, 1922	2:24 PM	LEO	Jul. 24, 1922	11:12 AM	LEO
Sep. 1, 1921	2:24 PM	V I R	Feb. 12, 1922	2:24 PM	V I R	Jul. 26, 1922	12:48 PM	V I R
Sep. 3, 1921	2:24 PM	L I B	Feb. 14, 1922	12:48 PM	L I B	Jul. 28, 1922	3:26 PM	L I B
Sep. 5, 1921	2:24 PM	SCO	Feb. 16, 1922	3:26 PM	SCO	Jul. 30, 1922	5:09 PM	SCO
Sep. 7, 1921	8:34 PM	SAG	Feb. 18, 1922	6:51 PM	SAG	Aug. 1, 1922	8:34 PM	SAG
Sep. 10, 1921	8:00 AM	CAP	Feb. 21, 1922	6:00 AM	CAP	Aug. 4, 1922	3:42 AM	CAP
Sep. 12, 1921	8:00 PM	AQU	Feb. 23, 1922	4:00 PM	AQU	Aug. 6, 1922	2:00 PM	AQU
Sep. 15, 1921	8:00 AM	P I S	Feb. 26, 1922	4:00 AM	P I S	Aug. 8, 1922	12:00 AM	P I S
Sep. 17, 1921	8:00 PM	A R I	Feb. 28, 1922	6:00 PM	A R I	Aug. 11, 1922	12:00 PM	A R I
Sep. 20, 1921	5:32 AM	T A U	Mar. 3, 1922	6:00 AM	T A U	Aug. 14, 1922	2:00 AM	T A U
Sep. 22, 1921	2:46 PM	GEM	Mar. 5, 1922	2:46 PM	GEM	Aug. 16, 1922	2:00 PM	GEM
Sep. 24, 1921	6:51 PM	CAN	Mar. 7, 1922	8:34 PM	CAN	Aug. 18, 1922	8:18 PM	CAN
Sep. 26, 1921	12:00 AM	LEO	Mar. 10, 1922	1:43 AM	LEO	Aug. 22, 1922	10:24 PM	V I R

Date	Time	Moon	Date	Time	Moon	Date	Time	Moon
Aug. 24, 1922	10:24 PM	L I B	Feb. 2, 1923	12:00 AM	V I R	Jul. 21, 1923	6:51 AM	SCO
Aug. 26, 1922	10:24 PM	SCO	Feb. 7, 1923	1:36 AM	SCO	Jul. 23, 1923	10:17 AM	SAG
Aug. 29, 1922	3:26 AM	SAG	Feb. 9, 1923	5:09 AM	SAG	Jul. 25, 1923	12:00 PM	CAP
Aug. 31, 1922	9:14 AM	CAP	Feb. 11, 1923	10:17 AM	CAP	Jul. 27, 1923	3:26 PM	AQU
Sep. 2, 1922	8:00 PM	AQU	Feb. 13, 1923	6:28 PM	AQU	Jul. 29, 1923	12:00 AM	P I S
Sep. 5, 1922	6:00 AM	P I S	Feb. 16, 1923	4:00 AM	P I S	Aug. 1, 1923	10:00 AM	A R I
Sep. 7, 1922	9:49 PM	A R I	Feb. 18, 1923	4:00 PM	A R I	Aug. 3, 1923	10:00 PM	T A U
Sep. 10, 1922	8:00 AM	T A U	Feb. 21, 1923	4:00 AM	T A U	Aug. 6, 1923	10:00 AM	GEM
Sep. 12, 1922	8:00 PM	GEM	Feb. 23, 1923	4:00 PM	GEM	Aug. 8, 1923	10:00 PM	CAN
Sep. 15, 1922	3:42 AM	CAN	Feb. 26, 1923	1:51 AM	CAN	Aug. 11, 1923	3:42 AM	LEO
Sep. 17, 1922	8:34 AM	LEO	Feb. 28, 1923	6:51 AM	LEO	Aug. 13, 1923	6:51 AM	V I R
Sep. 19, 1922	9:36 AM	V I R	Mar. 2, 1923	10:17 AM	V I R	Aug. 15, 1923	10:17 AM	L I B
Sep. 21, 1922	9:36 AM	L I B	Mar. 4, 1923	9:36 AM	L I B	Aug. 17, 1923	11:12 AM	SCO
Sep. 23, 1922	9:36 AM	SCO	Mar. 6, 1923	9:36 AM	SCO	Aug. 19, 1923	3:26 PM	SAG
Sep. 25, 1922	12:00 PM	SAG	Mar. 8, 1923	12:00 PM	SAG	Aug. 21, 1923	6:51 PM	CAP
Sep. 27, 1922	4:37 PM	CAP	Mar. 10, 1923	3:26 PM	CAP	Aug. 23, 1923	10:17 PM	AQU
Sep. 30, 1922	2:00 AM	AQU	Mar. 12, 1923	12:00 AM	AQU	Aug. 26, 1923	7:23 AM	P I S
Oct. 2, 1922	12:00 PM	P I S	Mar. 15, 1923	10:00 AM	P I S	Aug. 28, 1923	6:00 PM	A R I
Oct. 5, 1922	2:00 AM	A R I	Mar. 17, 1923	10:00 PM	A R I	Aug. 31, 1923	6:00 AM	T A U
Oct. 7, 1922	2:00 AM	T A U	Mar. 20, 1923	10:00 AM	T A U	Sep. 2, 1923	6:00 PM	GEM
Oct. 10, 1922	2:00 AM	GEM	Mar. 22, 1923	12:00 AM	GEM	Sep. 5, 1923	6:00 AM	CAN
Oct. 12, 1922	12:00 PM	CAN	Mar. 25, 1923	9:14 AM	CAN	Sep. 7, 1923	12:55 PM	LEO
Oct. 14, 1922	6:28 PM	LEO	Mar. 27, 1923	6:28 PM	LEO	Sep. 9, 1923	5:09 PM	V I R
Oct. 16, 1922	8:34 PM	V I R	Mar. 29, 1923	8:34 PM	V I R	Sep. 11, 1923	8:34 PM	L I B
Oct. 18, 1922	8:48 PM	L I B	Mar. 31, 1923	8:48 PM	L I B	Sep. 13, 1923	7:12 PM	SCO
Oct. 20, 1922	8:48 PM	SCO	Apr. 2, 1923	8:48 PM	SCO	Sep. 15, 1923	10:17 PM	SAG
Oct. 22, 1922	8:48 PM	SAG	Apr. 4, 1923	8:48 PM	SAG	Sep. 17, 1923	12:00 AM	CAP
Oct. 24, 1922	12:00 AM	CAP	Apr. 6, 1923	8:48 PM	CAP	Sep. 20, 1923	5:32 AM	AQU
Oct. 27, 1922	7:23 AM	AQU	Apr. 9, 1923	5:32 AM	AQU	Sep. 22, 1923	12:55 PM	P I S
Oct. 29, 1922	8:00 PM	P I S	Apr. 11, 1923	4:00 PM	P I S	Sep. 24, 1923	10:09 PM	A R I
Nov. 1, 1922	8:00 AM	A R I	Apr. 14, 1923	4:00 AM	A R I	Sep. 27, 1923	12:00 PM	T A U
Nov. 3, 1922	8:00 PM	T A U	Apr. 16, 1923	4:00 PM	T A U	Sep. 30, 1923	2:11 AM	GEM
Nov. 6, 1922	8:00 AM	GEM	Apr. 19, 1923	6:00 AM	GEM	Oct. 2, 1923	2:00 PM	CAN
Nov. 8, 1922	6:00 PM	CAN	Apr. 21, 1923	2:46 PM	CAN	Oct. 4, 1923	12:00 AM	LEO
Nov. 10, 1922	12:00 AM	LEO	Apr. 23, 1923	12:00 AM	LEO	Oct. 7, 1923	3:26 AM	V I R
Nov. 13, 1922	3:26 AM	V I R	Apr. 26, 1923	5:09 AM	V I R	Oct. 9, 1923	4:48 AM	L I B
Nov. 15, 1922	6:51 AM	L I B	Apr. 28, 1923	8:34 AM	L I B	Oct. 11, 1923	4:48 AM	SCO
Nov. 17, 1922	6:24 AM	SCO	Apr. 30, 1923	8:00 AM	SCO	Oct. 13, 1923	4:48 AM	SAG
Nov. 19, 1922	8:34 AM	SAG	May. 2, 1923	6:24 AM	SAG	Oct. 15, 1923	6:51 AM	CAP
Nov. 21, 1922	10:17 AM	CAP	May. 4, 1923	8:34 AM	CAP	Oct. 17, 1923	10:17 AM	AQU
Nov. 23, 1922	4:37 PM	AQU	May. 6, 1923	12:00 AM	AQU	Oct. 19, 1923	6:28 PM	P I S
Nov. 26, 1922	1:51 AM	P I S	May. 8, 1923	8:18 PM	P I S	Oct. 22, 1923	6:00 AM	A R I
Nov. 28, 1922	5:27 AM	A R I	May. 11, 1923	10:00 AM	A R I	Oct. 24, 1923	6:00 PM	T A U
Dec. 1, 1922	4:00 AM	T A U	May. 13, 1923	10:00 PM	T A U	Oct. 27, 1923	8:00 AM	GEM
Dec. 3, 1922	4:00 PM	GEM	May. 16, 1923	12:00 PM	GEM	Oct. 29, 1923	8:00 PM	CAN
Dec. 5, 1922	10:09 PM	CAN	May. 18, 1923	8:18 PM	CAN	Nov. 1, 1923	5:32 AM	LEO
Dec. 8, 1922	3:26 AM	LEO	May. 21, 1923	8:00 AM	LEO	Nov. 3, 1923	12:55 PM	V I R
Dec. 10, 1922	8:34 AM	V I R	May. 23, 1923	12:00 PM	V I R	Nov. 5, 1923	5:09 PM	L I B
Dec. 12, 1922	12:00 PM	L I B	May. 25, 1923	5:09 PM	L I B	Nov. 7, 1923	4:00 PM	SCO
Dec. 14, 1922	3:26 PM	SCO	May. 27, 1923	6:51 PM	SCO	Nov. 9, 1923	4:00 PM	SAG
Dec. 16, 1922	4:00 PM	SAG	May. 29, 1923	5:36 PM	SAG	Nov. 11, 1923	1:30 PM	CAP
Dec. 18, 1922	8:34 PM	CAP	May. 31, 1923	5:36 PM	CAP	Nov. 13, 1923	6:51 PM	AQU
Dec. 21, 1922	1:51 AM	AQU	Jun. 2, 1923	7:12 PM	AQU	Nov. 16, 1923	1:51 AM	P I S
Dec. 23, 1922	12:00 PM	P I S	Jun. 5, 1923	5:32 AM	P I S	Nov. 18, 1923	12:00 PM	A R I
Dec. 25, 1922	12:00 AM	A R I	Jun. 7, 1923	2:46 PM	A R I	Nov. 20, 1923	12:00 AM	T A U
Dec. 28, 1922	12:00 PM	T A U	Jun. 10, 1923	6:00 AM	T A U	Nov. 23, 1923	2:00 PM	GEM
Dec. 30, 1922	12:00 AM	GEM	Jun. 12, 1923	6:00 PM	GEM	Nov. 26, 1923	2:00 AM	CAN
Jan. 2, 1923	7:23 AM	CAN	Jun. 15, 1923	3:42 AM	CAN	Nov. 28, 1923	11:05 AM	LEO
Jan. 4, 1923	12:55 PM	LEO	Jun. 17, 1923	2:00 PM	LEO	Nov. 30, 1923	8:18 PM	V I R
Jan. 6, 1923	3:26 PM	V I R	Jun. 19, 1923	5:09 PM	V I R	Dec. 3, 1923	1:43 AM	L I B
Jan. 8, 1923	4:00 PM	L I B	Jun. 21, 1923	10:17 PM	L I B	Dec. 5, 1923	3:12 AM	SCO
Jan. 10, 1923	8:34 PM	SCO	Jun. 24, 1923	1:43 AM	SCO	Dec. 7, 1923	3:12 AM	SAG
Jan. 12, 1923	12:00 AM	SAG	Jun. 26, 1923	3:26 AM	SAG	Dec. 9, 1923	1:30 AM	CAP
Jan. 15, 1923	5:32 AM	CAP	Jun. 28, 1923	3:12 AM	CAP	Dec. 11, 1923	3:12 AM	AQU
Jan. 17, 1923	11:05 AM	AQU	Jun. 30, 1923	6:51 AM	AQU	Dec. 13, 1923	8:34 AM	P I S
Jan. 19, 1923	6:28 PM	P I S	Jul. 2, 1923	2:46 PM	P I S	Dec. 15, 1923	8:00 PM	A R I
Jan. 22, 1923	8:00 AM	A R I	Jul. 7, 1923	3:16 PM	T A U	Dec. 18, 1923	8:00 AM	T A U
Jan. 24, 1923	8:00 PM	T A U	Jul. 10, 1923	2:00 AM	GEM	Dec. 20, 1923	8:00 PM	GEM
Jan. 27, 1923	8:00 AM	GEM	Jul. 12, 1923	11:05 AM	CAN	Dec. 23, 1923	8:00 AM	CAN
Jan. 29, 1923	4:37 PM	CAN	Jul. 14, 1923	6:28 PM	LEO	Dec. 25, 1923	4:37 PM	LEO
Jan. 31, 1923	8:34 PM	LEO	Jul. 19, 1923	3:26 AM	L I B	Dec. 28, 1923	1:51 AM	V I R

Date	Time	Moon	Date	Time	Moon	Date	Time	Moon
Dec. 30, 1923	6:51 AM	L I B	Jun. 11, 1924	8:34 AM	L I B	Nov. 19, 1924	12:00 AM	V I R
Jan. 1, 1924	12:00 PM	SCO	Jun. 13, 1924	1:43 PM	SCO	Nov. 22, 1924	7:23 AM	L I B
Jan. 3, 1924	1:43 PM	SAG	Jun. 15, 1924	12:48 PM	SAG	Nov. 24, 1924	12:00 PM	SCO
Jan. 5, 1924	12:48 PM	CAP	Jun. 17, 1924	12:48 PM	CAP	Nov. 26, 1924	11:12 AM	SAG
Jan. 7, 1924	3:26 PM	AQU	Jun. 19, 1924	12:48 PM	AQU	Nov. 28, 1924	11:12 AM	CAP
Jan. 9, 1924	6:51 PM	PIS	Jun. 21, 1924	3:26 PM	PIS	Nov. 30, 1924	11:12 AM	AQU
Jan. 12, 1924	4:00 AM	A R I	Jun. 23, 1924	10:09 PM	A R I	Dec. 2, 1924	1:43 PM	PIS
Jan. 14, 1924	2:00 PM	T A U	Jun. 26, 1924	10:00 AM	T A U	Dec. 4, 1924	6:51 PM	A R I
Jan. 17, 1924	4:00 AM	GEM	Jun. 28, 1924	10:00 PM	GEM	Dec. 7, 1924	5:32 AM	T A U
Jan. 19, 1924	4:00 PM	CAN	Jul. 1, 1924	10:00 AM	CAN	Dec. 9, 1924	6:00 PM	GEM
Jan. 24, 1924	7:23 AM	V I R	Jul. 3, 1924	10:00 PM	LEO	Dec. 12, 1924	6:00 AM	CAN
Jan. 26, 1924	12:00 PM	L I B	Jul. 6, 1924	7:23 AM	V I R	Dec. 14, 1924	6:00 PM	LEO
Jan. 28, 1924	5:09 PM	SCO	Jul. 8, 1924	4:37 PM	L I B	Dec. 17, 1924	8:00 AM	V I R
Jan. 30, 1924	8:34 PM	SAG	Jul. 10, 1924	10:09 PM	SCO	Dec. 19, 1924	6:00 PM	L I B
Feb. 1, 1924	10:17 PM	CAP	Jul. 12, 1924	12:00 AM	SAG	Dec. 21, 1924	8:34 PM	SCO
Feb. 3, 1924	10:24 PM	AQU	Jul. 14, 1924	10:24 PM	CAP	Dec. 23, 1924	12:00 AM	SAG
Feb. 6, 1924	5:32 AM	P I S	Jul. 16, 1924	10:24 PM	AQU	Dec. 25, 1924	10:24 PM	CAP
Feb. 8, 1924	12:55 PM	A R I	Jul. 19, 1924	1:43 PM	P I S	Dec. 27, 1924	10:24 PM	AQU
Feb. 10, 1924	12:00 AM	T A U	Jul. 21, 1924	7:23 AM	A R I	Dec. 29, 1924	12:00 AM	PIS
Feb. 13, 1924	12:00 PM	GEM	Jul. 23, 1924	2:46 PM	T A U	Jan. 1, 1925	3:26 AM	A R I
Feb. 15, 1924	12:00 AM	CAN	Jul. 26, 1924	4:00 AM	GEM	Jan. 3, 1925	11:05 AM	T A U
Feb. 18, 1924	10:00 AM	LEO	Jul. 28, 1924	7:38 PM	CAN	Jan. 5, 1925	12:00 AM	GEM
Feb. 20, 1924	4:37 PM	V I R	Jul. 31, 1924	3:42 AM	LEO	Jan. 8, 1925	12:00 PM	CAN
Feb. 22, 1924	10:09 PM	L I B	Aug. 2, 1924	12:55 PM	V I R	Jan. 11, 1925	2:00 AM	LEO
Feb. 24, 1924	8:48 PM	SCO	Aug. 4, 1924	10:09 PM	L I B	Jan. 13, 1925	2:00 PM	V I R
Feb. 27, 1924	1:43 AM	SAG	Aug. 7, 1924	1:43 AM	SCO	Jan. 15, 1925	12:00 AM	L I B
Feb. 29, 1924	3:26 AM	CAP	Aug. 9, 1924	5:09 AM	SAG	Jan. 18, 1925	5:32 AM	SCO
Mar. 2, 1924	9:14 AM	AQU	Aug. 11, 1924	6:24 AM	CAP	Jan. 20, 1925	8:34 AM	SAG
Mar. 4, 1924	2:46 PM	P I S	Aug. 13, 1924	8:00 AM	AQU	Jan. 22, 1925	9:36 AM	CAP
Mar. 6, 1924	8:18 PM	A R I	Aug. 15, 1924	12:00 PM	P I S	Jan. 24, 1925	9:36 AM	AQU
Mar. 9, 1924	8:00 AM	T A U	Aug. 17, 1924	3:26 PM	A R I	Jan. 26, 1925	9:36 AM	P I S
Mar. 11, 1924	8:00 PM	GEM	Aug. 19, 1924	12:00 AM	T A U	Jan. 28, 1925	12:00 PM	A R I
Mar. 14, 1924	8:00 AM	CAN	Aug. 22, 1924	12:00 AM	GEM	Jan. 30, 1925	8:18 PM	T A U
Mar. 16, 1924	8:00 PM	LEO	Aug. 24, 1924	12:00 AM	CAN	Feb. 2, 1925	6:00 AM	GEM
Mar. 19, 1924	1:51 AM	V I R	Aug. 27, 1924	12:00 PM	LEO	Feb. 4, 1925	6:00 PM	CAN
Mar. 21, 1924	5:09 AM	L I B	Aug. 29, 1924	8:18 PM	V I R	Feb. 7, 1925	8:00 AM	LEO
Mar. 23, 1924	6:51 AM	SCO	Sep. 1, 1924	3:42 AM	L I B	Feb. 9, 1925	8:00 PM	V I R
Mar. 25, 1924	6:24 AM	SAG	Sep. 3, 1924	9:14 AM	SCO	Feb. 12, 1925	3:42 AM	L I B
Mar. 27, 1924	10:17 AM	CAP	Sep. 5, 1924	9:36 AM	SAG	Feb. 14, 1925	11:05 AM	SCO
Mar. 29, 1924	1:43 AM	AQU	Sep. 7, 1924	1:43 PM	CAP	Feb. 16, 1925	3:26 PM	SAG
Mar. 31, 1924	8:18 PM	P I S	Sep. 9, 1924	5:09 PM	AQU	Feb. 18, 1925	6:51 PM	CAP
Apr. 3, 1924	3:42 AM	A R I	Sep. 11, 1924	8:34 PM	P I S	Feb. 20, 1925	8:34 PM	AQU
Apr. 5, 1924	4:00 PM	T A U	Sep. 14, 1924	1:51 AM	A R I	Feb. 22, 1925	7:12 PM	P I S
Apr. 8, 1924	4:00 AM	GEM	Sep. 16, 1924	9:14 AM	T A U	Feb. 24, 1925	12:00 AM	A R I
Apr. 10, 1924	4:00 PM	CAN	Sep. 18, 1924	6:28 PM	GEM	Feb. 27, 1925	5:32 AM	T A U
Apr. 13, 1924	4:00 AM	LEO	Sep. 21, 1924	8:00 AM	CAN	Mar. 1, 1925	12:55 PM	GEM
Apr. 15, 1924	11:05 AM	V I R	Sep. 23, 1924	10:00 PM	LEO	Mar. 4, 1925	2:00 AM	CAN
Apr. 17, 1924	3:26 PM	L I B	Sep. 26, 1924	5:32 AM	V I R	Mar. 6, 1925	5:27 PM	LEO
Apr. 19, 1924	4:00 PM	SCO	Sep. 28, 1924	12:55 PM	L I B	Mar. 9, 1925	1:51 AM	V I R
Apr. 21, 1924	4:00 PM	SAG	Sep. 30, 1924	3:26 PM	SCO	Mar. 11, 1925	11:05 AM	SCO
Apr. 23, 1924	4:00 PM	CAP	Oct. 2, 1924	4:00 PM	SAG	Mar. 13, 1925	3:26 PM	SCO
Apr. 25, 1924	6:51 PM	AQU	Oct. 4, 1924	5:36 PM	CAP	Mar. 15, 1925	8:34 PM	SAG
Apr. 28, 1924	1:51 AM	P I S	Oct. 6, 1924	10:17 PM	AQU	Mar. 17, 1925	12:00 AM	CAP
Apr. 30, 1924	9:14 AM	A R I	Oct. 9, 1924	3:42 AM	P I S	Mar. 20, 1925	3:26 AM	AQU
May. 2, 1924	10:00 PM	T A U	Oct. 11, 1924	9:14 AM	A R I	Mar. 22, 1925	5:09 AM	P I S
May. 5, 1924	10:00 AM	GEM	Oct. 13, 1924	4:37 PM	T A U	Mar. 24, 1925	8:34 AM	A R I
May. 7, 1924	10:00 PM	CAN	Oct. 16, 1924	4:00 AM	GEM	Mar. 26, 1925	2:46 PM	T A U
May. 10, 1924	10:00 AM	LEO	Oct. 18, 1924	4:00 PM	CAN	Mar. 28, 1925	10:09 PM	GEM
May. 12, 1924	10:00 PM	V I R	Oct. 21, 1924	6:00 AM	LEO	Mar. 31, 1925	10:00 AM	CAN
May. 15, 1924	1:43 AM	L I B	Oct. 23, 1924	2:46 PM	V I R	Apr. 5, 1925	12:00 PM	V I R
May. 17, 1924	3:12 AM	SCO	Oct. 25, 1924	10:09 PM	L I B	Apr. 7, 1925	6:28 PM	L I B
May. 19, 1924	1:30 AM	SAG	Oct. 29, 1924	12:00 AM	SCO	Apr. 12, 1925	3:26 AM	SAG
May. 21, 1924	1:36 AM	CAP	Oct. 30, 1924	1:43 AM	SAG	Apr. 14, 1925	5:09 AM	CAP
May. 23, 1924	3:26 AM	AQU	Nov. 1, 1924	1:36 AM	CAP	Apr. 16, 1925	8:34 AM	AQU
May. 25, 1924	6:51 AM	P I S	Nov. 3, 1924	3:26 AM	AQU	Apr. 18, 1925	12:00 PM	P I S
May. 27, 1924	2:46 PM	A R I	Nov. 5, 1924	9:14 AM	P I S	Apr. 20, 1925	3:26 PM	A R I
May. 30, 1924	4:00 AM	T A U	Nov. 7, 1924	2:46 PM	A R I	Apr. 22, 1925	12:00 AM	T A U
Jun. 1, 1924	4:00 PM	GEM	Nov. 9, 1924	12:00 AM	T A U	Apr. 25, 1925	7:23 AM	GEM
Jun. 4, 1924	4:00 AM	CAN	Nov. 12, 1924	12:00 PM	GEM	Apr. 27, 1925	4:37 PM	CAN
Jun. 6, 1924	4:00 PM	LEO	Nov. 14, 1924	12:00 AM	CAN	Apr. 30, 1925	8:00 AM	LEO
Jun. 9, 1924	1:51 AM	V I R	Nov. 17, 1924	12:00 PM	LEO	May. 2, 1925	8:00 PM	V I R

Date	Time	Moon	Date	Time	Moon	Date	Time	Moon
May. 5, 1925	3:42 AM	L I B	Oct. 18, 1925	5:09 AM	S C O	Mar. 28, 1926	8:00 PM	L I B
May. 7, 1925	8:34 AM	S C O	Oct. 20, 1925	10:17 AM	S A G	Mar. 31, 1926	6:00 AM	S C O
May. 9, 1925	12:00 PM	S A G	Oct. 22, 1925	3:26 PM	C A P	Apr. 2, 1926	12:55 PM	S A G
May. 11, 1925	1:43 PM	C A P	Oct. 24, 1925	6:51 PM	A Q U	Apr. 4, 1926	8:18 PM	C A P
May. 13, 1925	12:48 PM	A Q U	Oct. 26, 1925	7:12 PM	P I S	Apr. 6, 1926	10:17 PM	A Q U
May. 15, 1925	5:09 PM	P I S	Oct. 28, 1925	12:00 AM	A R I	Apr. 9, 1926	1:43 AM	P I S
May. 17, 1925	12:00 AM	A R I	Oct. 31, 1925	3:26 AM	T A U	Apr. 11, 1926	1:36 AM	A R I
May. 20, 1925	5:32 AM	T A U	Nov. 1, 1925	11:05 AM	G E M	Apr. 13, 1926	3:26 AM	T A U
May. 22, 1925	4:00 PM	G E M	Nov. 4, 1925	6:28 PM	C A N	Apr. 15, 1926	6:51 AM	G E M
May. 25, 1925	2:00 AM	C A N	Nov. 7, 1925	8:00 AM	L E O	Apr. 17, 1926	2:46 PM	C A N
May. 27, 1925	2:00 PM	L E O	Nov. 9, 1925	8:00 PM	V I R	Apr. 20, 1926	2:00 AM	L E O
May. 30, 1925	4:00 AM	V I R	Nov. 12, 1925	8:00 AM	L I B	Apr. 22, 1926	2:00 PM	V I R
Jun. 1, 1925	12:55 PM	L I B	Nov. 14, 1925	2:46 PM	S C O	Apr. 25, 1926	1:51 AM	L I B
Jun. 3, 1925	8:18 PM	S C O	Nov. 16, 1925	6:51 PM	S A G	Apr. 27, 1926	2:00 PM	S C O
Jun. 5, 1925	10:17 PM	S A G	Nov. 18, 1925	10:17 PM	C A P	Apr. 29, 1926	8:18 PM	S A G
Jun. 7, 1925	8:48 PM	C A P	Nov. 20, 1925	12:00 AM	A Q U	May. 4, 1926	5:32 AM	A Q U
Jun. 9, 1925	8:48 PM	A Q U	Nov. 23, 1925	1:36 AM	P I S	May. 6, 1926	6:24 AM	P I S
Jun. 11, 1925	10:24 PM	P I S	Nov. 25, 1925	7:23 AM	A R I	May. 8, 1926	10:17 AM	A R I
Jun. 14, 1925	3:26 AM	A R I	Nov. 27, 1925	10:17 AM	T A U	May. 10, 1926	11:12 AM	T A U
Jun. 16, 1925	11:05 AM	T A U	Nov. 29, 1925	6:28 PM	G E M	May. 12, 1926	3:26 PM	G E M
Jun. 18, 1925	10:00 PM	G E M	Dec. 2, 1925	3:42 AM	C A N	May. 14, 1926	12:00 AM	C A N
Jun. 21, 1925	8:00 AM	C A N	Dec. 4, 1925	4:00 PM	L E O	May. 17, 1926	10:00 AM	L E O
Jun. 23, 1925	12:00 AM	L E O	Dec. 7, 1925	6:33 AM	V I R	May. 19, 1926	10:00 PM	V I R
Jun. 26, 1925	10:00 AM	V I R	Dec. 9, 1925	6:00 PM	L I B	May. 22, 1926	12:00 PM	L I B
Jun. 28, 1925	10:00 PM	L I B	Dec. 12, 1925	1:51 AM	S C O	May. 24, 1926	10:00 PM	S C O
Jul. 1, 1925	3:26 AM	S C O	Dec. 14, 1925	5:09 AM	S A G	May. 27, 1926	3:42 AM	S A G
Jul. 3, 1925	8:34 AM	S A G	Dec. 16, 1925	6:24 AM	C A P	May. 29, 1926	6:51 AM	C A P
Jul. 5, 1925	8:00 AM	C A P	Dec. 18, 1925	8:34 AM	A Q U	May. 31, 1926	10:17 AM	A Q U
Jul. 7, 1925	8:00 AM	A Q U	Dec. 20, 1925	8:00 AM	P I S	Jun. 2, 1926	1:43 PM	P I S
Jul. 9, 1925	8:00 AM	P I S	Dec. 22, 1925	12:00 PM	A R I	Jun. 4, 1926	3:26 PM	A R I
Jul. 11, 1925	10:17 AM	A R I	Dec. 24, 1925	6:28 PM	T A U	Jun. 6, 1926	6:51 PM	T A U
Jul. 13, 1925	4:37 PM	T A U	Dec. 27, 1925	2:00 AM	G E M	Jun. 11, 1926	7:23 AM	C A N
Jul. 16, 1925	1:51 AM	G E M	Dec. 29, 1925	12:00 PM	C A N	Jun. 13, 1926	4:37 PM	L E O
Jul. 18, 1925	2:00 PM	C A N	Dec. 31, 1925	12:00 AM	L E O	Jun. 16, 1926	6:00 AM	V I R
Jul. 21, 1925	4:00 AM	L E O	Jan. 3, 1926	12:00 PM	V I R	Jun. 18, 1926	8:00 PM	L I B
Jul. 23, 1925	4:00 PM	V I R	Jan. 5, 1926	12:00 AM	L I B	Jun. 21, 1926	6:00 AM	S C O
Jul. 26, 1925	4:00 AM	L I B	Jan. 8, 1926	9:14 AM	S C O	Jun. 23, 1926	12:55 PM	S A G
Jul. 28, 1925	11:05 AM	S C O	Jan. 10, 1926	3:26 PM	S A G	Jun. 25, 1926	6:28 PM	C A P
Jul. 30, 1925	6:28 PM	S A G	Jan. 12, 1926	6:51 PM	C A P	Jun. 27, 1926	6:51 PM	A Q U
Aug. 1, 1925	5:36 PM	C A P	Jan. 14, 1926	5:36 PM	A Q U	Jun. 29, 1926	8:34 PM	P I S
Aug. 3, 1925	7:12 PM	A Q U	Jan. 16, 1926	5:36 PM	P I S	Jul. 1, 1926	10:17 PM	A R I
Aug. 5, 1925	4:30 PM	P I S	Jan. 18, 1926	5:36 PM	A R I	Jul. 3, 1926	12:00 AM	T A U
Aug. 7, 1925	8:34 AM	A R I	Jan. 20, 1926	10:17 PM	T A U	Jul. 6, 1926	7:23 AM	G E M
Aug. 12, 1925	10:00 AM	G E M	Jan. 23, 1926	8:00 AM	G E M	Jul. 8, 1926	2:46 PM	C A N
Aug. 14, 1925	8:00 PM	C A N	Jan. 25, 1926	6:00 PM	C A N	Jul. 11, 1926	2:00 AM	L E O
Aug. 17, 1925	10:00 AM	L E O	Jan. 28, 1926	6:00 AM	L E O	Jul. 13, 1926	2:00 PM	V I R
Aug. 19, 1925	10:00 PM	V I R	Jan. 30, 1926	6:00 PM	V I R	Jul. 16, 1926	2:00 AM	L I B
Aug. 22, 1925	10:00 AM	L I B	Feb. 2, 1926	8:00 AM	L I B	Jul. 18, 1926	2:00 PM	S C O
Aug. 24, 1925	8:00 PM	S C O	Feb. 4, 1926	6:00 PM	S C O	Jul. 20, 1926	10:09 PM	S A G
Aug. 26, 1925	10:17 PM	S A G	Feb. 7, 1926	1:51 AM	S A G	Jul. 23, 1926	1:43 AM	C A P
Aug. 29, 1925	3:26 AM	C A P	Feb. 9, 1926	5:09 AM	C A P	Jul. 25, 1926	3:12 AM	A Q U
Aug. 31, 1925	5:09 AM	A Q U	Feb. 11, 1926	4:48 AM	A Q U	Jul. 27, 1926	3:12 AM	P I S
Sep. 2, 1925	4:48 AM	P I S	Feb. 13, 1926	4:48 AM	P I S	Jul. 29, 1926	3:12 AM	A R I
Sep. 4, 1925	6:51 AM	A R I	Feb. 15, 1926	4:48 AM	A R I	Jul. 31, 1926	6:51 AM	T A U
Sep. 6, 1925	8:34 AM	T A U	Feb. 17, 1926	6:51 AM	T A U	Aug. 2, 1926	12:55 PM	G E M
Sep. 8, 1925	4:37 PM	G E M	Feb. 19, 1926	12:55 PM	G E M	Aug. 4, 1926	8:18 PM	C A N
Sep. 11, 1925	4:00 AM	C A N	Feb. 21, 1926	12:00 AM	C A N	Aug. 7, 1926	8:00 AM	L E O
Sep. 13, 1925	4:00 PM	L E O	Feb. 24, 1926	12:00 PM	L E O	Aug. 9, 1926	8:00 PM	V I R
Sep. 16, 1925	4:00 AM	V I R	Feb. 26, 1926	12:00 AM	V I R	Aug. 12, 1926	10:00 AM	L I B
Sep. 18, 1925	4:00 PM	L I B	Mar. 1, 1926	2:00 PM	L I B	Aug. 14, 1926	10:00 PM	S C O
Sep. 23, 1925	5:32 AM	S A G	Mar. 3, 1926	12:00 AM	S C O	Aug. 17, 1926	8:00 AM	S A G
Sep. 25, 1925	11:05 AM	C A P	Mar. 6, 1926	7:23 AM	S A G	Aug. 19, 1926	12:00 PM	C A P
Sep. 27, 1925	11:12 AM	A Q U	Mar. 8, 1926	12:00 PM	C A P	Aug. 21, 1926	3:26 PM	A Q U
Sep. 29, 1925	3:26 PM	P I S	Mar. 10, 1926	2:24 PM	A Q U	Aug. 23, 1926	2:24 PM	P I S
Oct. 1, 1925	5:09 PM	A R I	Mar. 12, 1926	4:00 PM	P I S	Aug. 25, 1926	12:00 PM	A R I
Oct. 3, 1925	6:51 PM	T A U	Mar. 14, 1926	4:00 PM	A R I	Aug. 27, 1926	3:26 PM	T A U
Oct. 6, 1925	1:51 AM	G E M	Mar. 16, 1926	4:00 PM	T A U	Aug. 29, 1926	5:09 PM	G E M
Oct. 8, 1925	12:00 PM	C A N	Mar. 18, 1926	8:34 PM	G E M	Sep. 1, 1926	1:51 AM	C A N
Oct. 10, 1925	12:00 AM	L E O	Mar. 21, 1926	5:32 AM	C A N	Sep. 3, 1926	2:00 PM	L E O
Oct. 13, 1925	12:00 PM	V I R	Mar. 23, 1926	6:00 PM	L E O	Sep. 6, 1926	2:00 AM	V I R
Oct. 15, 1925	12:00 AM	L I B	Mar. 26, 1926	8:00 AM	V I R	Sep. 8, 1926	5:27 PM	L I B

119

Date	Time	Moon	Date	Time	Moon	Date	Time	Moon
Sep. 11, 1926	4:00 AM	SCO	Feb. 19, 1927	12:00 PM	LIB	Aug. 2, 1927	6:00 AM	LIB
Sep. 13, 1926	2:00 PM	SAG	Feb. 21, 1927	12:00 AM	SCO	Aug. 4, 1927	6:00 PM	SCO
Sep. 15, 1926	8:18 PM	CAP	Feb. 24, 1927	12:00 PM	SAG	Aug. 7, 1927	6:00 AM	SAG
Sep. 17, 1926	12:00 AM	AQU	Feb. 26, 1927	8:18 PM	CAP	Aug. 9, 1927	2:46 PM	CAP
Sep. 20, 1926	1:36 AM	PIS	Feb. 28, 1927	12:00 AM	AQU	Aug. 11, 1927	10:09 PM	AQU
Sep. 21, 1926	10:30 PM	ARI	Mar. 3, 1927	1:36 AM	PIS	Aug. 13, 1927	12:00 AM	PIS
Sep. 23, 1926	12:00 AM	TAU	Mar. 4, 1927	10:30 PM	ARI	Aug. 17, 1927	12:00 AM	ARI
Sep. 26, 1926	3:26 AM	GEM	Mar. 6, 1927	12:00 AM	TAU	Aug. 18, 1927	1:43 AM	TAU
Sep. 28, 1926	9:14 AM	CAN	Mar. 9, 1927	1:43 AM	GEM	Aug. 20, 1927	3:26 AM	GEM
Sep. 30, 1926	8:00 PM	LEO	Mar. 11, 1927	9:14 AM	CAN	Aug. 22, 1927	8:34 AM	CAN
Oct. 3, 1926	8:00 AM	VIR	Mar. 13, 1927	4:37 PM	LEO	Aug. 24, 1927	4:37 PM	LEO
Oct. 5, 1926	10:00 PM	LIB	Mar. 16, 1927	6:00 AM	VIR	Aug. 27, 1927	2:00 AM	VIR
Oct. 8, 1926	10:00 AM	SCO	Mar. 18, 1927	6:00 PM	LIB	Aug. 29, 1927	2:00 PM	LIB
Oct. 10, 1926	8:00 PM	SAG	Mar. 21, 1927	6:00 AM	SCO	Sep. 1, 1927	2:00 AM	SCO
Oct. 13, 1926	1:51 AM	CAP	Mar. 23, 1927	6:00 PM	SAG	Sep. 3, 1927	2:00 PM	SAG
Oct. 15, 1926	9:14 AM	AQU	Mar. 26, 1927	3:42 AM	CAP	Sep. 8, 1927	7:23 AM	AQU
Oct. 17, 1926	9:36 AM	PIS	Mar. 28, 1927	8:34 AM	AQU	Sep. 10, 1927	10:17 AM	PIS
Oct. 19, 1926	11:12 AM	ARI	Mar. 30, 1927	11:12 AM	PIS	Sep. 12, 1927	9:36 AM	ARI
Oct. 21, 1926	11:12 AM	TAU	Apr. 1, 1927	11:12 AM	ARI	Sep. 14, 1927	9:36 AM	TAU
Oct. 23, 1926	11:12 AM	GEM	Apr. 3, 1927	11:12 AM	TAU	Sep. 16, 1927	9:36 AM	GEM
Oct. 25, 1926	6:28 PM	CAN	Apr. 5, 1927	12:00 PM	GEM	Sep. 18, 1927	1:43 PM	CAN
Oct. 28, 1926	4:00 AM	LEO	Apr. 7, 1927	4:37 PM	CAN	Sep. 20, 1927	10:09 PM	LEO
Oct. 30, 1926	4:00 AM	VIR	Apr. 12, 1927	12:00 PM	VIR	Sep. 23, 1927	8:00 AM	VIR
Nov. 2, 1926	4:00 AM	LIB	Apr. 14, 1927	12:00 AM	LIB	Sep. 25, 1927	8:00 PM	LIB
Nov. 4, 1926	4:00 AM	SCO	Apr. 17, 1927	12:00 PM	SCO	Sep. 28, 1927	8:00 AM	SCO
Nov. 6, 1926	12:00 AM	SAG	Apr. 19, 1927	12:00 AM	SAG	Sep. 30, 1927	8:00 PM	SAG
Nov. 9, 1926	6:51 AM	CAP	Apr. 22, 1927	9:14 AM	CAP	Oct. 3, 1927	8:00 AM	CAP
Nov. 11, 1926	2:46 PM	AQU	Apr. 24, 1927	4:37 PM	AQU	Oct. 5, 1927	4:37 PM	AQU
Nov. 13, 1926	5:09 PM	PIS	Apr. 26, 1927	8:34 PM	PIS	Oct. 7, 1927	8:34 PM	PIS
Nov. 15, 1926	8:34 AM	ARI	Apr. 28, 1927	8:48 PM	ARI	Oct. 9, 1927	10:17 PM	ARI
Nov. 17, 1926	10:17 PM	TAU	Apr. 30, 1927	8:48 PM	TAU	Oct. 11, 1927	7:12 PM	TAU
Nov. 19, 1926	12:00 AM	GEM	May. 2, 1927	8:48 PM	GEM	Oct. 13, 1927	7:12 PM	GEM
Nov. 22, 1926	3:26 AM	CAN	May. 4, 1927	10:24 PM	CAN	Oct. 15, 1927	10:17 PM	CAN
Nov. 24, 1926	11:05 AM	LEO	May. 7, 1927	7:23 AM	LEO	Oct. 18, 1927	3:42 AM	LEO
Nov. 26, 1926	12:00 AM	VIR	May. 9, 1927	6:00 PM	VIR	Oct. 20, 1927	2:00 PM	VIR
Nov. 29, 1926	12:00 PM	LIB	May. 12, 1927	6:00 AM	LIB	Oct. 23, 1927	2:00 AM	LIB
Dec. 1, 1926	12:00 AM	SCO	May. 14, 1927	6:00 PM	SCO	Oct. 25, 1927	2:00 PM	SCO
Dec. 4, 1926	10:00 AM	SAG	May. 17, 1927	6:00 AM	SAG	Oct. 28, 1927	2:00 AM	SAG
Dec. 6, 1926	1:43 AM	CAP	May. 19, 1927	2:46 PM	CAP	Oct. 30, 1927	2:00 PM	CAP
Dec. 8, 1926	6:51 PM	AQU	May. 21, 1927	10:09 PM	AQU	Nov. 4, 1927	5:32 AM	PIS
Dec. 10, 1926	10:17 PM	PIS	May. 24, 1927	3:42 AM	PIS	Nov. 6, 1927	6:24 AM	ARI
Dec. 13, 1926	1:43 AM	ARI	May. 26, 1927	4:48 AM	ARI	Nov. 8, 1927	6:24 AM	TAU
Dec. 15, 1926	3:12 AM	TAU	May. 28, 1927	6:24 AM	TAU	Nov. 10, 1927	6:24 AM	GEM
Dec. 17, 1926	9:14 AM	GEM	May. 30, 1927	8:34 AM	GEM	Nov. 12, 1927	6:24 AM	CAN
Dec. 19, 1926	12:00 PM	CAN	Jun. 1, 1927	10:17 AM	CAN	Nov. 14, 1927	10:17 AM	LEO
Dec. 21, 1926	8:18 PM	LEO	Jun. 3, 1927	4:37 PM	LEO	Nov. 16, 1927	10:00 PM	VIR
Dec. 24, 1926	8:00 AM	VIR	Jun. 6, 1927	2:00 AM	VIR	Nov. 19, 1927	8:00 AM	LIB
Dec. 26, 1926	8:00 PM	LIB	Jun. 8, 1927	2:00 PM	LIB	Nov. 21, 1927	8:00 PM	SCO
Dec. 29, 1926	8:00 AM	SCO	Jun. 11, 1927	2:00 AM	SCO	Nov. 24, 1927	8:00 AM	SAG
Dec. 31, 1926	4:37 PM	SAG	Jun. 13, 1927	2:00 PM	SAG	Nov. 26, 1927	8:00 PM	CAP
Jan. 2, 1927	10:17 PM	CAP	Jun. 15, 1927	12:00 AM	CAP	Nov. 29, 1927	6:00 AM	AQU
Jan. 5, 1927	3:26 AM	AQU	Jun. 18, 1927	3:26 AM	AQU	Dec. 1, 1927	10:17 AM	PIS
Jan. 7, 1927	5:09 AM	PIS	Jun. 20, 1927	8:34 AM	PIS	Dec. 3, 1927	3:26 PM	ARI
Jan. 9, 1927	6:51 AM	ARI	Jun. 22, 1927	12:00 PM	ARI	Dec. 5, 1927	4:00 PM	TAU
Jan. 11, 1927	10:17 AM	TAU	Jun. 24, 1927	1:43 PM	TAU	Dec. 7, 1927	6:51 PM	GEM
Jan. 13, 1927	1:43 PM	GEM	Jun. 26, 1927	5:09 PM	GEM	Dec. 9, 1927	5:36 PM	CAN
Jan. 15, 1927	6:51 PM	CAN	Jun. 28, 1927	6:51 PM	CAN	Dec. 11, 1927	8:34 PM	LEO
Jan. 18, 1927	6:00 AM	LEO	Jul. 1, 1927	1:51 AM	LEO	Dec. 14, 1927	3:42 AM	VIR
Jan. 20, 1927	4:00 PM	VIR	Jul. 3, 1927	9:14 AM	VIR	Dec. 16, 1927	4:00 PM	LIB
Jan. 23, 1927	4:00 AM	LIB	Jul. 5, 1927	10:00 PM	LIB	Dec. 19, 1927	4:00 AM	SCO
Jan. 25, 1927	4:00 PM	SCO	Jul. 8, 1927	10:00 AM	SCO	Dec. 21, 1927	4:00 PM	SAG
Jan. 28, 1927	4:00 AM	SAG	Jul. 10, 1927	10:00 PM	SAG	Dec. 24, 1927	1:51 AM	CAP
Jan. 30, 1927	11:05 AM	CAP	Jul. 13, 1927	5:32 AM	CAP	Dec. 26, 1927	11:05 AM	AQU
Feb. 1, 1927	1:43 PM	AQU	Jul. 15, 1927	12:55 PM	AQU	Dec. 28, 1927	3:26 PM	PIS
Feb. 3, 1927	3:26 PM	PIS	Jul. 17, 1927	3:26 PM	PIS	Dec. 30, 1927	8:34 PM	ARI
Feb. 5, 1927	2:24 PM	ARI	Jul. 19, 1927	5:09 PM	ARI	Jan. 1, 1928	12:00 AM	TAU
Feb. 7, 1927	2:24 PM	TAU	Jul. 21, 1927	5:36 PM	TAU	Jan. 4, 1928	1:36 AM	GEM
Feb. 9, 1927	6:51 PM	GEM	Jul. 23, 1927	10:17 PM	GEM	Jan. 6, 1928	5:09 AM	CAN
Feb. 12, 1927	1:51 AM	CAN	Jul. 26, 1927	3:42 AM	CAN	Jan. 8, 1928	6:51 AM	LEO
Feb. 14, 1927	11:05 AM	LEO	Jul. 28, 1927	8:34 AM	LEO	Jan. 10, 1928	12:00 PM	VIR
Feb. 16, 1927	12:00 AM	VIR	Jul. 30, 1927	8:00 PM	VIR	Jan. 12, 1928	10:09 PM	LIB

120

Date	Time	Moon	Date	Time	Moon	Date	Time	Moon
Jan. 15, 1928	12:00 PM	SCO	Jun. 27, 1928	6:00 AM	SCO	Dec. 7, 1928	10:09 PM	SCO
Jan. 17, 1928	12:00 AM	SAG	Jun. 29, 1928	6:00 PM	SAG	Dec. 10, 1928	3:16 PM	SAG
Jan. 20, 1928	12:00 PM	CAP	Jul. 2, 1928	6:00 AM	CAP	Dec. 13, 1928	2:00 AM	CAP
Jan. 22, 1928	6:28 PM	AQU	Jul. 4, 1928	6:00 PM	AQU	Dec. 15, 1928	2:00 PM	AQU
Jan. 24, 1928	10:17 PM	P I S	Jul. 6, 1928	12:00 AM	P I S	Dec. 20, 1928	9:14 AM	A R I
Jan. 27, 1928	3:26 AM	A R I	Jul. 9, 1928	5:09 AM	A R I	Dec. 22, 1928	12:00 PM	TAU
Jan. 29, 1928	5:09 AM	TAU	Jul. 11, 1928	10:17 AM	TAU	Dec. 24, 1928	12:48 PM	GEM
Jan. 31, 1928	8:34 AM	GEM	Jul. 13, 1928	11:12 AM	GEM	Dec. 26, 1928	12:48 PM	CAN
Feb. 2, 1928	12:00 PM	CAN	Jul. 15, 1928	12:48 PM	CAN	Dec. 28, 1928	12:48 PM	LEO
Feb. 4, 1928	3:26 PM	LEO	Jul. 17, 1928	3:26 PM	LEO	Dec. 30, 1928	3:26 PM	VIR
Feb. 6, 1928	12:00 AM	VIR	Jul. 19, 1928	6:51 PM	VIR	Jan. 1, 1929	6:51 PM	LIB
Feb. 9, 1928	7:23 AM	LIB	Jul. 22, 1928	1:51 AM	LIB	Jan. 4, 1929	8:00 AM	SCO
Feb. 11, 1928	8:00 PM	SCO	Jul. 24, 1928	11:05 AM	SCO	Jan. 6, 1929	8:00 PM	SAG
Feb. 14, 1928	8:00 AM	SAG	Jul. 27, 1928	2:00 AM	SAG	Jan. 9, 1929	8:00 AM	CAP
Feb. 16, 1928	8:00 PM	CAP	Jul. 29, 1928	2:00 PM	CAP	Jan. 11, 1929	8:00 PM	AQU
Feb. 19, 1928	3:42 AM	AQU	Jul. 31, 1928	10:09 PM	AQU	Jan. 14, 1929	5:32 AM	P I S
Feb. 21, 1928	8:34 AM	P I S	Aug. 3, 1928	7:23 AM	P I S	Jan. 16, 1929	2:46 PM	A R I
Feb. 23, 1928	10:17 AM	A R I	Aug. 5, 1928	12:55 PM	A R I	Jan. 18, 1929	6:51 PM	TAU
Feb. 25, 1928	12:00 PM	TAU	Aug. 7, 1928	3:26 PM	TAU	Jan. 20, 1329	10:17 PM	GEM
Feb. 27, 1928	12:48 PM	GEM	Aug. 9, 1928	6:51 PM	GEM	Jan. 24, 1929	12:00 AM	LEO
Feb. 29, 1928	5:09 PM	CAN	Aug. 11, 1928	7:12 PM	CAN	Jan. 27, 1929	1:43 AM	VIR
Mar. 2, 1928	10:17 PM	LEO	Aug. 13, 1928	12:00 AM	LEO	Jan. 29, 1929	5:09 AM	LIB
Mar. 5, 1928	7:23 AM	VIR	Aug. 16, 1928	3:26 AM	VIR	Jan. 31, 1929	4:00 PM	SCO
Mar. 7, 1928	2:46 PM	LIB	Aug. 18, 1928	11:05 AM	LIB	Feb. 3, 1929	2:00 AM	SAG
Mar. 10, 1928	4:00 PM	SCO	Aug. 20, 1928	10:00 PM	SCO	Feb. 5, 1929	4:00 PM	CAP
Mar. 12, 1928	4:00 PM	SAG	Aug. 23, 1928	10:00 AM	SAG	Feb. 8, 1929	4:00 AM	AQU
Mar. 15, 1928	4:00 AM	CAP	Aug. 25, 1928	10:00 PM	CAP	Feb. 10, 1929	2:00 PM	P I S
Mar. 17, 1928	12:55 PM	AQU	Aug. 28, 1928	7:23 AM	AQU	Feb. 12, 1929	8:18 PM	A R I
Mar. 19, 1928	8:18 PM	P I S	Aug. 30, 1928	2:46 PM	P I S	Feb. 15, 1929	1:51 AM	TAU
Mar. 21, 1928	7:12 PM	A R I	Sep. 1, 1928	6:51 PM	A R I	Feb. 17, 1929	5:09 AM	GEM
Mar. 23, 1928	7:12 PM	TAU	Sep. 3, 1928	7:12 PM	TAU	Feb. 19, 1929	8:34 AM	CAN
Mar. 25, 1928	10:17 PM	GEM	Sep. 5, 1928	12:00 AM	GEM	Feb. 21, 1929	10:17 AM	LEO
Mar. 27, 1928	12:00 AM	CAN	Sep. 8, 1928	3:26 AM	CAN	Feb. 23, 1929	12:00 PM	VIR
Mar. 30, 1928	5:32 AM	LEO	Sep. 10, 1928	6:51 PM	LEO	Feb. 25, 1929	3:26 PM	LIB
Apr. 1, 1928	12:55 PM	VIR	Sep. 12, 1928	12:55 PM	VIR	Feb. 27, 1929	12:00 AM	SCO
Apr. 3, 1928	12:00 AM	LIB	Sep. 14, 1928	6:28 PM	LIB	Mar. 2, 1929	12:00 PM	SAG
Apr. 6, 1928	10:00 AM	SCO	Sep. 17, 1928	6:00 AM	SCO	Mar. 4, 1929	12:00 AM	CAP
Apr. 8, 1928	10:00 PM	SAG	Sep. 19, 1928	7:38 PM	SAG	Mar. 7, 1929	12:00 PM	AQU
Apr. 11, 1928	12:00 PM	CAP	Sep. 22, 1928	6:00 AM	CAP	Mar. 9, 1929	8:18 PM	P I S
Apr. 13, 1928	12:00 AM	AQU	Sep. 24, 1928	6:00 PM	AQU	Mar. 12, 1929	3:42 AM	A R I
Apr. 16, 1928	3:26 AM	P I S	Sep. 26, 1928	12:00 PM	P I S	Mar. 14, 1929	6:51 AM	TAU
Apr. 18, 1928	6:51 AM	A R I	Sep. 29, 1928	3:26 AM	A R I	Mar. 16, 1929	10:17 AM	GEM
Apr. 20, 1928	6:24 AM	TAU	Oct. 1, 1928	4:48 AM	TAU	Mar. 18, 1929	1:43 PM	CAN
Apr. 22, 1928	6:24 AM	GEM	Oct. 3, 1928	6:51 AM	GEM	Mar. 20, 1929	5:09 PM	LEO
Apr. 24, 1928	6:24 AM	CAN	Oct. 5, 1928	8:34 AM	CAN	Mar. 22, 1929	8:34 PM	VIR
Apr. 26, 1928	10:17 AM	LEO	Oct. 7, 1928	12:00 PM	LEO	Mar. 25, 1929	1:51 AM	LIB
Apr. 28, 1928	6:28 PM	VIR	Oct. 9, 1928	6:28 PM	VIR	Mar. 27, 1929	10:00 AM	SCO
May. 1, 1928	3:42 AM	LIB	Oct. 12, 1928	1:51 AM	LIB	Mar. 29, 1929	8:00 PM	SAG
May. 3, 1928	4:00 PM	SCO	Oct. 14, 1928	11:05 AM	SCO	Apr. 1, 1929	8:00 AM	CAP
May. 6, 1928	6:00 AM	SAG	Oct. 16, 1928	12:00 AM	SAG	Apr. 3, 1929	8:00 PM	AQU
May. 8, 1928	6:00 PM	CAP	Oct. 19, 1928	2:00 PM	CAP	Apr. 6, 1929	5:32 AM	P I S
May. 11, 1928	6:00 AM	AQU	Oct. 22, 1928	2:00 AM	AQU	Apr. 8, 1929	12:55 PM	A R I
May. 13, 1928	12:55 PM	P I S	Oct. 24, 1928	9:14 AM	P I S	Apr. 10, 1929	3:26 PM	TAU
May. 15, 1928	5:09 PM	A R I	Oct. 26, 1928	1:43 PM	A R I	Apr. 12, 1929	4:00 PM	GEM
May. 17, 1928	6:51 PM	TAU	Oct. 28, 1928	2:24 PM	TAU	Apr. 14, 1929	5:36 PM	CAN
May. 19, 1928	5:36 PM	GEM	Oct. 30, 1928	2:24 PM	GEM	Apr. 16, 1929	10:17 PM	LEO
May. 21, 1928	4:00 PM	CAN	Nov. 1, 1928	2:24 PM	CAN	Apr. 19, 1929	1:43 AM	VIR
May. 23, 1928	5:36 PM	LEO	Nov. 3, 1928	6:51 PM	LEO	Apr. 21, 1929	6:51 AM	LIB
May. 26, 1928	1:51 AM	VIR	Nov. 5, 1928	10:17 PM	VIR	Apr. 23, 1929	6:00 PM	SCO
May. 28, 1928	9:14 AM	LIB	Nov. 8, 1928	7:23 AM	LIB	Apr. 26, 1929	4:00 AM	SAG
May. 30, 1928	10:00 PM	SCO	Nov. 10, 1928	8:00 PM	SCO	Apr. 28, 1929	4:00 PM	CAP
Jun. 2, 1928	12:00 PM	SAG	Nov. 13, 1928	8:44 PM	SAG	May. 1, 1929	4:00 AM	AQU
Jun. 4, 1928	12:00 AM	CAP	Nov. 15, 1928	8:00 PM	CAP	May. 3, 1929	4:00 PM	P I S
Jun. 7, 1928	12:00 PM	AQU	Nov. 18, 1928	8:00 AM	AQU	May. 5, 1929	10:09 PM	A R I
Jun. 9, 1928	6:28 PM	P I S	Nov. 20, 1928	8:00 PM	P I S	May. 8, 1929	1:43 AM	TAU
Jun. 14, 1928	3:26 AM	TAU	Nov. 25, 1928	1:36 AM	TAU	May. 10, 1929	1:36 AM	GEM
Jun. 16, 1928	3:12 AM	GEM	Nov. 27, 1928	1:30 AM	GEM	May. 12, 1929	3:26 AM	CAN
Jun. 18, 1928	3:12 AM	CAN	Nov. 29, 1928	1:36 AM	CAN	May. 14, 1929	3:12 AM	LEO
Jun. 20, 1928	5:09 AM	LEO	Dec. 1, 1928	1:36 AM	LEO	May. 16, 1929	6:51 AM	VIR
Jun. 22, 1928	8:34 AM	VIR	Dec. 3, 1928	5:09 AM	VIR	May. 18, 1929	12:00 PM	LIB
Jun. 24, 1928	4:37 PM	LIB	Dec. 5, 1928	12:55 PM	LIB	May. 20, 1929	10:09 PM	SCO

121

Date	Time	Moon	Date	Time	Moon	Date	Time	Moon
May. 23, 1929	10:00 AM	SAG	Nov. 5, 1929	2:46 PM	CAP	Apr. 18, 1930	12:00 PM	CAP
May. 25, 1929	10:00 PM	CAP	Nov. 8, 1929	6:00 AM	AQU	Apr. 20, 1930	10:00 PM	AQU
May. 28, 1929	1:05 PM	AQU	Nov. 10, 1929	6:00 PM	PIS	Apr. 23, 1930	12:00 PM	PIS
May. 30, 1929	12:00 AM	PIS	Nov. 13, 1929	1:51 AM	ARI	Apr. 25, 1930	8:18 PM	ARI
Jun. 2, 1929	7:23 AM	ARI	Nov. 15, 1929	9:14 AM	TAU	Apr. 28, 1930	5:32 AM	TAU
Jun. 4, 1929	12:55 PM	TAU	Nov. 17, 1929	9:36 AM	GEM	Apr. 30, 1930	10:17 AM	GEM
Jun. 6, 1929	12:48 PM	GEM	Nov. 19, 1929	11:12 AM	CAN	May. 2, 1930	3:26 PM	CAN
Jun. 8, 1929	12:48 PM	CAN	Nov. 21, 1929	1:43 PM	LEO	May. 4, 1930	4:00 PM	LEO
Jun. 10, 1929	12:48 PM	LEO	Nov. 23, 1929	3:26 PM	VIR	May. 6, 1930	8:34 PM	VIR
Jun. 12, 1929	12:48 PM	VIR	Nov. 25, 1929	6:51 PM	LIB	May. 8, 1930	12:00 AM	LIB
Jun. 14, 1929	8:18 PM	LIB	Nov. 28, 1929	3:42 AM	SCO	May. 11, 1930	3:26 AM	SCO
Jun. 17, 1929	3:42 AM	SCO	Nov. 30, 1929	2:00 PM	SAG	May. 13, 1930	11:05 AM	SAG
Jun. 19, 1929	4:00 PM	SAG	Dec. 2, 1929	12:00 AM	CAP	May. 15, 1930	6:28 PM	CAP
Jun. 22, 1929	4:00 AM	CAP	Dec. 5, 1929	12:00 PM	AQU	May. 18, 1930	8:00 AM	AQU
Jun. 24, 1929	6:00 PM	AQU	Dec. 8, 1929	2:00 AM	PIS	May. 20, 1930	8:00 PM	PIS
Jun. 27, 1929	6:00 AM	PIS	Dec. 10, 1929	11:05 AM	ARI	May. 23, 1930	8:00 AM	ARI
Jun. 29, 1929	4:00 PM	ARI	Dec. 12, 1929	5:09 PM	TAU	May. 25, 1930	2:46 PM	TAU
Jul. 1, 1929	10:09 PM	TAU	Dec. 14, 1929	10:17 PM	GEM	May. 27, 1930	10:09 PM	GEM
Jul. 3, 1929	12:00 AM	GEM	Dec. 16, 1929	10:24 PM	CAN	May. 29, 1930	8:48 PM	CAN
Jul. 7, 1929	10:24 PM	LEO	Dec. 18, 1929	7:30 PM	LEO	May. 31, 1930	10:24 PM	LEO
Jul. 9, 1929	10:24 PM	VIR	Dec. 20, 1929	8:48 PM	VIR	Jun. 3, 1930	1:43 AM	VIR
Jul. 12, 1929	3:42 AM	LIB	Dec. 23, 1929	1:43 AM	LIB	Jun. 5, 1930	5:09 AM	LIB
Jul. 14, 1929	12:00 PM	SCO	Dec. 25, 1929	9:14 AM	SCO	Jun. 7, 1930	11:05 AM	SCO
Jul. 16, 1929	10:00 PM	SAG	Dec. 27, 1929	8:00 PM	SAG	Jun. 9, 1930	6:28 PM	SAG
Jul. 19, 1929	10:00 AM	CAP	Dec. 30, 1929	6:00 AM	CAP	Jun. 12, 1930	4:00 AM	CAP
Jul. 24, 1929	9:14 AM	PIS	Jan. 1, 1930	8:00 AM	AQU	Jun. 14, 1930	2:00 PM	AQU
Jul. 26, 1929	10:00 PM	ARI	Jan. 4, 1930	8:00 AM	PIS	Jun. 17, 1930	4:22 AM	PIS
Jul. 29, 1929	3:42 AM	TAU	Jan. 6, 1930	8:00 PM	ARI	Jun. 19, 1930	4:00 PM	ARI
Jul. 31, 1929	6:51 AM	GEM	Jan. 9, 1930	3:42 AM	TAU	Jun. 21, 1930	12:00 AM	TAU
Aug. 2, 1929	10:17 AM	CAN	Jan. 11, 1930	8:34 AM	GEM	Jun. 24, 1930	5:09 AM	GEM
Aug. 4, 1929	9:36 AM	LEO	Jan. 13, 1930	9:36 AM	CAN	Jun. 26, 1930	8:34 AM	CAN
Aug. 6, 1929	9:36 AM	VIR	Jan. 15, 1930	7:30 AM	LEO	Jun. 28, 1930	8:00 AM	LEO
Aug. 8, 1929	12:00 PM	LIB	Jan. 17, 1930	8:00 AM	VIR	Jun. 30, 1930	8:00 AM	VIR
Aug. 10, 1929	6:28 PM	SCO	Jan. 19, 1930	10:17 AM	LIB	Jul. 2, 1930	10:17 AM	LIB
Aug. 13, 1929	3:42 AM	SAG	Jan. 21, 1930	1:43 PM	SCO	Jul. 4, 1930	4:37 PM	SCO
Aug. 15, 1929	7:38 PM	CAP	Jan. 26, 1930	12:00 PM	CAP	Jul. 6, 1930	12:00 AM	SAG
Aug. 18, 1929	6:00 AM	AQU	Jan. 29, 1930	2:00 AM	AQU	Jul. 9, 1930	10:00 AM	CAP
Aug. 20, 1929	6:00 PM	PIS	Jan. 31, 1930	2:00 PM	PIS	Jul. 11, 1930	10:00 PM	AQU
Aug. 23, 1929	1:51 AM	ARI	Feb. 3, 1930	2:00 AM	ARI	Jul. 14, 1930	10:00 AM	PIS
Aug. 25, 1929	9:14 AM	TAU	Feb. 5, 1930	12:00 PM	TAU	Jul. 16, 1930	10:00 PM	ARI
Aug. 27, 1929	1:43 PM	GEM	Feb. 7, 1930	6:28 PM	GEM	Jul. 19, 1930	10:00 AM	TAU
Aug. 29, 1929	5:09 PM	CAN	Feb. 9, 1930	8:34 PM	CAN	Jul. 21, 1930	4:37 PM	GEM
Aug. 31, 1929	5:36 PM	LEO	Feb. 11, 1930	7:12 PM	LEO	Jul. 23, 1930	6:51 PM	CAN
Sep. 2, 1929	8:34 PM	VIR	Feb. 13, 1930	7:12 PM	VIR	Jul. 25, 1930	5:36 PM	LEO
Sep. 4, 1929	10:17 PM	LIB	Feb. 15, 1930	7:12 PM	LIB	Jul. 27, 1930	5:36 PM	VIR
Sep. 7, 1929	3:42 AM	SCO	Feb. 17, 1930	10:17 PM	SCO	Jul. 29, 1930	5:36 PM	LIB
Sep. 9, 1929	11:05 AM	SAG	Feb. 20, 1930	7:23 AM	SAG	Jul. 31, 1930	7:12 PM	SCO
Sep. 11, 1929	12:00 AM	CAP	Feb. 22, 1930	8:00 PM	CAP	Aug. 3, 1930	5:32 AM	SAG
Sep. 14, 1929	2:00 AM	AQU	Feb. 25, 1930	8:00 AM	AQU	Aug. 5, 1930	4:00 PM	CAP
Sep. 16, 1929	10:09 PM	PIS	Feb. 27, 1930	8:00 PM	PIS	Aug. 8, 1930	4:00 AM	AQU
Sep. 19, 1929	10:00 AM	ARI	Mar. 2, 1930	8:00 AM	ARI	Aug. 10, 1930	4:00 PM	PIS
Sep. 21, 1929	2:46 PM	TAU	Mar. 4, 1930	6:00 PM	TAU	Aug. 13, 1930	4:00 AM	ARI
Sep. 23, 1929	6:51 PM	GEM	Mar. 6, 1930	12:00 AM	GEM	Aug. 15, 1930	4:00 PM	TAU
Sep. 25, 1929	10:17 PM	CAN	Mar. 9, 1930	3:26 AM	CAN	Aug. 17, 1930	12:00 AM	GEM
Sep. 28, 1929	1:43 AM	LEO	Mar. 11, 1930	4:48 AM	LEO	Aug. 20, 1930	3:26 AM	CAN
Sep. 30, 1929	3:26 AM	VIR	Mar. 13, 1930	6:51 AM	VIR	Aug. 22, 1930	4:48 AM	LEO
Oct. 2, 1929	6:51 AM	LIB	Mar. 15, 1930	6:24 AM	LIB	Aug. 24, 1930	4:48 AM	VIR
Oct. 4, 1929	12:55 PM	SCO	Mar. 17, 1930	10:17 AM	SCO	Aug. 26, 1930	3:12 AM	LIB
Oct. 6, 1929	8:18 PM	SAG	Mar. 19, 1930	4:37 PM	SAG	Aug. 28, 1930	6:51 AM	SCO
Oct. 9, 1929	8:00 AM	CAP	Mar. 22, 1930	1:51 AM	CAP	Aug. 30, 1930	10:17 AM	SAG
Oct. 11, 1929	12:00 AM	AQU	Mar. 24, 1930	2:00 PM	AQU	Sep. 1, 1930	8:18 PM	CAP
Oct. 14, 1929	7:23 AM	PIS	Mar. 27, 1930	4:00 AM	PIS	Sep. 4, 1930	10:00 AM	AQU
Oct. 16, 1929	4:37 PM	ARI	Mar. 29, 1930	12:55 PM	ARI	Sep. 6, 1930	10:00 PM	PIS
Oct. 18, 1929	12:00 AM	TAU	Mar. 31, 1930	10:09 PM	TAU	Sep. 9, 1930	10:00 AM	ARI
Oct. 21, 1929	1:43 AM	GEM	Apr. 3, 1930	5:32 AM	GEM	Sep. 11, 1930	10:00 PM	TAU
Oct. 23, 1929	5:09 AM	CAN	Apr. 5, 1930	8:34 AM	CAN	Sep. 14, 1930	5:32 AM	GEM
Oct. 25, 1929	6:51 AM	LEO	Apr. 7, 1930	12:00 PM	LEO	Sep. 16, 1930	12:55 PM	CAN
Oct. 27, 1929	10:17 AM	VIR	Apr. 9, 1930	12:48 PM	VIR	Sep. 18, 1930	3:26 PM	LEO
Oct. 29, 1929	1:43 PM	LIB	Apr. 11, 1930	5:09 PM	LIB	Sep. 20, 1930	2:24 PM	VIR
Oct. 31, 1929	6:51 PM	SCO	Apr. 13, 1930	6:51 PM	SCO	Sep. 22, 1930	2:24 PM	LIB
Nov. 3, 1929	5:32 AM	SAG	Apr. 16, 1930	1:51 AM	SAG	Sep. 24, 1930	5:09 PM	SCO

Date	Time	Moon	Date	Time	Moon	Date	Time	Moon
Sep. 26, 1930	6:51 PM	SAG	Mar. 7, 1931	2:24 PM	SCO	Aug. 20, 1931	6:51 PM	SAG
Sep. 29, 1930	3:42 AM	CAP	Mar. 9, 1931	4:00 PM	SAG	Aug. 25, 1931	9:14 AM	AQU
Oct. 1, 1930	4:00 PM	AQU	Mar. 12, 1931	1:51 AM	CAP	Aug. 27, 1931	6:28 PM	PIS
Oct. 4, 1930	4:00 AM	PIS	Mar. 14, 1931	12:00 PM	AQU	Aug. 30, 1931	8:00 AM	ARI
Oct. 6, 1930	4:00 AM	ARI	Mar. 16, 1931	12:00 AM	PIS	Sep. 1, 1931	10:00 PM	TAU
Oct. 9, 1930	4:00 AM	TAU	Mar. 19, 1931	3:16 AM	ARI	Sep. 4, 1931	10:00 AM	GEM
Oct. 11, 1930	11:05 AM	GEM	Mar. 22, 1931	2:00 AM	TAU	Sep. 6, 1931	6:28 PM	CAN
Oct. 13, 1930	6:28 PM	CAN	Mar. 24, 1931	11:05 AM	GEM	Sep. 8, 1931	10:17 PM	LEO
Oct. 15, 1930	8:34 PM	LEO	Mar. 26, 1931	8:18 PM	CAN	Sep. 12, 1931	12:00 AM	LIB
Oct. 17, 1930	12:00 AM	VIR	Mar. 28, 1931	12:00 AM	LEO	Sep. 14, 1931	12:00 AM	SCO
Oct. 19, 1930	12:00 AM	LIB	Mar. 31, 1931	1:36 AM	VIR	Sep. 17, 1931	1:43 AM	SAG
Oct. 22, 1930	1:36 AM	SCO	Apr. 2, 1931	1:36 AM	LIB	Sep. 19, 1931	7:23 AM	CAP
Oct. 24, 1930	7:23 AM	SAG	Apr. 4, 1931	1:36 AM	SCO	Sep. 21, 1931	2:46 PM	AQU
Oct. 26, 1930	12:55 PM	CAP	Apr. 6, 1931	3:26 AM	SAG	Sep. 24, 1931	2:00 AM	PIS
Oct. 28, 1930	12:00 AM	AQU	Apr. 8, 1931	9:14 AM	CAP	Sep. 26, 1931	2:00 PM	ARI
Oct. 31, 1930	12:00 PM	PIS	Apr. 10, 1931	8:00 PM	AQU	Sep. 29, 1931	4:00 AM	TAU
Nov. 2, 1930	12:00 AM	ARI	Apr. 13, 1931	6:00 AM	PIS	Oct. 1, 1931	4:00 PM	GEM
Nov. 5, 1930	12:00 PM	TAU	Apr. 15, 1931	8:00 PM	ARI	Oct. 4, 1931	1:51 AM	CAN
Nov. 7, 1930	6:28 PM	GEM	Apr. 18, 1931	8:00 AM	TAU	Oct. 6, 1931	6:51 AM	LEO
Nov. 9, 1930	10:17 PM	CAN	Apr. 20, 1931	4:37 PM	GEM	Oct. 8, 1931	9:36 AM	VIR
Nov. 12, 1930	3:26 AM	LEO	Apr. 23, 1931	1:51 AM	CAN	Oct. 10, 1931	11:12 AM	LIB
Nov. 14, 1930	5:09 AM	VIR	Apr. 25, 1931	6:51 AM	LEO	Oct. 12, 1931	9:00 AM	SCO
Nov. 16, 1930	8:34 AM	LIB	Apr. 27, 1931	10:17 AM	VIR	Oct. 14, 1931	9:36 AM	SAG
Nov. 18, 1930	12:00 PM	SCO	Apr. 29, 1931	11:12 AM	LIB	Oct. 16, 1931	1:43 PM	CAP
Nov. 20, 1930	3:26 PM	SAG	May. 1, 1931	1:43 PM	SCO	Oct. 18, 1931	6:51 PM	AQU
Nov. 22, 1930	10:09 PM	CAP	May. 3, 1931	12:48 PM	SAG	Oct. 21, 1931	8:00 AM	PIS
Nov. 25, 1930	7:23 AM	AQU	May. 5, 1931	5:09 PM	CAP	Oct. 23, 1931	8:00 PM	ARI
Nov. 27, 1930	8:00 PM	PIS	May. 8, 1931	1:51 AM	AQU	Oct. 26, 1931	10:00 AM	TAU
Nov. 30, 1930	10:55 AM	ARI	May. 10, 1931	2:00 PM	PIS	Oct. 28, 1931	10:00 PM	GEM
Dec. 2, 1930	8:00 PM	TAU	May. 13, 1931	2:00 AM	ARI	Oct. 31, 1931	8:00 AM	CAN
Dec. 5, 1930	1:43 AM	GEM	May. 15, 1931	4:00 PM	TAU	Nov. 2, 1931	2:46 PM	LEO
Dec. 7, 1930	6:51 AM	CAN	May. 20, 1931	7:23 AM	CAN	Nov. 4, 1931	6:51 PM	VIR
Dec. 9, 1930	8:00 AM	LEO	May. 22, 1931	12:00 PM	LEO	Nov. 6, 1931	10:17 PM	LIB
Dec. 11, 1930	9:36 AM	VIR	May. 24, 1931	3:26 PM	VIR	Nov. 8, 1931	8:48 PM	SCO
Dec. 13, 1930	1:43 PM	LIB	May. 26, 1931	6:51 PM	LIB	Nov. 10, 1931	8:48 PM	SAG
Dec. 15, 1930	5:09 PM	SCO	May. 28, 1931	10:17 PM	SCO	Nov. 12, 1931	12:00 AM	CAP
Dec. 17, 1930	10:17 PM	SAG	May. 30, 1931	12:00 AM	SAG	Nov. 15, 1931	5:32 AM	AQU
Dec. 20, 1930	7:23 AM	CAP	Jun. 2, 1931	3:26 AM	CAP	Nov. 17, 1931	4:00 PM	PIS
Dec. 22, 1930	6:00 PM	AQU	Jun. 4, 1931	11:05 AM	AQU	Nov. 20, 1931	4:00 AM	ARI
Dec. 25, 1930	4:00 AM	PIS	Jun. 6, 1931	10:00 PM	PIS	Nov. 22, 1931	4:00 PM	TAU
Dec. 27, 1930	7:38 PM	ARI	Jun. 9, 1931	10:00 AM	ARI	Nov. 25, 1931	4:00 AM	GEM
Dec. 30, 1930	6:00 AM	TAU	Jun. 14, 1931	7:23 AM	GEM	Nov. 27, 1931	12:55 PM	CAN
Jan. 1, 1931	12:55 PM	GEM	Jun. 16, 1931	2:46 PM	CAN	Nov. 29, 1931	8:18 PM	LEO
Jan. 3, 1931	6:28 PM	CAN	Jun. 18, 1931	6:51 PM	LEO	Dec. 2, 1931	1:51 AM	VIR
Jan. 5, 1931	6:51 PM	LEO	Jun. 20, 1931	10:17 PM	VIR	Dec. 4, 1931	5:09 AM	LIB
Jan. 7, 1931	5:36 PM	VIR	Jun. 22, 1931	12:00 AM	LIB	Dec. 6, 1931	6:51 AM	SCO
Jan. 9, 1931	8:34 PM	LIB	Jun. 25, 1931	3:26 AM	SCO	Dec. 8, 1931	8:34 AM	SAG
Jan. 11, 1931	10:17 PM	SCO	Jun. 27, 1931	6:51 AM	SAG	Dec. 10, 1931	10:17 AM	CAP
Jan. 14, 1931	5:32 AM	SAG	Jun. 29, 1931	12:55 PM	CAP	Dec. 12, 1931	1:43 PM	AQU
Jan. 16, 1931	12:55 PM	CAP	Jul. 1, 1931	8:18 PM	AQU	Dec. 14, 1931	10:09 PM	PIS
Jan. 18, 1931	10:09 PM	AQU	Jul. 4, 1931	6:00 AM	PIS	Dec. 17, 1931	12:00 PM	ARI
Jan. 21, 1931	12:00 PM	PIS	Jul. 6, 1931	6:00 PM	ARI	Dec. 19, 1931	12:00 AM	TAU
Jan. 23, 1931	12:00 AM	ARI	Jul. 9, 1931	8:00 AM	TAU	Dec. 22, 1931	12:00 PM	GEM
Jan. 26, 1931	2:00 PM	TAU	Jul. 11, 1931	6:00 PM	GEM	Dec. 24, 1931	8:18 PM	CAN
Jan. 28, 1931	12:00 AM	GEM	Jul. 13, 1931	12:00 AM	CAN	Dec. 27, 1931	1:43 AM	LEO
Jan. 31, 1931	3:26 AM	CAN	Jul. 16, 1931	3:26 AM	LEO	Dec. 29, 1931	6:51 AM	VIR
Feb. 2, 1931	5:09 AM	LEO	Jul. 18, 1931	5:09 AM	VIR	Dec. 31, 1931	10:17 AM	LIB
Feb. 4, 1931	3:00 AM	VIR	Jul. 20, 1931	6:51 AM	LIB	Jan. 2, 1932	1:43 PM	SCO
Feb. 6, 1931	3:12 AM	LIB	Jul. 22, 1931	8:34 AM	SCO	Jan. 4, 1932	2:24 PM	SAG
Feb. 8, 1931	4:48 AM	SCO	Jul. 24, 1931	12:00 PM	SAG	Jan. 6, 1932	6:51 PM	CAP
Feb. 10, 1931	10:17 AM	SAG	Jul. 26, 1931	8:18 PM	CAP	Jan. 11, 1932	10:00 AM	PIS
Feb. 12, 1931	6:28 PM	CAP	Jul. 29, 1931	4:00 AM	AQU	Jan. 13, 1932	8:00 PM	ARI
Feb. 15, 1931	6:00 AM	AQU	Jul. 31, 1931	2:00 PM	PIS	Jan. 16, 1932	8:00 AM	TAU
Feb. 17, 1931	6:00 PM	PIS	Aug. 3, 1931	2:00 AM	ARI	Jan. 18, 1932	10:00 PM	GEM
Feb. 20, 1931	8:44 AM	ARI	Aug. 5, 1931	2:00 PM	TAU	Jan. 21, 1932	5:32 AM	CAN
Feb. 22, 1931	8:00 PM	TAU	Aug. 8, 1931	2:00 AM	GEM	Jan. 23, 1932	10:17 AM	LEO
Feb. 25, 1931	5:32 AM	GEM	Aug. 10, 1931	9:14 AM	CAN	Jan. 25, 1932	1:43 PM	VIR
Feb. 27, 1931	12:55 PM	CAN	Aug. 12, 1931	12:00 PM	LEO	Jan. 27, 1932	5:09 PM	LIB
Mar. 1, 1931	3:26 PM	LEO	Aug. 14, 1931	12:48 PM	VIR	Jan. 29, 1932	6:51 PM	SCO
Mar. 3, 1931	4:00 PM	VIR	Aug. 16, 1931	12:48 PM	LIB	Jan. 31, 1932	10:17 PM	SAG
Mar. 5, 1931	2:24 PM	LIB	Aug. 18, 1931	2:24 PM	SCO	Feb. 3, 1932	1:43 AM	CAP

Date	Time	Moon	Date	Time	Moon	Date	Time	Moon
Feb. 5, 1932	9:14 AM	AQU	Jul. 18, 1932	6:51 AM	AQU	Dec. 27, 1932	3:12 AM	CAP
Feb. 7, 1932	4:37 PM	PIS	Jul. 20, 1932	12:55 PM	PIS	Dec. 29, 1932	5:09 AM	AQU
Feb. 10, 1932	4:00 AM	ARI	Jul. 22, 1932	8:18 PM	ARI	Dec. 31, 1932	9:14 AM	PIS
Feb. 12, 1932	4:00 PM	TAU	Jul. 25, 1932	10:00 AM	TAU	Jan. 2, 1933	2:46 PM	ARI
Feb. 15, 1932	6:00 AM	GEM	Jul. 27, 1932	10:00 PM	GEM	Jan. 5, 1933	4:00 AM	TAU
Feb. 17, 1932	2:46 PM	CAN	Jul. 30, 1932	10:00 AM	CAN	Jan. 7, 1933	4:00 PM	GEM
Feb. 19, 1932	10:09 PM	LEO	Aug. 1, 1932	4:37 PM	LEO	Jan. 10, 1933	4:00 AM	CAN
Feb. 21, 1932	12:00 AM	VIR	Aug. 3, 1932	12:00 AM	VIR	Jan. 12, 1933	4:00 PM	LEO
Feb. 23, 1932	12:00 AM	LIB	Aug. 6, 1932	1:43 AM	LIB	Jan. 14, 1933	10:09 PM	VIR
Feb. 26, 1932	1:43 AM	SCO	Aug. 8, 1932	5:09 AM	SCO	Jan. 17, 1933	5:32 AM	LIB
Feb. 28, 1932	3:26 AM	SAG	Aug. 10, 1932	6:24 AM	SAG	Jan. 19, 1933	8:34 AM	SCO
Mar. 1, 1932	6:51 AM	CAP	Aug. 12, 1932	10:17 AM	CAP	Jan. 21, 1933	12:00 PM	SAG
Mar. 3, 1932	2:46 PM	AQU	Aug. 14, 1932	1:43 PM	AQU	Jan. 23, 1933	12:48 PM	CAP
Mar. 8, 1932	12:00 PM	ARI	Aug. 16, 1932	10:09 PM	PIS	Jan. 25, 1933	3:26 PM	AQU
Mar. 10, 1932	12:00 AM	TAU	Aug. 19, 1932	5:32 AM	ARI	Jan. 27, 1933	6:51 PM	PIS
Mar. 13, 1932	3:16 PM	GEM	Aug. 21, 1932	6:00 PM	TAU	Jan. 30, 1933	1:51 AM	ARI
Mar. 15, 1932	10:09 PM	CAN	Aug. 24, 1932	6:00 AM	GEM	Feb. 1, 1933	12:00 PM	TAU
Mar. 18, 1932	7:23 AM	LEO	Aug. 26, 1932	6:00 PM	CAN	Feb. 3, 1933	12:00 AM	GEM
Mar. 20, 1932	10:17 AM	VIR	Aug. 29, 1932	1:51 AM	LEO	Feb. 6, 1933	12:00 PM	CAN
Mar. 22, 1932	11:12 AM	LIB	Aug. 31, 1932	6:51 AM	VIR	Feb. 8, 1933	12:00 AM	LEO
Mar. 24, 1932	11:12 AM	SCO	Sep. 2, 1932	10:17 AM	LIB	Feb. 11, 1933	5:32 AM	VIR
Mar. 26, 1932	12:00 PM	SAG	Sep. 4, 1932	12:00 PM	SCO	Feb. 13, 1933	10:17 AM	LIB
Mar. 28, 1932	1:43 PM	CAP	Sep. 6, 1932	1:43 PM	SAG	Feb. 15, 1933	4:37 PM	SCO
Mar. 30, 1932	8:18 PM	AQU	Sep. 8, 1932	3:26 PM	CAP	Feb. 17, 1933	4:00 PM	SAG
Apr. 2, 1932	6:00 AM	PIS	Sep. 10, 1932	10:09 PM	AQU	Feb. 19, 1933	8:34 PM	CAP
Apr. 4, 1932	6:00 PM	ARI	Sep. 13, 1932	3:42 AM	PIS	Feb. 21, 1933	12:00 AM	AQU
Apr. 7, 1932	6:00 AM	TAU	Sep. 15, 1932	12:55 PM	ARI	Feb. 24, 1933	3:26 AM	PIS
Apr. 9, 1932	8:00 PM	GEM	Sep. 18, 1932	2:00 AM	TAU	Feb. 26, 1933	11:05 AM	ARI
Apr. 12, 1932	5:32 AM	CAN	Sep. 20, 1932	2:00 PM	GEM	Feb. 28, 1933	6:28 PM	TAU
Apr. 14, 1932	2:46 PM	LEO	Sep. 23, 1932	2:00 AM	CAN	Mar. 3, 1933	8:00 AM	GEM
Apr. 16, 1932	10:09 PM	VIR	Sep. 25, 1932	11:05 AM	LEO	Mar. 5, 1933	8:00 PM	CAN
Apr. 18, 1932	8:48 PM	LIB	Sep. 27, 1932	6:28 PM	VIR	Mar. 8, 1933	8:00 AM	LEO
Apr. 20, 1932	10:24 PM	SCO	Sep. 29, 1932	8:34 PM	LIB	Mar. 10, 1933	2:46 PM	VIR
Apr. 22, 1932	8:48 PM	SAG	Oct. 1, 1932	7:12 PM	SCO	Mar. 12, 1933	6:51 PM	LIB
Apr. 24, 1932	8:48 PM	CAP	Oct. 3, 1932	7:12 PM	SAG	Mar. 14, 1933	10:17 PM	SCO
Apr. 27, 1932	3:42 AM	AQU	Oct. 5, 1932	10:17 PM	CAP	Mar. 16, 1933	12:00 AM	SAG
Apr. 29, 1932	11:05 AM	PIS	Oct. 8, 1932	1:43 AM	AQU	Mar. 19, 1933	1:43 AM	CAP
May. 1, 1932	12:00 AM	ARI	Oct. 10, 1932	9:14 AM	PIS	Mar. 21, 1933	5:09 AM	AQU
May. 4, 1932	12:00 PM	TAU	Oct. 12, 1932	6:28 PM	ARI	Mar. 23, 1933	10:17 PM	PIS
May. 7, 1932	2:00 AM	GEM	Oct. 15, 1932	8:00 AM	TAU	Mar. 25, 1933	6:28 PM	ARI
May. 9, 1932	11:05 AM	CAN	Oct. 17, 1932	8:00 PM	GEM	Mar. 28, 1933	3:42 AM	TAU
May. 11, 1932	12:00 AM	LEO	Oct. 20, 1932	10:00 AM	CAN	Mar. 30, 1933	4:00 PM	GEM
May. 14, 1932	3:26 AM	VIR	Oct. 22, 1932	6:28 PM	LEO	Apr. 2, 1933	4:00 AM	CAN
May. 16, 1932	6:24 AM	LIB	Oct. 25, 1932	3:42 AM	VIR	Apr. 4, 1933	4:00 PM	LEO
May. 18, 1932	8:00 AM	SCO	Oct. 27, 1932	6:51 AM	LIB	Apr. 6, 1933	12:00 AM	VIR
May. 20, 1932	8:00 AM	SAG	Oct. 29, 1932	6:24 AM	SCO	Apr. 9, 1933	5:09 AM	LIB
May. 22, 1932	8:00 AM	CAP	Oct. 31, 1932	4:30 AM	SAG	Apr. 11, 1933	6:24 AM	SCO
May. 24, 1932	10:17 AM	AQU	Nov. 2, 1932	4:48 AM	CAP	Apr. 13, 1933	6:24 AM	SAG
May. 26, 1932	6:28 PM	PIS	Nov. 4, 1932	8:34 AM	AQU	Apr. 15, 1933	8:34 AM	CAP
May. 29, 1932	6:00 AM	ARI	Nov. 6, 1932	4:37 PM	PIS	Apr. 17, 1933	10:17 AM	AQU
May. 31, 1932	6:00 PM	TAU	Nov. 9, 1932	2:00 AM	ARI	Apr. 19, 1933	3:26 PM	PIS
Jun. 3, 1932	8:00 AM	GEM	Nov. 11, 1932	2:00 PM	TAU	Apr. 22, 1933	2:00 AM	ARI
Jun. 5, 1932	4:37 PM	CAN	Nov. 14, 1932	4:22 AM	GEM	Apr. 24, 1933	12:00 PM	TAU
Jun. 8, 1932	4:00 AM	LEO	Nov. 16, 1932	4:00 PM	CAN	Apr. 26, 1933	12:00 AM	GEM
Jun. 10, 1932	11:05 AM	VIR	Nov. 19, 1932	1:51 AM	LEO	Apr. 29, 1933	12:00 PM	CAN
Jun. 12, 1932	1:43 PM	LIB	Nov. 21, 1932	11:05 AM	VIR	May. 1, 1933	12:00 AM	LEO
Jun. 14, 1932	5:09 PM	SCO	Nov. 23, 1932	3:26 PM	LIB	May. 4, 1933	9:14 AM	VIR
Jun. 16, 1932	5:36 PM	SAG	Nov. 25, 1932	6:51 PM	SCO	May. 6, 1933	4:37 PM	LIB
Jun. 18, 1932	5:36 PM	CAP	Nov. 27, 1932	5:36 PM	SAG	May. 8, 1933	4:00 PM	SCO
Jun. 20, 1932	7:12 PM	AQU	Nov. 29, 1932	4:00 PM	CAP	May. 10, 1933	3:00 PM	SAG
Jun. 23, 1932	3:42 AM	PIS	Dec. 1, 1932	4:00 PM	AQU	May. 12, 1933	4:00 PM	CAP
Jun. 25, 1932	2:00 PM	ARI	Dec. 3, 1932	12:00 AM	PIS	May. 14, 1933	4:00 PM	AQU
Jun. 28, 1932	2:00 AM	TAU	Dec. 6, 1932	7:23 AM	ARI	May. 16, 1933	12:00 AM	PIS
Jun. 30, 1932	2:00 PM	GEM	Dec. 8, 1932	8:00 PM	TAU	May. 19, 1933	8:00 AM	ARI
Jul. 3, 1932	2:00 AM	CAN	Dec. 11, 1932	10:00 AM	GEM	May. 21, 1933	6:00 PM	TAU
Jul. 5, 1932	9:14 AM	LEO	Dec. 13, 1932	10:00 PM	CAN	May. 24, 1933	6:00 AM	GEM
Jul. 7, 1932	4:37 PM	VIR	Dec. 16, 1932	7:23 AM	LEO	May. 26, 1933	6:00 PM	CAN
Jul. 9, 1932	10:09 PM	LIB	Dec. 18, 1932	4:37 PM	VIR	May. 29, 1933	6:00 AM	LEO
Jul. 11, 1932	12:00 AM	SCO	Dec. 20, 1932	12:00 AM	LIB	May. 31, 1933	6:00 PM	VIR
Jul. 14, 1932	1:43 AM	SAG	Dec. 23, 1932	3:26 AM	SCO	Jun. 2, 1933	12:00 AM	LIB
Jul. 16, 1932	3:26 AM	CAP	Dec. 25, 1932	3:12 AM	SAG	Jun. 5, 1933	3:26 AM	SCO

Date	Time	Moon	Date	Time	Moon	Date	Time	Moon
Jun. 7, 1933	3:12 AM	SAG	Nov. 20, 1933	1:36 AM	CAP	May. 3, 1934	3:12 AM	CAP
Jun. 9, 1933	1:30 AM	CAP	Nov. 22, 1933	1:36 AM	AQU	May. 5, 1934	6:51 AM	AQU
Jun. 11, 1933	3:26 AM	AQU	Nov. 24, 1933	5:09 AM	PIS	May. 7, 1934	8:34 AM	PIS
Jun. 13, 1933	5:09 AM	PIS	Nov. 26, 1933	12:55 PM	ARI	May. 9, 1934	1:43 PM	ARI
Jun. 15, 1933	12:55 PM	ARI	Nov. 28, 1933	8:18 PM	TAU	May. 11, 1934	8:18 PM	TAU
Jun. 17, 1933	12:00 AM	TAU	Dec. 1, 1933	8:00 AM	GEM	May. 14, 1934	3:42 AM	GEM
Jun. 20, 1933	12:00 PM	GEM	Dec. 3, 1933	8:00 PM	CAN	May. 16, 1934	4:00 PM	CAN
Jun. 22, 1933	12:00 AM	CAN	Dec. 6, 1933	8:00 AM	LEO	May. 19, 1934	4:00 AM	LEO
Jun. 25, 1933	12:00 PM	LEO	Dec. 8, 1933	10:00 PM	VIR	May. 21, 1934	4:00 PM	VIR
Jun. 27, 1933	12:00 AM	VIR	Dec. 11, 1933	5:32 AM	LIB	May. 24, 1934	1:51 AM	LIB
Jun. 30, 1933	7:23 AM	LIB	Dec. 13, 1933	12:55 PM	SCO	May. 26, 1934	9:14 AM	SCO
Jul. 2, 1933	12:00 PM	SCO	Dec. 15, 1933	1:43 PM	SAG	May. 28, 1934	12:00 PM	SAG
Jul. 4, 1933	12:48 PM	SAG	Dec. 17, 1933	12:48 PM	CAP	May. 30, 1934	11:12 AM	CAP
Jul. 6, 1933	12:48 PM	CAP	Dec. 19, 1933	11:12 AM	AQU	Jun. 1, 1934	12:48 PM	AQU
Jul. 8, 1933	12:48 PM	AQU	Dec. 21, 1933	1:43 PM	PIS	Jun. 3, 1934	3:26 PM	PIS
Jul. 10, 1933	3:26 PM	PIS	Dec. 23, 1933	5:09 PM	ARI	Jun. 5, 1934	6:51 PM	ARI
Jul. 12, 1933	6:51 PM	ARI	Dec. 26, 1933	1:51 AM	TAU	Jun. 8, 1934	1:51 AM	TAU
Jul. 15, 1933	6:00 AM	TAU	Dec. 28, 1933	2:00 PM	GEM	Jun. 10, 1934	12:00 PM	GEM
Jul. 17, 1933	6:00 AM	GEM	Dec. 31, 1933	2:00 AM	CAN	Jun. 12, 1934	10:00 PM	CAN
Jul. 20, 1933	6:00 AM	CAN	Jan. 2, 1934	2:00 PM	LEO	Jun. 15, 1934	10:00 AM	LEO
Jul. 22, 1933	6:00 PM	LEO	Jan. 5, 1934	4:00 AM	VIR	Jun. 17, 1934	12:00 AM	VIR
Jul. 25, 1933	3:42 AM	VIR	Jan. 7, 1934	2:00 PM	LIB	Jun. 20, 1934	12:00 PM	LIB
Jul. 27, 1933	12:55 PM	LIB	Jan. 9, 1934	8:18 PM	SCO	Jun. 22, 1934	6:28 PM	SCO
Jul. 29, 1933	5:09 PM	SCO	Jan. 11, 1934	12:00 AM	SAG	Jun. 24, 1934	10:17 PM	SAG
Jul. 31, 1933	10:17 PM	SAG	Jan. 15, 1934	9:00 PM	AQU	Jun. 26, 1934	10:24 PM	CAP
Aug. 2, 1933	12:00 AM	CAP	Jan. 17, 1934	10:24 PM	PIS	Jun. 28, 1934	10:24 PM	AQU
Aug. 4, 1933	10:24 PM	AQU	Jan. 20, 1934	1:43 AM	ARI	Jun. 30, 1934	10:24 PM	PIS
Aug. 7, 1933	1:43 AM	PIS	Jan. 22, 1934	9:14 AM	TAU	Jul. 3, 1934	1:43 AM	ARI
Aug. 9, 1933	5:09 AM	ARI	Jan. 24, 1934	8:00 PM	GEM	Jul. 5, 1934	7:23 AM	TAU
Aug. 11, 1933	12:55 PM	TAU	Jan. 27, 1934	8:00 AM	CAN	Jul. 7, 1934	6:00 PM	GEM
Aug. 13, 1933	10:09 PM	GEM	Jan. 29, 1934	8:00 PM	LEO	Jul. 10, 1934	4:00 AM	CAN
Aug. 16, 1933	2:00 PM	CAN	Feb. 1, 1934	10:00 AM	VIR	Jul. 12, 1934	4:00 PM	LEO
Aug. 19, 1933	2:00 AM	LEO	Feb. 3, 1934	8:00 PM	LIB	Jul. 15, 1934	6:00 AM	VIR
Aug. 21, 1933	12:00 PM	VIR	Feb. 6, 1934	1:51 AM	SCO	Jul. 17, 1934	6:00 PM	LIB
Aug. 23, 1933	6:28 PM	LIB	Feb. 8, 1934	6:51 AM	SAG	Jul. 20, 1934	1:51 AM	SCO
Aug. 25, 1933	10:17 PM	SCO	Feb. 10, 1934	10:17 AM	CAP	Jul. 22, 1934	6:51 AM	SAG
Aug. 28, 1933	3:26 AM	SAG	Feb. 12, 1934	9:36 AM	AQU	Jul. 24, 1934	8:00 AM	CAP
Aug. 30, 1933	4:48 AM	CAP	Feb. 14, 1934	9:36 AM	PIS	Jul. 26, 1934	7:30 AM	AQU
Sep. 1, 1933	8:34 AM	AQU	Feb. 16, 1934	11:12 AM	ARI	Jul. 28, 1934	8:00 AM	PIS
Sep. 3, 1933	10:17 AM	PIS	Feb. 18, 1934	6:28 PM	TAU	Jul. 30, 1934	10:17 AM	ARI
Sep. 5, 1933	4:37 PM	ARI	Feb. 21, 1934	4:00 AM	GEM	Aug. 1, 1934	1:43 PM	TAU
Sep. 7, 1933	10:09 PM	TAU	Feb. 23, 1934	4:00 PM	CAN	Aug. 3, 1934	10:09 PM	GEM
Sep. 10, 1933	10:00 AM	GEM	Feb. 26, 1934	4:00 AM	LEO	Aug. 6, 1934	10:00 AM	CAN
Sep. 12, 1933	10:00 PM	CAN	Feb. 28, 1934	4:00 PM	VIR	Aug. 8, 1934	10:00 PM	LEO
Sep. 15, 1933	10:00 AM	LEO	Mar. 3, 1934	2:00 AM	LIB	Aug. 11, 1934	12:00 PM	VIR
Sep. 17, 1933	6:28 PM	VIR	Mar. 5, 1934	6:51 AM	SCO	Aug. 13, 1934	12:00 AM	LIB
Sep. 20, 1933	1:51 AM	LIB	Mar. 7, 1934	12:00 PM	SAG	Aug. 16, 1934	10:00 AM	SCO
Sep. 22, 1933	5:09 AM	SCO	Mar. 9, 1934	5:09 PM	CAP	Aug. 18, 1934	4:37 PM	SAG
Sep. 24, 1933	8:34 AM	SAG	Mar. 11, 1934	6:51 PM	AQU	Aug. 20, 1934	6:51 PM	CAP
Sep. 26, 1933	12:00 PM	CAP	Mar. 13, 1934	7:12 PM	PIS	Aug. 22, 1934	7:12 PM	AQU
Sep. 28, 1933	1:43 PM	AQU	Mar. 15, 1934	8:48 PM	ARI	Aug. 24, 1934	7:12 PM	PIS
Sep. 30, 1933	5:09 PM	PIS	Mar. 18, 1934	3:26 AM	TAU	Aug. 26, 1934	7:12 PM	ARI
Oct. 2, 1933	10:17 PM	ARI	Mar. 20, 1934	11:05 AM	GEM	Aug. 28, 1934	10:17 PM	TAU
Oct. 5, 1933	7:23 AM	TAU	Mar. 22, 1934	12:00 AM	CAN	Aug. 31, 1934	5:32 AM	GEM
Oct. 7, 1933	6:00 PM	GEM	Mar. 25, 1934	12:00 PM	LEO	Sep. 2, 1934	2:46 PM	CAN
Oct. 10, 1933	6:00 AM	CAN	Mar. 27, 1934	12:00 AM	VIR	Sep. 5, 1934	6:00 AM	LEO
Oct. 12, 1933	6:00 PM	LEO	Mar. 30, 1934	10:00 AM	LIB	Sep. 7, 1934	6:00 PM	VIR
Oct. 15, 1933	3:42 AM	VIR	Apr. 1, 1934	1:43 PM	SCO	Sep. 10, 1934	6:00 AM	LIB
Oct. 17, 1933	11:05 AM	LIB	Apr. 3, 1934	6:51 PM	SAG	Sep. 12, 1934	4:00 PM	SCO
Oct. 19, 1933	3:26 PM	SCO	Apr. 5, 1934	10:17 PM	CAP	Sep. 14, 1934	10:09 PM	SAG
Oct. 21, 1933	5:09 PM	SAG	Apr. 7, 1934	10:24 PM	AQU	Sep. 17, 1934	1:43 AM	CAP
Oct. 23, 1933	4:00 PM	CAP	Apr. 10, 1934	3:26 AM	PIS	Sep. 19, 1934	3:12 AM	AQU
Oct. 25, 1933	8:34 PM	AQU	Apr. 12, 1934	6:51 AM	ARI	Sep. 21, 1934	4:48 AM	PIS
Oct. 30, 1933	7:23 AM	ARI	Apr. 14, 1934	12:00 PM	TAU	Sep. 23, 1934	6:51 AM	ARI
Nov. 1, 1933	2:46 PM	TAU	Apr. 16, 1934	8:18 PM	GEM	Sep. 25, 1934	8:34 AM	TAU
Nov. 4, 1933	2:00 AM	GEM	Apr. 19, 1934	8:00 AM	CAN	Sep. 27, 1934	2:46 PM	GEM
Nov. 6, 1933	12:00 PM	CAN	Apr. 21, 1934	8:00 PM	LEO	Sep. 29, 1934	10:09 PM	CAN
Nov. 9, 1933	2:00 AM	LEO	Apr. 24, 1934	8:00 AM	VIR	Oct. 2, 1934	12:00 PM	LEO
Nov. 11, 1933	2:00 PM	VIR	Apr. 26, 1934	4:37 PM	LIB	Oct. 5, 1934	2:00 AM	VIR
Nov. 13, 1933	12:00 AM	LIB	Apr. 28, 1934	12:00 AM	SCO	Oct. 7, 1934	11:05 AM	LIB
Nov. 18, 1933	1:36 AM	SAG	May. 1, 1934	1:43 AM	SAG	Oct. 9, 1934	8:18 PM	SCO

125

Date	Time	Moon	Date	Time	Moon	Date	Time	Moon
Oct. 12, 1934	1:43 AM	SAG	Mar. 27, 1935	11:05 AM	CAP	Sep. 5, 1935	4:00 AM	SAG
Oct. 14, 1934	6:51 AM	CAP	Mar. 29, 1935	4:37 PM	AQU	Sep. 7, 1935	11:05 AM	CAP
Oct. 16, 1934	10:17 AM	AQU	Mar. 31, 1935	5:09 PM	PIS	Sep. 9, 1935	3:26 PM	AQU
Oct. 18, 1934	1:43 PM	PIS	Apr. 2, 1935	4:00 PM	ARI	Sep. 11, 1935	2:24 PM	PIS
Oct. 20, 1934	3:26 PM	ARI	Apr. 4, 1935	4:00 PM	TAU	Sep. 13, 1935	2:24 PM	ARI
Oct. 22, 1934	6:51 PM	TAU	Apr. 6, 1935	8:34 PM	GEM	Sep. 15, 1935	2:24 PM	TAU
Oct. 24, 1934	10:17 PM	GEM	Apr. 9, 1935	3:42 AM	CAN	Sep. 17, 1935	5:09 PM	GEM
Oct. 27, 1934	7:23 AM	CAN	Apr. 11, 1935	12:55 PM	LEO	Sep. 19, 1935	12:00 AM	CAN
Oct. 29, 1934	8:00 PM	LEO	Apr. 14, 1935	4:00 AM	VIR	Sep. 22, 1935	10:00 AM	LEO
Nov. 1, 1934	10:00 AM	VIR	Apr. 16, 1935	4:00 PM	LIB	Sep. 24, 1935	10:00 PM	VIR
Nov. 3, 1934	10:00 PM	LIB	Apr. 19, 1935	1:51 AM	SCO	Sep. 27, 1935	10:00 AM	LIB
Nov. 6, 1934	3:26 AM	SCO	Apr. 21, 1935	9:14 AM	SAG	Sep. 29, 1935	12:00 AM	SCO
Nov. 8, 1934	8:34 AM	SAG	Apr. 23, 1935	4:37 PM	CAP	Oct. 2, 1935	10:00 AM	SAG
Nov. 10, 1934	1:43 PM	CAP	Apr. 25, 1935	8:34 PM	AQU	Oct. 4, 1935	8:00 PM	CAP
Nov. 12, 1934	3:26 PM	AQU	Apr. 27, 1935	12:00 AM	PIS	Oct. 6, 1935	10:17 PM	AQU
Nov. 14, 1934	6:51 PM	PIS	Apr. 30, 1935	1:43 AM	ARI	Oct. 9, 1935	1:43 AM	PIS
Nov. 16, 1934	10:17 PM	ARI	May. 2, 1935	3:26 AM	TAU	Oct. 11, 1935	1:36 AM	ARI
Nov. 19, 1934	3:42 AM	TAU	May. 4, 1935	6:51 AM	GEM	Oct. 15, 1935	1:36 AM	GEM
Nov. 21, 1934	9:14 AM	GEM	May. 6, 1935	12:55 PM	CAN	Oct. 17, 1935	7:23 AM	CAN
Nov. 23, 1934	4:37 PM	CAN	May. 8, 1935	12:00 AM	LEO	Oct. 19, 1935	2:46 PM	LEO
Nov. 26, 1934	4:00 AM	LEO	May. 11, 1935	1:05 PM	VIR	Oct. 22, 1935	4:00 AM	VIR
Nov. 28, 1934	6:00 PM	VIR	May. 13, 1935	12:00 AM	LIB	Oct. 24, 1935	6:00 PM	LIB
Dec. 1, 1934	6:00 AM	LIB	May. 16, 1935	9:14 AM	SCO	Oct. 27, 1935	6:00 AM	SCO
Dec. 3, 1934	4:00 PM	SCO	May. 18, 1935	4:37 PM	SAG	Oct. 29, 1935	4:00 PM	SAG
Dec. 5, 1934	8:18 PM	SAG	May. 20, 1935	12:00 AM	CAP	Nov. 3, 1935	5:09 AM	AQU
Dec. 7, 1934	10:17 PM	CAP	May. 23, 1935	1:43 AM	AQU	Nov. 5, 1935	8:34 AM	PIS
Dec. 9, 1934	12:00 AM	AQU	May. 25, 1935	5:09 AM	PIS	Nov. 7, 1935	12:00 PM	ARI
Dec. 14, 1934	3:26 AM	ARI	May. 27, 1935	3:42 AM	ARI	Nov. 9, 1935	11:12 AM	TAU
Dec. 16, 1934	9:14 AM	TAU	May. 29, 1935	10:17 AM	TAU	Nov. 11, 1935	1:43 PM	GEM
Dec. 18, 1934	4:37 PM	GEM	May. 31, 1935	4:37 PM	GEM	Nov. 13, 1935	3:26 PM	CAN
Dec. 21, 1934	2:00 AM	CAN	Jun. 2, 1935	10:09 PM	CAN	Nov. 15, 1935	12:00 AM	LEO
Dec. 23, 1934	12:00 PM	LEO	Jun. 5, 1935	8:00 AM	LEO	Nov. 18, 1935	12:00 PM	VIR
Dec. 26, 1934	2:00 AM	VIR	Jun. 7, 1935	8:00 PM	VIR	Nov. 20, 1935	12:00 AM	LIB
Dec. 28, 1934	2:00 PM	LIB	Jun. 10, 1935	8:00 AM	LIB	Nov. 23, 1935	12:00 PM	SCO
Jan. 2, 1935	5:09 AM	SAG	Jun. 12, 1935	8:00 PM	SCO	Nov. 25, 1935	12:00 AM	SAG
Jan. 4, 1935	8:34 AM	CAP	Jun. 15, 1935	1:51 AM	SAG	Nov. 28, 1935	5:32 AM	CAP
Jan. 6, 1935	8:00 AM	AQU	Jun. 17, 1935	7:23 AM	CAP	Nov. 30, 1935	10:17 AM	AQU
Jan. 8, 1935	8:00 AM	PIS	Jun. 19, 1935	8:00 AM	AQU	Dec. 2, 1935	3:26 PM	PIS
Jan. 10, 1935	10:17 AM	ARI	Jun. 21, 1935	9:36 AM	PIS	Dec. 4, 1935	6:51 PM	ARI
Jan. 12, 1935	1:43 PM	TAU	Jun. 23, 1935	1:43 AM	ARI	Dec. 8, 1935	8:34 PM	TAU
Jan. 14, 1935	10:09 PM	GEM	Jun. 25, 1935	5:09 PM	TAU	Dec. 8, 1935	8:48 PM	GEM
Jan. 17, 1935	8:00 AM	CAN	Jun. 27, 1935	8:34 PM	GEM	Dec. 11, 1935	3:42 AM	CAN
Jan. 19, 1935	8:00 PM	LEO	Jun. 30, 1935	5:32 AM	CAN	Dec. 13, 1935	9:14 AM	LEO
Jan. 22, 1935	8:00 AM	VIR	Jul. 2, 1935	4:00 PM	LEO	Dec. 15, 1935	6:28 PM	VIR
Jan. 24, 1935	8:00 PM	LIB	Jul. 5, 1935	4:22 AM	VIR	Dec. 18, 1935	8:00 AM	LIB
Jan. 27, 1935	8:00 AM	SCO	Jul. 7, 1935	4:00 PM	LIB	Dec. 20, 1935	10:00 PM	SCO
Jan. 29, 1935	2:46 PM	SAG	Jul. 10, 1935	4:00 AM	SCO	Dec. 23, 1935	8:00 AM	SAG
Jan. 31, 1935	6:51 PM	CAP	Jul. 12, 1935	11:05 AM	SAG	Dec. 25, 1935	12:00 PM	CAP
Feb. 2, 1935	7:12 AM	AQU	Jul. 14, 1935	3:26 PM	CAP	Dec. 27, 1935	5:09 PM	AQU
Feb. 4, 1935	7:12 AM	PIS	Jul. 16, 1935	6:51 PM	AQU	Dec. 29, 1935	8:34 PM	PIS
Feb. 6, 1935	7:12 AM	ARI	Jul. 18, 1935	5:36 PM	PIS	Dec. 31, 1935	12:00 AM	ARI
Feb. 8, 1935	7:12 AM	TAU	Jul. 20, 1935	8:34 PM	ARI	Jan. 3, 1936	1:43 AM	TAU
Feb. 11, 1935	3:42 AM	GEM	Jul. 22, 1935	10:17 PM	TAU	Jan. 5, 1936	5:09 AM	GEM
Feb. 13, 1935	2:00 PM	CAN	Jul. 25, 1935	3:42 AM	GEM	Jan. 7, 1936	10:17 AM	CAN
Feb. 16, 1935	2:00 AM	LEO	Jul. 27, 1935	11:05 AM	CAN	Jan. 9, 1936	6:28 PM	LEO
Feb. 18, 1935	2:00 PM	VIR	Jul. 29, 1935	8:18 PM	LEO	Jan. 12, 1936	6:00 AM	VIR
Feb. 21, 1935	4:22 AM	LIB	Aug. 1, 1935	10:00 AM	VIR	Jan. 14, 1936	7:38 PM	LIB
Feb. 23, 1935	2:00 PM	SCO	Aug. 3, 1935	10:00 PM	LIB	Jan. 17, 1936	6:00 AM	SCO
Feb. 25, 1935	10:09 PM	SAG	Aug. 6, 1935	12:00 PM	SCO	Jan. 19, 1936	2:46 PM	SAG
Feb. 28, 1935	3:26 AM	CAP	Aug. 8, 1935	10:00 PM	SAG	Jan. 21, 1936	12:00 AM	CAP
Mar. 2, 1935	6:51 AM	AQU	Aug. 11, 1935	1:43 AM	CAP	Jan. 24, 1936	3:26 AM	AQU
Mar. 4, 1935	6:24 AM	PIS	Aug. 13, 1935	5:09 AM	AQU	Jan. 26, 1936	5:09 AM	PIS
Mar. 6, 1935	4:30 AM	ARI	Aug. 15, 1935	4:48 AM	PIS	Jan. 28, 1936	4:48 AM	ARI
Mar. 8, 1935	6:51 AM	TAU	Aug. 17, 1935	3:12 AM	ARI	Jan. 30, 1936	6:24 AM	TAU
Mar. 10, 1935	10:17 AM	GEM	Aug. 19, 1935	5:09 AM	TAU	Feb. 1, 1936	12:55 PM	GEM
Mar. 12, 1935	6:28 PM	CAN	Aug. 21, 1935	8:34 AM	GEM	Feb. 3, 1936	6:28 PM	CAN
Mar. 15, 1935	8:00 AM	LEO	Aug. 23, 1935	4:37 PM	CAN	Feb. 6, 1936	1:51 AM	LEO
Mar. 17, 1935	8:00 PM	VIR	Aug. 26, 1935	4:00 AM	LEO	Feb. 8, 1936	11:05 AM	VIR
Mar. 20, 1935	10:00 AM	LIB	Aug. 28, 1935	4:00 PM	VIR	Feb. 10, 1936	12:00 AM	LIB
Mar. 22, 1935	8:00 PM	SCO	Aug. 31, 1935	6:33 AM	LIB	Feb. 13, 1936	2:00 PM	SCO
Mar. 25, 1935	3:42 AM	SAG	Sep. 2, 1935	6:00 PM	SCO	Feb. 18, 1936	9:14 AM	CAP

Date	Time	Moon	Date	Time	Moon	Date	Time	Moon
Feb. 20, 1936	1:43 PM	A Q U	Aug. 4, 1936	1:43 PM	P I S	Jan. 15, 1937	2:46 PM	P I S
Feb. 22, 1936	2:24 PM	P I S	Aug. 6, 1936	2:24 PM	A R I	Jan. 17, 1937	6:51 PM	A R I
Feb. 24, 1936	2:24 PM	A R I	Aug. 8, 1936	4:00 PM	T A U	Jan. 19, 1937	10:17 PM	T A U
Feb. 26, 1936	2:24 PM	T A U	Aug. 10, 1936	8:34 PM	G E M	Jan. 24, 1937	3:26 AM	C A N
Feb. 28, 1936	5:09 PM	G E M	Aug. 12, 1936	12:00 AM	C A N	Jan. 26, 1937	6:51 AM	L E O
Mar. 1, 1936	12:00 AM	C A N	Aug. 15, 1936	7:23 AM	L E O	Jan. 28, 1937	12:55 PM	V I R
Mar. 4, 1936	7:23 AM	L E O	Aug. 17, 1936	2:46 PM	V I R	Jan. 30, 1937	8:18 PM	L I B
Mar. 6, 1936	8:00 PM	V I R	Aug. 20, 1936	2:00 AM	L I B	Feb. 2, 1937	8:00 AM	S C O
Mar. 9, 1936	8:00 AM	L I B	Aug. 22, 1936	2:00 PM	S C O	Feb. 4, 1937	8:00 PM	S A G
Mar. 11, 1936	8:00 PM	S C O	Aug. 25, 1936	4:00 AM	S A G	Feb. 7, 1937	7:23 AM	C A P
Mar. 14, 1936	8:00 AM	S A G	Aug. 27, 1936	2:00 PM	C A P	Feb. 9, 1937	4:37 PM	A Q U
Mar. 16, 1936	4:37 PM	C A P	Aug. 29, 1936	8:18 PM	A Q U	Feb. 11, 1937	12:00 AM	P I S
Mar. 18, 1936	10:17 PM	A Q U	Aug. 31, 1936	12:00 AM	P I S	Feb. 14, 1937	1:43 AM	A R I
Mar. 21, 1936	1:36 AM	P I S	Sep. 4, 1936	12:00 AM	T A U	Feb. 16, 1937	3:26 AM	T A U
Mar. 23, 1936	1:36 AM	A R I	Sep. 7, 1936	1:43 AM	G E M	Feb. 18, 1937	6:51 AM	G E M
Mar. 24, 1936	10:30 PM	T A U	Sep. 9, 1936	5:09 AM	C A N	Feb. 20, 1937	10:17 AM	C A N
Mar. 27, 1936	1:43 AM	G E M	Sep. 11, 1936	12:55 PM	L E O	Feb. 22, 1937	1:43 PM	L E O
Mar. 29, 1936	5:09 AM	C A N	Sep. 13, 1936	12:00 AM	V I R	Feb. 24, 1937	6:51 PM	V I R
Mar. 31, 1936	12:55 PM	L E O	Sep. 16, 1936	10:00 AM	L I B	Feb. 27, 1937	6:00 AM	L I B
Apr. 3, 1936	2:00 AM	V I R	Sep. 18, 1936	10:00 PM	S C O	Mar. 1, 1937	4:00 PM	S C O
Apr. 5, 1936	2:00 PM	L I B	Sep. 21, 1936	10:00 AM	S A G	Mar. 4, 1937	6:33 AM	S A G
Apr. 8, 1936	2:00 AM	S C O	Sep. 23, 1936	10:00 PM	C A P	Mar. 6, 1937	6:00 PM	C A P
Apr. 10, 1936	2:00 PM	S A G	Sep. 26, 1936	5:32 AM	A Q U	Mar. 9, 1937	1:51 AM	A Q U
Apr. 15, 1936	7:23 AM	A Q U	Sep. 28, 1936	10:17 PM	P I S	Mar. 11, 1937	6:51 PM	P I S
Apr. 17, 1936	12:00 PM	P I S	Sep. 30, 1936	9:36 AM	A R I	Mar. 13, 1937	10:17 AM	A R I
Apr. 19, 1936	1:43 PM	A R I	Oct. 2, 1936	9:36 AM	T A U	Mar. 15, 1937	12:00 PM	T A U
Apr. 21, 1936	10:30 AM	T A U	Oct. 4, 1936	9:36 AM	G E M	Mar. 17, 1937	11:12 AM	G E M
Apr. 23, 1936	11:12 AM	G E M	Oct. 6, 1936	12:00 PM	C A N	Mar. 19, 1937	3:26 PM	C A N
Apr. 25, 1936	1:43 PM	C A N	Oct. 8, 1936	6:28 PM	L E O	Mar. 21, 1937	6:51 PM	L E O
Apr. 27, 1936	8:18 PM	L E O	Oct. 11, 1936	4:00 AM	V I R	Mar. 24, 1937	3:42 AM	V I R
Apr. 30, 1936	8:00 AM	V I R	Oct. 13, 1936	4:00 PM	L I B	Mar. 26, 1937	2:00 PM	L I B
May. 2, 1936	8:00 PM	L I B	Oct. 16, 1936	4:00 AM	S C O	Mar. 28, 1937	12:00 AM	S C O
May. 5, 1936	8:00 AM	S C O	Oct. 18, 1936	4:00 PM	S A G	Mar. 31, 1937	12:00 PM	S A G
May. 7, 1936	8:00 PM	S A G	Oct. 21, 1936	4:00 AM	C A P	Apr. 3, 1937	2:00 AM	C A P
May. 10, 1936	5:32 AM	C A P	Oct. 23, 1936	12:55 PM	A Q U	Apr. 5, 1937	11:05 AM	A Q U
May. 12, 1936	12:55 PM	A Q U	Oct. 25, 1936	6:51 PM	P I S	Apr. 7, 1937	6:28 PM	P I S
May. 14, 1936	8:18 PM	P I S	Oct. 27, 1936	10:17 PM	A R I	Apr. 9, 1937	8:34 PM	A R I
May. 16, 1936	10:17 PM	A R I	Oct. 29, 1936	8:48 PM	T A U	Apr. 11, 1937	8:48 PM	T A U
May. 18, 1936	8:48 PM	T A U	Oct. 31, 1936	6:00 PM	G E M	Apr. 13, 1937	8:48 PM	G E M
May. 20, 1936	10:24 PM	G E M	Nov. 2, 1936	7:12 PM	C A N	Apr. 15, 1937	8:48 PM	C A N
May. 22, 1936	10:24 PM	C A N	Nov. 5, 1936	1:51 AM	L E O	Apr. 18, 1937	1:43 AM	L E O
May. 25, 1936	5:32 AM	L E O	Nov. 7, 1936	9:14 AM	V I R	Apr. 20, 1937	9:14 AM	V I R
May. 27, 1936	4:00 PM	V I R	Nov. 9, 1936	10:00 PM	L I B	Apr. 22, 1937	8:00 PM	L I B
May. 30, 1936	2:00 AM	L I B	Nov. 12, 1936	10:00 AM	S C O	Apr. 25, 1937	6:00 AM	S C O
Jun. 1, 1936	5:27 PM	S C O	Nov. 14, 1936	10:00 PM	S A G	Apr. 27, 1937	6:00 PM	S A G
Jun. 4, 1936	1:51 AM	S A G	Nov. 17, 1936	10:00 AM	C A P	Apr. 30, 1937	8:00 AM	C A P
Jun. 6, 1936	11:05 AM	C A P	Nov. 19, 1936	10:00 PM	A Q U	May. 2, 1937	8:00 PM	A Q U
Jun. 8, 1936	8:18 PM	A Q U	Nov. 22, 1936	3:42 AM	P I S	May. 5, 1937	3:42 AM	P I S
Jun. 13, 1936	3:26 AM	A R I	Nov. 24, 1936	6:51 AM	A R I	May. 7, 1937	6:51 AM	A R I
Jun. 15, 1936	4:48 AM	T A U	Nov. 26, 1936	8:34 AM	T A U	May. 9, 1937	8:34 AM	T A U
Jun. 17, 1936	6:24 AM	G E M	Nov. 28, 1936	6:00 AM	G E M	May. 11, 1937	6:24 AM	G E M
Jun. 19, 1936	10:17 AM	C A N	Nov. 30, 1936	8:34 AM	C A N	May. 13, 1937	6:24 AM	C A N
Jun. 21, 1936	1:43 PM	L E O	Dec. 2, 1936	10:17 AM	L E O	May. 15, 1937	8:00 AM	L E O
Jun. 23, 1936	10:09 PM	V I R	Dec. 4, 1936	4:37 PM	V I R	May. 17, 1937	1:43 PM	V I R
Jun. 26, 1936	10:00 AM	L I B	Dec. 7, 1936	4:00 AM	L I B	May. 22, 1937	12:00 PM	S C O
Jun. 28, 1936	10:00 PM	S C O	Dec. 9, 1936	4:00 PM	S C O	May. 27, 1937	2:00 PM	C A P
Jul. 1, 1936	10:00 AM	S A G	Dec. 12, 1936	6:33 AM	S A G	May. 30, 1937	2:00 AM	A Q U
Jul. 3, 1936	6:28 PM	C A P	Dec. 14, 1936	2:46 PM	C A P	Jun. 1, 1937	9:14 AM	P I S
Jul. 6, 1936	1:51 AM	A Q U	Dec. 17, 1936	1:51 AM	A Q U	Jun. 3, 1937	4:37 PM	A R I
Jul. 8, 1936	7:23 AM	P I S	Dec. 19, 1936	9:14 AM	P I S	Jun. 5, 1937	6:51 PM	T A U
Jul. 10, 1936	8:34 AM	A R I	Dec. 21, 1936	2:46 PM	A R I	Jun. 7, 1937	5:36 PM	G E M
Jul. 12, 1936	12:00 PM	T A U	Dec. 23, 1936	5:09 PM	T A U	Jun. 9, 1937	5:36 PM	C A N
Jul. 14, 1936	3:26 PM	G E M	Dec. 25, 1936	6:51 PM	G E M	Jun. 11, 1937	5:36 PM	L E O
Jul. 16, 1936	8:18 PM	C A N	Dec. 27, 1936	5:36 PM	C A N	Jun. 13, 1937	10:17 PM	V I R
Jul. 18, 1936	10:17 PM	L E O	Dec. 29, 1936	7:12 PM	L E O	Jun. 16, 1937	8:00 AM	L I B
Jul. 21, 1936	7:23 AM	V I R	Jan. 1, 1937	1:43 AM	V I R	Jun. 18, 1937	6:00 PM	S C O
Jul. 23, 1936	4:37 PM	L I B	Jan. 3, 1937	11:05 AM	L I B	Jun. 21, 1937	8:44 AM	S A G
Jul. 26, 1936	6:00 AM	S C O	Jan. 5, 1937	12:00 AM	S C O	Jun. 23, 1937	8:00 PM	C A P
Jul. 28, 1936	8:00 PM	S A G	Jan. 8, 1937	12:00 PM	S A G	Jun. 26, 1937	8:00 AM	A Q U
Jul. 31, 1936	3:42 AM	C A P	Jan. 10, 1937	12:00 AM	C A P	Jun. 28, 1937	2:46 PM	P I S
Aug. 2, 1936	11:05 AM	A Q U	Jan. 13, 1937	10:00 AM	A Q U	Jun. 30, 1937	10:09 PM	A R I

Date	Time	Moon	Date	Time	Moon	Date	Time	Moon
Jul. 3, 1937	1:43 AM	T A U	Dec. 16, 1937	3:12 AM	G E M	May. 27, 1938	1:43 AM	T A U
Jul. 5, 1937	3:26 AM	G E M	Dec. 18, 1937	3:12 AM	C A N	May. 29, 1938	3:26 AM	G E M
Jul. 7, 1937	3:12 AM	C A N	Dec. 20, 1937	3:12 AM	L E O	May. 31, 1938	3:12 AM	C A N
Jul. 9, 1937	4:48 AM	L E O	Dec. 22, 1937	5:09 AM	V I R	Jun. 2, 1938	3:12 AM	L E O
Jul. 11, 1937	8:34 AM	V I R	Dec. 24, 1937	11:05 AM	L I B	Jun. 4, 1938	5:09 AM	V I R
Jul. 13, 1937	2:46 AM	L I B	Dec. 26, 1937	10:00 PM	S C O	Jun. 6, 1938	11:05 AM	L I B
Jul. 16, 1937	2:00 AM	S C O	Dec. 29, 1937	10:55 AM	S A G	Jun. 8, 1938	6:28 PM	S C O
Jul. 18, 1937	2:00 AM	S A G	Dec. 31, 1937	10:00 PM	C A P	Jun. 11, 1938	6:00 AM	S A G
Jul. 21, 1937	2:00 AM	C A P	Jan. 3, 1938	10:00 AM	A Q U	Jun. 13, 1938	6:00 PM	C A P
Jul. 23, 1937	2:00 PM	A Q U	Jan. 5, 1938	10:00 PM	P I S	Jun. 16, 1938	8:44 AM	A Q U
Jul. 25, 1937	12:00 AM	P I S	Jan. 8, 1938	5:32 AM	A R I	Jun. 18, 1938	8:00 PM	P I S
Jul. 28, 1937	3:42 AM	A R I	Jan. 10, 1938	10:17 AM	T A U	Jun. 21, 1938	3:42 AM	A R I
Jul. 30, 1937	6:51 AM	T A U	Jan. 12, 1938	1:43 PM	G E M	Jun. 23, 1938	11:05 AM	T A U
Aug. 1, 1937	10:17 AM	G E M	Jan. 14, 1938	2:24 PM	C A N	Jun. 25, 1938	1:43 PM	G E M
Aug. 3, 1937	11:12 AM	C A N	Jan. 16, 1938	2:24 PM	L E O	Jun. 27, 1938	12:48 PM	C A N
Aug. 5, 1937	3:26 PM	L E O	Jan. 18, 1938	2:24 PM	V I R	Jun. 29, 1938	12:48 PM	L E O
Aug. 7, 1937	5:09 PM	V I R	Jan. 20, 1938	6:51 PM	L I B	Jul. 1, 1938	12:48 PM	V I R
Aug. 9, 1937	12:00 AM	L I B	Jan. 23, 1938	3:42 AM	S C O	Jul. 3, 1938	5:09 PM	L I B
Aug. 12, 1937	10:00 AM	S C O	Jan. 25, 1938	4:00 PM	S A G	Jul. 5, 1938	12:00 AM	S C O
Aug. 14, 1937	10:00 PM	S A G	Jan. 28, 1938	4:00 AM	C A P	Jul. 8, 1938	12:00 PM	S A G
Aug. 17, 1937	10:00 AM	C A P	Jan. 30, 1938	6:00 PM	A Q U	Jul. 10, 1938	12:00 AM	C A P
Aug. 19, 1937	10:00 PM	A Q U	Feb. 2, 1938	4:00 AM	P I S	Jul. 13, 1938	12:00 PM	A Q U
Aug. 22, 1937	3:26 AM	P I S	Feb. 4, 1938	11:05 AM	A R I	Jul. 18, 1938	12:00 PM	A R I
Aug. 24, 1937	8:34 AM	A R I	Feb. 6, 1938	3:26 PM	T A U	Jul. 20, 1938	6:28 PM	T A U
Aug. 26, 1937	12:00 PM	T A U	Feb. 8, 1938	8:34 PM	G E M	Jul. 23, 1938	10:17 AM	G E M
Aug. 28, 1937	3:26 PM	G E M	Feb. 10, 1938	12:00 AM	C A N	Jul. 26, 1938	12:00 AM	L E O
Aug. 30, 1937	6:51 PM	C A N	Feb. 12, 1938	12:00 AM	L E O	Jul. 28, 1938	9:00 PM	V I R
Sep. 1, 1937	10:17 PM	L E O	Feb. 15, 1938	1:36 AM	V I R	Jul. 31, 1938	1:43 AM	L I B
Sep. 4, 1937	1:43 AM	V I R	Feb. 17, 1938	5:09 AM	L I B	Aug. 2, 1938	7:23 AM	S C O
Sep. 6, 1937	9:14 AM	L I B	Feb. 19, 1938	12:55 PM	S C O	Aug. 4, 1938	6:00 PM	S A G
Sep. 8, 1937	4:37 PM	S C O	Feb. 21, 1938	12:00 AM	S A G	Aug. 7, 1938	6:00 AM	C A P
Sep. 11, 1937	6:00 AM	S A G	Feb. 24, 1938	12:00 PM	C A P	Aug. 9, 1938	9:49 PM	A Q U
Sep. 13, 1937	6:00 PM	C A P	Feb. 26, 1938	12:00 AM	A Q U	Aug. 12, 1938	5:32 AM	P I S
Sep. 16, 1937	6:00 AM	A Q U	Mar. 1, 1938	9:14 AM	P I S	Aug. 14, 1938	6:00 PM	A R I
Sep. 18, 1937	12:55 PM	P I S	Mar. 3, 1938	3:26 PM	A R I	Aug. 16, 1938	12:00 AM	T A U
Sep. 20, 1937	5:09 PM	A R I	Mar. 5, 1938	12:00 AM	T A U	Aug. 19, 1938	5:09 AM	G E M
Sep. 22, 1937	8:34 PM	T A U	Mar. 8, 1938	1:43 AM	G E M	Aug. 21, 1938	8:34 AM	C A N
Sep. 24, 1937	10:17 PM	G E M	Mar. 10, 1938	5:09 AM	C A N	Aug. 23, 1938	9:36 AM	L E O
Sep. 26, 1937	10:24 PM	C A N	Mar. 12, 1938	8:34 AM	L E O	Aug. 25, 1938	9:36 AM	V I R
Sep. 29, 1937	3:26 AM	L E O	Mar. 14, 1938	9:36 AM	V I R	Aug. 27, 1938	12:00 PM	L I B
Oct. 1, 1937	8:34 AM	V I R	Mar. 16, 1938	4:37 PM	L I B	Aug. 29, 1938	3:26 PM	S C O
Oct. 3, 1937	4:37 PM	L I B	Mar. 18, 1938	10:09 PM	S C O	Sep. 3, 1938	2:00 PM	C A P
Oct. 8, 1937	2:00 PM	S A G	Mar. 21, 1938	8:00 AM	S A G	Sep. 6, 1938	2:00 AM	A Q U
Oct. 11, 1937	2:00 AM	C A P	Mar. 23, 1938	8:00 PM	C A P	Sep. 8, 1938	2:00 PM	P I S
Oct. 13, 1937	12:55 PM	A Q U	Mar. 26, 1938	8:00 AM	A Q U	Sep. 10, 1938	10:09 PM	A R I
Oct. 15, 1937	10:09 PM	P I S	Mar. 28, 1938	8:00 PM	P I S	Sep. 13, 1938	5:32 AM	T A U
Oct. 18, 1937	3:26 AM	A R I	Mar. 31, 1938	1:51 AM	A R I	Sep. 15, 1938	10:17 AM	G E M
Oct. 20, 1937	4:48 AM	T A U	Apr. 2, 1938	5:09 AM	T A U	Sep. 17, 1938	3:26 PM	C A N
Oct. 22, 1937	4:48 AM	G E M	Apr. 4, 1938	8:34 AM	G E M	Sep. 19, 1938	4:00 PM	L E O
Oct. 24, 1937	6:24 AM	C A N	Apr. 6, 1938	12:00 PM	C A N	Sep. 21, 1938	5:36 PM	V I R
Oct. 26, 1937	10:17 AM	L E O	Apr. 8, 1938	1:43 PM	L E O	Sep. 23, 1938	10:17 PM	L I B
Oct. 28, 1937	1:43 PM	V I R	Apr. 10, 1938	5:09 PM	V I R	Sep. 26, 1938	1:43 AM	S C O
Oct. 30, 1937	10:09 PM	L I B	Apr. 12, 1938	12:00 AM	L I B	Sep. 28, 1938	9:14 AM	S A G
Nov. 2, 1937	7:23 AM	S C O	Apr. 15, 1938	5:32 AM	S C O	Sep. 30, 1938	10:00 PM	C A P
Nov. 4, 1937	8:00 PM	S A G	Apr. 17, 1938	2:46 PM	S A G	Oct. 3, 1938	10:00 AM	A Q U
Nov. 7, 1937	10:00 AM	C A P	Apr. 20, 1938	4:00 AM	C A P	Oct. 5, 1938	10:00 PM	P I S
Nov. 9, 1937	10:00 PM	A Q U	Apr. 22, 1938	7:38 PM	A Q U	Oct. 8, 1938	5:32 AM	A R I
Nov. 12, 1937	7:23 AM	P I S	Apr. 25, 1938	4:00 AM	P I S	Oct. 10, 1938	12:55 PM	T A U
Nov. 14, 1937	2:46 PM	A R I	Apr. 27, 1938	11:05 AM	A R I	Oct. 12, 1938	5:09 PM	G E M
Nov. 16, 1937	5:09 PM	T A U	Apr. 29, 1938	3:26 PM	T A U	Oct. 14, 1938	8:34 PM	C A N
Nov. 18, 1937	4:00 PM	G E M	May. 1, 1938	4:00 PM	G E M	Oct. 16, 1938	12:00 AM	L E O
Nov. 20, 1937	4:00 PM	C A N	May. 3, 1938	6:51 PM	C A N	Oct. 21, 1938	5:09 AM	L I B
Nov. 22, 1937	4:00 PM	L E O	May. 5, 1938	8:34 PM	L E O	Oct. 23, 1938	10:17 AM	S C O
Nov. 24, 1937	8:34 PM	V I R	May. 7, 1938	10:17 PM	V I R	Oct. 25, 1938	6:28 PM	S A G
Nov. 27, 1937	3:42 AM	L I B	May. 10, 1938	5:32 AM	L I B	Oct. 28, 1938	6:00 AM	C A P
Nov. 29, 1937	12:55 PM	S C O	May. 12, 1938	12:55 PM	S C O	Oct. 30, 1938	6:00 PM	A Q U
Dec. 2, 1937	4:22 AM	S A G	May. 14, 1938	12:00 AM	S A G	Nov. 2, 1938	6:00 AM	P I S
Dec. 4, 1937	4:00 PM	C A P	May. 17, 1938	12:00 PM	C A P	Nov. 4, 1938	2:46 PM	A R I
Dec. 7, 1937	4:00 AM	A Q U	May. 19, 1938	12:00 AM	A Q U	Nov. 6, 1938	10:09 PM	T A U
Dec. 9, 1937	4:00 PM	P I S	May. 22, 1938	12:00 PM	P I S	Nov. 9, 1938	1:43 AM	G E M
Dec. 14, 1937	3:26 AM	T A U	May. 24, 1938	8:18 PM	A R I	Nov. 11, 1938	3:26 AM	C A N

128

Date	Time	Moon	Date	Time	Moon	Date	Time	Moon
Nov. 13, 1938	5:09 AM	LEO	Apr. 28, 1939	11:12 AM	VIR	Oct. 13, 1939	5:09 PM	SCO
Nov. 15, 1938	6:51 AM	VIR	Apr. 30, 1939	3:26 PM	LIB	Oct. 15, 1939	6:51 PM	SAG
Nov. 17, 1938	12:55 PM	LIB	May. 2, 1939	6:51 PM	SCO	Oct. 18, 1939	1:51 AM	CAP
Nov. 19, 1938	6:28 PM	SCO	May. 4, 1939	10:17 PM	SAG	Oct. 20, 1939	11:05 AM	AQU
Nov. 22, 1938	4:00 AM	SAG	May. 7, 1939	7:23 AM	CAP	Oct. 25, 1939	2:00 PM	ARI
Nov. 24, 1938	2:00 PM	CAP	May. 9, 1939	8:00 PM	AQU	Oct. 27, 1939	10:09 PM	TAU
Nov. 27, 1938	2:00 AM	AQU	May. 12, 1939	8:00 AM	PIS	Oct. 30, 1939	10:00 AM	GEM
Nov. 29, 1938	2:00 PM	PIS	May. 14, 1939	8:00 PM	ARI	Nov. 1, 1939	2:46 PM	CAN
Dec. 2, 1938	2:00 AM	ARI	May. 17, 1939	3:42 AM	TAU	Nov. 3, 1939	6:51 PM	LEO
Dec. 4, 1938	6:51 AM	TAU	May. 19, 1939	11:05 AM	GEM	Nov. 5, 1939	10:17 PM	VIR
Dec. 6, 1938	12:00 PM	GEM	May. 21, 1939	1:43 PM	CAN	Nov. 7, 1939	10:24 PM	LIB
Dec. 8, 1938	11:12 AM	CAN	May. 23, 1939	2:24 PM	LEO	Nov. 10, 1939	1:36 AM	SCO
Dec. 10, 1938	1:43 PM	LEO	May. 25, 1939	6:51 PM	VIR	Nov. 12, 1939	5:09 AM	SAG
Dec. 12, 1938	12:48 PM	VIR	May. 27, 1939	8:34 PM	LIB	Nov. 14, 1939	10:17 AM	CAP
Dec. 14, 1938	5:09 PM	LIB	May. 30, 1939	1:43 AM	SCO	Nov. 16, 1939	10:00 PM	AQU
Dec. 16, 1938	12:00 PM	SCO	Jun. 1, 1939	6:51 AM	SAG	Nov. 19, 1939	8:00 AM	PIS
Dec. 19, 1938	10:00 AM	SAG	Jun. 3, 1939	6:00 PM	CAP	Nov. 21, 1939	10:00 PM	ARI
Dec. 21, 1938	6:28 PM	CAP	Jun. 6, 1939	4:00 AM	AQU	Nov. 24, 1939	7:23 AM	TAU
Dec. 24, 1938	8:00 AM	AQU	Jun. 8, 1939	4:00 PM	PIS	Nov. 26, 1939	4:37 PM	GEM
Dec. 26, 1938	10:00 PM	PIS	Jun. 11, 1939	4:00 AM	ARI	Nov. 28, 1939	8:34 PM	CAN
Dec. 29, 1938	10:00 AM	ARI	Jun. 13, 1939	12:55 PM	TAU	Nov. 30, 1939	12:00 AM	LEO
Dec. 31, 1938	8:00 PM	TAU	Jun. 15, 1939	8:18 PM	GEM	Dec. 3, 1939	3:26 AM	VIR
Jan. 2, 1939	10:17 PM	GEM	Jun. 17, 1939	10:17 PM	CAN	Dec. 5, 1939	6:51 AM	LIB
Jan. 4, 1939	10:24 PM	CAN	Jun. 19, 1939	10:24 PM	LEO	Dec. 7, 1939	10:17 AM	SCO
Jan. 6, 1939	10:24 PM	LEO	Jun. 21, 1939	10:24 PM	VIR	Dec. 9, 1939	1:43 PM	SAG
Jan. 8, 1939	10:24 PM	VIR	Jun. 26, 1939	6:51 AM	SCO	Dec. 11, 1939	6:51 PM	CAP
Jan. 10, 1939	10:24 PM	LIB	Jun. 28, 1939	2:46 PM	SAG	Dec. 14, 1939	6:00 AM	AQU
Jan. 13, 1939	5:32 AM	SCO	Jun. 30, 1939	10:09 PM	CAP	Dec. 16, 1939	6:00 PM	PIS
Jan. 15, 1939	4:00 PM	SAG	Jul. 3, 1939	9:14 AM	AQU	Dec. 19, 1939	6:00 AM	ARI
Jan. 18, 1939	2:00 AM	CAP	Jul. 8, 1939	12:00 PM	ARI	Dec. 21, 1939	6:00 PM	TAU
Jan. 20, 1939	5:27 PM	AQU	Jul. 10, 1939	12:00 AM	TAU	Dec. 24, 1939	1:51 AM	GEM
Jan. 23, 1939	4:00 AM	PIS	Jul. 13, 1939	5:32 AM	GEM	Dec. 26, 1939	5:09 AM	CAN
Jan. 25, 1939	4:00 AM	ARI	Jul. 15, 1939	8:34 AM	CAN	Dec. 28, 1939	8:34 AM	LEO
Jan. 30, 1939	6:51 AM	GEM	Jul. 17, 1939	8:00 AM	LEO	Dec. 30, 1939	10:17 AM	VIR
Feb. 1, 1939	9:36 AM	CAN	Jul. 19, 1939	8:00 AM	VIR	Jan. 1, 1940	2:00 PM	LIB
Feb. 3, 1939	9:36 AM	LEO	Jul. 21, 1939	8:00 AM	LIB	Jan. 3, 1940	3:26 PM	SCO
Feb. 5, 1939	9:36 AM	VIR	Jul. 23, 1939	12:00 PM	SCO	Jan. 5, 1940	10:09 PM	SAG
Feb. 7, 1939	10:17 AM	LIB	Jul. 25, 1939	8:18 PM	SAG	Jan. 8, 1940	3:42 AM	CAP
Feb. 9, 1939	12:00 PM	SCO	Jul. 28, 1939	6:00 AM	CAP	Jan. 10, 1940	12:55 PM	AQU
Feb. 11, 1939	8:18 PM	SAG	Jul. 30, 1939	6:00 PM	AQU	Jan. 13, 1940	2:00 AM	PIS
Feb. 14, 1939	8:00 AM	CAP	Aug. 2, 1939	6:00 AM	PIS	Jan. 15, 1940	2:00 PM	ARI
Feb. 16, 1939	12:00 AM	AQU	Aug. 4, 1939	6:00 PM	ARI	Jan. 18, 1940	2:00 AM	TAU
Feb. 19, 1939	10:00 AM	PIS	Aug. 7, 1939	6:00 AM	TAU	Jan. 20, 1940	11:05 AM	GEM
Feb. 21, 1939	10:00 PM	ARI	Aug. 9, 1939	4:00 PM	GEM	Jan. 22, 1940	6:28 PM	CAN
Feb. 24, 1939	8:00 AM	TAU	Aug. 11, 1939	8:18 PM	CAN	Jan. 24, 1940	5:36 PM	LEO
Feb. 26, 1939	2:46 PM	GEM	Aug. 13, 1939	7:12 PM	LEO	Jan. 26, 1940	5:36 PM	VIR
Feb. 28, 1939	6:51 PM	CAN	Aug. 15, 1939	7:12 PM	VIR	Jan. 28, 1940	5:36 PM	LIB
Mar. 2, 1939	10:17 PM	LEO	Aug. 17, 1939	5:36 PM	LIB	Jan. 30, 1940	7:12 PM	SCO
Mar. 4, 1939	8:48 PM	VIR	Aug. 19, 1939	8:34 PM	SCO	Feb. 2, 1940	1:43 AM	SAG
Mar. 6, 1939	6:00 PM	LIB	Aug. 24, 1939	12:00 PM	CAP	Feb. 4, 1940	9:14 AM	CAP
Mar. 8, 1939	8:48 PM	SCO	Aug. 26, 1939	12:00 AM	AQU	Feb. 6, 1940	6:28 PM	AQU
Mar. 11, 1939	5:32 AM	SAG	Aug. 29, 1939	12:00 PM	PIS	Feb. 9, 1940	8:00 AM	PIS
Mar. 13, 1939	4:00 PM	CAP	Aug. 31, 1939	12:00 AM	ARI	Feb. 11, 1940	8:00 PM	ARI
Mar. 16, 1939	4:00 AM	AQU	Sep. 3, 1939	12:00 PM	TAU	Feb. 14, 1940	10:00 AM	TAU
Mar. 18, 1939	4:00 PM	PIS	Sep. 5, 1939	8:18 PM	GEM	Feb. 16, 1940	10:00 PM	GEM
Mar. 21, 1939	4:00 AM	ARI	Sep. 8, 1939	3:42 AM	CAN	Feb. 19, 1940	3:42 AM	CAN
Mar. 23, 1939	2:00 PM	TAU	Sep. 10, 1939	4:48 AM	LEO	Feb. 21, 1940	4:48 AM	LEO
Mar. 25, 1939	8:18 PM	GEM	Sep. 12, 1939	4:48 AM	VIR	Feb. 23, 1940	4:48 AM	VIR
Mar. 30, 1939	3:12 AM	LEO	Sep. 14, 1939	4:48 AM	LIB	Feb. 25, 1940	4:48 AM	LIB
Apr. 1, 1939	4:48 AM	VIR	Sep. 16, 1939	4:48 AM	SCO	Feb. 27, 1940	4:48 AM	SCO
Apr. 3, 1939	6:24 AM	LIB	Sep. 18, 1939	11:05 AM	SAG	Feb. 29, 1940	8:34 AM	SAG
Apr. 5, 1939	8:00 AM	SCO	Sep. 20, 1939	4:37 PM	CAP	Mar. 2, 1940	4:37 PM	CAP
Apr. 7, 1939	1:43 PM	SAG	Sep. 23, 1939	6:00 AM	AQU	Mar. 7, 1940	2:00 PM	PIS
Apr. 9, 1939	10:09 PM	CAP	Sep. 25, 1939	6:00 PM	PIS	Mar. 10, 1940	2:00 AM	ARI
Apr. 12, 1939	12:00 PM	AQU	Sep. 28, 1939	6:00 AM	ARI	Mar. 12, 1940	4:00 PM	TAU
Apr. 14, 1939	12:00 AM	PIS	Sep. 30, 1939	6:00 PM	TAU	Mar. 15, 1940	1:51 AM	GEM
Apr. 17, 1939	12:00 PM	ARI	Oct. 3, 1939	1:51 AM	GEM	Mar. 17, 1940	11:05 AM	CAN
Apr. 19, 1939	10:00 PM	TAU	Oct. 5, 1939	9:14 AM	CAN	Mar. 19, 1940	3:26 PM	LEO
Apr. 22, 1939	1:43 AM	GEM	Oct. 7, 1939	1:43 PM	LEO	Mar. 21, 1940	4:00 PM	VIR
Apr. 24, 1939	6:51 AM	CAN	Oct. 9, 1939	3:26 PM	VIR	Mar. 23, 1940	4:00 PM	LIB
Apr. 26, 1939	10:17 AM	LEO	Oct. 11, 1939	2:24 PM	LIB	Mar. 25, 1940	4:00 PM	SCO

Date	Time	Moon	Date	Time	Moon	Date	Time	Moon
Mar. 27, 1940	4:00 PM	SAG	Sep. 7, 1940	5:09 PM	SAG	Feb. 23, 1941	5:32 AM	AQU
Mar. 29, 1940	12:00 AM	CAP	Sep. 9, 1940	8:34 PM	CAP	Feb. 25, 1941	12:55 PM	PIS
Apr. 1, 1940	7:23 AM	AQU	Sep. 12, 1940	5:32 AM	AQU	Mar. 2, 1941	3:16 PM	TAU
Apr. 3, 1940	8:00 PM	PIS	Sep. 14, 1940	2:46 PM	PIS	Mar. 5, 1941	2:00 AM	GEM
Apr. 6, 1940	10:55 AM	ARI	Sep. 17, 1940	4:00 AM	ARI	Mar. 7, 1941	2:00 PM	CAN
Apr. 8, 1940	10:00 PM	TAU	Sep. 19, 1940	6:00 PM	TAU	Mar. 9, 1941	8:18 PM	LEO
Apr. 11, 1940	7:23 AM	GEM	Sep. 22, 1940	6:00 AM	GEM	Mar. 11, 1941	12:00 AM	VIR
Apr. 13, 1940	4:37 PM	CAN	Sep. 24, 1940	2:46 PM	CAN	Mar. 13, 1941	12:00 AM	LIB
Apr. 15, 1940	12:00 AM	LEO	Sep. 26, 1940	8:34 PM	LEO	Mar. 18, 1941	1:36 AM	SAG
Apr. 18, 1940	1:43 AM	VIR	Sep. 30, 1940	12:00 AM	LIB	Mar. 20, 1941	5:09 AM	CAP
Apr. 20, 1940	1:36 AM	LIB	Oct. 2, 1940	12:00 AM	SCO	Mar. 22, 1941	11:05 AM	AQU
Apr. 22, 1940	1:36 AM	SCO	Oct. 4, 1940	12:00 AM	SAG	Mar. 24, 1941	10:00 PM	PIS
Apr. 24, 1940	3:12 AM	SAG	Oct. 7, 1940	3:26 AM	CAP	Mar. 27, 1941	8:00 AM	ARI
Apr. 26, 1940	6:51 AM	CAP	Oct. 9, 1940	11:05 AM	AQU	Mar. 29, 1941	8:00 PM	TAU
Apr. 28, 1940	2:46 PM	AQU	Oct. 11, 1940	8:18 PM	PIS	Apr. 1, 1941	10:55 AM	GEM
May. 3, 1940	4:00 PM	ARI	Oct. 14, 1940	10:00 AM	ARI	Apr. 3, 1941	10:00 PM	CAN
May. 6, 1940	4:00 AM	TAU	Oct. 16, 1940	12:00 AM	TAU	Apr. 6, 1941	5:32 AM	LEO
May. 8, 1940	4:00 PM	GEM	Oct. 19, 1940	12:00 PM	GEM	Apr. 8, 1941	10:17 AM	VIR
May. 10, 1940	10:09 PM	CAN	Oct. 21, 1940	12:00 AM	CAN	Apr. 10, 1941	11:12 AM	LIB
May. 13, 1940	3:26 AM	LEO	Oct. 24, 1940	5:32 AM	LEO	Apr. 12, 1941	11:12 AM	SCO
May. 15, 1940	8:34 AM	VIR	Oct. 26, 1940	10:17 AM	VIR	Apr. 14, 1941	11:12 AM	SAG
May. 17, 1940	9:36 AM	LIB	Oct. 28, 1940	11:12 AM	LIB	Apr. 16, 1941	11:12 AM	CAP
May. 19, 1940	11:12 AM	SCO	Oct. 30, 1940	11:12 AM	SCO	Apr. 18, 1941	6:28 PM	AQU
May. 21, 1940	12:48 PM	SAG	Nov. 1, 1940	11:12 AM	SAG	Apr. 21, 1941	1:51 AM	PIS
May. 23, 1940	5:09 PM	CAP	Nov. 3, 1940	1:43 PM	CAP	Apr. 23, 1941	2:00 PM	ARI
May. 25, 1940	12:00 AM	AQU	Nov. 5, 1940	5:09 PM	AQU	Apr. 26, 1941	2:00 AM	TAU
May. 28, 1940	9:14 AM	PIS	Nov. 8, 1940	3:42 AM	PIS	Apr. 28, 1941	5:27 PM	GEM
May. 30, 1940	10:00 PM	ARI	Nov. 10, 1940	4:00 PM	ARI	May. 1, 1941	1:51 AM	CAN
Jun. 2, 1940	12:00 PM	TAU	Nov. 13, 1940	6:00 AM	TAU	May. 3, 1941	2:00 PM	LEO
Jun. 4, 1940	8:18 PM	GEM	Nov. 15, 1940	6:00 PM	GEM	May. 5, 1941	8:18 PM	VIR
Jun. 7, 1940	5:32 AM	CAN	Nov. 18, 1940	3:42 AM	CAN	May. 7, 1941	10:17 PM	LIB
Jun. 9, 1940	11:05 AM	LEO	Nov. 20, 1940	11:05 AM	LEO	May. 9, 1941	10:24 PM	SCO
Jun. 11, 1940	1:43 PM	VIR	Nov. 22, 1940	6:28 PM	VIR	May. 11, 1941	10:24 PM	SAG
Jun. 13, 1940	5:09 PM	LIB	Nov. 24, 1940	8:34 PM	LIB	May. 13, 1941	8:48 PM	CAP
Jun. 15, 1940	5:36 PM	SCO	Nov. 26, 1940	8:48 PM	SCO	May. 16, 1941	1:51 AM	AQU
Jun. 17, 1940	10:17 PM	SAG	Nov. 28, 1940	12:00 AM	SAG	May. 18, 1941	7:23 AM	PIS
Jun. 20, 1940	1:43 AM	CAP	Nov. 30, 1940	10:24 PM	CAP	May. 20, 1941	8:00 PM	ARI
Jun. 22, 1940	9:14 AM	AQU	Dec. 3, 1940	3:26 AM	AQU	May. 23, 1941	8:00 AM	TAU
Jun. 24, 1940	8:00 PM	PIS	Dec. 5, 1940	11:05 AM	PIS	May. 25, 1941	12:00 AM	GEM
Jun. 27, 1940	8:44 AM	ARI	Dec. 7, 1940	12:00 AM	ARI	May. 28, 1941	7:23 AM	CAN
Jun. 29, 1940	8:00 PM	TAU	Dec. 10, 1940	3:16 PM	TAU	May. 30, 1941	8:00 PM	LEO
Jul. 2, 1940	5:32 AM	GEM	Dec. 13, 1940	2:00 AM	GEM	Jun. 2, 1941	1:51 AM	VIR
Jul. 4, 1940	12:55 PM	CAN	Dec. 15, 1940	9:14 AM	CAN	Jun. 4, 1941	7:23 AM	LIB
Jul. 6, 1940	5:09 PM	LEO	Dec. 17, 1940	3:26 PM	LEO	Jun. 6, 1941	8:34 AM	SCO
Jul. 8, 1940	8:34 PM	VIR	Dec. 19, 1940	12:00 AM	VIR	Jun. 8, 1941	8:00 AM	SAG
Jul. 10, 1940	10:17 PM	LIB	Dec. 22, 1940	1:43 AM	LIB	Jun. 10, 1941	8:00 AM	CAP
Jul. 13, 1940	1:43 AM	SCO	Dec. 24, 1940	5:09 AM	SCO	Jun. 12, 1941	10:17 AM	AQU
Jul. 15, 1940	5:09 AM	SAG	Dec. 26, 1940	6:24 AM	SAG	Jun. 14, 1941	4:37 PM	PIS
Jul. 17, 1940	11:05 AM	CAP	Dec. 28, 1940	10:17 AM	CAP	Jun. 17, 1941	2:00 AM	ARI
Jul. 19, 1940	4:37 PM	AQU	Dec. 30, 1940	1:43 PM	AQU	Jun. 19, 1941	2:00 PM	TAU
Jul. 22, 1940	4:00 PM	PIS	Jan. 1, 1941	8:18 PM	PIS	Jun. 22, 1941	4:00 AM	GEM
Jul. 24, 1940	2:00 PM	ARI	Jan. 4, 1941	8:00 AM	ARI	Jun. 24, 1941	4:00 PM	CAN
Jul. 27, 1940	4:00 AM	TAU	Jan. 6, 1941	12:00 AM	TAU	Jun. 29, 1941	7:23 AM	VIR
Jul. 29, 1940	4:00 PM	GEM	Jan. 9, 1941	10:00 AM	GEM	Jul. 1, 1941	12:00 PM	LIB
Jul. 31, 1940	10:09 PM	CAN	Jan. 11, 1941	6:28 PM	CAN	Jul. 3, 1941	3:26 PM	SCO
Aug. 3, 1940	1:43 AM	LEO	Jan. 16, 1941	5:09 AM	VIR	Jul. 5, 1941	4:00 PM	SAG
Aug. 5, 1940	3:12 AM	VIR	Jan. 18, 1941	8:34 AM	LIB	Jul. 7, 1941	5:36 PM	CAP
Aug. 7, 1940	4:48 AM	LIB	Jan. 20, 1941	9:36 AM	SCO	Jul. 9, 1941	8:34 PM	AQU
Aug. 9, 1940	6:51 AM	SCO	Jan. 22, 1941	1:43 PM	SAG	Jul. 12, 1941	1:51 AM	PIS
Aug. 11, 1940	10:17 AM	SAG	Jan. 24, 1941	5:09 PM	CAP	Jul. 14, 1941	9:14 AM	ARI
Aug. 13, 1940	4:37 PM	CAP	Jan. 26, 1941	12:00 AM	AQU	Jul. 16, 1941	10:00 PM	TAU
Aug. 15, 1940	12:00 AM	AQU	Jan. 29, 1941	5:32 AM	PIS	Jul. 19, 1941	1:05 PM	GEM
Aug. 18, 1940	9:14 AM	PIS	Jan. 31, 1941	6:00 PM	ARI	Jul. 21, 1941	8:18 PM	CAN
Aug. 20, 1940	10:00 PM	ARI	Feb. 3, 1941	6:00 AM	TAU	Jul. 24, 1941	8:00 AM	LEO
Aug. 23, 1940	1:05 PM	TAU	Feb. 5, 1941	6:00 PM	GEM	Jul. 26, 1941	12:00 PM	VIR
Aug. 25, 1940	12:00 AM	GEM	Feb. 8, 1941	3:42 AM	CAN	Jul. 28, 1941	5:09 PM	LIB
Aug. 28, 1940	7:23 AM	CAN	Feb. 10, 1941	11:05 AM	LEO	Jul. 30, 1941	8:34 PM	SCO
Aug. 30, 1940	12:00 PM	LEO	Feb. 12, 1941	1:43 PM	VIR	Aug. 1, 1941	12:00 AM	SAG
Sep. 1, 1940	12:48 PM	VIR	Feb. 14, 1941	2:24 PM	LIB	Aug. 4, 1941	1:36 AM	CAP
Sep. 3, 1940	2:24 PM	LIB	Feb. 16, 1941	4:00 PM	SCO	Aug. 6, 1941	5:09 AM	AQU
Sep. 5, 1940	2:24 PM	SCO	Feb. 18, 1941	5:36 PM	SAG	Aug. 8, 1941	11:05 AM	PIS

Date	Time	Moon	Date	Time	Moon	Date	Time	Moon
Aug. 10, 1941	6:28 PM	A R I	Jan. 21, 1942	2:46 PM	A R I	Jul. 2, 1942	5:09 AM	P I S
Aug. 13, 1941	6:00 AM	T A U	Jan. 23, 1942	10:09 PM	T A U	Jul. 4, 1942	8:34 AM	A R I
Aug. 15, 1941	6:00 PM	GEM	Jan. 26, 1942	12:00 PM	GEM	Jul. 6, 1942	6:28 PM	T A U
Aug. 18, 1941	5:32 AM	C A N	Jan. 29, 1942	2:00 AM	C A N	Jul. 9, 1942	8:00 AM	GEM
Aug. 20, 1941	2:46 PM	L E O	Jan. 31, 1942	12:00 PM	L E O	Jul. 11, 1942	8:00 PM	C A N
Aug. 22, 1941	10:09 PM	V I R	Feb. 2, 1942	10:00 PM	V I R	Jul. 14, 1942	8:00 AM	L E O
Aug. 24, 1941	12:00 AM	L I B	Feb. 5, 1942	1:43 AM	L I B	Jul. 16, 1942	8:00 PM	V I R
Aug. 27, 1941	3:26 AM	SCO	Feb. 7, 1942	6:51 AM	SCO	Jul. 19, 1942	3:42 AM	L I B
Aug. 29, 1941	5:09 AM	SAG	Feb. 9, 1942	10:17 AM	SAG	Jul. 21, 1942	11:05 AM	SCO
Aug. 31, 1941	8:34 AM	CAP	Feb. 11, 1942	11:12 AM	CAP	Jul. 23, 1942	1:43 PM	SAG
Sep. 2, 1941	12:00 PM	AQU	Feb. 13, 1942	3:26 PM	AQU	Jul. 25, 1942	12:48 PM	CAP
Sep. 4, 1941	5:09 PM	P I S	Feb. 15, 1942	5:09 PM	P I S	Jul. 27, 1942	12:48 PM	AQU
Sep. 7, 1941	4:00 AM	A R I	Feb. 17, 1942	12:00 AM	A R I	Jul. 29, 1942	3:26 PM	P I S
Sep. 9, 1941	2:00 PM	T A U	Feb. 20, 1942	10:00 AM	T A U	Jul. 31, 1942	8:18 PM	A R I
Sep. 12, 1941	4:22 AM	GEM	Feb. 22, 1942	8:00 PM	GEM	Aug. 3, 1942	1:51 AM	T A U
Sep. 14, 1941	4:00 PM	C A N	Feb. 25, 1942	10:00 AM	C A N	Aug. 5, 1942	2:00 PM	GEM
Sep. 19, 1941	7:23 AM	V I R	Feb. 27, 1942	6:28 PM	L E O	Aug. 8, 1942	2:00 AM	C A N
Sep. 21, 1941	8:00 AM	L I B	Mar. 2, 1942	3:42 AM	V I R	Aug. 10, 1942	2:00 PM	L E O
Sep. 23, 1941	9:36 AM	SCO	Mar. 4, 1942	8:34 AM	L I B	Aug. 13, 1942	2:00 AM	V I R
Sep. 25, 1941	11:12 AM	SAG	Mar. 6, 1942	12:00 PM	SCO	Aug. 15, 1942	9:14 AM	L I B
Sep. 27, 1941	1:43 PM	CAP	Mar. 8, 1942	3:26 PM	SAG	Aug. 17, 1942	4:37 PM	SCO
Sep. 29, 1941	5:09 PM	AQU	Mar. 10, 1942	6:51 PM	CAP	Aug. 19, 1942	6:51 PM	SAG
Oct. 2, 1941	1:51 AM	P I S	Mar. 12, 1942	8:34 PM	AQU	Aug. 21, 1942	10:17 PM	CAP
Oct. 4, 1941	9:14 AM	A R I	Mar. 15, 1942	1:43 AM	P I S	Aug. 23, 1942	10:24 PM	AQU
Oct. 6, 1941	10:00 PM	T A U	Mar. 17, 1942	9:14 AM	A R I	Aug. 28, 1942	5:32 AM	A R I
Oct. 9, 1941	10:00 AM	GEM	Mar. 19, 1942	4:37 PM	T A U	Aug. 30, 1942	11:05 AM	T A U
Oct. 11, 1941	10:00 PM	C A N	Mar. 22, 1942	3:42 AM	GEM	Sep. 1, 1942	10:00 PM	GEM
Oct. 14, 1941	10:00 AM	L E O	Mar. 24, 1942	6:00 PM	C A N	Sep. 4, 1942	10:00 AM	C A N
Oct. 16, 1941	4:37 PM	V I R	Mar. 27, 1942	6:00 AM	L E O	Sep. 6, 1942	10:00 PM	L E O
Oct. 18, 1941	8:34 PM	L I B	Mar. 29, 1942	12:55 PM	V I R	Sep. 9, 1942	7:23 AM	V I R
Oct. 20, 1941	10:17 PM	SCO	Mar. 31, 1942	8:18 PM	L I B	Sep. 11, 1942	4:37 PM	L I B
Oct. 22, 1941	6:00 PM	SAG	Apr. 2, 1942	10:17 PM	SCO	Sep. 13, 1942	8:34 PM	SCO
Oct. 24, 1941	7:12 PM	CAP	Apr. 4, 1942	8:48 PM	SAG	Sep. 18, 1942	3:26 AM	CAP
Oct. 26, 1941	12:00 AM	AQU	Apr. 6, 1942	10:24 PM	CAP	Sep. 20, 1942	6:51 AM	AQU
Oct. 29, 1941	7:23 AM	P I S	Apr. 9, 1942	3:26 AM	AQU	Sep. 22, 1942	8:00 AM	P I S
Oct. 31, 1941	2:46 PM	A R I	Apr. 11, 1942	9:14 AM	P I S	Sep. 24, 1942	1:43 PM	A R I
Nov. 3, 1941	4:00 AM	T A U	Apr. 13, 1942	2:46 PM	A R I	Sep. 26, 1942	8:18 PM	T A U
Nov. 5, 1941	4:00 PM	GEM	Apr. 16, 1942	2:00 AM	T A U	Sep. 29, 1942	6:00 AM	GEM
Nov. 8, 1941	6:00 AM	C A N	Apr. 18, 1942	12:00 PM	GEM	Oct. 1, 1942	6:00 PM	C A N
Nov. 10, 1941	6:00 PM	L E O	Apr. 21, 1942	2:11 AM	C A N	Oct. 4, 1942	6:00 AM	L E O
Nov. 13, 1941	1:51 AM	V I R	Apr. 23, 1942	2:00 PM	L E O	Oct. 6, 1942	6:00 PM	V I R
Nov. 15, 1941	7:23 AM	L I B	Apr. 25, 1942	10:09 PM	V I R	Oct. 11, 1942	5:09 AM	SCO
Nov. 17, 1941	8:34 AM	SCO	Apr. 28, 1942	5:32 AM	L I B	Oct. 13, 1942	6:24 AM	SAG
Nov. 19, 1941	6:00 AM	SAG	Apr. 30, 1942	6:24 AM	SCO	Oct. 15, 1942	8:00 AM	CAP
Nov. 21, 1941	6:24 AM	CAP	May. 2, 1942	6:24 AM	SAG	Oct. 17, 1942	12:00 PM	AQU
Nov. 23, 1941	6:24 AM	AQU	May. 4, 1942	6:24 AM	CAP	Oct. 19, 1942	3:26 PM	P I S
Nov. 25, 1941	12:00 PM	P I S	May. 6, 1942	8:00 AM	AQU	Oct. 21, 1942	10:09 PM	A R I
Nov. 27, 1941	12:00 AM	A R I	May. 8, 1942	2:46 PM	P I S	Oct. 24, 1942	5:32 AM	T A U
Nov. 30, 1941	10:00 AM	T A U	May. 10, 1942	8:18 PM	A R I	Oct. 26, 1942	12:55 PM	GEM
Dec. 2, 1941	10:00 PM	GEM	May. 13, 1942	8:00 AM	T A U	Oct. 29, 1942	2:00 AM	C A N
Dec. 5, 1941	12:00 PM	C A N	May. 15, 1942	8:00 PM	GEM	Oct. 31, 1942	2:00 PM	L E O
Dec. 7, 1941	12:00 AM	L E O	May. 18, 1942	8:00 AM	C A N	Nov. 3, 1942	2:00 AM	V I R
Dec. 10, 1941	7:23 AM	V I R	May. 20, 1942	8:00 PM	L E O	Nov. 5, 1942	11:05 AM	L I B
Dec. 12, 1941	2:46 PM	L I B	May. 23, 1942	8:00 AM	V I R	Nov. 7, 1942	1:43 PM	SCO
Dec. 14, 1941	6:51 PM	SCO	May. 25, 1942	2:46 PM	L I B	Nov. 9, 1942	5:09 PM	SAG
Dec. 16, 1941	5:36 PM	SAG	May. 27, 1942	5:09 PM	SCO	Nov. 11, 1942	4:00 PM	CAP
Dec. 18, 1941	5:36 PM	CAP	May. 29, 1942	5:36 PM	SAG	Nov. 13, 1942	6:51 PM	AQU
Dec. 20, 1941	5:36 PM	AQU	May. 31, 1942	5:36 PM	CAP	Nov. 15, 1942	8:34 PM	P I S
Dec. 22, 1941	8:34 PM	P I S	Jun. 2, 1942	4:00 PM	AQU	Nov. 18, 1942	3:42 AM	A R I
Dec. 25, 1941	6:00 AM	A R I	Jun. 4, 1942	8:34 PM	P I S	Nov. 20, 1942	11:05 AM	T A U
Dec. 27, 1941	4:00 PM	T A U	Jun. 7, 1942	3:42 AM	A R I	Nov. 22, 1942	10:00 PM	GEM
Dec. 30, 1941	6:00 AM	GEM	Jun. 9, 1942	2:00 PM	T A U	Nov. 25, 1942	10:00 AM	C A N
Jan. 1, 1942	6:00 PM	C A N	Jun. 12, 1942	2:00 AM	GEM	Nov. 27, 1942	10:00 PM	L E O
Jan. 4, 1942	3:42 AM	L E O	Jun. 14, 1942	2:00 PM	C A N	Nov. 30, 1942	10:00 AM	V I R
Jan. 6, 1942	12:55 PM	V I R	Jun. 17, 1942	2:00 AM	L E O	Dec. 2, 1942	10:00 PM	L I B
Jan. 8, 1942	8:18 PM	L I B	Jun. 19, 1942	2:00 PM	V I R	Dec. 5, 1942	1:51 AM	SCO
Jan. 11, 1942	1:43 AM	SCO	Jun. 21, 1942	10:09 PM	L I B	Dec. 7, 1942	1:36 AM	SAG
Jan. 13, 1942	3:12 AM	SAG	Jun. 24, 1942	3:42 AM	SCO	Dec. 9, 1942	1:36 AM	CAP
Jan. 15, 1942	3:12 AM	CAP	Jun. 26, 1942	3:12 AM	SAG	Dec. 11, 1942	1:36 AM	AQU
Jan. 17, 1942	4:48 AM	AQU	Jun. 28, 1942	3:12 AM	CAP	Dec. 13, 1942	3:26 PM	P I S
Jan. 19, 1942	6:51 AM	P I S	Jun. 30, 1942	3:12 AM	AQU	Dec. 15, 1942	9:14 AM	A R I

Date	Time	Moon	Date	Time	Moon	Date	Time	Moon
Dec. 17, 1942	4:37 PM	T A U	Jun. 4, 1943	12:00 PM	C A N	Nov. 17, 1943	6:00 PM	L E O
Dec. 20, 1942	4:00 AM	G E M	Jun. 6, 1943	12:00 AM	L E O	Nov. 20, 1943	6:00 AM	V I R
Dec. 22, 1942	4:00 PM	C A N	Jun. 9, 1943	12:00 PM	V I R	Nov. 22, 1943	6:00 PM	L I B
Dec. 25, 1942	4:00 AM	L E O	Jun. 14, 1943	7:23 AM	S C O	Nov. 25, 1943	3:42 AM	S C O
Dec. 27, 1942	7:38 PM	V I R	Jun. 16, 1943	12:00 PM	S A G	Nov. 27, 1943	9:14 AM	S A G
Dec. 30, 1942	4:00 AM	L I B	Jun. 18, 1943	1:43 PM	C A P	Nov. 29, 1943	12:00 PM	C A P
Jan. 1, 1943	11:05 AM	S C O	Jun. 20, 1943	12:48 PM	A Q U	Dec. 1, 1943	12:48 PM	A Q U
Jan. 3, 1943	1:43 PM	S A G	Jun. 22, 1943	12:48 PM	P I S	Dec. 3, 1943	5:09 PM	P I S
Jan. 5, 1943	12:48 PM	C A P	Jun. 24, 1943	5:09 PM	A R I	Dec. 5, 1943	8:34 PM	A R I
Jan. 7, 1943	12:48 PM	A Q U	Jun. 26, 1943	8:34 PM	T A U	Dec. 7, 1943	12:00 AM	T A U
Jan. 9, 1943	12:48 PM	P I S	Jun. 29, 1943	8:00 AM	G E M	Dec. 10, 1943	7:23 AM	G E M
Jan. 11, 1943	3:26 PM	A R I	Jul. 1, 1943	6:00 PM	C A N	Dec. 12, 1943	2:46 PM	C A N
Jan. 13, 1943	8:34 PM	T A U	Jul. 4, 1943	6:00 AM	L E O	Dec. 15, 1943	2:00 AM	L E O
Jan. 16, 1943	10:00 AM	G E M	Jul. 6, 1943	9:49 PM	V I R	Dec. 17, 1943	2:00 PM	V I R
Jan. 18, 1943	10:00 PM	C A N	Jul. 9, 1943	8:00 AM	L I B	Dec. 20, 1943	2:00 AM	L I B
Jan. 21, 1943	10:00 AM	L E O	Jul. 11, 1943	4:37 PM	S C O	Dec. 22, 1943	2:00 PM	S C O
Jan. 26, 1943	10:00 AM	L I B	Jul. 13, 1943	8:34 PM	S A G	Dec. 24, 1943	8:18 PM	S A G
Jan. 28, 1943	6:28 PM	S C O	Jul. 15, 1943	10:24 PM	C A P	Dec. 26, 1943	10:17 PM	C A P
Jan. 30, 1943	10:17 PM	S A G	Jul. 17, 1943	10:24 PM	A Q U	Dec. 28, 1943	12:00 AM	A Q U
Feb. 3, 1943	12:00 AM	A Q U	Jul. 19, 1943	10:24 PM	P I S	Dec. 30, 1943	10:24 PM	P I S
Feb. 5, 1943	12:00 AM	P I S	Jul. 21, 1943	10:24 PM	A R I	Jan. 2, 1944	1:43 AM	A R I
Feb. 8, 1943	1:43 AM	A R I	Jul. 24, 1943	5:32 AM	T A U	Jan. 4, 1944	5:09 AM	T A U
Feb. 10, 1943	7:23 AM	T A U	Jul. 26, 1943	12:55 PM	G E M	Jan. 6, 1944	12:55 PM	G E M
Feb. 12, 1943	2:46 PM	G E M	Jul. 28, 1943	12:00 AM	C A N	Jan. 8, 1944	8:18 PM	C A N
Feb. 15, 1943	4:00 AM	C A N	Jul. 31, 1943	12:00 PM	L E O	Jan. 11, 1944	7:23 AM	L E O
Feb. 17, 1943	7:38 PM	L E O	Aug. 3, 1943	2:00 AM	V I R	Jan. 13, 1944	10:00 PM	V I R
Feb. 20, 1943	6:00 AM	V I R	Aug. 5, 1943	2:00 PM	L I B	Jan. 16, 1944	10:00 AM	L I B
Feb. 22, 1943	4:00 PM	L I B	Aug. 7, 1943	10:09 PM	S C O	Jan. 18, 1944	10:00 PM	S C O
Feb. 27, 1943	5:32 AM	S A G	Aug. 10, 1943	5:09 AM	S A G	Jan. 21, 1944	5:32 AM	S A G
Mar. 1, 1943	8:34 AM	C A P	Aug. 12, 1943	8:00 AM	C A P	Jan. 23, 1944	8:34 AM	C A P
Mar. 3, 1943	9:36 AM	A Q U	Aug. 14, 1943	9:36 AM	A Q U	Jan. 25, 1944	10:17 AM	A Q U
Mar. 5, 1943	12:00 PM	P I S	Aug. 16, 1943	9:36 AM	P I S	Jan. 27, 1944	7:30 AM	P I S
Mar. 7, 1943	11:12 AM	A R I	Aug. 18, 1943	9:36 AM	A R I	Jan. 29, 1944	10:17 AM	A R I
Mar. 9, 1943	3:26 PM	T A U	Aug. 20, 1943	12:00 PM	T A U	Jan. 31, 1944	12:00 PM	T A U
Mar. 11, 1943	12:00 AM	G E M	Aug. 22, 1943	5:09 PM	G E M	Feb. 2, 1944	6:28 PM	G E M
Mar. 14, 1943	12:00 PM	C A N	Aug. 25, 1943	6:00 AM	C A N	Feb. 5, 1944	4:00 AM	C A N
Mar. 16, 1943	12:00 AM	L E O	Aug. 27, 1943	6:00 PM	L E O	Feb. 7, 1944	4:00 PM	L E O
Mar. 19, 1943	12:00 PM	V I R	Aug. 30, 1943	8:00 AM	V I R	Feb. 10, 1944	4:00 AM	V I R
Mar. 21, 1943	12:00 AM	L I B	Sep. 1, 1943	8:00 PM	L I B	Feb. 12, 1944	4:00 PM	L I B
Mar. 24, 1943	5:32 AM	S C O	Sep. 4, 1943	6:00 AM	S C O	Feb. 15, 1944	4:00 AM	S C O
Mar. 26, 1943	10:17 AM	S A G	Sep. 6, 1943	12:55 PM	S A G	Feb. 17, 1944	12:55 PM	S A G
Mar. 28, 1943	1:43 PM	C A P	Sep. 8, 1943	5:09 PM	C A P	Feb. 19, 1944	8:18 PM	C A P
Mar. 30, 1943	5:09 PM	A Q U	Sep. 10, 1943	8:34 PM	A Q U	Feb. 21, 1944	7:12 PM	A Q U
Apr. 1, 1943	5:36 PM	P I S	Sep. 12, 1943	7:12 PM	P I S	Feb. 23, 1944	8:48 PM	P I S
Apr. 3, 1943	10:17 PM	A R I	Sep. 14, 1943	7:12 PM	A R I	Feb. 25, 1944	7:12 PM	A R I
Apr. 6, 1943	1:43 AM	T A U	Sep. 16, 1943	8:48 PM	T A U	Feb. 27, 1944	7:12 PM	T A U
Apr. 8, 1943	9:14 AM	G E M	Sep. 19, 1943	3:42 AM	G E M	Mar. 1, 1944	1:51 AM	G E M
Apr. 10, 1943	8:00 PM	C A N	Sep. 21, 1943	2:00 PM	C A N	Mar. 3, 1944	9:14 AM	C A N
Apr. 13, 1943	8:00 AM	L E O	Sep. 24, 1943	2:00 AM	L E O	Mar. 5, 1944	10:00 PM	L E O
Apr. 15, 1943	12:00 AM	V I R	Sep. 26, 1943	2:00 PM	V I R	Mar. 8, 1944	10:00 AM	V I R
Apr. 18, 1943	8:00 AM	L I B	Sep. 29, 1943	2:00 AM	L I B	Mar. 10, 1944	10:00 PM	L I B
Apr. 20, 1943	12:00 PM	S C O	Oct. 1, 1943	11:05 AM	S C O	Mar. 13, 1944	10:00 AM	S C O
Apr. 22, 1943	5:09 PM	S A G	Oct. 3, 1943	6:28 PM	S A G	Mar. 15, 1944	6:28 PM	S A G
Apr. 24, 1943	8:34 PM	C A P	Oct. 5, 1943	10:17 PM	C A P	Mar. 18, 1944	1:43 AM	C A P
Apr. 26, 1943	10:17 PM	A Q U	Oct. 8, 1943	1:36 AM	A Q U	Mar. 20, 1944	5:09 AM	A Q U
Apr. 29, 1943	1:43 AM	P I S	Oct. 10, 1943	5:09 AM	P I S	Mar. 22, 1944	6:24 AM	P I S
May. 1, 1943	5:09 AM	A R I	Oct. 12, 1943	6:51 AM	A R I	Mar. 24, 1944	6:24 AM	A R I
May. 3, 1943	10:17 AM	T A U	Oct. 14, 1943	8:34 AM	T A U	Mar. 26, 1944	6:24 AM	T A U
May. 5, 1943	6:28 PM	G E M	Oct. 16, 1943	12:00 PM	G E M	Mar. 28, 1944	10:17 AM	G E M
May. 8, 1943	4:00 AM	C A N	Oct. 18, 1943	8:18 PM	C A N	Mar. 30, 1944	4:37 PM	C A N
May. 10, 1943	4:00 PM	L E O	Oct. 21, 1943	10:00 AM	L E O	Apr. 2, 1944	4:00 AM	L E O
May. 13, 1943	6:00 AM	V I R	Oct. 23, 1943	10:00 PM	V I R	Apr. 4, 1944	4:00 PM	V I R
May. 15, 1943	2:46 PM	L I B	Oct. 26, 1943	10:00 AM	L I B	Apr. 7, 1944	6:00 AM	L I B
May. 17, 1943	8:34 PM	S C O	Oct. 28, 1943	6:28 PM	S C O	Apr. 9, 1944	2:46 PM	S C O
May. 20, 1943	1:43 AM	S A G	Nov. 2, 1943	5:32 AM	C A P	Apr. 12, 1944	2:00 AM	S A G
May. 22, 1943	3:26 PM	C A P	Nov. 4, 1943	8:34 AM	A Q U	Apr. 14, 1944	6:51 AM	C A P
May. 24, 1943	5:09 AM	A Q U	Nov. 6, 1943	12:00 PM	P I S	Apr. 16, 1944	12:00 PM	A Q U
May. 26, 1943	6:51 AM	P I S	Nov. 8, 1943	1:43 PM	A R I	Apr. 18, 1944	3:26 PM	P I S
May. 28, 1943	10:17 AM	A R I	Nov. 10, 1943	5:09 PM	T A U	Apr. 20, 1944	4:00 PM	A R I
May. 30, 1943	3:26 PM	T A U	Nov. 12, 1943	12:00 AM	G E M	Apr. 22, 1944	6:51 AM	T A U
Jun. 2, 1943	2:00 AM	G E M	Nov. 15, 1943	5:32 AM	C A N	Apr. 24, 1944	8:34 PM	G E M

Date	Time	Moon	Date	Time	Moon	Date	Time	Moon
Apr. 27, 1944	1:51 AM	CAN	Oct. 5, 1944	2:24 PM	GEM	Mar. 18, 1945	5:09 PM	GEM
Apr. 29, 1944	12:00 PM	LEO	Oct. 7, 1944	10:09 PM	CAN	Mar. 20, 1945	6:51 PM	CAN
May. 1, 1944	12:00 AM	VIR	Oct. 10, 1944	5:32 AM	LEO	Mar. 23, 1945	3:42 AM	LEO
May. 4, 1944	12:00 PM	LIB	Oct. 12, 1944	6:00 PM	VIR	Mar. 25, 1945	4:00 PM	VIR
May. 6, 1944	12:00 AM	SCO	Oct. 15, 1944	6:00 AM	LIB	Mar. 28, 1945	4:00 AM	LIB
May. 9, 1944	7:23 AM	SAG	Oct. 17, 1944	8:00 PM	SCO	Mar. 30, 1945	4:00 PM	SCO
May. 11, 1944	2:46 PM	CAP	Oct. 20, 1944	6:00 AM	SAG	Apr. 2, 1945	4:00 AM	SAG
May. 13, 1944	5:09 PM	AQU	Oct. 22, 1944	2:46 PM	CAP	Apr. 4, 1945	4:00 PM	CAP
May. 15, 1944	10:17 PM	PIS	Oct. 24, 1944	10:09 PM	AQU	Apr. 6, 1945	10:09 PM	AQU
May. 17, 1944	12:00 AM	ARI	Oct. 29, 1944	1:36 AM	ARI	Apr. 9, 1945	1:43 AM	PIS
May. 20, 1944	1:36 AM	TAU	Oct. 31, 1944	1:36 AM	TAU	Apr. 11, 1945	3:12 AM	ARI
May. 22, 1944	5:09 AM	GEM	Nov. 2, 1944	1:36 AM	GEM	Apr. 13, 1945	1:36 AM	TAU
May. 24, 1944	11:05 AM	CAN	Nov. 4, 1944	5:09 AM	CAN	Apr. 15, 1945	1:36 AM	GEM
May. 26, 1944	6:28 PM	LEO	Nov. 6, 1944	12:55 PM	LEO	Apr. 17, 1945	3:26 AM	CAN
May. 29, 1944	8:00 AM	VIR	Nov. 8, 1944	10:09 PM	VIR	Apr. 19, 1945	11:05 AM	LEO
May. 31, 1944	8:00 PM	LIB	Nov. 11, 1944	2:00 PM	LIB	Apr. 21, 1945	10:00 PM	VIR
Jun. 3, 1944	8:00 AM	SCO	Nov. 14, 1944	2:00 AM	SCO	Apr. 24, 1945	10:00 AM	LIB
Jun. 5, 1944	2:46 PM	SAG	Nov. 16, 1944	11:05 AM	SAG	Apr. 26, 1945	10:00 PM	SCO
Jun. 7, 1944	10:09 PM	CAP	Nov. 18, 1944	8:18 PM	CAP	Apr. 29, 1945	10:00 AM	SAG
Jun. 9, 1944	12:00 AM	AQU	Nov. 21, 1944	3:42 AM	AQU	May. 1, 1945	10:00 PM	CAP
Jun. 12, 1944	3:26 AM	PIS	Nov. 23, 1944	6:51 AM	PIS	May. 4, 1945	5:32 AM	AQU
Jun. 14, 1944	5:09 AM	ARI	Nov. 25, 1944	10:17 AM	ARI	May. 6, 1945	10:17 PM	PIS
Jun. 16, 1944	8:34 AM	TAU	Nov. 27, 1944	12:00 PM	TAU	May. 8, 1945	11:12 AM	ARI
Jun. 18, 1944	12:00 PM	GEM	Nov. 29, 1944	1:43 PM	GEM	May. 10, 1945	12:48 PM	TAU
Jun. 20, 1944	8:18 PM	CAN	Dec. 1, 1944	3:26 PM	CAN	May. 12, 1945	10:30 AM	GEM
Jun. 23, 1944	3:42 AM	LEO	Dec. 3, 1944	8:34 PM	LEO	May. 14, 1945	12:48 PM	CAN
Jun. 25, 1944	4:00 PM	VIR	Dec. 6, 1944	10:00 AM	VIR	May. 16, 1945	5:09 PM	LEO
Jun. 28, 1944	4:00 AM	LIB	Dec. 8, 1944	10:00 PM	LIB	May. 19, 1945	4:00 AM	VIR
Jun. 30, 1944	4:00 PM	SCO	Dec. 11, 1944	10:00 AM	SCO	May. 21, 1945	4:00 PM	LIB
Jul. 2, 1944	12:00 AM	SAG	Dec. 13, 1944	6:28 PM	SAG	May. 24, 1945	4:00 AM	SCO
Jul. 5, 1944	5:09 AM	CAP	Dec. 16, 1944	3:42 AM	CAP	May. 26, 1945	4:00 PM	SAG
Jul. 7, 1944	8:34 AM	AQU	Dec. 18, 1944	9:14 AM	AQU	May. 29, 1945	1:51 AM	CAP
Jul. 9, 1944	10:17 AM	PIS	Dec. 20, 1944	12:00 PM	PIS	May. 31, 1945	11:05 AM	AQU
Jul. 11, 1944	12:00 PM	ARI	Dec. 22, 1944	3:26 PM	ARI	Jun. 2, 1945	3:26 PM	PIS
Jul. 13, 1944	1:43 PM	TAU	Dec. 24, 1944	6:51 PM	TAU	Jun. 4, 1945	8:34 PM	ARI
Jul. 15, 1944	8:18 PM	GEM	Dec. 26, 1944	7:12 PM	GEM	Jun. 6, 1945	10:17 PM	TAU
Jul. 18, 1944	1:51 AM	CAN	Dec. 29, 1944	1:43 AM	CAN	Jun. 8, 1945	12:00 AM	GEM
Jul. 20, 1944	11:05 AM	LEO	Dec. 31, 1944	6:51 AM	LEO	Jun. 10, 1945	10:24 PM	CAN
Jul. 22, 1944	12:00 AM	VIR	Jan. 2, 1945	4:37 PM	VIR	Jun. 13, 1945	3:26 AM	LEO
Jul. 25, 1944	12:00 PM	LIB	Jan. 5, 1945	6:00 AM	LIB	Jun. 15, 1945	11:05 AM	VIR
Jul. 27, 1944	12:00 AM	SCO	Jan. 7, 1945	6:00 PM	SCO	Jun. 17, 1945	12:00 AM	LIB
Jul. 30, 1944	9:14 AM	SAG	Jan. 10, 1945	6:00 AM	SAG	Jun. 20, 1945	12:00 PM	SCO
Aug. 1, 1944	4:37 PM	CAP	Jan. 12, 1945	12:55 PM	CAP	Jun. 22, 1945	12:00 AM	SAG
Aug. 3, 1944	6:51 PM	AQU	Jan. 14, 1945	6:28 PM	AQU	Jun. 25, 1945	10:00 AM	CAP
Aug. 5, 1944	5:36 PM	PIS	Jan. 16, 1945	8:34 PM	PIS	Jun. 27, 1945	4:37 PM	AQU
Aug. 7, 1944	5:36 PM	ARI	Jan. 18, 1945	10:17 PM	ARI	Jun. 29, 1945	8:34 PM	PIS
Aug. 9, 1944	7:12 PM	TAU	Jan. 20, 1945	12:00 AM	TAU	Jul. 2, 1945	1:43 AM	ARI
Aug. 11, 1944	12:00 AM	GEM	Jan. 23, 1945	3:26 AM	GEM	Jul. 4, 1945	3:12 AM	TAU
Aug. 14, 1944	7:23 AM	CAN	Jan. 25, 1945	9:14 AM	CAN	Jul. 6, 1945	6:51 AM	GEM
Aug. 16, 1944	4:37 PM	LEO	Jan. 27, 1945	4:37 PM	LEO	Jul. 8, 1945	8:34 AM	CAN
Aug. 19, 1944	6:00 AM	VIR	Jan. 30, 1945	2:00 AM	VIR	Jul. 10, 1945	2:46 PM	LEO
Aug. 21, 1944	6:00 PM	LIB	Feb. 1, 1945	2:00 PM	LIB	Jul. 12, 1945	8:18 PM	VIR
Aug. 24, 1944	8:00 AM	SCO	Feb. 4, 1945	2:00 AM	SCO	Jul. 15, 1945	8:00 AM	LIB
Aug. 26, 1944	4:37 PM	SAG	Feb. 6, 1945	2:00 PM	SAG	Jul. 17, 1945	8:00 PM	SCO
Aug. 29, 1944	1:51 AM	CAP	Feb. 8, 1945	10:09 PM	CAP	Jul. 20, 1945	8:00 AM	SAG
Aug. 31, 1944	5:09 AM	AQU	Feb. 11, 1945	3:26 AM	AQU	Jul. 22, 1945	4:37 PM	CAP
Sep. 2, 1944	4:48 AM	PIS	Feb. 13, 1945	4:48 AM	PIS	Jul. 24, 1945	12:00 AM	AQU
Sep. 4, 1944	4:48 AM	ARI	Feb. 15, 1945	4:48 AM	ARI	Jul. 27, 1945	5:32 AM	PIS
Sep. 6, 1944	4:48 AM	TAU	Feb. 17, 1945	6:51 AM	TAU	Jul. 29, 1945	6:51 AM	ARI
Sep. 8, 1944	6:51 AM	GEM	Feb. 19, 1945	8:34 AM	GEM	Jul. 31, 1945	10:17 AM	TAU
Sep. 10, 1944	12:55 PM	CAN	Feb. 21, 1945	2:46 PM	CAN	Aug. 2, 1945	12:00 PM	GEM
Sep. 12, 1944	10:09 PM	LEO	Feb. 23, 1945	10:09 PM	LEO	Aug. 4, 1945	3:26 PM	CAN
Sep. 15, 1944	12:00 PM	VIR	Feb. 26, 1945	10:00 AM	VIR	Aug. 6, 1945	8:34 PM	LEO
Sep. 17, 1944	12:00 AM	LIB	Feb. 28, 1945	6:28 PM	LIB	Aug. 9, 1945	5:32 AM	VIR
Sep. 20, 1944	2:00 PM	SCO	Mar. 3, 1945	10:00 AM	SCO	Aug. 11, 1945	4:00 PM	LIB
Sep. 22, 1944	10:09 PM	SAG	Mar. 5, 1945	10:00 PM	SAG	Aug. 14, 1945	4:00 AM	SCO
Sep. 25, 1944	9:14 AM	CAP	Mar. 8, 1945	7:23 AM	CAP	Aug. 16, 1945	4:00 PM	SAG
Sep. 27, 1944	1:43 PM	AQU	Mar. 10, 1945	2:46 PM	AQU	Aug. 19, 1945	1:51 AM	CAP
Sep. 29, 1944	5:09 PM	PIS	Mar. 12, 1945	5:09 PM	PIS	Aug. 21, 1945	9:14 AM	AQU
Oct. 1, 1944	4:00 PM	ARI	Mar. 14, 1945	4:00 PM	ARI	Aug. 23, 1945	1:43 PM	PIS
Oct. 3, 1944	2:24 PM	TAU	Mar. 16, 1945	2:24 PM	TAU	Aug. 25, 1945	3:26 PM	ARI

Date	Time	Moon	Date	Time	Moon	Date	Time	Moon
Aug. 27, 1945	2:24 PM	T A U	Feb. 14, 1946	5:09 AM	L E O	Jul. 30, 1946	6:51 AM	V I R
Aug. 29, 1945	4:00 PM	G E M	Feb. 16, 1946	10:17 AM	V I R	Aug. 1, 1946	12:55 PM	L I B
Aug. 31, 1945	8:34 PM	C A N	Feb. 18, 1946	6:28 PM	L I B	Aug. 3, 1946	8:18 PM	S C O
Sep. 3, 1945	3:42 AM	L E O	Feb. 21, 1946	6:00 AM	S C O	Aug. 6, 1946	10:00 AM	S A G
Sep. 5, 1945	2:00 PM	V I R	Feb. 23, 1946	6:00 PM	S A G	Aug. 11, 1946	9:14 AM	A Q U
Sep. 7, 1945	12:00 PM	L I B	Feb. 26, 1946	6:00 AM	C A P	Aug. 13, 1946	6:28 PM	P I S
Sep. 10, 1945	10:00 AM	S C O	Feb. 28, 1946	2:46 PM	A Q U	Aug. 18, 1946	5:09 AM	T A U
Sep. 15, 1945	12:00 PM	C A P	Mar. 2, 1946	10:09 PM	P I S	Aug. 20, 1946	8:34 AM	G E M
Sep. 17, 1945	10:00 PM	A Q U	Mar. 4, 1946	12:00 AM	A R I	Aug. 22, 1946	9:36 AM	C A N
Sep. 23, 1945	12:00 AM	T A U	Mar. 7, 1946	1:36 AM	T A U	Aug. 24, 1946	1:43 PM	L E O
Sep. 25, 1945	12:00 AM	G E M	Mar. 9, 1946	3:12 AM	G E M	Aug. 26, 1946	5:09 PM	V I R
Sep. 28, 1945	3:26 AM	C A N	Mar. 11, 1946	6:51 AM	C A N	Aug. 28, 1946	8:34 PM	L I B
Sep. 30, 1945	9:14 AM	L E O	Mar. 13, 1946	12:55 PM	L E O	Aug. 31, 1946	8:00 AM	S C O
Oct. 2, 1945	8:00 PM	V I R	Mar. 15, 1946	6:28 PM	V I R	Sep. 2, 1946	6:00 PM	S A G
Oct. 5, 1945	6:00 AM	L I B	Mar. 18, 1946	1:51 AM	L I B	Sep. 5, 1946	8:44 AM	C A P
Oct. 7, 1945	6:00 PM	S C O	Mar. 20, 1946	2:00 AM	S C O	Sep. 7, 1946	8:00 PM	A Q U
Oct. 10, 1945	6:00 AM	S A G	Mar. 23, 1946	2:00 AM	S A G	Sep. 10, 1946	1:43 AM	P I S
Oct. 12, 1945	6:00 PM	C A P	Mar. 25, 1946	2:00 AM	C A P	Sep. 12, 1946	6:51 AM	A R I
Oct. 15, 1945	3:42 AM	A Q U	Mar. 30, 1946	6:51 AM	P I S	Sep. 14, 1946	9:36 AM	T A U
Oct. 17, 1945	8:34 AM	P I S	Apr. 1, 1946	10:17 AM	A R I	Sep. 16, 1946	1:43 PM	G E M
Oct. 19, 1945	12:00 PM	A R I	Apr. 3, 1946	11:12 AM	T A U	Sep. 18, 1946	5:09 PM	C A N
Oct. 21, 1945	11:12 AM	T A U	Apr. 5, 1946	11:12 AM	G E M	Sep. 20, 1946	8:34 PM	L E O
Oct. 23, 1945	9:36 AM	G E M	Apr. 7, 1946	1:43 PM	C A N	Sep. 22, 1946	12:00 AM	V I R
Oct. 25, 1945	12:00 PM	C A N	Apr. 9, 1946	5:09 PM	L E O	Sep. 25, 1946	7:23 AM	L I B
Oct. 27, 1945	4:37 PM	L E O	Apr. 11, 1946	12:00 AM	V I R	Sep. 27, 1946	2:46 PM	S C O
Oct. 29, 1945	12:00 AM	V I R	Apr. 14, 1946	10:00 AM	L I B	Sep. 30, 1946	2:00 AM	S A G
Nov. 1, 1945	12:00 PM	L I B	Apr. 16, 1946	8:00 PM	S C O	Oct. 2, 1946	5:27 PM	C A P
Nov. 3, 1945	12:00 AM	S C O	Apr. 19, 1946	8:00 AM	S A G	Oct. 5, 1946	4:00 AM	A Q U
Nov. 6, 1945	12:00 PM	S A G	Apr. 21, 1946	12:00 AM	C A P	Oct. 7, 1946	2:00 PM	P I S
Nov. 8, 1945	12:00 AM	C A P	Apr. 24, 1946	10:00 AM	A Q U	Oct. 9, 1946	6:28 PM	A R I
Nov. 11, 1945	12:00 PM	A Q U	Apr. 26, 1946	4:37 PM	P I S	Oct. 11, 1946	8:34 PM	T A U
Nov. 13, 1945	6:28 PM	P I S	Apr. 28, 1946	8:34 PM	A R I	Oct. 13, 1946	7:12 PM	G E M
Nov. 15, 1945	10:17 PM	A R I	Apr. 30, 1946	8:48 PM	T A U	Oct. 15, 1946	8:48 PM	C A N
Nov. 17, 1945	12:00 AM	T A U	May. 2, 1946	8:48 PM	G E M	Oct. 18, 1946	1:43 AM	L E O
Nov. 19, 1945	8:48 PM	G E M	May. 4, 1946	8:48 PM	C A N	Oct. 20, 1946	7:23 AM	V I R
Nov. 21, 1945	8:48 PM	C A N	May. 6, 1946	12:00 AM	L E O	Oct. 22, 1946	12:55 PM	L I B
Nov. 23, 1945	12:00 AM	L E O	May. 9, 1946	5:32 AM	V I R	Oct. 24, 1946	12:00 AM	S C O
Nov. 26, 1945	7:23 AM	V I R	May. 11, 1946	4:00 PM	L I B	Oct. 27, 1946	10:00 AM	S A G
Nov. 28, 1945	6:00 PM	L I B	May. 14, 1946	2:00 AM	S C O	Oct. 29, 1946	10:00 PM	C A P
Dec. 1, 1945	6:00 AM	S C O	May. 16, 1946	2:00 PM	S A G	Nov. 1, 1946	12:00 PM	A Q U
Dec. 3, 1945	6:00 PM	S A G	May. 19, 1946	4:00 AM	C A P	Nov. 3, 1946	8:18 PM	P I S
Dec. 6, 1945	6:00 AM	C A P	May. 21, 1946	4:00 PM	A Q U	Nov. 6, 1946	3:26 AM	A R I
Dec. 8, 1945	6:00 PM	A Q U	May. 23, 1946	12:00 AM	P I S	Nov. 8, 1946	4:48 AM	T A U
Dec. 10, 1945	12:00 AM	P I S	May. 26, 1946	5:09 AM	A R I	Nov. 10, 1946	6:24 AM	G E M
Dec. 13, 1945	5:09 AM	A R I	May. 28, 1946	8:34 AM	T A U	Nov. 12, 1946	6:24 AM	C A N
Dec. 15, 1945	6:24 AM	T A U	May. 30, 1946	8:00 AM	G E M	Nov. 14, 1946	8:34 AM	L E O
Dec. 17, 1945	8:00 AM	G E M	Jun. 1, 1946	8:00 AM	C A N	Nov. 16, 1946	12:55 PM	V I R
Dec. 19, 1945	8:00 AM	C A N	Jun. 3, 1946	8:00 AM	L E O	Nov. 18, 1946	6:28 PM	L I B
Dec. 21, 1945	10:17 AM	L E O	Jun. 5, 1946	12:00 PM	V I R	Nov. 21, 1946	6:00 AM	S C O
Dec. 23, 1945	4:37 PM	V I R	Jun. 7, 1946	8:18 PM	L I B	Nov. 23, 1946	4:00 PM	S A G
Dec. 28, 1945	12:00 PM	S C O	Jun. 10, 1946	8:00 AM	S C O	Nov. 26, 1946	6:00 AM	C A P
Dec. 31, 1945	2:00 AM	S A G	Jun. 12, 1946	8:00 PM	S A G	Nov. 28, 1946	6:00 PM	A Q U
Jan. 2, 1946	2:00 PM	C A P	Jun. 15, 1946	10:00 AM	C A P	Dec. 1, 1946	6:00 AM	P I S
Jan. 4, 1946	12:00 AM	A Q U	Jun. 17, 1946	10:00 PM	A Q U	Dec. 3, 1946	12:55 PM	A R I
Jan. 7, 1946	5:32 AM	P I S	Jun. 20, 1946	8:00 AM	P I S	Dec. 5, 1946	5:09 PM	T A U
Jan. 9, 1946	10:17 AM	A R I	Jun. 22, 1946	12:00 PM	A R I	Dec. 7, 1946	5:36 PM	G E M
Jan. 11, 1946	1:43 PM	T A U	Jun. 24, 1946	5:09 PM	T A U	Dec. 9, 1946	5:36 PM	C A N
Jan. 13, 1946	5:09 PM	G E M	Jun. 26, 1946	5:36 PM	G E M	Dec. 11, 1946	4:00 PM	L E O
Jan. 15, 1946	5:36 PM	C A N	Jun. 28, 1946	5:36 PM	C A N	Dec. 13, 1946	6:51 PM	V I R
Jan. 17, 1946	7:12 PM	L E O	Jun. 30, 1946	5:36 PM	L E O	Dec. 16, 1946	1:51 AM	L I B
Jan. 20, 1946	1:51 AM	V I R	Jul. 2, 1946	7:12 PM	V I R	Dec. 18, 1946	9:14 AM	S C O
Jan. 22, 1946	9:14 AM	L I B	Jul. 5, 1946	3:42 AM	L I B	Dec. 20, 1946	10:00 PM	S A G
Jan. 24, 1946	6:28 PM	S C O	Jul. 7, 1946	12:55 PM	S C O	Dec. 23, 1946	12:00 PM	C A P
Jan. 27, 1946	10:55 AM	S A G	Jul. 10, 1946	4:22 AM	S A G	Dec. 25, 1946	12:00 AM	A Q U
Jan. 29, 1946	10:00 PM	C A P	Jul. 12, 1946	4:00 PM	C A P	Dec. 28, 1946	12:00 PM	P I S
Feb. 1, 1946	5:32 AM	A Q U	Jul. 15, 1946	4:00 AM	A Q U	Dec. 30, 1946	8:18 PM	A R I
Feb. 3, 1946	12:55 PM	P I S	Jul. 17, 1946	2:00 PM	P I S	Jan. 2, 1947	1:43 AM	T A U
Feb. 5, 1946	6:28 PM	A R I	Jul. 19, 1946	5:09 PM	A R I	Jan. 4, 1947	5:09 AM	G E M
Feb. 7, 1946	8:34 PM	T A U	Jul. 24, 1946	1:36 AM	G E M	Jan. 6, 1947	4:48 AM	C A N
Feb. 9, 1946	10:17 PM	G E M	Jul. 26, 1946	3:12 AM	C A N	Jan. 8, 1947	3:12 AM	L E O
Feb. 12, 1946	1:43 AM	C A N	Jul. 28, 1946	4:48 AM	L E O	Jan. 10, 1947	5:09 AM	V I R

Date	Time	Moon	Date	Time	Moon	Date	Time	Moon
Jan. 12, 1947	8:34 AM	L I B	Jun. 25, 1947	6:51 AM	L I B	Dec. 6, 1947	8:34 AM	L I B
Jan. 14, 1947	4:37 PM	SCO	Jun. 27, 1947	2:46 PM	SCO	Dec. 8, 1947	1:43 PM	SCO
Jan. 17, 1947	6:33 AM	SAG	Jun. 30, 1947	2:00 AM	SAG	Dec. 13, 1947	10:00 AM	CAP
Jan. 19, 1947	6:00 PM	CAP	Jul. 2, 1947	2:00 PM	CAP	Dec. 15, 1947	10:00 PM	AQU
Jan. 22, 1947	6:00 AM	AQU	Jul. 5, 1947	2:00 AM	AQU	Dec. 18, 1947	10:00 AM	P I S
Jan. 24, 1947	6:00 PM	P I S	Jul. 7, 1947	4:00 PM	P I S	Dec. 20, 1947	12:00 AM	A R I
Jan. 27, 1947	1:51 AM	A R I	Jul. 10, 1947	2:00 AM	A R I	Dec. 23, 1947	7:23 AM	T A U
Jan. 29, 1947	9:14 AM	T A U	Jul. 12, 1947	9:14 AM	T A U	Dec. 25, 1947	12:00 PM	GEM
Jan. 31, 1947	12:00 PM	GEM	Jul. 14, 1947	1:43 PM	GEM	Dec. 27, 1947	12:48 PM	CAN
Feb. 2, 1947	3:26 PM	CAN	Jul. 16, 1947	3:26 PM	CAN	Dec. 29, 1947	12:48 PM	LEO
Feb. 4, 1947	2:24 AM	LEO	Jul. 18, 1947	2:24 PM	LEO	Dec. 31, 1947	12:48 PM	V I R
Feb. 6, 1947	2:24 AM	V I R	Jul. 20, 1947	12:48 PM	V I R	Jan. 2, 1948	3:26 PM	L I B
Feb. 8, 1947	6:51 PM	L I B	Jul. 22, 1947	3:26 PM	L I B	Jan. 4, 1948	6:51 PM	SCO
Feb. 11, 1947	1:51 AM	SCO	Jul. 24, 1947	10:09 PM	SCO	Jan. 7, 1948	6:00 AM	SAG
Feb. 13, 1947	12:00 PM	SAG	Jul. 27, 1947	8:00 AM	SAG	Jan. 9, 1948	2:46 PM	CAP
Feb. 16, 1947	2:11 AM	CAP	Jul. 29, 1947	8:00 PM	CAP	Jan. 12, 1948	4:00 AM	AQU
Feb. 18, 1947	2:00 PM	AQU	Aug. 1, 1947	8:00 AM	AQU	Jan. 14, 1948	6:00 PM	P I S
Feb. 20, 1947	10:09 PM	P I S	Aug. 3, 1947	8:00 PM	P I S	Jan. 17, 1948	6:00 AM	A R I
Feb. 23, 1947	7:23 AM	A R I	Aug. 6, 1947	8:00 AM	A R I	Jan. 19, 1948	2:46 PM	T A U
Feb. 25, 1947	2:46 PM	T A U	Aug. 8, 1947	2:46 PM	T A U	Jan. 21, 1948	8:34 PM	GEM
Feb. 27, 1947	8:18 PM	GEM	Aug. 10, 1947	10:09 PM	GEM	Jan. 25, 1948	12:00 AM	LEO
Mar. 1, 1947	10:17 PM	CAN	Aug. 12, 1947	12:00 AM	CAN	Jan. 27, 1948	9:00 PM	V I R
Mar. 3, 1947	10:24 PM	LEO	Aug. 14, 1947	12:00 AM	LEO	Jan. 29, 1948	10:24 PM	L I B
Mar. 6, 1947	1:43 AM	V I R	Aug. 16, 1947	12:00 AM	V I R	Feb. 1, 1948	3:42 AM	SCO
Mar. 8, 1947	5:09 AM	L I B	Aug. 19, 1947	1:43 AM	L I B	Feb. 3, 1948	11:05 AM	SAG
Mar. 10, 1947	11:05 AM	SCO	Aug. 21, 1947	5:09 AM	SCO	Feb. 5, 1948	8:18 PM	CAP
Mar. 12, 1947	6:28 PM	SAG	Aug. 23, 1947	12:55 PM	SAG	Feb. 8, 1948	10:00 AM	AQU
Mar. 15, 1947	8:00 AM	CAP	Aug. 26, 1947	2:00 AM	CAP	Feb. 10, 1948	12:00 AM	P I S
Mar. 17, 1947	10:00 AM	AQU	Aug. 28, 1947	5:27 PM	AQU	Feb. 13, 1948	12:00 PM	A R I
Mar. 20, 1947	7:23 AM	P I S	Aug. 31, 1947	4:00 AM	P I S	Feb. 15, 1948	8:18 PM	T A U
Mar. 22, 1947	2:46 PM	A R I	Sep. 2, 1947	2:00 PM	A R I	Feb. 18, 1948	5:32 AM	GEM
Mar. 24, 1947	10:09 PM	T A U	Sep. 4, 1947	8:18 PM	T A U	Feb. 20, 1948	10:17 AM	CAN
Mar. 26, 1947	12:00 AM	GEM	Sep. 7, 1947	3:42 AM	GEM	Feb. 22, 1948	11:12 AM	LEO
Mar. 29, 1947	3:26 AM	CAN	Sep. 9, 1947	6:51 AM	CAN	Feb. 24, 1948	9:00 AM	V I R
Mar. 31, 1947	6:51 AM	LEO	Sep. 11, 1947	8:00 AM	LEO	Feb. 26, 1948	9:36 AM	L I B
Apr. 2, 1947	8:00 AM	V I R	Sep. 13, 1947	9:36 AM	V I R	Feb. 28, 1948	12:00 PM	SCO
Apr. 4, 1947	1:43 PM	L I B	Sep. 15, 1947	12:00 PM	L I B	Mar. 1, 1948	6:28 PM	SAG
Apr. 6, 1947	8:18 PM	SCO	Sep. 17, 1947	4:37 PM	SCO	Mar. 4, 1948	3:42 AM	CAP
Apr. 9, 1947	6:00 AM	SAG	Sep. 19, 1947	10:09 PM	SAG	Mar. 6, 1948	7:38 PM	AQU
Apr. 11, 1947	4:00 PM	CAP	Sep. 22, 1947	10:00 AM	CAP	Mar. 9, 1948	6:00 AM	P I S
Apr. 14, 1947	6:00 AM	AQU	Sep. 24, 1947	10:00 PM	AQU	Mar. 11, 1948	6:00 PM	A R I
Apr. 16, 1947	6:00 PM	P I S	Sep. 27, 1947	10:00 AM	P I S	Mar. 14, 1948	4:00 AM	T A U
Apr. 18, 1947	12:00 AM	A R I	Sep. 29, 1947	10:00 PM	A R I	Mar. 16, 1948	11:05 AM	GEM
Apr. 21, 1947	5:09 AM	T A U	Oct. 2, 1947	3:42 AM	T A U	Mar. 18, 1948	6:28 PM	CAN
Apr. 23, 1947	6:24 AM	GEM	Oct. 4, 1947	9:14 AM	GEM	Mar. 20, 1948	8:34 PM	LEO
Apr. 25, 1947	10:17 AM	CAN	Oct. 6, 1947	12:00 PM	CAN	Mar. 22, 1948	10:17 PM	V I R
Apr. 27, 1947	12:00 PM	LEO	Oct. 8, 1947	3:26 PM	LEO	Mar. 24, 1948	8:48 PM	L I B
Apr. 29, 1947	3:26 PM	V I R	Oct. 10, 1947	6:51 PM	V I R	Mar. 26, 1948	8:48 PM	SCO
May. 1, 1947	6:51 PM	L I B	Oct. 12, 1947	8:34 PM	L I B	Mar. 29, 1948	3:42 AM	SAG
May. 4, 1947	3:42 AM	SCO	Oct. 14, 1947	12:00 AM	SCO	Mar. 31, 1948	11:05 AM	CAP
May. 6, 1947	2:00 PM	SAG	Oct. 17, 1947	7:23 AM	SAG	Apr. 2, 1948	12:00 AM	AQU
May. 8, 1947	12:00 AM	CAP	Oct. 19, 1947	4:37 PM	CAP	Apr. 5, 1948	12:00 PM	P I S
May. 11, 1947	2:00 AM	AQU	Oct. 22, 1947	6:00 AM	AQU	Apr. 7, 1948	12:00 AM	A R I
May. 14, 1947	2:00 AM	P I S	Oct. 24, 1947	6:00 PM	P I S	Apr. 10, 1948	9:14 AM	T A U
May. 16, 1947	9:14 AM	A R I	Oct. 27, 1947	3:42 AM	A R I	Apr. 12, 1948	4:37 PM	GEM
May. 18, 1947	4:37 PM	T A U	Oct. 29, 1947	11:05 AM	T A U	Apr. 14, 1948	12:00 AM	CAN
May. 20, 1947	4:00 PM	GEM	Oct. 31, 1947	3:26 PM	GEM	Apr. 17, 1948	1:43 AM	LEO
May. 22, 1947	5:36 PM	CAN	Nov. 2, 1947	6:51 PM	CAN	Apr. 19, 1948	5:09 AM	V I R
May. 24, 1947	5:36 PM	LEO	Nov. 4, 1947	7:12 PM	LEO	Apr. 21, 1948	6:51 AM	L I B
May. 26, 1947	8:34 PM	V I R	Nov. 6, 1947	12:00 AM	V I R	Apr. 23, 1948	8:34 AM	SCO
May. 29, 1947	1:51 AM	L I B	Nov. 9, 1947	3:26 AM	L I B	Apr. 25, 1948	12:00 PM	SAG
May. 31, 1947	9:14 AM	SCO	Nov. 11, 1947	9:14 AM	SCO	Apr. 27, 1948	8:18 PM	CAP
Jun. 2, 1947	6:28 PM	SAG	Nov. 13, 1947	4:37 PM	SAG	Apr. 30, 1948	8:00 AM	AQU
Jun. 5, 1947	8:00 AM	CAP	Nov. 16, 1947	1:51 AM	CAP	May. 2, 1948	8:00 PM	P I S
Jun. 7, 1947	8:00 PM	AQU	Nov. 18, 1947	2:00 PM	AQU	May. 5, 1948	8:00 AM	A R I
Jun. 10, 1947	8:00 AM	P I S	Nov. 21, 1947	4:00 AM	P I S	May. 7, 1948	4:37 PM	T A U
Jun. 12, 1947	8:00 PM	A R I	Nov. 23, 1947	12:55 PM	A R I	May. 12, 1948	5:32 AM	CAN
Jun. 17, 1947	3:26 AM	GEM	Nov. 25, 1947	10:09 PM	T A U	May. 14, 1948	6:24 AM	LEO
Jun. 19, 1947	3:12 AM	CAN	Nov. 30, 1947	1:36 AM	CAN	May. 16, 1948	10:17 AM	V I R
Jun. 21, 1947	3:12 AM	LEO	Dec. 2, 1947	3:12 AM	LEO	May. 18, 1948	1:43 PM	L I B
Jun. 23, 1947	3:12 AM	V I R	Dec. 4, 1947	5:09 AM	V I R	May. 20, 1948	5:09 PM	SCO

135

Date	Time	Moon	Date	Time	Moon	Date	Time	Moon
May. 22, 1948	8:34 PM	SAG	Nov. 7, 1948	10:00 AM	AQU	Apr. 20, 1949	6:00 AM	AQU
May. 25, 1948	5:32 AM	CAP	Nov. 9, 1948	10:00 PM	PIS	Apr. 22, 1949	4:00 PM	PIS
May. 27, 1948	2:46 PM	AQU	Nov. 12, 1948	10:00 AM	ARI	Apr. 25, 1949	4:00 AM	ARI
May. 30, 1948	4:00 AM	PIS	Nov. 14, 1948	10:00 PM	TAU	Apr. 27, 1949	6:00 PM	TAU
Jun. 1, 1948	7:38 PM	ARI	Nov. 17, 1948	5:32 AM	GEM	Apr. 30, 1949	3:42 AM	GEM
Jun. 4, 1948	1:51 AM	TAU	Nov. 19, 1948	12:55 PM	CAN	May. 2, 1949	12:55 PM	CAN
Jun. 6, 1948	9:14 AM	GEM	Nov. 21, 1948	3:26 PM	LEO	May. 4, 1949	8:18 PM	LEO
Jun. 8, 1948	12:00 PM	CAN	Nov. 23, 1948	8:34 PM	VIR	May. 6, 1949	12:00 AM	VIR
Jun. 10, 1948	3:26 PM	LEO	Nov. 25, 1948	10:17 PM	LIB	May. 9, 1949	1:36 AM	LIB
Jun. 12, 1948	2:24 PM	VIR	Nov. 28, 1948	1:43 AM	SCO	May. 11, 1949	3:26 AM	SCO
Jun. 14, 1948	6:51 PM	LIB	Nov. 30, 1948	5:09 AM	SAG	May. 13, 1949	3:12 AM	SAG
Jun. 16, 1948	10:17 PM	SCO	Dec. 2, 1948	11:05 AM	CAP	May. 15, 1949	6:51 AM	CAP
Jun. 19, 1948	5:32 AM	SAG	Dec. 4, 1948	8:00 PM	AQU	May. 17, 1949	12:55 PM	AQU
Jun. 21, 1948	12:55 PM	CAP	Dec. 7, 1948	6:00 AM	PIS	May. 19, 1949	12:00 AM	PIS
Jun. 23, 1948	10:09 PM	AQU	Dec. 9, 1948	6:00 PM	ARI	May. 22, 1949	12:00 PM	ARI
Jun. 26, 1948	12:00 PM	PIS	Dec. 12, 1948	6:00 AM	TAU	May. 24, 1949	12:00 AM	TAU
Jun. 28, 1948	12:00 AM	ARI	Dec. 14, 1948	2:46 PM	GEM	May. 27, 1949	12:00 PM	GEM
Jul. 1, 1948	12:00 PM	TAU	Dec. 16, 1948	6:51 PM	CAN	May. 29, 1949	10:00 PM	CAN
Jul. 3, 1948	6:28 PM	GEM	Dec. 18, 1948	12:00 AM	LEO	Jun. 1, 1949	1:51 AM	LEO
Jul. 5, 1948	10:17 PM	CAN	Dec. 21, 1948	1:43 AM	VIR	Jun. 3, 1949	5:09 AM	VIR
Jul. 7, 1948	10:24 PM	LEO	Dec. 23, 1948	3:26 AM	LIB	Jun. 5, 1949	8:34 AM	LIB
Jul. 9, 1948	10:24 PM	VIR	Dec. 25, 1948	6:51 AM	SCO	Jun. 7, 1949	12:00 PM	SCO
Jul. 14, 1948	3:26 AM	SCO	Dec. 27, 1948	12:00 PM	SAG	Jun. 9, 1949	1:43 PM	SAG
Jul. 16, 1948	11:05 AM	SAG	Dec. 29, 1948	5:09 PM	CAP	Jun. 11, 1949	5:09 PM	CAP
Jul. 18, 1948	6:28 PM	CAP	Jan. 1, 1949	4:00 AM	AQU	Jun. 13, 1949	8:34 PM	AQU
Jul. 21, 1948	8:00 AM	AQU	Jan. 3, 1949	2:00 PM	PIS	Jun. 16, 1949	8:00 AM	PIS
Jul. 23, 1948	9:49 PM	PIS	Jan. 6, 1949	2:00 AM	ARI	Jun. 18, 1949	8:00 PM	ARI
Jul. 26, 1948	8:00 AM	ARI	Jan. 8, 1949	4:00 PM	TAU	Jun. 21, 1949	8:00 AM	TAU
Jul. 28, 1948	8:00 PM	TAU	Jan. 13, 1949	5:09 AM	CAN	Jun. 23, 1949	8:00 PM	GEM
Jul. 31, 1948	3:42 AM	GEM	Jan. 15, 1949	8:34 AM	LEO	Jun. 26, 1949	3:42 AM	CAN
Aug. 2, 1948	8:34 AM	CAN	Jan. 17, 1949	8:00 AM	VIR	Jun. 28, 1949	9:14 AM	LEO
Aug. 4, 1948	10:17 AM	LEO	Jan. 19, 1949	9:36 AM	LIB	Jun. 30, 1949	12:00 PM	VIR
Aug. 6, 1948	7:30 AM	VIR	Jan. 21, 1949	11:12 AM	SCO	Jul. 2, 1949	12:48 PM	LIB
Aug. 8, 1948	8:00 AM	LIB	Jan. 23, 1949	5:09 PM	SAG	Jul. 4, 1949	5:09 PM	SCO
Aug. 10, 1948	10:17 AM	SCO	Jan. 26, 1949	1:51 AM	CAP	Jul. 6, 1949	8:34 PM	SAG
Aug. 12, 1948	4:37 PM	SAG	Jan. 28, 1949	9:14 AM	AQU	Jul. 9, 1949	1:51 AM	CAP
Aug. 15, 1948	2:00 AM	CAP	Jan. 30, 1949	10:00 PM	PIS	Jul. 11, 1949	7:23 AM	AQU
Aug. 17, 1948	2:00 AM	AQU	Feb. 2, 1949	10:00 AM	ARI	Jul. 13, 1949	2:46 PM	PIS
Aug. 20, 1948	2:00 AM	PIS	Feb. 4, 1949	10:00 PM	TAU	Jul. 16, 1949	4:00 AM	ARI
Aug. 22, 1948	2:00 AM	ARI	Feb. 7, 1949	10:00 AM	GEM	Jul. 18, 1949	4:00 PM	TAU
Aug. 25, 1948	2:00 AM	TAU	Feb. 9, 1949	4:37 PM	CAN	Jul. 21, 1949	4:00 AM	GEM
Aug. 27, 1948	11:05 AM	GEM	Feb. 11, 1949	5:36 PM	LEO	Jul. 23, 1949	11:05 AM	CAN
Aug. 29, 1948	6:28 PM	CAN	Feb. 13, 1949	7:12 PM	VIR	Jul. 25, 1949	3:26 PM	LEO
Aug. 31, 1948	8:34 PM	LEO	Feb. 15, 1949	7:12 PM	LIB	Jul. 27, 1949	6:51 PM	VIR
Sep. 2, 1948	7:12 PM	VIR	Feb. 17, 1949	7:12 PM	SCO	Jul. 29, 1949	7:12 PM	LIB
Sep. 4, 1948	7:12 PM	LIB	Feb. 19, 1949	10:17 PM	SAG	Jul. 31, 1949	8:48 PM	SCO
Sep. 6, 1948	8:34 PM	SCO	Feb. 22, 1949	7:23 AM	CAP	Aug. 3, 1949	1:43 AM	SAG
Sep. 8, 1948	10:17 PM	SAG	Feb. 24, 1949	2:46 PM	AQU	Aug. 5, 1949	6:51 AM	CAP
Sep. 11, 1948	7:23 AM	CAP	Feb. 27, 1949	4:00 AM	PIS	Aug. 7, 1949	2:46 PM	AQU
Sep. 13, 1948	8:00 PM	AQU	Mar. 1, 1949	4:00 PM	ARI	Aug. 9, 1949	10:09 PM	PIS
Sep. 16, 1948	8:00 AM	PIS	Mar. 4, 1949	6:00 AM	TAU	Aug. 12, 1949	12:00 PM	ARI
Sep. 18, 1948	8:00 PM	ARI	Mar. 6, 1949	6:00 PM	GEM	Aug. 14, 1949	12:00 AM	TAU
Sep. 21, 1948	8:00 AM	TAU	Mar. 9, 1949	1:51 AM	CAN	Aug. 17, 1949	12:00 PM	GEM
Sep. 23, 1948	4:37 PM	GEM	Mar. 11, 1949	5:09 AM	LEO	Aug. 19, 1949	8:18 PM	CAN
Sep. 28, 1948	5:09 AM	LEO	Mar. 13, 1949	6:24 AM	VIR	Aug. 22, 1949	1:43 AM	LEO
Sep. 30, 1948	4:48 AM	VIR	Mar. 15, 1949	4:30 AM	LIB	Aug. 24, 1949	3:12 AM	VIR
Oct. 2, 1948	4:48 AM	LIB	Mar. 17, 1949	4:48 AM	SCO	Aug. 26, 1949	5:09 AM	LIB
Oct. 4, 1948	6:51 AM	SCO	Mar. 19, 1949	6:24 AM	SAG	Aug. 28, 1949	4:48 AM	SCO
Oct. 6, 1948	8:34 AM	SAG	Mar. 21, 1949	12:55 PM	CAP	Aug. 30, 1949	8:34 AM	SAG
Oct. 8, 1948	2:46 PM	CAP	Mar. 23, 1949	8:18 PM	AQU	Sep. 1, 1949	12:00 PM	CAP
Oct. 11, 1948	2:00 AM	AQU	Mar. 26, 1949	10:00 AM	PIS	Sep. 3, 1949	8:18 PM	AQU
Oct. 13, 1948	2:00 PM	PIS	Mar. 28, 1949	10:00 PM	ARI	Sep. 6, 1949	5:32 AM	PIS
Oct. 16, 1948	2:00 AM	ARI	Mar. 31, 1949	12:00 PM	TAU	Sep. 8, 1949	6:00 PM	ARI
Oct. 18, 1948	2:00 PM	TAU	Apr. 2, 1949	12:00 AM	GEM	Sep. 11, 1949	8:44 AM	TAU
Oct. 20, 1948	10:09 PM	GEM	Apr. 5, 1949	7:23 AM	CAN	Sep. 13, 1949	8:00 PM	GEM
Oct. 23, 1948	5:09 AM	CAN	Apr. 7, 1949	2:46 PM	LEO	Sep. 16, 1949	5:32 AM	CAN
Oct. 25, 1948	10:17 AM	LEO	Apr. 9, 1949	5:09 PM	VIR	Sep. 18, 1949	12:55 PM	LEO
Oct. 27, 1948	1:43 PM	VIR	Apr. 11, 1949	4:00 PM	LIB	Sep. 20, 1949	3:26 PM	VIR
Oct. 29, 1948	2:24 PM	LIB	Apr. 13, 1949	4:00 PM	SCO	Sep. 22, 1949	2:24 PM	LIB
Oct. 31, 1948	4:00 PM	SCO	Apr. 15, 1949	4:00 PM	SAG	Sep. 24, 1949	2:24 PM	SCO
Nov. 2, 1948	6:51 PM	SAG	Apr. 17, 1949	8:34 PM	CAP	Sep. 26, 1949	2:24 PM	SAG

Date	Time	Moon	Date	Time	Moon	Date	Time	Moon
Sep. 28, 1949	6:51 PM	CAP	Mar. 11, 1950	8:34 PM	CAP	Aug. 25, 1950	3:26 AM	AQU
Oct. 1, 1949	1:51 AM	AQU	Mar. 14, 1950	3:42 AM	AQU	Aug. 27, 1950	9:14 AM	PIS
Oct. 3, 1949	11:05 AM	PIS	Mar. 16, 1950	11:05 AM	PIS	Aug. 29, 1950	4:37 PM	ARI
Oct. 5, 1949	12:00 AM	ARI	Mar. 18, 1950	10:00 PM	ARI	Sep. 1, 1950	4:00 AM	TAU
Oct. 8, 1949	3:16 PM	TAU	Mar. 21, 1950	10:00 AM	TAU	Sep. 3, 1950	4:00 PM	GEM
Oct. 11, 1949	2:00 AM	GEM	Mar. 23, 1950	10:00 PM	GEM	Sep. 6, 1950	4:00 AM	CAN
Oct. 13, 1949	2:00 PM	CAN	Mar. 26, 1950	10:00 AM	CAN	Sep. 8, 1950	12:55 PM	LEO
Oct. 15, 1949	8:18 PM	LEO	Mar. 28, 1950	6:28 PM	LEO	Sep. 10, 1950	8:18 PM	VIR
Oct. 17, 1949	12:00 AM	VIR	Apr. 2, 1950	1:36 AM	LIB	Sep. 12, 1950	12:00 AM	LIB
Oct. 20, 1949	1:36 AM	LIB	Apr. 4, 1950	1:36 AM	SCO	Sep. 15, 1950	1:43 AM	SCO
Oct. 22, 1949	1:36 AM	SCO	Apr. 6, 1950	1:36 AM	SAG	Sep. 17, 1950	3:26 AM	SAG
Oct. 24, 1949	1:36 AM	SAG	Apr. 8, 1950	3:26 AM	CAP	Sep. 19, 1950	5:09 AM	CAP
Oct. 26, 1949	3:26 AM	CAP	Apr. 10, 1950	9:14 AM	AQU	Sep. 21, 1950	11:05 AM	AQU
Oct. 28, 1949	9:14 AM	AQU	Apr. 12, 1950	6:00 PM	PIS	Sep. 23, 1950	4:37 PM	PIS
Oct. 30, 1949	4:37 PM	PIS	Apr. 15, 1950	4:00 AM	ARI	Sep. 25, 1950	12:00 AM	ARI
Nov. 2, 1949	6:00 AM	ARI	Apr. 17, 1950	4:00 PM	TAU	Sep. 28, 1950	12:00 PM	TAU
Nov. 4, 1949	9:49 PM	TAU	Apr. 20, 1950	4:00 AM	GEM	Sep. 30, 1950	12:00 AM	GEM
Nov. 7, 1949	8:00 AM	GEM	Apr. 22, 1950	6:00 PM	CAN	Oct. 3, 1950	12:00 PM	CAN
Nov. 9, 1949	8:00 PM	CAN	Apr. 25, 1950	4:00 AM	LEO	Oct. 5, 1950	12:00 AM	LEO
Nov. 12, 1949	4:00 AM	LEO	Apr. 27, 1950	8:34 AM	VIR	Oct. 8, 1950	5:32 AM	VIR
Nov. 14, 1949	9:14 AM	VIR	Apr. 29, 1950	11:12 AM	LIB	Oct. 10, 1950	10:17 AM	LIB
Nov. 16, 1949	12:00 PM	LIB	May. 1, 1950	12:48 PM	SCO	Oct. 12, 1950	9:36 AM	SCO
Nov. 18, 1949	1:43 PM	SCO	May. 3, 1950	10:30 AM	SAG	Oct. 14, 1950	12:00 PM	SAG
Nov. 20, 1949	12:48 PM	SAG	May. 5, 1950	11:12 AM	CAP	Oct. 16, 1950	11:12 AM	CAP
Nov. 22, 1949	12:48 PM	CAP	May. 7, 1950	3:26 PM	AQU	Oct. 18, 1950	3:26 PM	AQU
Nov. 24, 1949	5:09 PM	AQU	May. 9, 1950	10:09 PM	PIS	Oct. 20, 1950	10:09 PM	PIS
Nov. 27, 1949	2:00 AM	PIS	May. 12, 1950	10:00 AM	ARI	Oct. 23, 1950	8:00 AM	ARI
Nov. 29, 1949	2:00 AM	ARI	May. 14, 1950	10:00 PM	TAU	Oct. 25, 1950	6:00 PM	TAU
Dec. 2, 1949	2:00 AM	TAU	May. 17, 1950	10:00 AM	GEM	Oct. 28, 1950	6:00 AM	GEM
Dec. 4, 1949	2:00 PM	GEM	May. 22, 1950	10:00 AM	LEO	Oct. 30, 1950	6:00 PM	CAN
Dec. 9, 1949	9:14 AM	LEO	May. 24, 1950	4:37 PM	VIR	Nov. 2, 1950	5:32 AM	LEO
Dec. 11, 1949	2:46 PM	VIR	May. 26, 1950	8:34 PM	LIB	Nov. 4, 1950	2:46 PM	VIR
Dec. 13, 1949	6:51 PM	LIB	May. 28, 1950	12:00 AM	SCO	Nov. 6, 1950	10:09 PM	LIB
Dec. 15, 1949	10:17 PM	SCO	May. 30, 1950	10:24 PM	SAG	Nov. 8, 1950	8:48 PM	SCO
Dec. 17, 1949	12:00 AM	SAG	Jun. 1, 1950	10:24 PM	CAP	Nov. 10, 1950	8:48 PM	SAG
Dec. 19, 1949	10:24 PM	CAP	Jun. 3, 1950	10:24 PM	AQU	Nov. 12, 1950	8:48 PM	CAP
Dec. 22, 1949	3:26 AM	AQU	Jun. 6, 1950	5:32 AM	PIS	Nov. 14, 1950	8:48 PM	AQU
Dec. 24, 1949	9:14 AM	PIS	Jun. 8, 1950	4:00 PM	ARI	Nov. 17, 1950	3:42 AM	PIS
Dec. 26, 1949	10:00 PM	ARI	Jun. 11, 1950	4:00 AM	TAU	Nov. 19, 1950	2:00 PM	ARI
Dec. 29, 1949	10:00 AM	TAU	Jun. 13, 1950	4:00 PM	GEM	Nov. 21, 1950	12:00 AM	TAU
Dec. 31, 1949	10:00 PM	GEM	Jun. 16, 1950	3:42 AM	CAN	Nov. 24, 1950	12:00 PM	GEM
Jan. 3, 1950	7:23 AM	CAN	Jun. 18, 1950	4:00 PM	LEO	Nov. 27, 1950	2:00 AM	CAN
Jan. 5, 1950	2:46 PM	LEO	Jun. 20, 1950	10:09 PM	VIR	Nov. 29, 1950	2:00 PM	LEO
Jan. 7, 1950	6:51 PM	VIR	Jun. 23, 1950	3:26 AM	LIB	Dec. 1, 1950	12:00 AM	VIR
Jan. 9, 1950	12:00 AM	LIB	Jun. 25, 1950	6:51 AM	SCO	Dec. 4, 1950	5:32 AM	LIB
Jan. 12, 1950	3:26 AM	SCO	Jun. 27, 1950	8:00 AM	SAG	Dec. 6, 1950	8:34 AM	SCO
Jan. 14, 1950	6:51 AM	SAG	Jun. 29, 1950	8:00 AM	CAP	Dec. 8, 1950	8:00 AM	SAG
Jan. 16, 1950	8:34 AM	CAP	Jul. 1, 1950	9:36 AM	AQU	Dec. 10, 1950	6:00 AM	CAP
Jan. 18, 1950	12:00 PM	AQU	Jul. 3, 1950	1:43 PM	PIS	Dec. 12, 1950	6:24 AM	AQU
Jan. 20, 1950	8:18 PM	PIS	Jul. 5, 1950	10:09 PM	ARI	Dec. 14, 1950	10:17 AM	PIS
Jan. 23, 1950	6:00 AM	ARI	Jul. 8, 1950	12:00 PM	TAU	Dec. 16, 1950	6:28 PM	ARI
Jan. 25, 1950	6:00 PM	TAU	Jul. 10, 1950	12:00 AM	GEM	Dec. 19, 1950	6:00 AM	TAU
Jan. 28, 1950	6:00 AM	GEM	Jul. 13, 1950	12:00 PM	CAN	Dec. 21, 1950	6:00 PM	GEM
Jan. 30, 1950	6:00 PM	CAN	Jul. 15, 1950	8:18 PM	LEO	Dec. 24, 1950	8:00 AM	CAN
Feb. 1, 1950	12:00 AM	LEO	Jul. 18, 1950	3:42 AM	VIR	Dec. 26, 1950	8:00 PM	LEO
Feb. 4, 1950	3:26 AM	VIR	Jul. 20, 1950	8:34 AM	LIB	Dec. 29, 1950	3:42 AM	VIR
Feb. 6, 1950	6:51 AM	LIB	Jul. 22, 1950	1:43 PM	SCO	Dec. 31, 1950	12:55 PM	LIB
Feb. 8, 1950	8:34 AM	SCO	Jul. 24, 1950	2:24 PM	SAG	Jan. 2, 1951	6:28 PM	SCO
Feb. 10, 1950	12:00 PM	SAG	Jul. 26, 1950	6:51 PM	CAP	Jan. 4, 1951	5:36 PM	SAG
Feb. 12, 1950	3:26 PM	CAP	Jul. 28, 1950	8:34 PM	AQU	Jan. 6, 1951	7:12 PM	CAP
Feb. 14, 1950	10:09 PM	AQU	Jul. 30, 1950	12:00 AM	PIS	Jan. 8, 1951	5:36 PM	AQU
Feb. 17, 1950	3:42 AM	PIS	Aug. 2, 1950	7:23 AM	ARI	Jan. 10, 1951	7:12 PM	PIS
Feb. 19, 1950	12:55 PM	ARI	Aug. 4, 1950	8:00 PM	TAU	Jan. 13, 1951	3:42 AM	ARI
Feb. 22, 1950	2:00 AM	TAU	Aug. 7, 1950	8:00 AM	GEM	Jan. 15, 1951	2:00 PM	TAU
Feb. 24, 1950	2:00 PM	GEM	Aug. 9, 1950	8:00 PM	CAN	Jan. 18, 1951	2:00 AM	GEM
Feb. 27, 1950	2:00 AM	CAN	Aug. 12, 1950	3:42 AM	LEO	Jan. 20, 1951	2:00 PM	CAN
Mar. 1, 1950	9:14 AM	LEO	Aug. 14, 1950	11:05 AM	VIR	Jan. 23, 1951	2:00 AM	LEO
Mar. 3, 1950	1:43 PM	VIR	Aug. 16, 1950	3:26 PM	LIB	Jan. 25, 1951	12:00 PM	VIR
Mar. 5, 1950	2:24 PM	LIB	Aug. 18, 1950	6:51 PM	SCO	Jan. 27, 1951	6:28 PM	LIB
Mar. 7, 1950	5:09 PM	SCO	Aug. 20, 1950	10:17 PM	SAG	Jan. 29, 1951	12:00 AM	SCO
Mar. 9, 1950	4:00 PM	SAG	Aug. 22, 1950	12:00 AM	CAP	Feb. 1, 1951	1:43 AM	SAG

137

Date	Time	Moon	Date	Time	Moon	Date	Time	Moon
Feb. 3, 1951	3:12 AM	C A P	Jul. 15, 1951	3:12 AM	S A G	Dec. 28, 1951	3:12 AM	C A P
Feb. 5, 1951	4:48 AM	A Q U	Jul. 17, 1951	4:48 AM	C A P	Dec. 30, 1951	3:12 AM	A Q U
Feb. 7, 1951	6:51 AM	P I S	Jul. 19, 1951	3:12 AM	A Q U	Jan. 1, 1952	3:26 AM	P I S
Feb. 9, 1951	12:55 PM	A R I	Jul. 21, 1951	5:09 AM	P I S	Jan. 3, 1952	6:51 AM	A R I
Feb. 11, 1951	8:18 PM	T A U	Jul. 23, 1951	9:14 AM	A R I	Jan. 5, 1952	12:55 PM	T A U
Feb. 14, 1951	10:00 AM	G E M	Jul. 25, 1951	2:46 PM	T A U	Jan. 7, 1952	10:09 PM	G E M
Feb. 16, 1951	10:00 PM	C A N	Jul. 28, 1951	4:00 AM	G E M	Jan. 10, 1952	12:00 PM	C A N
Feb. 19, 1951	10:00 AM	L E O	Jul. 30, 1951	4:00 PM	C A N	Jan. 12, 1952	12:00 AM	L E O
Feb. 21, 1951	4:37 PM	V I R	Aug. 2, 1951	4:00 AM	L E O	Jan. 15, 1952	12:00 PM	V I R
Feb. 23, 1951	10:17 PM	L I B	Aug. 4, 1951	4:00 PM	V I R	Jan. 17, 1952	10:09 PM	L I B
Feb. 26, 1951	5:32 AM	S C O	Aug. 6, 1951	12:00 AM	L I B	Jan. 20, 1952	9:14 AM	S C O
Feb. 28, 1951	8:34 AM	S A G	Aug. 9, 1951	7:23 AM	S C O	Jan. 22, 1952	2:46 PM	S A G
Mar. 2, 1951	10:17 AM	C A P	Aug. 11, 1951	12:00 PM	S A G	Jan. 24, 1952	2:24 PM	C A P
Mar. 4, 1951	1:43 PM	A Q U	Aug. 13, 1951	1:43 PM	C A P	Jan. 26, 1952	2:24 PM	A Q U
Mar. 6, 1951	5:09 PM	P I S	Aug. 15, 1951	12:48 PM	A Q U	Jan. 28, 1952	12:00 PM	P I S
Mar. 8, 1951	8:34 AM	A R I	Aug. 17, 1951	2:24 PM	P I S	Jan. 30, 1952	2:24 PM	A R I
Mar. 11, 1951	5:32 AM	T A U	Aug. 19, 1951	5:09 PM	A R I	Feb. 1, 1952	6:51 PM	T A U
Mar. 13, 1951	6:00 PM	G E M	Aug. 21, 1951	10:17 PM	T A U	Feb. 4, 1952	6:00 AM	G E M
Mar. 16, 1951	6:00 AM	C A N	Aug. 24, 1951	9:14 AM	G E M	Feb. 6, 1952	6:00 PM	C A N
Mar. 18, 1951	6:00 PM	L E O	Aug. 26, 1951	10:00 PM	C A N	Feb. 9, 1952	6:00 AM	L E O
Mar. 21, 1951	1:51 AM	V I R	Aug. 29, 1951	12:00 PM	L E O	Feb. 11, 1952	9:49 PM	V I R
Mar. 23, 1951	9:14 AM	L I B	Aug. 31, 1951	8:18 PM	V I R	Feb. 14, 1952	6:00 AM	L I B
Mar. 25, 1951	12:00 PM	S C O	Sep. 3, 1951	5:32 AM	L I B	Feb. 16, 1952	2:46 PM	S C O
Mar. 27, 1951	12:48 PM	S A G	Sep. 5, 1951	12:55 PM	S C O	Feb. 18, 1952	10:09 PM	S A G
Mar. 29, 1951	2:24 PM	C A P	Sep. 7, 1951	5:09 PM	S A G	Feb. 20, 1952	12:00 AM	C A P
Mar. 31, 1951	6:51 PM	A Q U	Sep. 9, 1951	8:34 PM	C A P	Feb. 22, 1952	12:00 AM	A Q U
Apr. 2, 1951	10:17 PM	P I S	Sep. 11, 1951	8:48 PM	A Q U	Feb. 25, 1952	1:43 AM	P I S
Apr. 5, 1951	5:32 AM	A R I	Sep. 13, 1951	10:24 PM	P I S	Feb. 27, 1952	1:36 AM	A R I
Apr. 7, 1951	4:00 PM	T A U	Sep. 16, 1951	3:26 AM	A R I	Feb. 29, 1952	5:09 AM	T A U
Apr. 10, 1951	2:00 AM	G E M	Sep. 18, 1951	9:14 AM	T A U	Mar. 2, 1952	12:55 PM	G E M
Apr. 12, 1951	2:00 PM	C A N	Sep. 20, 1951	8:00 PM	G E M	Mar. 4, 1952	10:09 PM	C A N
Apr. 15, 1951	2:00 AM	L E O	Sep. 23, 1951	6:00 AM	C A N	Mar. 7, 1952	3:16 PM	L E O
Apr. 17, 1951	11:05 AM	V I R	Sep. 25, 1951	9:49 PM	L E O	Mar. 10, 1952	2:00 AM	V I R
Apr. 19, 1951	5:09 PM	L I B	Sep. 28, 1951	6:00 AM	V I R	Mar. 12, 1952	11:05 AM	L I B
Apr. 21, 1951	7:12 PM	S C O	Sep. 30, 1951	2:46 PM	L I B	Mar. 14, 1952	8:18 PM	S C O
Apr. 23, 1951	8:48 PM	S A G	Oct. 2, 1951	8:18 PM	S C O	Mar. 17, 1952	1:43 AM	S A G
Apr. 25, 1951	12:00 AM	C A P	Oct. 4, 1951	10:17 PM	S A G	Mar. 19, 1952	6:51 AM	C A P
Apr. 27, 1951	10:24 PM	A Q U	Oct. 7, 1951	1:43 AM	C A P	Mar. 21, 1952	8:00 AM	A Q U
Apr. 30, 1951	5:32 AM	P I S	Oct. 9, 1951	3:12 AM	A Q U	Mar. 23, 1952	9:36 AM	P I S
May. 2, 1951	12:55 PM	A R I	Oct. 11, 1951	6:51 AM	P I S	Mar. 25, 1952	11:12 AM	A R I
May. 4, 1951	8:18 PM	T A U	Oct. 13, 1951	12:00 PM	A R I	Mar. 27, 1952	3:26 PM	T A U
May. 7, 1951	7:23 AM	G E M	Oct. 15, 1951	6:28 PM	T A U	Mar. 29, 1952	10:09 PM	G E M
May. 9, 1951	12:00 AM	C A N	Oct. 18, 1951	4:00 AM	G E M	Apr. 1, 1952	7:23 AM	C A N
May. 12, 1951	10:00 AM	L E O	Oct. 20, 1951	2:00 PM	C A N	Apr. 3, 1952	8:00 PM	L E O
May. 14, 1951	10:00 PM	V I R	Oct. 23, 1951	4:00 AM	L E O	Apr. 6, 1952	10:00 AM	V I R
May. 17, 1951	3:42 AM	L I B	Oct. 25, 1951	4:00 PM	V I R	Apr. 8, 1952	6:28 PM	L I B
May. 19, 1951	6:24 AM	S C O	Oct. 30, 1951	3:26 AM	S C O	Apr. 11, 1952	3:42 AM	S C O
May. 21, 1951	8:00 AM	S A G	Nov. 1, 1951	6:51 AM	S A G	Apr. 13, 1952	9:14 AM	S A G
May. 23, 1951	6:00 AM	C A P	Nov. 3, 1951	8:34 AM	C A P	Apr. 15, 1952	12:00 PM	C A P
May. 25, 1951	8:34 AM	A Q U	Nov. 5, 1951	10:17 AM	A Q U	Apr. 17, 1952	3:26 PM	A Q U
May. 27, 1951	10:17 AM	P I S	Nov. 7, 1951	1:43 PM	P I S	Apr. 19, 1952	5:09 PM	P I S
May. 29, 1951	6:28 PM	A R I	Nov. 9, 1951	5:09 PM	A R I	Apr. 21, 1952	8:34 PM	A R I
Jun. 1, 1951	4:00 AM	T A U	Nov. 12, 1951	1:51 AM	T A U	Apr. 24, 1952	1:51 AM	T A U
Jun. 3, 1951	4:00 PM	G E M	Nov. 14, 1951	12:00 PM	G E M	Apr. 26, 1952	7:23 AM	G E M
Jun. 6, 1951	4:00 AM	C A N	Nov. 16, 1951	10:00 PM	C A N	Apr. 28, 1952	6:00 PM	C A N
Jun. 8, 1951	4:00 PM	L E O	Nov. 19, 1951	1:05 PM	L E O	May. 1, 1952	6:33 AM	L E O
Jun. 11, 1951	4:00 AM	V I R	Nov. 21, 1951	12:00 AM	V I R	May. 3, 1952	6:00 PM	V I R
Jun. 13, 1951	12:55 PM	L I B	Nov. 24, 1951	9:14 AM	L I B	May. 6, 1952	3:42 AM	L I B
Jun. 15, 1951	5:09 PM	S C O	Nov. 26, 1951	1:43 PM	S C O	May. 8, 1952	12:55 PM	S C O
Jun. 17, 1951	5:36 PM	S A G	Nov. 28, 1951	5:09 PM	S A G	May. 10, 1952	3:26 PM	S A G
Jun. 19, 1951	5:36 PM	C A P	Nov. 30, 1951	4:00 PM	C A P	May. 12, 1952	6:51 PM	C A P
Jun. 21, 1951	5:36 PM	A Q U	Dec. 2, 1951	4:00 PM	A Q U	May. 14, 1952	8:34 PM	A Q U
Jun. 23, 1951	5:36 PM	P I S	Dec. 4, 1951	6:51 PM	P I S	May. 16, 1952	8:48 PM	P I S
Jun. 25, 1951	10:17 PM	A R I	Dec. 6, 1951	10:17 PM	A R I	May. 19, 1952	3:42 AM	A R I
Jun. 28, 1951	10:00 AM	T A U	Dec. 9, 1951	7:23 AM	T A U	May. 21, 1952	9:14 AM	T A U
Jun. 30, 1951	8:00 PM	G E M	Dec. 11, 1951	4:37 PM	G E M	May. 23, 1952	2:46 PM	G E M
Jul. 3, 1951	10:00 AM	C A N	Dec. 14, 1951	6:00 AM	C A N	May. 26, 1952	2:00 AM	C A N
Jul. 5, 1951	10:00 PM	L E O	Dec. 16, 1951	6:00 PM	L E O	May. 28, 1952	12:00 PM	L E O
Jul. 8, 1951	10:00 AM	V I R	Dec. 19, 1951	6:00 AM	V I R	May. 31, 1952	2:00 AM	V I R
Jul. 10, 1951	6:28 PM	L I B	Dec. 21, 1951	6:00 PM	L I B	Jun. 2, 1952	2:00 PM	L I B
Jul. 13, 1951	1:51 AM	S C O	Dec. 26, 1951	3:26 AM	S A G	Jun. 4, 1952	12:00 AM	S C O

Date	Time	Moon	Date	Time	Moon	Date	Time	Moon
Jun. 7, 1952	1:43 AM	SAG	Nov. 15, 1952	6:00 PM	SCO	Apr. 30, 1953	12:00 AM	SAG
Jun. 9, 1952	3:26 AM	CAP	Nov. 17, 1952	12:00 AM	SAG	May. 3, 1953	5:32 AM	CAP
Jun. 11, 1952	3:12 AM	AQU	Nov. 20, 1952	1:43 AM	CAP	May. 5, 1953	11:05 AM	AQU
Jun. 13, 1952	5:09 AM	PIS	Nov. 22, 1952	5:09 AM	AQU	May. 7, 1953	1:43 PM	PIS
Jun. 15, 1952	8:34 AM	ARI	Nov. 24, 1952	8:34 AM	PIS	May. 9, 1953	2:24 PM	ARI
Jun. 17, 1952	2:46 PM	TAU	Nov. 26, 1952	12:00 PM	ARI	May. 11, 1953	4:00 PM	TAU
Jun. 19, 1952	10:09 PM	GEM	Nov. 28, 1952	3:26 PM	TAU	May. 13, 1953	5:36 PM	GEM
Jun. 22, 1952	8:00 AM	CAN	Nov. 30, 1952	10:09 PM	GEM	May. 15, 1953	10:17 PM	CAN
Jun. 24, 1952	8:00 PM	LEO	Dec. 3, 1952	3:42 AM	CAN	May. 18, 1953	10:00 AM	LEO
Jun. 27, 1952	8:00 AM	VIR	Dec. 5, 1952	12:55 PM	LEO	May. 20, 1953	8:00 PM	VIR
Jun. 29, 1952	10:00 PM	LIB	Dec. 8, 1952	2:00 AM	VIR	May. 23, 1953	10:55 AM	LIB
Jul. 2, 1952	5:32 AM	SCO	Dec. 10, 1952	4:00 PM	LIB	May. 25, 1953	10:00 PM	SCO
Jul. 4, 1952	12:55 PM	SAG	Dec. 13, 1952	2:00 AM	SCO	May. 28, 1953	5:32 AM	SAG
Jul. 6, 1952	1:43 PM	CAP	Dec. 15, 1952	6:51 AM	SAG	May. 30, 1953	10:17 AM	CAP
Jul. 8, 1952	12:48 PM	AQU	Dec. 17, 1952	12:00 PM	CAP	Jun. 1, 1953	3:26 PM	AQU
Jul. 10, 1952	12:48 PM	PIS	Dec. 19, 1952	1:43 PM	AQU	Jun. 3, 1953	6:51 PM	PIS
Jul. 12, 1952	3:26 PM	ARI	Dec. 21, 1952	3:26 PM	PIS	Jun. 5, 1953	10:17 PM	ARI
Jul. 14, 1952	6:51 PM	TAU	Dec. 23, 1952	5:09 PM	ARI	Jun. 10, 1953	3:26 AM	GEM
Jul. 17, 1952	3:42 AM	GEM	Dec. 25, 1952	8:34 PM	TAU	Jun. 12, 1953	8:34 AM	CAN
Jul. 19, 1952	2:00 PM	CAN	Dec. 28, 1952	3:42 AM	GEM	Jun. 14, 1953	4:37 PM	LEO
Jul. 22, 1952	2:00 AM	LEO	Dec. 30, 1952	11:05 AM	CAN	Jun. 17, 1953	4:00 AM	VIR
Jul. 24, 1952	5:27 PM	VIR	Jan. 1, 1953	8:18 PM	LEO	Jun. 19, 1953	7:38 PM	LIB
Jul. 27, 1952	4:00 AM	LIB	Jan. 4, 1953	10:00 AM	VIR	Jun. 22, 1953	6:00 AM	SCO
Jul. 29, 1952	12:55 PM	SCO	Jan. 9, 1953	12:00 PM	SCO	Jun. 24, 1953	12:55 PM	SAG
Jul. 31, 1952	10:09 PM	SAG	Jan. 11, 1953	6:28 PM	SAG	Jun. 26, 1953	8:18 PM	CAP
Aug. 2, 1952	12:00 AM	CAP	Jan. 13, 1953	10:17 PM	CAP	Jun. 28, 1953	10:17 PM	AQU
Aug. 4, 1952	12:00 AM	AQU	Jan. 15, 1953	10:24 PM	AQU	Jul. 1, 1953	1:43 AM	PIS
Aug. 6, 1952	9:00 PM	PIS	Jan. 17, 1953	10:24 PM	PIS	Jul. 3, 1953	3:26 AM	ARI
Aug. 8, 1952	10:24 PM	ARI	Jan. 22, 1953	3:26 AM	TAU	Jul. 5, 1953	6:51 AM	TAU
Aug. 11, 1952	3:42 AM	TAU	Jan. 24, 1953	9:14 AM	GEM	Jul. 7, 1953	10:17 AM	GEM
Aug. 13, 1952	9:14 AM	GEM	Jan. 26, 1953	4:37 PM	CAN	Jul. 9, 1953	4:37 PM	CAN
Aug. 15, 1952	8:00 PM	CAN	Jan. 29, 1953	6:00 AM	LEO	Jul. 12, 1953	2:00 AM	LEO
Aug. 18, 1952	8:00 AM	LEO	Jan. 31, 1953	6:00 PM	VIR	Jul. 14, 1953	12:00 PM	VIR
Aug. 20, 1952	12:00 AM	VIR	Feb. 3, 1953	6:00 AM	LIB	Jul. 17, 1953	2:11 AM	LIB
Aug. 23, 1952	10:00 AM	LIB	Feb. 5, 1953	6:00 PM	SCO	Jul. 19, 1953	2:00 PM	SCO
Aug. 25, 1952	6:28 PM	SCO	Feb. 8, 1953	3:42 AM	SAG	Jul. 21, 1953	10:09 PM	SAG
Aug. 28, 1952	3:42 AM	SAG	Feb. 10, 1953	8:34 AM	CAP	Jul. 24, 1953	5:32 AM	CAP
Aug. 30, 1952	8:34 AM	CAP	Feb. 12, 1953	9:36 AM	AQU	Jul. 26, 1953	8:34 AM	AQU
Sep. 1, 1952	9:36 AM	AQU	Feb. 14, 1953	9:36 AM	PIS	Jul. 28, 1953	10:17 AM	PIS
Sep. 3, 1952	9:36 AM	PIS	Feb. 16, 1953	9:36 AM	ARI	Jul. 30, 1953	9:36 AM	ARI
Sep. 5, 1952	9:36 AM	ARI	Feb. 18, 1953	9:36 AM	TAU	Aug. 1, 1953	12:00 PM	TAU
Sep. 7, 1952	12:00 PM	TAU	Feb. 20, 1953	4:37 PM	GEM	Aug. 3, 1953	3:26 PM	GEM
Sep. 9, 1952	3:26 PM	GEM	Feb. 22, 1953	10:09 PM	CAN	Aug. 5, 1953	8:34 PM	CAN
Sep. 12, 1952	1:51 AM	CAN	Feb. 25, 1953	12:00 PM	LEO	Aug. 8, 1953	7:23 AM	LEO
Sep. 14, 1952	2:00 PM	LEO	Feb. 27, 1953	12:00 AM	VIR	Aug. 10, 1953	8:00 PM	VIR
Sep. 17, 1952	4:00 AM	VIR	Mar. 2, 1953	12:00 PM	LIB	Aug. 13, 1953	8:00 AM	LIB
Sep. 19, 1952	4:00 PM	LIB	Mar. 4, 1953	12:00 AM	SCO	Aug. 15, 1953	8:00 PM	SCO
Sep. 22, 1952	2:00 AM	SCO	Mar. 7, 1953	9:14 AM	SAG	Aug. 18, 1953	8:00 AM	SAG
Sep. 24, 1952	9:14 AM	SAG	Mar. 9, 1953	6:28 PM	CAP	Aug. 20, 1953	2:46 PM	CAP
Sep. 26, 1952	4:37 PM	CAP	Mar. 11, 1953	8:34 PM	AQU	Aug. 22, 1953	6:51 PM	AQU
Sep. 28, 1952	6:51 PM	AQU	Mar. 13, 1953	8:48 PM	PIS	Aug. 24, 1953	7:12 PM	PIS
Sep. 30, 1952	7:12 PM	PIS	Mar. 15, 1953	8:48 PM	ARI	Aug. 26, 1953	7:12 PM	ARI
Oct. 2, 1952	10:17 PM	ARI	Mar. 17, 1953	8:48 PM	TAU	Aug. 28, 1953	7:12 PM	TAU
Oct. 4, 1952	8:48 PM	TAU	Mar. 19, 1953	12:00 AM	GEM	Aug. 30, 1953	10:17 PM	GEM
Oct. 7, 1952	1:43 AM	GEM	Mar. 22, 1953	5:32 AM	CAN	Sep. 2, 1953	3:42 AM	CAN
Oct. 9, 1952	9:14 AM	CAN	Mar. 24, 1953	6:00 AM	LEO	Sep. 4, 1953	12:55 PM	LEO
Oct. 11, 1952	10:00 PM	LEO	Mar. 27, 1953	6:00 AM	VIR	Sep. 7, 1953	2:00 AM	VIR
Oct. 14, 1952	10:00 AM	VIR	Mar. 29, 1953	6:00 AM	LIB	Sep. 9, 1953	2:00 PM	LIB
Oct. 16, 1952	12:00 AM	LIB	Apr. 1, 1953	6:00 AM	SCO	Sep. 12, 1953	4:22 AM	SCO
Oct. 19, 1952	7:23 AM	SCO	Apr. 3, 1953	2:46 PM	SAG	Sep. 14, 1953	12:55 PM	SAG
Oct. 21, 1952	2:46 PM	SAG	Apr. 5, 1953	12:00 AM	CAP	Sep. 19, 1953	5:32 AM	AQU
Oct. 23, 1952	10:09 PM	CAP	Apr. 8, 1953	5:32 AM	AQU	Sep. 21, 1953	6:51 AM	PIS
Oct. 25, 1952	12:00 AM	AQU	Apr. 10, 1953	6:51 AM	PIS	Sep. 23, 1953	4:30 AM	ARI
Oct. 28, 1952	3:26 PM	PIS	Apr. 12, 1953	6:24 AM	ARI	Sep. 25, 1953	4:48 AM	TAU
Oct. 30, 1952	4:48 AM	ARI	Apr. 14, 1953	8:34 AM	TAU	Sep. 27, 1953	4:48 AM	GEM
Nov. 1, 1952	8:34 AM	TAU	Apr. 16, 1953	8:00 AM	GEM	Sep. 29, 1953	11:05 AM	CAN
Nov. 3, 1952	12:00 PM	GEM	Apr. 18, 1953	1:43 PM	CAN	Oct. 1, 1953	6:28 PM	LEO
Nov. 5, 1952	6:28 PM	CAN	Apr. 20, 1953	10:09 PM	LEO	Oct. 4, 1953	8:00 AM	VIR
Nov. 8, 1952	6:00 AM	LEO	Apr. 23, 1953	12:00 PM	VIR	Oct. 6, 1953	8:00 PM	LIB
Nov. 10, 1952	6:00 PM	VIR	Apr. 26, 1953	2:00 AM	LIB	Oct. 9, 1953	8:00 AM	SCO
Nov. 13, 1952	8:00 AM	LIB	Apr. 28, 1953	2:00 PM	SCO	Oct. 11, 1953	8:00 PM	SAG

Date	Time	Moon	Date	Time	Moon	Date	Time	Moon
Oct. 14, 1953	5:32 AM	C A P	Mar. 27, 1954	6:00 AM	C A P	Sep. 6, 1954	12:00 AM	C A P
Oct. 16, 1953	12:55 PM	A Q U	Mar. 29, 1954	12:55 PM	A Q U	Sep. 9, 1954	9:14 AM	A Q U
Oct. 18, 1953	3:26 PM	P I S	Mar. 31, 1954	5:09 PM	P I S	Sep. 11, 1954	2:46 PM	P I S
Oct. 20, 1953	4:00 PM	A R I	Apr. 2, 1954	4:00 PM	A R I	Sep. 13, 1954	3:26 PM	A R I
Oct. 22, 1953	4:00 PM	T A U	Apr. 4, 1954	4:00 PM	T A U	Sep. 15, 1954	2:24 PM	T A U
Oct. 24, 1953	4:00 PM	G E M	Apr. 6, 1954	4:00 PM	G E M	Sep. 17, 1954	2:24 PM	G E M
Oct. 26, 1953	6:51 PM	C A N	Apr. 8, 1954	6:51 PM	C A N	Sep. 19, 1954	6:51 PM	C A N
Oct. 29, 1953	4:00 AM	L E O	Apr. 11, 1954	2:00 AM	L E O	Sep. 22, 1954	1:51 AM	L E O
Oct. 31, 1953	2:00 PM	V I R	Apr. 13, 1954	12:00 PM	V I R	Sep. 24, 1954	9:14 AM	V I R
Nov. 3, 1953	2:00 AM	L I B	Apr. 15, 1954	10:00 PM	L I B	Sep. 26, 1954	8:00 PM	L I B
Nov. 5, 1953	4:00 PM	S C O	Apr. 18, 1954	12:00 PM	S C O	Sep. 29, 1954	6:00 AM	S C O
Nov. 8, 1953	2:00 AM	S A G	Apr. 20, 1954	12:00 AM	S A G	Oct. 1, 1954	8:00 PM	S A G
Nov. 10, 1953	11:05 AM	C A P	Apr. 23, 1954	12:00 PM	C A P	Oct. 4, 1954	8:00 AM	C A P
Nov. 12, 1953	6:28 PM	A Q U	Apr. 25, 1954	10:00 PM	A Q U	Oct. 6, 1954	4:37 PM	A Q U
Nov. 14, 1953	10:17 PM	P I S	Apr. 28, 1954	1:51 AM	P I S	Oct. 8, 1954	10:17 PM	P I S
Nov. 17, 1953	1:43 AM	A R I	Apr. 30, 1954	3:26 AM	A R I	Oct. 12, 1954	12:00 AM	T A U
Nov. 19, 1953	1:36 AM	T A U	May. 2, 1954	3:12 AM	T A U	Oct. 14, 1954	12:00 AM	G E M
Nov. 21, 1953	3:26 AM	G E M	May. 4, 1954	1:36 AM	G E M	Oct. 17, 1954	1:43 AM	C A N
Nov. 23, 1953	5:09 AM	C A N	May. 6, 1954	3:26 AM	C A N	Oct. 19, 1954	7:23 AM	L E O
Nov. 25, 1953	11:05 AM	L E O	May. 8, 1954	9:14 AM	L E O	Oct. 21, 1954	2:46 PM	V I R
Nov. 27, 1953	10:00 PM	V I R	May. 10, 1954	4:37 PM	V I R	Oct. 24, 1954	2:00 AM	L I B
Nov. 30, 1953	10:00 AM	L I B	May. 13, 1954	6:33 AM	L I B	Oct. 26, 1954	2:00 PM	S C O
Dec. 2, 1953	10:00 PM	S C O	May. 15, 1954	6:00 PM	S C O	Oct. 29, 1954	2:00 AM	S A G
Dec. 5, 1953	10:00 AM	S A G	May. 18, 1954	6:00 AM	S A G	Oct. 31, 1954	2:00 PM	C A P
Dec. 7, 1953	4:37 PM	C A P	May. 20, 1954	6:00 PM	C A P	Nov. 3, 1954	2:00 AM	A Q U
Dec. 9, 1953	12:00 AM	A Q U	May. 23, 1954	1:51 AM	A Q U	Nov. 5, 1954	9:14 AM	P I S
Dec. 12, 1953	5:32 AM	P I S	May. 25, 1954	9:14 AM	P I S	Nov. 7, 1954	12:00 PM	A R I
Dec. 14, 1953	8:34 AM	A R I	May. 27, 1954	12:00 PM	A R I	Nov. 9, 1954	11:12 AM	T A U
Dec. 16, 1953	10:17 AM	T A U	May. 29, 1954	1:43 PM	T A U	Nov. 11, 1954	11:12 AM	G E M
Dec. 18, 1953	11:12 AM	G E M	May. 31, 1954	12:48 PM	G E M	Nov. 13, 1954	11:12 AM	C A N
Dec. 20, 1953	3:26 PM	C A N	Jun. 2, 1954	12:48 PM	C A N	Nov. 15, 1954	1:43 PM	L E O
Dec. 22, 1953	10:09 PM	L E O	Jun. 4, 1954	5:09 PM	L E O	Nov. 17, 1954	8:18 PM	V I R
Dec. 25, 1953	5:32 AM	V I R	Jun. 7, 1954	2:00 AM	V I R	Nov. 20, 1954	8:00 AM	L I B
Dec. 27, 1953	6:00 PM	L I B	Jun. 9, 1954	12:00 PM	L I B	Nov. 22, 1954	9:49 PM	S C O
Dec. 30, 1953	6:00 AM	S C O	Jun. 11, 1954	12:00 AM	S C O	Nov. 25, 1954	8:00 AM	S A G
Jan. 1, 1954	6:00 PM	S A G	Jun. 14, 1954	12:00 PM	S A G	Nov. 27, 1954	8:00 PM	C A P
Jan. 4, 1954	1:51 AM	C A P	Jun. 16, 1954	12:00 AM	C A P	Nov. 30, 1954	8:00 AM	A Q U
Jan. 6, 1954	6:51 AM	A Q U	Jun. 19, 1954	7:23 AM	A Q U	Dec. 2, 1954	2:46 PM	P I S
Jan. 8, 1954	10:17 AM	P I S	Jun. 21, 1954	2:46 PM	P I S	Dec. 4, 1954	10:09 PM	A R I
Jan. 10, 1954	1:43 PM	A R I	Jun. 23, 1954	5:09 PM	A R I	Dec. 6, 1954	12:00 AM	T A U
Jan. 12, 1954	2:24 PM	T A U	Jun. 25, 1954	8:34 PM	T A U	Dec. 8, 1954	10:24 PM	G E M
Jan. 14, 1954	6:51 PM	G E M	Jun. 27, 1954	8:48 PM	G E M	Dec. 10, 1954	10:24 PM	C A N
Jan. 19, 1954	5:09 AM	L E O	Jun. 29, 1954	12:00 AM	C A N	Dec. 12, 1954	10:24 PM	L E O
Jan. 21, 1954	2:46 PM	V I R	Jul. 2, 1954	3:26 AM	L E O	Dec. 15, 1954	5:32 AM	V I R
Jan. 24, 1954	2:00 AM	L I B	Jul. 4, 1954	9:14 AM	V I R	Dec. 17, 1954	12:55 PM	L I B
Jan. 26, 1954	2:00 PM	S C O	Jul. 6, 1954	6:28 PM	L I B	Dec. 20, 1954	2:00 AM	S C O
Jan. 29, 1954	1:51 AM	S A G	Jul. 9, 1954	8:00 AM	S C O	Dec. 22, 1954	2:00 PM	S A G
Jan. 31, 1954	11:05 AM	C A P	Jul. 11, 1954	8:00 PM	S A G	Dec. 25, 1954	2:00 AM	C A P
Feb. 2, 1954	6:28 PM	A Q U	Jul. 14, 1954	5:32 AM	C A P	Dec. 27, 1954	2:00 PM	A Q U
Feb. 4, 1954	5:36 PM	P I S	Jul. 16, 1954	2:46 PM	A Q U	Dec. 29, 1954	8:18 PM	P I S
Feb. 6, 1954	7:12 PM	A R I	Jul. 18, 1954	6:51 PM	P I S	Jan. 1, 1955	3:42 AM	A R I
Feb. 8, 1954	8:48 PM	T A U	Jul. 20, 1954	10:17 PM	A R I	Jan. 3, 1955	6:51 AM	T A U
Feb. 10, 1954	10:24 PM	G E M	Jul. 23, 1954	1:43 AM	T A U	Jan. 5, 1955	8:34 AM	G E M
Feb. 13, 1954	5:09 AM	C A N	Jul. 25, 1954	5:09 AM	G E M	Jan. 7, 1955	8:00 AM	C A N
Feb. 15, 1954	12:55 PM	L E O	Jul. 27, 1954	6:51 AM	C A N	Jan. 9, 1955	9:36 AM	L E O
Feb. 17, 1954	12:00 AM	V I R	Jul. 29, 1954	12:00 PM	L E O	Jan. 11, 1955	1:43 PM	V I R
Feb. 20, 1954	10:00 AM	L I B	Jul. 31, 1954	6:28 PM	V I R	Jan. 13, 1955	10:09 PM	L I B
Feb. 22, 1954	10:00 PM	S C O	Aug. 3, 1954	3:42 AM	L I B	Jan. 16, 1955	10:00 AM	S C O
Feb. 25, 1954	1:05 AM	S A G	Aug. 5, 1954	4:00 PM	S C O	Jan. 18, 1955	10:00 PM	S A G
Feb. 27, 1954	10:00 PM	C A P	Aug. 8, 1954	4:00 AM	S A G	Jan. 21, 1955	10:00 AM	C A P
Mar. 2, 1954	3:42 AM	A Q U	Aug. 10, 1954	4:00 PM	C A P	Jan. 23, 1955	10:00 PM	A Q U
Mar. 4, 1954	4:48 PM	P I S	Aug. 15, 1954	3:26 AM	P I S	Jan. 26, 1955	3:42 AM	P I S
Mar. 6, 1954	4:48 AM	A R I	Aug. 17, 1954	4:48 AM	A R I	Jan. 28, 1955	9:14 AM	A R I
Mar. 8, 1954	4:48 AM	T A U	Aug. 19, 1954	6:24 AM	T A U	Jan. 30, 1955	12:00 PM	T A U
Mar. 10, 1954	6:24 AM	G E M	Aug. 21, 1954	10:17 AM	G E M	Feb. 1, 1955	3:26 PM	G E M
Mar. 12, 1954	10:17 AM	C A N	Aug. 23, 1954	1:43 PM	C A N	Feb. 3, 1955	4:00 PM	C A N
Mar. 14, 1954	6:28 PM	L E O	Aug. 25, 1954	8:18 PM	L E O	Feb. 5, 1955	8:34 PM	L E O
Mar. 17, 1954	6:00 AM	V I R	Aug. 28, 1954	1:51 AM	V I R	Feb. 7, 1955	12:00 AM	V I R
Mar. 19, 1954	2:46 PM	L I B	Aug. 30, 1954	11:05 AM	L I B	Feb. 10, 1955	7:23 AM	L I B
Mar. 22, 1954	6:00 AM	S C O	Sep. 1, 1954	12:00 AM	S C O	Feb. 12, 1955	6:00 PM	S C O
Mar. 24, 1954	6:00 AM	S A G	Sep. 4, 1954	12:00 PM	S A G	Feb. 15, 1955	6:00 AM	S A G

Date	Time	Moon	Date	Time	Moon	Date	Time	Moon
Feb. 17, 1955	6:00 PM	CAP	Jul. 31, 1955	12:00 PM	CAP	Jan. 8, 1956	6:00 PM	SAG
Feb. 20, 1955	3:42 AM	AQU	Aug. 2, 1955	12:00 AM	AQU	Jan. 11, 1956	8:44 AM	CAP
Feb. 22, 1955	11:05 AM	PIS	Aug. 5, 1955	10:00 AM	PIS	Jan. 13, 1956	8:00 PM	AQU
Feb. 24, 1955	3:26 PM	ARI	Aug. 7, 1955	4:37 PM	ARI	Jan. 16, 1956	8:00 AM	PIS
Feb. 26, 1955	4:00 PM	TAU	Aug. 9, 1955	10:09 PM	TAU	Jan. 18, 1956	4:37 PM	ARI
Feb. 28, 1955	8:34 PM	GEM	Aug. 11, 1955	12:00 AM	GEM	Jan. 20, 1956	12:00 AM	TAU
Mar. 2, 1955	12:00 AM	CAN	Aug. 14, 1955	3:26 AM	CAN	Jan. 23, 1956	3:26 AM	GEM
Mar. 5, 1955	3:26 AM	LEO	Aug. 16, 1955	5:09 AM	LEO	Jan. 25, 1956	4:48 AM	CAN
Mar. 7, 1955	9:14 AM	VIR	Aug. 18, 1955	6:51 AM	VIR	Jan. 27, 1956	4:48 AM	LEO
Mar. 9, 1955	4:37 PM	LIB	Aug. 20, 1955	10:17 AM	LIB	Jan. 29, 1956	4:48 AM	VIR
Mar. 12, 1955	2:00 AM	SCO	Aug. 22, 1955	6:28 PM	SCO	Jan. 31, 1956	6:24 AM	LIB
Mar. 14, 1955	2:00 PM	SAG	Aug. 25, 1955	8:00 AM	SAG	Feb. 2, 1956	2:46 PM	SCO
Mar. 17, 1955	4:22 AM	CAP	Aug. 27, 1955	8:00 PM	CAP	Feb. 5, 1956	2:00 AM	SAG
Mar. 19, 1955	2:00 PM	AQU	Aug. 30, 1955	8:00 AM	AQU	Feb. 7, 1956	2:00 PM	CAP
Mar. 21, 1955	10:09 PM	PIS	Sep. 1, 1955	6:00 PM	PIS	Feb. 10, 1956	2:00 AM	AQU
Mar. 23, 1955	12:00 AM	ARI	Sep. 3, 1955	12:00 AM	ARI	Feb. 12, 1956	2:00 PM	PIS
Mar. 26, 1955	1:43 AM	TAU	Sep. 6, 1955	1:43 AM	TAU	Feb. 14, 1956	10:09 PM	ARI
Mar. 28, 1955	3:26 AM	GEM	Sep. 8, 1955	5:09 AM	GEM	Feb. 17, 1956	5:32 AM	TAU
Mar. 30, 1955	5:09 AM	CAN	Sep. 10, 1955	8:34 AM	CAN	Feb. 19, 1956	10:17 AM	GEM
Apr. 1, 1955	8:34 AM	LEO	Sep. 12, 1955	12:00 PM	LEO	Feb. 21, 1956	1:43 PM	CAN
Apr. 3, 1955	1:43 PM	VIR	Sep. 14, 1955	3:26 PM	VIR	Feb. 23, 1956	2:24 PM	LEO
Apr. 5, 1955	10:09 PM	LIB	Sep. 16, 1955	6:51 PM	LIB	Feb. 25, 1956	5:09 PM	VIR
Apr. 8, 1955	10:00 AM	SCO	Sep. 19, 1955	3:42 AM	SCO	Feb. 27, 1956	6:51 PM	LIB
Apr. 10, 1955	10:00 PM	SAG	Sep. 21, 1955	4:00 PM	SAG	Feb. 29, 1956	10:17 PM	SCO
Apr. 13, 1955	10:00 AM	CAP	Sep. 24, 1955	4:00 AM	CAP	Mar. 3, 1956	10:00 AM	SAG
Apr. 15, 1955	10:00 PM	AQU	Sep. 26, 1955	4:00 PM	AQU	Mar. 5, 1956	10:00 PM	CAP
Apr. 18, 1955	7:23 AM	PIS	Sep. 29, 1955	2:00 AM	PIS	Mar. 8, 1956	10:00 AM	AQU
Apr. 20, 1955	10:17 AM	ARI	Oct. 1, 1955	7:23 AM	ARI	Mar. 10, 1956	10:00 PM	PIS
Apr. 22, 1955	11:12 AM	TAU	Oct. 3, 1955	10:17 AM	TAU	Mar. 13, 1956	5:32 AM	ARI
Apr. 24, 1955	11:12 AM	GEM	Oct. 5, 1955	12:00 PM	GEM	Mar. 15, 1956	10:17 AM	TAU
Apr. 26, 1955	11:12 AM	CAN	Oct. 7, 1955	12:48 PM	CAN	Mar. 17, 1956	3:26 PM	GEM
Apr. 28, 1955	3:26 PM	LEO	Oct. 9, 1955	5:09 PM	LEO	Mar. 19, 1956	6:51 PM	CAN
Apr. 30, 1955	6:51 PM	VIR	Oct. 11, 1955	12:00 AM	VIR	Mar. 21, 1956	10:17 PM	LEO
May. 3, 1955	6:00 AM	LIB	Oct. 14, 1955	3:42 AM	LIB	Mar. 26, 1956	3:26 AM	LIB
May. 5, 1955	4:00 PM	SCO	Oct. 16, 1955	11:05 AM	SCO	Mar. 28, 1956	9:14 AM	SCO
May. 8, 1955	4:00 AM	SAG	Oct. 18, 1955	12:00 AM	SAG	Mar. 30, 1956	4:37 PM	SAG
May. 10, 1955	7:38 PM	CAP	Oct. 21, 1955	12:00 PM	CAP	Apr. 2, 1956	6:00 AM	CAP
May. 13, 1955	6:00 AM	AQU	Oct. 23, 1955	12:00 AM	AQU	Apr. 4, 1956	6:00 PM	AQU
May. 15, 1955	2:46 PM	PIS	Oct. 26, 1955	12:00 PM	PIS	Apr. 9, 1956	6:00 AM	PIS
May. 17, 1955	10:09 PM	ARI	Oct. 28, 1955	3:26 PM	ARI	Apr. 9, 1956	12:55 PM	ARI
May. 19, 1955	8:48 PM	TAU	Oct. 30, 1955	8:34 PM	TAU	Apr. 11, 1956	8:18 PM	TAU
May. 21, 1955	10:24 PM	GEM	Nov. 1, 1955	7:12 PM	GEM	Apr. 13, 1956	10:17 PM	GEM
May. 23, 1955	7:30 PM	CAN	Nov. 3, 1955	8:48 PM	CAN	Apr. 16, 1956	1:43 AM	CAN
May. 25, 1955	12:00 AM	LEO	Nov. 5, 1955	12:00 AM	LEO	Apr. 18, 1956	3:26 AM	LEO
May. 28, 1955	3:42 AM	VIR	Nov. 8, 1955	3:26 AM	VIR	Apr. 20, 1956	6:51 AM	VIR
May. 30, 1955	11:05 AM	LIB	Nov. 10, 1955	8:34 AM	LIB	Apr. 22, 1956	12:55 PM	LIB
Jun. 1, 1955	10:00 PM	SCO	Nov. 12, 1955	6:28 PM	SCO	Apr. 24, 1956	6:28 PM	SCO
Jun. 4, 1955	10:00 AM	SAG	Nov. 15, 1955	6:00 AM	SAG	Apr. 27, 1956	1:51 AM	SAG
Jun. 9, 1955	12:00 PM	AQU	Nov. 17, 1955	6:00 PM	CAP	Apr. 29, 1956	2:00 PM	CAP
Jun. 11, 1955	8:18 PM	PIS	Nov. 20, 1955	8:00 AM	AQU	May. 2, 1956	2:00 AM	AQU
Jun. 14, 1955	3:26 AM	ARI	Nov. 22, 1955	8:00 PM	PIS	May. 4, 1956	2:00 PM	PIS
Jun. 16, 1955	8:34 AM	TAU	Nov. 25, 1955	3:42 AM	ARI	May. 6, 1956	10:09 PM	ARI
Jun. 18, 1955	8:00 AM	GEM	Nov. 27, 1955	6:51 AM	TAU	May. 9, 1956	3:26 AM	TAU
Jun. 20, 1955	8:00 AM	CAN	Nov. 29, 1955	6:24 AM	GEM	May. 11, 1956	6:51 AM	GEM
Jun. 22, 1955	8:00 AM	LEO	Dec. 1, 1955	6:24 AM	CAN	May. 13, 1956	8:00 AM	CAN
Jun. 24, 1955	12:00 PM	VIR	Dec. 3, 1955	6:24 AM	LEO	May. 15, 1956	10:17 AM	LEO
Jun. 26, 1955	6:28 PM	LIB	Dec. 5, 1955	10:17 AM	VIR	May. 17, 1956	12:00 PM	VIR
Jun. 29, 1955	4:00 AM	SCO	Dec. 7, 1955	4:37 PM	LIB	May. 19, 1956	6:28 PM	LIB
Jul. 1, 1955	4:00 PM	SAG	Dec. 9, 1955	12:00 PM	SCO	May. 21, 1956	12:00 AM	SCO
Jul. 4, 1955	6:00 AM	CAP	Dec. 12, 1955	12:00 PM	SAG	May. 24, 1956	9:14 AM	SAG
Jul. 6, 1955	6:00 PM	AQU	Dec. 15, 1955	2:11 AM	CAP	May. 26, 1956	10:00 PM	CAP
Jul. 9, 1955	4:00 AM	PIS	Dec. 17, 1955	2:00 PM	AQU	May. 29, 1956	10:00 AM	AQU
Jul. 11, 1955	11:05 AM	ARI	Dec. 20, 1955	2:00 AM	PIS	May. 31, 1956	10:00 PM	PIS
Jul. 13, 1955	4:37 PM	TAU	Dec. 22, 1955	11:05 AM	ARI	Jun. 3, 1956	7:23 AM	ARI
Jul. 15, 1955	6:51 PM	GEM	Dec. 24, 1955	3:26 PM	TAU	Jun. 5, 1956	2:46 PM	TAU
Jul. 17, 1955	5:36 PM	CAN	Dec. 26, 1955	5:36 PM	GEM	Jun. 7, 1956	5:09 PM	GEM
Jul. 19, 1955	8:34 PM	LEO	Dec. 28, 1955	4:30 PM	CAN	Jun. 9, 1956	5:36 PM	CAN
Jul. 21, 1955	7:12 PM	VIR	Dec. 30, 1955	5:36 PM	LEO	Jun. 11, 1956	5:36 PM	LEO
Jul. 24, 1955	1:51 AM	LIB	Jan. 1, 1956	5:36 PM	VIR	Jun. 13, 1956	5:36 PM	VIR
Jul. 26, 1955	12:00 PM	SCO	Jan. 3, 1956	10:17 AM	LIB	Jun. 15, 1956	10:17 PM	LIB
Jul. 28, 1955	12:00 AM	SAG	Jan. 6, 1956	8:00 AM	SCO	Jun. 18, 1956	5:32 AM	SCO

The Sun, Moon and Venus

Date	Time	Moon	Date	Time	Moon	Date	Time	Moon
Jun. 20, 1956	2:46 PM	SAG	Dec. 3, 1956	10:09 PM	CAP	May. 16, 1957	6:28 PM	CAP
Jun. 23, 1956	4:00 AM	CAP	Dec. 6, 1956	12:00 PM	AQU	May. 19, 1957	6:00 AM	AQU
Jun. 25, 1956	4:00 PM	AQU	Dec. 8, 1956	12:00 AM	PIS	May. 21, 1957	6:00 PM	PIS
Jun. 28, 1956	4:00 AM	PIS	Dec. 11, 1956	12:00 PM	ARI	May. 24, 1957	6:00 AM	ARI
Jun. 30, 1956	4:00 PM	ARI	Dec. 13, 1956	8:18 PM	TAU	May. 26, 1957	2:46 PM	TAU
Jul. 2, 1956	12:00 AM	TAU	Dec. 16, 1956	1:51 AM	GEM	May. 28, 1957	12:00 AM	GEM
Jul. 5, 1956	3:26 AM	GEM	Dec. 18, 1956	3:26 AM	CAN	May. 31, 1957	3:26 AM	CAN
Jul. 7, 1956	5:09 AM	CAN	Dec. 20, 1956	3:12 AM	LEO	Jun. 2, 1957	4:48 AM	LEO
Jul. 9, 1956	3:12 AM	LEO	Dec. 22, 1956	3:12 AM	VIR	Jun. 4, 1957	8:34 AM	VIR
Jul. 11, 1956	3:12 AM	VIR	Dec. 24, 1956	6:51 AM	LIB	Jun. 6, 1957	10:17 AM	LIB
Jul. 13, 1956	5:09 AM	LIB	Dec. 26, 1956	12:55 PM	SCO	Jun. 8, 1957	1:43 PM	SCO
Jul. 15, 1956	10:17 AM	SCO	Dec. 28, 1956	8:18 PM	SAG	Jun. 10, 1957	6:51 PM	SAG
Jul. 17, 1956	8:18 PM	SAG	Dec. 31, 1956	5:32 AM	CAP	Jun. 13, 1957	3:42 AM	CAP
Jul. 20, 1956	10:00 AM	CAP	Jan. 2, 1957	6:00 PM	AQU	Jun. 15, 1957	2:00 PM	AQU
Jul. 22, 1956	10:00 AM	AQU	Jan. 5, 1957	8:44 AM	PIS	Jun. 18, 1957	2:00 AM	PIS
Jul. 25, 1956	10:00 AM	PIS	Jan. 7, 1957	8:00 PM	ARI	Jun. 20, 1957	2:00 PM	ARI
Jul. 27, 1956	10:00 PM	ARI	Jan. 10, 1957	6:00 AM	TAU	Jun. 25, 1957	6:51 AM	GEM
Jul. 30, 1956	8:00 AM	TAU	Jan. 12, 1957	12:55 PM	GEM	Jun. 27, 1957	12:00 PM	CAN
Aug. 1, 1956	12:55 PM	GEM	Jan. 14, 1957	3:26 PM	CAN	Jun. 29, 1957	12:48 PM	LEO
Aug. 3, 1956	3:26 PM	CAN	Jan. 16, 1957	2:24 PM	LEO	Jul. 1, 1957	3:26 PM	VIR
Aug. 5, 1956	2:24 PM	LEO	Jan. 18, 1957	12:48 PM	VIR	Jul. 3, 1957	5:09 PM	LIB
Aug. 7, 1956	2:24 PM	VIR	Jan. 20, 1957	12:48 PM	LIB	Jul. 5, 1957	6:51 PM	SCO
Aug. 9, 1956	2:24 PM	LIB	Jan. 22, 1957	5:09 PM	SCO	Jul. 8, 1957	1:51 AM	SAG
Aug. 11, 1956	6:51 PM	SCO	Jan. 25, 1957	1:51 AM	SAG	Jul. 10, 1957	12:00 PM	CAP
Aug. 14, 1956	3:42 AM	SAG	Jan. 27, 1957	11:05 AM	CAP	Jul. 12, 1957	10:00 PM	AQU
Aug. 16, 1956	4:00 PM	CAP	Jan. 29, 1957	12:00 AM	AQU	Jul. 15, 1957	8:00 AM	PIS
Aug. 19, 1956	4:00 AM	AQU	Feb. 1, 1957	3:16 PM	PIS	Jul. 17, 1957	12:00 AM	ARI
Aug. 21, 1956	4:00 PM	PIS	Feb. 4, 1957	2:00 AM	ARI	Jul. 20, 1957	10:00 AM	TAU
Aug. 24, 1956	4:00 AM	ARI	Feb. 6, 1957	2:00 PM	TAU	Jul. 22, 1957	8:00 PM	GEM
Aug. 26, 1956	2:00 PM	TAU	Feb. 8, 1957	8:18 PM	GEM	Jul. 24, 1957	12:00 AM	CAN
Aug. 28, 1956	8:18 PM	GEM	Feb. 10, 1957	12:00 AM	CAN	Jul. 26, 1957	10:24 PM	LEO
Aug. 30, 1956	10:17 PM	CAN	Feb. 13, 1957	1:36 AM	LEO	Jul. 28, 1957	10:24 PM	VIR
Sep. 3, 1956	12:00 AM	VIR	Feb. 14, 1957	10:30 PM	VIR	Jul. 30, 1957	10:24 PM	LIB
Sep. 6, 1956	1:43 AM	LIB	Feb. 16, 1957	12:00 AM	LIB	Aug. 2, 1957	1:43 AM	SCO
Sep. 8, 1956	3:26 AM	SCO	Feb. 19, 1957	1:43 AM	SCO	Aug. 4, 1957	7:23 AM	SAG
Sep. 10, 1956	11:05 AM	SAG	Feb. 21, 1957	6:51 AM	SAG	Aug. 6, 1957	6:00 PM	CAP
Sep. 12, 1956	8:18 PM	CAP	Feb. 23, 1957	4:37 PM	CAP	Aug. 9, 1957	4:00 AM	AQU
Sep. 15, 1956	12:00 PM	AQU	Feb. 26, 1957	6:00 AM	AQU	Aug. 11, 1957	2:00 PM	PIS
Sep. 17, 1956	12:00 AM	PIS	Feb. 28, 1957	9:49 PM	PIS	Aug. 14, 1957	4:00 AM	ARI
Sep. 20, 1956	9:14 AM	ARI	Mar. 3, 1957	8:00 AM	ARI	Aug. 16, 1957	4:00 PM	TAU
Sep. 22, 1956	8:00 PM	TAU	Mar. 5, 1957	4:37 PM	TAU	Aug. 19, 1957	1:51 AM	GEM
Sep. 27, 1956	5:09 AM	CAN	Mar. 8, 1957	4:00 AM	GEM	Aug. 21, 1957	6:51 AM	CAN
Sep. 29, 1956	8:34 AM	LEO	Mar. 10, 1957	9:14 AM	CAN	Aug. 23, 1957	10:17 AM	LEO
Oct. 1, 1956	10:17 AM	VIR	Mar. 12, 1957	12:00 PM	LEO	Aug. 25, 1957	9:36 AM	VIR
Oct. 3, 1956	12:00 PM	LIB	Mar. 14, 1957	11:12 AM	VIR	Aug. 27, 1957	7:30 AM	LIB
Oct. 5, 1956	1:43 PM	SCO	Mar. 16, 1957	11:12 AM	LIB	Aug. 29, 1957	10:17 AM	SCO
Oct. 7, 1956	8:18 PM	SAG	Mar. 18, 1957	11:12 AM	SCO	Aug. 31, 1957	1:43 AM	SAG
Oct. 10, 1956	5:32 AM	CAP	Mar. 20, 1957	3:26 PM	SAG	Sep. 2, 1957	10:09 PM	CAP
Oct. 12, 1956	6:00 PM	AQU	Mar. 23, 1957	2:00 AM	CAP	Sep. 5, 1957	7:23 AM	AQU
Oct. 15, 1956	8:00 AM	PIS	Mar. 25, 1957	2:00 AM	AQU	Sep. 7, 1957	8:00 PM	PIS
Oct. 17, 1956	4:37 PM	ARI	Mar. 28, 1957	2:00 AM	PIS	Sep. 10, 1957	10:00 AM	ARI
Oct. 20, 1956	1:51 AM	TAU	Mar. 30, 1957	2:00 PM	ARI	Sep. 12, 1957	10:00 PM	TAU
Oct. 22, 1956	7:23 AM	GEM	Apr. 4, 1957	10:00 AM	GEM	Sep. 15, 1957	7:23 AM	GEM
Oct. 24, 1956	10:17 AM	CAN	Apr. 6, 1957	2:46 PM	CAN	Sep. 17, 1957	4:37 PM	CAN
Oct. 26, 1956	1:43 PM	LEO	Apr. 8, 1957	6:51 PM	LEO	Sep. 19, 1957	6:51 PM	LEO
Oct. 28, 1956	2:24 PM	VIR	Apr. 10, 1957	7:12 PM	VIR	Sep. 21, 1957	7:12 PM	VIR
Oct. 30, 1956	6:51 PM	LIB	Apr. 12, 1957	8:48 PM	LIB	Sep. 23, 1957	7:12 PM	LIB
Nov. 1, 1956	10:17 PM	SCO	Apr. 14, 1957	12:00 AM	SCO	Sep. 25, 1957	7:12 PM	SCO
Nov. 4, 1956	5:32 AM	SAG	Apr. 17, 1957	1:43 AM	SAG	Sep. 27, 1957	10:17 PM	SAG
Nov. 6, 1956	4:00 PM	CAP	Apr. 19, 1957	9:14 AM	CAP	Sep. 30, 1957	5:32 AM	CAP
Nov. 9, 1956	4:00 AM	AQU	Apr. 21, 1957	10:00 PM	AQU	Oct. 2, 1957	4:00 PM	AQU
Nov. 11, 1956	4:00 PM	PIS	Apr. 24, 1957	10:00 AM	PIS	Oct. 5, 1957	4:00 AM	PIS
Nov. 14, 1956	1:51 AM	ARI	Apr. 26, 1957	10:00 PM	ARI	Oct. 7, 1957	4:00 PM	ARI
Nov. 16, 1956	11:05 AM	TAU	Apr. 29, 1957	8:00 AM	TAU	Oct. 10, 1957	4:00 AM	TAU
Nov. 18, 1956	1:43 PM	GEM	May. 1, 1957	2:46 PM	GEM	Oct. 12, 1957	12:55 PM	GEM
Nov. 20, 1956	5:09 PM	CAN	May. 3, 1957	6:51 PM	CAN	Oct. 14, 1957	10:09 PM	CAN
Nov. 22, 1956	5:36 PM	LEO	May. 5, 1957	12:00 AM	LEO	Oct. 17, 1957	3:42 AM	LEO
Nov. 24, 1956	10:17 PM	VIR	May. 8, 1957	1:36 AM	VIR	Oct. 19, 1957	4:48 AM	VIR
Nov. 27, 1956	1:51 AM	LIB	May. 10, 1957	5:09 AM	LIB	Oct. 21, 1957	6:51 AM	LIB
Nov. 29, 1956	7:23 AM	SCO	May. 12, 1957	6:24 AM	SCO	Oct. 23, 1957	6:24 AM	SCO
Dec. 1, 1956	12:55 PM	SAG	May. 14, 1957	12:00 PM	SAG	Oct. 25, 1957	8:34 AM	SAG

Date	Time	Moon	Date	Time	Moon	Date	Time	Moon
Oct. 27, 1957	12:00 PM	CAP	Apr. 7, 1958	6:24 AM	SAG	Sep. 18, 1958	6:51 AM	SAG
Oct. 29, 1957	12:00 AM	AQU	Apr. 9, 1958	10:17 AM	CAP	Sep. 20, 1958	11:05 AM	CAP
Nov. 1, 1957	10:00 AM	PIS	Apr. 11, 1958	6:28 PM	AQU	Sep. 22, 1958	4:37 PM	AQU
Nov. 3, 1957	10:00 PM	ARI	Apr. 14, 1958	6:00 AM	PIS	Sep. 25, 1958	1:51 AM	PIS
Nov. 6, 1957	9:14 AM	TAU	Apr. 16, 1958	6:00 PM	ARI	Sep. 27, 1958	2:00 PM	ARI
Nov. 8, 1957	10:00 PM	GEM	Apr. 19, 1958	8:44 AM	TAU	Sep. 30, 1958	2:00 AM	TAU
Nov. 11, 1957	3:42 AM	CAN	Apr. 21, 1958	8:00 PM	GEM	Oct. 2, 1958	4:00 PM	GEM
Nov. 13, 1957	9:14 AM	LEO	Apr. 24, 1958	6:00 AM	CAN	Oct. 5, 1958	4:00 AM	CAN
Nov. 15, 1957	12:00 PM	VIR	Apr. 26, 1958	10:17 AM	LEO	Oct. 7, 1958	11:05 AM	LEO
Nov. 17, 1957	3:26 PM	LIB	Apr. 28, 1958	3:26 PM	VIR	Oct. 9, 1958	3:26 PM	VIR
Nov. 19, 1957	5:09 PM	SCO	Apr. 30, 1958	4:00 PM	LIB	Oct. 11, 1958	5:09 PM	LIB
Nov. 21, 1957	6:51 PM	SAG	May. 2, 1958	5:36 PM	SCO	Oct. 13, 1958	1:30 PM	SCO
Nov. 23, 1957	10:17 PM	CAP	May. 4, 1958	5:36 PM	SAG	Oct. 15, 1958	2:24 PM	SAG
Nov. 26, 1957	7:23 AM	AQU	May. 6, 1958	8:34 PM	CAP	Oct. 17, 1958	5:09 PM	CAP
Nov. 28, 1957	6:00 PM	PIS	May. 9, 1958	1:51 AM	AQU	Oct. 19, 1958	12:00 AM	AQU
Dec. 1, 1957	6:00 AM	ARI	May. 11, 1958	11:05 AM	PIS	Oct. 22, 1958	7:23 AM	PIS
Dec. 3, 1957	8:00 PM	TAU	May. 13, 1958	12:00 AM	ARI	Oct. 24, 1958	8:00 PM	ARI
Dec. 6, 1957	3:42 AM	GEM	May. 16, 1958	2:00 PM	TAU	Oct. 27, 1958	8:00 AM	TAU
Dec. 8, 1957	11:05 AM	CAN	May. 19, 1958	2:00 AM	GEM	Oct. 29, 1958	10:00 PM	GEM
Dec. 10, 1957	1:43 PM	LEO	May. 21, 1958	12:00 PM	CAN	Nov. 1, 1958	10:00 AM	CAN
Dec. 12, 1957	5:09 PM	VIR	May. 23, 1958	6:28 PM	LEO	Nov. 3, 1958	8:00 PM	LEO
Dec. 14, 1957	8:34 PM	LIB	May. 25, 1958	12:00 AM	VIR	Nov. 5, 1958	10:17 PM	VIR
Dec. 16, 1957	12:00 AM	SCO	May. 30, 1958	1:36 AM	SCO	Nov. 8, 1958	1:36 AM	LIB
Dec. 19, 1957	3:26 AM	SAG	Jun. 1, 1958	3:12 AM	SAG	Nov. 10, 1958	1:36 AM	SCO
Dec. 21, 1957	9:14 AM	CAP	Jun. 3, 1958	6:51 AM	CAP	Nov. 12, 1958	1:36 AM	SAG
Dec. 23, 1957	4:37 PM	AQU	Jun. 5, 1958	10:17 AM	AQU	Nov. 14, 1958	3:26 AM	CAP
Dec. 26, 1957	1:51 AM	PIS	Jun. 7, 1958	10:00 PM	PIS	Nov. 16, 1958	7:23 AM	AQU
Dec. 28, 1957	5:27 AM	ARI	Jun. 10, 1958	8:00 AM	ARI	Nov. 18, 1958	2:46 PM	PIS
Dec. 31, 1957	4:00 AM	TAU	Jun. 12, 1958	8:00 PM	TAU	Nov. 21, 1958	2:00 AM	ARI
Jan. 2, 1958	12:55 PM	GEM	Jun. 15, 1958	7:23 AM	GEM	Nov. 23, 1958	5:27 PM	TAU
Jan. 4, 1958	8:18 PM	CAN	Jun. 17, 1958	4:37 PM	CAN	Nov. 26, 1958	4:00 AM	GEM
Jan. 6, 1958	10:17 PM	LEO	Jun. 19, 1958	12:00 AM	LEO	Nov. 28, 1958	4:00 PM	CAN
Jan. 8, 1958	10:24 PM	VIR	Jun. 22, 1958	3:26 AM	VIR	Dec. 3, 1958	5:09 AM	VIR
Jan. 11, 1958	1:43 AM	LIB	Jun. 24, 1958	6:51 AM	LIB	Dec. 5, 1958	10:17 AM	LIB
Jan. 13, 1958	5:09 AM	SCO	Jun. 26, 1958	10:17 AM	SCO	Dec. 7, 1958	11:12 AM	SCO
Jan. 15, 1958	8:34 AM	SAG	Jun. 28, 1958	12:00 AM	SAG	Dec. 9, 1958	12:48 PM	SAG
Jan. 17, 1958	4:37 PM	CAP	Jun. 30, 1958	3:26 AM	CAP	Dec. 11, 1958	12:48 PM	CAP
Jan. 19, 1958	12:00 AM	AQU	Jul. 2, 1958	6:51 PM	AQU	Dec. 13, 1958	5:09 PM	AQU
Jan. 22, 1958	9:14 AM	PIS	Jul. 5, 1958	6:00 AM	PIS	Dec. 15, 1958	8:34 PM	PIS
Jan. 24, 1958	10:00 PM	ARI	Jul. 7, 1958	4:00 PM	ARI	Dec. 18, 1958	10:00 AM	ARI
Jan. 27, 1958	12:00 PM	TAU	Jul. 10, 1958	6:33 AM	TAU	Dec. 20, 1958	10:00 PM	TAU
Jan. 29, 1958	12:00 AM	GEM	Jul. 12, 1958	6:00 PM	GEM	Dec. 23, 1958	12:00 PM	GEM
Feb. 1, 1958	5:32 AM	CAN	Jul. 15, 1958	1:51 AM	CAN	Dec. 25, 1958	8:18 PM	CAN
Feb. 3, 1958	8:34 AM	LEO	Jul. 17, 1958	7:23 AM	LEO	Dec. 28, 1958	5:32 AM	LEO
Feb. 5, 1958	10:17 AM	VIR	Jul. 19, 1958	10:17 AM	VIR	Dec. 30, 1958	10:17 AM	VIR
Feb. 7, 1958	9:36 AM	LIB	Jul. 21, 1958	12:00 PM	LIB	Jan. 1, 1959	3:26 PM	LIB
Feb. 9, 1958	9:36 AM	SCO	Jul. 23, 1958	3:26 PM	SCO	Jan. 3, 1959	8:34 PM	SCO
Feb. 11, 1958	4:37 PM	SAG	Jul. 25, 1958	6:51 PM	SAG	Jan. 5, 1959	10:17 PM	SAG
Feb. 13, 1958	10:09 PM	CAP	Jul. 27, 1958	10:17 PM	CAP	Jan. 7, 1959	10:24 PM	CAP
Feb. 16, 1958	8:00 AM	AQU	Jul. 30, 1958	5:32 AM	AQU	Jan. 10, 1959	3:26 AM	AQU
Feb. 18, 1958	6:00 PM	PIS	Aug. 1, 1958	12:55 PM	PIS	Jan. 12, 1959	9:14 AM	PIS
Feb. 21, 1958	6:00 AM	ARI	Aug. 3, 1958	12:00 AM	ARI	Jan. 14, 1959	4:37 PM	ARI
Feb. 23, 1958	6:00 PM	TAU	Aug. 6, 1958	12:00 PM	TAU	Jan. 17, 1959	6:00 AM	TAU
Feb. 26, 1958	8:00 AM	GEM	Aug. 9, 1958	2:00 AM	GEM	Jan. 19, 1959	9:49 PM	GEM
Feb. 28, 1958	2:46 PM	CAN	Aug. 11, 1958	12:00 PM	CAN	Jan. 22, 1959	6:00 AM	CAN
Mar. 2, 1958	6:51 PM	LEO	Aug. 13, 1958	3:26 PM	LEO	Jan. 24, 1959	12:55 PM	LEO
Mar. 4, 1958	10:17 PM	VIR	Aug. 15, 1958	6:51 PM	VIR	Jan. 26, 1959	5:09 PM	VIR
Mar. 6, 1958	6:00 PM	LIB	Aug. 17, 1958	8:34 PM	LIB	Jan. 28, 1959	10:17 PM	LIB
Mar. 8, 1958	7:12 PM	SCO	Aug. 19, 1958	7:12 PM	SCO	Jan. 31, 1959	1:43 AM	SCO
Mar. 10, 1958	10:17 PM	SAG	Aug. 21, 1958	12:00 AM	SAG	Feb. 2, 1959	3:26 AM	SAG
Mar. 13, 1958	3:42 AM	CAP	Aug. 24, 1958	5:32 AM	CAP	Feb. 4, 1959	6:51 AM	CAP
Mar. 15, 1958	11:05 AM	AQU	Aug. 26, 1958	11:05 AM	AQU	Feb. 6, 1959	12:55 PM	AQU
Mar. 17, 1958	12:00 PM	PIS	Aug. 28, 1958	10:00 PM	PIS	Feb. 8, 1959	6:28 PM	PIS
Mar. 20, 1958	12:00 PM	ARI	Aug. 31, 1958	8:00 AM	ARI	Feb. 11, 1959	1:51 AM	ARI
Mar. 23, 1958	2:11 AM	TAU	Sep. 2, 1958	8:00 PM	TAU	Feb. 13, 1959	2:00 PM	TAU
Mar. 25, 1958	2:00 PM	GEM	Sep. 5, 1958	10:55 AM	GEM	Feb. 16, 1959	4:00 AM	GEM
Mar. 27, 1958	10:09 PM	CAN	Sep. 7, 1958	8:00 PM	CAN	Feb. 18, 1959	4:00 PM	CAN
Mar. 30, 1958	5:32 AM	LEO	Sep. 10, 1958	1:51 AM	LEO	Feb. 20, 1959	10:09 PM	LEO
Apr. 1, 1958	6:24 AM	VIR	Sep. 12, 1958	5:09 PM	VIR	Feb. 23, 1959	3:26 AM	VIR
Apr. 3, 1958	6:24 AM	LIB	Sep. 14, 1958	4:48 AM	LIB	Feb. 25, 1959	4:48 AM	LIB
Apr. 5, 1958	6:24 AM	SCO	Sep. 16, 1958	4:48 AM	SCO	Feb. 27, 1959	6:24 AM	SCO

Date	Time	Moon	Date	Time	Moon	Date	Time	Moon
Mar. 1, 1959	10:17 AM	SAG	Aug. 10, 1959	10:17 AM	SCO	Jan. 21, 1960	1:43 PM	SCO
Mar. 3, 1959	12:00 PM	CAP	Aug. 12, 1959	1:43 PM	SAG	Jan. 23, 1960	6:51 PM	SAG
Mar. 5, 1959	5:09 PM	AQU	Aug. 14, 1959	5:09 PM	CAP	Jan. 25, 1960	8:34 PM	CAP
Mar. 8, 1959	1:51 AM	PIS	Aug. 16, 1959	6:51 PM	AQU	Jan. 27, 1960	7:12 PM	AQU
Mar. 10, 1959	12:00 PM	ARI	Aug. 18, 1959	10:17 PM	PIS	Jan. 29, 1960	7:12 PM	PIS
Mar. 12, 1959	10:00 PM	TAU	Aug. 21, 1959	5:32 AM	ARI	Feb. 1, 1960	1:51 AM	ARI
Mar. 15, 1959	1:05 PM	GEM	Aug. 23, 1959	4:00 PM	TAU	Feb. 3, 1960	9:14 AM	TAU
Mar. 17, 1959	12:00 PM	CAN	Aug. 26, 1959	4:00 AM	GEM	Feb. 5, 1960	10:00 PM	GEM
Mar. 20, 1959	10:00 AM	LEO	Aug. 28, 1959	4:00 PM	CAN	Feb. 8, 1960	10:00 AM	CAN
Mar. 22, 1959	2:46 PM	VIR	Aug. 31, 1959	1:51 AM	LEO	Feb. 10, 1960	10:00 PM	LEO
Mar. 24, 1959	2:24 PM	LIB	Sep. 2, 1959	9:14 AM	VIR	Feb. 13, 1960	7:23 AM	VIR
Mar. 26, 1959	4:00 PM	SCO	Sep. 4, 1959	1:43 PM	LIB	Feb. 15, 1960	2:46 PM	LIB
Mar. 28, 1959	4:00 PM	SAG	Sep. 6, 1959	5:09 PM	SCO	Feb. 17, 1960	10:09 PM	SCO
Mar. 30, 1959	6:51 PM	CAP	Sep. 8, 1959	5:36 PM	SAG	Feb. 19, 1960	12:00 AM	SAG
Apr. 1, 1959	10:17 PM	AQU	Sep. 10, 1959	10:17 PM	CAP	Feb. 22, 1960	1:36 AM	CAP
Apr. 4, 1959	7:23 AM	PIS	Sep. 13, 1959	1:43 AM	AQU	Feb. 24, 1960	5:09 AM	AQU
Apr. 6, 1959	6:00 AM	ARI	Sep. 15, 1959	7:23 AM	PIS	Feb. 26, 1960	6:51 AM	PIS
Apr. 9, 1959	6:00 AM	TAU	Sep. 17, 1959	2:46 PM	ARI	Feb. 28, 1960	10:17 AM	ARI
Apr. 11, 1959	6:00 AM	GEM	Sep. 19, 1959	10:09 PM	TAU	Mar. 1, 1960	6:28 PM	TAU
Apr. 14, 1959	6:00 AM	CAN	Sep. 22, 1959	12:00 PM	GEM	Mar. 4, 1960	6:00 AM	GEM
Apr. 16, 1959	6:00 AM	LEO	Sep. 24, 1959	12:00 AM	CAN	Mar. 6, 1960	6:00 PM	CAN
Apr. 18, 1959	12:00 AM	VIR	Sep. 27, 1959	12:00 PM	LEO	Mar. 9, 1960	6:00 AM	LEO
Apr. 21, 1959	1:36 AM	LIB	Sep. 29, 1959	6:28 PM	VIR	Mar. 11, 1960	2:46 PM	VIR
Apr. 23, 1959	1:30 AM	SCO	Oct. 1, 1959	10:17 PM	LIB	Mar. 13, 1960	8:34 PM	LIB
Apr. 25, 1959	1:36 AM	SAG	Oct. 6, 1959	1:36 AM	SAG	Mar. 16, 1960	1:43 AM	SCO
Apr. 27, 1959	1:36 AM	CAP	Oct. 8, 1959	3:26 AM	CAP	Mar. 18, 1960	5:09 AM	SAG
Apr. 29, 1959	5:09 AM	AQU	Oct. 10, 1959	6:51 AM	AQU	Mar. 20, 1960	8:34 AM	CAP
May. 1, 1959	12:55 PM	PIS	Oct. 12, 1959	12:55 PM	PIS	Mar. 22, 1960	9:36 AM	AQU
May. 3, 1959	12:00 AM	ARI	Oct. 14, 1959	8:18 PM	ARI	Mar. 24, 1960	4:37 PM	PIS
May. 6, 1959	12:00 PM	TAU	Oct. 17, 1959	8:00 AM	TAU	Mar. 26, 1960	6:51 PM	ARI
May. 8, 1959	12:00 AM	GEM	Oct. 19, 1959	8:00 PM	GEM	Mar. 29, 1960	3:42 AM	TAU
May. 11, 1959	12:00 PM	CAN	Oct. 22, 1959	8:00 AM	CAN	Mar. 31, 1960	12:55 PM	GEM
May. 13, 1959	12:00 AM	LEO	Oct. 24, 1959	8:00 PM	LEO	Apr. 3, 1960	2:00 AM	CAN
May. 16, 1959	7:23 AM	VIR	Oct. 27, 1959	6:00 AM	VIR	Apr. 5, 1960	5:27 PM	LEO
May. 18, 1959	12:00 PM	LIB	Oct. 29, 1959	11:05 AM	LIB	Apr. 8, 1960	2:00 AM	VIR
May. 20, 1959	12:48 PM	SCO	Oct. 31, 1959	12:00 PM	SCO	Apr. 10, 1960	6:51 AM	LIB
May. 22, 1959	12:48 PM	SAG	Nov. 2, 1959	11:12 AM	SAG	Apr. 12, 1960	9:36 AM	SCO
May. 24, 1959	12:48 PM	CAP	Nov. 4, 1959	11:12 AM	CAP	Apr. 14, 1960	1:43 PM	SAG
May. 26, 1959	12:48 PM	AQU	Nov. 6, 1959	1:43 PM	AQU	Apr. 16, 1960	12:48 PM	CAP
May. 28, 1959	8:18 PM	PIS	Nov. 8, 1959	5:09 PM	PIS	Apr. 18, 1960	5:09 PM	AQU
May. 31, 1959	6:00 AM	ARI	Nov. 11, 1959	4:00 AM	ARI	Apr. 20, 1960	8:34 PM	PIS
Jun. 2, 1959	6:00 PM	TAU	Nov. 13, 1959	2:00 PM	TAU	Apr. 23, 1960	3:42 AM	ARI
Jun. 5, 1959	6:00 AM	GEM	Nov. 16, 1959	2:00 AM	GEM	Apr. 25, 1960	11:05 AM	TAU
Jun. 7, 1959	6:00 AM	CAN	Nov. 18, 1959	2:00 PM	CAN	Apr. 27, 1960	8:18 PM	GEM
Jun. 10, 1959	6:00 AM	LEO	Nov. 21, 1959	4:00 AM	LEO	Apr. 30, 1960	10:00 AM	CAN
Jun. 12, 1959	12:55 PM	VIR	Nov. 23, 1959	2:00 PM	VIR	May. 2, 1960	10:00 PM	LEO
Jun. 14, 1959	8:18 PM	LIB	Nov. 25, 1959	8:18 PM	LIB	May. 5, 1960	10:00 AM	VIR
Jun. 16, 1959	10:17 PM	SCO	Nov. 27, 1959	10:17 PM	SCO	May. 7, 1960	6:28 PM	LIB
Jun. 18, 1959	10:24 PM	SAG	Nov. 29, 1959	10:24 PM	SAG	May. 9, 1960	8:34 PM	SCO
Jun. 20, 1959	10:24 PM	CAP	Dec. 1, 1959	7:30 PM	CAP	May. 11, 1960	12:00 AM	SAG
Jun. 22, 1959	10:24 PM	AQU	Dec. 3, 1959	8:48 PM	AQU	May. 13, 1960	10:24 PM	CAP
Jun. 25, 1959	3:26 AM	PIS	Dec. 6, 1959	1:51 AM	PIS	May. 15, 1960	10:24 PM	AQU
Jun. 27, 1959	11:05 AM	ARI	Dec. 8, 1959	10:00 AM	ARI	May. 18, 1960	1:43 AM	PIS
Jun. 29, 1959	12:00 AM	TAU	Dec. 10, 1959	8:00 PM	TAU	May. 20, 1960	9:14 AM	ARI
Jul. 2, 1959	12:00 PM	GEM	Dec. 13, 1959	8:00 AM	GEM	May. 22, 1960	4:37 PM	TAU
Jul. 5, 1959	2:00 AM	CAN	Dec. 15, 1959	8:00 PM	CAN	May. 25, 1960	3:42 AM	GEM
Jul. 7, 1959	12:00 PM	LEO	Dec. 18, 1959	10:00 AM	LEO	May. 27, 1960	4:00 PM	CAN
Jul. 9, 1959	6:28 PM	VIR	Dec. 20, 1959	8:00 PM	VIR	May. 30, 1960	6:00 AM	LEO
Jul. 12, 1959	1:51 AM	LIB	Dec. 23, 1959	3:42 AM	LIB	Jun. 1, 1960	6:00 PM	VIR
Jul. 14, 1959	5:09 AM	SCO	Dec. 25, 1959	9:14 AM	SCO	Jun. 4, 1960	1:51 AM	LIB
Jul. 16, 1959	8:34 AM	SAG	Dec. 27, 1959	10:17 AM	SAG	Jun. 6, 1960	6:51 AM	SCO
Jul. 18, 1959	8:00 AM	CAP	Dec. 29, 1959	7:30 AM	CAP	Jun. 8, 1960	8:00 AM	SAG
Jul. 20, 1959	9:36 AM	AQU	Dec. 31, 1959	8:00 AM	AQU	Jun. 10, 1960	8:00 AM	CAP
Jul. 22, 1959	1:43 PM	PIS	Jan. 2, 1960	10:17 PM	PIS	Jun. 12, 1960	6:00 AM	AQU
Jul. 24, 1959	8:18 PM	ARI	Jan. 4, 1960	4:37 PM	ARI	Jun. 14, 1960	8:00 AM	PIS
Jul. 27, 1959	8:00 AM	TAU	Jan. 7, 1960	2:00 AM	TAU	Jun. 16, 1960	2:46 PM	ARI
Jul. 29, 1959	8:00 PM	GEM	Jan. 9, 1960	2:00 PM	GEM	Jun. 18, 1960	10:09 PM	TAU
Aug. 1, 1959	8:00 AM	CAN	Jan. 12, 1960	4:00 AM	CAN	Jun. 21, 1960	9:14 AM	GEM
Aug. 3, 1959	8:00 PM	LEO	Jan. 14, 1960	4:00 PM	LEO	Jun. 23, 1960	10:00 PM	CAN
Aug. 6, 1959	1:51 AM	VIR	Jan. 17, 1960	2:00 AM	VIR	Jun. 26, 1960	12:00 PM	LEO
Aug. 8, 1959	7:23 AM	LIB	Jan. 19, 1960	9:14 AM	LIB	Jun. 28, 1960	12:00 AM	VIR

Date	Time	Moon	Date	Time	Moon	Date	Time	Moon
Jul. 1, 1960	9:14 AM	L I B	Dec. 12, 1960	8:00 AM	L I B	May. 25, 1961	2:00 AM	L I B
Jul. 3, 1960	4:37 PM	SCO	Dec. 14, 1960	2:46 PM	SCO	May. 27, 1961	11:05 AM	SCO
Jul. 5, 1960	6:51 PM	SAG	Dec. 16, 1960	5:09 PM	SAG	May. 29, 1961	4:37 PM	SAG
Jul. 7, 1960	7:12 PM	CAP	Dec. 18, 1960	5:36 PM	CAP	May. 31, 1961	4:00 PM	CAP
Jul. 9, 1960	5:36 PM	AQU	Dec. 20, 1960	3:00 PM	AQU	Jun. 2, 1961	5:36 PM	AQU
Jul. 11, 1960	5:36 PM	P I S	Dec. 22, 1960	6:51 PM	P I S	Jun. 4, 1961	7:12 PM	P I S
Jul. 13, 1960	7:12 PM	A R I	Dec. 24, 1960	8:34 PM	A R I	Jun. 6, 1961	12:00 AM	A R I
Jul. 16, 1960	5:32 AM	T A U	Dec. 27, 1960	3:42 AM	T A U	Jun. 9, 1961	5:09 AM	T A U
Jul. 18, 1960	2:46 PM	GEM	Dec. 29, 1960	12:55 PM	GEM	Jun. 11, 1961	12:55 PM	GEM
Jul. 21, 1960	6:33 AM	CAN	Jan. 1, 1961	2:00 AM	CAN	Jun. 13, 1961	8:18 PM	CAN
Jul. 23, 1960	6:00 PM	LEO	Jan. 3, 1961	2:00 PM	LEO	Jun. 16, 1961	10:00 AM	LEO
Jul. 26, 1960	6:00 AM	V I R	Jan. 6, 1961	2:00 AM	V I R	Jun. 18, 1961	10:00 PM	V I R
Jul. 28, 1960	2:46 PM	L I B	Jan. 8, 1961	2:00 PM	L I B	Jun. 21, 1961	10:00 AM	L I B
Aug. 2, 1960	3:26 AM	SAG	Jan. 10, 1961	10:09 PM	SCO	Jun. 23, 1961	10:00 PM	SCO
Aug. 4, 1960	5:09 AM	CAP	Jan. 13, 1961	3:26 AM	SAG	Jun. 26, 1961	1:51 AM	SAG
Aug. 6, 1960	4:48 AM	AQU	Jan. 15, 1961	4:48 AM	CAP	Jun. 28, 1961	3:26 AM	CAP
Aug. 8, 1960	4:48 AM	P I S	Jan. 17, 1961	3:00 AM	AQU	Jun. 30, 1961	3:12 AM	AQU
Aug. 10, 1960	6:51 AM	A R I	Jan. 19, 1961	3:12 AM	P I S	Jul. 2, 1961	3:12 AM	P I S
Aug. 12, 1960	12:00 PM	T A U	Jan. 21, 1961	5:09 AM	A R I	Jul. 4, 1961	6:51 AM	A R I
Aug. 14, 1960	12:00 PM	GEM	Jan. 23, 1961	11:05 AM	T A U	Jul. 6, 1961	10:17 AM	T A U
Aug. 17, 1960	12:00 PM	CAN	Jan. 25, 1961	6:28 PM	GEM	Jul. 8, 1961	6:28 PM	GEM
Aug. 19, 1960	12:00 AM	LEO	Jan. 28, 1961	8:00 AM	CAN	Jul. 11, 1961	4:00 AM	CAN
Aug. 22, 1960	12:00 AM	V I R	Jan. 30, 1961	8:00 PM	LEO	Jul. 13, 1961	4:00 PM	LEO
Aug. 24, 1960	8:18 PM	L I B	Feb. 2, 1961	8:00 AM	V I R	Jul. 16, 1961	4:00 AM	V I R
Aug. 27, 1960	3:26 AM	SCO	Feb. 4, 1961	8:00 PM	L I B	Jul. 18, 1961	6:00 PM	L I B
Aug. 29, 1960	8:34 AM	SAG	Feb. 7, 1961	5:32 AM	SCO	Jul. 21, 1961	3:42 AM	SCO
Aug. 31, 1960	12:00 PM	CAP	Feb. 9, 1961	12:55 PM	SAG	Jul. 23, 1961	11:05 AM	SAG
Sep. 2, 1960	12:48 PM	AQU	Feb. 11, 1961	3:26 PM	CAP	Jul. 25, 1961	1:43 PM	CAP
Sep. 4, 1960	2:24 PM	P I S	Feb. 13, 1961	2:24 PM	AQU	Jul. 27, 1961	12:48 PM	AQU
Sep. 6, 1960	5:09 PM	A R I	Feb. 15, 1961	2:24 PM	P I S	Jul. 29, 1961	12:48 PM	P I S
Sep. 8, 1960	12:00 AM	T A U	Feb. 17, 1961	2:24 AM	A R I	Jul. 31, 1961	12:48 PM	A R I
Sep. 11, 1960	8:00 AM	GEM	Feb. 19, 1961	6:51 PM	T A U	Aug. 2, 1961	5:09 PM	T A U
Sep. 13, 1960	8:00 PM	CAN	Feb. 22, 1961	1:51 AM	GEM	Aug. 4, 1961	12:00 AM	GEM
Sep. 16, 1960	8:00 AM	LEO	Feb. 24, 1961	2:00 PM	CAN	Aug. 7, 1961	10:00 AM	CAN
Sep. 18, 1960	8:00 PM	V I R	Feb. 27, 1961	2:00 AM	LEO	Aug. 9, 1961	10:00 PM	LEO
Sep. 21, 1960	3:42 AM	L I B	Mar. 1, 1961	5:27 PM	V I R	Aug. 12, 1961	10:00 AM	V I R
Sep. 23, 1960	11:05 AM	SCO	Mar. 4, 1961	2:00 AM	L I B	Aug. 14, 1961	12:00 AM	L I B
Sep. 25, 1960	1:43 PM	SAG	Mar. 6, 1961	11:05 AM	SCO	Aug. 17, 1961	12:00 PM	SCO
Sep. 27, 1960	4:00 PM	CAP	Mar. 8, 1961	6:28 PM	SAG	Aug. 19, 1961	6:28 PM	SAG
Sep. 29, 1960	8:34 PM	AQU	Mar. 10, 1961	10:17 PM	CAP	Aug. 21, 1961	10:17 PM	CAP
Oct. 1, 1960	12:00 AM	P I S	Mar. 15, 1961	1:36 AM	P I S	Aug. 25, 1961	12:00 AM	P I S
Oct. 4, 1960	3:42 AM	A R I	Mar. 17, 1961	1:36 AM	A R I	Aug. 27, 1961	12:00 AM	A R I
Oct. 6, 1960	6:51 AM	T A U	Mar. 19, 1961	5:09 AM	T A U	Aug. 30, 1961	1:43 AM	T A U
Oct. 8, 1960	6:00 PM	GEM	Mar. 21, 1961	11:05 AM	GEM	Sep. 1, 1961	7:23 AM	GEM
Oct. 11, 1960	4:00 AM	CAN	Mar. 23, 1961	10:00 PM	CAN	Sep. 3, 1961	2:46 PM	CAN
Oct. 13, 1960	4:00 AM	LEO	Mar. 26, 1961	10:00 AM	LEO	Sep. 6, 1961	4:00 AM	LEO
Oct. 16, 1960	4:00 AM	V I R	Mar. 28, 1961	10:00 PM	V I R	Sep. 8, 1961	4:00 PM	V I R
Oct. 18, 1960	2:00 PM	L I B	Mar. 31, 1961	10:00 AM	L I B	Sep. 11, 1961	6:00 AM	L I B
Oct. 20, 1960	5:09 PM	SCO	Apr. 2, 1961	8:00 PM	SCO	Sep. 13, 1961	2:46 PM	SCO
Oct. 22, 1960	10:17 PM	SAG	Apr. 4, 1961	12:00 AM	SAG	Sep. 15, 1961	12:00 AM	SAG
Oct. 24, 1960	12:00 AM	CAP	Apr. 7, 1961	3:26 AM	CAP	Sep. 18, 1961	7:23 AM	CAP
Oct. 27, 1960	1:43 AM	AQU	Apr. 9, 1961	6:51 AM	AQU	Sep. 20, 1961	10:17 AM	AQU
Oct. 29, 1960	5:09 AM	P I S	Apr. 11, 1961	10:17 AM	P I S	Sep. 22, 1961	9:36 AM	P I S
Oct. 31, 1960	11:05 AM	A R I	Apr. 13, 1961	12:00 PM	A R I	Sep. 24, 1961	11:12 AM	A R I
Nov. 2, 1960	4:37 PM	T A U	Apr. 15, 1961	3:26 PM	T A U	Sep. 26, 1961	11:12 AM	T A U
Nov. 4, 1960	12:00 AM	GEM	Apr. 17, 1961	6:51 PM	GEM	Sep. 28, 1961	3:26 PM	GEM
Nov. 7, 1960	12:00 PM	CAN	Apr. 20, 1961	6:00 AM	CAN	Sep. 30, 1961	10:09 PM	CAN
Nov. 9, 1960	12:00 AM	LEO	Apr. 22, 1961	6:00 PM	LEO	Oct. 3, 1961	10:00 AM	LEO
Nov. 12, 1960	12:00 PM	V I R	Apr. 25, 1961	6:00 AM	V I R	Oct. 8, 1961	12:00 PM	L I B
Nov. 14, 1960	12:00 AM	L I B	Apr. 27, 1961	6:00 PM	L I B	Oct. 10, 1961	12:00 AM	SCO
Nov. 17, 1960	3:26 AM	SCO	Apr. 30, 1961	1:51 AM	SCO	Oct. 13, 1961	5:32 AM	SAG
Nov. 19, 1960	6:51 AM	SAG	May. 2, 1961	7:23 AM	SAG	Oct. 15, 1961	12:55 PM	CAP
Nov. 21, 1960	6:24 AM	CAP	May. 4, 1961	10:17 AM	CAP	Oct. 17, 1961	6:28 PM	AQU
Nov. 23, 1960	8:34 AM	AQU	May. 6, 1961	12:00 PM	AQU	Oct. 19, 1961	5:36 PM	P I S
Nov. 25, 1960	10:17 AM	P I S	May. 8, 1961	3:26 PM	P I S	Oct. 21, 1961	7:12 PM	A R I
Nov. 27, 1960	4:37 PM	A R I	May. 10, 1961	6:51 PM	A R I	Oct. 23, 1961	8:48 PM	T A U
Nov. 29, 1960	10:09 PM	T A U	May. 12, 1961	10:17 PM	T A U	Oct. 26, 1961	1:43 AM	GEM
Dec. 2, 1960	7:23 AM	GEM	May. 15, 1961	5:32 AM	GEM	Oct. 28, 1961	7:23 AM	CAN
Dec. 4, 1960	8:00 PM	CAN	May. 17, 1961	12:55 PM	CAN	Oct. 30, 1961	4:37 PM	LEO
Dec. 7, 1960	8:44 AM	LEO	May. 20, 1961	2:00 AM	LEO	Nov. 2, 1961	8:44 AM	V I R
Dec. 9, 1960	8:00 PM	V I R	May. 22, 1961	2:00 PM	V I R	Nov. 4, 1961	8:00 PM	L I B

145

Date	Time	Moon	Date	Time	Moon	Date	Time	Moon
Nov. 7, 1961	5:32 AM	SCO	Apr. 24, 1962	8:18 PM	CAP	Oct. 3, 1962	10:00 AM	SAG
Nov. 9, 1961	12:55 PM	SAG	Apr. 27, 1962	1:43 AM	AQU	Oct. 5, 1962	10:00 PM	CAP
Nov. 11, 1961	5:09 PM	CAP	Apr. 29, 1962	5:09 AM	PIS	Oct. 8, 1962	3:42 AM	AQU
Nov. 13, 1961	12:00 AM	AQU	May. 1, 1962	6:24 AM	ARI	Oct. 10, 1962	6:51 AM	PIS
Nov. 16, 1961	1:43 AM	PIS	May. 3, 1962	8:00 AM	TAU	Oct. 12, 1962	6:24 AM	ARI
Nov. 18, 1961	3:12 AM	ARI	May. 5, 1962	8:00 AM	GEM	Oct. 14, 1962	6:24 AM	TAU
Nov. 20, 1961	6:51 AM	TAU	May. 7, 1962	12:00 PM	CAN	Oct. 16, 1962	4:48 AM	GEM
Nov. 22, 1961	10:17 AM	GEM	May. 9, 1962	8:18 PM	LEO	Oct. 18, 1962	8:34 AM	CAN
Nov. 24, 1961	3:26 AM	CAN	May. 12, 1962	10:00 AM	VIR	Oct. 20, 1962	4:37 PM	LEO
Nov. 27, 1961	4:00 AM	LEO	May. 14, 1962	10:00 PM	LIB	Oct. 23, 1962	4:00 AM	VIR
Nov. 29, 1961	5:27 PM	VIR	May. 17, 1962	10:00 AM	SCO	Oct. 25, 1962	4:00 PM	LIB
Dec. 2, 1961	4:00 AM	LIB	May. 19, 1962	6:28 PM	SAG	Oct. 28, 1962	4:00 AM	SCO
Dec. 4, 1961	4:00 PM	SCO	May. 22, 1962	1:51 AM	CAP	Oct. 30, 1962	4:00 PM	SAG
Dec. 6, 1961	10:09 PM	SAG	May. 24, 1962	6:51 AM	AQU	Nov. 2, 1962	1:51 AM	CAP
Dec. 9, 1961	1:43 AM	CAP	May. 26, 1962	12:55 PM	PIS	Nov. 4, 1962	9:14 AM	AQU
Dec. 11, 1961	3:12 AM	AQU	May. 28, 1962	12:48 PM	ARI	Nov. 6, 1962	4:37 PM	PIS
Dec. 13, 1961	6:51 AM	PIS	May. 30, 1962	5:09 PM	TAU	Nov. 8, 1962	4:00 PM	ARI
Dec. 15, 1961	10:17 AM	ARI	Jun. 1, 1962	6:51 PM	GEM	Nov. 10, 1962	4:00 PM	TAU
Dec. 17, 1961	1:43 PM	TAU	Jun. 3, 1962	10:17 PM	CAN	Nov. 12, 1962	4:00 PM	GEM
Dec. 19, 1961	5:09 PM	GEM	Jun. 6, 1962	5:32 AM	LEO	Nov. 14, 1962	6:51 PM	CAN
Dec. 22, 1961	1:51 AM	CAN	Jun. 8, 1962	6:00 PM	VIR	Nov. 16, 1962	10:17 PM	LEO
Dec. 24, 1961	12:00 PM	LEO	Jun. 11, 1962	6:00 AM	LIB	Nov. 19, 1962	9:14 AM	VIR
Dec. 26, 1961	12:00 AM	VIR	Jun. 13, 1962	6:00 PM	SCO	Nov. 21, 1962	10:00 PM	LIB
Dec. 29, 1961	12:00 PM	LIB	Jun. 16, 1962	4:00 AM	SAG	Nov. 24, 1962	12:00 PM	SCO
Dec. 31, 1961	12:00 AM	SCO	Jun. 18, 1962	8:34 AM	CAP	Nov. 26, 1962	12:00 AM	SAG
Jan. 3, 1962	7:23 AM	SAG	Jun. 20, 1962	1:43 PM	AQU	Nov. 29, 1962	7:23 AM	CAP
Jan. 5, 1962	12:00 PM	CAP	Jun. 22, 1962	5:09 PM	PIS	Dec. 1, 1962	2:46 PM	AQU
Jan. 7, 1962	1:43 PM	AQU	Jun. 24, 1962	8:34 PM	ARI	Dec. 3, 1962	10:09 PM	PIS
Jan. 9, 1962	12:48 PM	PIS	Jun. 26, 1962	10:17 PM	TAU	Dec. 5, 1962	12:00 AM	ARI
Jan. 11, 1962	2:24 PM	ARI	Jun. 29, 1962	1:43 AM	GEM	Dec. 8, 1962	1:36 AM	TAU
Jan. 13, 1962	6:51 PM	TAU	Jul. 1, 1962	7:23 AM	CAN	Dec. 10, 1962	3:26 AM	GEM
Jan. 18, 1962	10:00 AM	CAN	Jul. 3, 1962	2:46 PM	LEO	Dec. 12, 1962	5:09 AM	CAN
Jan. 20, 1962	8:00 PM	LEO	Jul. 6, 1962	2:00 AM	VIR	Dec. 14, 1962	11:05 AM	LEO
Jan. 23, 1962	6:00 AM	VIR	Jul. 8, 1962	2:00 PM	LIB	Dec. 16, 1962	6:28 PM	VIR
Jan. 25, 1962	8:00 PM	LIB	Jul. 11, 1962	2:00 AM	SCO	Dec. 19, 1962	6:00 AM	LIB
Jan. 28, 1962	8:00 AM	SCO	Jul. 13, 1962	11:05 AM	SAG	Dec. 21, 1962	9:49 PM	SCO
Jan. 30, 1962	4:37 PM	SAG	Jul. 15, 1962	5:09 PM	CAP	Dec. 24, 1962	5:32 AM	SAG
Feb. 1, 1962	12:00 AM	CAP	Jul. 17, 1962	10:17 PM	AQU	Dec. 26, 1962	2:46 PM	CAP
Feb. 5, 1962	12:00 AM	PIS	Jul. 19, 1962	10:24 PM	PIS	Dec. 28, 1962	10:09 PM	AQU
Feb. 7, 1962	12:00 AM	ARI	Jul. 22, 1962	1:43 AM	ARI	Dec. 31, 1962	1:43 AM	PIS
Feb. 10, 1962	1:43 AM	TAU	Jul. 24, 1962	3:26 AM	TAU	Jan. 2, 1963	5:09 AM	ARI
Feb. 12, 1962	5:09 AM	GEM	Jul. 26, 1962	6:51 AM	GEM	Jan. 4, 1963	8:34 AM	TAU
Feb. 14, 1962	12:55 PM	CAN	Jul. 28, 1962	2:46 PM	CAN	Jan. 6, 1963	12:00 PM	GEM
Feb. 17, 1962	2:00 AM	LEO	Jul. 30, 1962	10:09 PM	LEO	Jan. 8, 1963	1:43 PM	CAN
Feb. 19, 1962	2:00 PM	VIR	Aug. 2, 1962	10:00 AM	VIR	Jan. 10, 1963	6:51 PM	LEO
Feb. 22, 1962	2:00 AM	LIB	Aug. 4, 1962	12:00 AM	LIB	Jan. 13, 1963	3:42 AM	VIR
Feb. 24, 1962	2:00 PM	SCO	Aug. 7, 1962	10:00 AM	SCO	Jan. 15, 1963	4:00 PM	LIB
Mar. 1, 1962	6:51 AM	CAP	Aug. 9, 1962	10:00 PM	SAG	Jan. 18, 1963	4:00 AM	SCO
Mar. 3, 1962	9:36 AM	AQU	Aug. 12, 1962	3:26 AM	CAP	Jan. 20, 1963	4:00 PM	SAG
Mar. 5, 1962	11:12 AM	PIS	Aug. 14, 1962	8:34 AM	AQU	Jan. 23, 1963	12:00 AM	CAP
Mar. 7, 1962	11:12 AM	ARI	Aug. 16, 1962	10:17 AM	PIS	Jan. 25, 1963	5:09 AM	AQU
Mar. 9, 1962	9:36 AM	TAU	Aug. 18, 1962	9:36 AM	ARI	Jan. 27, 1963	10:17 AM	PIS
Mar. 11, 1962	1:43 PM	GEM	Aug. 20, 1962	9:36 AM	TAU	Jan. 29, 1963	12:00 PM	ARI
Mar. 13, 1962	8:18 PM	CAN	Aug. 22, 1962	1:43 PM	GEM	Jan. 31, 1963	12:48 PM	TAU
Mar. 16, 1962	5:32 AM	LEO	Aug. 24, 1962	8:18 PM	CAN	Feb. 2, 1963	5:09 PM	GEM
Mar. 18, 1962	9:49 PM	VIR	Aug. 27, 1962	3:42 AM	LEO	Feb. 4, 1963	8:34 PM	CAN
Mar. 21, 1962	8:00 AM	LIB	Aug. 29, 1962	4:00 PM	VIR	Feb. 7, 1963	3:42 AM	LEO
Mar. 23, 1962	8:00 PM	SCO	Sep. 1, 1962	4:00 AM	LIB	Feb. 9, 1963	2:00 PM	VIR
Mar. 26, 1962	8:00 AM	SAG	Sep. 3, 1962	4:00 PM	SCO	Feb. 11, 1963	12:00 AM	LIB
Mar. 28, 1962	2:46 PM	CAP	Sep. 6, 1962	4:00 AM	SAG	Feb. 14, 1963	12:00 PM	SCO
Mar. 30, 1962	6:51 PM	AQU	Sep. 8, 1962	12:55 PM	CAP	Feb. 16, 1963	12:00 AM	SAG
Apr. 1, 1962	10:17 PM	PIS	Sep. 10, 1962	8:18 PM	AQU	Feb. 19, 1963	9:14 AM	CAP
Apr. 3, 1962	12:00 AM	ARI	Sep. 12, 1962	7:12 PM	PIS	Feb. 21, 1963	4:37 PM	AQU
Apr. 5, 1962	8:48 PM	TAU	Sep. 14, 1962	7:12 PM	ARI	Feb. 23, 1963	5:36 PM	PIS
Apr. 7, 1962	12:00 AM	GEM	Sep. 16, 1962	7:12 PM	TAU	Feb. 25, 1963	7:12 PM	ARI
Apr. 10, 1962	3:26 AM	CAN	Sep. 18, 1962	7:12 PM	GEM	Feb. 27, 1963	10:17 PM	TAU
Apr. 12, 1962	2:00 PM	LEO	Sep. 21, 1962	1:51 AM	CAN	Mar. 1, 1963	8:48 PM	GEM
Apr. 15, 1962	2:00 AM	VIR	Sep. 23, 1962	9:14 AM	LEO	Mar. 4, 1963	3:42 AM	CAN
Apr. 17, 1962	2:00 PM	LIB	Sep. 25, 1962	10:00 PM	VIR	Mar. 6, 1963	9:14 AM	LEO
Apr. 20, 1962	2:00 PM	SCO	Sep. 28, 1962	10:00 AM	LIB	Mar. 8, 1963	6:28 PM	VIR
Apr. 22, 1962	2:00 PM	SAG	Sep. 30, 1962	10:00 PM	SCO	Mar. 11, 1963	6:00 AM	LIB

Date	Time	Moon	Date	Time	Moon	Date	Time	Moon
Mar. 13, 1963	6:00 PM	SCO	Aug. 22, 1963	2:00 AM	LIB	Feb. 4, 1964	6:00 AM	SCO
Mar. 16, 1963	8:00 AM	SAG	Aug. 24, 1963	12:00 PM	SCO	Feb. 6, 1964	6:00 PM	SAG
Mar. 18, 1963	8:00 PM	CAP	Aug. 27, 1963	2:11 AM	SAG	Feb. 9, 1964	8:00 AM	CAP
Mar. 21, 1963	1:51 AM	AQU	Aug. 29, 1963	2:00 PM	CAP	Feb. 11, 1964	4:37 PM	AQU
Mar. 23, 1963	6:51 AM	PIS	Aug. 31, 1963	12:00 AM	AQU	Feb. 14, 1964	1:51 AM	PIS
Mar. 25, 1963	6:24 AM	ARI	Sep. 3, 1963	1:43 AM	PIS	Feb. 16, 1964	5:09 AM	ARI
Mar. 27, 1963	6:24 AM	TAU	Sep. 5, 1963	5:09 AM	ARI	Feb. 18, 1964	10:17 AM	TAU
Mar. 29, 1963	6:24 AM	GEM	Sep. 7, 1963	6:51 AM	TAU	Feb. 20, 1964	11:12 AM	GEM
Mar. 31, 1963	8:34 AM	CAN	Sep. 9, 1963	8:34 AM	GEM	Feb. 22, 1964	3:26 PM	CAN
Apr. 2, 1963	1:43 PM	LEO	Sep. 11, 1963	10:17 AM	CAN	Feb. 24, 1964	6:51 PM	LEO
Apr. 5, 1963	2:00 AM	VIR	Sep. 13, 1963	3:26 PM	LEO	Feb. 26, 1964	10:17 PM	VIR
Apr. 7, 1963	12:00 PM	LIB	Sep. 15, 1963	12:00 AM	VIR	Feb. 29, 1964	5:32 AM	LIB
Apr. 10, 1963	2:00 AM	SCO	Sep. 18, 1963	10:00 AM	LIB	Mar. 2, 1964	4:00 PM	SCO
Apr. 12, 1963	2:00 PM	SAG	Sep. 20, 1963	8:00 PM	SCO	Mar. 5, 1964	2:00 AM	SAG
Apr. 15, 1963	2:00 AM	CAP	Sep. 23, 1963	8:00 AM	SAG	Mar. 7, 1964	4:00 PM	CAP
Apr. 17, 1963	12:00 PM	AQU	Sep. 25, 1963	10:00 PM	CAP	Mar. 10, 1964	1:51 AM	AQU
Apr. 19, 1963	3:26 PM	PIS	Sep. 28, 1963	8:00 AM	AQU	Mar. 12, 1964	11:05 AM	PIS
Apr. 21, 1963	6:51 PM	ARI	Sep. 30, 1963	12:00 PM	PIS	Mar. 14, 1964	1:43 PM	ARI
Apr. 23, 1963	5:36 PM	TAU	Oct. 2, 1963	3:26 PM	ARI	Mar. 16, 1964	5:09 PM	TAU
Apr. 25, 1963	4:00 PM	GEM	Oct. 4, 1963	2:24 PM	TAU	Mar. 18, 1964	6:51 PM	GEM
Apr. 27, 1963	4:00 PM	CAN	Oct. 6, 1963	2:24 PM	GEM	Mar. 20, 1964	7:12 PM	CAN
Apr. 29, 1963	8:34 PM	LEO	Oct. 8, 1963	5:09 PM	CAN	Mar. 23, 1964	1:51 AM	LEO
May. 2, 1963	8:00 AM	VIR	Oct. 10, 1963	8:34 PM	LEO	Mar. 25, 1964	7:23 AM	VIR
May. 4, 1963	6:00 PM	LIB	Oct. 13, 1963	5:32 AM	VIR	Mar. 27, 1964	12:55 PM	LIB
May. 7, 1963	8:44 AM	SCO	Oct. 15, 1963	4:00 PM	LIB	Mar. 29, 1964	10:09 PM	SCO
May. 9, 1963	8:00 PM	SAG	Oct. 18, 1963	2:00 AM	SCO	Apr. 1, 1964	10:00 AM	SAG
May. 12, 1963	8:00 AM	CAP	Oct. 20, 1963	4:00 PM	SAG	Apr. 6, 1964	12:00 PM	AQU
May. 14, 1963	6:00 PM	AQU	Oct. 23, 1963	4:00 AM	CAP	Apr. 8, 1964	10:00 PM	PIS
May. 16, 1963	12:00 AM	PIS	Oct. 25, 1963	4:00 PM	AQU	Apr. 10, 1964	12:00 AM	ARI
May. 19, 1963	3:26 AM	ARI	Oct. 30, 1963	1:43 AM	ARI	Apr. 13, 1964	1:36 AM	TAU
May. 21, 1963	3:12 AM	TAU	Nov. 1, 1963	1:36 AM	TAU	Apr. 15, 1964	1:36 AM	GEM
May. 23, 1963	3:12 AM	GEM	Nov. 4, 1963	12:00 AM	GEM	Apr. 17, 1964	3:26 AM	CAN
May. 25, 1963	3:12 AM	CAN	Nov. 5, 1963	1:43 AM	CAN	Apr. 19, 1964	6:51 AM	LEO
May. 27, 1963	6:51 AM	LEO	Nov. 7, 1963	3:26 AM	LEO	Apr. 21, 1964	12:55 PM	VIR
May. 29, 1963	2:46 PM	VIR	Nov. 9, 1963	11:05 AM	VIR	Apr. 23, 1964	8:18 PM	LIB
Jun. 1, 1963	2:00 AM	LIB	Nov. 11, 1963	10:00 PM	LIB	Apr. 26, 1964	6:00 AM	SCO
Jun. 3, 1963	2:00 PM	SCO	Nov. 14, 1963	8:00 AM	SCO	Apr. 28, 1964	6:00 PM	SAG
Jun. 6, 1963	2:00 AM	SAG	Nov. 16, 1963	10:00 PM	SAG	May. 1, 1964	6:00 AM	CAP
Jun. 8, 1963	2:00 PM	CAP	Nov. 19, 1963	10:00 AM	CAP	May. 3, 1964	9:49 PM	AQU
Jun. 10, 1963	12:00 AM	AQU	Nov. 21, 1963	10:00 PM	AQU	May. 6, 1964	6:00 AM	PIS
Jun. 13, 1963	5:32 AM	PIS	Nov. 24, 1963	8:00 AM	PIS	May. 8, 1964	11:05 AM	ARI
Jun. 15, 1963	11:05 AM	ARI	Nov. 26, 1963	12:55 PM	ARI	May. 10, 1964	11:12 AM	TAU
Jun. 17, 1963	11:12 AM	TAU	Nov. 28, 1963	1:43 PM	TAU	May. 12, 1964	10:30 AM	GEM
Jun. 19, 1963	12:48 PM	GEM	Nov. 30, 1963	12:48 PM	GEM	May. 14, 1964	11:12 AM	CAN
Jun. 21, 1963	12:48 PM	CAN	Dec. 2, 1963	11:12 AM	CAN	May. 16, 1964	1:43 PM	LEO
Jun. 23, 1963	5:09 PM	LEO	Dec. 4, 1963	1:43 PM	LEO	May. 18, 1964	5:09 PM	VIR
Jun. 25, 1963	8:34 PM	VIR	Dec. 6, 1963	5:09 PM	VIR	May. 21, 1964	1:51 AM	LIB
Jun. 28, 1963	7:23 AM	LIB	Dec. 9, 1963	4:00 AM	LIB	May. 23, 1964	12:00 PM	SCO
Jun. 30, 1963	8:00 PM	SCO	Dec. 11, 1963	12:55 PM	SCO	May. 25, 1964	12:00 AM	SAG
Jul. 3, 1963	10:00 AM	SAG	Dec. 14, 1963	4:00 AM	SAG	May. 28, 1964	12:00 PM	CAP
Jul. 5, 1963	6:28 PM	CAP	Dec. 16, 1963	4:00 PM	CAP	May. 31, 1964	2:00 AM	AQU
Jul. 8, 1963	3:42 AM	AQU	Dec. 19, 1963	4:00 AM	AQU	Jun. 2, 1964	11:05 AM	PIS
Jul. 10, 1963	11:05 AM	PIS	Dec. 21, 1963	2:00 PM	PIS	Jun. 4, 1964	8:18 PM	ARI
Jul. 12, 1963	3:26 PM	ARI	Dec. 23, 1963	5:09 PM	ARI	Jun. 6, 1964	10:17 PM	TAU
Jul. 14, 1963	6:51 PM	TAU	Dec. 25, 1963	10:17 PM	TAU	Jun. 8, 1964	10:24 PM	GEM
Jul. 16, 1963	8:34 PM	GEM	Dec. 27, 1963	10:24 PM	GEM	Jun. 10, 1964	10:24 PM	CAN
Jul. 18, 1963	8:48 PM	CAN	Dec. 29, 1963	10:24 PM	CAN	Jun. 12, 1964	10:24 PM	LEO
Jul. 21, 1963	1:43 AM	LEO	Jan. 3, 1964	3:26 AM	VIR	Jun. 15, 1964	1:43 AM	VIR
Jul. 23, 1963	6:51 AM	VIR	Jan. 5, 1964	11:05 AM	LIB	Jun. 17, 1964	7:23 AM	LIB
Jul. 25, 1963	6:00 PM	LIB	Jan. 7, 1964	10:00 PM	SCO	Jun. 19, 1964	6:00 PM	SCO
Jul. 28, 1963	4:00 AM	SCO	Jan. 10, 1964	10:00 AM	SAG	Jun. 22, 1964	6:00 AM	SAG
Jul. 30, 1963	7:38 PM	SAG	Jan. 12, 1964	12:00 AM	CAP	Jun. 24, 1964	6:00 PM	CAP
Aug. 2, 1963	4:00 AM	CAP	Jan. 15, 1964	10:00 AM	AQU	Jun. 27, 1964	6:00 AM	AQU
Aug. 4, 1963	12:55 AM	AQU	Jan. 17, 1964	6:28 PM	PIS	Jun. 29, 1964	4:37 PM	PIS
Aug. 6, 1963	5:09 PM	PIS	Jan. 19, 1964	10:17 PM	ARI	Jul. 2, 1964	1:51 AM	ARI
Aug. 8, 1963	8:34 AM	ARI	Jan. 22, 1964	3:26 AM	TAU	Jul. 4, 1964	6:51 AM	TAU
Aug. 10, 1963	12:00 AM	TAU	Jan. 24, 1964	6:51 AM	GEM	Jul. 6, 1964	8:00 AM	GEM
Aug. 13, 1963	1:43 AM	GEM	Jan. 26, 1964	8:00 AM	CAN	Jul. 8, 1964	8:00 AM	CAN
Aug. 15, 1963	5:09 AM	CAN	Jan. 28, 1964	9:36 AM	LEO	Jul. 10, 1964	8:00 AM	LEO
Aug. 17, 1963	11:05 AM	LEO	Jan. 30, 1964	1:43 AM	VIR	Jul. 12, 1964	9:36 AM	VIR
Aug. 19, 1963	4:37 PM	VIR	Feb. 1, 1964	8:18 PM	LIB	Jul. 14, 1964	4:37 PM	LIB

Date	Time	Moon	Date	Time	Moon	Date	Time	Moon
Jul. 19, 1964	12:00 PM	SAG	Dec. 27, 1964	8:18 PM	SCO	Jun. 7, 1965	1:43 PM	LIB
Jul. 22, 1964	2:00 AM	CAP	Dec. 30, 1964	8:00 AM	SAG	Jun. 9, 1965	6:51 PM	SCO
Jul. 24, 1964	2:00 AM	AQU	Jan. 1, 1965	8:00 PM	CAP	Jun. 12, 1965	5:32 AM	SAG
Jul. 26, 1964	10:09 PM	PIS	Jan. 4, 1965	10:00 AM	AQU	Jun. 14, 1965	6:00 PM	CAP
Jul. 29, 1964	7:23 AM	ARI	Jan. 6, 1965	10:00 PM	PIS	Jun. 17, 1965	6:00 AM	AQU
Jul. 31, 1964	12:00 PM	TAU	Jan. 9, 1965	7:23 AM	ARI	Jun. 19, 1965	6:00 PM	PIS
Aug. 2, 1964	5:09 PM	GEM	Jan. 11, 1965	1:43 PM	TAU	Jun. 22, 1965	6:00 AM	ARI
Aug. 4, 1964	6:51 PM	CAN	Jan. 13, 1965	6:51 PM	GEM	Jun. 24, 1965	12:55 PM	TAU
Aug. 6, 1964	8:34 PM	LEO	Jan. 15, 1965	7:12 PM	CAN	Jun. 26, 1965	5:09 PM	GEM
Aug. 8, 1964	7:12 PM	VIR	Jan. 17, 1965	7:12 PM	LEO	Jun. 28, 1965	5:36 PM	CAN
Aug. 10, 1964	12:00 AM	LIB	Jan. 19, 1965	7:12 PM	VIR	Jun. 30, 1965	5:36 PM	LEO
Aug. 13, 1964	7:23 AM	SCO	Jan. 21, 1965	7:12 PM	LIB	Jul. 2, 1965	5:36 PM	VIR
Aug. 15, 1964	8:00 PM	SAG	Jan. 24, 1965	3:42 AM	SCO	Jul. 4, 1965	8:34 PM	LIB
Aug. 18, 1964	8:00 AM	CAP	Jan. 26, 1965	12:55 PM	SAG	Jul. 7, 1965	1:43 PM	SCO
Aug. 20, 1964	8:00 PM	AQU	Jan. 29, 1965	4:22 AM	CAP	Jul. 9, 1965	11:05 AM	SAG
Aug. 23, 1964	5:32 AM	PIS	Jan. 31, 1965	4:00 PM	AQU	Jul. 11, 1965	12:00 AM	CAP
Aug. 25, 1964	12:55 PM	ARI	Feb. 3, 1965	4:00 AM	PIS	Jul. 14, 1965	12:00 PM	AQU
Aug. 27, 1964	5:09 PM	TAU	Feb. 5, 1965	12:55 PM	ARI	Jul. 16, 1965	12:00 AM	PIS
Aug. 29, 1964	10:17 PM	GEM	Feb. 7, 1965	10:09 PM	TAU	Jul. 19, 1965	12:00 PM	ARI
Sep. 1, 1964	1:43 AM	CAN	Feb. 10, 1965	1:43 AM	GEM	Jul. 21, 1965	8:18 PM	TAU
Sep. 3, 1964	3:26 AM	LEO	Feb. 12, 1965	5:09 AM	CAN	Jul. 24, 1965	3:42 AM	GEM
Sep. 5, 1964	6:51 AM	VIR	Feb. 14, 1965	6:51 AM	LEO	Jul. 26, 1965	5:09 AM	CAN
Sep. 7, 1964	10:17 AM	LIB	Feb. 16, 1965	6:24 AM	VIR	Jul. 28, 1965	4:48 AM	LEO
Sep. 9, 1964	4:37 PM	SCO	Feb. 18, 1965	6:24 AM	LIB	Jul. 30, 1965	3:00 AM	VIR
Sep. 12, 1964	4:00 AM	SAG	Feb. 20, 1965	12:55 PM	SCO	Aug. 1, 1965	5:09 AM	LIB
Sep. 14, 1964	4:00 PM	CAP	Feb. 22, 1965	8:18 PM	SAG	Aug. 3, 1965	8:34 AM	SCO
Sep. 17, 1964	4:00 AM	AQU	Feb. 25, 1965	10:00 AM	CAP	Aug. 5, 1965	4:37 PM	SAG
Sep. 19, 1964	4:00 PM	PIS	Feb. 27, 1965	10:00 PM	AQU	Aug. 8, 1965	6:00 AM	CAP
Sep. 21, 1964	10:09 PM	ARI	Mar. 2, 1965	9:14 AM	PIS	Aug. 10, 1965	6:00 PM	AQU
Sep. 23, 1964	12:00 AM	TAU	Mar. 4, 1965	6:28 PM	ARI	Aug. 13, 1965	6:00 AM	PIS
Sep. 26, 1964	3:26 AM	GEM	Mar. 7, 1965	3:42 AM	TAU	Aug. 15, 1965	6:00 PM	ARI
Sep. 28, 1964	6:51 AM	CAN	Mar. 9, 1965	9:14 AM	GEM	Aug. 18, 1965	4:00 AM	TAU
Sep. 30, 1964	10:17 AM	LEO	Mar. 11, 1965	12:00 PM	CAN	Aug. 20, 1965	11:05 AM	GEM
Oct. 2, 1964	1:43 PM	VIR	Mar. 13, 1965	3:26 PM	LEO	Aug. 22, 1965	1:43 PM	CAN
Oct. 4, 1964	5:09 PM	LIB	Mar. 15, 1965	5:09 PM	VIR	Aug. 24, 1965	2:24 PM	LEO
Oct. 7, 1964	1:51 AM	SCO	Mar. 17, 1965	6:51 PM	LIB	Aug. 26, 1965	2:24 PM	VIR
Oct. 9, 1964	12:00 PM	SAG	Mar. 19, 1965	12:00 AM	SCO	Aug. 28, 1965	2:24 PM	LIB
Oct. 11, 1964	12:00 AM	CAP	Mar. 22, 1965	5:32 AM	SAG	Aug. 30, 1965	5:09 PM	SCO
Oct. 14, 1964	3:16 PM	AQU	Mar. 24, 1965	6:00 PM	CAP	Sep. 2, 1965	2:00 AM	SAG
Oct. 16, 1964	10:09 PM	PIS	Mar. 27, 1965	6:00 AM	AQU	Sep. 4, 1965	12:00 PM	CAP
Oct. 19, 1964	5:09 AM	ARI	Mar. 29, 1965	4:37 PM	PIS	Sep. 6, 1965	12:00 AM	AQU
Oct. 21, 1964	10:17 AM	TAU	Apr. 1, 1965	3:42 AM	ARI	Sep. 9, 1965	12:00 PM	PIS
Oct. 23, 1964	12:00 PM	GEM	Apr. 3, 1965	8:34 AM	TAU	Sep. 11, 1965	12:00 AM	ARI
Oct. 25, 1964	1:43 PM	CAN	Apr. 5, 1965	1:43 PM	GEM	Sep. 14, 1965	10:00 AM	TAU
Oct. 27, 1964	3:26 PM	LEO	Apr. 7, 1965	5:09 PM	CAN	Sep. 16, 1965	4:37 PM	GEM
Oct. 29, 1964	6:51 PM	VIR	Apr. 9, 1965	8:34 PM	LEO	Sep. 18, 1965	8:34 PM	CAN
Nov. 1, 1964	1:51 AM	LIB	Apr. 11, 1965	12:00 AM	VIR	Sep. 20, 1965	12:00 AM	LEO
Nov. 3, 1964	9:14 AM	SCO	Apr. 14, 1965	1:43 AM	LIB	Sep. 22, 1965	12:00 AM	VIR
Nov. 5, 1964	8:00 PM	SAG	Apr. 16, 1965	6:51 AM	SCO	Sep. 25, 1965	1:43 AM	LIB
Nov. 8, 1964	8:00 AM	CAP	Apr. 18, 1965	2:46 PM	SAG	Sep. 27, 1965	3:26 AM	SCO
Nov. 10, 1964	8:00 PM	AQU	Apr. 21, 1965	2:00 AM	CAP	Sep. 29, 1965	9:14 AM	SAG
Nov. 13, 1964	7:23 AM	PIS	Apr. 23, 1965	2:00 PM	AQU	Oct. 1, 1965	8:00 PM	CAP
Nov. 15, 1964	4:37 PM	ARI	Apr. 26, 1965	4:00 AM	PIS	Oct. 4, 1965	8:00 AM	AQU
Nov. 17, 1964	8:34 PM	TAU	Apr. 28, 1965	2:00 PM	ARI	Oct. 6, 1965	8:00 PM	PIS
Nov. 19, 1964	10:17 PM	GEM	Apr. 30, 1965	5:09 PM	TAU	Oct. 9, 1965	8:00 AM	ARI
Nov. 21, 1964	8:48 PM	CAN	May. 2, 1965	10:17 PM	GEM	Oct. 11, 1965	2:46 PM	TAU
Nov. 23, 1964	8:48 PM	LEO	May. 4, 1965	12:00 AM	CAN	Oct. 13, 1965	10:09 PM	GEM
Nov. 26, 1964	1:51 AM	VIR	May. 7, 1965	1:43 AM	LEO	Oct. 16, 1965	1:43 AM	CAN
Nov. 28, 1964	7:23 AM	LIB	May. 9, 1965	5:09 AM	VIR	Oct. 18, 1965	5:09 AM	LEO
Nov. 30, 1964	2:46 PM	SCO	May. 11, 1965	8:34 AM	LIB	Oct. 20, 1965	8:34 AM	VIR
Dec. 3, 1964	2:00 AM	SAG	May. 13, 1965	1:43 PM	SCO	Oct. 22, 1965	10:17 AM	LIB
Dec. 5, 1964	2:00 PM	CAP	May. 15, 1965	10:09 PM	SAG	Oct. 24, 1965	1:43 PM	SCO
Dec. 8, 1964	4:00 AM	AQU	May. 18, 1965	10:00 AM	CAP	Oct. 26, 1965	5:09 PM	SAG
Dec. 10, 1964	4:00 PM	PIS	May. 20, 1965	10:00 PM	AQU	Oct. 29, 1965	3:42 AM	CAP
Dec. 13, 1964	2:00 AM	ARI	May. 23, 1965	12:00 PM	PIS	Oct. 31, 1965	4:00 PM	AQU
Dec. 15, 1964	7:23 AM	TAU	May. 25, 1965	8:18 PM	ARI	Nov. 3, 1965	4:00 AM	PIS
Dec. 17, 1964	8:00 AM	GEM	May. 28, 1965	3:26 AM	TAU	Nov. 5, 1965	4:00 PM	ARI
Dec. 19, 1964	8:00 AM	CAN	May. 30, 1965	6:51 AM	GEM	Nov. 10, 1965	5:32 AM	GEM
Dec. 21, 1964	8:00 AM	LEO	Jun. 1, 1965	8:00 AM	CAN	Nov. 12, 1965	8:34 AM	CAN
Dec. 23, 1964	8:00 AM	VIR	Jun. 3, 1965	8:00 AM	LEO	Nov. 14, 1965	12:00 PM	LEO
Dec. 25, 1964	12:00 PM	LIB	Jun. 5, 1965	9:36 AM	VIR	Nov. 16, 1965	1:43 PM	VIR

Date	Time	Moon	Date	Time	Moon	Date	Time	Moon
Nov. 18, 1965	5:09 PM	LIB	May. 1, 1966	7:12 PM	LIB	Oct. 14, 1966	8:48 PM	SCO
Nov. 20, 1965	8:34 PM	SCO	May. 3, 1966	8:48 PM	SCO	Oct. 16, 1966	8:48 PM	SAG
Nov. 23, 1965	3:42 AM	SAG	May. 6, 1966	1:43 AM	SAG	Oct. 19, 1966	3:42 AM	CAP
Nov. 25, 1965	2:00 PM	CAP	May. 8, 1966	6:51 AM	CAP	Oct. 21, 1966	11:05 AM	AQU
Nov. 27, 1965	12:00 AM	AQU	May. 10, 1966	4:37 PM	AQU	Oct. 23, 1966	12:00 AM	PIS
Nov. 30, 1965	12:00 PM	PIS	May. 13, 1966	6:00 AM	PIS	Oct. 26, 1966	12:00 PM	ARI
Dec. 2, 1965	12:00 AM	ARI	May. 15, 1966	6:00 AM	ARI	Oct. 28, 1966	12:00 AM	TAU
Dec. 5, 1965	9:14 AM	TAU	May. 18, 1966	6:00 AM	TAU	Oct. 31, 1966	9:14 AM	GEM
Dec. 7, 1965	1:43 PM	GEM	May. 20, 1966	12:55 PM	GEM	Nov. 2, 1966	6:28 PM	CAN
Dec. 9, 1965	5:09 PM	CAN	May. 22, 1966	5:09 PM	CAN	Nov. 7, 1966	3:26 AM	VIR
Dec. 11, 1965	5:36 PM	LEO	May. 24, 1966	12:00 AM	LEO	Nov. 9, 1966	4:48 AM	LIB
Dec. 13, 1965	8:34 PM	VIR	May. 26, 1966	10:24 PM	VIR	Nov. 11, 1966	6:24 AM	SCO
Dec. 15, 1965	10:17 PM	LIB	May. 29, 1966	3:26 AM	LIB	Nov. 13, 1966	8:34 AM	SAG
Dec. 18, 1965	3:42 AM	SCO	May. 31, 1966	6:51 AM	SCO	Nov. 15, 1966	12:00 PM	CAP
Dec. 20, 1965	11:05 AM	SAG	Jun. 2, 1966	10:17 AM	SAG	Nov. 17, 1966	8:18 PM	AQU
Dec. 22, 1965	10:00 PM	CAP	Jun. 4, 1966	4:37 PM	CAP	Nov. 20, 1966	5:32 AM	PIS
Dec. 25, 1965	8:00 AM	AQU	Jun. 7, 1966	1:51 AM	AQU	Nov. 22, 1966	9:49 PM	ARI
Dec. 27, 1965	8:00 PM	PIS	Jun. 9, 1966	2:00 PM	PIS	Nov. 25, 1966	8:00 AM	TAU
Dec. 30, 1965	8:00 AM	ARI	Jun. 12, 1966	2:00 AM	ARI	Nov. 27, 1966	4:37 PM	GEM
Jan. 1, 1966	8:00 PM	TAU	Jun. 14, 1966	2:00 PM	TAU	Dec. 2, 1966	5:09 AM	LEO
Jan. 4, 1966	1:51 AM	GEM	Jun. 16, 1966	12:00 AM	GEM	Dec. 4, 1966	10:17 AM	VIR
Jan. 6, 1966	3:12 AM	CAN	Jun. 19, 1966	1:43 AM	CAN	Dec. 6, 1966	11:12 AM	LIB
Jan. 8, 1966	3:12 AM	LEO	Jun. 21, 1966	5:09 AM	LEO	Dec. 8, 1966	3:26 PM	SCO
Jan. 10, 1966	3:12 AM	VIR	Jun. 23, 1966	6:51 AM	VIR	Dec. 10, 1966	6:51 PM	SAG
Jan. 12, 1966	5:09 AM	LIB	Jun. 25, 1966	8:34 AM	LIB	Dec. 12, 1966	10:17 PM	CAP
Jan. 14, 1966	8:34 AM	SCO	Jun. 27, 1966	12:00 PM	SCO	Dec. 15, 1966	5:32 AM	AQU
Jan. 16, 1966	4:37 PM	SAG	Jun. 29, 1966	6:28 PM	SAG	Dec. 17, 1966	4:00 PM	PIS
Jan. 19, 1966	1:51 AM	CAP	Jul. 1, 1966	12:00 AM	CAP	Dec. 20, 1966	4:00 AM	ARI
Jan. 21, 1966	2:00 PM	AQU	Jul. 4, 1966	9:14 AM	AQU	Dec. 22, 1966	4:00 PM	TAU
Jan. 24, 1966	2:00 AM	PIS	Jul. 6, 1966	10:00 PM	PIS	Dec. 25, 1966	1:51 AM	GEM
Jan. 26, 1966	4:00 PM	ARI	Jul. 9, 1966	10:00 AM	ARI	Dec. 27, 1966	9:14 AM	CAN
Jan. 29, 1966	1:51 AM	TAU	Jul. 11, 1966	10:00 PM	TAU	Dec. 29, 1966	2:46 PM	LEO
Jan. 31, 1966	11:05 AM	GEM	Jul. 14, 1966	7:23 AM	GEM	Dec. 31, 1966	3:26 PM	VIR
Feb. 2, 1966	4:37 PM	CAN	Jul. 16, 1966	12:55 PM	CAN	Jan. 2, 1967	6:51 PM	LIB
Feb. 4, 1966	2:24 PM	LEO	Jul. 18, 1966	12:48 PM	LEO	Jan. 4, 1967	8:34 PM	SCO
Feb. 6, 1966	2:24 PM	VIR	Jul. 20, 1966	12:48 PM	VIR	Jan. 7, 1967	1:51 AM	SAG
Feb. 8, 1966	12:00 PM	LIB	Jul. 22, 1966	2:24 PM	LIB	Jan. 9, 1967	7:23 AM	CAP
Feb. 10, 1966	2:24 PM	SCO	Jul. 24, 1966	5:09 PM	SCO	Jan. 11, 1967	2:46 PM	AQU
Feb. 12, 1966	8:34 PM	SAG	Jul. 26, 1966	12:00 AM	SAG	Jan. 13, 1967	10:09 PM	PIS
Feb. 15, 1966	7:23 AM	CAP	Jul. 29, 1966	8:00 AM	CAP	Jan. 16, 1967	12:00 PM	ARI
Feb. 17, 1966	8:00 PM	AQU	Jul. 31, 1966	6:00 PM	AQU	Jan. 18, 1967	12:00 AM	TAU
Feb. 20, 1966	10:55 AM	PIS	Aug. 3, 1966	4:00 AM	PIS	Jan. 21, 1967	12:00 PM	GEM
Feb. 22, 1966	10:00 PM	ARI	Aug. 5, 1966	7:38 PM	ARI	Jan. 23, 1967	6:28 PM	CAN
Feb. 25, 1966	10:00 AM	TAU	Aug. 8, 1966	6:00 AM	TAU	Jan. 25, 1967	10:17 PM	LEO
Feb. 27, 1966	8:00 PM	GEM	Aug. 10, 1966	2:46 PM	GEM	Jan. 27, 1967	10:24 PM	VIR
Mar. 1, 1966	10:17 PM	CAN	Aug. 12, 1966	10:09 PM	CAN	Jan. 29, 1967	12:00 AM	LIB
Mar. 4, 1966	1:36 AM	LEO	Aug. 14, 1966	10:24 PM	LEO	Feb. 1, 1967	3:26 AM	SCO
Mar. 6, 1966	1:36 AM	VIR	Aug. 16, 1966	12:00 AM	VIR	Feb. 3, 1967	6:51 AM	SAG
Mar. 9, 1966	12:00 AM	LIB	Aug. 18, 1966	9:00 PM	LIB	Feb. 5, 1967	12:55 PM	CAP
Mar. 10, 1966	1:43 AM	SCO	Aug. 23, 1966	5:32 AM	SAG	Feb. 7, 1967	8:18 PM	AQU
Mar. 12, 1966	5:09 AM	SAG	Aug. 25, 1966	2:00 PM	CAP	Feb. 10, 1967	8:00 AM	PIS
Mar. 14, 1966	4:00 PM	CAP	Aug. 27, 1966	12:00 AM	AQU	Feb. 12, 1967	8:00 PM	ARI
Mar. 17, 1966	2:00 AM	AQU	Aug. 30, 1966	10:00 AM	PIS	Feb. 15, 1967	8:00 AM	TAU
Mar. 19, 1966	5:27 PM	PIS	Sep. 4, 1966	12:00 PM	TAU	Feb. 17, 1967	8:00 PM	GEM
Mar. 22, 1966	4:00 AM	ARI	Sep. 6, 1966	12:00 AM	GEM	Feb. 22, 1967	8:34 AM	LEO
Mar. 24, 1966	12:55 PM	TAU	Sep. 9, 1966	7:23 AM	CAN	Feb. 24, 1967	9:36 AM	VIR
Mar. 29, 1966	7:23 AM	CAN	Sep. 11, 1966	10:17 AM	LEO	Feb. 26, 1967	9:36 AM	LIB
Mar. 31, 1966	10:17 AM	LEO	Sep. 13, 1966	9:36 AM	VIR	Feb. 28, 1967	9:36 AM	SCO
Apr. 2, 1966	11:12 AM	VIR	Sep. 15, 1966	9:36 AM	LIB	Mar. 2, 1967	11:12 AM	SAG
Apr. 4, 1966	11:12 AM	LIB	Sep. 17, 1966	9:36 AM	SCO	Mar. 4, 1967	5:09 PM	CAP
Apr. 6, 1966	11:12 AM	SCO	Sep. 19, 1966	12:00 PM	SAG	Mar. 7, 1967	4:00 AM	AQU
Apr. 8, 1966	3:26 PM	SAG	Sep. 21, 1966	6:28 PM	CAP	Mar. 9, 1967	2:00 PM	PIS
Apr. 10, 1966	10:09 PM	CAP	Sep. 24, 1966	3:42 AM	AQU	Mar. 12, 1967	2:00 AM	ARI
Apr. 13, 1966	10:00 AM	AQU	Sep. 26, 1966	4:00 PM	PIS	Mar. 14, 1967	2:00 PM	TAU
Apr. 15, 1966	10:00 PM	PIS	Sep. 29, 1966	6:00 AM	ARI	Mar. 17, 1967	4:00 AM	GEM
Apr. 18, 1966	10:00 AM	ARI	Oct. 1, 1966	6:00 PM	TAU	Mar. 19, 1967	2:00 PM	CAN
Apr. 20, 1966	10:00 PM	TAU	Oct. 4, 1966	3:42 AM	GEM	Mar. 21, 1967	8:18 PM	LEO
Apr. 23, 1966	5:32 AM	GEM	Oct. 6, 1966	12:55 PM	CAN	Mar. 23, 1967	10:17 PM	VIR
Apr. 25, 1966	12:55 PM	CAN	Oct. 8, 1966	8:18 PM	LEO	Mar. 25, 1967	8:48 PM	LIB
Apr. 27, 1966	3:26 PM	LEO	Oct. 10, 1966	7:12 PM	VIR	Mar. 27, 1967	8:48 PM	SCO
Apr. 29, 1966	6:51 PM	VIR	Oct. 12, 1966	8:48 PM	LIB			

149

Date	Time	Moon	Date	Time	Moon	Date	Time	Moon
Mar. 29, 1967	10:17 PM	SAG	Sep. 7, 1967	7:12 PM	SCO	Feb. 16, 1968	8:34 PM	L I B
Apr. 1, 1967	1:51 AM	CAP	Sep. 9, 1967	10:17 PM	SAG	Feb. 18, 1968	12:00 AM	SCO
Apr. 3, 1967	10:00 AM	AQU	Sep. 12, 1967	1:43 AM	CAP	Feb. 21, 1968	1:43 AM	SAG
Apr. 5, 1967	8:00 PM	P I S	Sep. 14, 1967	6:51 AM	AQU	Feb. 23, 1968	5:09 AM	CAP
Apr. 8, 1967	8:00 AM	A R I	Sep. 16, 1967	6:00 PM	P I S	Feb. 25, 1968	8:34 AM	AQU
Apr. 10, 1967	8:00 PM	TAU	Sep. 19, 1967	4:00 AM	A R I	Feb. 27, 1968	4:37 PM	P I S
Apr. 13, 1967	10:00 AM	GEM	Sep. 21, 1967	4:00 PM	TAU	Mar. 3, 1968	12:00 PM	TAU
Apr. 15, 1967	6:28 PM	CAN	Sep. 24, 1967	6:33 AM	GEM	Mar. 5, 1968	12:00 AM	GEM
Apr. 18, 1967	3:42 AM	LEO	Sep. 26, 1967	6:00 PM	CAN	Mar. 8, 1968	12:00 PM	CAN
Apr. 20, 1967	6:51 AM	V I R	Sep. 28, 1967	12:00 AM	LEO	Mar. 10, 1968	8:18 PM	LEO
Apr. 22, 1967	8:34 AM	L I B	Oct. 1, 1967	5:09 AM	V I R	Mar. 13, 1968	3:42 AM	V I R
Apr. 24, 1967	6:00 AM	SCO	Oct. 3, 1967	4:48 AM	L I B	Mar. 15, 1968	4:48 AM	L I B
Apr. 26, 1967	6:24 AM	SAG	Oct. 5, 1967	4:48 AM	SCO	Mar. 17, 1968	6:24 AM	SCO
Apr. 28, 1967	10:17 AM	CAP	Oct. 7, 1967	4:48 AM	SAG	Mar. 19, 1968	8:34 AM	SAG
Apr. 30, 1967	4:37 PM	AQU	Oct. 9, 1967	8:34 AM	CAP	Mar. 21, 1968	10:17 AM	CAP
May. 3, 1967	2:00 AM	P I S	Oct. 11, 1967	12:00 PM	AQU	Mar. 23, 1968	4:37 PM	AQU
May. 5, 1967	2:00 AM	A R I	Oct. 13, 1967	12:00 AM	P I S	Mar. 25, 1968	10:09 PM	P I S
May. 8, 1967	4:22 AM	TAU	Oct. 16, 1967	10:00 AM	A R I	Mar. 28, 1968	8:00 AM	A R I
May. 10, 1967	4:00 PM	GEM	Oct. 18, 1967	10:00 PM	TAU	Mar. 30, 1968	4:37 PM	TAU
May. 13, 1967	2:00 AM	CAN	Oct. 21, 1967	12:00 PM	GEM	Apr. 2, 1968	8:00 AM	GEM
May. 15, 1967	9:14 AM	LEO	Oct. 23, 1967	12:00 AM	CAN	Apr. 4, 1968	8:00 PM	CAN
May. 17, 1967	1:43 PM	V I R	Oct. 26, 1967	10:00 AM	LEO	Apr. 7, 1968	5:32 AM	LEO
May. 19, 1967	5:09 PM	L I B	Oct. 28, 1967	1:43 PM	V I R	Apr. 9, 1968	12:00 PM	V I R
May. 21, 1967	6:51 PM	SCO	Oct. 30, 1967	5:09 PM	L I B	Apr. 11, 1968	5:09 PM	L I B
May. 23, 1967	5:36 PM	SAG	Nov. 1, 1967	4:00 PM	SCO	Apr. 13, 1968	4:00 PM	SCO
May. 25, 1967	8:34 PM	CAP	Nov. 3, 1967	4:00 PM	SAG	Apr. 15, 1968	4:00 PM	SAG
May. 27, 1967	12:00 AM	AQU	Nov. 5, 1967	4:00 PM	CAP	Apr. 17, 1968	4:00 PM	CAP
May. 30, 1967	10:00 AM	P I S	Nov. 7, 1967	8:34 PM	AQU	Apr. 19, 1968	8:34 PM	AQU
Jun. 1, 1967	6:28 PM	A R I	Nov. 10, 1967	3:42 AM	P I S	Apr. 22, 1968	3:42 AM	P I S
Jun. 4, 1967	10:00 AM	TAU	Nov. 12, 1967	4:00 PM	A R I	Apr. 24, 1968	2:00 PM	A R I
Jun. 6, 1967	10:00 PM	GEM	Nov. 15, 1967	4:00 AM	TAU	Apr. 27, 1968	2:00 AM	TAU
Jun. 9, 1967	8:00 AM	CAN	Nov. 17, 1967	6:00 PM	GEM	Apr. 29, 1968	2:00 PM	GEM
Jun. 11, 1967	2:46 PM	LEO	Nov. 20, 1967	6:00 AM	CAN	May. 2, 1968	2:00 AM	CAN
Jun. 13, 1967	6:51 PM	V I R	Nov. 22, 1967	4:00 PM	LEO	May. 4, 1968	2:00 PM	LEO
Jun. 15, 1967	10:17 PM	L I B	Nov. 24, 1967	10:09 PM	V I R	May. 6, 1968	10:09 PM	V I R
Jun. 18, 1967	1:43 AM	SCO	Nov. 27, 1967	1:43 AM	L I B	May. 9, 1968	1:43 AM	L I B
Jun. 20, 1967	3:26 AM	SAG	Nov. 29, 1967	3:12 AM	SCO	May. 11, 1968	3:12 AM	SCO
Jun. 22, 1967	4:48 AM	CAP	Dec. 1, 1967	3:12 AM	SAG	May. 13, 1968	3:12 AM	SAG
Jun. 24, 1967	11:05 AM	AQU	Dec. 3, 1967	3:12 AM	CAP	May. 15, 1968	1:36 AM	CAP
Jun. 26, 1967	4:37 PM	P I S	Dec. 5, 1967	5:09 AM	AQU	May. 17, 1968	3:12 AM	AQU
Jun. 29, 1967	4:00 AM	A R I	Dec. 7, 1967	12:55 PM	P I S	May. 19, 1968	8:34 AM	P I S
Jul. 1, 1967	6:00 PM	TAU	Dec. 9, 1967	8:18 PM	A R I	May. 21, 1968	8:00 AM	A R I
Jul. 4, 1967	6:00 AM	GEM	Dec. 12, 1967	1:05 PM	TAU	May. 24, 1968	8:00 AM	TAU
Jul. 6, 1967	2:46 PM	CAN	Dec. 14, 1967	12:00 AM	GEM	May. 26, 1968	8:00 PM	GEM
Jul. 8, 1967	10:09 PM	LEO	Dec. 17, 1967	12:00 PM	CAN	May. 29, 1968	8:00 AM	CAN
Jul. 11, 1967	1:51 AM	V I R	Dec. 19, 1967	10:00 PM	LEO	May. 31, 1968	8:00 PM	LEO
Jul. 13, 1967	3:12 AM	L I B	Dec. 22, 1967	3:42 AM	V I R	Jun. 3, 1968	6:00 AM	V I R
Jul. 15, 1967	6:51 AM	SCO	Dec. 24, 1967	9:14 AM	L I B	Jun. 5, 1968	10:17 AM	L I B
Jul. 17, 1967	10:17 AM	SAG	Dec. 26, 1967	12:00 PM	SCO	Jun. 7, 1968	1:43 PM	SCO
Jul. 19, 1967	1:43 PM	CAP	Dec. 28, 1967	1:43 PM	SAG	Jun. 9, 1968	3:26 PM	SAG
Jul. 21, 1967	8:18 PM	AQU	Dec. 30, 1967	3:26 PM	CAP	Jun. 11, 1968	12:48 PM	CAP
Jul. 24, 1967	1:51 AM	P I S	Jan. 1, 1968	5:09 PM	AQU	Jun. 13, 1968	12:48 PM	AQU
Jul. 26, 1967	2:00 AM	A R I	Jan. 3, 1968	8:34 PM	P I S	Jun. 15, 1968	5:09 PM	P I S
Jul. 29, 1967	2:00 AM	TAU	Jan. 6, 1968	5:32 AM	A R I	Jun. 18, 1968	1:51 AM	A R I
Jul. 31, 1967	2:00 PM	GEM	Jan. 8, 1968	6:00 PM	TAU	Jun. 20, 1968	2:00 PM	TAU
Aug. 2, 1967	10:09 PM	CAN	Jan. 11, 1968	8:00 AM	GEM	Jun. 23, 1968	2:00 AM	GEM
Aug. 5, 1967	5:09 AM	LEO	Jan. 13, 1968	8:00 PM	CAN	Jun. 25, 1968	2:00 PM	CAN
Aug. 7, 1967	8:34 AM	V I R	Jan. 16, 1968	3:42 AM	LEO	Jun. 28, 1968	2:00 AM	LEO
Aug. 9, 1967	9:36 AM	L I B	Jan. 18, 1968	9:14 AM	V I R	Jun. 30, 1968	12:00 PM	V I R
Aug. 11, 1967	11:12 AM	SCO	Jan. 20, 1968	1:43 PM	L I B	Jul. 2, 1968	6:28 PM	L I B
Aug. 13, 1967	3:26 PM	SAG	Jan. 22, 1968	5:09 PM	SCO	Jul. 4, 1968	8:34 PM	SCO
Aug. 15, 1967	6:51 PM	CAP	Jan. 24, 1968	8:34 PM	SAG	Jul. 6, 1968	12:00 AM	SAG
Aug. 18, 1967	1:51 AM	AQU	Jan. 26, 1968	12:00 AM	CAP	Jul. 8, 1968	10:24 PM	CAP
Aug. 20, 1967	9:14 AM	P I S	Jan. 29, 1968	1:43 AM	AQU	Jul. 10, 1968	12:00 AM	AQU
Aug. 22, 1967	10:00 PM	A R I	Jan. 31, 1968	7:23 AM	P I S	Jul. 13, 1968	3:26 AM	P I S
Aug. 25, 1967	10:55 AM	TAU	Feb. 2, 1968	2:46 PM	A R I	Jul. 15, 1968	9:14 AM	A R I
Aug. 27, 1967	10:00 PM	GEM	Feb. 5, 1968	4:00 AM	TAU	Jul. 17, 1968	6:28 PM	TAU
Aug. 30, 1967	10:00 AM	CAN	Feb. 7, 1968	4:00 PM	GEM	Jul. 20, 1968	10:55 AM	GEM
Sep. 1, 1967	1:43 PM	LEO	Feb. 10, 1968	4:00 AM	CAN	Jul. 22, 1968	10:00 PM	CAN
Sep. 3, 1967	6:51 PM	V I R	Feb. 12, 1968	11:05 AM	LEO	Jul. 25, 1968	7:23 AM	LEO
Sep. 5, 1967	8:34 PM	L I B	Feb. 14, 1968	6:28 PM	V I R	Jul. 27, 1968	4:37 PM	V I R

Date	Time	Moon	Date	Time	Moon	Date	Time	Moon
Jul. 29, 1968	12:00 AM	L I B	Jan. 12, 1969	7:23 AM	S C O	Jun. 29, 1969	7:30 AM	C A P
Aug. 1, 1968	3:26 AM	S C O	Jan. 14, 1969	10:17 AM	S A G	Jul. 1, 1969	8:00 AM	A Q U
Aug. 3, 1968	6:51 AM	S A G	Jan. 16, 1969	9:36 AM	C A P	Jul. 3, 1969	8:00 AM	P I S
Aug. 5, 1968	8:34 AM	C A P	Jan. 18, 1969	9:36 AM	A Q U	Jul. 5, 1969	12:00 PM	A R I
Aug. 7, 1968	10:17 AM	A Q U	Jan. 20, 1969	9:36 AM	P I S	Jul. 7, 1969	6:28 PM	T A U
Aug. 9, 1968	12:00 PM	P I S	Jan. 22, 1969	1:43 PM	A R I	Jul. 10, 1969	6:00 AM	G E M
Aug. 11, 1968	5:09 PM	A R I	Jan. 24, 1969	10:09 PM	T A U	Jul. 12, 1969	6:00 PM	C A N
Aug. 14, 1968	3:42 AM	T A U	Jan. 27, 1969	10:00 AM	G E M	Jul. 15, 1969	8:00 AM	L E O
Aug. 16, 1968	4:00 PM	G E M	Jan. 29, 1969	12:00 AM	C A N	Jul. 17, 1969	8:00 PM	V I R
Aug. 19, 1968	6:00 AM	C A N	Feb. 1, 1969	12:00 PM	L E O	Jul. 20, 1969	5:32 AM	L I B
Aug. 21, 1968	2:46 PM	L E O	Feb. 3, 1969	8:18 PM	V I R	Jul. 22, 1969	2:46 PM	S C O
Aug. 23, 1968	12:00 AM	V I R	Feb. 6, 1969	5:32 AM	L I B	Jul. 24, 1969	8:18 PM	S A G
Aug. 26, 1968	5:32 AM	L I B	Feb. 8, 1969	12:55 PM	S C O	Jul. 26, 1969	8:34 PM	C A P
Aug. 28, 1968	8:34 AM	S C O	Feb. 10, 1969	6:28 PM	S A G	Jul. 28, 1969	7:12 PM	A Q U
Aug. 30, 1968	12:00 PM	S A G	Feb. 12, 1969	6:51 PM	C A P	Jul. 30, 1969	5:36 PM	P I S
Sep. 1, 1968	12:48 PM	C A P	Feb. 14, 1969	7:12 PM	A Q U	Aug. 1, 1969	7:12 PM	A R I
Sep. 3, 1968	5:09 PM	A Q U	Feb. 16, 1969	10:17 PM	P I S	Aug. 4, 1969	3:42 AM	T A U
Sep. 5, 1968	8:34 PM	P I S	Feb. 18, 1969	12:00 AM	A R I	Aug. 6, 1969	2:00 PM	G E M
Sep. 8, 1968	3:42 AM	A R I	Feb. 21, 1969	7:23 AM	T A U	Aug. 8, 1969	12:00 AM	C A N
Sep. 10, 1968	2:00 PM	T A U	Feb. 23, 1969	4:37 PM	G E M	Aug. 11, 1969	2:00 PM	L E O
Sep. 12, 1968	12:00 AM	G E M	Feb. 26, 1969	8:44 AM	C A N	Aug. 14, 1969	2:00 AM	V I R
Sep. 15, 1968	2:00 PM	C A N	Feb. 28, 1969	8:00 PM	L E O	Aug. 16, 1969	11:05 AM	L I B
Sep. 20, 1968	9:14 AM	V I R	Mar. 3, 1969	6:00 AM	V I R	Aug. 18, 1969	8:18 PM	S C O
Sep. 22, 1968	12:00 PM	L I B	Mar. 5, 1969	12:55 PM	L I B	Aug. 21, 1969	1:51 AM	S A G
Sep. 24, 1968	3:26 PM	S C O	Mar. 7, 1969	5:09 PM	S C O	Aug. 23, 1969	3:12 AM	C A P
Sep. 26, 1968	4:00 PM	S A G	Mar. 9, 1969	12:00 AM	S A G	Aug. 25, 1969	4:48 AM	A Q U
Sep. 28, 1968	8:34 PM	C A P	Mar. 14, 1969	3:26 AM	A Q U	Aug. 27, 1969	4:48 AM	P I S
Sep. 30, 1968	10:17 PM	A Q U	Mar. 16, 1969	4:48 AM	P I S	Aug. 29, 1969	6:51 AM	A R I
Oct. 3, 1968	3:26 AM	P I S	Mar. 18, 1969	10:17 AM	A R I	Aug. 31, 1969	10:17 AM	T A U
Oct. 5, 1968	11:05 AM	A R I	Mar. 20, 1969	4:37 PM	T A U	Sep. 2, 1969	10:00 PM	G E M
Oct. 7, 1968	10:00 PM	T A U	Mar. 23, 1969	4:00 AM	G E M	Sep. 5, 1969	8:00 AM	C A N
Oct. 10, 1968	8:00 AM	G E M	Mar. 25, 1969	4:00 PM	C A N	Sep. 7, 1969	8:00 PM	L E O
Oct. 12, 1968	12:00 AM	C A N	Mar. 28, 1969	4:00 AM	L E O	Sep. 10, 1969	8:00 AM	V I R
Oct. 15, 1968	10:00 AM	L E O	Mar. 30, 1969	12:55 PM	V I R	Sep. 12, 1969	4:37 PM	L I B
Oct. 17, 1968	8:00 PM	V I R	Apr. 1, 1969	10:09 PM	L I B	Sep. 15, 1969	1:51 AM	S C O
Oct. 19, 1968	10:17 PM	L I B	Apr. 4, 1969	1:43 AM	S C O	Sep. 17, 1969	7:23 AM	S A G
Oct. 22, 1968	1:43 AM	S C O	Apr. 6, 1969	3:12 AM	S A G	Sep. 19, 1969	10:17 AM	C A P
Oct. 24, 1968	1:36 AM	S A G	Apr. 8, 1969	6:51 AM	C A P	Sep. 21, 1969	11:12 AM	A Q U
Oct. 26, 1968	1:36 AM	C A P	Apr. 10, 1969	8:34 AM	A Q U	Sep. 23, 1969	3:26 PM	P I S
Oct. 28, 1968	5:09 AM	A Q U	Apr. 12, 1969	12:00 PM	P I S	Sep. 25, 1969	5:09 PM	A R I
Oct. 30, 1968	8:34 AM	P I S	Apr. 14, 1969	5:09 PM	A R I	Sep. 27, 1969	8:34 PM	T A U
Nov. 1, 1968	4:37 PM	A R I	Apr. 17, 1969	1:51 AM	T A U	Sep. 30, 1969	6:00 AM	G E M
Nov. 4, 1968	4:00 AM	T A U	Apr. 19, 1969	12:00 PM	G E M	Oct. 2, 1969	4:00 PM	C A N
Nov. 6, 1968	4:00 PM	G E M	Apr. 21, 1969	12:00 AM	C A N	Oct. 5, 1969	4:00 AM	L E O
Nov. 9, 1968	4:00 AM	C A N	Apr. 24, 1969	12:00 PM	L E O	Oct. 7, 1969	4:00 PM	V I R
Nov. 11, 1968	4:00 PM	L E O	Apr. 26, 1969	12:00 AM	V I R	Oct. 10, 1969	1:51 AM	L I B
Nov. 14, 1968	4:00 AM	V I R	Apr. 29, 1969	7:23 AM	L I B	Oct. 12, 1969	9:14 AM	S C O
Nov. 16, 1968	8:34 AM	L I B	May. 1, 1969	10:17 AM	S C O	Oct. 14, 1969	12:00 PM	S A G
Nov. 18, 1968	11:12 AM	S C O	May. 3, 1969	11:12 AM	S A G	Oct. 16, 1969	3:26 PM	C A P
Nov. 20, 1968	12:48 PM	S A G	May. 5, 1969	12:48 PM	C A P	Oct. 18, 1969	6:51 PM	A Q U
Nov. 22, 1968	11:12 AM	C A P	May. 7, 1969	3:26 PM	A Q U	Oct. 20, 1969	7:12 PM	P I S
Nov. 24, 1968	11:12 AM	A Q U	May. 9, 1969	5:09 PM	P I S	Oct. 23, 1969	1:51 AM	A R I
Nov. 26, 1968	3:26 PM	P I S	May. 11, 1969	10:17 PM	A R I	Oct. 25, 1969	7:23 AM	T A U
Nov. 28, 1968	10:09 PM	A R I	May. 14, 1969	7:23 AM	T A U	Oct. 27, 1969	12:55 PM	G E M
Dec. 1, 1968	10:00 AM	T A U	May. 16, 1969	8:00 PM	G E M	Oct. 29, 1969	10:09 PM	C A N
Dec. 3, 1968	10:00 PM	G E M	May. 19, 1969	6:00 AM	C A N	Nov. 1, 1969	12:00 PM	L E O
Dec. 6, 1968	10:00 AM	C A N	May. 21, 1969	6:00 PM	L E O	Nov. 4, 1969	2:00 AM	V I R
Dec. 11, 1968	10:00 AM	V I R	May. 24, 1969	8:00 AM	V I R	Nov. 6, 1969	12:00 PM	L I B
Dec. 13, 1968	6:28 PM	L I B	May. 26, 1969	6:00 PM	L I B	Nov. 8, 1969	6:28 PM	S C O
Dec. 15, 1968	10:17 PM	S C O	May. 28, 1969	8:34 PM	S C O	Nov. 10, 1969	8:34 PM	S A G
Dec. 17, 1968	10:24 PM	S A G	May. 30, 1969	12:00 AM	S A G	Nov. 12, 1969	8:48 PM	C A P
Dec. 19, 1968	9:00 PM	C A P	Jun. 1, 1969	10:24 PM	C A P	Nov. 14, 1969	10:24 PM	A Q U
Dec. 21, 1968	10:24 PM	A Q U	Jun. 3, 1969	10:24 PM	A Q U	Nov. 17, 1969	3:26 AM	P I S
Dec. 23, 1968	10:24 PM	P I S	Jun. 5, 1969	10:24 PM	P I S	Nov. 19, 1969	6:51 AM	A R I
Dec. 26, 1968	5:32 AM	A R I	Jun. 8, 1969	5:32 AM	A R I	Nov. 21, 1969	2:46 PM	T A U
Dec. 28, 1968	4:00 PM	T A U	Jun. 10, 1969	12:55 PM	T A U	Nov. 23, 1969	12:00 AM	G E M
Dec. 31, 1968	4:00 AM	G E M	Jun. 15, 1969	12:00 PM	C A N	Nov. 26, 1969	8:00 AM	C A N
Jan. 2, 1969	4:00 PM	C A N	Jun. 18, 1969	2:00 AM	L E O	Nov. 28, 1969	8:00 PM	L E O
Jan. 5, 1969	3:42 AM	L E O	Jun. 20, 1969	2:00 PM	V I R	Dec. 1, 1969	10:55 AM	V I R
Jan. 7, 1969	4:00 PM	V I R	Jun. 25, 1969	7:23 AM	S C O	Dec. 3, 1969	6:28 PM	L I B
Jan. 9, 1969	12:00 AM	L I B	Jun. 27, 1969	8:00 AM	S A G	Dec. 6, 1969	3:42 AM	S C O

Date	Time	Moon	Date	Time	Moon	Date	Time	Moon
Dec. 8, 1969	6:51 AM	S A G	May. 21, 1970	5:09 AM	S A G	Nov. 7, 1970	5:09 PM	P I S
Dec. 10, 1969	6:24 AM	C A P	May. 23, 1970	8:34 AM	C A P	Nov. 9, 1970	8:34 PM	A R I
Dec. 12, 1969	8:34 AM	A Q U	May. 25, 1970	10:17 AM	A Q U	Nov. 11, 1970	10:17 PM	T A U
Dec. 14, 1969	8:00 AM	P I S	May. 27, 1970	1:43 PM	P I S	Nov. 13, 1970	10:24 PM	G E M
Dec. 16, 1969	12:00 PM	A R I	May. 29, 1970	3:26 PM	A R I	Nov. 16, 1970	5:09 AM	C A N
Dec. 18, 1969	8:18 PM	T A U	May. 31, 1970	8:34 PM	T A U	Nov. 18, 1970	2:46 PM	L E O
Dec. 21, 1969	3:42 AM	G E M	Jun. 3, 1970	3:42 AM	G E M	Nov. 21, 1970	4:00 AM	V I R
Dec. 23, 1969	4:00 PM	C A N	Jun. 5, 1970	11:05 AM	C A N	Nov. 23, 1970	4:00 PM	L I B
Dec. 26, 1969	4:00 AM	L E O	Jun. 7, 1970	10:00 PM	L E O	Nov. 26, 1970	4:00 AM	S C O
Dec. 28, 1969	4:00 PM	V I R	Jun. 10, 1970	10:00 AM	V I R	Nov. 28, 1970	11:05 AM	S A G
Dec. 31, 1969	4:00 AM	L I B	Jun. 12, 1970	12:00 AM	L I B	Nov. 30, 1970	3:26 PM	C A P
Jan. 2, 1970	12:55 PM	S C O	Jun. 15, 1970	10:00 AM	S C O	Dec. 2, 1970	6:51 PM	A Q U
Jan. 4, 1970	5:09 PM	S A G	Jun. 17, 1970	1:43 PM	S A G	Dec. 4, 1970	10:17 PM	P I S
Jan. 6, 1970	5:36 PM	C A P	Jun. 19, 1970	5:09 PM	C A P	Dec. 7, 1970	1:43 AM	A R I
Jan. 8, 1970	5:36 PM	A Q U	Jun. 21, 1970	5:36 PM	A Q U	Dec. 9, 1970	5:09 AM	T A U
Jan. 10, 1970	5:36 PM	P I S	Jun. 23, 1970	8:34 PM	P I S	Dec. 11, 1970	8:34 AM	G E M
Jan. 12, 1970	8:34 PM	A R I	Jun. 25, 1970	10:17 PM	A R I	Dec. 13, 1970	1:43 PM	C A N
Jan. 15, 1970	1:51 AM	T A U	Jun. 28, 1970	1:43 AM	T A U	Dec. 18, 1970	12:00 PM	V I R
Jan. 17, 1970	9:14 AM	G E M	Jun. 30, 1970	9:14 AM	G E M	Dec. 21, 1970	2:11 AM	L I B
Jan. 19, 1970	10:00 PM	C A N	Jul. 2, 1970	8:00 PM	C A N	Dec. 23, 1970	11:05 AM	S C O
Jan. 22, 1970	10:00 AM	L E O	Jul. 5, 1970	6:00 AM	L E O	Dec. 25, 1970	8:18 PM	S A G
Jan. 24, 1970	10:00 PM	V I R	Jul. 7, 1970	6:00 PM	V I R	Dec. 28, 1970	1:51 AM	C A P
Jan. 27, 1970	10:00 AM	L I B	Jul. 10, 1970	8:44 AM	L I B	Dec. 30, 1970	3:26 AM	A Q U
Jan. 29, 1970	10:00 PM	S C O	Jul. 12, 1970	6:00 PM	S C O	Jan. 1, 1971	5:09 AM	P I S
Feb. 1, 1970	3:42 AM	S A G	Jul. 17, 1970	3:26 AM	C A P	Jan. 3, 1971	6:24 AM	A R I
Feb. 3, 1970	4:48 AM	C A P	Jul. 19, 1970	3:12 AM	A Q U	Jan. 5, 1971	10:17 AM	T A U
Feb. 5, 1970	4:48 AM	A Q U	Jul. 21, 1970	3:12 AM	P I S	Jan. 7, 1971	3:26 PM	G E M
Feb. 7, 1970	4:48 AM	P I S	Jul. 23, 1970	5:09 AM	A R I	Jan. 9, 1971	8:34 PM	C A N
Feb. 9, 1970	4:48 AM	A R I	Jul. 25, 1970	8:34 AM	T A U	Jan. 12, 1971	7:23 AM	L E O
Feb. 11, 1970	8:34 AM	T A U	Jul. 27, 1970	2:46 PM	G E M	Jan. 14, 1971	8:00 PM	V I R
Feb. 13, 1970	4:37 PM	G E M	Aug. 1, 1970	12:00 PM	L E O	Jan. 17, 1971	8:00 AM	L I B
Feb. 16, 1970	4:00 AM	C A N	Aug. 3, 1970	12:00 AM	V I R	Jan. 19, 1971	10:00 PM	S C O
Feb. 18, 1970	4:00 PM	L E O	Aug. 6, 1970	2:00 PM	L I B	Jan. 22, 1971	5:32 AM	S A G
Feb. 21, 1970	4:00 AM	V I R	Aug. 11, 1970	9:14 AM	S A G	Jan. 24, 1971	12:55 PM	C A P
Feb. 23, 1970	4:00 PM	L I B	Aug. 13, 1970	1:43 PM	C A P	Jan. 26, 1971	12:48 PM	A Q U
Feb. 26, 1970	1:51 AM	S C O	Aug. 15, 1970	2:24 PM	A Q U	Jan. 28, 1971	3:26 PM	P I S
Feb. 28, 1970	9:14 AM	S A G	Aug. 17, 1970	2:24 PM	P I S	Jan. 30, 1971	2:24 PM	A R I
Mar. 2, 1970	1:43 PM	C A P	Aug. 19, 1970	12:00 AM	A R I	Feb. 1, 1971	5:09 PM	T A U
Mar. 4, 1970	2:24 AM	A Q U	Aug. 21, 1970	2:24 AM	T A U	Feb. 3, 1971	8:34 PM	G E M
Mar. 6, 1970	4:00 PM	P I S	Aug. 23, 1970	10:09 PM	G E M	Feb. 6, 1971	5:32 AM	C A N
Mar. 8, 1970	4:00 PM	A R I	Aug. 26, 1970	5:32 AM	C A N	Feb. 8, 1971	4:00 PM	L E O
Mar. 10, 1970	6:51 AM	T A U	Aug. 28, 1970	6:00 PM	L E O	Feb. 11, 1971	2:00 AM	V I R
Mar. 12, 1970	10:17 PM	G E M	Aug. 31, 1970	6:00 AM	V I R	Feb. 13, 1971	4:00 PM	L I B
Mar. 15, 1970	9:14 AM	C A N	Sep. 2, 1970	9:49 PM	L I B	Feb. 16, 1971	4:00 AM	S C O
Mar. 17, 1970	10:00 PM	L E O	Sep. 5, 1970	8:00 AM	S C O	Feb. 18, 1971	4:00 PM	S A G
Mar. 20, 1970	12:00 PM	V I R	Sep. 7, 1970	6:00 PM	S A G	Feb. 20, 1971	10:09 PM	C A P
Mar. 22, 1970	12:00 AM	L I B	Sep. 9, 1970	8:34 PM	C A P	Feb. 25, 1971	1:36 AM	P I S
Mar. 25, 1970	7:23 AM	S C O	Sep. 13, 1970	12:00 AM	P I S	Feb. 26, 1971	10:30 PM	A R I
Mar. 27, 1970	2:46 PM	S A G	Sep. 15, 1970	12:00 AM	A R I	Feb. 28, 1971	12:00 AM	T A U
Mar. 29, 1970	6:51 PM	C A P	Sep. 18, 1970	1:43 AM	T A U	Mar. 3, 1971	3:26 AM	G E M
Mar. 31, 1970	12:00 AM	A Q U	Sep. 20, 1970	5:09 AM	G E M	Mar. 5, 1971	11:05 AM	C A N
Apr. 3, 1970	1:43 AM	P I S	Sep. 22, 1970	2:00 PM	C A N	Mar. 7, 1971	10:00 PM	L E O
Apr. 5, 1970	1:36 AM	A R I	Sep. 24, 1970	12:00 AM	L E O	Mar. 10, 1971	10:55 AM	V I R
Apr. 7, 1970	5:09 AM	T A U	Sep. 27, 1970	12:00 PM	V I R	Mar. 12, 1971	10:00 PM	L I B
Apr. 9, 1970	8:34 AM	G E M	Sep. 30, 1970	2:00 AM	L I B	Mar. 15, 1971	10:00 AM	S C O
Apr. 11, 1970	8:00 PM	C A N	Oct. 2, 1970	11:05 AM	S C O	Mar. 17, 1971	10:00 PM	S A G
Apr. 14, 1970	6:00 AM	L E O	Oct. 4, 1970	8:18 PM	S A G	Mar. 20, 1971	5:32 AM	C A P
Apr. 16, 1970	6:00 PM	V I R	Oct. 7, 1970	3:26 AM	C A P	Mar. 22, 1971	10:17 AM	A Q U
Apr. 19, 1970	5:32 AM	L I B	Oct. 9, 1970	8:34 AM	A Q U	Mar. 24, 1971	11:12 AM	P I S
Apr. 21, 1970	2:46 PM	S C O	Oct. 11, 1970	9:36 AM	P I S	Mar. 26, 1971	11:12 AM	A R I
Apr. 23, 1970	10:09 PM	S A G	Oct. 13, 1970	11:12 AM	A R I	Mar. 28, 1971	11:12 AM	T A U
Apr. 26, 1970	1:43 AM	C A P	Oct. 15, 1970	11:12 AM	T A U	Mar. 30, 1971	11:12 AM	G E M
Apr. 28, 1970	5:09 AM	A Q U	Oct. 17, 1970	12:48 PM	G E M	Apr. 1, 1971	6:28 PM	C A N
Apr. 30, 1970	6:24 AM	P I S	Oct. 19, 1970	6:51 PM	C A N	Apr. 4, 1971	4:00 AM	L E O
May. 2, 1970	10:17 AM	A R I	Oct. 22, 1970	8:00 AM	L E O	Apr. 6, 1971	5:27 PM	V I R
May. 4, 1970	1:43 PM	T A U	Oct. 24, 1970	8:00 PM	V I R	Apr. 9, 1971	4:00 AM	L I B
May. 6, 1970	8:18 PM	G E M	Oct. 27, 1970	8:00 AM	L I B	Apr. 11, 1971	4:00 PM	S C O
May. 9, 1970	4:00 AM	C A N	Oct. 29, 1970	8:00 PM	S C O	Apr. 14, 1971	4:00 AM	S A G
May. 11, 1970	2:00 PM	L E O	Nov. 1, 1970	3:42 AM	S A G	Apr. 16, 1971	11:05 AM	C A P
May. 14, 1970	4:22 AM	V I R	Nov. 3, 1970	8:34 AM	C A P	Apr. 18, 1971	6:28 PM	A Q U
May. 16, 1970	4:00 PM	L I B	Nov. 5, 1970	1:43 PM	A Q U	Apr. 20, 1971	8:34 PM	P I S

Date	Time	Moon	Date	Time	Moon	Date	Time	Moon
Apr. 22, 1971	12:00 AM	A R I	Oct. 3, 1971	8:48 PM	A R I	Mar. 15, 1972	10:17 PM	A R I
Apr. 24, 1971	10:24 PM	T A U	Oct. 5, 1971	6:00 PM	T A U	Mar. 17, 1972	8:48 PM	T A U
Apr. 26, 1971	10:24 PM	GEM	Oct. 7, 1971	7:12 PM	GEM	Mar. 19, 1972	8:48 PM	GEM
Apr. 29, 1971	1:43 AM	CAN	Oct. 9, 1971	10:17 PM	CAN	Mar. 21, 1972	12:00 AM	CAN
May. 1, 1971	9:14 AM	LEO	Oct. 12, 1971	5:32 AM	LEO	Mar. 24, 1972	7:23 AM	LEO
May. 3, 1971	10:00 PM	V I R	Oct. 14, 1971	6:00 PM	V I R	Mar. 26, 1972	2:46 PM	V I R
May. 6, 1971	10:00 AM	L I B	Oct. 17, 1971	6:00 AM	L I B	Mar. 29, 1972	1:51 AM	L I B
May. 8, 1971	12:00 AM	SCO	Oct. 19, 1971	6:00 PM	SCO	Mar. 31, 1972	2:00 PM	SCO
May. 11, 1971	10:00 AM	SAG	Oct. 22, 1971	6:00 AM	SAG	Apr. 3, 1972	4:00 AM	SAG
May. 13, 1971	4:37 PM	CAP	Oct. 24, 1971	6:00 PM	CAP	Apr. 5, 1972	4:00 PM	CAP
May. 15, 1971	12:00 AM	AQU	Oct. 27, 1971	1:51 AM	AQU	Apr. 7, 1972	12:00 AM	AQU
May. 18, 1971	3:26 AM	P I S	Oct. 29, 1971	5:09 AM	P I S	Apr. 10, 1972	5:09 AM	P I S
May. 20, 1971	6:51 AM	A R I	Oct. 31, 1971	8:34 AM	A R I	Apr. 12, 1972	8:34 AM	A R I
May. 22, 1971	6:24 AM	T A U	Nov. 2, 1971	6:24 AM	T A U	Apr. 14, 1972	6:00 AM	T A U
May. 24, 1971	8:00 AM	GEM	Nov. 4, 1971	6:24 AM	GEM	Apr. 16, 1972	6:24 AM	GEM
May. 26, 1971	12:00 PM	CAN	Nov. 6, 1971	8:34 AM	CAN	Apr. 18, 1972	6:24 AM	CAN
May. 28, 1971	6:28 PM	LEO	Nov. 8, 1971	2:46 PM	LEO	Apr. 20, 1972	12:00 PM	LEO
May. 31, 1971	6:00 AM	V I R	Nov. 10, 1971	10:09 PM	V I R	Apr. 22, 1972	8:18 PM	V I R
Jun. 2, 1971	6:00 PM	L I B	Nov. 13, 1971	12:00 PM	L I B	Apr. 25, 1972	8:00 AM	L I B
Jun. 5, 1971	6:00 AM	SCO	Nov. 15, 1971	12:00 AM	SCO	Apr. 27, 1972	8:00 PM	SCO
Jun. 7, 1971	6:00 PM	SAG	Nov. 18, 1971	12:00 PM	SAG	Apr. 30, 1972	10:00 AM	SAG
Jun. 9, 1971	12:00 AM	CAP	Nov. 20, 1971	12:00 AM	CAP	May. 2, 1972	10:00 PM	CAP
Jun. 12, 1971	5:32 AM	AQU	Nov. 23, 1971	7:23 AM	AQU	May. 5, 1972	8:00 AM	AQU
Jun. 14, 1971	8:34 AM	P I S	Nov. 25, 1971	12:00 PM	P I S	May. 7, 1972	2:46 PM	P I S
Jun. 16, 1971	12:00 PM	A R I	Nov. 27, 1971	2:24 PM	A R I	May. 9, 1972	5:09 PM	A R I
Jun. 18, 1971	3:26 PM	T A U	Nov. 29, 1971	4:00 PM	T A U	May. 11, 1972	5:36 PM	T A U
Jun. 20, 1971	5:09 PM	GEM	Dec. 1, 1971	5:36 PM	GEM	May. 13, 1972	5:36 PM	GEM
Jun. 22, 1971	8:34 PM	CAN	Dec. 3, 1971	5:36 PM	CAN	May. 15, 1972	4:00 PM	CAN
Jun. 25, 1971	3:42 AM	LEO	Dec. 5, 1971	10:17 PM	LEO	May. 17, 1972	8:34 PM	LEO
Jun. 27, 1971	12:55 PM	V I R	Dec. 8, 1971	7:23 AM	V I R	May. 20, 1972	3:42 AM	V I R
Jun. 30, 1971	2:00 AM	L I B	Dec. 10, 1971	8:00 PM	L I B	May. 22, 1972	12:55 PM	L I B
Jul. 2, 1971	2:00 PM	SCO	Dec. 13, 1971	8:00 AM	SCO	May. 25, 1972	4:22 AM	SCO
Jul. 7, 1971	6:51 AM	CAP	Dec. 15, 1971	8:00 PM	SAG	May. 27, 1972	4:00 PM	SAG
Jul. 9, 1971	12:00 PM	AQU	Dec. 18, 1971	6:00 AM	CAP	May. 30, 1972	4:00 AM	CAP
Jul. 11, 1971	3:26 PM	P I S	Dec. 20, 1971	12:55 PM	AQU	Jun. 1, 1972	2:00 PM	AQU
Jul. 13, 1971	4:00 PM	A R I	Dec. 22, 1971	5:09 PM	P I S	Jun. 3, 1972	8:18 PM	P I S
Jul. 15, 1971	8:34 PM	T A U	Dec. 24, 1971	10:17 PM	A R I	Jun. 6, 1972	1:43 AM	A R I
Jul. 17, 1971	12:00 AM	GEM	Dec. 29, 1971	1:36 AM	GEM	Jun. 8, 1972	3:26 AM	T A U
Jul. 20, 1971	5:32 AM	CAN	Dec. 31, 1971	5:09 AM	CAN	Jun. 10, 1972	3:12 AM	GEM
Jul. 22, 1971	2:00 PM	LEO	Jan. 2, 1972	8:34 AM	LEO	Jun. 12, 1972	3:12 AM	CAN
Jul. 24, 1971	8:18 PM	V I R	Jan. 4, 1972	4:37 PM	V I R	Jun. 14, 1972	4:48 AM	LEO
Jul. 27, 1971	10:00 AM	L I B	Jan. 7, 1972	4:00 AM	L I B	Jun. 16, 1972	10:17 AM	V I R
Jul. 29, 1971	10:00 PM	SCO	Jan. 9, 1972	4:00 PM	SCO	Jun. 18, 1972	8:18 PM	L I B
Aug. 1, 1971	10:00 AM	SAG	Jan. 12, 1972	4:00 AM	SAG	Jun. 21, 1972	10:00 AM	SCO
Aug. 3, 1971	6:28 PM	CAP	Jan. 14, 1972	12:55 PM	CAP	Jun. 23, 1972	10:00 PM	SAG
Aug. 5, 1971	12:00 AM	AQU	Jan. 16, 1972	8:18 PM	AQU	Jun. 26, 1972	10:00 AM	CAP
Aug. 7, 1971	10:24 PM	P I S	Jan. 18, 1972	12:00 AM	P I S	Jun. 28, 1972	6:28 PM	AQU
Aug. 9, 1971	12:00 AM	A R I	Jan. 21, 1972	3:26 AM	A R I	Jul. 1, 1972	1:51 AM	P I S
Aug. 12, 1971	1:36 AM	T A U	Jan. 23, 1972	6:51 AM	T A U	Jul. 3, 1972	6:51 AM	A R I
Aug. 14, 1971	5:09 AM	GEM	Jan. 25, 1972	8:34 AM	GEM	Jul. 5, 1972	10:17 AM	T A U
Aug. 16, 1971	11:05 AM	CAN	Jan. 27, 1972	12:00 PM	CAN	Jul. 7, 1972	11:12 AM	GEM
Aug. 18, 1971	6:28 PM	LEO	Jan. 29, 1972	5:09 PM	LEO	Jul. 9, 1972	12:48 PM	CAN
Aug. 21, 1971	6:00 AM	V I R	Feb. 1, 1972	1:51 AM	V I R	Jul. 11, 1972	2:24 PM	LEO
Aug. 23, 1971	6:00 PM	L I B	Feb. 3, 1972	12:00 PM	L I B	Jul. 13, 1972	10:09 PM	V I R
Aug. 26, 1971	6:00 AM	SCO	Feb. 5, 1972	12:00 AM	SCO	Jul. 16, 1972	5:32 AM	L I B
Aug. 28, 1971	6:00 PM	SAG	Feb. 8, 1972	12:00 PM	SAG	Jul. 18, 1972	6:00 PM	SCO
Aug. 31, 1971	4:00 AM	CAP	Feb. 10, 1972	12:00 AM	CAP	Jul. 21, 1972	6:00 AM	SAG
Sep. 2, 1971	9:14 AM	AQU	Feb. 13, 1972	5:32 AM	AQU	Jul. 23, 1972	6:00 PM	CAP
Sep. 4, 1971	10:17 AM	P I S	Feb. 15, 1972	8:34 AM	P I S	Jul. 26, 1972	1:51 AM	AQU
Sep. 6, 1971	9:36 AM	A R I	Feb. 17, 1972	9:36 AM	A R I	Jul. 28, 1972	9:14 AM	P I S
Sep. 8, 1971	9:36 AM	T A U	Feb. 19, 1972	11:12 AM	T A U	Jul. 30, 1972	12:00 PM	A R I
Sep. 10, 1971	12:00 PM	GEM	Feb. 21, 1972	12:48 PM	GEM	Aug. 1, 1972	3:26 PM	T A U
Sep. 12, 1971	3:26 PM	CAN	Feb. 23, 1972	8:18 PM	CAN	Aug. 3, 1972	6:51 PM	GEM
Sep. 14, 1971	12:00 AM	LEO	Feb. 26, 1972	1:51 AM	LEO	Aug. 5, 1972	7:12 PM	CAN
Sep. 17, 1971	12:00 PM	V I R	Feb. 28, 1972	9:14 AM	V I R	Aug. 7, 1972	12:00 AM	LEO
Sep. 19, 1971	12:00 AM	L I B	Mar. 1, 1972	6:28 PM	L I B	Aug. 10, 1972	5:09 AM	V I R
Sep. 22, 1971	12:00 PM	SCO	Mar. 4, 1972	8:00 AM	SCO	Aug. 12, 1972	4:00 PM	L I B
Sep. 24, 1971	12:00 AM	SAG	Mar. 6, 1972	8:00 AM	SAG	Aug. 15, 1972	2:00 AM	SCO
Sep. 27, 1971	12:00 PM	CAP	Mar. 9, 1972	8:00 AM	CAP	Aug. 17, 1972	2:00 PM	SAG
Sep. 29, 1971	6:28 PM	AQU	Mar. 11, 1972	4:37 PM	AQU	Aug. 20, 1972	2:00 AM	CAP
Oct. 1, 1971	8:34 PM	P I S	Mar. 13, 1972	10:09 PM	P I S	Aug. 22, 1972	12:00 PM	AQU

Date	Time	Moon	Date	Time	Moon	Date	Time	Moon
Aug. 24, 1972	3:26 PM	P I S	Feb. 2, 1973	8:00 AM	A Q U	Jul. 20, 1973	10:09 PM	A R I
Aug. 26, 1972	8:34 PM	A R I	Feb. 4, 1973	2:46 PM	P I S	Jul. 23, 1973	5:32 AM	T A U
Aug. 28, 1972	10:17 PM	T A U	Feb. 6, 1973	10:09 PM	A R I	Jul. 25, 1973	8:34 AM	G E M
Aug. 30, 1972	10:24 PM	G E M	Feb. 9, 1973	1:43 AM	T A U	Jul. 27, 1973	10:17 AM	C A N
Sep. 2, 1972	3:26 AM	C A N	Feb. 11, 1973	5:09 AM	G E M	Jul. 29, 1973	9:36 AM	L E O
Sep. 4, 1972	6:51 AM	L E O	Feb. 13, 1973	8:34 AM	C A N	Jul. 31, 1973	9:36 AM	V I R
Sep. 6, 1972	2:46 PM	V I R	Feb. 15, 1973	10:17 AM	L E O	Aug. 2, 1973	1:43 PM	L I B
Sep. 8, 1972	10:09 PM	L I B	Feb. 17, 1973	1:43 PM	V I R	Aug. 4, 1973	8:18 PM	S C O
Sep. 11, 1972	10:00 AM	S C O	Feb. 19, 1973	5:09 PM	L I B	Aug. 7, 1973	8:00 AM	S A G
Sep. 13, 1972	10:00 AM	S A G	Feb. 22, 1973	4:00 AM	S C O	Aug. 9, 1973	12:00 AM	C A P
Sep. 16, 1972	10:00 AM	C A P	Feb. 24, 1973	4:00 AM	S A G	Aug. 12, 1973	10:00 AM	A Q U
Sep. 18, 1972	10:00 PM	A Q U	Feb. 27, 1973	4:00 AM	C A P	Aug. 14, 1973	10:00 PM	P I S
Sep. 21, 1972	1:43 AM	P I S	Mar. 1, 1973	4:00 PM	A Q U	Aug. 17, 1973	3:42 AM	A R I
Sep. 23, 1972	5:09 AM	A R I	Mar. 6, 1973	5:32 AM	A R I	Aug. 19, 1973	11:05 AM	T A U
Sep. 25, 1972	4:48 AM	T A U	Mar. 8, 1973	8:34 AM	T A U	Aug. 21, 1973	1:43 PM	G E M
Sep. 27, 1972	6:51 AM	G E M	Mar. 10, 1973	10:17 AM	G E M	Aug. 23, 1973	5:09 PM	C A N
Sep. 29, 1972	8:34 AM	C A N	Mar. 12, 1973	1:43 PM	C A N	Aug. 25, 1973	5:36 PM	L E O
Oct. 1, 1972	12:00 PM	L E O	Mar. 14, 1973	5:09 PM	L E O	Aug. 27, 1973	7:12 PM	V I R
Oct. 3, 1972	8:18 PM	V I R	Mar. 16, 1973	8:34 PM	V I R	Aug. 29, 1973	12:00 AM	L I B
Oct. 6, 1972	6:00 AM	L I B	Mar. 19, 1973	3:42 AM	L I B	Sep. 1, 1973	5:32 AM	S C O
Oct. 8, 1972	2:46 PM	S C O	Mar. 21, 1973	11:05 AM	S C O	Sep. 3, 1973	2:46 PM	S A G
Oct. 11, 1972	4:00 AM	S A G	Mar. 23, 1973	12:00 AM	S A G	Sep. 6, 1973	4:00 AM	C A P
Oct. 13, 1972	6:00 PM	C A P	Mar. 26, 1973	12:00 AM	C A P	Sep. 8, 1973	6:00 PM	A Q U
Oct. 16, 1972	6:00 AM	A Q U	Mar. 28, 1973	12:00 AM	A Q U	Sep. 11, 1973	4:00 PM	P I S
Oct. 18, 1972	12:55 PM	P I S	Mar. 31, 1973	9:14 AM	P I S	Sep. 13, 1973	11:05 AM	A R I
Oct. 20, 1972	3:26 PM	A R I	Apr. 2, 1973	1:43 PM	A R I	Sep. 15, 1973	3:26 PM	T A U
Oct. 22, 1972	4:00 PM	T A U	Apr. 4, 1973	5:09 PM	T A U	Sep. 17, 1973	6:51 PM	G E M
Oct. 24, 1972	1:30 PM	G E M	Apr. 6, 1973	4:00 PM	G E M	Sep. 19, 1973	10:17 PM	C A N
Oct. 26, 1972	2:24 PM	C A N	Apr. 8, 1973	5:36 PM	C A N	Sep. 22, 1973	1:43 AM	L E O
Oct. 28, 1972	6:51 PM	L E O	Apr. 10, 1973	10:17 PM	L E O	Sep. 24, 1973	5:09 AM	V I R
Oct. 31, 1972	1:51 AM	V I R	Apr. 13, 1973	3:42 AM	V I R	Sep. 26, 1973	8:34 AM	L I B
Nov. 2, 1972	12:00 PM	L I B	Apr. 15, 1973	11:05 AM	L I B	Sep. 28, 1973	1:43 PM	S C O
Nov. 4, 1972	8:18 PM	S C O	Apr. 17, 1973	6:28 PM	S C O	Oct. 3, 1973	12:00 PM	C A P
Nov. 7, 1972	1:05 PM	S A G	Apr. 20, 1973	8:00 AM	S A G	Oct. 6, 1973	2:00 AM	A Q U
Nov. 9, 1972	12:00 AM	C A P	Apr. 22, 1973	8:00 PM	C A P	Oct. 8, 1973	11:05 AM	P I S
Nov. 12, 1972	12:00 PM	A Q U	Apr. 25, 1973	8:00 AM	A Q U	Oct. 10, 1973	8:18 PM	A R I
Nov. 14, 1972	8:18 PM	P I S	Apr. 27, 1973	8:00 PM	P I S	Oct. 14, 1973	12:00 AM	T A U
Nov. 17, 1972	1:43 AM	A R I	May 2, 1973	1:36 AM	T A U	Oct. 15, 1973	1:43 AM	G E M
Nov. 19, 1972	3:12 AM	T A U	May 4, 1973	1:36 AM	G E M	Oct. 17, 1973	5:09 AM	C A N
Nov. 21, 1972	1:30 AM	G E M	May 6, 1973	1:36 AM	C A N	Oct. 19, 1973	6:51 AM	L E O
Nov. 23, 1972	1:36 AM	C A N	May 8, 1973	5:09 AM	L E O	Oct. 21, 1973	10:17 AM	V I R
Nov. 25, 1972	3:26 AM	L E O	May 10, 1973	8:34 AM	V I R	Oct. 23, 1973	3:26 PM	L I B
Nov. 27, 1972	9:14 AM	V I R	May 12, 1973	4:37 PM	L I B	Oct. 25, 1973	12:00 AM	S C O
Nov. 29, 1972	4:37 PM	L I B	May 15, 1973	2:00 AM	S C O	Oct. 28, 1973	10:00 AM	S A G
Dec. 2, 1972	4:00 AM	S C O	May 17, 1973	2:00 PM	S A G	Oct. 30, 1973	8:00 PM	C A P
Dec. 4, 1972	7:38 PM	S A G	May 20, 1973	2:00 AM	C A P	Nov. 2, 1973	10:00 AM	A Q U
Dec. 7, 1972	6:00 AM	C A P	May 22, 1973	5:27 PM	A Q U	Nov. 4, 1973	10:00 PM	P I S
Dec. 9, 1972	6:00 PM	A Q U	May 25, 1973	2:00 AM	P I S	Nov. 7, 1973	5:32 AM	A R I
Dec. 12, 1972	4:00 AM	P I S	May 27, 1973	9:14 AM	A R I	Nov. 9, 1973	8:34 AM	T A U
Dec. 14, 1972	11:05 AM	A R I	May 29, 1973	11:12 AM	T A U	Nov. 11, 1973	12:00 PM	G E M
Dec. 16, 1972	1:43 PM	T A U	May 31, 1973	12:48 PM	G E M	Nov. 13, 1973	11:12 AM	C A N
Dec. 18, 1972	12:48 PM	G E M	Jun. 2, 1973	12:48 PM	C A N	Nov. 15, 1973	1:43 PM	L E O
Dec. 20, 1972	12:48 PM	C A N	Jun. 4, 1973	12:48 PM	L E O	Nov. 17, 1973	5:09 PM	V I R
Dec. 22, 1972	12:48 PM	L E O	Jun. 6, 1973	3:26 PM	V I R	Nov. 19, 1973	8:34 PM	L I B
Dec. 24, 1972	5:09 PM	V I R	Jun. 8, 1973	10:09 PM	L I B	Nov. 22, 1973	5:32 AM	S C O
Dec. 26, 1972	12:00 AM	L I B	Jun. 11, 1973	8:00 AM	S C O	Nov. 24, 1973	2:46 PM	S A G
Dec. 29, 1972	12:00 AM	S C O	Jun. 13, 1973	8:00 AM	S A G	Nov. 27, 1973	4:00 AM	C A P
Dec. 31, 1972	12:00 AM	S A G	Jun. 16, 1973	8:00 AM	C A P	Nov. 29, 1973	4:00 PM	A Q U
Jan. 3, 1973	12:00 AM	C A P	Jun. 18, 1973	12:00 AM	A Q U	Dec. 2, 1973	6:00 AM	P I S
Jan. 5, 1973	12:00 AM	A Q U	Jun. 21, 1973	7:23 AM	P I S	Dec. 4, 1973	2:46 PM	A R I
Jan. 8, 1973	10:00 AM	P I S	Jun. 23, 1973	4:37 PM	A R I	Dec. 6, 1973	10:09 PM	T A U
Jan. 10, 1973	4:37 PM	A R I	Jun. 25, 1973	8:34 PM	T A U	Dec. 8, 1973	8:48 PM	G E M
Jan. 12, 1973	10:09 PM	T A U	Jun. 27, 1973	10:24 PM	G E M	Dec. 10, 1973	10:24 PM	C A N
Jan. 14, 1973	12:00 AM	G E M	Jun. 29, 1973	10:24 PM	C A N	Dec. 12, 1973	7:30 PM	L E O
Jan. 16, 1973	10:24 PM	C A N	Jul. 1, 1973	10:24 PM	L E O	Dec. 14, 1973	12:00 AM	V I R
Jan. 18, 1973	12:00 AM	L E O	Jul. 6, 1973	5:32 AM	L I B	Dec. 17, 1973	3:26 AM	L I B
Jan. 21, 1973	3:26 AM	V I R	Jul. 8, 1973	12:55 PM	S C O	Dec. 19, 1973	11:05 AM	S C O
Jan. 23, 1973	9:14 AM	L I B	Jul. 11, 1973	2:00 AM	S A G	Dec. 21, 1973	8:18 PM	S A G
Jan. 25, 1973	8:00 AM	S C O	Jul. 13, 1973	2:00 PM	C A P	Dec. 24, 1973	10:00 AM	C A P
Jan. 28, 1973	8:44 AM	S A G	Jul. 16, 1973	4:00 AM	A Q U	Dec. 29, 1973	12:00 PM	P I S
Jan. 30, 1973	8:00 PM	C A P	Jul. 18, 1973	12:55 PM	P I S	Dec. 31, 1973	12:00 AM	A R I

Date	Time	Moon	Date	Time	Moon	Date	Time	Moon
Jan. 3, 1974	5:32 AM	TAU	Jun. 18, 1974	6:51 AM	GEM	Nov. 29, 1974	3:26 AM	GEM
Jan. 5, 1974	8:34 AM	GEM	Jun. 20, 1974	8:00 AM	CAN	Dec. 1, 1974	6:51 AM	CAN
Jan. 7, 1974	9:36 AM	CAN	Jun. 22, 1974	8:00 AM	LEO	Dec. 3, 1974	10:17 AM	LEO
Jan. 9, 1974	7:30 AM	LEO	Jun. 24, 1974	8:00 AM	VIR	Dec. 5, 1974	12:00 PM	VIR
Jan. 11, 1974	8:00 AM	VIR	Jun. 26, 1974	12:00 PM	LIB	Dec. 7, 1974	12:48 PM	LIB
Jan. 13, 1974	9:36 AM	LIB	Jun. 28, 1974	6:28 PM	SCO	Dec. 9, 1974	6:51 PM	SCO
Jan. 15, 1974	6:28 PM	SCO	Jul. 1, 1974	1:51 AM	SAG	Dec. 12, 1974	1:51 AM	SAG
Jan. 18, 1974	4:00 AM	SAG	Jul. 3, 1974	2:00 PM	CAP	Dec. 14, 1974	9:14 AM	CAP
Jan. 20, 1974	4:00 PM	CAP	Jul. 6, 1974	2:00 AM	AQU	Dec. 16, 1974	6:28 PM	AQU
Jan. 23, 1974	6:00 AM	AQU	Jul. 8, 1974	2:00 PM	PIS	Dec. 19, 1974	10:55 AM	PIS
Jan. 25, 1974	6:00 PM	PIS	Jul. 11, 1974	2:00 AM	ARI	Dec. 21, 1974	10:00 PM	ARI
Jan. 28, 1974	3:42 AM	ARI	Jul. 13, 1974	11:05 AM	TAU	Dec. 24, 1974	7:23 AM	TAU
Jan. 30, 1974	12:55 PM	TAU	Jul. 15, 1974	6:28 PM	GEM	Dec. 26, 1974	2:46 PM	GEM
Feb. 1, 1974	5:09 PM	GEM	Jul. 17, 1974	5:36 PM	CAN	Dec. 28, 1974	5:09 PM	CAN
Feb. 3, 1974	8:34 PM	CAN	Jul. 19, 1974	7:12 PM	LEO	Dec. 30, 1974	5:36 PM	LEO
Feb. 5, 1974	10:17 PM	LEO	Jul. 21, 1974	4:30 PM	VIR	Jan. 1, 1975	5:36 PM	VIR
Feb. 7, 1974	7:12 PM	VIR	Jul. 23, 1974	5:36 PM	LIB	Jan. 3, 1975	7:12 PM	LIB
Feb. 9, 1974	10:17 PM	LIB	Jul. 25, 1974	10:17 PM	SCO	Jan. 5, 1975	12:00 AM	SCO
Feb. 12, 1974	1:51 AM	SCO	Jul. 28, 1974	7:23 AM	SAG	Jan. 8, 1975	7:23 AM	SAG
Feb. 14, 1974	12:00 PM	SAG	Jul. 30, 1974	8:00 PM	CAP	Jan. 10, 1975	6:00 PM	CAP
Feb. 16, 1974	10:00 PM	CAP	Aug. 2, 1974	8:00 AM	AQU	Jan. 13, 1975	4:00 AM	AQU
Feb. 19, 1974	12:00 PM	AQU	Aug. 4, 1974	8:00 PM	PIS	Jan. 15, 1975	4:00 PM	PIS
Feb. 21, 1974	12:00 AM	PIS	Aug. 7, 1974	8:00 AM	ARI	Jan. 18, 1975	6:33 AM	ARI
Feb. 24, 1974	9:14 AM	ARI	Aug. 9, 1974	8:00 PM	TAU	Jan. 20, 1975	2:46 PM	TAU
Feb. 26, 1974	6:28 PM	TAU	Aug. 12, 1974	1:51 AM	GEM	Jan. 22, 1975	12:00 AM	GEM
Mar. 3, 1974	3:26 AM	CAN	Aug. 14, 1974	5:09 AM	CAN	Jan. 25, 1975	5:09 AM	CAN
Mar. 5, 1974	4:48 AM	LEO	Aug. 16, 1974	4:48 AM	LEO	Jan. 27, 1975	4:48 AM	LEO
Mar. 7, 1974	6:24 AM	VIR	Aug. 18, 1974	4:48 AM	VIR	Jan. 29, 1975	4:48 AM	VIR
Mar. 9, 1974	8:34 AM	LIB	Aug. 20, 1974	4:48 AM	LIB	Jan. 31, 1975	3:12 AM	LIB
Mar. 11, 1974	12:55 PM	SCO	Aug. 22, 1974	6:51 AM	SCO	Feb. 2, 1975	6:51 AM	SCO
Mar. 13, 1974	6:28 PM	SAG	Aug. 24, 1974	2:46 PM	SAG	Feb. 4, 1975	12:55 PM	SAG
Mar. 16, 1974	6:00 AM	CAP	Aug. 27, 1974	2:00 AM	CAP	Feb. 6, 1975	12:00 AM	CAP
Mar. 18, 1974	9:49 PM	AQU	Aug. 29, 1974	2:00 PM	AQU	Feb. 9, 1975	10:00 AM	AQU
Mar. 21, 1974	8:00 AM	PIS	Sep. 1, 1974	2:00 AM	PIS	Feb. 11, 1975	10:00 PM	PIS
Mar. 23, 1974	4:37 PM	ARI	Sep. 3, 1974	2:00 PM	ARI	Feb. 14, 1975	12:00 PM	ARI
Mar. 25, 1974	12:00 AM	TAU	Sep. 5, 1974	10:09 PM	TAU	Feb. 16, 1975	12:00 AM	TAU
Mar. 28, 1974	5:09 AM	GEM	Sep. 8, 1974	7:23 AM	GEM	Feb. 19, 1975	10:00 AM	GEM
Mar. 30, 1974	11:05 AM	CAN	Sep. 10, 1974	12:00 PM	CAN	Feb. 21, 1975	1:43 PM	CAN
Apr. 1, 1974	11:12 AM	LEO	Sep. 12, 1974	3:26 PM	LEO	Feb. 23, 1975	5:09 PM	LEO
Apr. 3, 1974	3:26 PM	VIR	Sep. 14, 1974	2:24 PM	VIR	Feb. 25, 1975	4:00 PM	VIR
Apr. 5, 1974	5:09 PM	LIB	Sep. 16, 1974	2:24 PM	LIB	Feb. 27, 1975	2:24 PM	LIB
Apr. 7, 1974	8:34 PM	SCO	Sep. 18, 1974	4:00 PM	SCO	Mar. 1, 1975	2:24 PM	SCO
Apr. 10, 1974	3:42 AM	SAG	Sep. 20, 1974	8:34 PM	SAG	Mar. 3, 1975	6:51 PM	SAG
Apr. 12, 1974	4:00 PM	CAP	Sep. 23, 1974	7:23 AM	CAP	Mar. 6, 1975	3:42 AM	CAP
Apr. 15, 1974	4:00 AM	AQU	Sep. 25, 1974	8:00 PM	AQU	Mar. 8, 1975	4:00 PM	AQU
Apr. 17, 1974	4:00 PM	PIS	Sep. 28, 1974	10:00 AM	PIS	Mar. 11, 1975	4:00 PM	PIS
Apr. 20, 1974	2:00 AM	ARI	Sep. 30, 1974	6:28 PM	ARI	Mar. 13, 1975	6:00 PM	ARI
Apr. 22, 1974	6:51 AM	TAU	Oct. 3, 1974	5:32 AM	TAU	Mar. 16, 1975	3:42 AM	TAU
Apr. 24, 1974	12:00 PM	GEM	Oct. 5, 1974	12:55 PM	GEM	Mar. 18, 1975	4:00 PM	GEM
Apr. 26, 1974	3:26 PM	CAN	Oct. 7, 1974	5:09 PM	CAN	Mar. 20, 1975	10:09 PM	CAN
Apr. 28, 1974	6:51 PM	LEO	Oct. 9, 1974	10:17 PM	LEO	Mar. 23, 1975	1:43 AM	LEO
Apr. 30, 1974	8:34 PM	VIR	Oct. 11, 1974	10:24 PM	VIR	Mar. 25, 1975	1:36 AM	VIR
May. 2, 1974	12:00 AM	LIB	Oct. 14, 1974	1:43 AM	LIB	Mar. 27, 1975	1:36 AM	LIB
May. 5, 1974	5:09 AM	SCO	Oct. 16, 1974	3:26 AM	SCO	Mar. 29, 1975	1:36 AM	SCO
May. 7, 1974	12:55 PM	SAG	Oct. 18, 1974	9:14 AM	SAG	Mar. 31, 1975	5:09 AM	SAG
May. 9, 1974	12:00 AM	CAP	Oct. 20, 1974	6:00 PM	CAP	Apr. 2, 1975	11:05 AM	CAP
May. 12, 1974	12:00 PM	AQU	Oct. 23, 1974	4:00 AM	AQU	Apr. 4, 1975	8:18 PM	AQU
May. 14, 1974	12:00 AM	PIS	Oct. 25, 1974	4:00 PM	PIS	Apr. 7, 1975	1:05 PM	PIS
May. 17, 1974	9:14 AM	ARI	Oct. 28, 1974	4:00 AM	ARI	Apr. 9, 1975	12:00 AM	ARI
May. 19, 1974	6:28 PM	TAU	Oct. 30, 1974	12:55 PM	TAU	Apr. 12, 1975	12:00 PM	TAU
May. 21, 1974	8:34 PM	GEM	Nov. 1, 1974	8:18 PM	GEM	Apr. 14, 1975	10:00 PM	GEM
May. 23, 1974	12:00 AM	CAN	Nov. 6, 1974	3:26 AM	LEO	Apr. 17, 1975	3:42 AM	CAN
May. 28, 1974	1:36 AM	VIR	Nov. 8, 1974	6:51 AM	VIR	Apr. 19, 1975	9:14 AM	LEO
May. 30, 1974	7:23 AM	LIB	Nov. 10, 1974	8:34 AM	LIB	Apr. 21, 1975	9:36 AM	VIR
Jun. 1, 1974	12:55 PM	SCO	Nov. 12, 1974	12:00 PM	SCO	Apr. 23, 1975	11:12 AM	LIB
Jun. 3, 1974	8:18 PM	SAG	Nov. 14, 1974	6:28 PM	SAG	Apr. 25, 1975	1:43 PM	SCO
Jun. 6, 1974	5:32 AM	CAP	Nov. 17, 1974	1:51 AM	CAP	Apr. 27, 1975	3:26 PM	SAG
Jun. 8, 1974	6:00 PM	AQU	Nov. 19, 1974	12:00 PM	AQU	Apr. 29, 1975	6:51 PM	CAP
Jun. 11, 1974	8:00 AM	PIS	Nov. 22, 1974	2:11 AM	PIS	May. 2, 1975	5:32 AM	AQU
Jun. 13, 1974	8:00 PM	ARI	Nov. 24, 1974	2:00 PM	ARI	May. 4, 1975	6:00 PM	PIS
Jun. 16, 1974	1:43 AM	TAU	Nov. 26, 1974	12:00 AM	TAU	May. 7, 1975	8:44 AM	ARI

155

Date	Time	Moon	Date	Time	Moon	Date	Time	Moon
May. 9, 1975	6:00 PM	TAU	Oct. 20, 1975	2:00 PM	TAU	Apr. 8, 1976	6:28 PM	LEO
May. 12, 1975	1:51 AM	GEM	Oct. 25, 1975	9:14 AM	CAN	Apr. 10, 1976	12:00 AM	VIR
May. 14, 1975	9:14 AM	CAN	Oct. 27, 1975	4:37 PM	LEO	Apr. 12, 1976	12:00 AM	LIB
May. 16, 1975	1:43 PM	LEO	Oct. 29, 1975	8:34 PM	VIR	Apr. 14, 1976	7:30 PM	SCO
May. 18, 1975	5:09 PM	VIR	Oct. 31, 1975	10:17 PM	LIB	Apr. 16, 1976	8:48 PM	SAG
May. 20, 1975	5:36 PM	LIB	Nov. 2, 1975	8:48 PM	SCO	Apr. 18, 1976	12:00 AM	CAP
May. 22, 1975	10:17 PM	SCO	Nov. 4, 1975	8:48 PM	SAG	Apr. 21, 1976	5:32 AM	AQU
May. 24, 1975	12:00 AM	SAG	Nov. 7, 1975	1:43 AM	CAP	Apr. 23, 1976	4:00 PM	PIS
May. 27, 1975	7:23 AM	CAP	Nov. 9, 1975	9:14 AM	AQU	Apr. 26, 1976	4:00 AM	ARI
May. 29, 1975	2:46 PM	AQU	Nov. 11, 1975	8:00 PM	PIS	Apr. 28, 1976	4:00 PM	TAU
Jun. 1, 1975	2:00 AM	PIS	Nov. 14, 1975	8:00 AM	ARI	May. 1, 1976	6:00 AM	GEM
Jun. 3, 1975	2:00 PM	ARI	Nov. 16, 1975	8:00 PM	TAU	May. 3, 1976	4:00 PM	CAN
Jun. 6, 1975	2:00 AM	TAU	Nov. 19, 1975	8:00 AM	GEM	May. 5, 1976	12:00 AM	LEO
Jun. 8, 1975	11:05 AM	GEM	Nov. 21, 1975	2:46 PM	CAN	May. 8, 1976	5:09 AM	VIR
Jun. 10, 1975	3:26 PM	CAN	Nov. 23, 1975	10:09 PM	LEO	May. 10, 1976	8:34 AM	LIB
Jun. 12, 1975	8:34 PM	LEO	Nov. 26, 1975	1:43 AM	VIR	May. 12, 1976	8:00 AM	SCO
Jun. 14, 1975	10:17 PM	VIR	Nov. 28, 1975	5:09 AM	LIB	May. 14, 1976	8:00 AM	SAG
Jun. 19, 1975	3:26 AM	SCO	Nov. 30, 1975	6:51 AM	SCO	May. 16, 1976	10:17 AM	CAP
Jun. 21, 1975	9:14 AM	SAG	Dec. 2, 1975	8:34 AM	SAG	May. 18, 1976	2:46 PM	AQU
Jun. 23, 1975	2:46 PM	CAP	Dec. 4, 1975	12:00 PM	CAP	May. 20, 1976	10:09 PM	PIS
Jun. 25, 1975	10:09 PM	AQU	Dec. 6, 1975	6:28 PM	AQU	May. 23, 1976	10:00 AM	ARI
Jun. 28, 1975	10:00 AM	PIS	Dec. 9, 1975	4:00 AM	PIS	May. 25, 1976	10:00 PM	TAU
Jun. 30, 1975	10:00 AM	ARI	Dec. 11, 1975	4:00 AM	ARI	May. 28, 1976	12:00 PM	GEM
Jul. 3, 1975	12:00 PM	TAU	Dec. 14, 1975	4:00 AM	TAU	May. 30, 1976	8:18 PM	CAN
Jul. 5, 1975	10:00 PM	GEM	Dec. 16, 1975	4:00 PM	GEM	Jun. 2, 1976	5:32 AM	LEO
Jul. 8, 1975	1:51 AM	CAN	Dec. 18, 1975	10:09 PM	CAN	Jun. 4, 1976	10:17 AM	VIR
Jul. 10, 1975	3:12 PM	LEO	Dec. 21, 1975	3:26 AM	LEO	Jun. 6, 1976	3:26 PM	LIB
Jul. 12, 1975	4:48 AM	VIR	Dec. 23, 1975	6:51 AM	VIR	Jun. 8, 1976	4:00 PM	SCO
Jul. 14, 1975	6:51 AM	LIB	Dec. 25, 1975	10:17 AM	LIB	Jun. 10, 1976	5:36 PM	SAG
Jul. 16, 1975	8:34 PM	SCO	Dec. 27, 1975	1:43 PM	SCO	Jun. 12, 1976	8:34 PM	CAP
Jul. 18, 1975	1:43 PM	SAG	Dec. 29, 1975	5:09 PM	SAG	Jun. 14, 1976	10:17 PM	AQU
Jul. 20, 1975	10:09 PM	CAP	Dec. 31, 1975	8:34 PM	CAP	Jun. 17, 1976	8:00 AM	PIS
Jul. 23, 1975	8:00 AM	AQU	Jan. 3, 1976	3:42 AM	AQU	Jun. 19, 1976	6:00 PM	ARI
Jul. 25, 1975	6:00 PM	PIS	Jan. 5, 1976	11:05 AM	PIS	Jun. 22, 1976	6:00 AM	TAU
Jul. 28, 1975	6:00 AM	ARI	Jan. 7, 1976	12:00 AM	ARI	Jun. 24, 1976	6:00 PM	GEM
Jul. 30, 1975	6:00 PM	TAU	Jan. 10, 1976	3:16 PM	TAU	Jun. 27, 1976	3:42 AM	CAN
Aug. 2, 1975	6:00 AM	GEM	Jan. 15, 1976	7:23 AM	CAN	Jun. 29, 1976	10:17 AM	LEO
Aug. 4, 1975	10:17 AM	CAN	Jan. 17, 1976	12:00 PM	LEO	Jul. 1, 1976	6:28 PM	VIR
Aug. 6, 1975	12:48 PM	LEO	Jan. 19, 1976	3:26 PM	VIR	Jul. 3, 1976	8:34 PM	LIB
Aug. 8, 1975	2:24 PM	VIR	Jan. 21, 1976	5:09 PM	LIB	Jul. 5, 1976	12:00 AM	SCO
Aug. 10, 1975	12:00 PM	LIB	Jan. 23, 1976	6:51 PM	SCO	Jul. 8, 1976	1:43 AM	SAG
Aug. 12, 1975	2:24 PM	SCO	Jan. 25, 1976	10:17 PM	SAG	Jul. 10, 1976	5:09 AM	CAP
Aug. 14, 1975	6:51 PM	SAG	Jan. 28, 1976	3:26 AM	CAP	Jul. 12, 1976	8:34 AM	AQU
Aug. 17, 1975	3:42 AM	CAP	Jan. 30, 1976	11:05 AM	AQU	Jul. 14, 1976	2:46 PM	PIS
Aug. 19, 1975	2:00 PM	AQU	Feb. 1, 1976	10:00 PM	PIS	Jul. 17, 1976	2:00 AM	ARI
Aug. 21, 1975	12:00 AM	PIS	Feb. 4, 1976	8:00 AM	ARI	Jul. 19, 1976	2:00 PM	TAU
Aug. 24, 1975	12:00 AM	ARI	Feb. 6, 1976	8:00 PM	TAU	Jul. 22, 1976	2:00 AM	GEM
Aug. 27, 1975	2:00 AM	TAU	Feb. 9, 1976	10:00 AM	GEM	Jul. 24, 1976	2:00 PM	CAN
Aug. 29, 1975	2:00 PM	GEM	Feb. 11, 1976	8:00 PM	CAN	Jul. 26, 1976	8:18 PM	LEO
Aug. 31, 1975	8:18 PM	CAN	Feb. 13, 1976	10:17 PM	LEO	Jul. 30, 1976	12:00 AM	VIR
Sep. 2, 1975	12:00 AM	LEO	Feb. 17, 1976	12:00 AM	LIB	Jul. 31, 1976	1:43 AM	LIB
Sep. 4, 1975	12:00 AM	VIR	Feb. 20, 1976	1:43 AM	SCO	Aug. 2, 1976	5:09 AM	SCO
Sep. 6, 1975	12:00 AM	LIB	Feb. 22, 1976	3:26 AM	SAG	Aug. 4, 1976	8:34 AM	SAG
Sep. 8, 1975	12:00 AM	SCO	Feb. 24, 1976	8:34 AM	CAP	Aug. 6, 1976	12:00 PM	CAP
Sep. 11, 1975	1:43 AM	SAG	Feb. 26, 1976	4:37 PM	AQU	Aug. 8, 1976	3:26 PM	AQU
Sep. 13, 1975	9:14 AM	CAP	Feb. 29, 1976	4:00 AM	PIS	Aug. 10, 1976	12:00 AM	PIS
Sep. 15, 1975	8:00 AM	AQU	Mar. 2, 1976	4:00 AM	ARI	Aug. 13, 1976	10:00 AM	ARI
Sep. 18, 1975	6:00 AM	PIS	Mar. 5, 1976	4:00 AM	TAU	Aug. 15, 1976	10:00 PM	TAU
Sep. 20, 1975	6:00 AM	ARI	Mar. 7, 1976	4:00 PM	GEM	Aug. 18, 1976	10:00 AM	GEM
Sep. 23, 1975	8:00 AM	TAU	Mar. 10, 1976	4:00 AM	CAN	Aug. 20, 1976	10:00 PM	CAN
Sep. 25, 1975	8:00 PM	GEM	Mar. 12, 1976	8:34 AM	LEO	Aug. 23, 1976	3:26 AM	LEO
Sep. 28, 1975	3:42 AM	CAN	Mar. 14, 1976	12:00 PM	VIR	Aug. 25, 1976	8:34 AM	VIR
Sep. 30, 1975	8:34 AM	LEO	Mar. 16, 1976	11:12 AM	LIB	Aug. 27, 1976	10:17 AM	LIB
Oct. 2, 1975	12:00 PM	VIR	Mar. 18, 1976	9:36 AM	SCO	Aug. 29, 1976	12:00 PM	SCO
Oct. 4, 1975	11:12 AM	LIB	Mar. 20, 1976	12:00 PM	SAG	Aug. 31, 1976	1:43 PM	SAG
Oct. 6, 1975	9:36 AM	SCO	Mar. 22, 1976	3:26 PM	CAP	Sep. 2, 1976	5:09 PM	CAP
Oct. 8, 1975	12:00 PM	SAG	Mar. 24, 1976	10:09 PM	AQU	Sep. 4, 1976	12:00 AM	AQU
Oct. 10, 1975	3:26 PM	CAP	Mar. 27, 1976	10:00 AM	PIS	Sep. 7, 1976	7:23 AM	PIS
Oct. 13, 1975	2:00 AM	AQU	Mar. 29, 1976	10:00 PM	ARI	Sep. 9, 1976	6:00 PM	ARI
Oct. 15, 1975	12:00 PM	PIS	Apr. 1, 1976	10:00 AM	TAU	Sep. 12, 1976	6:00 AM	TAU
Oct. 18, 1975	2:00 AM	ARI	Apr. 6, 1976	9:14 AM	CAN	Sep. 14, 1976	6:00 PM	GEM

Date	Time	Moon	Date	Time	Moon	Date	Time	Moon
Sep. 17, 1976	6:00 AM	C A N	Feb. 28, 1977	2:00 AM	C A N	Aug. 8, 1977	6:00 AM	G E M
Sep. 19, 1976	2:46 PM	L E O	Mar. 2, 1977	12:00 PM	L E O	Aug. 10, 1977	6:00 PM	C A N
Sep. 21, 1976	8:18 PM	V I R	Mar. 4, 1977	3:26 PM	V I R	Aug. 13, 1977	6:00 AM	L E O
Sep. 23, 1976	8:34 PM	L I B	Mar. 6, 1977	8:34 PM	L I B	Aug. 15, 1977	12:55 PM	V I R
Sep. 25, 1976	7:12 PM	S C O	Mar. 8, 1977	10:17 PM	S C O	Aug. 17, 1977	8:18 PM	L I B
Sep. 27, 1976	7:12 PM	S A G	Mar. 10, 1977	12:00 AM	S A G	Aug. 19, 1977	12:00 AM	S C O
Sep. 29, 1976	8:48 PM	C A P	Mar. 13, 1977	1:36 AM	C A P	Aug. 22, 1977	3:26 AM	S A G
Oct. 2, 1976	5:32 AM	A Q U	Mar. 15, 1977	6:51 AM	A Q U	Aug. 24, 1977	6:51 AM	C A P
Oct. 4, 1976	12:55 PM	P I S	Mar. 17, 1977	12:55 PM	P I S	Aug. 26, 1977	8:34 AM	A Q U
Oct. 6, 1976	12:00 AM	A R I	Mar. 19, 1977	8:18 PM	A R I	Aug. 28, 1977	12:00 PM	P I S
Oct. 9, 1976	12:00 PM	T A U	Mar. 22, 1977	8:00 AM	T A U	Aug. 30, 1977	3:26 PM	A R I
Oct. 12, 1976	2:11 AM	G E M	Mar. 24, 1977	8:00 PM	G E M	Sep. 2, 1977	2:00 AM	T A U
Oct. 14, 1976	2:00 PM	C A N	Mar. 27, 1977	10:00 AM	C A N	Sep. 4, 1977	2:00 PM	G E M
Oct. 16, 1976	10:09 PM	L E O	Mar. 29, 1977	6:28 PM	L E O	Sep. 7, 1977	2:00 AM	C A N
Oct. 19, 1976	3:26 AM	V I R	Apr. 1, 1977	1:43 AM	V I R	Sep. 9, 1977	2:00 PM	L E O
Oct. 21, 1976	6:51 AM	L I B	Apr. 3, 1977	5:09 AM	L I B	Sep. 11, 1977	12:00 AM	V I R
Oct. 23, 1976	6:24 AM	S C O	Apr. 5, 1977	6:24 AM	S C O	Sep. 14, 1977	3:42 AM	L I B
Oct. 25, 1976	6:24 AM	S A G	Apr. 7, 1977	6:24 AM	S A G	Sep. 16, 1977	6:51 AM	S C O
Oct. 27, 1976	6:24 AM	C A P	Apr. 9, 1977	8:00 AM	C A P	Sep. 18, 1977	10:17 AM	S A G
Oct. 29, 1976	10:17 AM	A Q U	Apr. 11, 1977	12:00 PM	A Q U	Sep. 20, 1977	12:00 PM	C A P
Oct. 31, 1976	6:28 PM	P I S	Apr. 13, 1977	6:28 PM	P I S	Sep. 22, 1977	3:26 PM	A Q U
Nov. 3, 1976	6:00 AM	A R I	Apr. 16, 1977	4:00 AM	A R I	Sep. 24, 1977	6:51 PM	P I S
Nov. 5, 1976	6:00 PM	T A U	Apr. 18, 1977	4:00 PM	T A U	Sep. 27, 1977	1:51 AM	A R I
Nov. 8, 1976	8:44 AM	G E M	Apr. 21, 1977	4:00 AM	G E M	Sep. 29, 1977	9:14 AM	T A U
Nov. 10, 1976	8:00 PM	C A N	Apr. 23, 1977	4:00 PM	C A N	Oct. 1, 1977	10:00 PM	G E M
Nov. 13, 1976	6:00 AM	L E O	Apr. 26, 1977	4:00 AM	L E O	Oct. 4, 1977	10:00 AM	C A N
Nov. 15, 1976	12:55 PM	V I R	Apr. 28, 1977	11:05 AM	V I R	Oct. 6, 1977	10:00 PM	L E O
Nov. 17, 1976	5:09 PM	L I B	Apr. 30, 1977	3:26 PM	L I B	Oct. 9, 1977	7:23 AM	V I R
Nov. 19, 1976	6:51 PM	S C O	May. 2, 1977	6:51 PM	S C O	Oct. 11, 1977	12:00 PM	L I B
Nov. 21, 1976	5:36 PM	S A G	May. 4, 1977	5:36 PM	S A G	Oct. 13, 1977	3:26 PM	S C O
Nov. 23, 1976	4:00 PM	C A P	May. 6, 1977	4:00 PM	C A P	Oct. 15, 1977	4:00 PM	S A G
Nov. 25, 1976	5:36 PM	A Q U	May. 8, 1977	5:36 PM	A Q U	Oct. 17, 1977	6:51 PM	C A P
Nov. 28, 1976	1:51 AM	P I S	May. 10, 1977	10:17 PM	P I S	Oct. 19, 1977	8:34 PM	A Q U
Nov. 30, 1976	12:00 PM	A R I	May. 13, 1977	10:00 AM	A R I	Oct. 22, 1977	1:51 AM	P I S
Dec. 2, 1976	12:00 AM	T A U	May. 15, 1977	10:00 PM	T A U	Oct. 24, 1977	9:14 AM	A R I
Dec. 5, 1976	2:00 PM	G E M	May. 18, 1977	10:00 AM	G E M	Oct. 26, 1977	4:37 PM	T A U
Dec. 8, 1976	2:00 AM	C A N	May. 20, 1977	10:00 PM	C A N	Oct. 29, 1977	6:00 AM	G E M
Dec. 10, 1976	12:00 PM	L E O	May. 23, 1977	10:00 AM	L E O	Oct. 31, 1977	6:00 PM	C A N
Dec. 12, 1976	6:28 PM	V I R	May. 25, 1977	6:28 PM	V I R	Nov. 3, 1977	6:00 AM	L E O
Dec. 17, 1976	3:26 AM	S C O	May. 28, 1977	1:51 AM	L I B	Nov. 5, 1977	6:00 PM	V I R
Dec. 19, 1976	3:12 AM	S A G	May. 30, 1977	3:12 AM	S C O	Nov. 7, 1977	12:00 AM	L I B
Dec. 21, 1976	3:12 AM	C A P	Jun. 1, 1977	3:12 AM	S A G	Nov. 10, 1977	1:43 AM	S C O
Dec. 23, 1976	4:48 AM	A Q U	Jun. 3, 1977	3:12 AM	C A P	Nov. 12, 1977	1:36 AM	S A G
Dec. 25, 1976	11:05 AM	P I S	Jun. 5, 1977	3:12 AM	A Q U	Nov. 14, 1977	1:36 AM	C A P
Dec. 27, 1976	6:28 PM	A R I	Jun. 7, 1977	6:51 AM	P I S	Nov. 16, 1977	3:26 AM	A Q U
Dec. 30, 1976	8:00 AM	T A U	Jun. 9, 1977	2:46 AM	A R I	Nov. 18, 1977	6:51 AM	P I S
Jan. 1, 1977	8:00 PM	G E M	Jun. 12, 1977	2:00 AM	T A U	Nov. 20, 1977	2:46 PM	A R I
Jan. 4, 1977	8:00 AM	C A N	Jun. 14, 1977	4:00 PM	G E M	Nov. 22, 1977	10:09 PM	T A U
Jan. 6, 1977	4:37 PM	L E O	Jun. 17, 1977	4:00 AM	C A N	Nov. 25, 1977	12:00 PM	G E M
Jan. 8, 1977	12:00 AM	V I R	Jun. 19, 1977	4:00 PM	L E O	Nov. 27, 1977	12:00 AM	C A N
Jan. 11, 1977	5:09 AM	L I B	Jun. 22, 1977	2:00 AM	V I R	Nov. 30, 1977	12:00 PM	L E O
Jan. 13, 1977	10:17 AM	S C O	Jun. 24, 1977	9:14 AM	L I B	Dec. 2, 1977	12:00 AM	V I R
Jan. 15, 1977	11:12 AM	S A G	Jun. 26, 1977	12:00 PM	S C O	Dec. 5, 1977	10:00 AM	L I B
Jan. 17, 1977	12:48 PM	C A P	Jun. 28, 1977	3:26 PM	S A G	Dec. 7, 1977	12:00 PM	S C O
Jan. 19, 1977	5:09 PM	A Q U	Jun. 30, 1977	2:24 PM	C A P	Dec. 9, 1977	12:48 PM	S A G
Jan. 21, 1977	6:51 PM	P I S	Jul. 2, 1977	12:48 PM	A Q U	Dec. 11, 1977	12:48 PM	C A P
Jan. 24, 1977	3:42 AM	A R I	Jul. 4, 1977	2:24 PM	P I S	Dec. 13, 1977	11:12 AM	A Q U
Jan. 26, 1977	4:00 PM	T A U	Jul. 6, 1977	8:34 PM	A R I	Dec. 15, 1977	12:48 PM	P I S
Jan. 29, 1977	4:00 AM	G E M	Jul. 9, 1977	10:00 AM	T A U	Dec. 17, 1977	8:18 PM	A R I
Jan. 31, 1977	4:00 PM	C A N	Jul. 11, 1977	10:00 PM	G E M	Dec. 20, 1977	6:00 AM	T A U
Feb. 3, 1977	2:00 AM	L E O	Jul. 14, 1977	10:00 AM	C A N	Dec. 22, 1977	6:00 PM	G E M
Feb. 5, 1977	7:23 AM	V I R	Jul. 16, 1977	10:00 PM	L E O	Dec. 25, 1977	6:00 AM	C A N
Feb. 7, 1977	12:55 PM	L I B	Jul. 19, 1977	8:00 AM	V I R	Dec. 27, 1977	6:00 PM	L E O
Feb. 9, 1977	3:26 PM	S C O	Jul. 21, 1977	2:46 PM	L I B	Dec. 30, 1977	6:00 AM	V I R
Feb. 11, 1977	6:51 PM	S A G	Jul. 23, 1977	8:18 PM	S C O	Jan. 1, 1978	2:46 PM	L I B
Feb. 13, 1977	8:34 PM	C A P	Jul. 25, 1977	10:17 PM	S A G	Jan. 3, 1978	10:09 PM	S C O
Feb. 15, 1977	12:00 AM	A Q U	Jul. 27, 1977	10:24 PM	C A P	Jan. 5, 1978	10:24 PM	S A G
Feb. 18, 1977	5:09 AM	P I S	Jul. 31, 1977	12:00 AM	A Q U	Jan. 7, 1978	12:00 AM	C A P
Feb. 20, 1977	12:55 PM	A R I	Aug. 1, 1977	1:43 AM	P I S	Jan. 9, 1978	12:00 AM	A Q U
Feb. 22, 1977	12:00 AM	T A U	Aug. 3, 1977	6:51 AM	A R I	Jan. 11, 1978	10:24 PM	P I S
Feb. 25, 1977	12:00 PM	G E M	Aug. 5, 1977	6:00 PM	T A U	Jan. 14, 1978	3:26 AM	A R I

157

Date	Time	Moon	Date	Time	Moon	Date	Time	Moon
Jan. 16, 1978	11:05 AM	TAU	Jun. 29, 1978	9:14 AM	TAU	Dec. 10, 1978	11:05 AM	TAU
Jan. 18, 1978	12:00 AM	GEM	Jul. 1, 1978	6:28 PM	GEM	Dec. 12, 1978	6:28 PM	GEM
Jan. 21, 1978	12:00 PM	CAN	Jul. 4, 1978	8:00 AM	CAN	Dec. 15, 1978	3:42 AM	CAN
Jan. 24, 1978	2:00 AM	LEO	Jul. 6, 1978	8:00 PM	LEO	Dec. 17, 1978	4:00 PM	LEO
Jan. 26, 1978	12:00 PM	VIR	Jul. 9, 1978	10:00 AM	VIR	Dec. 20, 1978	6:00 AM	VIR
Jan. 28, 1978	8:18 PM	LIB	Jul. 11, 1978	10:00 PM	LIB	Dec. 22, 1978	6:00 PM	LIB
Jan. 31, 1978	3:42 AM	SCO	Jul. 14, 1978	5:32 AM	SCO	Dec. 25, 1978	1:51 AM	SCO
Feb. 2, 1978	8:34 AM	SAG	Jul. 16, 1978	8:34 AM	SAG	Dec. 27, 1978	6:51 AM	SAG
Feb. 4, 1978	9:36 AM	CAP	Jul. 18, 1978	9:36 AM	CAP	Dec. 29, 1978	8:00 AM	CAP
Feb. 6, 1978	9:36 AM	AQU	Jul. 20, 1978	7:30 AM	AQU	Dec. 31, 1978	8:00 AM	AQU
Feb. 8, 1978	9:36 AM	PIS	Jul. 22, 1978	8:00 AM	PIS	Jan. 2, 1979	8:00 AM	PIS
Feb. 10, 1978	1:43 PM	ARI	Jul. 24, 1978	10:17 AM	ARI	Jan. 4, 1979	10:17 AM	ARI
Feb. 12, 1978	8:18 PM	TAU	Jul. 26, 1978	4:37 PM	TAU	Jan. 6, 1979	4:37 PM	TAU
Feb. 15, 1978	8:00 AM	GEM	Jul. 29, 1978	1:51 AM	GEM	Jan. 8, 1979	12:00 AM	GEM
Feb. 17, 1978	8:00 PM	CAN	Jul. 31, 1978	2:00 PM	CAN	Jan. 11, 1979	12:00 PM	CAN
Feb. 20, 1978	8:00 AM	LEO	Aug. 3, 1978	4:22 AM	LEO	Jan. 13, 1979	12:00 AM	LEO
Feb. 22, 1978	8:00 PM	VIR	Aug. 5, 1978	4:00 PM	VIR	Jan. 16, 1979	12:00 PM	VIR
Feb. 25, 1978	3:42 AM	LIB	Aug. 8, 1978	1:51 AM	LIB	Jan. 18, 1979	12:00 AM	LIB
Feb. 27, 1978	8:34 AM	SCO	Aug. 10, 1978	11:05 AM	SCO	Jan. 21, 1979	12:00 PM	SCO
Mar. 1, 1978	1:43 PM	SAG	Aug. 12, 1978	6:28 PM	SAG	Jan. 23, 1979	6:28 PM	SAG
Mar. 3, 1978	5:09 PM	CAP	Aug. 14, 1978	5:36 PM	CAP	Jan. 25, 1979	8:34 PM	CAP
Mar. 5, 1978	5:36 PM	AQU	Aug. 16, 1978	7:12 PM	AQU	Jan. 27, 1979	7:12 PM	AQU
Mar. 7, 1978	7:12 PM	PIS	Aug. 18, 1978	7:12 PM	PIS	Jan. 29, 1979	7:12 PM	PIS
Mar. 9, 1978	12:00 AM	ARI	Aug. 20, 1978	7:12 PM	ARI	Jan. 31, 1979	8:34 PM	ARI
Mar. 12, 1978	5:09 AM	TAU	Aug. 23, 1978	1:51 AM	TAU	Feb. 2, 1979	10:17 PM	TAU
Mar. 14, 1978	2:46 PM	GEM	Aug. 25, 1978	9:14 AM	GEM	Feb. 5, 1979	5:32 AM	GEM
Mar. 17, 1978	4:00 AM	CAN	Aug. 27, 1978	6:28 PM	CAN	Feb. 7, 1979	6:00 PM	CAN
Mar. 19, 1978	4:00 PM	LEO	Aug. 30, 1978	10:00 AM	LEO	Feb. 10, 1979	6:00 AM	LEO
Mar. 22, 1978	1:51 AM	VIR	Sep. 1, 1978	10:00 PM	VIR	Feb. 12, 1979	6:00 PM	VIR
Mar. 24, 1978	11:05 AM	LIB	Sep. 4, 1978	7:23 AM	LIB	Feb. 15, 1979	6:00 AM	LIB
Mar. 26, 1978	3:26 PM	SCO	Sep. 6, 1978	4:37 PM	SCO	Feb. 17, 1979	6:00 PM	SCO
Mar. 28, 1978	6:51 PM	SAG	Sep. 8, 1978	12:00 AM	SAG	Feb. 22, 1979	5:09 AM	CAP
Mar. 30, 1978	10:17 PM	CAP	Sep. 11, 1978	1:43 AM	CAP	Feb. 24, 1979	6:51 AM	AQU
Apr. 2, 1978	1:43 AM	AQU	Sep. 13, 1978	3:12 AM	AQU	Feb. 26, 1979	6:24 PM	PIS
Apr. 4, 1978	3:26 AM	PIS	Sep. 15, 1978	4:48 AM	PIS	Feb. 28, 1979	6:51 AM	ARI
Apr. 6, 1978	8:34 AM	ARI	Sep. 17, 1978	6:51 AM	ARI	Mar. 2, 1979	8:34 AM	TAU
Apr. 8, 1978	2:46 PM	TAU	Sep. 19, 1978	10:17 AM	TAU	Mar. 4, 1979	2:46 PM	GEM
Apr. 13, 1978	12:00 AM	CAN	Sep. 21, 1978	3:26 PM	GEM	Mar. 6, 1979	10:09 PM	CAN
Apr. 15, 1978	12:00 AM	LEO	Sep. 24, 1978	4:00 AM	CAN	Mar. 9, 1979	12:00 PM	LEO
Apr. 18, 1978	12:00 PM	VIR	Sep. 26, 1978	4:00 PM	LEO	Mar. 11, 1979	12:00 AM	VIR
Apr. 20, 1978	8:18 PM	LIB	Sep. 29, 1978	6:00 AM	VIR	Mar. 14, 1979	12:00 PM	LIB
Apr. 22, 1978	12:00 AM	SCO	Oct. 1, 1978	4:00 PM	LIB	Mar. 16, 1979	12:00 AM	SCO
Apr. 25, 1978	3:26 AM	SAG	Oct. 3, 1978	10:09 PM	SCO	Mar. 19, 1979	7:23 AM	SAG
Apr. 27, 1978	5:09 PM	CAP	Oct. 6, 1978	3:26 AM	SAG	Mar. 21, 1979	12:55 PM	CAP
Apr. 29, 1978	6:51 AM	AQU	Oct. 8, 1978	9:14 AM	CAP	Mar. 23, 1979	3:26 PM	AQU
May. 1, 1978	10:17 AM	PIS	Oct. 10, 1978	10:17 AM	AQU	Mar. 25, 1979	5:09 PM	PIS
May. 3, 1978	4:37 PM	ARI	Oct. 12, 1978	1:43 PM	PIS	Mar. 27, 1979	4:00 PM	ARI
May. 5, 1978	10:09 PM	TAU	Oct. 14, 1978	2:24 PM	ARI	Mar. 29, 1979	6:51 PM	TAU
May. 8, 1978	7:23 AM	GEM	Oct. 16, 1978	6:51 PM	TAU	Mar. 31, 1979	10:17 PM	GEM
May. 10, 1978	8:00 AM	CAN	Oct. 19, 1978	3:42 AM	GEM	Apr. 3, 1979	8:00 AM	CAN
May. 13, 1978	8:00 AM	LEO	Oct. 21, 1978	2:00 PM	CAN	Apr. 5, 1979	6:00 PM	LEO
May. 15, 1978	8:00 PM	VIR	Oct. 24, 1978	2:11 AM	LEO	Apr. 8, 1979	8:00 AM	VIR
May. 18, 1978	5:32 AM	LIB	Oct. 26, 1978	2:00 PM	VIR	Apr. 10, 1979	8:00 PM	LIB
May. 20, 1978	10:17 AM	SCO	Oct. 28, 1978	10:09 PM	LIB	Apr. 13, 1979	6:00 AM	SCO
May. 22, 1978	1:43 PM	SAG	Oct. 31, 1978	7:23 AM	SCO	Apr. 15, 1979	12:55 PM	SAG
May. 24, 1978	12:48 PM	CAP	Nov. 2, 1978	10:17 AM	SAG	Apr. 17, 1979	6:28 PM	CAP
May. 26, 1978	12:48 PM	AQU	Nov. 4, 1978	1:43 PM	CAP	Apr. 19, 1979	8:34 PM	AQU
May. 28, 1978	3:26 PM	PIS	Nov. 6, 1978	2:24 PM	AQU	Apr. 21, 1979	12:00 AM	PIS
May. 30, 1978	10:09 PM	ARI	Nov. 8, 1978	6:51 PM	PIS	Apr. 24, 1979	1:43 AM	ARI
Jun. 2, 1978	6:00 AM	TAU	Nov. 10, 1978	10:17 PM	ARI	Apr. 26, 1979	5:09 AM	TAU
Jun. 4, 1978	4:00 PM	GEM	Nov. 13, 1978	3:26 AM	TAU	Apr. 28, 1979	8:34 AM	GEM
Jun. 7, 1978	2:00 AM	CAN	Nov. 15, 1978	11:05 AM	GEM	Apr. 30, 1979	4:37 PM	CAN
Jun. 9, 1978	2:00 PM	LEO	Nov. 17, 1978	10:00 PM	CAN	May. 3, 1979	1:51 AM	LEO
Jun. 12, 1978	4:00 AM	VIR	Nov. 20, 1978	10:55 AM	LEO	May. 5, 1979	4:00 PM	VIR
Jun. 14, 1978	12:55 PM	LIB	Nov. 22, 1978	10:00 PM	VIR	May. 8, 1979	4:00 AM	LIB
Jun. 16, 1978	6:51 PM	SCO	Nov. 25, 1978	10:00 AM	LIB	May. 10, 1979	12:55 PM	SCO
Jun. 18, 1978	12:00 AM	SAG	Nov. 27, 1978	4:37 PM	SCO	May. 12, 1979	8:18 PM	SAG
Jun. 20, 1978	10:24 PM	CAP	Nov. 29, 1978	8:34 PM	SAG	May. 16, 1979	12:00 AM	CAP
Jun. 22, 1978	10:24 PM	AQU	Dec. 1, 1978	8:48 PM	CAP	May. 17, 1979	1:43 AM	AQU
Jun. 24, 1978	10:24 PM	PIS	Dec. 3, 1978	12:00 AM	AQU	May. 19, 1979	5:09 AM	PIS
Jun. 27, 1978	3:42 AM	ARI	Dec. 8, 1978	5:32 AM	ARI	May. 21, 1979	8:34 AM	ARI

Date	Time	Moon	Date	Time	Moon	Date	Time	Moon
May. 23, 1979	12:00 PM	TAU	Nov. 3, 1979	11:12 AM	TAU	Apr. 15, 1980	12:48 PM	TAU
May. 25, 1979	6:28 PM	GEM	Nov. 5, 1979	12:48 PM	GEM	Apr. 17, 1980	1:43 PM	GEM
May. 27, 1979	12:00 AM	CAN	Nov. 7, 1979	8:18 PM	CAN	Apr. 19, 1980	3:26 PM	CAN
May. 30, 1979	12:00 PM	LEO	Nov. 10, 1979	3:42 AM	LEO	Apr. 21, 1980	12:00 AM	LEO
Jun. 1, 1979	12:00 AM	VIR	Nov. 12, 1979	4:00 PM	VIR	Apr. 24, 1980	12:00 PM	VIR
Jun. 4, 1979	12:00 PM	LIB	Nov. 15, 1979	6:33 AM	LIB	Apr. 26, 1980	12:00 AM	LIB
Jun. 6, 1979	12:00 AM	SCO	Nov. 17, 1979	2:46 PM	SCO	Apr. 29, 1980	12:00 PM	SCO
Jun. 9, 1979	3:26 AM	SAG	Nov. 19, 1979	12:00 AM	SAG	May. 1, 1980	12:00 AM	SAG
Jun. 11, 1979	6:51 AM	CAP	Nov. 22, 1979	7:23 AM	CAP	May. 4, 1980	7:23 AM	CAP
Jun. 13, 1979	8:00 AM	AQU	Nov. 24, 1979	12:55 PM	AQU	May. 6, 1980	2:46 AM	AQU
Jun. 15, 1979	9:36 AM	PIS	Nov. 26, 1979	3:26 PM	PIS	May. 8, 1980	6:51 PM	PIS
Jun. 17, 1979	1:43 PM	ARI	Nov. 28, 1979	6:51 PM	ARI	May. 10, 1980	10:17 PM	ARI
Jun. 19, 1979	5:09 PM	TAU	Nov. 30, 1979	7:12 PM	TAU	May. 12, 1980	10:24 PM	TAU
Jun. 21, 1979	10:17 PM	GEM	Dec. 2, 1979	12:00 AM	GEM	May. 14, 1980	10:24 PM	GEM
Jun. 24, 1979	7:23 AM	CAN	Dec. 5, 1979	5:32 AM	CAN	May. 17, 1980	1:43 AM	CAN
Jun. 26, 1979	8:00 PM	LEO	Dec. 7, 1979	12:55 PM	LEO	May. 19, 1980	7:23 AM	LEO
Jun. 29, 1979	8:44 AM	VIR	Dec. 9, 1979	12:00 AM	VIR	May. 21, 1980	4:37 PM	VIR
Jul. 1, 1979	8:00 PM	LIB	Dec. 12, 1979	3:16 PM	LIB	May. 24, 1980	8:44 AM	LIB
Jul. 4, 1979	8:00 AM	SCO	Dec. 15, 1979	2:00 AM	SCO	May. 26, 1980	8:00 PM	SCO
Jul. 6, 1979	2:46 PM	SAG	Dec. 17, 1979	9:14 AM	SAG	May. 29, 1980	5:32 AM	SAG
Jul. 8, 1979	5:09 PM	CAP	Dec. 19, 1979	1:43 PM	CAP	May. 31, 1980	2:46 PM	CAP
Jul. 10, 1979	5:36 PM	AQU	Dec. 21, 1979	6:51 PM	AQU	Jun. 2, 1980	6:51 PM	AQU
Jul. 12, 1979	5:36 PM	PIS	Dec. 23, 1979	8:34 PM	PIS	Jun. 5, 1980	1:51 AM	PIS
Jul. 14, 1979	8:34 PM	ARI	Dec. 25, 1979	12:00 AM	ARI	Jun. 7, 1980	5:09 AM	ARI
Jul. 16, 1979	8:48 PM	TAU	Dec. 28, 1979	3:26 AM	TAU	Jun. 9, 1980	6:51 AM	TAU
Jul. 19, 1979	5:32 AM	GEM	Dec. 30, 1979	6:51 AM	GEM	Jun. 11, 1980	8:34 AM	GEM
Jul. 21, 1979	4:00 PM	CAN	Jan. 1, 1980	12:00 PM	CAN	Jun. 13, 1980	12:00 PM	CAN
Jul. 24, 1979	2:00 AM	LEO	Jan. 3, 1980	8:18 PM	LEO	Jun. 15, 1980	3:26 PM	LEO
Jul. 26, 1979	2:00 PM	VIR	Jan. 6, 1980	7:23 AM	VIR	Jun. 18, 1980	1:51 AM	VIR
Jul. 29, 1979	4:22 AM	LIB	Jan. 8, 1980	12:00 AM	LIB	Jun. 20, 1980	2:00 PM	LIB
Jul. 31, 1979	4:00 PM	SCO	Jan. 11, 1980	10:00 AM	SCO	Jun. 23, 1980	4:00 AM	SCO
Aug. 5, 1979	3:26 AM	CAP	Jan. 13, 1980	6:28 PM	SAG	Jun. 25, 1980	12:55 PM	SAG
Aug. 7, 1979	5:09 AM	AQU	Jan. 18, 1980	3:26 AM	AQU	Jun. 27, 1980	10:09 PM	CAP
Aug. 9, 1979	3:00 AM	PIS	Jan. 20, 1980	5:09 AM	PIS	Jun. 30, 1980	3:42 AM	AQU
Aug. 11, 1979	3:12 AM	ARI	Jan. 22, 1980	4:48 AM	ARI	Jul. 2, 1980	6:51 AM	PIS
Aug. 13, 1979	6:51 AM	TAU	Jan. 24, 1980	8:34 AM	TAU	Jul. 4, 1980	10:17 AM	ARI
Aug. 15, 1979	10:17 AM	GEM	Jan. 26, 1980	12:00 PM	GEM	Jul. 6, 1980	11:12 AM	TAU
Aug. 17, 1979	10:00 PM	CAN	Jan. 28, 1980	8:18 PM	CAN	Jul. 8, 1980	3:26 PM	GEM
Aug. 20, 1979	8:00 AM	LEO	Jan. 31, 1980	6:00 AM	LEO	Jul. 10, 1980	6:51 PM	CAN
Aug. 22, 1979	8:00 PM	VIR	Feb. 2, 1980	4:00 PM	VIR	Jul. 13, 1980	1:51 AM	LEO
Aug. 25, 1979	10:55 AM	LIB	Feb. 5, 1980	6:33 AM	LIB	Jul. 15, 1980	12:00 PM	VIR
Aug. 27, 1979	10:00 PM	SCO	Feb. 7, 1980	6:00 PM	SCO	Jul. 17, 1980	10:00 PM	LIB
Aug. 30, 1979	8:00 AM	SAG	Feb. 10, 1980	3:42 AM	SAG	Jul. 20, 1980	12:00 PM	SCO
Sep. 1, 1979	12:00 PM	CAP	Feb. 12, 1980	11:05 AM	CAP	Jul. 22, 1980	12:00 AM	SAG
Sep. 3, 1979	3:26 PM	AQU	Feb. 14, 1980	3:26 PM	AQU	Jul. 25, 1980	7:23 AM	CAP
Sep. 5, 1979	2:24 PM	PIS	Feb. 16, 1980	2:24 PM	PIS	Jul. 27, 1980	12:55 PM	AQU
Sep. 7, 1979	2:24 PM	ARI	Feb. 18, 1980	2:24 PM	ARI	Jul. 29, 1980	12:48 PM	PIS
Sep. 9, 1979	2:24 PM	TAU	Feb. 20, 1980	2:24 PM	TAU	Jul. 31, 1980	5:09 PM	ARI
Sep. 11, 1979	6:51 PM	GEM	Feb. 22, 1980	6:51 PM	GEM	Aug. 2, 1980	6:51 PM	TAU
Sep. 14, 1979	1:51 AM	CAN	Feb. 25, 1980	1:51 AM	CAN	Aug. 4, 1980	8:34 PM	GEM
Sep. 16, 1979	2:00 PM	LEO	Feb. 27, 1980	12:00 PM	LEO	Aug. 7, 1980	1:43 AM	CAN
Sep. 19, 1979	2:00 AM	VIR	Feb. 29, 1980	10:00 PM	VIR	Aug. 9, 1980	9:14 AM	LEO
Sep. 21, 1979	5:27 PM	LIB	Mar. 3, 1980	12:00 PM	LIB	Aug. 11, 1980	8:00 PM	VIR
Sep. 24, 1979	1:51 AM	SCO	Mar. 5, 1980	12:00 AM	SCO	Aug. 14, 1980	6:00 AM	LIB
Sep. 26, 1979	2:00 PM	SAG	Mar. 8, 1980	12:00 PM	SAG	Aug. 16, 1980	9:49 PM	SCO
Sep. 28, 1979	8:18 PM	CAP	Mar. 10, 1980	8:18 PM	CAP	Aug. 19, 1980	8:00 AM	SAG
Sep. 30, 1979	12:00 AM	AQU	Mar. 12, 1980	12:00 AM	AQU	Aug. 21, 1980	6:00 PM	CAP
Oct. 3, 1979	1:43 AM	PIS	Mar. 15, 1980	1:36 AM	PIS	Aug. 23, 1980	8:34 PM	AQU
Oct. 5, 1979	1:36 AM	ARI	Mar. 17, 1980	1:36 AM	ARI	Aug. 25, 1980	12:00 AM	PIS
Oct. 7, 1979	1:36 AM	TAU	Mar. 19, 1980	1:36 AM	TAU	Aug. 27, 1980	12:00 AM	ARI
Oct. 9, 1979	3:26 AM	GEM	Mar. 21, 1980	3:26 AM	GEM	Aug. 29, 1980	12:00 AM	TAU
Oct. 11, 1979	8:34 AM	CAN	Mar. 23, 1980	6:51 AM	CAN	Sep. 1, 1980	3:26 AM	GEM
Oct. 13, 1979	6:28 PM	LEO	Mar. 25, 1980	6:00 PM	LEO	Sep. 3, 1980	6:51 AM	CAN
Oct. 16, 1979	8:00 AM	VIR	Mar. 28, 1980	4:00 AM	VIR	Sep. 5, 1980	2:46 PM	LEO
Oct. 18, 1979	10:00 PM	LIB	Mar. 30, 1980	6:00 PM	LIB	Sep. 8, 1980	2:00 AM	VIR
Oct. 21, 1979	10:00 AM	SCO	Apr. 2, 1980	6:00 AM	SCO	Sep. 10, 1980	2:00 PM	LIB
Oct. 23, 1979	8:00 PM	SAG	Apr. 4, 1980	6:00 PM	SAG	Sep. 13, 1980	2:00 AM	SCO
Oct. 26, 1979	1:51 AM	CAP	Apr. 7, 1980	1:51 AM	CAP	Sep. 15, 1980	2:00 PM	SAG
Oct. 28, 1979	7:23 AM	AQU	Apr. 9, 1980	9:14 AM	AQU	Sep. 20, 1980	7:23 AM	AQU
Oct. 30, 1979	10:17 AM	PIS	Apr. 11, 1980	12:00 PM	PIS	Sep. 22, 1980	10:17 AM	PIS
Nov. 1, 1979	12:00 PM	ARI	Apr. 13, 1980	12:48 PM	ARI	Sep. 24, 1980	11:12 AM	ARI

Date	Time	Moon	Date	Time	Moon	Date	Time	Moon
Sep. 26, 1980	9:36 AM	T A U	Mar. 9, 1981	11:12 AM	T A U	Aug. 22, 1981	5:09 PM	GEM
Sep. 28, 1980	9:36 AM	GEM	Mar. 11, 1981	1:43 PM	GEM	Aug. 24, 1981	6:51 PM	CAN
Sep. 30, 1980	1:43 PM	CAN	Mar. 13, 1981	3:26 PM	CAN	Aug. 26, 1981	10:17 PM	LEO
Oct. 2, 1980	8:18 PM	LEO	Mar. 15, 1981	10:09 PM	LEO	Aug. 29, 1981	3:26 AM	V I R
Oct. 5, 1980	8:00 AM	V I R	Mar. 18, 1981	5:32 AM	V I R	Aug. 31, 1981	11:05 AM	L I B
Oct. 7, 1980	8:00 AM	L I B	Mar. 20, 1981	2:46 PM	L I B	Sep. 2, 1981	8:18 PM	SCO
Oct. 10, 1980	8:00 AM	SCO	Mar. 23, 1981	4:00 AM	SCO	Sep. 5, 1981	10:00 AM	SAG
Oct. 12, 1980	8:00 PM	SAG	Mar. 25, 1981	4:00 PM	SAG	Sep. 7, 1981	10:00 PM	CAP
Oct. 15, 1980	8:00 AM	CAP	Mar. 28, 1981	3:42 AM	CAP	Sep. 10, 1981	10:00 AM	AQU
Oct. 17, 1980	6:00 PM	AQU	Mar. 30, 1981	4:00 PM	AQU	Sep. 12, 1981	4:37 PM	P I S
Oct. 19, 1980	10:09 PM	P I S	Apr. 1, 1981	6:51 PM	P I S	Sep. 14, 1981	6:51 PM	A R I
Oct. 21, 1980	8:48 PM	A R I	Apr. 3, 1981	10:17 PM	A R I	Sep. 16, 1981	7:12 PM	T A U
Oct. 23, 1980	8:48 PM	T A U	Apr. 5, 1981	8:48 PM	T A U	Sep. 18, 1981	8:48 PM	GEM
Oct. 25, 1980	8:48 PM	GEM	Apr. 7, 1981	8:48 PM	GEM	Sep. 20, 1981	10:24 PM	CAN
Oct. 27, 1980	8:48 PM	CAN	Apr. 9, 1981	8:48 PM	CAN	Sep. 23, 1981	5:32 AM	LEO
Oct. 30, 1980	3:42 AM	LEO	Apr. 12, 1981	3:42 AM	LEO	Sep. 25, 1981	11:05 AM	V I R
Nov. 1, 1980	2:00 PM	V I R	Apr. 14, 1981	11:05 AM	V I R	Sep. 27, 1981	6:28 PM	L I B
Nov. 4, 1980	2:00 AM	L I B	Apr. 16, 1981	8:18 PM	L I B	Sep. 30, 1981	6:00 AM	SCO
Nov. 6, 1980	2:00 PM	SCO	Apr. 19, 1981	10:00 AM	SCO	Oct. 2, 1981	6:00 PM	SAG
Nov. 9, 1980	2:00 AM	SAG	Apr. 24, 1981	12:00 PM	CAP	Oct. 5, 1981	6:00 AM	CAP
Nov. 11, 1980	2:00 PM	CAP	Apr. 26, 1981	8:18 PM	AQU	Oct. 7, 1981	6:00 PM	AQU
Nov. 13, 1980	12:00 AM	AQU	Apr. 29, 1981	5:32 AM	P I S	Oct. 10, 1981	1:51 AM	P I S
Nov. 16, 1980	3:26 PM	P I S	May. 1, 1981	8:34 AM	A R I	Oct. 12, 1981	5:09 AM	A R I
Nov. 18, 1980	6:24 AM	A R I	May. 3, 1981	8:00 AM	T A U	Oct. 14, 1981	4:48 AM	T A U
Nov. 20, 1980	8:00 AM	T A U	May. 5, 1981	6:00 AM	GEM	Oct. 16, 1981	4:48 AM	GEM
Nov. 22, 1980	8:00 AM	GEM	May. 7, 1981	6:24 AM	CAN	Oct. 18, 1981	6:24 AM	CAN
Nov. 24, 1980	8:00 AM	CAN	May. 9, 1981	10:17 AM	LEO	Oct. 20, 1981	10:17 AM	LEO
Nov. 26, 1980	12:00 PM	LEO	May. 11, 1981	3:26 PM	V I R	Oct. 22, 1981	4:37 PM	V I R
Nov. 28, 1980	8:18 PM	V I R	May. 14, 1981	4:00 AM	L I B	Oct. 25, 1981	1:51 AM	L I B
Dec. 1, 1980	8:00 AM	L I B	May. 16, 1981	4:00 PM	SCO	Oct. 27, 1981	11:05 AM	SCO
Dec. 3, 1980	8:00 PM	SCO	May. 19, 1981	6:33 AM	SAG	Oct. 29, 1981	12:00 AM	SAG
Dec. 6, 1980	10:00 AM	SAG	May. 21, 1981	6:00 PM	CAP	Nov. 1, 1981	2:00 PM	CAP
Dec. 8, 1980	8:00 PM	CAP	May. 24, 1981	4:00 AM	AQU	Nov. 4, 1981	2:00 AM	AQU
Dec. 11, 1980	3:42 AM	AQU	May. 26, 1981	2:00 PM	P I S	Nov. 6, 1981	11:05 AM	P I S
Dec. 13, 1980	11:05 AM	P I S	May. 28, 1981	6:28 PM	A R I	Nov. 8, 1981	3:26 PM	A R I
Dec. 15, 1980	1:43 PM	A R I	May. 30, 1981	5:36 PM	T A U	Nov. 10, 1981	4:00 PM	T A U
Dec. 17, 1980	5:09 PM	T A U	Jun. 1, 1981	5:36 PM	GEM	Nov. 12, 1981	4:00 PM	GEM
Dec. 19, 1980	6:51 PM	GEM	Jun. 3, 1981	5:36 PM	CAN	Nov. 14, 1981	4:00 PM	CAN
Dec. 21, 1980	5:36 PM	CAN	Jun. 5, 1981	5:36 PM	LEO	Nov. 16, 1981	4:00 PM	LEO
Dec. 23, 1980	10:17 PM	LEO	Jun. 8, 1981	1:51 AM	V I R	Nov. 18, 1981	12:00 AM	V I R
Dec. 26, 1980	5:32 AM	V I R	Jun. 10, 1981	12:00 PM	L I B	Nov. 21, 1981	8:00 AM	L I B
Dec. 28, 1980	4:00 PM	L I B	Jun. 12, 1981	10:00 PM	SCO	Nov. 23, 1981	4:37 PM	SCO
Dec. 31, 1980	4:00 AM	SCO	Jun. 15, 1981	12:00 PM	SAG	Nov. 26, 1981	6:00 AM	SAG
Jan. 2, 1981	4:00 PM	SAG	Jun. 17, 1981	12:00 AM	CAP	Nov. 28, 1981	8:00 PM	CAP
Jan. 5, 1981	1:51 AM	CAP	Jun. 20, 1981	10:00 AM	AQU	Dec. 1, 1981	8:00 AM	AQU
Jan. 7, 1981	11:05 AM	AQU	Jun. 22, 1981	8:00 PM	P I S	Dec. 3, 1981	8:00 PM	P I S
Jan. 9, 1981	4:37 PM	P I S	Jun. 24, 1981	10:17 PM	A R I	Dec. 8, 1981	3:26 AM	T A U
Jan. 11, 1981	6:51 PM	A R I	Jun. 27, 1981	1:36 AM	T A U	Dec. 10, 1981	3:12 AM	GEM
Jan. 13, 1981	10:17 PM	T A U	Jun. 29, 1981	3:12 AM	GEM	Dec. 12, 1981	3:12 AM	CAN
Jan. 16, 1981	1:43 PM	GEM	Jul. 1, 1981	3:12 AM	CAN	Dec. 14, 1981	3:12 AM	LEO
Jan. 18, 1981	3:26 AM	CAN	Jul. 3, 1981	4:48 AM	LEO	Dec. 16, 1981	6:51 AM	V I R
Jan. 20, 1981	9:14 AM	LEO	Jul. 5, 1981	11:05 AM	V I R	Dec. 18, 1981	12:55 PM	L I B
Jan. 22, 1981	2:46 PM	V I R	Jul. 7, 1981	6:28 PM	L I B	Dec. 20, 1981	10:09 PM	SCO
Jan. 27, 1981	12:00 PM	SCO	Jul. 10, 1981	6:00 AM	SCO	Dec. 23, 1981	3:16 PM	SAG
Jan. 30, 1981	2:00 AM	SAG	Jul. 12, 1981	6:00 PM	SAG	Dec. 26, 1981	2:00 AM	CAP
Feb. 1, 1981	12:00 PM	CAP	Jul. 15, 1981	6:00 AM	CAP	Dec. 28, 1981	2:00 PM	AQU
Feb. 3, 1981	6:28 PM	AQU	Jul. 17, 1981	2:46 PM	AQU	Jan. 2, 1982	7:23 AM	A R I
Feb. 5, 1981	10:17 PM	P I S	Jul. 19, 1981	12:00 AM	P I S	Jan. 4, 1982	12:00 PM	T A U
Feb. 8, 1981	1:43 AM	A R I	Jul. 22, 1981	5:32 AM	A R I	Jan. 6, 1982	12:48 PM	GEM
Feb. 10, 1981	3:12 AM	T A U	Jul. 24, 1981	8:34 AM	T A U	Jan. 8, 1982	2:24 PM	CAN
Feb. 12, 1981	6:51 AM	GEM	Jul. 26, 1981	9:36 AM	GEM	Jan. 10, 1982	2:24 PM	LEO
Feb. 14, 1981	10:17 AM	CAN	Jul. 28, 1981	1:43 PM	CAN	Jan. 12, 1982	5:09 PM	V I R
Feb. 16, 1981	4:37 PM	LEO	Jul. 30, 1981	3:26 PM	LEO	Jan. 14, 1982	8:34 PM	L I B
Feb. 18, 1981	12:00 AM	V I R	Aug. 1, 1981	6:51 PM	V I R	Jan. 17, 1982	8:00 AM	SCO
Feb. 21, 1981	10:00 AM	L I B	Aug. 4, 1981	3:42 AM	L I B	Jan. 19, 1982	8:00 PM	SAG
Feb. 23, 1981	8:00 PM	SCO	Aug. 6, 1981	2:00 PM	SCO	Jan. 22, 1982	8:00 AM	CAP
Feb. 26, 1981	10:00 AM	SAG	Aug. 9, 1981	2:00 AM	SAG	Jan. 24, 1982	8:00 AM	AQU
Feb. 28, 1981	10:00 PM	CAP	Aug. 11, 1981	2:00 PM	CAP	Jan. 27, 1982	5:32 AM	P I S
Mar. 3, 1981	5:32 AM	AQU	Aug. 16, 1981	7:23 AM	P I S	Jan. 29, 1982	12:55 AM	A R I
Mar. 5, 1981	8:34 AM	P I S	Aug. 18, 1981	10:17 AM	A R I	Jan. 31, 1982	5:09 PM	T A U
Mar. 7, 1981	12:00 PM	A R I	Aug. 20, 1981	1:43 PM	T A U	Feb. 2, 1982	10:17 PM	GEM

160

Date	Time	Moon	Date	Time	Moon	Date	Time	Moon
Feb. 4, 1982	12:00 AM	CAN	Jul. 22, 1982	12:00 AM	VIR	Jan. 5, 1983	1:43 AM	LIB
Feb. 9, 1982	3:26 AM	VIR	Jul. 25, 1982	3:26 AM	LIB	Jan. 7, 1983	7:23 AM	SCO
Feb. 11, 1982	6:51 AM	LIB	Jul. 27, 1982	11:05 AM	SCO	Jan. 9, 1983	4:37 PM	SAG
Feb. 13, 1982	2:46 PM	SCO	Jul. 29, 1982	10:00 PM	SAG	Jan. 12, 1983	6:00 AM	CAP
Feb. 16, 1982	4:00 AM	SAG	Aug. 1, 1982	10:00 AM	CAP	Jan. 14, 1983	9:49 PM	AQU
Feb. 18, 1982	4:00 PM	CAP	Aug. 6, 1982	9:14 AM	PIS	Jan. 17, 1983	8:00 AM	PIS
Feb. 21, 1982	4:00 AM	AQU	Aug. 8, 1982	6:28 PM	ARI	Jan. 19, 1983	8:00 PM	ARI
Feb. 23, 1982	12:55 PM	PIS	Aug. 11, 1982	1:51 AM	TAU	Jan. 22, 1983	3:42 AM	TAU
Feb. 25, 1982	8:18 PM	ARI	Aug. 13, 1982	7:23 AM	GEM	Jan. 24, 1983	8:34 AM	GEM
Mar. 2, 1982	3:26 AM	GEM	Aug. 15, 1982	8:00 AM	CAN	Jan. 26, 1983	9:36 AM	CAN
Mar. 4, 1982	5:09 AM	CAN	Aug. 17, 1982	9:36 AM	LEO	Jan. 28, 1983	9:36 AM	LEO
Mar. 6, 1982	8:34 AM	LEO	Aug. 19, 1982	9:36 AM	VIR	Jan. 30, 1983	9:36 AM	VIR
Mar. 8, 1982	12:00 PM	VIR	Aug. 21, 1982	1:43 PM	LIB	Feb. 1, 1983	9:36 AM	LIB
Mar. 10, 1982	6:28 PM	LIB	Aug. 23, 1982	5:09 PM	SCO	Feb. 3, 1983	4:37 PM	SCO
Mar. 13, 1982	2:00 AM	SCO	Aug. 26, 1982	6:00 AM	SAG	Feb. 8, 1983	12:00 PM	CAP
Mar. 15, 1982	12:00 PM	SAG	Aug. 28, 1982	6:00 PM	CAP	Feb. 11, 1983	2:00 AM	AQU
Mar. 17, 1982	12:00 AM	CAP	Aug. 31, 1982	6:00 AM	AQU	Feb. 13, 1983	2:00 PM	PIS
Mar. 20, 1982	2:00 PM	AQU	Sep. 2, 1982	6:00 PM	PIS	Feb. 18, 1983	9:14 AM	TAU
Mar. 22, 1982	12:00 AM	PIS	Sep. 5, 1982	1:51 AM	ARI	Feb. 20, 1983	4:37 PM	GEM
Mar. 25, 1982	3:26 AM	ARI	Sep. 7, 1982	6:51 AM	TAU	Feb. 22, 1983	6:51 PM	CAN
Mar. 27, 1982	6:51 AM	TAU	Sep. 9, 1982	12:00 PM	GEM	Feb. 24, 1983	10:17 PM	LEO
Mar. 29, 1982	8:00 AM	GEM	Sep. 11, 1982	3:26 PM	CAN	Feb. 26, 1983	8:48 PM	VIR
Mar. 31, 1982	12:00 PM	CAN	Sep. 13, 1982	6:51 PM	LEO	Feb. 28, 1983	8:48 PM	LIB
Apr. 2, 1982	1:43 PM	LEO	Sep. 15, 1982	8:34 PM	VIR	Mar. 2, 1983	12:00 AM	SCO
Apr. 4, 1982	6:51 PM	VIR	Sep. 17, 1982	8:48 PM	LIB	Mar. 5, 1983	7:23 AM	SAG
Apr. 7, 1982	1:51 AM	LIB	Sep. 20, 1982	3:26 AM	SCO	Mar. 7, 1983	8:00 PM	CAP
Apr. 9, 1982	9:14 AM	SCO	Sep. 22, 1982	12:55 PM	SAG	Mar. 10, 1983	8:00 AM	AQU
Apr. 11, 1982	8:00 PM	SAG	Sep. 25, 1982	2:00 AM	CAP	Mar. 12, 1983	8:00 PM	PIS
Apr. 14, 1982	8:00 AM	CAP	Sep. 27, 1982	2:00 AM	AQU	Mar. 15, 1983	8:00 AM	ARI
Apr. 16, 1982	12:00 AM	AQU	Sep. 30, 1982	2:00 AM	PIS	Mar. 17, 1983	2:46 PM	TAU
Apr. 19, 1982	8:00 AM	PIS	Oct. 2, 1982	9:14 AM	ARI	Mar. 19, 1983	10:09 PM	GEM
Apr. 21, 1982	2:46 PM	ARI	Oct. 4, 1982	1:43 PM	TAU	Mar. 22, 1983	1:43 AM	CAN
Apr. 23, 1982	5:09 PM	TAU	Oct. 6, 1982	5:09 PM	GEM	Mar. 24, 1983	5:09 AM	LEO
Apr. 25, 1982	4:00 PM	GEM	Oct. 8, 1982	8:34 PM	CAN	Mar. 26, 1983	6:51 AM	VIR
Apr. 27, 1982	6:51 PM	CAN	Oct. 10, 1982	12:00 AM	LEO	Mar. 28, 1983	8:34 AM	LIB
Apr. 29, 1982	8:34 PM	LEO	Oct. 13, 1982	3:26 AM	VIR	Mar. 30, 1983	10:17 AM	SCO
May. 1, 1982	12:00 AM	VIR	Oct. 15, 1982	6:51 AM	LIB	Apr. 1, 1983	3:26 PM	SAG
May. 4, 1982	7:23 AM	LIB	Oct. 17, 1982	12:00 PM	SCO	Apr. 4, 1983	4:00 AM	CAP
May. 6, 1982	6:00 PM	SCO	Oct. 19, 1982	8:18 PM	SAG	Apr. 6, 1983	4:00 PM	AQU
May. 9, 1982	4:00 AM	SAG	Oct. 22, 1982	10:00 AM	CAP	Apr. 9, 1983	4:00 AM	PIS
May. 11, 1982	4:00 PM	CAP	Oct. 24, 1982	10:00 PM	AQU	Apr. 11, 1983	4:00 PM	ARI
May. 14, 1982	4:00 AM	AQU	Oct. 27, 1982	10:00 AM	PIS	Apr. 13, 1983	10:09 PM	TAU
May. 16, 1982	4:00 PM	PIS	Oct. 29, 1982	6:28 PM	ARI	Apr. 16, 1983	3:42 AM	GEM
May. 18, 1982	12:00 AM	ARI	Oct. 31, 1982	10:17 PM	TAU	Apr. 18, 1983	6:51 AM	CAN
May. 21, 1982	1:36 AM	TAU	Nov. 3, 1982	1:43 AM	GEM	Apr. 20, 1983	10:17 AM	LEO
May. 23, 1982	3:12 AM	GEM	Nov. 5, 1982	3:26 AM	CAN	Apr. 22, 1983	1:43 PM	VIR
May. 25, 1982	3:12 AM	CAN	Nov. 7, 1982	5:09 AM	LEO	Apr. 24, 1983	2:24 PM	LIB
May. 27, 1982	3:12 AM	LEO	Nov. 9, 1982	8:34 AM	VIR	Apr. 26, 1983	6:51 PM	SCO
May. 29, 1982	6:51 AM	VIR	Nov. 11, 1982	2:46 PM	LIB	Apr. 29, 1983	1:51 AM	SAG
May. 31, 1982	12:55 PM	LIB	Nov. 13, 1982	8:18 PM	SCO	May. 1, 1983	11:05 AM	CAP
Jun. 2, 1982	8:18 PM	SCO	Nov. 16, 1982	6:00 AM	SAG	May. 3, 1983	12:00 AM	AQU
Jun. 5, 1982	10:00 AM	SAG	Nov. 18, 1982	6:00 PM	CAP	May. 6, 1983	12:00 PM	PIS
Jun. 7, 1982	10:00 PM	CAP	Nov. 21, 1982	6:00 AM	AQU	May. 8, 1983	12:00 AM	ARI
Jun. 10, 1982	1:05 PM	AQU	Nov. 23, 1982	6:00 PM	PIS	May. 11, 1983	7:23 AM	TAU
Jun. 12, 1982	12:00 PM	PIS	Nov. 26, 1982	3:42 AM	ARI	May. 13, 1983	10:17 PM	GEM
Jun. 15, 1982	7:23 AM	ARI	Nov. 28, 1982	8:34 AM	TAU	May. 15, 1983	1:43 PM	CAN
Jun. 17, 1982	12:00 PM	TAU	Nov. 30, 1982	12:00 PM	GEM	May. 17, 1983	2:24 PM	LEO
Jun. 19, 1982	12:48 PM	GEM	Dec. 2, 1982	11:12 AM	CAN	May. 19, 1983	6:51 PM	VIR
Jun. 21, 1982	12:48 PM	CAN	Dec. 4, 1982	1:43 PM	LEO	May. 21, 1983	10:17 PM	LIB
Jun. 23, 1982	12:48 PM	LEO	Dec. 6, 1982	12:48 PM	VIR	May. 24, 1983	3:42 AM	SCO
Jun. 25, 1982	3:26 PM	VIR	Dec. 8, 1982	8:18 PM	LIB	May. 26, 1983	11:05 AM	SAG
Jun. 27, 1982	8:18 PM	LIB	Dec. 11, 1982	1:51 AM	SCO	May. 28, 1983	6:28 PM	CAP
Jun. 30, 1982	3:42 AM	SCO	Dec. 13, 1982	11:05 AM	SAG	May. 31, 1983	8:00 AM	AQU
Jul. 2, 1982	4:00 PM	SAG	Dec. 15, 1982	12:00 AM	CAP	Jun. 2, 1983	8:00 PM	PIS
Jul. 5, 1982	4:00 AM	CAP	Dec. 18, 1982	12:00 PM	AQU	Jun. 5, 1983	8:00 AM	ARI
Jul. 7, 1982	4:00 PM	AQU	Dec. 21, 1982	2:00 AM	PIS	Jun. 7, 1983	4:37 PM	TAU
Jul. 10, 1982	3:42 AM	PIS	Dec. 23, 1982	2:00 PM	ARI	Jun. 9, 1983	8:34 PM	GEM
Jul. 12, 1982	12:55 PM	ARI	Dec. 25, 1982	8:18 PM	TAU	Jun. 11, 1983	12:00 AM	CAN
Jul. 14, 1982	8:18 PM	TAU	Dec. 29, 1982	10:24 PM	CAN	Jun. 13, 1983	10:24 PM	LEO
Jul. 16, 1982	12:00 AM	GEM	Dec. 31, 1982	10:24 PM	LEO	Jun. 18, 1983	3:26 AM	LIB
Jul. 20, 1982	12:00 AM	LEO	Jan. 2, 1983	10:24 PM	VIR	Jun. 20, 1983	9:14 AM	SCO

161

Date	Time	Moon	Date	Time	Moon	Date	Time	Moon
Jun. 22, 1983	4:37 PM	S A G	Dec. 3, 1983	4:37 PM	S A G	May. 17, 1984	6:51 PM	C A P
Jun. 25, 1983	4:00 AM	C A P	Dec. 5, 1983	8:34 PM	C A P	May. 20, 1984	3:42 AM	A Q U
Jun. 27, 1983	5:27 PM	A Q U	Dec. 8, 1983	10:00 AM	A Q U	May. 22, 1984	4:00 PM	P I S
Jun. 30, 1983	4:00 AM	P I S	Dec. 10, 1983	10:00 PM	P I S	May. 25, 1984	4:00 AM	A R I
Jul. 2, 1983	4:00 PM	A R I	Dec. 13, 1983	10:00 AM	A R I	May. 27, 1984	4:00 PM	T A U
Jul. 5, 1983	2:00 AM	T A U	Dec. 15, 1983	10:00 PM	T A U	Jun. 1, 1984	7:23 AM	C A N
Jul. 7, 1983	7:23 AM	G E M	Dec. 18, 1983	3:42 AM	G E M	Jun. 3, 1984	10:17 AM	L E O
Jul. 9, 1983	8:00 AM	C A N	Dec. 20, 1983	6:51 AM	C A N	Jun. 5, 1984	12:48 PM	V I R
Jul. 11, 1983	7:30 AM	L E O	Dec. 22, 1983	8:00 AM	L E O	Jun. 7, 1984	5:09 PM	L I B
Jul. 13, 1983	8:00 AM	V I R	Dec. 24, 1983	9:36 AM	V I R	Jun. 9, 1984	8:34 PM	S C O
Jul. 15, 1983	10:17 AM	L I B	Dec. 26, 1983	12:00 PM	L I B	Jun. 11, 1984	10:17 PM	S A G
Jul. 17, 1983	1:43 PM	S C O	Dec. 28, 1983	3:26 PM	S C O	Jun. 14, 1984	5:32 AM	C A P
Jul. 19, 1983	10:09 PM	S A G	Dec. 30, 1983	8:34 PM	S A G	Jun. 16, 1984	2:00 PM	A Q U
Jul. 22, 1983	10:00 AM	C A P	Jan. 2, 1984	8:00 AM	C A P	Jun. 18, 1984	12:00 AM	P I S
Jul. 24, 1983	10:00 PM	A Q U	Jan. 4, 1984	6:00 PM	A Q U	Jun. 21, 1984	12:00 PM	A R I
Jul. 27, 1983	10:00 AM	P I S	Jan. 7, 1984	6:00 AM	P I S	Jun. 23, 1984	12:00 AM	T A U
Jul. 29, 1983	10:00 PM	A R I	Jan. 9, 1984	6:00 PM	A R I	Jun. 26, 1984	10:00 AM	G E M
Aug. 1, 1983	10:00 AM	T A U	Jan. 12, 1984	6:00 AM	T A U	Jun. 28, 1984	4:37 PM	C A N
Aug. 3, 1983	4:37 PM	G E M	Jan. 14, 1984	12:55 PM	G E M	Jun. 30, 1984	6:51 PM	L E O
Aug. 5, 1983	6:51 PM	C A N	Jan. 16, 1984	5:09 PM	C A N	Jul. 2, 1984	7:12 PM	V I R
Aug. 7, 1983	7:12 PM	L E O	Jan. 18, 1984	8:34 PM	L E O	Jul. 4, 1984	8:48 PM	L I B
Aug. 9, 1983	7:12 PM	V I R	Jan. 20, 1984	7:12 PM	V I R	Jul. 7, 1984	1:43 AM	S C O
Aug. 11, 1983	7:12 PM	L I B	Jan. 22, 1984	8:34 PM	L I B	Jul. 9, 1984	5:09 AM	S A G
Aug. 13, 1983	7:12 PM	S C O	Jan. 24, 1984	10:17 PM	S C O	Jul. 11, 1984	12:55 PM	C A P
Aug. 16, 1983	3:42 AM	S A G	Jan. 27, 1984	3:42 AM	S A G	Jul. 13, 1984	8:18 PM	A Q U
Aug. 18, 1983	4:00 PM	C A P	Jan. 29, 1984	2:00 PM	C A P	Jul. 16, 1984	8:00 AM	P I S
Aug. 21, 1983	4:00 AM	A Q U	Jan. 31, 1984	12:00 AM	A Q U	Jul. 18, 1984	8:00 PM	A R I
Aug. 23, 1983	4:00 PM	P I S	Feb. 3, 1984	12:00 PM	P I S	Jul. 21, 1984	8:00 AM	T A U
Aug. 26, 1983	4:00 AM	A R I	Feb. 6, 1984	2:11 AM	A R I	Jul. 23, 1984	8:00 PM	G E M
Aug. 28, 1983	4:00 PM	T A U	Feb. 8, 1984	2:00 PM	T A U	Jul. 28, 1984	3:26 AM	L E O
Aug. 30, 1983	10:09 PM	G E M	Feb. 10, 1984	12:00 AM	G E M	Jul. 30, 1984	4:48 PM	V I R
Sep. 2, 1983	3:26 AM	C A N	Feb. 13, 1984	3:26 AM	C A N	Aug. 1, 1984	4:48 AM	L I B
Sep. 4, 1983	4:48 AM	L E O	Feb. 15, 1984	6:51 AM	L E O	Aug. 3, 1984	6:51 AM	S C O
Sep. 6, 1983	4:30 AM	V I R	Feb. 17, 1984	4:30 AM	V I R	Aug. 5, 1984	10:17 AM	S A G
Sep. 8, 1983	4:48 AM	L I B	Feb. 19, 1984	4:48 AM	L I B	Aug. 7, 1984	6:28 PM	C A P
Sep. 10, 1983	6:51 AM	S C O	Feb. 21, 1984	4:48 AM	S C O	Aug. 10, 1984	4:00 AM	A Q U
Sep. 12, 1983	12:55 PM	S A G	Feb. 23, 1984	11:05 AM	S A G	Aug. 12, 1984	2:00 PM	P I S
Sep. 14, 1983	8:18 PM	C A P	Feb. 25, 1984	6:28 PM	C A P	Aug. 15, 1984	2:00 AM	A R I
Sep. 17, 1983	10:00 AM	A Q U	Feb. 28, 1984	6:00 AM	A Q U	Aug. 17, 1984	5:27 PM	T A U
Sep. 19, 1983	10:00 PM	P I S	Mar. 1, 1984	6:00 PM	P I S	Aug. 20, 1984	1:51 AM	G E M
Sep. 22, 1983	10:00 AM	A R I	Mar. 4, 1984	8:44 AM	A R I	Aug. 22, 1984	11:05 AM	C A N
Sep. 24, 1983	10:00 PM	T A U	Mar. 6, 1984	8:00 PM	T A U	Aug. 24, 1984	1:43 PM	L E O
Sep. 27, 1983	3:42 AM	G E M	Mar. 9, 1984	6:00 AM	G E M	Aug. 26, 1984	2:24 PM	V I R
Sep. 29, 1983	11:05 AM	C A N	Mar. 11, 1984	12:55 PM	C A N	Aug. 28, 1984	2:24 PM	L I B
Oct. 1, 1983	1:43 PM	L E O	Mar. 13, 1984	5:09 PM	L E O	Aug. 30, 1984	2:24 PM	S C O
Oct. 3, 1983	2:24 PM	V I R	Mar. 15, 1984	4:00 PM	V I R	Sep. 1, 1984	5:09 PM	S A G
Oct. 5, 1983	5:09 PM	L I B	Mar. 17, 1984	4:00 PM	L I B	Sep. 3, 1984	12:00 AM	C A P
Oct. 7, 1983	4:00 PM	S C O	Mar. 19, 1984	4:00 PM	S C O	Sep. 6, 1984	10:00 AM	A Q U
Oct. 9, 1983	8:34 PM	S A G	Mar. 21, 1984	6:51 PM	S A G	Sep. 8, 1984	8:00 PM	P I S
Oct. 12, 1983	6:00 AM	C A P	Mar. 24, 1984	1:51 AM	C A P	Sep. 11, 1984	8:00 AM	A R I
Oct. 14, 1983	2:46 PM	A Q U	Mar. 26, 1984	12:00 PM	A Q U	Sep. 13, 1984	12:00 AM	T A U
Oct. 17, 1983	6:00 AM	P I S	Mar. 28, 1984	12:00 AM	P I S	Sep. 16, 1984	10:00 AM	G E M
Oct. 19, 1983	6:00 AM	A R I	Mar. 31, 1984	3:16 PM	A R I	Sep. 18, 1984	6:28 PM	C A N
Oct. 22, 1983	1:51 AM	T A U	Apr. 5, 1984	12:00 PM	G E M	Sep. 22, 1984	12:00 AM	L E O
Oct. 24, 1983	11:05 AM	G E M	Apr. 7, 1984	6:28 PM	C A N	Sep. 23, 1984	1:43 AM	V I R
Oct. 26, 1983	4:37 PM	C A N	Apr. 12, 1984	1:36 AM	V I R	Sep. 26, 1984	12:00 AM	S C O
Oct. 28, 1983	6:51 PM	L E O	Apr. 14, 1984	1:36 AM	L I B	Sep. 29, 1984	1:43 AM	S A G
Oct. 30, 1983	10:17 PM	V I R	Apr. 16, 1984	3:26 AM	S C O	Oct. 1, 1984	7:23 AM	C A P
Nov. 4, 1983	3:26 AM	S C O	Apr. 18, 1984	5:09 AM	S A G	Oct. 3, 1984	4:00 PM	A Q U
Nov. 6, 1983	6:51 AM	S A G	Apr. 20, 1984	11:05 AM	C A P	Oct. 6, 1984	2:00 AM	P I S
Nov. 8, 1983	2:46 PM	C A P	Apr. 22, 1984	6:28 PM	A Q U	Oct. 8, 1984	2:00 PM	A R I
Nov. 11, 1983	2:00 AM	A Q U	Apr. 25, 1984	8:00 AM	P I S	Oct. 11, 1984	4:00 AM	T A U
Nov. 13, 1983	2:00 PM	P I S	Apr. 27, 1984	8:00 PM	A R I	Oct. 13, 1984	4:00 PM	G E M
Nov. 16, 1983	2:00 AM	A R I	Apr. 30, 1984	8:00 AM	T A U	Oct. 16, 1984	2:00 AM	C A N
Nov. 18, 1983	12:00 PM	T A U	May. 2, 1984	6:00 PM	G E M	Oct. 18, 1984	6:51 AM	L E O
Nov. 20, 1983	6:28 PM	G E M	May. 4, 1984	12:00 AM	C A N	Oct. 20, 1984	9:36 AM	V I R
Nov. 22, 1983	12:00 AM	C A N	May. 7, 1984	5:09 AM	L E O	Oct. 22, 1984	11:12 AM	L I B
Nov. 25, 1983	1:43 AM	L E O	May. 9, 1984	8:34 AM	V I R	Oct. 24, 1984	11:12 AM	S C O
Nov. 27, 1983	3:12 AM	V I R	May. 11, 1984	12:00 PM	L I B	Oct. 26, 1984	11:12 AM	S A G
Nov. 29, 1983	6:51 AM	L I B	May. 13, 1984	11:12 AM	S C O	Oct. 28, 1984	3:26 PM	C A P
Dec. 1, 1983	10:17 AM	S C O	May. 15, 1984	3:26 PM	S A G	Oct. 30, 1984	10:09 PM	A Q U

Date	Time	Moon	Date	Time	Moon	Date	Time	Moon
Nov. 2, 1984	7:23 AM	P I S	Apr. 17, 1985	6:00 PM	A R I	Oct. 1, 1985	2:00 AM	T A U
Nov. 4, 1984	12:00 AM	A R I	Apr. 20, 1985	6:00 AM	T A U	Oct. 3, 1985	2:00 PM	G E M
Nov. 7, 1984	10:00 AM	T A U	Apr. 22, 1985	6:00 PM	G E M	Oct. 6, 1985	4:00 AM	C A N
Nov. 9, 1984	10:00 PM	G E M	Apr. 25, 1985	6:00 AM	C A N	Oct. 8, 1985	2:00 PM	L E O
Nov. 12, 1984	5:32 AM	C A N	Apr. 27, 1985	2:46 PM	L E O	Oct. 10, 1985	5:09 PM	V I R
Nov. 14, 1984	12:00 PM	L E O	Apr. 29, 1985	10:09 PM	V I R	Oct. 12, 1985	7:12 PM	L I B
Nov. 16, 1984	5:09 PM	V I R	May. 1, 1985	12:00 AM	L I B	Oct. 14, 1985	8:48 PM	S C O
Nov. 18, 1984	8:34 PM	L I B	May. 3, 1985	10:24 PM	S C O	Oct. 16, 1985	7:12 PM	S A G
Nov. 20, 1984	8:48 PM	S C O	May. 5, 1985	10:24 PM	S A G	Oct. 18, 1985	10:17 PM	C A P
Nov. 22, 1984	12:00 AM	S A G	May. 7, 1985	10:24 PM	C A P	Oct. 21, 1985	1:43 AM	A Q U
Nov. 25, 1984	1:43 AM	C A P	May. 10, 1985	3:42 AM	A Q U	Oct. 23, 1985	9:14 AM	P I S
Nov. 27, 1984	7:23 AM	A Q U	May. 12, 1985	11:05 AM	P I S	Oct. 25, 1985	8:00 PM	A R I
Nov. 29, 1984	2:46 PM	P I S	May. 14, 1985	12:00 AM	A R I	Oct. 28, 1985	8:00 AM	T A U
Dec. 2, 1984	4:00 AM	A R I	May. 17, 1985	12:00 PM	T A U	Oct. 30, 1985	8:00 PM	G E M
Dec. 4, 1984	7:38 PM	T A U	May. 20, 1985	2:11 AM	G E M	Nov. 2, 1985	10:00 AM	C A N
Dec. 7, 1984	3:42 AM	G E M	May. 22, 1985	12:00 PM	C A N	Nov. 4, 1985	6:28 PM	L E O
Dec. 9, 1984	12:55 PM	C A N	May. 24, 1985	8:18 PM	L E O	Nov. 7, 1985	3:42 AM	V I R
Dec. 11, 1984	8:18 PM	L E O	May. 27, 1985	3:42 AM	V I R	Nov. 9, 1985	6:51 AM	L I B
Dec. 16, 1984	3:26 AM	L I B	May. 29, 1985	6:51 AM	L I B	Nov. 11, 1985	8:34 AM	S C O
Dec. 18, 1984	5:09 AM	S C O	May. 31, 1985	8:00 AM	S C O	Nov. 13, 1985	6:24 AM	S A G
Dec. 20, 1984	8:34 AM	S A G	Jun. 2, 1985	8:00 AM	S A G	Nov. 15, 1985	6:24 AM	C A P
Dec. 22, 1984	10:17 AM	C A P	Jun. 4, 1985	10:17 AM	C A P	Nov. 17, 1985	8:00 AM	A Q U
Dec. 24, 1984	3:26 AM	A Q U	Jun. 6, 1985	12:00 PM	A Q U	Nov. 19, 1985	1:43 PM	P I S
Dec. 27, 1984	2:00 AM	P I S	Jun. 8, 1985	8:18 PM	P I S	Nov. 22, 1985	2:00 AM	A R I
Dec. 29, 1984	12:00 PM	A R I	Jun. 11, 1985	6:00 AM	A R I	Nov. 24, 1985	2:00 PM	T A U
Jan. 1, 1985	2:00 AM	T A U	Jun. 13, 1985	6:00 PM	T A U	Nov. 27, 1985	4:22 AM	G E M
Jan. 3, 1985	2:00 PM	G E M	Jun. 16, 1985	8:00 AM	G E M	Nov. 29, 1985	4:00 PM	C A N
Jan. 5, 1985	12:00 AM	C A N	Jun. 18, 1985	8:00 PM	C A N	Dec. 2, 1985	2:00 AM	L E O
Jan. 8, 1985	1:43 AM	L E O	Jun. 21, 1985	1:51 AM	L E O	Dec. 4, 1985	12:00 PM	V I R
Jan. 10, 1985	5:09 AM	V I R	Jun. 23, 1985	9:14 AM	V I R	Dec. 6, 1985	4:37 PM	L I B
Jan. 12, 1985	8:34 AM	L I B	Jun. 25, 1985	12:00 PM	L I B	Dec. 8, 1985	6:51 PM	S C O
Jan. 14, 1985	9:36 AM	S C O	Jun. 27, 1985	3:26 PM	S C O	Dec. 10, 1985	5:36 PM	S A G
Jan. 16, 1985	1:43 PM	S A G	Jun. 29, 1985	4:00 PM	S A G	Dec. 12, 1985	5:36 PM	C A P
Jan. 18, 1985	6:51 PM	C A P	Jul. 1, 1985	8:34 PM	C A P	Dec. 14, 1985	5:36 PM	A Q U
Jan. 21, 1985	1:51 AM	A Q U	Jul. 3, 1985	10:17 PM	A Q U	Dec. 16, 1985	10:17 PM	P I S
Jan. 23, 1985	9:14 AM	P I S	Jul. 6, 1985	3:26 AM	P I S	Dec. 19, 1985	7:23 AM	A R I
Jan. 25, 1985	10:00 PM	A R I	Jul. 8, 1985	12:55 PM	A R I	Dec. 21, 1985	8:00 PM	T A U
Jan. 28, 1985	10:00 AM	T A U	Jul. 11, 1985	2:00 AM	T A U	Dec. 24, 1985	10:00 AM	G E M
Jan. 30, 1985	10:00 PM	G E M	Jul. 13, 1985	4:00 PM	G E M	Dec. 26, 1985	10:00 PM	C A N
Feb. 2, 1985	7:23 AM	C A N	Jul. 16, 1985	2:00 AM	C A N	Dec. 29, 1985	7:23 AM	L E O
Feb. 4, 1985	12:00 PM	L E O	Jul. 18, 1985	9:14 AM	L E O	Dec. 31, 1985	2:46 PM	V I R
Feb. 6, 1985	12:48 PM	V I R	Jul. 20, 1985	1:43 PM	V I R	Jan. 2, 1986	10:09 PM	L I B
Feb. 8, 1985	2:24 PM	L I B	Jul. 22, 1985	8:18 PM	L I B	Jan. 5, 1986	1:43 AM	S C O
Feb. 10, 1985	4:00 PM	S C O	Jul. 24, 1985	7:12 PM	S C O	Jan. 7, 1986	3:12 AM	S A G
Feb. 12, 1985	8:34 PM	S A G	Jul. 26, 1985	12:00 AM	S A G	Jan. 9, 1986	4:48 AM	C A P
Feb. 15, 1985	1:51 AM	C A P	Jul. 29, 1985	3:26 AM	C A P	Jan. 11, 1986	6:51 AM	A Q U
Feb. 17, 1985	9:14 AM	A Q U	Jul. 31, 1985	6:51 AM	A Q U	Jan. 13, 1986	8:34 AM	P I S
Feb. 19, 1985	4:37 PM	P I S	Aug. 2, 1985	12:00 PM	P I S	Jan. 15, 1986	4:37 PM	A R I
Feb. 22, 1985	4:00 AM	A R I	Aug. 4, 1985	12:00 AM	A R I	Jan. 18, 1986	4:00 AM	T A U
Feb. 24, 1985	7:38 PM	T A U	Aug. 7, 1985	10:00 AM	T A U	Jan. 20, 1986	4:00 PM	G E M
Feb. 27, 1985	6:00 AM	G E M	Aug. 12, 1985	9:14 AM	C A N	Jan. 23, 1986	6:00 AM	C A N
Mar. 1, 1985	6:00 PM	C A N	Aug. 14, 1985	6:28 PM	L E O	Jan. 25, 1986	4:00 PM	L E O
Mar. 3, 1985	12:00 AM	L E O	Aug. 16, 1985	10:17 PM	V I R	Jan. 27, 1986	10:09 PM	V I R
Mar. 7, 1985	12:00 AM	L I B	Aug. 21, 1985	3:26 AM	S C O	Jan. 30, 1986	3:42 AM	L I B
Mar. 9, 1985	12:00 AM	S C O	Aug. 23, 1985	5:09 AM	S A G	Feb. 1, 1986	6:51 AM	S C O
Mar. 12, 1985	1:36 AM	S A G	Aug. 25, 1985	8:34 AM	C A P	Feb. 3, 1986	10:17 AM	S A G
Mar. 14, 1985	7:23 AM	C A P	Aug. 27, 1985	1:43 PM	A Q U	Feb. 5, 1986	1:43 PM	C A P
Mar. 16, 1985	2:46 PM	A Q U	Aug. 29, 1985	10:09 PM	P I S	Feb. 7, 1986	3:26 PM	A Q U
Mar. 18, 1985	10:09 PM	P I S	Sep. 1, 1985	5:32 AM	A R I	Feb. 9, 1986	6:51 PM	P I S
Mar. 21, 1985	12:00 PM	A R I	Sep. 3, 1985	6:00 PM	T A U	Feb. 12, 1986	1:51 AM	A R I
Mar. 23, 1985	12:00 AM	T A U	Sep. 6, 1985	8:44 AM	G E M	Feb. 14, 1986	11:05 AM	T A U
Mar. 26, 1985	12:00 PM	G E M	Sep. 8, 1985	8:00 PM	C A N	Feb. 17, 1986	2:11 PM	G E M
Mar. 28, 1985	10:09 PM	C A N	Sep. 11, 1985	3:42 AM	L E O	Feb. 19, 1986	2:00 PM	C A N
Mar. 31, 1985	7:23 AM	L E O	Sep. 13, 1985	9:14 AM	V I R	Feb. 21, 1986	10:09 PM	L E O
Apr. 2, 1985	12:00 PM	V I R	Sep. 15, 1985	10:17 AM	L I B	Feb. 24, 1986	5:09 AM	V I R
Apr. 4, 1985	11:12 AM	L I B	Sep. 17, 1985	9:36 AM	S C O	Feb. 26, 1986	10:17 AM	L I B
Apr. 6, 1985	11:12 AM	S C O	Sep. 19, 1985	12:00 PM	S A G	Feb. 28, 1986	1:43 PM	S C O
Apr. 8, 1985	11:12 AM	S A G	Sep. 21, 1985	12:48 PM	C A P	Mar. 2, 1986	3:26 PM	S A G
Apr. 10, 1985	1:43 PM	C A P	Sep. 23, 1985	6:51 PM	A Q U	Mar. 4, 1986	6:51 PM	C A P
Apr. 12, 1985	8:18 PM	A Q U	Sep. 26, 1985	3:42 AM	P I S	Mar. 6, 1986	10:17 PM	A Q U
Apr. 15, 1985	6:00 AM	P I S	Sep. 28, 1985	2:00 PM	A R I	Mar. 9, 1986	3:26 AM	P I S

163

Date	Time	Moon	Date	Time	Moon	Date	Time	Moon
Mar. 11, 1986	11:05 AM	A R I	Aug. 22, 1986	7:23 AM	A R I	Feb. 2, 1987	3:26 AM	A R I
Mar. 13, 1986	10:00 PM	TAU	Aug. 24, 1986	4:00 PM	TAU	Feb. 4, 1987	9:14 AM	TAU
Mar. 16, 1986	10:00 AM	GEM	Aug. 27, 1986	2:00 AM	GEM	Feb. 6, 1987	6:28 PM	GEM
Mar. 18, 1986	10:00 PM	CAN	Aug. 29, 1986	2:00 PM	CAN	Feb. 9, 1987	8:00 AM	CAN
Mar. 21, 1986	10:00 AM	LEO	Sep. 1, 1986	2:00 AM	LEO	Feb. 11, 1987	10:00 PM	LEO
Mar. 23, 1986	4:37 PM	VIR	Sep. 3, 1986	11:05 AM	VIR	Feb. 14, 1987	7:23 AM	VIR
Mar. 25, 1986	6:51 PM	L I B	Sep. 5, 1986	6:28 PM	L I B	Feb. 16, 1987	4:37 PM	L I B
Mar. 27, 1986	10:17 PM	SCO	Sep. 7, 1986	12:00 AM	SCO	Feb. 19, 1987	1:51 AM	SCO
Mar. 29, 1986	8:48 PM	SAG	Sep. 10, 1986	1:43 AM	SAG	Feb. 21, 1987	5:09 AM	SAG
Mar. 31, 1986	10:24 PM	CAP	Sep. 12, 1986	5:09 AM	CAP	Feb. 23, 1987	8:00 AM	CAP
Apr. 3, 1986	3:26 AM	AQU	Sep. 14, 1986	6:51 AM	AQU	Feb. 25, 1987	9:36 AM	AQU
Apr. 5, 1986	8:34 AM	P I S	Sep. 16, 1986	10:17 AM	P I S	Feb. 27, 1987	12:00 PM	P I S
Apr. 7, 1986	8:00 PM	A R I	Sep. 18, 1986	4:37 PM	A R I	Mar. 1, 1987	1:43 PM	A R I
Apr. 10, 1986	3:42 AM	TAU	Sep. 20, 1986	10:09 PM	TAU	Mar. 3, 1987	5:09 PM	TAU
Apr. 12, 1986	4:00 PM	GEM	Sep. 23, 1986	10:00 AM	GEM	Mar. 6, 1987	3:42 AM	GEM
Apr. 15, 1986	6:00 AM	CAN	Sep. 25, 1986	10:00 PM	CAN	Mar. 8, 1987	4:00 PM	CAN
Apr. 17, 1986	6:00 PM	LEO	Sep. 28, 1986	10:00 AM	LEO	Mar. 11, 1987	4:00 AM	LEO
Apr. 20, 1986	1:51 AM	VIR	Sep. 30, 1986	10:00 PM	VIR	Mar. 13, 1987	4:00 PM	VIR
Apr. 22, 1986	5:09 AM	L I B	Oct. 3, 1986	1:43 AM	L I B	Mar. 15, 1987	12:00 AM	L I B
Apr. 24, 1986	6:24 AM	SCO	Oct. 5, 1986	5:09 AM	SCO	Mar. 18, 1987	7:23 AM	SCO
Apr. 26, 1986	6:24 AM	SAG	Oct. 7, 1986	8:34 AM	SAG	Mar. 20, 1987	12:55 PM	SAG
Apr. 28, 1986	8:34 AM	CAP	Oct. 9, 1986	10:17 AM	CAP	Mar. 22, 1987	3:26 PM	CAP
Apr. 30, 1986	10:17 AM	AQU	Oct. 11, 1986	11:12 AM	AQU	Mar. 24, 1987	5:09 PM	AQU
May. 2, 1986	1:43 PM	P I S	Oct. 13, 1986	6:28 PM	P I S	Mar. 26, 1987	8:34 PM	P I S
May. 7, 1986	12:00 PM	TAU	Oct. 15, 1986	12:00 AM	A R I	Mar. 28, 1987	10:17 PM	A R I
May. 9, 1986	12:00 AM	GEM	Oct. 18, 1986	7:23 AM	TAU	Mar. 31, 1987	5:32 AM	TAU
May. 12, 1986	12:00 PM	CAN	Oct. 20, 1986	6:00 PM	GEM	Apr. 2, 1987	12:55 PM	GEM
May. 14, 1986	12:00 AM	LEO	Oct. 23, 1986	6:00 AM	CAN	Apr. 4, 1987	12:00 AM	CAN
May. 17, 1986	9:14 AM	VIR	Oct. 25, 1986	9:49 PM	LEO	Apr. 7, 1987	12:00 PM	LEO
May. 19, 1986	4:37 PM	L I B	Oct. 28, 1986	6:00 AM	VIR	Apr. 9, 1987	10:09 PM	VIR
May. 21, 1986	6:51 PM	SCO	Oct. 30, 1986	12:55 PM	L I B	Apr. 12, 1987	9:14 AM	L I B
May. 23, 1986	5:36 PM	SAG	Nov. 1, 1986	3:26 PM	SCO	Apr. 14, 1987	1:43 PM	SCO
May. 25, 1986	5:36 PM	CAP	Nov. 3, 1986	4:00 PM	SAG	Apr. 16, 1987	6:51 PM	SAG
May. 27, 1986	5:36 PM	AQU	Nov. 5, 1986	4:00 PM	CAP	Apr. 18, 1987	8:34 PM	CAP
May. 29, 1986	8:34 PM	P I S	Nov. 7, 1986	6:51 PM	AQU	Apr. 20, 1987	8:48 PM	AQU
Jun. 1, 1986	5:32 AM	A R I	Nov. 9, 1986	10:17 PM	P I S	Apr. 23, 1987	1:43 AM	P I S
Jun. 3, 1986	2:46 PM	TAU	Nov. 12, 1986	5:32 AM	A R I	Apr. 25, 1987	7:23 AM	A R I
Jun. 6, 1986	6:00 AM	GEM	Nov. 14, 1986	12:55 PM	TAU	Apr. 27, 1987	12:55 PM	TAU
Jun. 8, 1986	6:00 PM	CAN	Nov. 17, 1986	2:00 AM	GEM	Apr. 29, 1987	8:18 PM	GEM
Jun. 11, 1986	6:00 AM	LEO	Nov. 19, 1986	2:00 PM	CAN	May. 2, 1987	8:00 AM	CAN
Jun. 13, 1986	6:00 PM	VIR	Nov. 22, 1986	2:00 AM	LEO	May. 4, 1987	8:00 PM	LEO
Jun. 15, 1986	12:00 AM	L I B	Nov. 24, 1986	2:00 PM	VIR	May. 7, 1987	10:00 AM	VIR
Jun. 18, 1986	3:26 AM	SCO	Nov. 26, 1986	10:09 PM	L I B	May. 9, 1987	8:00 PM	L I B
Jun. 20, 1986	4:48 AM	SAG	Nov. 29, 1986	1:43 AM	SCO	May. 14, 1987	3:26 AM	SAG
Jun. 22, 1986	3:00 AM	CAP	Dec. 1, 1986	3:12 AM	SAG	May. 16, 1987	3:12 AM	CAP
Jun. 24, 1986	3:12 AM	AQU	Dec. 3, 1986	1:30 AM	CAP	May. 18, 1987	5:09 AM	AQU
Jun. 26, 1986	6:51 AM	P I S	Dec. 5, 1986	1:36 AM	AQU	May. 20, 1987	6:51 PM	P I S
Jun. 28, 1986	12:55 PM	A R I	Dec. 7, 1986	5:09 AM	P I S	May. 22, 1987	12:55 PM	A R I
Jun. 30, 1986	12:00 AM	TAU	Dec. 9, 1986	11:05 AM	A R I	May. 24, 1987	8:18 PM	TAU
Jul. 3, 1986	12:00 PM	GEM	Dec. 11, 1986	6:28 PM	TAU	May. 27, 1987	6:00 AM	GEM
Jul. 5, 1986	12:00 AM	CAN	Dec. 14, 1986	8:00 AM	GEM	May. 29, 1987	4:00 PM	CAN
Jul. 8, 1986	12:00 PM	LEO	Dec. 16, 1986	8:00 PM	CAN	Jun. 1, 1987	4:00 AM	LEO
Jul. 10, 1986	8:18 PM	VIR	Dec. 19, 1986	8:00 AM	LEO	Jun. 3, 1987	4:00 PM	VIR
Jul. 13, 1986	5:32 AM	L I B	Dec. 21, 1986	8:00 PM	VIR	Jun. 6, 1987	4:00 AM	L I B
Jul. 15, 1986	10:17 AM	SCO	Dec. 24, 1986	5:32 AM	L I B	Jun. 8, 1987	11:05 AM	SCO
Jul. 17, 1986	1:43 PM	SAG	Dec. 26, 1986	12:55 PM	SCO	Jun. 10, 1987	1:43 PM	SAG
Jul. 19, 1986	2:24 PM	CAP	Dec. 28, 1986	3:26 PM	SAG	Jun. 12, 1987	12:48 PM	CAP
Jul. 21, 1986	2:24 PM	AQU	Dec. 30, 1986	2:24 PM	CAP	Jun. 14, 1987	12:48 PM	AQU
Jul. 23, 1986	2:24 PM	P I S	Jan. 1, 1987	12:48 PM	AQU	Jun. 16, 1987	12:48 PM	P I S
Jul. 25, 1986	10:09 PM	A R I	Jan. 3, 1987	12:48 PM	P I S	Jun. 18, 1987	5:09 PM	A R I
Jul. 28, 1986	5:32 AM	TAU	Jan. 5, 1987	5:09 PM	A R I	Jun. 21, 1987	2:00 AM	TAU
Jul. 30, 1986	6:00 PM	GEM	Jan. 8, 1987	1:51 AM	TAU	Jun. 23, 1987	12:00 PM	GEM
Aug. 2, 1986	8:44 AM	CAN	Jan. 10, 1987	2:00 PM	GEM	Jun. 25, 1987	10:00 PM	CAN
Aug. 4, 1986	4:37 PM	LEO	Jan. 13, 1987	2:00 AM	CAN	Jun. 28, 1987	10:00 AM	LEO
Aug. 7, 1986	3:42 AM	VIR	Jan. 15, 1987	2:00 PM	LEO	Jun. 30, 1987	12:00 AM	VIR
Aug. 9, 1986	11:05 AM	L I B	Jan. 18, 1987	2:00 AM	VIR	Jul. 3, 1987	12:00 PM	L I B
Aug. 11, 1986	3:26 PM	SCO	Jan. 20, 1987	11:05 AM	L I B	Jul. 5, 1987	6:28 PM	SCO
Aug. 13, 1986	8:34 PM	SAG	Jan. 22, 1987	8:18 PM	SCO	Jul. 11, 1987	9:00 PM	AQU
Aug. 15, 1986	8:48 PM	CAP	Jan. 26, 1987	12:00 AM	CAP	Jul. 13, 1987	10:24 PM	P I S
Aug. 17, 1986	10:24 PM	AQU	Jan. 28, 1987	12:00 AM	AQU	Jul. 16, 1987	1:43 AM	A R I
Aug. 20, 1986	1:43 AM	P I S	Jan. 30, 1987	12:00 AM	P I S	Jul. 18, 1987	7:23 AM	TAU

Date	Time	Moon	Date	Time	Moon	Date	Time	Moon
Jul. 20, 1987	2:46 PM	GEM	Dec. 29, 1987	7:23 AM	TAU	Jun. 12, 1988	1:43 PM	GEM
Jul. 23, 1987	4:00 AM	CAN	Dec. 31, 1987	2:46 PM	GEM	Jun. 14, 1988	10:09 PM	CAN
Jul. 25, 1987	4:00 PM	LEO	Jan. 3, 1988	2:00 AM	CAN	Jun. 17, 1988	8:00 AM	LEO
Jul. 28, 1987	6:00 AM	VIR	Jan. 5, 1988	12:00 PM	LEO	Jun. 19, 1988	8:00 PM	VIR
Jul. 30, 1987	6:00 PM	LIB	Jan. 8, 1988	2:00 AM	VIR	Jun. 22, 1988	8:00 AM	LIB
Aug. 2, 1987	1:51 AM	SCO	Jan. 10, 1988	2:00 PM	LIB	Jun. 24, 1988	8:00 PM	SCO
Aug. 4, 1987	6:51 AM	SAG	Jan. 15, 1988	7:23 AM	SAG	Jun. 27, 1988	3:42 AM	SAG
Aug. 6, 1987	10:17 AM	CAP	Jan. 17, 1988	10:17 AM	CAP	Jun. 29, 1988	6:51 AM	CAP
Aug. 8, 1987	9:36 AM	AQU	Jan. 19, 1988	9:36 AM	AQU	Jul. 1, 1988	8:00 AM	AQU
Aug. 10, 1987	9:36 AM	PIS	Jan. 21, 1988	8:00 AM	PIS	Jul. 3, 1988	10:17 AM	PIS
Aug. 12, 1987	9:36 AM	ARI	Jan. 23, 1988	10:17 AM	ARI	Jul. 5, 1988	12:00 PM	ARI
Aug. 14, 1987	1:43 PM	TAU	Jan. 25, 1988	2:46 PM	TAU	Jul. 7, 1988	3:26 PM	TAU
Aug. 16, 1987	10:09 PM	GEM	Jan. 27, 1988	8:18 PM	GEM	Jul. 9, 1988	10:09 PM	GEM
Aug. 19, 1987	10:00 AM	CAN	Jan. 30, 1988	8:00 AM	CAN	Jul. 12, 1988	6:00 AM	CAN
Aug. 21, 1987	10:00 PM	LEO	Feb. 1, 1988	8:00 PM	LEO	Jul. 14, 1988	4:00 PM	LEO
Aug. 24, 1987	12:00 PM	VIR	Feb. 4, 1988	8:00 AM	VIR	Jul. 17, 1988	4:00 AM	VIR
Aug. 26, 1987	12:00 AM	LIB	Feb. 6, 1988	8:00 PM	LIB	Jul. 19, 1988	4:00 PM	LIB
Aug. 29, 1987	7:23 AM	SCO	Feb. 9, 1988	8:00 AM	SCO	Jul. 22, 1988	4:00 AM	SCO
Aug. 31, 1987	2:46 PM	SAG	Feb. 11, 1988	6:00 PM	SAG	Jul. 24, 1988	12:55 PM	SAG
Sep. 2, 1987	8:18 PM	CAP	Feb. 13, 1988	6:51 PM	CAP	Jul. 26, 1988	5:09 PM	CAP
Sep. 4, 1987	8:34 PM	AQU	Feb. 15, 1988	10:17 PM	AQU	Jul. 28, 1988	5:36 PM	AQU
Sep. 6, 1987	7:12 PM	PIS	Feb. 17, 1988	6:00 PM	PIS	Jul. 30, 1988	5:36 PM	PIS
Sep. 8, 1987	7:12 PM	ARI	Feb. 19, 1988	7:12 PM	ARI	Aug. 1, 1988	5:36 PM	ARI
Sep. 10, 1987	12:00 AM	TAU	Feb. 21, 1988	10:17 PM	TAU	Aug. 3, 1988	7:12 PM	TAU
Sep. 13, 1987	7:23 AM	GEM	Feb. 24, 1988	3:42 AM	GEM	Aug. 6, 1988	1:43 AM	GEM
Sep. 15, 1987	6:00 PM	CAN	Feb. 26, 1988	2:00 PM	CAN	Aug. 8, 1988	12:00 PM	CAN
Sep. 18, 1987	6:00 AM	LEO	Feb. 29, 1988	2:00 AM	LEO	Aug. 10, 1988	10:00 PM	LEO
Sep. 20, 1987	6:00 PM	VIR	Mar. 2, 1988	2:00 PM	VIR	Aug. 13, 1988	10:00 AM	VIR
Sep. 23, 1987	6:00 AM	LIB	Mar. 5, 1988	2:00 AM	LIB	Aug. 15, 1988	10:00 PM	LIB
Sep. 25, 1987	12:55 PM	SCO	Mar. 7, 1988	2:00 PM	SCO	Aug. 18, 1988	12:00 PM	SCO
Sep. 27, 1987	8:18 PM	SAG	Mar. 9, 1988	12:00 AM	SAG	Aug. 20, 1988	10:00 PM	SAG
Sep. 29, 1987	12:00 AM	CAP	Mar. 12, 1988	3:26 AM	CAP	Aug. 23, 1988	3:42 AM	CAP
Oct. 2, 1987	3:26 AM	AQU	Mar. 14, 1988	6:51 AM	AQU	Aug. 25, 1988	4:48 AM	AQU
Oct. 4, 1987	5:09 AM	PIS	Mar. 16, 1988	6:24 AM	PIS	Aug. 27, 1988	4:48 AM	PIS
Oct. 6, 1987	6:51 AM	ARI	Mar. 18, 1988	6:24 AM	ARI	Aug. 29, 1988	4:48 AM	ARI
Oct. 8, 1987	10:17 AM	TAU	Mar. 20, 1988	8:34 AM	TAU	Aug. 31, 1988	4:48 AM	TAU
Oct. 10, 1987	4:37 PM	GEM	Mar. 22, 1988	12:00 PM	GEM	Sep. 2, 1988	8:34 AM	GEM
Oct. 13, 1987	2:00 AM	CAN	Mar. 24, 1988	8:18 PM	CAN	Sep. 4, 1988	4:37 PM	CAN
Oct. 15, 1987	2:00 PM	LEO	Mar. 27, 1988	8:00 AM	LEO	Sep. 7, 1988	4:00 AM	LEO
Oct. 18, 1987	2:00 AM	VIR	Mar. 29, 1988	8:00 PM	VIR	Sep. 9, 1988	4:00 PM	VIR
Oct. 20, 1987	2:00 PM	LIB	Apr. 1, 1988	10:00 AM	LIB	Sep. 12, 1988	4:00 AM	LIB
Oct. 22, 1987	8:18 PM	SCO	Apr. 3, 1988	8:00 PM	SCO	Sep. 14, 1988	6:00 PM	SCO
Oct. 25, 1987	1:43 AM	SAG	Apr. 6, 1988	3:42 AM	SAG	Sep. 17, 1988	4:00 AM	SAG
Oct. 27, 1987	5:09 AM	CAP	Apr. 8, 1988	8:34 AM	CAP	Sep. 19, 1988	11:05 AM	CAP
Oct. 29, 1987	8:34 AM	AQU	Apr. 10, 1988	1:43 PM	AQU	Sep. 21, 1988	4:37 PM	AQU
Oct. 31, 1987	12:00 PM	PIS	Apr. 12, 1988	2:24 PM	PIS	Sep. 23, 1988	5:09 PM	PIS
Nov. 2, 1987	1:43 PM	ARI	Apr. 14, 1988	4:00 PM	ARI	Sep. 25, 1988	4:00 PM	ARI
Nov. 4, 1987	6:51 PM	TAU	Apr. 16, 1988	5:36 PM	TAU	Sep. 27, 1988	1:30 PM	TAU
Nov. 7, 1987	1:51 AM	GEM	Apr. 18, 1988	10:17 PM	GEM	Sep. 29, 1988	4:00 PM	GEM
Nov. 9, 1987	9:14 AM	CAN	Apr. 21, 1988	5:32 AM	CAN	Oct. 1, 1988	12:00 AM	CAN
Nov. 11, 1987	10:00 PM	LEO	Apr. 23, 1988	4:00 PM	LEO	Oct. 4, 1988	10:00 AM	LEO
Nov. 14, 1987	10:00 AM	VIR	Apr. 26, 1988	4:00 AM	VIR	Oct. 6, 1988	10:00 PM	VIR
Nov. 16, 1987	10:00 PM	LIB	Apr. 28, 1988	4:00 PM	LIB	Oct. 9, 1988	10:00 AM	LIB
Nov. 19, 1987	5:32 AM	SCO	May. 1, 1988	1:51 AM	SCO	Oct. 11, 1988	12:00 AM	SCO
Nov. 21, 1987	10:17 AM	SAG	May. 3, 1988	8:34 AM	SAG	Oct. 14, 1988	10:00 AM	SAG
Nov. 23, 1987	11:12 AM	CAP	May. 5, 1988	1:43 PM	CAP	Oct. 16, 1988	4:37 PM	CAP
Nov. 25, 1987	12:48 PM	AQU	May. 7, 1988	6:51 PM	AQU	Oct. 18, 1988	12:00 AM	AQU
Nov. 27, 1987	5:09 PM	PIS	May. 9, 1988	10:17 PM	PIS	Oct. 23, 1988	1:36 AM	ARI
Nov. 29, 1987	8:34 PM	ARI	May. 11, 1988	10:24 PM	ARI	Oct. 25, 1988	1:36 AM	TAU
Dec. 2, 1987	1:51 AM	TAU	May. 14, 1988	3:26 AM	TAU	Oct. 27, 1988	3:12 AM	GEM
Dec. 4, 1987	9:14 AM	GEM	May. 16, 1988	6:51 AM	GEM	Oct. 29, 1988	9:14 AM	CAN
Dec. 6, 1987	4:37 PM	CAN	May. 18, 1988	2:46 PM	CAN	Oct. 31, 1988	4:37 PM	LEO
Dec. 9, 1987	6:00 AM	LEO	May. 20, 1988	10:09 PM	LEO	Nov. 3, 1988	4:00 AM	VIR
Dec. 11, 1987	6:00 PM	VIR	May. 23, 1988	12:00 PM	VIR	Nov. 5, 1988	6:00 PM	LIB
Dec. 14, 1987	6:00 AM	LIB	May. 25, 1988	12:00 AM	LIB	Nov. 8, 1988	6:00 AM	SCO
Dec. 16, 1987	2:46 PM	SCO	May. 28, 1988	12:00 PM	SCO	Nov. 10, 1988	2:46 PM	SAG
Dec. 18, 1987	10:09 PM	SAG	May. 30, 1988	6:28 PM	SAG	Nov. 12, 1988	10:09 PM	CAP
Dec. 20, 1987	8:48 PM	CAP	Jun. 1, 1988	10:17 PM	CAP	Nov. 15, 1988	3:26 AM	AQU
Dec. 22, 1987	10:24 PM	AQU	Jun. 6, 1988	3:26 AM	PIS	Nov. 17, 1988	6:51 AM	PIS
Dec. 24, 1987	10:24 PM	PIS	Jun. 8, 1988	4:48 AM	ARI	Nov. 19, 1988	10:17 AM	ARI
Dec. 27, 1987	1:43 AM	ARI	Jun. 10, 1988	10:17 AM	TAU	Nov. 21, 1988	11:12 AM	TAU

Date	Time	Moon	Date	Time	Moon	Date	Time	Moon
Nov. 23, 1988	12:48 PM	GEM	May. 6, 1989	12:48 PM	GEM	Oct. 17, 1989	9:36 AM	GEM
Nov. 25, 1988	5:09 PM	CAN	May. 8, 1989	3:26 PM	CAN	Oct. 19, 1989	12:00 PM	CAN
Nov. 28, 1988	1:51 AM	LEO	May. 10, 1989	10:09 PM	LEO	Oct. 21, 1989	6:28 PM	LEO
Nov. 30, 1988	11:05 AM	VIR	May. 13, 1989	8:00 AM	VIR	Oct. 24, 1989	4:00 AM	VIR
Dec. 3, 1988	2:00 AM	LIB	May. 15, 1989	8:00 AM	LIB	Oct. 26, 1989	4:00 PM	LIB
Dec. 5, 1988	2:00 PM	SCO	May. 18, 1989	8:00 AM	SCO	Oct. 29, 1989	4:00 AM	SCO
Dec. 7, 1988	10:09 PM	SAG	May. 20, 1989	8:00 PM	SAG	Oct. 31, 1989	4:00 PM	SAG
Dec. 10, 1988	5:32 AM	CAP	May. 23, 1989	6:00 AM	CAP	Nov. 3, 1989	4:00 AM	CAP
Dec. 12, 1988	8:34 AM	AQU	May. 25, 1989	12:55 PM	AQU	Nov. 5, 1989	12:55 PM	AQU
Dec. 14, 1988	12:00 PM	PIS	May. 27, 1989	6:28 PM	PIS	Nov. 7, 1989	8:18 PM	PIS
Dec. 16, 1988	3:26 PM	ARI	May. 29, 1989	8:34 PM	ARI	Nov. 9, 1989	10:17 PM	ARI
Dec. 18, 1988	6:51 PM	TAU	May. 31, 1989	8:48 PM	TAU	Nov. 11, 1989	10:24 PM	TAU
Dec. 20, 1988	10:17 PM	GEM	Jun. 2, 1989	10:24 PM	GEM	Nov. 13, 1989	7:30 PM	GEM
Dec. 23, 1988	3:42 AM	CAN	Jun. 5, 1989	1:43 AM	CAN	Nov. 15, 1989	8:48 PM	CAN
Dec. 25, 1988	11:05 AM	LEO	Jun. 7, 1989	5:09 AM	LEO	Nov. 18, 1989	1:43 AM	LEO
Dec. 27, 1988	10:00 PM	VIR	Jun. 9, 1989	2:46 PM	VIR	Nov. 20, 1989	9:14 AM	VIR
Dec. 30, 1988	10:00 AM	LIB	Jun. 12, 1989	4:00 AM	LIB	Nov. 22, 1989	10:00 PM	LIB
Jan. 1, 1989	10:00 PM	SCO	Jun. 14, 1989	4:00 PM	SCO	Nov. 25, 1989	10:00 AM	SCO
Jan. 4, 1989	7:23 AM	SAG	Jun. 17, 1989	4:00 AM	SAG	Nov. 27, 1989	10:00 AM	SAG
Jan. 6, 1989	2:46 PM	CAP	Jun. 19, 1989	11:05 AM	CAP	Nov. 30, 1989	10:00 AM	CAP
Jan. 8, 1989	5:09 PM	AQU	Jun. 21, 1989	6:28 PM	AQU	Dec. 2, 1989	8:00 PM	AQU
Jan. 10, 1989	8:34 PM	PIS	Jun. 23, 1989	10:17 PM	PIS	Dec. 5, 1989	1:51 AM	PIS
Jan. 12, 1989	10:17 PM	ARI	Jun. 26, 1989	1:43 AM	ARI	Dec. 7, 1989	7:23 AM	ARI
Jan. 14, 1989	12:00 AM	TAU	Jun. 28, 1989	5:09 AM	TAU	Dec. 9, 1989	8:34 AM	TAU
Jan. 17, 1989	5:32 AM	GEM	Jun. 30, 1989	6:51 AM	GEM	Dec. 11, 1989	8:00 AM	GEM
Jan. 19, 1989	11:05 AM	CAN	Jul. 2, 1989	10:17 AM	CAN	Dec. 13, 1989	8:00 AM	CAN
Jan. 21, 1989	6:28 PM	LEO	Jul. 4, 1989	4:37 PM	LEO	Dec. 15, 1989	12:00 PM	LEO
Jan. 24, 1989	6:00 AM	VIR	Jul. 9, 1989	12:00 PM	LIB	Dec. 17, 1989	6:28 PM	VIR
Jan. 26, 1989	6:00 AM	LIB	Jul. 11, 1989	12:00 AM	SCO	Dec. 20, 1989	3:42 AM	LIB
Jan. 29, 1989	6:00 AM	SCO	Jul. 14, 1989	12:00 PM	SAG	Dec. 22, 1989	7:38 PM	SCO
Jan. 31, 1989	6:00 AM	SAG	Jul. 16, 1989	10:00 PM	CAP	Dec. 25, 1989	6:00 AM	SAG
Feb. 5, 1989	3:26 AM	AQU	Jul. 19, 1989	1:51 AM	AQU	Dec. 27, 1989	2:46 PM	CAP
Feb. 7, 1989	4:48 AM	PIS	Jul. 21, 1989	5:09 AM	PIS	Dec. 29, 1989	12:00 AM	AQU
Feb. 9, 1989	4:48 AM	ARI	Jul. 23, 1989	6:24 AM	ARI	Jan. 1, 1990	7:23 AM	PIS
Feb. 11, 1989	6:51 AM	TAU	Jul. 25, 1989	10:17 AM	TAU	Jan. 3, 1990	12:55 PM	ARI
Feb. 13, 1989	10:17 AM	GEM	Jul. 27, 1989	1:43 PM	GEM	Jan. 5, 1990	3:26 PM	TAU
Feb. 15, 1989	4:37 PM	CAN	Jul. 29, 1989	5:09 PM	CAN	Jan. 7, 1990	4:00 PM	GEM
Feb. 18, 1989	2:00 AM	LEO	Jul. 31, 1989	12:00 AM	LEO	Jan. 9, 1990	5:36 PM	CAN
Feb. 20, 1989	12:00 PM	VIR	Aug. 3, 1989	7:23 AM	VIR	Jan. 11, 1990	10:17 PM	LEO
Feb. 23, 1989	2:11 AM	LIB	Aug. 5, 1989	8:00 PM	LIB	Jan. 14, 1990	3:42 AM	VIR
Feb. 25, 1989	2:00 PM	SCO	Aug. 8, 1989	8:00 AM	SCO	Jan. 16, 1990	2:00 PM	LIB
Feb. 28, 1989	2:00 AM	SAG	Aug. 10, 1989	8:00 PM	SAG	Jan. 19, 1990	2:00 AM	SCO
Mar. 2, 1989	9:14 AM	CAP	Aug. 13, 1989	5:32 AM	CAP	Jan. 21, 1990	2:00 PM	SAG
Mar. 4, 1989	1:43 PM	AQU	Aug. 15, 1989	10:17 AM	AQU	Jan. 26, 1990	9:14 AM	AQU
Mar. 6, 1989	5:09 PM	PIS	Aug. 17, 1989	1:43 PM	PIS	Jan. 28, 1990	2:46 PM	PIS
Mar. 8, 1989	4:00 PM	ARI	Aug. 19, 1989	2:24 PM	ARI	Jan. 30, 1990	5:09 PM	ARI
Mar. 10, 1989	1:30 PM	TAU	Aug. 21, 1989	5:09 PM	TAU	Feb. 1, 1990	8:34 PM	TAU
Mar. 12, 1989	4:00 PM	GEM	Aug. 23, 1989	6:51 PM	GEM	Feb. 3, 1990	12:00 AM	GEM
Mar. 14, 1989	8:34 PM	CAN	Aug. 25, 1989	10:17 PM	CAN	Feb. 6, 1990	1:43 AM	CAN
Mar. 17, 1989	8:00 AM	LEO	Aug. 28, 1989	5:32 AM	LEO	Feb. 8, 1990	7:23 AM	LEO
Mar. 19, 1989	6:00 PM	VIR	Aug. 30, 1989	2:46 PM	VIR	Feb. 10, 1990	12:55 PM	VIR
Mar. 22, 1989	8:44 AM	LIB	Sep. 2, 1989	2:00 AM	LIB	Feb. 12, 1990	8:18 PM	LIB
Mar. 24, 1989	8:00 PM	SCO	Sep. 4, 1989	5:27 PM	SCO	Feb. 15, 1990	10:00 AM	SCO
Mar. 27, 1989	8:00 AM	SAG	Sep. 7, 1989	4:00 AM	SAG	Feb. 17, 1990	10:00 AM	SAG
Mar. 29, 1989	4:37 PM	CAP	Sep. 9, 1989	12:55 PM	CAP	Feb. 20, 1990	10:00 AM	CAP
Mar. 31, 1989	12:00 AM	AQU	Sep. 11, 1989	10:09 PM	AQU	Feb. 22, 1990	8:00 PM	AQU
Apr. 3, 1989	1:36 AM	PIS	Sep. 13, 1989	12:00 PM	PIS	Feb. 24, 1990	10:17 PM	PIS
Apr. 5, 1989	3:12 AM	ARI	Sep. 15, 1989	12:00 AM	ARI	Feb. 27, 1990	1:43 AM	ARI
Apr. 7, 1989	1:36 AM	TAU	Sep. 17, 1989	12:00 AM	TAU	Mar. 1, 1990	3:26 AM	TAU
Apr. 9, 1989	1:36 AM	GEM	Sep. 20, 1989	1:43 AM	GEM	Mar. 3, 1990	5:09 AM	GEM
Apr. 11, 1989	5:09 AM	CAN	Sep. 22, 1989	5:32 AM	CAN	Mar. 5, 1990	9:14 AM	CAN
Apr. 13, 1989	12:55 PM	LEO	Sep. 24, 1989	11:05 AM	LEO	Mar. 7, 1990	12:00 PM	LEO
Apr. 15, 1989	10:09 PM	VIR	Sep. 26, 1989	8:18 PM	VIR	Mar. 9, 1990	8:18 PM	VIR
Apr. 18, 1989	3:16 AM	LIB	Sep. 29, 1989	10:00 AM	LIB	Mar. 12, 1990	5:32 AM	LIB
Apr. 21, 1989	2:00 AM	SCO	Oct. 1, 1989	10:00 PM	SCO	Mar. 14, 1990	6:00 PM	SCO
Apr. 23, 1989	2:00 AM	SAG	Oct. 4, 1989	10:00 AM	SAG	Mar. 17, 1990	6:00 AM	SAG
Apr. 25, 1989	10:09 PM	CAP	Oct. 6, 1989	10:00 PM	CAP	Mar. 19, 1990	6:00 PM	CAP
Apr. 28, 1989	7:23 AM	AQU	Oct. 9, 1989	5:32 AM	AQU	Mar. 21, 1990	3:42 AM	AQU
Apr. 30, 1989	10:17 PM	PIS	Oct. 11, 1989	10:17 AM	PIS	Mar. 24, 1990	8:34 AM	PIS
May. 2, 1989	1:43 PM	ARI	Oct. 13, 1989	11:12 AM	ARI	Mar. 26, 1990	12:00 PM	ARI
May. 4, 1989	12:48 PM	TAU	Oct. 15, 1989	11:12 AM	TAU	Mar. 28, 1990	11:12 AM	TAU

Date	Time	Moon	Date	Time	Moon	Date	Time	Moon
Mar. 30, 1990	11:12 AM	GEM	Sep. 10, 1990	12:48 PM	GEM	Feb. 19, 1991	4:37 PM	TAU
Apr. 1, 1990	1:43 PM	CAN	Sep. 12, 1990	5:09 PM	CAN	Feb. 21, 1991	6:51 PM	GEM
Apr. 3, 1990	5:09 PM	LEO	Sep. 14, 1990	8:34 PM	LEO	Feb. 23, 1991	10:17 PM	CAN
Apr. 6, 1990	1:51 AM	VIR	Sep. 17, 1990	1:43 PM	VIR	Feb. 25, 1991	10:24 PM	LEO
Apr. 8, 1990	2:00 PM	LIB	Sep. 19, 1990	9:14 AM	LIB	Feb. 28, 1991	3:26 AM	VIR
Apr. 10, 1990	12:00 AM	SCO	Sep. 21, 1990	8:00 PM	SCO	Mar. 2, 1991	6:51 AM	LIB
Apr. 13, 1990	12:00 PM	SAG	Sep. 24, 1990	6:00 AM	SAG	Mar. 4, 1991	12:00 PM	SCO
Apr. 16, 1990	2:00 AM	CAP	Sep. 26, 1990	8:00 PM	CAP	Mar. 6, 1991	10:09 PM	SAG
Apr. 18, 1990	11:05 AM	AQU	Sep. 29, 1990	8:00 AM	AQU	Mar. 9, 1991	3:16 PM	CAP
Apr. 20, 1990	8:18 PM	PIS	Oct. 1, 1990	2:46 PM	PIS	Mar. 12, 1991	2:00 AM	AQU
Apr. 22, 1990	10:17 PM	ARI	Oct. 3, 1990	6:51 PM	ARI	Mar. 14, 1991	12:00 PM	PIS
Apr. 24, 1990	10:24 PM	TAU	Oct. 5, 1990	7:12 PM	TAU	Mar. 16, 1991	6:28 PM	ARI
Apr. 26, 1990	7:30 PM	GEM	Oct. 7, 1990	10:17 PM	GEM	Mar. 18, 1991	12:00 AM	TAU
Apr. 28, 1990	8:48 PM	CAN	Oct. 9, 1990	8:48 PM	CAN	Mar. 20, 1991	10:24 PM	GEM
May. 1, 1990	1:51 AM	LEO	Oct. 12, 1990	1:43 AM	LEO	Mar. 23, 1991	3:26 AM	CAN
May. 3, 1990	7:23 AM	VIR	Oct. 14, 1990	9:14 AM	VIR	Mar. 25, 1991	6:51 AM	LEO
May. 5, 1990	4:37 PM	LIB	Oct. 16, 1990	6:00 PM	LIB	Mar. 27, 1991	10:17 AM	VIR
May. 8, 1990	6:00 AM	SCO	Oct. 19, 1990	1:51 AM	SCO	Mar. 29, 1991	4:37 PM	LIB
May. 10, 1990	6:00 AM	SAG	Oct. 21, 1990	2:00 PM	SAG	Mar. 31, 1991	10:09 PM	SCO
May. 13, 1990	8:00 AM	CAP	Oct. 24, 1990	4:22 AM	CAP	Apr. 3, 1991	10:00 AM	SAG
May. 15, 1990	4:37 PM	AQU	Oct. 26, 1990	4:00 PM	AQU	Apr. 5, 1991	12:00 AM	CAP
May. 18, 1990	3:42 AM	PIS	Oct. 28, 1990	12:00 AM	PIS	Apr. 8, 1991	10:00 AM	AQU
May. 20, 1990	6:51 AM	ARI	Oct. 31, 1990	5:09 AM	ARI	Apr. 10, 1991	10:00 PM	PIS
May. 22, 1990	8:00 AM	TAU	Nov. 2, 1990	6:24 AM	TAU	Apr. 13, 1991	3:42 AM	ARI
May. 24, 1990	8:00 AM	GEM	Nov. 4, 1990	6:24 AM	GEM	Apr. 15, 1991	6:51 AM	TAU
May. 26, 1990	8:00 AM	CAN	Nov. 6, 1990	6:24 AM	CAN	Apr. 17, 1991	8:34 AM	GEM
May. 28, 1990	8:00 AM	LEO	Nov. 8, 1990	8:34 AM	LEO	Apr. 19, 1991	8:00 AM	CAN
May. 30, 1990	1:43 PM	VIR	Nov. 10, 1990	2:46 PM	VIR	Apr. 21, 1991	12:00 PM	LEO
Jun. 4, 1990	12:00 PM	SCO	Nov. 12, 1990	12:00 AM	LIB	Apr. 23, 1991	3:26 PM	VIR
Jun. 7, 1990	2:11 AM	SAG	Nov. 15, 1990	7:23 AM	SCO	Apr. 25, 1991	8:34 PM	LIB
Jun. 9, 1990	2:00 PM	CAP	Nov. 17, 1990	8:00 PM	SAG	Apr. 28, 1991	5:32 AM	SCO
Jun. 11, 1990	10:09 PM	AQU	Nov. 20, 1990	10:00 AM	CAP	Apr. 30, 1991	2:46 PM	SAG
Jun. 14, 1990	9:14 AM	PIS	Nov. 22, 1990	10:00 PM	AQU	May. 3, 1991	4:00 AM	CAP
Jun. 16, 1990	1:43 PM	ARI	Nov. 25, 1990	7:23 AM	PIS	May. 5, 1991	6:00 PM	AQU
Jun. 18, 1990	6:51 PM	TAU	Nov. 27, 1990	1:43 PM	ARI	May. 8, 1991	6:00 AM	PIS
Jun. 20, 1990	5:36 PM	GEM	Nov. 29, 1990	6:51 PM	TAU	May. 10, 1991	12:55 PM	ARI
Jun. 22, 1990	5:36 PM	CAN	Dec. 1, 1990	5:36 PM	GEM	May. 12, 1991	6:28 PM	TAU
Jun. 24, 1990	8:34 PM	LEO	Dec. 3, 1990	3:00 PM	CAN	May. 14, 1991	4:00 PM	GEM
Jun. 26, 1990	10:17 PM	VIR	Dec. 5, 1990	4:00 PM	LEO	May. 16, 1991	5:36 PM	CAN
Jun. 29, 1990	7:23 AM	LIB	Dec. 8, 1990	8:34 PM	VIR	May. 18, 1991	5:36 PM	LEO
Jul. 1, 1990	8:00 PM	SCO	Dec. 10, 1990	3:42 AM	LIB	May. 20, 1991	10:17 PM	VIR
Jul. 4, 1990	8:00 AM	SAG	Dec. 12, 1990	12:55 PM	SCO	May. 23, 1991	3:42 AM	LIB
Jul. 6, 1990	8:00 PM	CAP	Dec. 15, 1990	2:00 AM	SAG	May. 25, 1991	2:00 PM	SCO
Jul. 9, 1990	5:32 AM	AQU	Dec. 17, 1990	4:00 PM	CAP	May. 27, 1991	12:00 AM	SAG
Jul. 11, 1990	2:46 PM	PIS	Dec. 20, 1990	4:00 AM	AQU	May. 30, 1991	12:00 PM	CAP
Jul. 13, 1990	10:09 PM	ARI	Dec. 22, 1990	4:00 PM	PIS	Jun. 1, 1991	12:00 AM	AQU
Jul. 15, 1990	12:00 AM	TAU	Dec. 24, 1990	10:09 PM	ARI	Jun. 4, 1991	12:00 PM	PIS
Jul. 18, 1990	1:36 AM	GEM	Dec. 27, 1990	3:26 AM	TAU	Jun. 6, 1991	12:00 AM	ARI
Jul. 20, 1990	3:12 AM	CAN	Dec. 29, 1990	5:09 AM	GEM	Jun. 9, 1991	1:43 AM	TAU
Jul. 22, 1990	4:48 AM	LEO	Dec. 31, 1990	3:00 AM	CAN	Jun. 11, 1991	3:12 AM	GEM
Jul. 24, 1990	8:34 AM	VIR	Jan. 2, 1991	3:12 AM	LEO	Jun. 13, 1991	3:12 AM	CAN
Jul. 26, 1990	4:37 PM	LIB	Jan. 4, 1991	4:48 AM	VIR	Jun. 15, 1991	3:12 AM	LEO
Jul. 29, 1990	1:51 AM	SCO	Jan. 6, 1991	10:17 AM	LIB	Jun. 17, 1991	5:09 AM	VIR
Jul. 31, 1990	2:00 PM	SAG	Jan. 8, 1991	10:00 PM	SCO	Jun. 19, 1991	8:34 AM	LIB
Aug. 3, 1990	4:00 AM	CAP	Jan. 11, 1991	10:55 AM	SAG	Jun. 21, 1991	8:00 PM	SCO
Aug. 5, 1990	2:00 PM	AQU	Jan. 13, 1991	10:00 PM	CAP	Jun. 24, 1991	6:00 AM	SAG
Aug. 7, 1990	8:18 PM	PIS	Jan. 16, 1991	10:00 AM	AQU	Jun. 26, 1991	6:00 PM	CAP
Aug. 10, 1990	1:43 AM	ARI	Jan. 18, 1991	10:00 PM	PIS	Jun. 29, 1991	6:00 AM	AQU
Aug. 12, 1990	5:09 AM	TAU	Jan. 21, 1991	3:42 AM	ARI	Jul. 1, 1991	9:49 PM	PIS
Aug. 14, 1990	8:34 AM	GEM	Jan. 23, 1991	11:05 AM	TAU	Jul. 4, 1991	3:42 AM	ARI
Aug. 16, 1990	12:00 PM	CAN	Jan. 25, 1991	1:43 PM	GEM	Jul. 6, 1991	11:05 AM	TAU
Aug. 18, 1990	1:43 PM	LEO	Jan. 27, 1991	3:26 PM	CAN	Jul. 8, 1991	1:43 PM	GEM
Aug. 20, 1990	5:09 PM	VIR	Jan. 29, 1991	2:24 PM	LEO	Jul. 10, 1991	2:24 PM	CAN
Aug. 23, 1990	1:51 AM	LIB	Jan. 31, 1991	5:09 PM	VIR	Jul. 12, 1991	12:00 PM	LEO
Aug. 25, 1990	12:00 PM	SCO	Feb. 2, 1991	8:34 PM	LIB	Jul. 14, 1991	3:26 PM	VIR
Aug. 27, 1990	10:00 PM	SAG	Feb. 5, 1991	6:00 AM	SCO	Jul. 16, 1991	5:09 PM	LIB
Aug. 30, 1990	12:00 PM	CAP	Feb. 7, 1991	4:00 PM	SAG	Jul. 18, 1991	12:00 AM	SCO
Sep. 1, 1990	8:18 PM	AQU	Feb. 10, 1991	6:33 AM	CAP	Jul. 21, 1991	12:00 PM	SAG
Sep. 4, 1990	5:32 AM	PIS	Feb. 12, 1991	6:00 PM	AQU	Jul. 23, 1991	12:00 AM	CAP
Sep. 6, 1990	8:34 AM	ARI	Feb. 15, 1991	4:00 AM	PIS	Jul. 26, 1991	12:00 PM	AQU
Sep. 8, 1990	12:00 PM	TAU	Feb. 17, 1991	11:05 AM	ARI	Jul. 28, 1991	12:00 AM	PIS

167

Date	Time	Moon	Date	Time	Moon	Date	Time	Moon
Jul. 31, 1991	9:14 AM	A R I	Jan. 8, 1992	10:00 PM	P I S	Jun. 29, 1992	12:00 AM	C A N
Aug. 2, 1991	6:28 PM	T A U	Jan. 11, 1992	10:00 AM	A R I	Jul. 1, 1992	10:24 PM	L E O
Aug. 4, 1991	12:00 AM	G E M	Jan. 13, 1992	8:00 PM	T A U	Jul. 3, 1992	10:24 PM	V I R
Aug. 6, 1991	10:24 PM	C A N	Jan. 15, 1992	10:17 PM	G E M	Jul. 6, 1992	1:43 AM	L I B
Aug. 8, 1991	12:00 AM	L E O	Jan. 19, 1992	12:00 AM	L E O	Jul. 8, 1992	5:09 AM	S C O
Aug. 10, 1991	12:00 AM	V I R	Jan. 21, 1992	12:00 AM	V I R	Jul. 10, 1992	12:55 PM	S A G
Aug. 13, 1991	3:26 AM	L I B	Jan. 26, 1992	5:32 AM	S C O	Jul. 12, 1992	12:00 AM	C A P
Aug. 15, 1991	9:14 AM	S C O	Jan. 28, 1992	12:55 PM	S A G	Jul. 15, 1992	12:00 PM	A Q U
Aug. 17, 1991	4:37 PM	S A G	Jan. 31, 1992	2:00 AM	C A P	Jul. 17, 1992	12:00 AM	P I S
Aug. 20, 1991	6:00 AM	C A P	Feb. 2, 1992	2:00 PM	A Q U	Jul. 20, 1992	12:00 PM	A R I
Aug. 22, 1991	9:49 PM	A Q U	Feb. 5, 1992	4:00 AM	P I S	Jul. 22, 1992	12:00 AM	T A U
Aug. 25, 1991	8:00 AM	P I S	Feb. 7, 1992	4:00 PM	A R I	Jul. 25, 1992	5:32 AM	G E M
Aug. 27, 1991	6:00 PM	A R I	Feb. 12, 1992	7:23 AM	G E M	Jul. 27, 1992	8:00 AM	C A N
Aug. 29, 1991	12:00 AM	T A U	Feb. 14, 1992	10:17 AM	C A N	Jul. 29, 1992	9:36 AM	L E O
Sep. 1, 1991	3:26 AM	G E M	Feb. 16, 1992	11:12 AM	L E O	Jul. 31, 1992	9:36 AM	V I R
Sep. 3, 1991	6:51 AM	C A N	Feb. 18, 1992	11:12 AM	V I R	Aug. 2, 1992	10:17 AM	L I B
Sep. 5, 1991	8:00 AM	L E O	Feb. 20, 1992	11:12 AM	L I B	Aug. 4, 1992	12:00 PM	S C O
Sep. 7, 1991	9:36 AM	V I R	Feb. 22, 1992	1:43 PM	S C O	Aug. 6, 1992	6:28 PM	S A G
Sep. 9, 1991	11:12 AM	L I B	Feb. 24, 1992	8:18 PM	S A G	Aug. 9, 1992	6:00 AM	C A P
Sep. 11, 1991	6:28 PM	S C O	Feb. 27, 1992	8:00 AM	C A P	Aug. 11, 1992	4:00 PM	A Q U
Sep. 14, 1991	1:51 AM	S A G	Feb. 29, 1992	12:00 AM	A Q U	Aug. 14, 1992	6:00 AM	P I S
Sep. 16, 1991	2:00 PM	C A P	Mar. 3, 1992	10:00 AM	P I S	Aug. 16, 1992	6:00 PM	A R I
Sep. 19, 1991	2:00 AM	A Q U	Mar. 5, 1992	10:00 PM	A R I	Aug. 19, 1992	6:00 AM	T A U
Sep. 21, 1991	12:55 PM	P I S	Mar. 8, 1992	5:32 AM	T A U	Aug. 21, 1992	12:55 PM	G E M
Sep. 23, 1991	10:09 PM	A R I	Mar. 10, 1992	12:55 PM	G E M	Aug. 23, 1992	8:18 PM	C A N
Sep. 26, 1991	5:32 AM	T A U	Mar. 12, 1992	5:09 PM	C A N	Aug. 25, 1992	7:12 PM	L E O
Sep. 28, 1991	8:34 AM	G E M	Mar. 14, 1992	8:34 PM	L E O	Aug. 27, 1992	6:00 PM	V I R
Sep. 30, 1991	2:46 PM	C A N	Mar. 16, 1992	8:48 PM	V I R	Aug. 29, 1992	7:12 PM	L I B
Oct. 2, 1991	3:26 PM	L E O	Mar. 18, 1992	8:48 PM	L I B	Aug. 31, 1992	7:12 PM	S C O
Oct. 4, 1991	6:51 PM	V I R	Mar. 20, 1992	10:24 PM	S C O	Sep. 3, 1992	1:51 AM	S A G
Oct. 6, 1991	10:17 PM	L I B	Mar. 23, 1992	5:32 AM	S A G	Sep. 5, 1992	12:00 PM	C A P
Oct. 9, 1991	3:42 AM	S C O	Mar. 25, 1992	2:46 PM	C A P	Sep. 7, 1992	10:00 PM	A Q U
Oct. 11, 1991	12:00 PM	S A G	Mar. 28, 1992	4:00 AM	A Q U	Sep. 10, 1992	12:00 PM	P I S
Oct. 13, 1991	10:00 PM	C A P	Mar. 30, 1992	6:00 PM	P I S	Sep. 12, 1992	12:00 AM	A R I
Oct. 16, 1991	10:00 AM	A Q U	Apr. 2, 1992	3:42 AM	A R I	Sep. 15, 1992	12:00 PM	T A U
Oct. 18, 1991	12:00 AM	P I S	Apr. 4, 1992	2:00 PM	T A U	Sep. 17, 1992	6:28 PM	G E M
Oct. 21, 1991	7:23 AM	A R I	Apr. 6, 1992	5:09 PM	G E M	Sep. 20, 1992	1:43 AM	C A N
Oct. 23, 1991	12:00 PM	T A U	Apr. 8, 1992	10:17 PM	C A N	Sep. 22, 1992	5:09 AM	L E O
Oct. 25, 1991	2:24 PM	G E M	Apr. 11, 1992	3:26 AM	L E O	Sep. 24, 1992	6:24 AM	V I R
Oct. 27, 1991	6:51 PM	C A N	Apr. 13, 1992	5:09 AM	V I R	Sep. 26, 1992	6:24 AM	L I B
Oct. 29, 1991	7:12 PM	L E O	Apr. 15, 1992	6:24 AM	L I B	Sep. 28, 1992	6:24 AM	S C O
Oct. 31, 1991	12:00 AM	V I R	Apr. 17, 1992	10:17 AM	S C O	Sep. 30, 1992	10:17 AM	S A G
Nov. 3, 1991	5:09 AM	L I B	Apr. 19, 1992	4:37 PM	S A G	Oct. 2, 1992	6:28 PM	C A P
Nov. 5, 1991	11:05 AM	S C O	Apr. 24, 1992	12:00 PM	A Q U	Oct. 5, 1992	6:00 AM	A Q U
Nov. 7, 1991	6:28 PM	S A G	Apr. 27, 1992	2:00 AM	P I S	Oct. 7, 1992	6:00 PM	P I S
Nov. 10, 1991	6:00 AM	C A P	Apr. 29, 1992	11:05 AM	A R I	Oct. 10, 1992	6:00 AM	A R I
Nov. 12, 1991	6:00 PM	A Q U	May. 1, 1992	8:18 PM	T A U	Oct. 12, 1992	6:00 PM	T A U
Nov. 15, 1991	8:00 AM	P I S	May. 4, 1992	1:51 AM	G E M	Oct. 15, 1992	2:00 AM	G E M
Nov. 17, 1991	4:37 PM	A R I	May. 6, 1992	5:09 AM	C A N	Oct. 17, 1992	7:23 AM	C A N
Nov. 19, 1991	12:00 AM	T A U	May. 8, 1992	8:34 AM	L E O	Oct. 19, 1992	12:00 PM	L E O
Nov. 22, 1991	1:43 AM	G E M	May. 10, 1992	9:36 AM	V I R	Oct. 21, 1992	3:26 PM	V I R
Nov. 24, 1991	1:36 AM	C A N	May. 12, 1992	1:43 PM	L I B	Oct. 23, 1992	2:24 PM	L I B
Nov. 26, 1991	3:12 AM	L E O	May. 14, 1992	5:09 PM	S C O	Oct. 25, 1992	4:00 PM	S C O
Nov. 28, 1991	6:51 AM	V I R	May. 16, 1992	10:17 PM	S A G	Oct. 27, 1992	8:34 PM	S A G
Nov. 30, 1991	10:17 AM	L I B	May. 19, 1992	10:00 AM	C A P	Oct. 30, 1992	3:42 AM	C A P
Dec. 2, 1991	3:26 PM	S C O	May. 21, 1992	8:00 PM	A Q U	Nov. 1, 1992	2:00 PM	A Q U
Dec. 5, 1991	1:51 AM	S A G	May. 24, 1992	10:00 AM	P I S	Nov. 4, 1992	2:00 AM	P I S
Dec. 7, 1991	2:00 PM	C A P	May. 26, 1992	10:00 PM	A R I	Nov. 6, 1992	2:00 PM	A R I
Dec. 10, 1991	2:00 AM	A Q U	May. 29, 1992	5:32 AM	T A U	Nov. 11, 1992	7:23 AM	G E M
Dec. 12, 1991	5:27 PM	P I S	May. 31, 1992	10:17 AM	G E M	Nov. 13, 1992	12:00 PM	C A N
Dec. 15, 1991	1:51 AM	A R I	Jun. 2, 1992	1:43 PM	C A N	Nov. 15, 1992	5:09 PM	L E O
Dec. 17, 1991	9:14 AM	T A U	Jun. 4, 1992	3:26 PM	L E O	Nov. 17, 1992	8:34 PM	V I R
Dec. 19, 1991	12:00 PM	G E M	Jun. 6, 1992	5:09 PM	V I R	Nov. 19, 1992	12:00 AM	L I B
Dec. 21, 1991	12:48 PM	C A N	Jun. 8, 1992	6:51 PM	L I B	Nov. 22, 1992	1:43 AM	S C O
Dec. 23, 1991	12:48 PM	L E O	Jun. 13, 1992	7:23 AM	S A G	Nov. 24, 1992	5:09 AM	S A G
Dec. 25, 1991	12:48 PM	V I R	Jun. 15, 1992	6:00 PM	C A P	Nov. 26, 1992	12:55 PM	C A P
Dec. 27, 1991	2:24 PM	L I B	Jun. 18, 1992	4:00 AM	A Q U	Nov. 28, 1992	8:18 PM	A Q U
Dec. 29, 1991	8:34 PM	S C O	Jun. 20, 1992	4:00 PM	P I S	Dec. 1, 1992	10:00 AM	P I S
Jan. 1, 1992	7:23 AM	S A G	Jun. 23, 1992	6:00 AM	A R I	Dec. 3, 1992	10:00 PM	A R I
Jan. 3, 1992	8:00 PM	C A P	Jun. 25, 1992	4:00 AM	T A U	Dec. 6, 1992	10:00 AM	T A U
Jan. 6, 1992	8:00 AM	A Q U	Jun. 27, 1992	6:51 PM	G E M	Dec. 8, 1992	4:37 PM	G E M

Date	Time	Moon	Date	Time	Moon	Date	Time	Moon
Dec. 10, 1992	8:34 PM	CAN	May. 21, 1993	12:55 PM	GEM	Nov. 1, 1993	12:00 PM	GEM
Dec. 12, 1992	12:00 AM	LEO	May. 23, 1993	10:09 PM	CAN	Nov. 3, 1993	10:00 PM	CAN
Dec. 15, 1992	1:43 AM	VIR	May. 26, 1993	3:42 AM	LEO	Nov. 6, 1993	5:32 AM	LEO
Dec. 17, 1992	5:09 AM	LIB	May. 28, 1993	6:51 AM	VIR	Nov. 8, 1993	11:05 AM	VIR
Dec. 19, 1992	8:34 AM	SCO	May. 30, 1993	8:00 AM	LIB	Nov. 10, 1993	11:12 AM	LIB
Dec. 21, 1992	2:46 PM	SAG	Jun. 1, 1993	12:00 PM	SCO	Nov. 12, 1993	11:12 AM	SCO
Dec. 23, 1992	8:18 PM	CAP	Jun. 3, 1993	1:43 PM	SAG	Nov. 14, 1993	11:12 AM	SAG
Dec. 26, 1992	5:32 AM	AQU	Jun. 5, 1993	5:09 PM	CAP	Nov. 16, 1993	12:48 PM	CAP
Dec. 28, 1992	6:00 PM	PIS	Jun. 8, 1993	1:51 AM	AQU	Nov. 18, 1993	8:18 PM	AQU
Dec. 31, 1992	8:44 AM	ARI	Jun. 10, 1993	12:00 PM	PIS	Nov. 21, 1993	6:00 AM	PIS
Jan. 2, 1993	4:37 PM	TAU	Jun. 12, 1993	12:00 AM	ARI	Nov. 23, 1993	6:00 AM	ARI
Jan. 5, 1993	1:51 AM	GEM	Jun. 15, 1993	12:00 PM	TAU	Nov. 26, 1993	6:00 AM	TAU
Jan. 7, 1993	6:51 AM	CAN	Jun. 17, 1993	12:00 AM	GEM	Nov. 28, 1993	6:00 PM	GEM
Jan. 9, 1993	8:00 AM	LEO	Jun. 20, 1993	5:32 AM	CAN	Dec. 1, 1993	4:00 AM	CAN
Jan. 11, 1993	9:36 AM	VIR	Jun. 22, 1993	8:34 AM	LEO	Dec. 3, 1993	11:05 AM	LEO
Jan. 13, 1993	9:36 AM	LIB	Jun. 24, 1993	12:00 PM	VIR	Dec. 5, 1993	4:37 PM	VIR
Jan. 15, 1993	1:43 PM	SCO	Jun. 26, 1993	3:26 PM	LIB	Dec. 7, 1993	6:51 PM	LIB
Jan. 17, 1993	8:18 PM	SAG	Jun. 28, 1993	5:09 PM	SCO	Dec. 9, 1993	10:17 PM	SCO
Jan. 20, 1993	3:42 AM	CAP	Jun. 30, 1993	8:34 PM	SAG	Dec. 11, 1993	12:00 AM	SAG
Jan. 22, 1993	2:00 PM	AQU	Jul. 3, 1993	3:42 AM	CAP	Dec. 14, 1993	1:43 AM	CAP
Jan. 25, 1993	2:00 AM	PIS	Jul. 5, 1993	9:14 AM	AQU	Dec. 16, 1993	5:09 AM	AQU
Jan. 27, 1993	2:00 PM	ARI	Jul. 7, 1993	6:28 PM	PIS	Dec. 18, 1993	12:55 PM	PIS
Jan. 30, 1993	2:00 AM	TAU	Jul. 10, 1993	8:00 AM	ARI	Dec. 21, 1993	2:00 AM	ARI
Feb. 1, 1993	2:00 PM	GEM	Jul. 12, 1993	8:00 PM	TAU	Dec. 23, 1993	2:00 PM	TAU
Feb. 3, 1993	5:09 PM	CAN	Jul. 15, 1993	8:00 AM	GEM	Dec. 26, 1993	2:00 AM	GEM
Feb. 5, 1993	8:34 PM	LEO	Jul. 17, 1993	2:46 PM	CAN	Dec. 28, 1993	12:00 PM	CAN
Feb. 7, 1993	7:12 PM	VIR	Jul. 19, 1993	5:09 PM	LEO	Dec. 30, 1993	3:26 PM	LEO
Feb. 9, 1993	7:12 PM	LIB	Jul. 21, 1993	8:34 PM	VIR	Jan. 1, 1994	8:34 PM	VIR
Feb. 11, 1993	7:12 PM	SCO	Jul. 23, 1993	7:12 PM	LIB	Jan. 3, 1994	12:00 AM	LIB
Feb. 14, 1993	1:51 AM	SAG	Jul. 25, 1993	12:00 AM	SCO	Jan. 6, 1994	3:26 AM	SCO
Feb. 16, 1993	9:14 AM	CAP	Jul. 28, 1993	3:42 AM	SAG	Jan. 8, 1994	6:51 AM	SAG
Feb. 18, 1993	8:00 PM	AQU	Jul. 30, 1993	9:14 AM	CAP	Jan. 10, 1994	10:17 AM	CAP
Feb. 21, 1993	8:00 AM	PIS	Aug. 1, 1993	4:37 PM	AQU	Jan. 12, 1994	4:37 PM	AQU
Feb. 23, 1993	8:00 PM	ARI	Aug. 4, 1993	4:00 AM	PIS	Jan. 14, 1994	10:09 PM	PIS
Feb. 26, 1993	10:00 AM	TAU	Aug. 6, 1993	4:00 PM	ARI	Jan. 17, 1994	10:00 AM	ARI
Feb. 28, 1993	6:28 PM	GEM	Aug. 9, 1993	4:00 AM	TAU	Jan. 19, 1994	10:00 PM	TAU
Mar. 3, 1993	3:42 AM	CAN	Aug. 11, 1993	4:00 PM	GEM	Jan. 22, 1994	10:00 AM	GEM
Mar. 5, 1993	6:51 AM	LEO	Aug. 13, 1993	12:00 AM	CAN	Jan. 24, 1994	10:00 PM	CAN
Mar. 7, 1993	6:24 AM	VIR	Aug. 16, 1993	3:26 AM	LEO	Jan. 27, 1994	1:43 AM	LEO
Mar. 9, 1993	6:24 AM	LIB	Aug. 18, 1993	4:48 AM	VIR	Jan. 29, 1994	5:09 AM	VIR
Mar. 11, 1993	4:48 AM	SCO	Aug. 20, 1993	4:48 AM	LIB	Jan. 31, 1994	6:51 AM	LIB
Mar. 13, 1993	8:34 AM	SAG	Aug. 22, 1993	4:48 AM	SCO	Feb. 2, 1994	8:34 AM	SCO
Mar. 15, 1993	2:46 PM	CAP	Aug. 24, 1993	8:34 AM	SAG	Feb. 4, 1994	12:00 PM	SAG
Mar. 18, 1993	2:00 AM	AQU	Aug. 26, 1993	2:46 PM	CAP	Feb. 6, 1994	6:28 PM	CAP
Mar. 20, 1993	2:00 PM	PIS	Aug. 28, 1993	10:09 PM	AQU	Feb. 8, 1994	12:00 AM	AQU
Mar. 23, 1993	2:00 AM	ARI	Aug. 31, 1993	10:00 AM	PIS	Feb. 11, 1994	7:23 AM	PIS
Mar. 25, 1993	4:00 PM	TAU	Sep. 2, 1993	10:00 PM	ARI	Feb. 13, 1994	6:00 PM	ARI
Mar. 28, 1993	2:00 AM	GEM	Sep. 5, 1993	1:05 PM	TAU	Feb. 16, 1994	6:00 AM	TAU
Mar. 30, 1993	12:00 PM	CAN	Sep. 7, 1993	12:00 AM	GEM	Feb. 18, 1994	9:49 PM	GEM
Apr. 1, 1993	4:37 PM	LEO	Sep. 10, 1993	10:00 AM	CAN	Feb. 21, 1994	6:00 AM	CAN
Apr. 3, 1993	4:00 PM	VIR	Sep. 12, 1993	1:43 PM	LEO	Feb. 23, 1994	12:55 PM	LEO
Apr. 5, 1993	5:36 PM	LIB	Sep. 14, 1993	2:24 PM	VIR	Feb. 25, 1994	3:26 PM	VIR
Apr. 7, 1993	4:00 PM	SCO	Sep. 16, 1993	2:24 PM	LIB	Feb. 27, 1994	2:24 PM	LIB
Apr. 9, 1993	6:51 PM	SAG	Sep. 18, 1993	2:24 PM	SCO	Mar. 1, 1994	5:09 PM	SCO
Apr. 11, 1993	10:17 PM	CAP	Sep. 20, 1993	2:24 PM	SAG	Mar. 3, 1994	4:00 PM	SAG
Apr. 14, 1993	7:23 AM	AQU	Sep. 22, 1993	10:09 PM	CAP	Mar. 5, 1994	12:00 AM	CAP
Apr. 16, 1993	8:00 PM	PIS	Sep. 25, 1993	6:00 AM	AQU	Mar. 8, 1994	5:32 AM	AQU
Apr. 19, 1993	10:55 AM	ARI	Sep. 27, 1993	4:00 PM	PIS	Mar. 10, 1994	12:55 PM	PIS
Apr. 21, 1993	10:00 PM	TAU	Sep. 30, 1993	4:00 AM	ARI	Mar. 15, 1994	2:00 PM	TAU
Apr. 24, 1993	8:00 AM	GEM	Oct. 2, 1993	7:38 PM	TAU	Mar. 18, 1994	2:00 AM	GEM
Apr. 26, 1993	2:46 PM	CAN	Oct. 5, 1993	6:00 AM	GEM	Mar. 20, 1994	2:00 AM	CAN
Apr. 28, 1993	10:09 PM	LEO	Oct. 7, 1993	2:46 PM	CAN	Mar. 22, 1994	10:09 PM	LEO
May. 1, 1993	1:43 AM	VIR	Oct. 9, 1993	12:00 AM	LEO	Mar. 25, 1994	1:43 AM	VIR
May. 3, 1993	1:36 AM	LIB	Oct. 12, 1993	1:43 AM	VIR	Mar. 27, 1994	1:36 AM	LIB
May. 5, 1993	3:12 AM	SCO	Oct. 14, 1993	1:36 AM	LIB	Mar. 29, 1994	1:36 AM	SCO
May. 7, 1993	5:09 AM	SAG	Oct. 16, 1993	1:36 AM	SCO	Mar. 31, 1994	1:36 AM	SAG
May. 9, 1993	8:34 AM	CAP	Oct. 18, 1993	1:43 AM	SAG	Apr. 2, 1994	5:09 AM	CAP
May. 11, 1993	4:37 PM	AQU	Oct. 20, 1993	5:32 AM	CAP	Apr. 4, 1994	11:05 AM	AQU
May. 14, 1993	4:00 PM	PIS	Oct. 22, 1993	11:05 AM	AQU	Apr. 6, 1994	6:28 PM	PIS
May. 16, 1993	4:00 PM	ARI	Oct. 24, 1993	8:18 PM	PIS	Apr. 9, 1994	8:00 AM	ARI
May. 19, 1993	4:00 AM	TAU	Oct. 27, 1993	10:00 AM	ARI	Apr. 11, 1994	8:00 PM	TAU

169

Date	Time	Moon	Date	Time	Moon	Date	Time	Moon
Apr. 14, 1994	8:00 AM	GEM	Sep. 25, 1994	4:00 AM	GEM	Mar. 7, 1995	10:00 PM	GEM
Apr. 16, 1994	8:00 PM	CAN	Sep. 27, 1994	4:00 PM	CAN	Mar. 10, 1995	10:00 AM	CAN
Apr. 19, 1994	5:32 AM	LEO	Sep. 30, 1994	1:51 AM	LEO	Mar. 12, 1995	10:00 PM	LEO
Apr. 21, 1994	10:17 AM	VIR	Oct. 2, 1994	6:51 AM	VIR	Mar. 15, 1995	5:32 AM	VIR
Apr. 23, 1994	1:43 PM	LIB	Oct. 4, 1994	10:17 AM	LIB	Mar. 17, 1995	8:34 AM	LIB
Apr. 25, 1994	12:48 PM	SCO	Oct. 6, 1994	9:36 AM	SCO	Mar. 19, 1995	12:00 PM	SCO
Apr. 27, 1994	11:12 AM	SAG	Oct. 8, 1994	12:00 PM	SAG	Mar. 21, 1995	12:48 PM	SAG
Apr. 29, 1994	1:43 PM	CAP	Oct. 10, 1994	11:12 AM	CAP	Mar. 23, 1995	5:09 PM	CAP
May. 1, 1994	5:09 PM	AQU	Oct. 12, 1994	6:28 PM	AQU	Mar. 25, 1995	8:34 PM	AQU
May. 4, 1994	1:51 AM	PIS	Oct. 14, 1994	12:00 AM	PIS	Mar. 28, 1995	1:51 AM	PIS
May. 6, 1994	2:00 PM	ARI	Oct. 17, 1994	9:14 AM	ARI	Mar. 30, 1995	7:23 AM	ARI
May. 9, 1994	2:00 AM	TAU	Oct. 19, 1994	10:00 PM	TAU	Apr. 1, 1995	4:37 PM	TAU
May. 11, 1994	2:00 PM	GEM	Oct. 22, 1994	10:00 AM	GEM	Apr. 4, 1995	6:00 AM	GEM
May. 14, 1994	2:00 AM	CAN	Oct. 27, 1994	9:14 AM	LEO	Apr. 6, 1995	6:00 PM	CAN
May. 16, 1994	11:05 AM	LEO	Oct. 29, 1994	6:28 PM	VIR	Apr. 9, 1995	6:00 AM	LEO
May. 18, 1994	5:09 PM	VIR	Oct. 31, 1994	8:34 PM	LIB	Apr. 11, 1995	2:46 PM	VIR
May. 20, 1994	10:17 PM	LIB	Nov. 2, 1994	8:48 PM	SCO	Apr. 13, 1995	6:51 PM	LIB
May. 22, 1994	10:24 PM	SCO	Nov. 4, 1994	8:48 PM	SAG	Apr. 15, 1995	10:17 PM	SCO
May. 24, 1994	10:24 PM	SAG	Nov. 6, 1994	8:48 PM	CAP	Apr. 17, 1995	8:48 PM	SAG
May. 26, 1994	10:24 PM	CAP	Nov. 8, 1994	12:00 AM	AQU	Apr. 19, 1995	10:24 PM	CAP
May. 29, 1994	1:43 AM	AQU	Nov. 11, 1994	5:32 AM	PIS	Apr. 22, 1995	1:43 AM	AQU
May. 31, 1994	9:14 AM	PIS	Nov. 13, 1994	4:00 PM	ARI	Apr. 24, 1995	7:23 AM	PIS
Jun. 2, 1994	8:00 PM	ARI	Nov. 16, 1994	4:00 AM	TAU	Apr. 26, 1995	2:46 PM	ARI
Jun. 5, 1994	8:00 AM	TAU	Nov. 18, 1994	4:00 PM	GEM	May. 1, 1995	12:00 PM	GEM
Jun. 7, 1994	8:00 PM	GEM	Nov. 21, 1994	6:00 AM	CAN	May. 4, 1995	2:00 AM	CAN
Jun. 10, 1994	8:00 AM	CAN	Nov. 23, 1994	2:46 PM	LEO	May. 6, 1995	2:00 PM	LEO
Jun. 12, 1994	4:37 AM	LEO	Nov. 26, 1994	1:51 AM	VIR	May. 8, 1995	10:09 PM	VIR
Jun. 14, 1994	12:00 AM	VIR	Nov. 28, 1994	7:23 AM	LIB	May. 11, 1995	5:09 AM	LIB
Jun. 17, 1994	5:09 AM	LIB	Nov. 30, 1994	8:00 AM	SCO	May. 13, 1995	8:34 AM	SCO
Jun. 19, 1994	6:24 AM	SCO	Dec. 2, 1994	8:00 AM	SAG	May. 15, 1995	8:00 AM	SAG
Jun. 21, 1994	8:00 AM	SAG	Dec. 4, 1994	8:00 AM	CAP	May. 17, 1995	8:00 AM	CAP
Jun. 23, 1994	10:17 AM	CAP	Dec. 6, 1994	8:00 AM	AQU	May. 19, 1995	8:00 AM	AQU
Jun. 25, 1994	12:00 PM	AQU	Dec. 8, 1994	12:00 PM	PIS	May. 21, 1995	12:00 PM	PIS
Jun. 27, 1994	6:28 PM	PIS	Dec. 10, 1994	8:18 PM	ARI	May. 23, 1995	8:18 PM	ARI
Jun. 30, 1994	4:00 AM	ARI	Dec. 13, 1994	10:00 AM	TAU	May. 26, 1995	5:32 AM	TAU
Jul. 2, 1994	5:27 AM	TAU	Dec. 15, 1994	10:00 PM	GEM	May. 28, 1995	6:00 PM	GEM
Jul. 5, 1994	4:00 AM	GEM	Dec. 18, 1994	12:00 PM	CAN	May. 31, 1995	8:00 AM	CAN
Jul. 7, 1994	4:00 PM	CAN	Dec. 20, 1994	8:18 PM	LEO	Jun. 2, 1995	8:00 PM	LEO
Jul. 12, 1994	5:09 AM	VIR	Dec. 23, 1994	7:23 AM	VIR	Jun. 5, 1995	8:00 AM	VIR
Jul. 14, 1994	10:17 AM	LIB	Dec. 25, 1994	12:00 PM	LIB	Jun. 7, 1995	2:46 PM	LIB
Jul. 16, 1994	1:43 PM	SCO	Dec. 27, 1994	5:09 PM	SCO	Jun. 9, 1995	8:18 PM	SCO
Jul. 18, 1994	5:09 PM	SAG	Dec. 29, 1994	5:36 PM	SAG	Jun. 11, 1995	8:34 PM	SAG
Jul. 20, 1994	6:51 PM	CAP	Dec. 31, 1994	7:12 PM	CAP	Jun. 13, 1995	4:30 PM	CAP
Jul. 22, 1994	10:17 AM	AQU	Jan. 2, 1995	7:12 PM	AQU	Jun. 15, 1995	5:36 PM	AQU
Jul. 25, 1994	3:42 AM	PIS	Jan. 4, 1995	10:17 PM	PIS	Jun. 17, 1995	8:34 PM	PIS
Jul. 27, 1994	11:05 AM	ARI	Jan. 7, 1995	5:32 AM	ARI	Jun. 20, 1995	1:51 AM	ARI
Jul. 29, 1994	12:00 AM	TAU	Jan. 9, 1995	2:46 PM	TAU	Jun. 22, 1995	11:05 AM	TAU
Aug. 1, 1994	12:00 PM	GEM	Jan. 12, 1995	6:00 AM	GEM	Jun. 25, 1995	2:11 AM	GEM
Aug. 3, 1994	12:00 AM	CAN	Jan. 14, 1995	6:00 PM	CAN	Jun. 27, 1995	2:00 PM	CAN
Aug. 6, 1994	7:23 AM	LEO	Jan. 17, 1995	3:42 AM	LEO	Jun. 30, 1995	2:00 AM	LEO
Aug. 8, 1994	12:00 PM	VIR	Jan. 19, 1995	12:55 PM	VIR	Jul. 2, 1995	2:00 PM	VIR
Aug. 10, 1994	3:26 PM	LIB	Jan. 21, 1995	8:18 PM	LIB	Jul. 4, 1995	8:18 PM	LIB
Aug. 12, 1994	6:51 PM	SCO	Jan. 23, 1995	10:17 PM	SCO	Jul. 7, 1995	1:43 AM	SCO
Aug. 14, 1994	10:17 PM	SAG	Jan. 26, 1995	1:36 AM	SAG	Jul. 9, 1995	5:09 AM	SAG
Aug. 17, 1994	1:43 AM	CAP	Jan. 28, 1995	5:09 AM	CAP	Jul. 11, 1995	4:48 AM	CAP
Aug. 19, 1994	5:09 AM	AQU	Jan. 30, 1995	6:51 AM	AQU	Jul. 13, 1995	4:48 AM	AQU
Aug. 21, 1994	10:17 AM	PIS	Feb. 1, 1995	8:34 AM	PIS	Jul. 15, 1995	4:48 AM	PIS
Aug. 23, 1994	6:28 PM	ARI	Feb. 3, 1995	2:46 PM	ARI	Jul. 17, 1995	11:05 AM	ARI
Aug. 26, 1994	8:00 AM	TAU	Feb. 6, 1995	2:00 AM	TAU	Jul. 19, 1995	6:28 PM	TAU
Aug. 28, 1994	8:00 PM	GEM	Feb. 8, 1995	2:00 PM	GEM	Jul. 22, 1995	8:00 AM	GEM
Aug. 31, 1994	8:00 AM	CAN	Feb. 11, 1995	2:00 AM	CAN	Jul. 24, 1995	8:00 AM	CAN
Sep. 2, 1994	4:37 PM	LEO	Feb. 13, 1995	2:00 PM	LEO	Jul. 27, 1995	8:00 AM	LEO
Sep. 4, 1994	8:34 PM	VIR	Feb. 15, 1995	8:18 PM	VIR	Jul. 29, 1995	4:37 PM	VIR
Sep. 6, 1994	12:00 AM	LIB	Feb. 18, 1995	1:51 AM	LIB	Aug. 1, 1995	1:51 AM	LIB
Sep. 9, 1994	1:43 AM	SCO	Feb. 20, 1995	5:09 AM	SCO	Aug. 3, 1995	9:14 AM	SCO
Sep. 11, 1994	3:26 AM	SAG	Feb. 22, 1995	8:34 AM	SAG	Aug. 5, 1995	12:00 PM	SAG
Sep. 13, 1994	6:51 AM	CAP	Feb. 24, 1995	12:00 PM	CAP	Aug. 7, 1995	12:48 PM	CAP
Sep. 15, 1994	10:17 AM	AQU	Feb. 26, 1995	1:43 PM	AQU	Aug. 9, 1995	2:24 PM	AQU
Sep. 17, 1994	6:28 PM	PIS	Feb. 28, 1995	5:09 PM	PIS	Aug. 11, 1995	2:24 PM	PIS
Sep. 20, 1994	4:00 AM	ARI	Mar. 2, 1995	10:17 PM	ARI	Aug. 13, 1995	6:51 PM	ARI
Sep. 22, 1994	2:00 PM	TAU	Mar. 5, 1995	10:00 AM	TAU	Aug. 16, 1995	4:00 AM	TAU

170

Date	Time	Moon	Date	Time	Moon	Date	Time	Moon
Aug. 18, 1995	2:00 PM	GEM	Jan. 29, 1996	10:00 AM	GEM	Jul. 11, 1996	8:00 AM	GEM
Aug. 21, 1995	4:00 AM	CAN	Jan. 31, 1996	10:00 PM	CAN	Jul. 13, 1996	6:00 PM	CAN
Aug. 23, 1995	4:00 PM	LEO	Feb. 3, 1996	10:00 AM	LEO	Jul. 16, 1996	6:00 AM	LEO
Aug. 28, 1995	6:51 AM	L I B	Feb. 5, 1996	10:00 PM	VIR	Jul. 18, 1996	9:49 PM	VIR
Aug. 30, 1995	2:46 PM	SCO	Feb. 8, 1996	7:23 AM	L I B	Jul. 21, 1996	8:00 AM	L I B
Sep. 1, 1995	5:09 PM	SAG	Feb. 10, 1996	4:37 PM	SCO	Jul. 23, 1996	6:00 PM	SCO
Sep. 3, 1995	8:34 PM	CAP	Feb. 12, 1996	8:34 PM	SAG	Jul. 25, 1996	12:00 AM	SAG
Sep. 5, 1995	12:00 AM	AQU	Feb. 16, 1996	12:00 AM	CAP	Jul. 29, 1996	12:00 AM	AQU
Sep. 8, 1995	1:43 AM	P I S	Feb. 17, 1996	1:43 AM	AQU	Jul. 31, 1996	9:00 PM	P I S
Sep. 10, 1995	5:09 AM	A R I	Feb. 19, 1996	1:36 AM	P I S	Aug. 2, 1996	10:24 PM	A R I
Sep. 12, 1995	12:55 PM	TAU	Feb. 21, 1996	3:26 AM	A R I	Aug. 5, 1996	3:26 AM	TAU
Sep. 14, 1995	12:00 AM	GEM	Feb. 23, 1996	6:51 AM	TAU	Aug. 7, 1996	2:00 PM	GEM
Sep. 17, 1995	1:05 PM	CAN	Feb. 25, 1996	6:00 PM	GEM	Aug. 9, 1996	12:00 AM	CAN
Sep. 19, 1995	12:00 AM	LEO	Feb. 28, 1996	6:33 AM	CAN	Aug. 12, 1996	12:00 PM	LEO
Sep. 22, 1995	10:00 AM	VIR	Mar. 1, 1996	6:00 PM	LEO	Aug. 15, 1996	2:11 AM	VIR
Sep. 24, 1995	4:37 PM	L I B	Mar. 4, 1996	6:00 AM	VIR	Aug. 17, 1996	2:00 PM	L I B
Sep. 26, 1995	10:09 PM	SCO	Mar. 6, 1996	4:00 PM	L I B	Aug. 19, 1996	12:00 AM	SCO
Sep. 28, 1995	12:00 AM	SAG	Mar. 8, 1996	10:09 PM	SCO	Aug. 22, 1996	5:32 AM	SAG
Oct. 1, 1995	1:43 AM	CAP	Mar. 11, 1996	3:26 AM	SAG	Aug. 24, 1996	10:17 AM	CAP
Oct. 3, 1995	5:09 AM	AQU	Mar. 13, 1996	6:51 AM	CAP	Aug. 26, 1996	9:36 AM	AQU
Oct. 5, 1995	8:34 AM	P I S	Mar. 15, 1996	8:00 AM	AQU	Aug. 28, 1996	9:36 AM	P I S
Oct. 7, 1995	2:46 PM	A R I	Mar. 17, 1996	9:36 AM	P I S	Aug. 30, 1996	9:36 AM	A R I
Oct. 9, 1995	8:18 PM	TAU	Mar. 19, 1996	1:43 PM	A R I	Sep. 1, 1996	1:43 PM	TAU
Oct. 12, 1995	8:00 AM	GEM	Mar. 21, 1996	5:09 PM	TAU	Sep. 3, 1996	8:18 PM	GEM
Oct. 14, 1995	8:00 PM	CAN	Mar. 24, 1996	1:51 AM	GEM	Sep. 6, 1996	6:00 AM	CAN
Oct. 17, 1995	8:00 AM	LEO	Mar. 26, 1996	2:00 PM	CAN	Sep. 8, 1996	6:00 PM	LEO
Oct. 19, 1995	8:00 PM	VIR	Mar. 29, 1996	2:00 AM	LEO	Sep. 11, 1996	8:00 AM	VIR
Oct. 22, 1995	1:51 AM	L I B	Mar. 31, 1996	2:00 PM	VIR	Sep. 13, 1996	8:00 PM	L I B
Oct. 24, 1995	5:09 AM	SCO	Apr. 2, 1996	12:00 AM	L I B	Sep. 16, 1996	3:42 AM	SCO
Oct. 26, 1995	6:24 AM	SAG	Apr. 5, 1996	5:32 AM	SCO	Sep. 18, 1996	11:05 AM	SAG
Oct. 28, 1995	8:00 AM	CAP	Apr. 7, 1996	8:34 AM	SAG	Sep. 20, 1996	3:26 PM	CAP
Oct. 30, 1995	10:17 AM	AQU	Apr. 9, 1996	12:00 PM	CAP	Sep. 22, 1996	6:51 PM	AQU
Nov. 1, 1995	1:43 PM	P I S	Apr. 11, 1996	3:26 PM	AQU	Sep. 24, 1996	7:12 PM	P I S
Nov. 3, 1995	8:18 PM	A R I	Apr. 13, 1996	6:51 PM	P I S	Sep. 26, 1996	10:17 PM	A R I
Nov. 6, 1995	3:42 AM	TAU	Apr. 15, 1996	8:34 PM	A R I	Sep. 28, 1996	12:00 AM	TAU
Nov. 8, 1995	4:00 PM	GEM	Apr. 18, 1996	3:42 AM	TAU	Oct. 1, 1996	5:32 AM	GEM
Nov. 11, 1995	2:00 AM	CAN	Apr. 20, 1996	11:05 AM	GEM	Oct. 3, 1996	12:55 PM	CAN
Nov. 13, 1995	4:00 PM	LEO	Apr. 22, 1996	10:00 PM	CAN	Oct. 6, 1996	2:00 AM	LEO
Nov. 16, 1995	4:00 AM	VIR	Apr. 25, 1996	10:00 AM	LEO	Oct. 8, 1996	2:00 PM	VIR
Nov. 18, 1995	11:05 AM	L I B	Apr. 27, 1996	10:00 PM	VIR	Oct. 11, 1996	2:00 AM	L I B
Nov. 20, 1995	3:26 PM	SCO	Apr. 30, 1996	7:23 AM	L I B	Oct. 13, 1996	11:05 AM	SCO
Nov. 22, 1995	4:00 PM	SAG	May. 2, 1996	2:46 PM	SCO	Oct. 15, 1996	6:28 PM	SAG
Nov. 24, 1995	4:00 PM	CAP	May. 4, 1996	5:09 PM	SAG	Oct. 17, 1996	8:34 PM	CAP
Nov. 26, 1995	4:00 PM	AQU	May. 6, 1996	5:36 PM	CAP	Oct. 22, 1996	3:26 AM	P I S
Nov. 28, 1995	8:34 PM	P I S	May. 8, 1996	7:12 PM	AQU	Oct. 24, 1996	4:48 AM	A R I
Dec. 1, 1995	1:51 AM	A R I	May. 10, 1996	12:00 AM	P I S	Oct. 26, 1996	8:34 AM	TAU
Dec. 3, 1995	12:00 PM	TAU	May. 13, 1996	3:26 AM	A R I	Oct. 28, 1996	2:46 PM	GEM
Dec. 5, 1995	10:00 PM	GEM	May. 15, 1996	11:05 AM	TAU	Oct. 30, 1996	10:09 PM	CAN
Dec. 8, 1995	10:00 AM	CAN	May. 17, 1996	6:28 PM	GEM	Nov. 2, 1996	10:00 AM	LEO
Dec. 10, 1995	10:00 PM	LEO	May. 20, 1996	6:00 AM	CAN	Nov. 4, 1996	10:00 PM	VIR
Dec. 13, 1995	10:00 AM	VIR	May. 22, 1996	6:00 PM	LEO	Nov. 7, 1996	9:14 AM	L I B
Dec. 15, 1995	10:00 PM	L I B	May. 25, 1996	6:00 AM	VIR	Nov. 9, 1996	6:28 PM	SCO
Dec. 18, 1995	1:43 AM	SCO	May. 27, 1996	6:00 PM	L I B	Nov. 14, 1996	3:26 AM	CAP
Dec. 20, 1995	3:12 AM	SAG	May. 29, 1996	12:00 AM	SCO	Nov. 16, 1996	6:51 AM	AQU
Dec. 22, 1995	3:00 AM	CAP	Jun. 1, 1996	3:26 AM	SAG	Nov. 18, 1996	8:34 AM	P I S
Dec. 24, 1995	3:12 AM	AQU	Jun. 3, 1996	3:12 AM	CAP	Nov. 20, 1996	12:00 PM	A R I
Dec. 26, 1995	3:12 AM	P I S	Jun. 5, 1996	3:12 AM	AQU	Nov. 22, 1996	6:28 PM	TAU
Dec. 28, 1995	6:51 AM	A R I	Jun. 7, 1996	5:09 AM	P I S	Nov. 24, 1996	12:00 AM	GEM
Dec. 30, 1995	6:00 PM	TAU	Jun. 9, 1996	8:34 AM	A R I	Nov. 27, 1996	7:23 AM	CAN
Jan. 2, 1996	4:00 AM	GEM	Jun. 11, 1996	4:37 PM	TAU	Nov. 29, 1996	4:37 PM	LEO
Jan. 4, 1996	4:00 PM	CAN	Jun. 14, 1996	2:00 AM	GEM	Dec. 2, 1996	8:44 AM	VIR
Jan. 7, 1996	4:00 AM	LEO	Jun. 16, 1996	12:00 PM	CAN	Dec. 4, 1996	8:00 PM	L I B
Jan. 9, 1996	4:00 PM	VIR	Jun. 18, 1996	12:00 AM	LEO	Dec. 7, 1996	3:42 AM	SCO
Jan. 12, 1996	4:00 AM	L I B	Jun. 21, 1996	3:16 PM	VIR	Dec. 9, 1996	11:05 AM	SAG
Jan. 14, 1996	11:05 AM	SCO	Jun. 26, 1996	9:14 AM	SCO	Dec. 11, 1996	11:12 AM	CAP
Jan. 16, 1996	1:43 AM	SAG	Jun. 28, 1996	2:46 PM	SAG	Dec. 13, 1996	12:48 PM	AQU
Jan. 18, 1996	2:24 PM	CAP	Jun. 30, 1996	3:26 PM	CAP	Dec. 15, 1996	3:26 PM	P I S
Jan. 20, 1996	2:24 PM	AQU	Jul. 2, 1996	12:48 PM	AQU	Dec. 17, 1996	5:09 PM	A R I
Jan. 22, 1996	2:24 PM	P I S	Jul. 4, 1996	12:48 PM	P I S	Dec. 19, 1996	12:00 AM	TAU
Jan. 24, 1996	5:09 PM	A R I	Jul. 6, 1996	3:26 PM	A R I	Dec. 22, 1996	5:32 AM	GEM
Jan. 26, 1996	8:34 PM	TAU	Jul. 8, 1996	10:09 PM	TAU	Dec. 24, 1996	2:46 PM	CAN

Date	Time	Moon	Date	Time	Moon	Date	Time	Moon
Dec. 27, 1996	2:00 AM	LEO	Jun. 8, 1997	8:18 PM	LEO	Nov. 17, 1997	6:51 AM	CAN
Dec. 29, 1996	2:00 PM	VIR	Jun. 11, 1997	8:00 AM	VIR	Nov. 19, 1997	2:46 PM	LEO
Jan. 1, 1997	4:00 AM	LIB	Jun. 13, 1997	12:00 AM	LIB	Nov. 22, 1997	2:00 AM	VIR
Jan. 3, 1997	12:55 PM	SCO	Jun. 16, 1997	10:00 AM	SCO	Nov. 24, 1997	2:00 PM	LIB
Jan. 5, 1997	10:09 PM	SAG	Jun. 18, 1997	4:37 PM	SAG	Nov. 27, 1997	2:00 AM	SCO
Jan. 7, 1997	12:00 AM	CAP	Jun. 20, 1997	8:34 PM	CAP	Nov. 29, 1997	2:00 PM	SAG
Jan. 9, 1997	10:24 AM	AQU	Jun. 22, 1997	12:00 AM	AQU	Dec. 1, 1997	8:18 PM	CAP
Jan. 11, 1997	10:24 PM	PIS	Jun. 25, 1997	1:43 AM	PIS	Dec. 3, 1997	12:00 AM	AQU
Jan. 13, 1997	10:24 PM	ARI	Jun. 27, 1997	3:26 AM	ARI	Dec. 6, 1997	5:09 AM	PIS
Jan. 16, 1997	5:32 AM	TAU	Jun. 29, 1997	6:51 AM	TAU	Dec. 8, 1997	8:34 AM	ARI
Jan. 18, 1997	11:05 AM	GEM	Jul. 1, 1997	12:55 PM	GEM	Dec. 10, 1997	9:36 AM	TAU
Jan. 20, 1997	8:18 PM	CAN	Jul. 3, 1997	8:18 PM	CAN	Dec. 12, 1997	1:43 PM	GEM
Jan. 23, 1997	7:23 AM	LEO	Jul. 6, 1997	3:42 AM	LEO	Dec. 14, 1997	5:09 PM	CAN
Jan. 25, 1997	12:00 AM	VIR	Jul. 8, 1997	4:00 PM	VIR	Dec. 16, 1997	12:00 AM	LEO
Jan. 28, 1997	10:00 AM	LIB	Jul. 11, 1997	6:33 AM	LIB	Dec. 19, 1997	10:00 AM	VIR
Jan. 30, 1997	10:00 PM	SCO	Jul. 13, 1997	6:00 PM	SCO	Dec. 21, 1997	10:00 PM	LIB
Feb. 2, 1997	5:32 AM	SAG	Jul. 16, 1997	1:51 AM	SAG	Dec. 24, 1997	12:00 PM	SCO
Feb. 4, 1997	10:17 AM	CAP	Jul. 18, 1997	6:51 AM	CAP	Dec. 26, 1997	10:00 PM	SAG
Feb. 6, 1997	9:36 AM	AQU	Jul. 20, 1997	8:00 AM	AQU	Dec. 29, 1997	3:42 AM	CAP
Feb. 8, 1997	9:36 AM	PIS	Jul. 22, 1997	8:00 AM	PIS	Dec. 31, 1997	9:14 AM	AQU
Feb. 10, 1997	9:36 AM	ARI	Jul. 24, 1997	9:36 AM	ARI	Jan. 2, 1998	9:36 AM	PIS
Feb. 12, 1997	12:00 PM	TAU	Jul. 26, 1997	11:12 AM	TAU	Jan. 4, 1998	1:43 PM	ARI
Feb. 14, 1997	6:28 PM	GEM	Jul. 28, 1997	5:09 PM	GEM	Jan. 6, 1998	5:09 PM	TAU
Feb. 17, 1997	4:00 AM	CAN	Jul. 31, 1997	1:51 AM	CAN	Jan. 8, 1998	8:34 PM	GEM
Feb. 19, 1997	2:00 PM	LEO	Aug. 2, 1997	12:00 PM	LEO	Jan. 11, 1998	1:51 AM	CAN
Feb. 22, 1997	4:00 AM	VIR	Aug. 4, 1997	12:00 AM	VIR	Jan. 13, 1998	9:14 AM	LEO
Feb. 24, 1997	4:00 PM	LIB	Aug. 7, 1997	12:00 PM	LIB	Jan. 15, 1998	4:37 PM	VIR
Feb. 27, 1997	4:00 AM	SCO	Aug. 9, 1997	12:00 AM	SCO	Jan. 18, 1998	6:00 AM	LIB
Mar. 1, 1997	12:55 PM	SAG	Aug. 12, 1997	12:00 PM	SAG	Jan. 20, 1998	8:00 PM	SCO
Mar. 3, 1997	8:18 PM	CAP	Aug. 14, 1997	3:26 PM	CAP	Jan. 23, 1998	5:32 AM	SAG
Mar. 5, 1997	10:17 AM	AQU	Aug. 16, 1997	5:36 PM	AQU	Jan. 25, 1998	2:46 PM	CAP
Mar. 7, 1997	8:48 PM	PIS	Aug. 18, 1997	7:12 PM	PIS	Jan. 27, 1998	5:09 PM	AQU
Mar. 9, 1997	8:48 PM	ARI	Aug. 20, 1997	7:12 PM	ARI	Jan. 29, 1998	8:34 PM	PIS
Mar. 11, 1997	8:48 PM	TAU	Aug. 22, 1997	7:12 PM	TAU	Jan. 31, 1998	7:12 PM	ARI
Mar. 14, 1997	1:43 AM	GEM	Aug. 24, 1997	12:00 AM	GEM	Feb. 2, 1998	8:48 PM	TAU
Mar. 16, 1997	9:14 AM	CAN	Aug. 27, 1997	7:23 AM	CAN	Feb. 5, 1998	1:43 AM	GEM
Mar. 18, 1997	10:00 PM	LEO	Aug. 29, 1997	6:00 PM	LEO	Feb. 7, 1998	6:51 AM	CAN
Mar. 21, 1997	10:00 AM	VIR	Sep. 1, 1997	6:00 AM	VIR	Feb. 9, 1998	2:46 PM	LEO
Mar. 23, 1997	10:00 PM	LIB	Sep. 3, 1997	6:00 PM	LIB	Feb. 12, 1998	2:00 AM	VIR
Mar. 26, 1997	10:00 AM	SCO	Sep. 6, 1997	8:44 AM	SCO	Feb. 14, 1998	2:00 PM	LIB
Mar. 28, 1997	6:28 PM	SAG	Sep. 8, 1997	4:37 PM	SAG	Feb. 17, 1998	4:22 AM	SCO
Mar. 31, 1997	1:51 AM	CAP	Sep. 11, 1997	1:51 AM	CAP	Feb. 19, 1998	4:00 PM	SAG
Apr. 2, 1997	5:09 AM	AQU	Sep. 13, 1997	5:09 AM	AQU	Feb. 24, 1998	3:26 AM	AQU
Apr. 4, 1997	6:24 AM	PIS	Sep. 15, 1997	6:51 AM	PIS	Feb. 26, 1998	4:48 AM	PIS
Apr. 6, 1997	6:24 AM	ARI	Sep. 17, 1997	4:30 AM	ARI	Feb. 28, 1998	4:48 AM	ARI
Apr. 8, 1997	8:00 AM	TAU	Sep. 19, 1997	4:48 AM	TAU	Mar. 2, 1998	6:51 AM	TAU
Apr. 10, 1997	12:00 PM	GEM	Sep. 21, 1997	6:24 AM	GEM	Mar. 4, 1998	8:34 AM	GEM
Apr. 12, 1997	6:28 PM	CAN	Sep. 23, 1997	12:00 PM	CAN	Mar. 6, 1998	12:00 PM	CAN
Apr. 15, 1997	4:00 AM	LEO	Sep. 25, 1997	12:00 AM	LEO	Mar. 8, 1998	8:18 PM	LEO
Apr. 17, 1997	4:00 PM	VIR	Sep. 28, 1997	12:00 PM	VIR	Mar. 11, 1998	8:00 AM	VIR
Apr. 20, 1997	6:00 AM	LIB	Sep. 30, 1997	12:00 AM	LIB	Mar. 13, 1998	8:00 PM	LIB
Apr. 22, 1997	2:46 PM	SCO	Oct. 3, 1997	12:00 PM	SCO	Mar. 16, 1998	10:00 AM	SCO
Apr. 24, 1997	12:00 AM	SAG	Oct. 5, 1997	12:00 AM	SAG	Mar. 18, 1998	10:00 PM	SAG
Apr. 27, 1997	7:23 AM	CAP	Oct. 8, 1997	7:23 AM	CAP	Mar. 21, 1998	7:23 AM	CAP
Apr. 29, 1997	10:17 AM	AQU	Oct. 10, 1997	2:46 PM	AQU	Mar. 23, 1998	2:46 PM	AQU
May. 1, 1997	1:43 PM	PIS	Oct. 12, 1997	5:09 PM	PIS	Mar. 25, 1998	5:09 PM	PIS
May. 3, 1997	5:09 AM	ARI	Oct. 14, 1997	4:00 PM	ARI	Mar. 27, 1998	4:00 PM	ARI
May. 5, 1997	6:51 AM	TAU	Oct. 16, 1997	4:00 PM	TAU	Mar. 29, 1998	4:00 PM	TAU
May. 7, 1997	8:34 PM	GEM	Oct. 18, 1997	4:00 PM	GEM	Mar. 31, 1998	4:00 PM	GEM
May. 10, 1997	3:42 AM	CAN	Oct. 20, 1997	8:34 PM	CAN	Apr. 2, 1998	6:51 PM	CAN
May. 12, 1997	11:05 AM	LEO	Oct. 23, 1997	5:32 AM	LEO	Apr. 5, 1998	3:42 AM	LEO
May. 14, 1997	12:00 AM	VIR	Oct. 25, 1997	6:00 PM	VIR	Apr. 7, 1998	2:00 PM	VIR
May. 17, 1997	2:00 PM	LIB	Oct. 28, 1997	8:44 AM	LIB	Apr. 10, 1998	4:22 AM	LIB
May. 22, 1997	7:23 AM	SAG	Oct. 30, 1997	8:00 PM	SCO	Apr. 12, 1998	4:00 PM	SCO
May. 24, 1997	12:00 PM	CAP	Nov. 2, 1997	6:00 AM	SAG	Apr. 15, 1998	4:00 AM	SAG
May. 26, 1997	3:26 AM	AQU	Nov. 4, 1997	12:55 PM	CAP	Apr. 17, 1998	12:55 PM	CAP
May. 28, 1997	6:51 PM	PIS	Nov. 6, 1997	8:18 PM	AQU	Apr. 19, 1998	10:09 PM	AQU
May. 30, 1997	10:17 AM	ARI	Nov. 10, 1997	12:00 AM	PIS	Apr. 22, 1998	1:43 AM	PIS
Jun. 2, 1997	1:43 AM	TAU	Nov. 11, 1997	1:43 AM	ARI	Apr. 24, 1998	3:12 AM	ARI
Jun. 4, 1997	5:09 AM	GEM	Nov. 13, 1997	3:26 AM	TAU	Apr. 26, 1998	3:12 AM	TAU
Jun. 6, 1997	12:55 PM	CAN	Nov. 15, 1997	3:12 AM	GEM	Apr. 28, 1998	3:12 AM	GEM

Date	Time	Moon
Apr. 30, 1998	5:09 AM	CAN
May. 2, 1998	11:05 AM	LEO
May. 4, 1998	10:00 PM	VIR
May. 7, 1998	10:55 AM	LIB
May. 9, 1998	10:00 PM	SCO
May. 12, 1998	10:00 AM	SAG
May. 14, 1998	6:28 PM	CAP
May. 17, 1998	3:42 AM	AQU
May. 19, 1998	8:34 AM	PIS
May. 21, 1998	12:00 PM	ARI
May. 23, 1998	12:48 PM	TAU
May. 25, 1998	12:48 PM	GEM
May. 27, 1998	3:26 PM	CAN
May. 29, 1998	6:51 PM	LEO
Jun. 1, 1998	3:42 AM	VIR
Jun. 3, 1998	4:00 PM	LIB
Jun. 6, 1998	6:33 AM	SCO
Jun. 8, 1998	2:46 PM	SAG
Jun. 11, 1998	1:51 AM	CAP
Jun. 13, 1998	9:14 AM	AQU
Jun. 15, 1998	1:43 PM	PIS
Jun. 17, 1998	6:51 PM	ARI
Jun. 19, 1998	7:12 PM	TAU
Jun. 21, 1998	8:48 PM	GEM
Jun. 26, 1998	5:32 AM	LEO
Jun. 28, 1998	12:55 PM	VIR
Jun. 30, 1998	12:00 AM	LIB
Jul. 3, 1998	12:00 PM	SCO
Jul. 5, 1998	12:00 AM	SAG
Jul. 8, 1998	9:14 AM	CAP
Jul. 10, 1998	4:37 PM	AQU
Jul. 12, 1998	10:09 PM	PIS
Jul. 14, 1998	12:00 AM	ARI
Jul. 17, 1998	1:36 AM	TAU
Jul. 19, 1998	5:09 AM	GEM
Jul. 21, 1998	8:34 AM	CAN
Jul. 23, 1998	2:46 PM	LEO
Jul. 25, 1998	8:18 PM	VIR
Jul. 28, 1998	8:00 AM	LIB
Jul. 30, 1998	8:00 PM	SCO
Aug. 2, 1998	8:00 AM	SAG
Aug. 4, 1998	8:00 PM	CAP
Aug. 9, 1998	3:26 AM	PIS
Aug. 11, 1998	6:51 AM	ARI
Aug. 13, 1998	8:34 AM	TAU
Aug. 15, 1998	10:17 AM	GEM
Aug. 17, 1998	1:43 PM	CAN
Aug. 19, 1998	6:51 PM	LEO
Aug. 22, 1998	6:00 AM	VIR
Aug. 24, 1998	4:00 PM	LIB
Aug. 27, 1998	4:00 AM	SCO
Aug. 29, 1998	4:00 PM	SAG
Sep. 1, 1998	4:00 AM	CAP
Sep. 3, 1998	11:05 AM	AQU
Sep. 5, 1998	1:43 PM	PIS
Sep. 7, 1998	2:24 PM	ARI
Sep. 9, 1998	2:24 PM	TAU
Sep. 11, 1998	4:00 PM	GEM
Sep. 13, 1998	8:34 PM	CAN
Sep. 16, 1998	1:43 AM	LEO
Sep. 18, 1998	11:05 AM	VIR
Sep. 20, 1998	12:00 AM	LIB
Sep. 23, 1998	12:00 PM	SCO
Sep. 25, 1998	12:00 AM	SAG
Sep. 28, 1998	12:00 PM	CAP
Sep. 30, 1998	8:18 PM	AQU
Oct. 2, 1998	12:00 AM	PIS
Oct. 5, 1998	1:36 AM	ARI
Oct. 8, 1998	12:00 AM	GEM
Oct. 11, 1998	3:26 AM	CAN
Oct. 13, 1998	9:14 AM	LEO
Oct. 15, 1998	4:37 PM	VIR
Oct. 18, 1998	6:00 AM	LIB
Oct. 20, 1998	6:00 PM	SCO
Oct. 23, 1998	6:00 AM	SAG
Oct. 25, 1998	6:00 PM	CAP
Oct. 28, 1998	3:42 AM	AQU
Oct. 30, 1998	11:05 AM	PIS
Nov. 1, 1998	11:12 AM	ARI
Nov. 3, 1998	12:48 PM	TAU
Nov. 5, 1998	11:12 AM	GEM
Nov. 7, 1998	11:12 AM	CAN
Nov. 9, 1998	3:26 PM	LEO
Nov. 11, 1998	10:09 PM	VIR
Nov. 14, 1998	9:14 AM	LIB
Nov. 16, 1998	12:00 AM	SCO
Nov. 19, 1998	12:00 AM	SAG
Nov. 21, 1998	12:00 AM	CAP
Nov. 24, 1998	9:14 AM	AQU
Nov. 26, 1998	4:37 PM	PIS
Nov. 28, 1998	12:00 AM	ARI
Nov. 30, 1998	12:00 AM	TAU
Dec. 2, 1998	10:24 PM	GEM
Dec. 4, 1998	10:24 PM	CAN
Dec. 6, 1998	10:24 PM	LEO
Dec. 9, 1998	7:23 AM	VIR
Dec. 11, 1998	6:00 PM	LIB
Dec. 14, 1998	6:00 AM	SCO
Dec. 16, 1998	6:00 PM	SAG
Dec. 19, 1998	6:00 AM	CAP
Dec. 21, 1998	2:46 PM	AQU
Dec. 23, 1998	10:09 PM	PIS
Dec. 26, 1998	3:26 AM	ARI
Dec. 28, 1998	6:51 AM	TAU
Dec. 30, 1998	8:00 AM	GEM
Jan. 1, 1999	10:17 AM	CAN
Jan. 3, 1999	12:00 PM	LEO
Jan. 5, 1999	3:26 PM	VIR
Jan. 8, 1999	2:00 AM	LIB
Jan. 10, 1999	2:00 PM	SCO
Jan. 13, 1999	2:00 AM	SAG
Jan. 15, 1999	2:00 PM	CAP
Jan. 17, 1999	10:09 PM	AQU
Jan. 20, 1999	5:32 AM	PIS
Jan. 22, 1999	8:34 AM	ARI
Jan. 24, 1999	12:00 PM	TAU
Jan. 26, 1999	3:26 PM	GEM
Jan. 28, 1999	6:51 PM	CAN
Jan. 30, 1999	8:34 PM	LEO
Feb. 2, 1999	1:43 AM	VIR
Feb. 4, 1999	12:00 PM	LIB
Feb. 6, 1999	10:00 PM	SCO
Feb. 9, 1999	10:00 AM	SAG
Feb. 11, 1999	10:00 PM	CAP
Feb. 14, 1999	7:23 AM	AQU
Feb. 16, 1999	12:00 PM	PIS
Feb. 18, 1999	3:26 PM	ARI
Feb. 20, 1999	6:51 PM	TAU
Feb. 22, 1999	7:12 PM	GEM
Feb. 24, 1999	12:00 AM	CAN
Feb. 27, 1999	5:32 AM	LEO
Mar. 1, 1999	11:05 AM	VIR
Mar. 3, 1999	6:28 PM	LIB
Mar. 6, 1999	6:00 AM	SCO
Mar. 8, 1999	6:00 PM	SAG
Mar. 11, 1999	5:32 AM	CAP
Mar. 13, 1999	6:00 PM	AQU
Mar. 15, 1999	12:00 AM	PIS
Mar. 18, 1999	1:43 AM	ARI
Mar. 20, 1999	1:36 AM	TAU
Mar. 22, 1999	3:26 AM	GEM
Mar. 24, 1999	5:09 AM	CAN
Mar. 26, 1999	11:05 AM	LEO
Mar. 28, 1999	4:37 PM	VIR
Mar. 31, 1999	1:51 AM	LIB
Apr. 2, 1999	2:00 PM	SCO
Apr. 5, 1999	2:00 AM	SAG
Apr. 7, 1999	2:00 PM	CAP
Apr. 10, 1999	2:00 AM	AQU
Apr. 12, 1999	9:14 AM	PIS
Apr. 14, 1999	12:00 PM	ARI
Apr. 16, 1999	1:43 PM	TAU
Apr. 18, 1999	11:12 AM	GEM
Apr. 20, 1999	11:12 AM	CAN
Apr. 22, 1999	3:26 PM	LEO
Apr. 24, 1999	8:34 PM	VIR
Apr. 27, 1999	7:23 AM	LIB
Apr. 29, 1999	8:00 PM	SCO
May. 2, 1999	8:00 AM	SAG
May. 4, 1999	12:00 AM	CAP
May. 7, 1999	7:23 AM	AQU
May. 9, 1999	4:37 PM	PIS
May. 11, 1999	12:00 AM	ARI
May. 13, 1999	10:24 PM	TAU
May. 15, 1999	10:24 PM	GEM
May. 17, 1999	7:30 PM	CAN
May. 19, 1999	12:00 AM	LEO
May. 22, 1999	5:32 AM	VIR
May. 24, 1999	12:55 PM	LIB
May. 27, 1999	2:00 AM	SCO
May. 29, 1999	2:00 PM	SAG
Jun. 1, 1999	4:22 AM	CAP
Jun. 3, 1999	12:55 PM	AQU
Jun. 8, 1999	5:09 AM	ARI
Jun. 10, 1999	8:00 AM	TAU
Jun. 12, 1999	8:00 AM	GEM
Jun. 14, 1999	8:00 AM	CAN
Jun. 16, 1999	8:00 AM	LEO
Jun. 18, 1999	12:00 PM	VIR
Jun. 20, 1999	8:18 PM	LIB
Jun. 23, 1999	8:00 AM	SCO
Jun. 25, 1999	8:00 PM	SAG
Jun. 28, 1999	10:00 AM	CAP
Jun. 30, 1999	6:28 PM	AQU
Jul. 3, 1999	5:32 AM	PIS
Jul. 5, 1999	12:55 PM	ARI
Jul. 7, 1999	6:28 PM	TAU
Jul. 9, 1999	6:51 PM	GEM
Jul. 11, 1999	5:36 PM	CAN
Jul. 13, 1999	8:34 PM	LEO
Jul. 15, 1999	10:17 PM	VIR
Jul. 18, 1999	5:32 AM	LIB
Jul. 20, 1999	4:00 PM	SCO
Jul. 23, 1999	4:00 AM	SAG
Jul. 25, 1999	4:00 PM	CAP
Jul. 28, 1999	1:51 AM	AQU
Jul. 30, 1999	11:05 AM	PIS
Aug. 1, 1999	6:28 PM	ARI
Aug. 3, 1999	12:00 AM	TAU
Aug. 8, 1999	3:26 AM	CAN
Aug. 10, 1999	5:09 AM	LEO
Aug. 14, 1999	2:46 PM	LIB
Aug. 16, 1999	10:09 PM	SCO
Aug. 19, 1999	12:00 PM	SAG
Aug. 21, 1999	12:00 AM	CAP
Aug. 24, 1999	12:00 PM	AQU
Aug. 26, 1999	6:28 PM	PIS
Aug. 31, 1999	3:26 AM	TAU
Sep. 2, 1999	6:51 AM	GEM
Sep. 4, 1999	8:00 AM	CAN
Sep. 6, 1999	12:00 PM	LEO
Sep. 8, 1999	6:28 PM	VIR

173

Date	Time	Moon	Date	Time	Moon	Date	Time	Moon
Sep. 10, 1999	12:00 AM	L I B	Feb. 19, 2000	4:00 PM	V I R	Aug. 1, 2000	2:24 PM	V I R
Sep. 13, 1999	7:23 AM	SCO	Feb. 21, 2000	8:34 PM	L I B	Aug. 3, 2000	5:09 PM	L I B
Sep. 15, 1999	8:00 PM	SAG	Feb. 24, 2000	3:42 AM	SCO	Aug. 5, 2000	8:34 PM	SCO
Sep. 18, 1999	8:00 AM	CAP	Feb. 26, 2000	2:00 PM	SAG	Aug. 8, 2000	8:00 AM	SAG
Sep. 20, 1999	8:00 PM	AQU	Feb. 29, 2000	2:00 AM	CAP	Aug. 10, 2000	8:00 PM	CAP
Sep. 23, 1999	3:42 AM	P I S	Mar. 2, 2000	2:00 PM	AQU	Aug. 13, 2000	8:00 AM	AQU
Sep. 25, 1999	8:34 AM	A R I	Mar. 7, 2000	7:23 AM	A R I	Aug. 15, 2000	8:00 PM	P I S
Sep. 27, 1999	9:36 AM	TAU	Mar. 9, 2000	12:00 PM	TAU	Aug. 18, 2000	8:00 AM	A R I
Sep. 29, 1999	11:12 AM	GEM	Mar. 11, 2000	5:09 PM	GEM	Aug. 20, 2000	2:46 PM	TAU
Oct. 1, 1999	3:26 PM	CAN	Mar. 13, 2000	8:34 PM	CAN	Aug. 22, 2000	6:51 PM	GEM
Oct. 3, 1999	5:09 PM	LEO	Mar. 15, 2000	10:17 PM	LEO	Aug. 24, 2000	12:00 AM	CAN
Oct. 5, 1999	10:17 PM	V I R	Mar. 18, 2000	1:43 AM	V I R	Aug. 28, 2000	12:00 AM	V I R
Oct. 8, 1999	7:23 AM	L I B	Mar. 20, 2000	5:09 AM	L I B	Aug. 31, 2000	1:36 AM	L I B
Oct. 10, 1999	2:46 PM	SCO	Mar. 22, 2000	12:55 PM	SCO	Sep. 2, 2000	7:23 AM	SCO
Oct. 13, 1999	4:00 AM	SAG	Mar. 24, 2000	8:18 PM	SAG	Sep. 4, 2000	2:46 PM	SAG
Oct. 15, 1999	4:00 PM	CAP	Mar. 27, 2000	10:00 AM	CAP	Sep. 7, 2000	2:00 AM	CAP
Oct. 18, 1999	4:00 AM	AQU	Mar. 29, 2000	10:00 PM	AQU	Sep. 9, 2000	4:00 PM	AQU
Oct. 20, 1999	12:55 PM	P I S	Apr. 1, 2000	10:00 AM	P I S	Sep. 12, 2000	4:00 AM	P I S
Oct. 22, 1999	8:18 PM	A R I	Apr. 3, 2000	4:37 PM	A R I	Sep. 14, 2000	2:00 PM	A R I
Oct. 24, 1999	7:12 PM	TAU	Apr. 5, 2000	8:34 PM	TAU	Sep. 16, 2000	8:18 PM	TAU
Oct. 26, 1999	8:48 PM	GEM	Apr. 7, 2000	12:00 AM	GEM	Sep. 19, 2000	1:51 AM	GEM
Oct. 28, 1999	8:48 PM	CAN	Apr. 10, 2000	1:43 AM	CAN	Sep. 21, 2000	5:09 AM	CAN
Oct. 30, 1999	12:00 AM	LEO	Apr. 12, 2000	3:26 AM	LEO	Sep. 23, 2000	8:34 AM	LEO
Nov. 2, 1999	5:32 AM	V I R	Apr. 14, 2000	9:14 AM	V I R	Sep. 25, 2000	10:17 AM	V I R
Nov. 4, 1999	12:55 PM	L I B	Apr. 16, 2000	2:46 PM	L I B	Sep. 27, 2000	11:12 AM	L I B
Nov. 6, 1999	12:00 AM	SCO	Apr. 18, 2000	8:18 PM	SCO	Sep. 29, 2000	3:26 PM	SCO
Nov. 9, 1999	10:00 AM	SAG	Apr. 21, 2000	6:00 AM	SAG	Oct. 1, 2000	12:00 AM	SAG
Nov. 11, 1999	10:00 PM	CAP	Apr. 23, 2000	6:00 PM	CAP	Oct. 4, 2000	10:00 AM	CAP
Nov. 14, 1999	12:00 PM	AQU	Apr. 26, 2000	6:00 AM	AQU	Oct. 9, 2000	12:00 PM	P I S
Nov. 16, 1999	12:00 AM	P I S	Apr. 28, 2000	6:00 PM	P I S	Oct. 11, 2000	8:18 PM	A R I
Nov. 19, 1999	5:32 AM	A R I	May. 1, 2000	1:51 AM	A R I	Oct. 14, 2000	3:42 AM	TAU
Nov. 21, 1999	6:24 AM	TAU	May. 3, 2000	5:09 AM	TAU	Oct. 16, 2000	6:51 AM	GEM
Nov. 23, 1999	6:00 AM	GEM	May. 5, 2000	6:24 AM	GEM	Oct. 18, 2000	10:17 AM	CAN
Nov. 25, 1999	6:24 AM	CAN	May. 7, 2000	8:00 AM	CAN	Oct. 20, 2000	1:43 PM	LEO
Nov. 27, 1999	6:24 AM	LEO	May. 9, 2000	10:17 AM	LEO	Oct. 22, 2000	5:09 PM	V I R
Nov. 29, 1999	10:17 AM	V I R	May. 11, 2000	1:43 PM	V I R	Oct. 24, 2000	8:34 PM	L I B
Dec. 1, 1999	6:28 PM	L I B	May. 13, 2000	8:18 PM	L I B	Oct. 27, 2000	1:51 AM	SCO
Dec. 4, 1999	3:42 AM	SCO	May. 16, 2000	4:00 AM	SCO	Oct. 29, 2000	9:14 AM	SAG
Dec. 6, 1999	4:00 PM	SAG	May. 18, 2000	2:00 PM	SAG	Oct. 31, 2000	8:00 PM	CAP
Dec. 9, 1999	6:33 AM	CAP	May. 21, 2000	2:11 AM	CAP	Nov. 3, 2000	8:00 AM	AQU
Dec. 11, 1999	6:00 PM	AQU	May. 23, 2000	2:00 PM	AQU	Nov. 5, 2000	8:00 PM	P I S
Dec. 14, 1999	6:00 AM	P I S	May. 26, 2000	2:00 AM	P I S	Nov. 8, 2000	5:32 AM	A R I
Dec. 16, 1999	12:55 PM	A R I	May. 28, 2000	11:05 AM	A R I	Nov. 10, 2000	12:55 PM	TAU
Dec. 18, 1999	5:09 PM	TAU	May. 30, 2000	3:26 PM	TAU	Nov. 12, 2000	3:26 PM	GEM
Dec. 20, 1999	8:34 PM	GEM	Jun. 1, 2000	6:51 PM	GEM	Nov. 14, 2000	4:00 PM	CAN
Dec. 22, 1999	4:30 PM	CAN	Jun. 3, 2000	5:36 PM	CAN	Nov. 16, 2000	5:36 PM	LEO
Dec. 24, 1999	5:36 PM	LEO	Jun. 5, 2000	5:36 PM	LEO	Nov. 18, 2000	10:17 PM	V I R
Dec. 26, 1999	5:36 PM	V I R	Jun. 7, 2000	8:34 PM	V I R	Nov. 21, 2000	1:43 AM	L I B
Dec. 29, 1999	1:51 AM	L I B	Jun. 9, 2000	12:00 AM	L I B	Nov. 23, 2000	9:14 AM	SCO
Dec. 31, 1999	9:14 AM	SCO	Jun. 12, 2000	10:00 AM	SCO	Nov. 25, 2000	4:37 PM	SAG
Jan. 2, 2000	10:00 PM	SAG	Jun. 14, 2000	8:00 PM	SAG	Nov. 28, 2000	1:51 AM	CAP
Jan. 5, 2000	1:05 PM	CAP	Jun. 17, 2000	8:00 AM	CAP	Nov. 30, 2000	5:27 PM	AQU
Jan. 7, 2000	12:00 AM	AQU	Jun. 19, 2000	8:00 PM	AQU	Dec. 3, 2000	4:00 AM	P I S
Jan. 10, 2000	12:00 PM	P I S	Jun. 22, 2000	8:00 AM	P I S	Dec. 5, 2000	4:00 PM	A R I
Jan. 12, 2000	10:00 PM	A R I	Jun. 24, 2000	8:00 PM	A R I	Dec. 7, 2000	10:09 PM	TAU
Jan. 15, 2000	1:51 AM	TAU	Jun. 27, 2000	1:51 AM	TAU	Dec. 10, 2000	1:43 AM	GEM
Jan. 17, 2000	5:09 AM	GEM	Jun. 29, 2000	3:12 AM	GEM	Dec. 12, 2000	3:26 AM	CAN
Jan. 19, 2000	4:48 AM	CAN	Jul. 1, 2000	4:48 AM	CAN	Dec. 14, 2000	3:12 AM	LEO
Jan. 21, 2000	4:48 AM	LEO	Jul. 3, 2000	3:12 AM	LEO	Dec. 16, 2000	5:09 AM	V I R
Jan. 23, 2000	6:51 AM	V I R	Jul. 5, 2000	5:09 AM	V I R	Dec. 18, 2000	9:14 AM	L I B
Jan. 25, 2000	11:05 AM	L I B	Jul. 7, 2000	6:51 AM	L I B	Dec. 20, 2000	2:46 PM	SCO
Jan. 27, 2000	4:37 PM	SCO	Jul. 9, 2000	2:46 PM	SCO	Dec. 22, 2000	10:09 PM	SAG
Jan. 30, 2000	6:00 AM	SAG	Jul. 12, 2000	2:00 AM	SAG	Dec. 25, 2000	10:00 AM	CAP
Feb. 1, 2000	6:00 PM	CAP	Jul. 14, 2000	2:00 PM	CAP	Dec. 27, 2000	10:00 PM	AQU
Feb. 4, 2000	6:00 AM	AQU	Jul. 17, 2000	2:00 AM	AQU	Dec. 30, 2000	1:05 PM	P I S
Feb. 6, 2000	6:00 PM	P I S	Jul. 19, 2000	2:00 PM	P I S	Jan. 1, 2001	12:00 AM	A R I
Feb. 9, 2000	1:51 AM	A R I	Jul. 22, 2000	2:00 AM	A R I	Jan. 4, 2001	7:23 AM	TAU
Feb. 11, 2000	7:23 AM	TAU	Jul. 24, 2000	9:14 AM	TAU	Jan. 6, 2001	12:00 PM	GEM
Feb. 13, 2000	12:55 PM	GEM	Jul. 26, 2000	2:46 PM	GEM	Jan. 8, 2001	3:26 PM	CAN
Feb. 15, 2000	1:43 PM	CAN	Jul. 28, 2000	3:26 PM	CAN	Jan. 10, 2001	2:24 PM	LEO
Feb. 17, 2000	2:24 PM	LEO	Jul. 30, 2000	2:24 PM	LEO	Jan. 12, 2001	12:48 PM	V I R

174

Date	Time	Moon
Jan. 14, 2001	3:26 PM	L I B
Jan. 16, 2001	6:51 PM	SCO
Jan. 19, 2001	3:42 AM	SAG
Jan. 21, 2001	4:00 PM	CAP
Jan. 24, 2001	4:00 AM	AQU
Jan. 26, 2001	6:00 PM	P I S
Jan. 29, 2001	6:00 AM	A R I
Jan. 31, 2001	2:46 PM	TAU
Feb. 2, 2001	10:09 PM	GEM
Feb. 5, 2001	1:43 AM	CAN
Feb. 7, 2001	1:36 AM	LEO
Feb. 8, 2001	10:30 PM	V I R
Feb. 10, 2001	12:00 AM	L I B
Feb. 13, 2001	3:26 AM	SCO
Feb. 15, 2001	11:05 AM	SAG
Feb. 17, 2001	10:00 PM	CAP
Feb. 20, 2001	10:00 AM	AQU
Feb. 22, 2001	12:00 AM	P I S
Feb. 25, 2001	12:00 PM	A R I
Feb. 27, 2001	8:18 PM	TAU
Mar. 2, 2001	5:32 AM	GEM
Mar. 4, 2001	8:34 AM	CAN
Mar. 6, 2001	12:00 PM	LEO
Mar. 8, 2001	11:12 AM	V I R
Mar. 10, 2001	11:12 AM	L I B
Mar. 12, 2001	1:43 AM	SCO
Mar. 14, 2001	5:09 PM	SAG
Mar. 17, 2001	6:00 AM	CAP
Mar. 19, 2001	6:00 AM	AQU
Mar. 22, 2001	6:00 AM	P I S
Mar. 24, 2001	6:00 AM	A R I
Mar. 27, 2001	1:51 AM	TAU
Mar. 29, 2001	8:34 AM	GEM
Mar. 31, 2001	4:37 PM	CAN
Apr. 2, 2001	6:51 PM	LEO
Apr. 4, 2001	7:12 PM	V I R
Apr. 6, 2001	8:48 PM	L I B
Apr. 8, 2001	10:24 PM	SCO
Apr. 11, 2001	5:32 AM	SAG
Apr. 13, 2001	12:55 PM	CAP
Apr. 16, 2001	2:11 AM	AQU
Apr. 18, 2001	2:00 PM	P I S
Apr. 21, 2001	2:00 AM	A R I
Apr. 23, 2001	9:14 AM	TAU
Apr. 25, 2001	4:37 PM	GEM
Apr. 27, 2001	8:34 AM	CAN
Apr. 29, 2001	12:00 AM	LEO
May. 2, 2001	3:26 AM	V I R
May. 4, 2001	4:48 AM	L I B
May. 6, 2001	8:34 AM	SCO
May. 8, 2001	2:46 PM	SAG
May. 10, 2001	10:09 PM	CAP
May. 13, 2001	10:00 AM	AQU
May. 15, 2001	10:00 PM	P I S
May. 18, 2001	10:00 AM	A R I
May. 20, 2001	6:28 PM	TAU
May. 25, 2001	3:26 AM	CAN
May. 27, 2001	6:51 AM	LEO
May. 29, 2001	8:34 AM	V I R
May. 31, 2001	12:00 PM	L I B
Jun. 2, 2001	3:26 PM	SCO
Jun. 4, 2001	10:09 PM	SAG
Jun. 7, 2001	5:32 AM	CAP
Jun. 9, 2001	6:00 AM	AQU
Jun. 12, 2001	6:00 AM	P I S
Jun. 14, 2001	6:00 AM	A R I
Jun. 17, 2001	3:42 AM	TAU
Jun. 19, 2001	8:34 AM	GEM
Jun. 21, 2001	1:43 AM	CAN
Jun. 23, 2001	12:48 PM	LEO
Jun. 25, 2001	2:24 PM	V I R
Jun. 27, 2001	5:09 PM	L I B
Jun. 29, 2001	8:34 PM	SCO
Jul. 2, 2001	3:42 AM	SAG
Jul. 4, 2001	2:00 PM	CAP
Jul. 6, 2001	10:09 PM	AQU
Jul. 9, 2001	12:00 PM	P I S
Jul. 12, 2001	2:00 AM	A R I
Jul. 14, 2001	11:05 AM	TAU
Jul. 16, 2001	8:18 PM	GEM
Jul. 22, 2001	12:00 AM	V I R
Jul. 24, 2001	12:00 AM	L I B
Jul. 27, 2001	3:26 AM	SCO
Jul. 29, 2001	9:14 AM	SAG
Jul. 31, 2001	8:00 PM	CAP
Aug. 3, 2001	6:00 AM	AQU
Aug. 5, 2001	8:00 PM	P I S
Aug. 8, 2001	8:00 AM	A R I
Aug. 10, 2001	8:00 PM	TAU
Aug. 13, 2001	3:42 AM	GEM
Aug. 15, 2001	8:34 AM	CAN
Aug. 17, 2001	9:36 AM	LEO
Aug. 19, 2001	9:36 AM	V I R
Aug. 21, 2001	9:36 AM	L I B
Aug. 23, 2001	9:36 AM	SCO
Aug. 25, 2001	4:37 PM	SAG
Aug. 28, 2001	2:00 AM	CAP
Aug. 30, 2001	12:00 PM	AQU
Sep. 2, 2001	2:00 AM	P I S
Sep. 4, 2001	2:00 AM	A R I
Sep. 7, 2001	2:00 AM	TAU
Sep. 9, 2001	12:00 PM	GEM
Sep. 11, 2001	6:28 PM	CAN
Sep. 13, 2001	8:34 PM	LEO
Sep. 15, 2001	8:48 PM	V I R
Sep. 17, 2001	8:48 PM	L I B
Sep. 19, 2001	7:12 PM	SCO
Sep. 21, 2001	12:00 AM	SAG
Sep. 24, 2001	7:23 AM	CAP
Sep. 26, 2001	8:00 PM	AQU
Sep. 29, 2001	8:00 AM	P I S
Oct. 1, 2001	8:00 PM	A R I
Oct. 4, 2001	8:00 AM	TAU
Oct. 6, 2001	6:00 PM	GEM
Oct. 8, 2001	12:00 AM	CAN
Oct. 11, 2001	3:26 AM	LEO
Oct. 13, 2001	6:51 AM	V I R
Oct. 15, 2001	6:24 AM	L I B
Oct. 17, 2001	6:24 AM	SCO
Oct. 19, 2001	10:17 AM	SAG
Oct. 21, 2001	4:37 PM	CAP
Oct. 24, 2001	2:00 AM	AQU
Oct. 26, 2001	2:00 PM	P I S
Oct. 29, 2001	4:00 AM	A R I
Oct. 31, 2001	2:00 PM	TAU
Nov. 2, 2001	10:09 PM	GEM
Nov. 5, 2001	5:32 AM	CAN
Nov. 7, 2001	8:34 AM	LEO
Nov. 9, 2001	1:43 PM	V I R
Nov. 11, 2001	3:26 PM	L I B
Nov. 13, 2001	5:09 PM	SCO
Nov. 15, 2001	5:36 PM	SAG
Nov. 18, 2001	1:51 AM	CAP
Nov. 20, 2001	12:00 PM	AQU
Nov. 22, 2001	10:00 PM	P I S
Nov. 25, 2001	12:00 PM	A R I
Nov. 27, 2001	8:18 PM	TAU
Nov. 30, 2001	5:32 AM	GEM
Dec. 2, 2001	10:17 AM	CAN
Dec. 4, 2001	3:26 PM	LEO
Dec. 6, 2001	6:51 PM	V I R
Dec. 8, 2001	8:34 PM	L I B
Dec. 10, 2001	12:00 AM	SCO
Dec. 13, 2001	3:26 AM	SAG
Dec. 15, 2001	11:05 AM	CAP
Dec. 17, 2001	6:28 PM	AQU
Dec. 20, 2001	8:00 AM	P I S
Dec. 22, 2001	8:00 PM	A R I
Dec. 25, 2001	8:00 AM	TAU
Dec. 27, 2001	2:46 PM	GEM
Dec. 29, 2001	10:09 PM	CAN
Dec. 31, 2001	12:00 AM	LEO
Jan. 5, 2002	1:36 AM	L I B
Jan. 7, 2002	5:09 AM	SCO
Jan. 9, 2002	11:05 AM	SAG
Jan. 11, 2002	6:28 PM	CAP
Jan. 14, 2002	4:00 AM	AQU
Jan. 16, 2002	4:00 PM	P I S
Jan. 19, 2002	4:00 AM	A R I
Jan. 21, 2002	4:00 PM	TAU
Jan. 24, 2002	2:00 AM	GEM
Jan. 26, 2002	6:51 AM	CAN
Jan. 28, 2002	10:17 AM	LEO
Jan. 30, 2002	9:36 AM	V I R
Feb. 1, 2002	9:36 AM	L I B
Feb. 3, 2002	12:00 PM	SCO
Feb. 5, 2002	3:26 PM	SAG
Feb. 7, 2002	12:00 AM	CAP
Feb. 10, 2002	9:14 AM	AQU
Feb. 12, 2002	10:00 PM	P I S
Feb. 15, 2002	10:00 AM	A R I
Feb. 17, 2002	10:00 PM	TAU
Feb. 20, 2002	10:00 AM	GEM
Feb. 22, 2002	6:28 PM	CAN
Feb. 24, 2002	8:34 PM	LEO
Feb. 26, 2002	8:48 PM	V I R
Feb. 28, 2002	6:00 PM	L I B
Mar. 2, 2002	7:12 PM	SCO
Mar. 4, 2002	10:17 PM	SAG
Mar. 7, 2002	5:32 AM	CAP
Mar. 9, 2002	4:00 PM	AQU
Mar. 12, 2002	4:00 AM	P I S
Mar. 14, 2002	4:00 PM	A R I
Mar. 17, 2002	6:33 AM	TAU
Mar. 19, 2002	4:00 PM	GEM
Mar. 22, 2002	2:00 AM	CAN
Mar. 24, 2002	7:23 AM	LEO
Mar. 26, 2002	8:34 AM	V I R
Mar. 28, 2002	6:00 AM	L I B
Mar. 30, 2002	6:24 AM	SCO
Apr. 1, 2002	8:34 AM	SAG
Apr. 3, 2002	12:00 PM	CAP
Apr. 5, 2002	8:18 PM	AQU
Apr. 8, 2002	10:00 AM	P I S
Apr. 10, 2002	10:00 PM	A R I
Apr. 13, 2002	10:00 AM	TAU
Apr. 15, 2002	10:00 PM	GEM
Apr. 18, 2002	8:00 AM	CAN
Apr. 20, 2002	12:00 PM	LEO
Apr. 22, 2002	5:09 PM	V I R
Apr. 24, 2002	6:51 PM	L I B
Apr. 26, 2002	5:36 PM	SCO
Apr. 28, 2002	5:36 PM	SAG
Apr. 30, 2002	8:34 PM	CAP
May. 3, 2002	5:32 AM	AQU
May. 5, 2002	2:46 PM	P I S
May. 8, 2002	6:00 AM	A R I
May. 10, 2002	6:00 PM	TAU
May. 13, 2002	3:42 AM	GEM
May. 15, 2002	12:55 PM	CAN
May. 17, 2002	8:18 PM	LEO
May. 19, 2002	10:17 PM	V I R
May. 22, 2002	1:43 AM	L I B

Date	Time	Moon	Date	Time	Moon	Date	Time	Moon
May. 24, 2002	3:26 AM	SCO	Nov. 8, 2002	3:26 AM	CAP	Apr. 21, 2003	3:26 AM	CAP
May. 26, 2002	3:12 AM	SAG	Nov. 10, 2002	9:14 AM	AQU	Apr. 23, 2003	6:51 AM	AQU
May. 28, 2002	6:51 AM	CAP	Nov. 12, 2002	8:00 PM	PIS	Apr. 25, 2003	2:46 PM	PIS
May. 30, 2002	2:46 PM	AQU	Nov. 15, 2002	6:00 AM	ARI	Apr. 28, 2003	1:51 AM	ARI
Jun. 4, 2002	12:00 PM	ARI	Nov. 17, 2002	9:49 PM	TAU	Apr. 30, 2003	5:27 PM	TAU
Jun. 7, 2002	2:00 AM	TAU	Nov. 20, 2002	8:00 AM	GEM	May. 3, 2003	4:00 AM	GEM
Jun. 9, 2002	12:00 PM	GEM	Nov. 22, 2002	4:37 PM	CAN	May. 5, 2003	4:00 PM	CAN
Jun. 11, 2002	6:28 PM	CAN	Nov. 25, 2002	1:51 AM	LEO	May. 8, 2003	1:51 AM	LEO
Jun. 16, 2002	3:26 AM	VIR	Nov. 27, 2002	6:51 AM	VIR	May. 10, 2003	8:34 AM	VIR
Jun. 18, 2002	6:51 AM	LIB	Nov. 29, 2002	9:36 AM	LIB	May. 12, 2003	1:43 PM	LIB
Jun. 20, 2002	10:17 AM	SCO	Dec. 1, 2002	11:12 AM	SCO	May. 14, 2003	12:48 PM	SCO
Jun. 22, 2002	12:00 PM	SAG	Dec. 3, 2002	12:48 PM	SAG	May. 16, 2003	12:48 PM	SAG
Jun. 24, 2002	6:28 PM	CAP	Dec. 5, 2002	3:26 PM	CAP	May. 18, 2003	12:48 PM	CAP
Jun. 26, 2002	12:00 AM	AQU	Dec. 7, 2002	8:18 PM	AQU	May. 20, 2003	3:26 PM	AQU
Jun. 29, 2002	10:00 AM	PIS	Dec. 10, 2002	1:51 AM	PIS	May. 22, 2003	10:09 PM	PIS
Jul. 1, 2002	8:00 PM	ARI	Dec. 12, 2002	2:00 PM	ARI	May. 25, 2003	10:00 AM	ARI
Jul. 4, 2002	10:00 AM	TAU	Dec. 15, 2002	2:00 AM	TAU	May. 27, 2003	12:00 AM	TAU
Jul. 6, 2002	6:28 PM	GEM	Dec. 17, 2002	2:00 PM	GEM	May. 30, 2003	10:00 AM	GEM
Jul. 9, 2002	3:42 AM	CAN	Dec. 22, 2002	7:23 AM	LEO	Jun. 1, 2003	10:00 PM	CAN
Jul. 11, 2002	9:14 AM	LEO	Dec. 24, 2002	12:00 PM	VIR	Jun. 4, 2003	7:23 AM	LEO
Jul. 13, 2002	9:36 AM	VIR	Dec. 26, 2002	5:09 PM	LIB	Jun. 6, 2003	4:37 PM	VIR
Jul. 15, 2002	11:12 AM	LIB	Dec. 28, 2002	8:34 PM	SCO	Jun. 8, 2003	10:09 PM	LIB
Jul. 17, 2002	3:26 PM	SCO	Dec. 30, 2002	10:17 PM	SAG	Jun. 10, 2003	12:00 AM	SCO
Jul. 19, 2002	6:51 PM	SAG	Jan. 1, 2003	10:24 PM	CAP	Jun. 12, 2003	10:24 PM	SAG
Jul. 24, 2002	7:23 AM	AQU	Jan. 4, 2003	5:32 AM	AQU	Jun. 14, 2003	10:24 PM	CAP
Jul. 26, 2002	6:00 PM	PIS	Jan. 6, 2003	11:05 AM	PIS	Jun. 17, 2003	1:43 AM	AQU
Jul. 29, 2002	4:00 AM	ARI	Jan. 8, 2003	8:18 PM	ARI	Jun. 19, 2003	7:23 AM	PIS
Jul. 31, 2002	7:38 PM	TAU	Jan. 11, 2003	10:00 AM	TAU	Jun. 21, 2003	2:46 PM	ARI
Aug. 3, 2002	3:42 AM	GEM	Jan. 13, 2003	12:00 AM	GEM	Jun. 24, 2003	4:00 AM	TAU
Aug. 5, 2002	12:55 PM	CAN	Jan. 16, 2003	10:00 AM	CAN	Jun. 26, 2003	7:38 PM	GEM
Aug. 7, 2002	5:09 PM	LEO	Jan. 18, 2003	4:37 PM	LEO	Jun. 29, 2003	3:42 AM	CAN
Aug. 9, 2002	8:34 PM	VIR	Jan. 20, 2003	6:51 PM	VIR	Jul. 1, 2003	4:00 PM	LEO
Aug. 11, 2002	7:12 PM	LIB	Jan. 22, 2003	10:17 PM	LIB	Jul. 3, 2003	10:09 PM	VIR
Aug. 13, 2002	10:17 PM	SCO	Jan. 25, 2003	1:43 AM	SCO	Jul. 6, 2003	1:43 AM	LIB
Aug. 15, 2002	12:00 AM	SAG	Jan. 27, 2003	5:09 AM	SAG	Jul. 8, 2003	5:09 AM	SCO
Aug. 18, 2002	5:09 AM	CAP	Jan. 29, 2003	8:34 AM	CAP	Jul. 10, 2003	8:34 AM	SAG
Aug. 20, 2002	4:00 PM	AQU	Jan. 31, 2003	2:46 PM	AQU	Jul. 12, 2003	10:17 AM	CAP
Aug. 22, 2002	10:09 PM	PIS	Feb. 2, 2003	8:18 PM	PIS	Jul. 14, 2003	12:00 PM	AQU
Aug. 25, 2002	12:00 PM	ARI	Feb. 5, 2003	5:32 AM	ARI	Jul. 16, 2003	3:26 PM	PIS
Aug. 27, 2002	12:00 AM	TAU	Feb. 7, 2003	6:00 PM	TAU	Jul. 18, 2003	12:00 AM	ARI
Aug. 30, 2002	12:00 PM	GEM	Feb. 10, 2003	8:00 AM	GEM	Jul. 21, 2003	12:00 PM	TAU
Sep. 1, 2002	12:00 AM	CAN	Feb. 12, 2003	8:00 PM	CAN	Jul. 23, 2003	12:00 AM	GEM
Sep. 4, 2002	3:26 AM	LEO	Feb. 15, 2003	1:51 AM	LEO	Jul. 26, 2003	12:00 PM	CAN
Sep. 6, 2002	4:48 AM	VIR	Feb. 17, 2003	5:09 AM	VIR	Jul. 28, 2003	8:18 PM	LEO
Sep. 8, 2002	4:48 AM	LIB	Feb. 19, 2003	4:48 AM	LIB	Jul. 31, 2003	3:42 AM	VIR
Sep. 10, 2002	4:48 AM	SCO	Feb. 21, 2003	6:24 AM	SCO	Aug. 2, 2003	6:51 AM	LIB
Sep. 12, 2002	6:51 AM	SAG	Feb. 23, 2003	10:17 AM	SAG	Aug. 4, 2003	9:36 AM	SCO
Sep. 14, 2002	10:17 AM	CAP	Feb. 25, 2003	1:43 PM	CAP	Aug. 6, 2003	1:43 PM	SAG
Sep. 16, 2002	6:28 PM	AQU	Feb. 27, 2003	8:18 PM	AQU	Aug. 8, 2003	5:09 PM	CAP
Sep. 19, 2002	6:00 AM	PIS	Mar. 2, 2003	3:42 PM	PIS	Aug. 10, 2003	8:34 PM	AQU
Sep. 21, 2002	6:00 PM	ARI	Mar. 4, 2003	12:55 PM	ARI	Aug. 13, 2003	1:51 AM	PIS
Sep. 24, 2002	6:00 AM	TAU	Mar. 7, 2003	2:00 AM	TAU	Aug. 15, 2003	9:14 AM	ARI
Sep. 26, 2002	8:00 PM	GEM	Mar. 9, 2003	5:27 PM	GEM	Aug. 17, 2003	8:00 PM	TAU
Sep. 29, 2002	5:32 AM	CAN	Mar. 12, 2003	4:00 AM	CAN	Aug. 20, 2003	8:00 AM	GEM
Oct. 1, 2002	12:55 PM	LEO	Mar. 14, 2003	11:05 AM	LEO	Aug. 22, 2003	8:00 PM	CAN
Oct. 3, 2002	2:24 PM	VIR	Mar. 16, 2003	3:26 PM	VIR	Aug. 25, 2003	5:32 AM	LEO
Oct. 5, 2002	4:00 PM	LIB	Mar. 18, 2003	5:09 PM	LIB	Aug. 27, 2003	10:17 AM	VIR
Oct. 7, 2002	1:30 PM	SCO	Mar. 20, 2003	4:00 PM	SCO	Aug. 29, 2003	3:26 PM	LIB
Oct. 9, 2002	2:24 PM	SAG	Mar. 22, 2003	4:00 PM	SAG	Aug. 31, 2003	5:09 PM	SCO
Oct. 11, 2002	6:51 PM	CAP	Mar. 24, 2003	6:51 PM	CAP	Sep. 2, 2003	5:36 PM	SAG
Oct. 14, 2002	1:51 AM	AQU	Mar. 27, 2003	1:51 AM	AQU	Sep. 4, 2003	10:17 PM	CAP
Oct. 16, 2002	12:00 PM	PIS	Mar. 29, 2003	9:14 AM	PIS	Sep. 7, 2003	3:42 AM	AQU
Oct. 18, 2002	12:00 AM	ARI	Mar. 31, 2003	10:00 AM	ARI	Sep. 9, 2003	9:14 AM	PIS
Oct. 21, 2002	12:00 PM	TAU	Apr. 3, 2003	10:00 AM	TAU	Sep. 11, 2003	4:37 PM	ARI
Oct. 24, 2002	2:00 AM	GEM	Apr. 5, 2003	10:00 PM	GEM	Sep. 14, 2003	4:00 AM	TAU
Oct. 26, 2002	11:05 AM	CAN	Apr. 8, 2003	10:00 AM	CAN	Sep. 16, 2003	4:00 PM	GEM
Oct. 28, 2002	8:18 PM	LEO	Apr. 10, 2003	10:00 PM	LEO	Sep. 19, 2003	6:00 AM	CAN
Oct. 31, 2002	1:51 AM	VIR	Apr. 13, 2003	1:51 AM	VIR	Sep. 21, 2003	4:00 PM	LEO
Nov. 2, 2002	1:36 AM	LIB	Apr. 15, 2003	3:26 AM	LIB	Sep. 23, 2003	10:09 PM	VIR
Nov. 4, 2002	1:36 AM	SCO	Apr. 17, 2003	1:30 AM	SCO	Sep. 25, 2003	12:00 AM	LIB
Nov. 6, 2002	1:36 AM	SAG	Apr. 19, 2003	1:36 AM	SAG	Sep. 27, 2003	12:00 AM	SCO

176

Date	Time	Moon	Date	Time	Moon	Date	Time	Moon
Sep. 30, 2003	1:36 AM	SAG	Mar. 12, 2004	4:48 AM	SAG	Aug. 21, 2004	5:32 AM	SCO
Oct. 2, 2003	3:12 AM	CAP	Mar. 14, 2004	8:34 AM	CAP	Aug. 23, 2004	10:17 AM	SAG
Oct. 4, 2003	8:34 AM	AQU	Mar. 16, 2004	12:00 PM	AQU	Aug. 25, 2004	1:43 PM	CAP
Oct. 6, 2003	2:46 PM	PIS	Mar. 18, 2004	3:26 PM	PIS	Aug. 27, 2004	3:26 PM	AQU
Oct. 11, 2003	12:00 PM	TAU	Mar. 20, 2004	8:34 PM	ARI	Aug. 29, 2004	2:24 PM	PIS
Oct. 13, 2003	12:00 AM	GEM	Mar. 23, 2004	8:00 AM	TAU	Aug. 31, 2004	6:51 PM	ARI
Oct. 16, 2003	12:00 PM	CAN	Mar. 25, 2004	6:00 PM	GEM	Sep. 3, 2004	1:51 AM	TAU
Oct. 18, 2003	12:00 AM	LEO	Mar. 28, 2004	8:44 AM	CAN	Sep. 5, 2004	12:00 PM	GEM
Oct. 21, 2003	7:23 AM	VIR	Mar. 30, 2004	8:00 PM	LEO	Sep. 7, 2004	12:00 AM	CAN
Oct. 23, 2003	10:17 AM	LIB	Apr. 2, 2004	3:42 AM	VIR	Sep. 10, 2004	12:00 PM	LEO
Oct. 25, 2003	11:12 AM	SCO	Apr. 4, 2004	8:34 AM	LIB	Sep. 12, 2004	12:00 AM	VIR
Oct. 27, 2003	11:12 AM	SAG	Apr. 6, 2004	12:00 PM	SCO	Sep. 15, 2004	5:32 AM	LIB
Oct. 29, 2003	11:12 AM	CAP	Apr. 8, 2004	1:43 PM	SAG	Sep. 17, 2004	10:17 AM	SCO
Oct. 31, 2003	1:43 PM	AQU	Apr. 10, 2004	3:26 PM	CAP	Sep. 19, 2004	3:26 PM	SAG
Nov. 2, 2003	6:51 PM	PIS	Apr. 12, 2004	5:09 PM	AQU	Sep. 21, 2004	6:51 PM	CAP
Nov. 5, 2003	5:32 AM	ARI	Apr. 14, 2004	12:00 AM	PIS	Sep. 23, 2004	7:12 PM	AQU
Nov. 7, 2003	6:00 PM	TAU	Apr. 17, 2004	5:32 AM	ARI	Sep. 25, 2004	12:00 AM	PIS
Nov. 10, 2003	6:00 AM	GEM	Apr. 19, 2004	4:00 PM	TAU	Sep. 28, 2004	3:26 AM	ARI
Nov. 12, 2003	6:00 PM	CAN	Apr. 22, 2004	2:00 AM	GEM	Sep. 30, 2004	11:05 AM	TAU
Nov. 15, 2003	5:32 AM	LEO	Apr. 24, 2004	2:00 PM	CAN	Oct. 2, 2004	6:28 PM	GEM
Nov. 17, 2003	2:46 PM	VIR	Apr. 27, 2004	4:00 AM	LEO	Oct. 5, 2004	8:00 AM	CAN
Nov. 19, 2003	10:09 PM	LIB	Apr. 29, 2004	2:00 PM	VIR	Oct. 7, 2004	8:00 PM	LEO
Nov. 21, 2003	12:00 AM	SCO	May 1, 2004	8:18 PM	LIB	Oct. 10, 2004	8:00 AM	VIR
Nov. 23, 2003	10:24 PM	SAG	May 3, 2004	10:17 PM	SCO	Oct. 12, 2004	2:46 PM	LIB
Nov. 25, 2003	7:30 PM	CAP	May 5, 2004	12:00 AM	SAG	Oct. 14, 2004	6:51 PM	SCO
Nov. 27, 2003	12:00 AM	AQU	May 7, 2004	10:24 PM	CAP	Oct. 16, 2004	10:17 PM	SAG
Nov. 30, 2003	3:42 AM	PIS	May 9, 2004	10:24 PM	AQU	Oct. 18, 2004	10:24 PM	CAP
Dec. 2, 2003	11:05 AM	ARI	May 12, 2004	3:26 AM	PIS	Oct. 21, 2004	1:36 AM	AQU
Dec. 4, 2003	12:00 AM	TAU	May 14, 2004	11:05 AM	ARI	Oct. 23, 2004	7:23 AM	PIS
Dec. 7, 2003	12:00 PM	GEM	May 16, 2004	10:00 PM	TAU	Oct. 25, 2004	10:17 AM	ARI
Dec. 10, 2003	2:00 AM	CAN	May 19, 2004	8:00 AM	GEM	Oct. 27, 2004	6:28 PM	TAU
Dec. 12, 2003	11:05 AM	LEO	May 21, 2004	12:00 AM	CAN	Oct. 30, 2004	3:42 AM	GEM
Dec. 14, 2003	12:00 AM	VIR	May 24, 2004	10:00 AM	LEO	Nov. 1, 2004	4:00 PM	CAN
Dec. 17, 2003	5:32 AM	LIB	May 26, 2004	10:00 PM	VIR	Nov. 4, 2004	4:00 AM	LEO
Dec. 19, 2003	8:34 AM	SCO	May 29, 2004	3:26 AM	LIB	Nov. 6, 2004	4:00 PM	VIR
Dec. 21, 2003	10:17 AM	SAG	May 31, 2004	8:34 AM	SCO	Nov. 8, 2004	12:00 AM	LIB
Dec. 23, 2003	9:36 AM	CAP	Jun. 2, 2004	8:00 AM	SAG	Nov. 11, 2004	5:09 AM	SCO
Dec. 25, 2003	10:17 AM	AQU	Jun. 4, 2004	8:00 AM	CAP	Nov. 13, 2004	6:24 AM	SAG
Dec. 27, 2003	12:00 PM	PIS	Jun. 6, 2004	8:00 AM	AQU	Nov. 15, 2004	8:34 AM	CAP
Dec. 29, 2003	6:28 PM	ARI	Jun. 8, 2004	10:17 AM	PIS	Nov. 17, 2004	8:00 AM	AQU
Jan. 1, 2004	6:00 AM	TAU	Jun. 10, 2004	4:37 PM	ARI	Nov. 19, 2004	12:00 PM	PIS
Jan. 3, 2004	6:00 PM	GEM	Jun. 13, 2004	1:51 AM	TAU	Nov. 21, 2004	3:26 PM	ARI
Jan. 6, 2004	8:00 AM	CAN	Jun. 15, 2004	2:00 PM	GEM	Nov. 24, 2004	2:00 AM	TAU
Jan. 8, 2004	8:00 PM	LEO	Jun. 18, 2004	4:00 AM	CAN	Nov. 26, 2004	12:00 PM	GEM
Jan. 11, 2004	3:42 AM	VIR	Jun. 20, 2004	4:00 PM	LEO	Nov. 28, 2004	12:00 AM	CAN
Jan. 13, 2004	11:05 AM	LIB	Jun. 23, 2004	4:00 AM	VIR	Dec. 1, 2004	12:00 PM	LEO
Jan. 15, 2004	4:37 PM	SCO	Jun. 25, 2004	11:05 AM	LIB	Dec. 3, 2004	12:00 AM	VIR
Jan. 17, 2004	6:51 PM	SAG	Jun. 27, 2004	6:28 PM	SCO	Dec. 6, 2004	9:14 AM	LIB
Jan. 19, 2004	8:34 PM	CAP	Jun. 29, 2004	8:34 AM	SAG	Dec. 8, 2004	4:37 PM	SCO
Jan. 21, 2004	7:12 PM	AQU	Jul. 1, 2004	7:12 PM	CAP	Dec. 10, 2004	6:51 PM	SAG
Jan. 23, 2004	8:48 PM	PIS	Jul. 3, 2004	4:30 PM	AQU	Dec. 12, 2004	5:36 PM	CAP
Jan. 26, 2004	3:42 AM	ARI	Jul. 5, 2004	8:34 PM	PIS	Dec. 14, 2004	5:36 PM	AQU
Jan. 28, 2004	2:00 PM	TAU	Jul. 7, 2004	10:17 PM	ARI	Dec. 16, 2004	5:36 PM	PIS
Jan. 31, 2004	2:00 AM	GEM	Jul. 10, 2004	10:00 AM	TAU	Dec. 18, 2004	10:17 PM	ARI
Feb. 2, 2004	5:27 PM	CAN	Jul. 12, 2004	8:00 PM	GEM	Dec. 21, 2004	8:00 AM	TAU
Feb. 5, 2004	2:00 AM	LEO	Jul. 15, 2004	10:00 AM	CAN	Dec. 23, 2004	6:00 PM	GEM
Feb. 7, 2004	9:14 AM	VIR	Jul. 17, 2004	10:00 PM	LEO	Dec. 26, 2004	6:00 AM	CAN
Feb. 9, 2004	4:37 PM	LIB	Jul. 20, 2004	10:00 AM	VIR	Dec. 28, 2004	6:00 PM	LEO
Feb. 11, 2004	8:34 PM	SCO	Jul. 22, 2004	4:37 PM	LIB	Dec. 31, 2004	6:00 AM	VIR
Feb. 13, 2004	12:00 AM	SAG	Jul. 24, 2004	10:17 PM	SCO	Jan. 2, 2005	6:00 PM	LIB
Feb. 16, 2004	3:26 AM	CAP	Jul. 27, 2004	3:26 AM	SAG	Jan. 5, 2005	1:51 AM	SCO
Feb. 18, 2004	4:48 AM	AQU	Jul. 29, 2004	4:48 AM	CAP	Jan. 7, 2005	5:09 AM	SAG
Feb. 20, 2004	8:34 AM	PIS	Jul. 31, 2004	4:48 AM	AQU	Jan. 9, 2005	4:48 AM	CAP
Feb. 22, 2004	2:46 PM	ARI	Aug. 2, 2004	4:48 AM	PIS	Jan. 11, 2005	4:48 AM	AQU
Feb. 24, 2004	12:00 AM	TAU	Aug. 4, 2004	8:34 AM	ARI	Jan. 13, 2005	3:12 AM	PIS
Feb. 27, 2004	10:00 AM	GEM	Aug. 6, 2004	4:37 PM	TAU	Jan. 15, 2005	6:51 AM	ARI
Feb. 29, 2004	10:00 PM	CAN	Aug. 9, 2004	4:00 AM	GEM	Jan. 17, 2005	12:55 PM	TAU
Mar. 3, 2004	9:14 AM	LEO	Aug. 11, 2004	4:00 PM	CAN	Jan. 19, 2005	12:00 AM	GEM
Mar. 5, 2004	6:28 PM	VIR	Aug. 14, 2004	4:00 AM	LEO	Jan. 22, 2005	12:00 AM	CAN
Mar. 7, 2004	10:17 PM	LIB	Aug. 16, 2004	4:00 PM	VIR	Jan. 24, 2005	12:00 AM	LEO
Mar. 10, 2004	3:26 AM	SCO	Aug. 18, 2004	10:09 PM	LIB	Jan. 27, 2005	12:00 PM	VIR

177

Date	Time	Moon	Date	Time	Moon	Date	Time	Moon
Jan. 29, 2005	12:00 AM	L I B	Jul. 17, 2005	12:00 PM	SAG	Dec. 26, 2005	4:00 AM	SCO
Feb. 1, 2005	7:23 AM	SCO	Jul. 19, 2005	3:26 PM	CAP	Dec. 28, 2005	8:34 AM	SAG
Feb. 3, 2005	2:46 PM	SAG	Jul. 21, 2005	2:24 PM	AQU	Dec. 30, 2005	1:43 PM	CAP
Feb. 5, 2005	2:24 PM	CAP	Jul. 23, 2005	12:48 PM	P I S	Jan. 1, 2006	12:48 PM	AQU
Feb. 7, 2005	4:00 PM	AQU	Jul. 25, 2005	12:48 PM	A R I	Jan. 3, 2006	12:48 PM	P I S
Feb. 9, 2005	2:24 PM	P I S	Jul. 27, 2005	5:09 PM	TAU	Jan. 5, 2006	2:24 PM	A R I
Feb. 11, 2005	5:09 PM	A R I	Jul. 30, 2005	4:00 AM	GEM	Jan. 7, 2006	6:51 PM	TAU
Feb. 13, 2005	10:09 PM	TAU	Aug. 1, 2005	2:00 PM	CAN	Jan. 10, 2006	3:42 AM	GEM
Feb. 16, 2005	5:32 AM	GEM	Aug. 4, 2005	2:00 AM	LEO	Jan. 12, 2006	11:05 AM	CAN
Feb. 18, 2005	6:00 PM	CAN	Aug. 6, 2005	2:00 PM	V I R	Jan. 14, 2006	8:18 PM	LEO
Feb. 21, 2005	6:00 AM	LEO	Aug. 9, 2005	4:00 AM	L I B	Jan. 17, 2006	10:00 AM	V I R
Feb. 23, 2005	4:37 PM	V I R	Aug. 11, 2005	2:00 PM	SCO	Jan. 19, 2006	12:00 AM	L I B
Feb. 26, 2005	6:00 AM	L I B	Aug. 13, 2005	12:00 AM	SAG	Jan. 22, 2006	12:00 PM	SCO
Feb. 28, 2005	12:55 PM	SCO	Aug. 15, 2005	12:00 AM	CAP	Jan. 24, 2006	10:00 PM	SAG
Mar. 2, 2005	8:18 PM	SAG	Aug. 17, 2005	12:00 AM	AQU	Jan. 26, 2006	12:00 AM	CAP
Mar. 9, 2005	1:36 AM	P I S	Aug. 19, 2005	12:00 AM	P I S	Jan. 28, 2006	12:00 AM	AQU
Mar. 11, 2005	3:26 AM	A R I	Aug. 21, 2005	12:00 AM	A R I	Jan. 30, 2006	12:00 AM	P I S
Mar. 13, 2005	6:51 AM	TAU	Aug. 24, 2005	3:26 AM	TAU	Feb. 1, 2006	12:00 AM	A R I
Mar. 15, 2005	2:46 PM	GEM	Aug. 26, 2005	9:14 AM	GEM	Feb. 4, 2006	1:43 AM	TAU
Mar. 18, 2005	2:00 AM	CAN	Aug. 28, 2005	8:00 PM	CAN	Feb. 6, 2006	9:14 AM	GEM
Mar. 20, 2005	2:00 PM	LEO	Aug. 31, 2005	8:00 AM	LEO	Feb. 8, 2006	4:37 PM	CAN
Mar. 23, 2005	2:00 AM	V I R	Sep. 2, 2005	8:00 PM	V I R	Feb. 11, 2006	4:00 AM	LEO
Mar. 25, 2005	11:05 AM	L I B	Sep. 5, 2005	7:23 AM	L I B	Feb. 13, 2006	7:38 PM	V I R
Mar. 27, 2005	8:18 PM	SCO	Sep. 7, 2005	8:00 PM	SCO	Feb. 16, 2006	6:00 AM	L I B
Apr. 1, 2005	5:09 AM	CAP	Sep. 10, 2005	3:42 AM	SAG	Feb. 18, 2006	6:00 PM	SCO
Apr. 3, 2005	6:24 AM	AQU	Sep. 12, 2005	9:14 AM	CAP	Feb. 21, 2006	3:42 AM	SAG
Apr. 5, 2005	10:17 AM	P I S	Sep. 14, 2005	10:17 AM	AQU	Feb. 23, 2006	8:34 AM	CAP
Apr. 7, 2005	12:00 PM	A R I	Sep. 16, 2005	9:36 AM	P I S	Feb. 25, 2006	12:00 PM	AQU
Apr. 9, 2005	3:26 PM	TAU	Sep. 18, 2005	9:36 AM	A R I	Feb. 27, 2006	11:12 AM	P I S
Apr. 11, 2005	12:00 AM	GEM	Sep. 20, 2005	11:12 AM	TAU	Mar. 1, 2006	9:00 AM	A R I
Apr. 14, 2005	10:00 AM	CAN	Sep. 22, 2005	6:28 PM	GEM	Mar. 3, 2006	12:00 PM	TAU
Apr. 16, 2005	10:00 PM	LEO	Sep. 25, 2005	4:00 AM	CAN	Mar. 5, 2006	4:37 PM	GEM
Apr. 19, 2005	10:00 AM	V I R	Sep. 27, 2005	2:00 PM	LEO	Mar. 7, 2006	10:09 PM	CAN
Apr. 21, 2005	10:00 PM	L I B	Sep. 30, 2005	4:00 AM	V I R	Mar. 10, 2006	10:00 AM	LEO
Apr. 24, 2005	3:42 AM	SCO	Oct. 2, 2005	4:00 PM	L I B	Mar. 15, 2006	12:00 PM	L I B
Apr. 26, 2005	6:51 AM	SAG	Oct. 5, 2005	2:00 AM	SCO	Mar. 17, 2006	12:00 AM	SCO
Apr. 28, 2005	10:17 AM	CAP	Oct. 7, 2005	9:14 AM	SAG	Mar. 20, 2006	9:14 AM	SAG
Apr. 30, 2005	1:43 PM	AQU	Oct. 9, 2005	2:46 PM	CAP	Mar. 22, 2006	4:37 PM	CAP
May. 2, 2005	3:26 PM	P I S	Oct. 11, 2005	5:09 PM	AQU	Mar. 24, 2006	8:34 AM	AQU
May. 4, 2005	6:51 PM	A R I	Oct. 13, 2005	5:36 PM	P I S	Mar. 26, 2006	8:48 PM	P I S
May. 7, 2005	1:51 AM	TAU	Oct. 15, 2005	7:12 PM	A R I	Mar. 28, 2006	8:48 PM	A R I
May. 9, 2005	7:23 AM	GEM	Oct. 17, 2005	12:00 AM	TAU	Mar. 30, 2006	8:48 PM	TAU
May. 11, 2005	4:37 PM	CAN	Oct. 20, 2005	3:26 AM	GEM	Apr. 1, 2006	10:24 PM	GEM
May. 14, 2005	6:00 AM	LEO	Oct. 22, 2005	11:05 AM	CAN	Apr. 4, 2006	7:23 AM	CAN
May. 16, 2005	6:00 PM	V I R	Oct. 24, 2005	8:18 PM	LEO	Apr. 6, 2006	6:00 PM	LEO
May. 19, 2005	6:00 AM	L I B	Oct. 27, 2005	12:00 PM	V I R	Apr. 9, 2006	6:00 AM	V I R
May. 21, 2005	12:55 PM	SCO	Oct. 29, 2005	12:00 AM	L I B	Apr. 11, 2006	6:00 PM	L I B
May. 23, 2005	5:09 PM	SAG	Nov. 1, 2005	10:00 AM	SCO	Apr. 14, 2006	6:00 AM	SCO
May. 25, 2005	5:36 PM	CAP	Nov. 3, 2005	1:43 PM	SAG	Apr. 16, 2006	2:46 PM	SAG
May. 27, 2005	8:34 PM	AQU	Nov. 5, 2005	6:51 PM	CAP	Apr. 18, 2006	10:09 PM	CAP
May. 29, 2005	7:12 PM	P I S	Nov. 7, 2005	10:17 PM	AQU	Apr. 21, 2006	3:42 AM	AQU
Jun. 1, 2005	1:51 AM	A R I	Nov. 10, 2005	1:43 AM	P I S	Apr. 23, 2006	4:48 PM	P I S
Jun. 3, 2005	7:23 AM	TAU	Nov. 12, 2005	3:12 AM	A R I	Apr. 25, 2006	6:24 AM	A R I
Jun. 5, 2005	2:46 PM	GEM	Nov. 14, 2005	9:14 AM	TAU	Apr. 27, 2006	8:00 AM	TAU
Jun. 8, 2005	2:00 AM	CAN	Nov. 16, 2005	12:00 PM	GEM	Apr. 29, 2006	9:36 AM	GEM
Jun. 10, 2005	2:00 PM	LEO	Nov. 18, 2005	8:18 PM	CAN	May. 1, 2006	4:37 PM	CAN
Jun. 13, 2005	2:00 AM	V I R	Nov. 21, 2005	8:00 AM	LEO	May. 4, 2006	2:00 AM	LEO
Jun. 15, 2005	2:00 PM	L I B	Nov. 23, 2005	8:00 PM	V I R	May. 6, 2006	2:00 PM	V I R
Jun. 17, 2005	10:09 PM	SCO	Nov. 26, 2005	8:00 AM	L I B	May. 9, 2006	2:00 AM	L I B
Jun. 20, 2005	3:26 AM	SAG	Nov. 28, 2005	4:37 PM	SCO	May. 11, 2006	2:00 PM	SCO
Jun. 22, 2005	3:12 AM	CAP	Nov. 30, 2005	12:00 AM	SAG	May. 13, 2006	12:00 AM	SAG
Jun. 24, 2005	3:12 AM	AQU	Dec. 3, 2005	3:26 AM	CAP	May. 16, 2006	3:26 AM	CAP
Jun. 26, 2005	3:12 AM	P I S	Dec. 5, 2005	5:09 AM	AQU	May. 18, 2006	8:34 AM	AQU
Jun. 28, 2005	6:51 AM	A R I	Dec. 7, 2005	6:51 AM	P I S	May. 20, 2006	12:00 PM	P I S
Jun. 30, 2005	12:55 PM	TAU	Dec. 9, 2005	10:17 AM	A R I	May. 22, 2006	12:48 PM	A R I
Jul. 2, 2005	8:18 PM	GEM	Dec. 11, 2005	1:43 PM	TAU	May. 24, 2006	5:09 PM	TAU
Jul. 5, 2005	8:00 AM	CAN	Dec. 13, 2005	6:51 PM	GEM	May. 26, 2006	8:34 PM	GEM
Jul. 7, 2005	8:00 PM	LEO	Dec. 16, 2005	6:00 AM	CAN	May. 29, 2006	1:51 AM	CAN
Jul. 10, 2005	8:00 AM	V I R	Dec. 18, 2005	4:00 PM	LEO	May. 31, 2006	9:14 AM	LEO
Jul. 12, 2005	10:00 PM	L I B	Dec. 21, 2005	4:00 AM	V I R	Jun. 2, 2006	10:00 PM	V I R
Jul. 15, 2005	8:00 AM	SCO	Dec. 23, 2005	4:00 PM	L I B	Jun. 5, 2006	10:00 AM	L I B

Date	Time	Moon	Date	Time	Moon	Date	Time	Moon
Jun. 7, 2006	10:00 PM	SCO	Nov. 18, 2006	4:00 PM	SCO	Apr. 28, 2007	10:00 PM	L I B
Jun. 10, 2006	5:32 AM	SAG	Nov. 21, 2006	1:51 AM	SAG	May. 1, 2007	12:00 PM	SCO
Jun. 12, 2006	10:17 AM	CAP	Nov. 23, 2006	12:00 PM	CAP	May. 3, 2007	12:00 AM	SAG
Jun. 14, 2006	3:26 PM	AQU	Nov. 25, 2006	3:26 PM	AQU	May. 6, 2007	9:14 AM	CAP
Jun. 16, 2006	5:09 PM	P I S	Nov. 27, 2006	8:34 PM	P I S	May. 8, 2007	6:28 PM	AQU
Jun. 18, 2006	8:34 PM	A R I	Nov. 29, 2006	12:00 AM	A R I	May. 13, 2007	3:26 AM	A R I
Jun. 20, 2006	8:48 PM	T A U	Dec. 2, 2006	1:36 AM	T A U	May. 15, 2007	3:12 AM	T A U
Jun. 23, 2006	3:26 AM	GEM	Dec. 4, 2006	3:12 AM	GEM	May. 17, 2007	3:12 AM	GEM
Jun. 25, 2006	8:34 AM	CAN	Dec. 6, 2006	6:51 AM	CAN	May. 19, 2007	5:09 AM	CAN
Jun. 27, 2006	4:37 PM	LEO	Dec. 8, 2006	12:55 PM	LEO	May. 21, 2007	8:34 AM	LEO
Jun. 30, 2006	6:00 AM	VIR	Dec. 10, 2006	8:18 PM	VIR	May. 23, 2007	4:37 PM	VIR
Jul. 2, 2006	6:00 PM	L I B	Dec. 13, 2006	10:00 AM	L I B	May. 26, 2007	6:00 AM	L I B
Jul. 5, 2006	6:00 AM	SCO	Dec. 15, 2006	12:00 AM	SCO	May. 28, 2007	6:00 PM	SCO
Jul. 7, 2006	2:46 PM	SAG	Dec. 18, 2006	9:14 AM	SAG	May. 31, 2007	6:00 AM	SAG
Jul. 9, 2006	10:09 PM	CAP	Dec. 20, 2006	6:28 PM	CAP	Jun. 2, 2007	2:46 PM	CAP
Jul. 11, 2006	12:00 AM	AQU	Dec. 22, 2006	12:00 AM	AQU	Jun. 4, 2007	12:00 AM	AQU
Jul. 15, 2006	12:00 AM	P I S	Dec. 25, 2006	3:42 AM	P I S	Jun. 7, 2007	7:23 AM	P I S
Jul. 16, 2006	1:43 AM	A R I	Dec. 27, 2006	4:48 AM	A R I	Jun. 9, 2007	10:17 AM	A R I
Jul. 18, 2006	5:09 AM	T A U	Dec. 29, 2006	8:34 AM	T A U	Jun. 11, 2007	11:12 AM	T A U
Jul. 20, 2006	8:34 AM	GEM	Dec. 31, 2006	12:00 PM	GEM	Jun. 13, 2007	12:48 PM	GEM
Jul. 22, 2006	4:37 PM	CAN	Jan. 2, 2007	3:26 PM	CAN	Jun. 15, 2007	3:26 PM	CAN
Jul. 25, 2006	2:00 AM	LEO	Jan. 4, 2007	8:34 PM	LEO	Jun. 17, 2007	5:09 PM	LEO
Jul. 27, 2006	12:00 PM	VIR	Jan. 7, 2007	8:00 AM	VIR	Jun. 20, 2007	1:51 AM	VIR
Jul. 30, 2006	2:00 AM	L I B	Jan. 9, 2007	8:00 PM	L I B	Jun. 22, 2007	12:00 PM	L I B
Aug. 1, 2006	2:00 PM	SCO	Jan. 12, 2007	8:00 AM	SCO	Jun. 25, 2007	2:00 AM	SCO
Aug. 6, 2006	7:23 AM	CAP	Jan. 14, 2007	8:00 PM	SAG	Jun. 27, 2007	2:00 PM	SAG
Aug. 8, 2006	8:00 AM	AQU	Jan. 17, 2007	3:42 AM	CAP	Jun. 29, 2007	10:09 PM	CAP
Aug. 10, 2006	9:36 AM	P I S	Jan. 19, 2007	6:51 AM	AQU	Jul. 2, 2007	5:09 AM	AQU
Aug. 12, 2006	9:36 AM	A R I	Jan. 21, 2007	10:17 AM	P I S	Jul. 4, 2007	12:55 PM	P I S
Aug. 14, 2006	9:36 AM	T A U	Jan. 23, 2007	12:00 PM	A R I	Jul. 6, 2007	3:26 PM	A R I
Aug. 16, 2006	1:43 PM	GEM	Jan. 25, 2007	12:48 PM	T A U	Jul. 8, 2007	6:51 PM	T A U
Aug. 18, 2006	10:09 PM	CAN	Jan. 27, 2007	5:09 PM	GEM	Jul. 10, 2007	10:17 PM	GEM
Aug. 21, 2006	8:00 AM	LEO	Jan. 29, 2007	10:17 PM	CAN	Jul. 12, 2007	12:00 AM	CAN
Aug. 23, 2006	8:00 PM	VIR	Feb. 1, 2007	5:32 AM	LEO	Jul. 15, 2007	3:26 AM	LEO
Aug. 26, 2006	8:00 AM	L I B	Feb. 3, 2007	2:46 PM	VIR	Jul. 17, 2007	11:05 AM	VIR
Aug. 28, 2006	8:00 PM	SCO	Feb. 6, 2007	4:00 AM	L I B	Jul. 19, 2007	10:00 PM	L I B
Aug. 31, 2006	8:00 AM	SAG	Feb. 8, 2007	4:00 PM	SCO	Jul. 22, 2007	10:55 AM	SCO
Sep. 2, 2006	4:37 PM	CAP	Feb. 11, 2007	4:00 AM	SAG	Jul. 24, 2007	10:00 PM	SAG
Sep. 4, 2006	6:51 PM	AQU	Feb. 13, 2007	12:55 PM	CAP	Jul. 27, 2007	8:00 AM	CAP
Sep. 6, 2006	7:12 PM	P I S	Feb. 15, 2007	5:09 PM	AQU	Jul. 29, 2007	2:46 PM	AQU
Sep. 8, 2006	7:12 PM	A R I	Feb. 17, 2007	8:34 PM	P I S	Jul. 31, 2007	8:18 PM	P I S
Sep. 10, 2006	7:12 PM	T A U	Feb. 19, 2007	7:12 PM	A R I	Aug. 2, 2007	10:17 PM	A R I
Sep. 12, 2006	10:17 PM	GEM	Feb. 21, 2007	10:17 PM	T A U	Aug. 4, 2007	10:24 PM	T A U
Sep. 15, 2006	3:42 AM	CAN	Feb. 23, 2007	12:00 AM	GEM	Aug. 7, 2007	3:26 AM	GEM
Sep. 17, 2006	2:00 PM	LEO	Feb. 26, 2007	5:32 AM	CAN	Aug. 9, 2007	6:51 AM	CAN
Sep. 20, 2006	2:11 AM	VIR	Feb. 28, 2007	2:00 PM	LEO	Aug. 11, 2007	10:17 AM	LEO
Sep. 22, 2006	2:00 PM	L I B	Mar. 2, 2007	12:00 AM	VIR	Aug. 13, 2007	6:28 PM	VIR
Sep. 25, 2006	2:00 AM	SCO	Mar. 5, 2007	10:00 AM	L I B	Aug. 16, 2007	6:00 AM	L I B
Sep. 27, 2006	2:00 PM	SAG	Mar. 7, 2007	10:00 PM	SCO	Aug. 18, 2007	7:38 PM	SCO
Sep. 29, 2006	10:09 PM	CAP	Mar. 10, 2007	12:00 PM	SAG	Aug. 21, 2007	6:00 AM	SAG
Oct. 2, 2006	3:26 AM	AQU	Mar. 12, 2007	8:18 PM	CAP	Aug. 23, 2007	6:00 PM	CAP
Oct. 4, 2006	6:51 AM	P I S	Mar. 15, 2007	3:26 AM	AQU	Aug. 25, 2007	12:00 AM	AQU
Oct. 6, 2006	6:24 AM	A R I	Mar. 17, 2007	6:51 AM	P I S	Aug. 28, 2007	3:26 AM	P I S
Oct. 8, 2006	6:24 AM	T A U	Mar. 19, 2007	6:24 AM	A R I	Aug. 30, 2007	4:48 AM	A R I
Oct. 10, 2006	6:24 AM	GEM	Mar. 21, 2007	6:24 AM	T A U	Sep. 1, 2007	6:24 AM	T A U
Oct. 12, 2006	10:17 AM	CAN	Mar. 23, 2007	6:24 AM	GEM	Sep. 3, 2007	8:34 AM	GEM
Oct. 14, 2006	6:28 PM	LEO	Mar. 25, 2007	10:17 AM	CAN	Sep. 5, 2007	12:00 PM	CAN
Oct. 17, 2006	8:00 AM	VIR	Mar. 27, 2007	6:28 PM	LEO	Sep. 7, 2007	6:28 PM	LEO
Oct. 19, 2006	8:00 PM	L I B	Mar. 30, 2007	4:00 PM	VIR	Sep. 10, 2007	1:51 AM	VIR
Oct. 22, 2006	8:00 PM	SCO	Apr. 1, 2007	4:00 PM	L I B	Sep. 12, 2007	11:05 AM	L I B
Oct. 24, 2006	8:00 PM	SAG	Apr. 4, 2007	6:00 AM	SCO	Sep. 14, 2007	12:00 AM	SCO
Oct. 27, 2006	6:00 AM	CAP	Apr. 6, 2007	6:00 PM	SAG	Sep. 17, 2007	3:16 PM	SAG
Oct. 29, 2006	10:17 AM	AQU	Apr. 9, 2007	3:42 AM	CAP	Sep. 22, 2007	9:14 AM	AQU
Oct. 31, 2006	3:26 PM	P I S	Apr. 11, 2007	12:55 PM	AQU	Sep. 24, 2007	1:43 PM	P I S
Nov. 2, 2006	4:00 PM	A R I	Apr. 13, 2007	6:28 PM	P I S	Sep. 26, 2007	2:24 PM	A R I
Nov. 4, 2006	6:51 PM	T A U	Apr. 15, 2007	5:36 PM	A R I	Sep. 28, 2007	1:30 PM	T A U
Nov. 6, 2006	5:36 PM	GEM	Apr. 17, 2007	5:36 PM	T A U	Sep. 30, 2007	2:24 PM	GEM
Nov. 8, 2006	8:34 PM	CAN	Apr. 19, 2007	3:00 PM	GEM	Oct. 2, 2007	4:00 PM	CAN
Nov. 11, 2006	3:42 AM	LEO	Apr. 21, 2007	6:51 PM	CAN	Oct. 4, 2007	12:00 AM	LEO
Nov. 13, 2006	2:00 PM	VIR	Apr. 23, 2007	10:17 PM	LEO	Oct. 7, 2007	7:23 AM	VIR
Nov. 16, 2006	4:22 AM	L I B	Apr. 26, 2007	9:14 AM	VIR	Oct. 9, 2007	8:00 PM	L I B

179

Date	Time	Moon	Date	Time	Moon	Date	Time	Moon
Oct. 12, 2007	8:44 AM	SCO	Mar. 29, 2008	4:00 AM	CAP	Sep. 8, 2008	8:00 PM	CAP
Oct. 14, 2007	8:00 PM	SAG	Mar. 31, 2008	4:00 PM	AQU	Sep. 11, 2008	8:00 AM	AQU
Oct. 17, 2007	8:00 AM	CAP	Apr. 2, 2008	10:09 PM	PIS	Sep. 13, 2008	4:37 PM	PIS
Oct. 19, 2007	4:37 PM	AQU	Apr. 5, 2008	1:43 AM	ARI	Sep. 15, 2008	12:00 AM	ARI
Oct. 24, 2007	1:36 AM	ARI	Apr. 7, 2008	1:36 AM	TAU	Sep. 18, 2008	1:43 AM	TAU
Oct. 26, 2007	1:36 AM	TAU	Apr. 9, 2008	1:36 AM	GEM	Sep. 20, 2008	3:12 AM	GEM
Oct. 28, 2007	1:36 AM	GEM	Apr. 11, 2008	3:12 AM	CAN	Sep. 22, 2008	6:51 AM	CAN
Oct. 30, 2007	1:36 AM	CAN	Apr. 13, 2008	6:51 AM	LEO	Sep. 24, 2008	10:17 AM	LEO
Nov. 1, 2007	5:09 AM	LEO	Apr. 15, 2008	2:46 PM	VIR	Sep. 26, 2008	1:43 PM	VIR
Nov. 3, 2007	12:55 PM	VIR	Apr. 17, 2008	10:09 PM	LIB	Sep. 28, 2008	10:09 PM	LIB
Nov. 5, 2007	10:09 PM	LIB	Apr. 20, 2008	10:00 AM	SCO	Oct. 1, 2008	6:00 AM	SCO
Nov. 8, 2007	3:16 PM	SCO	Apr. 22, 2008	10:00 PM	SAG	Oct. 3, 2008	4:00 PM	SAG
Nov. 11, 2007	2:00 AM	SAG	Apr. 25, 2008	10:00 AM	CAP	Oct. 6, 2008	4:00 AM	CAP
Nov. 13, 2007	2:00 PM	CAP	Apr. 27, 2008	10:00 PM	AQU	Oct. 8, 2008	6:00 PM	AQU
Nov. 18, 2007	9:14 AM	PIS	Apr. 30, 2008	7:23 AM	PIS	Oct. 11, 2008	1:51 AM	PIS
Nov. 20, 2007	12:00 PM	ARI	May. 2, 2008	12:00 PM	ARI	Oct. 13, 2008	9:14 AM	ARI
Nov. 22, 2007	12:48 PM	TAU	May. 4, 2008	12:48 PM	TAU	Oct. 15, 2008	9:36 AM	TAU
Nov. 24, 2007	12:48 PM	GEM	May. 6, 2008	12:48 PM	GEM	Oct. 17, 2008	11:12 AM	GEM
Nov. 26, 2007	10:30 AM	CAN	May. 8, 2008	11:12 AM	CAN	Oct. 19, 2008	1:43 PM	CAN
Nov. 28, 2007	12:48 PM	LEO	May. 10, 2008	12:48 PM	LEO	Oct. 21, 2008	3:26 PM	LEO
Nov. 30, 2007	8:18 PM	VIR	May. 12, 2008	8:18 PM	VIR	Oct. 23, 2008	6:51 PM	VIR
Dec. 3, 2007	8:00 AM	LIB	May. 15, 2008	3:42 AM	LIB	Oct. 26, 2008	3:42 AM	LIB
Dec. 5, 2007	8:00 PM	SCO	May. 17, 2008	4:00 PM	SCO	Oct. 28, 2008	2:00 PM	SCO
Dec. 8, 2007	8:00 AM	SAG	May. 20, 2008	4:00 AM	SAG	Oct. 30, 2008	12:00 AM	SAG
Dec. 10, 2007	8:00 PM	CAP	May. 22, 2008	4:00 PM	CAP	Nov. 2, 2008	12:00 PM	CAP
Dec. 13, 2007	5:32 AM	AQU	May. 25, 2008	3:42 AM	AQU	Nov. 5, 2008	2:11 AM	AQU
Dec. 15, 2007	2:46 PM	PIS	May. 27, 2008	4:00 PM	PIS	Nov. 7, 2008	12:00 PM	PIS
Dec. 17, 2007	6:51 PM	ARI	May. 29, 2008	10:09 PM	ARI	Nov. 9, 2008	6:28 PM	ARI
Dec. 19, 2007	8:48 PM	TAU	May. 31, 2008	12:00 AM	TAU	Nov. 11, 2008	10:17 PM	TAU
Dec. 21, 2007	10:24 PM	GEM	Jun. 4, 2008	10:24 PM	CAN	Nov. 13, 2008	8:48 PM	GEM
Dec. 23, 2007	10:24 PM	CAN	Jun. 6, 2008	10:24 PM	LEO	Nov. 15, 2008	8:48 PM	CAN
Dec. 28, 2007	5:09 AM	VIR	Jun. 9, 2008	3:42 AM	VIR	Nov. 17, 2008	8:48 PM	LEO
Dec. 30, 2007	4:00 PM	LIB	Jun. 11, 2008	12:00 PM	LIB	Nov. 20, 2008	1:43 AM	VIR
Jan. 2, 2008	2:00 AM	SCO	Jun. 13, 2008	10:00 PM	SCO	Nov. 22, 2008	9:14 AM	LIB
Jan. 4, 2008	5:27 PM	SAG	Jun. 16, 2008	10:00 AM	SAG	Nov. 24, 2008	8:00 PM	SCO
Jan. 7, 2008	1:51 AM	CAP	Jun. 18, 2008	10:00 PM	CAP	Nov. 27, 2008	6:00 AM	SAG
Jan. 9, 2008	11:05 AM	AQU	Jun. 21, 2008	10:00 AM	AQU	Nov. 29, 2008	6:00 PM	CAP
Jan. 11, 2008	8:18 PM	PIS	Jun. 23, 2008	10:00 PM	PIS	Dec. 2, 2008	8:00 AM	AQU
Jan. 14, 2008	1:51 AM	ARI	Jun. 26, 2008	3:42 AM	ARI	Dec. 4, 2008	8:00 PM	PIS
Jan. 16, 2008	5:09 AM	TAU	Jun. 28, 2008	8:34 AM	TAU	Dec. 7, 2008	3:42 AM	ARI
Jan. 18, 2008	6:24 AM	GEM	Jun. 30, 2008	10:17 AM	GEM	Dec. 9, 2008	8:34 AM	TAU
Jan. 20, 2008	8:00 AM	CAN	Jul. 2, 2008	7:30 AM	CAN	Dec. 11, 2008	8:00 AM	GEM
Jan. 22, 2008	12:00 PM	LEO	Jul. 4, 2008	10:17 AM	LEO	Dec. 13, 2008	8:00 AM	CAN
Jan. 24, 2008	3:26 PM	VIR	Jul. 6, 2008	12:00 PM	VIR	Dec. 15, 2008	6:24 AM	LEO
Jan. 26, 2008	10:09 PM	LIB	Jul. 8, 2008	6:28 PM	LIB	Dec. 17, 2008	10:17 PM	VIR
Jan. 29, 2008	10:00 AM	SCO	Jul. 11, 2008	3:42 AM	SCO	Dec. 19, 2008	1:43 PM	LIB
Jan. 31, 2008	10:00 PM	SAG	Jul. 13, 2008	4:00 PM	SAG	Dec. 24, 2008	12:00 PM	SAG
Feb. 3, 2008	12:00 PM	CAP	Jul. 16, 2008	6:00 AM	CAP	Dec. 26, 2008	12:00 AM	CAP
Feb. 5, 2008	10:00 PM	AQU	Jul. 18, 2008	6:00 PM	AQU	Dec. 29, 2008	2:00 PM	AQU
Feb. 8, 2008	3:42 AM	PIS	Jul. 21, 2008	1:51 AM	PIS	Jan. 1, 2009	2:00 AM	PIS
Feb. 10, 2008	6:51 AM	ARI	Jul. 23, 2008	9:14 AM	ARI	Jan. 3, 2009	12:00 PM	ARI
Feb. 12, 2008	10:17 AM	TAU	Jul. 25, 2008	1:43 PM	TAU	Jan. 5, 2009	3:26 PM	TAU
Feb. 14, 2008	1:43 PM	GEM	Jul. 27, 2008	5:09 PM	GEM	Jan. 7, 2009	8:34 PM	GEM
Feb. 16, 2008	2:24 PM	CAN	Jul. 29, 2008	5:36 PM	CAN	Jan. 9, 2009	7:12 PM	CAN
Feb. 18, 2008	6:51 PM	LEO	Jul. 31, 2008	8:34 PM	LEO	Jan. 11, 2009	7:12 PM	LEO
Feb. 21, 2008	1:51 AM	VIR	Aug. 2, 2008	10:17 PM	VIR	Jan. 13, 2009	7:12 PM	VIR
Feb. 23, 2008	10:00 AM	LIB	Aug. 5, 2008	3:42 AM	LIB	Jan. 15, 2009	10:17 PM	LIB
Feb. 25, 2008	8:00 PM	SCO	Aug. 7, 2008	11:05 AM	SCO	Jan. 18, 2009	7:23 AM	SCO
Feb. 28, 2008	8:00 AM	SAG	Aug. 9, 2008	12:00 AM	SAG	Jan. 20, 2009	6:00 PM	SAG
Mar. 1, 2008	8:00 PM	CAP	Aug. 12, 2008	12:00 PM	CAP	Jan. 23, 2009	8:44 AM	CAP
Mar. 4, 2008	6:00 AM	AQU	Aug. 14, 2008	12:00 AM	AQU	Jan. 25, 2009	8:00 PM	AQU
Mar. 6, 2008	12:55 PM	PIS	Aug. 17, 2008	10:00 AM	PIS	Jan. 28, 2009	8:00 AM	PIS
Mar. 8, 2008	3:26 PM	ARI	Aug. 19, 2008	1:43 PM	ARI	Jan. 30, 2009	6:00 PM	ARI
Mar. 10, 2008	4:00 PM	TAU	Aug. 21, 2008	6:51 PM	TAU	Feb. 1, 2009	12:00 AM	TAU
Mar. 12, 2008	5:36 PM	GEM	Aug. 23, 2008	10:17 PM	GEM	Feb. 4, 2009	3:26 AM	GEM
Mar. 14, 2008	10:17 PM	CAN	Aug. 26, 2008	1:43 AM	CAN	Feb. 6, 2009	4:48 AM	CAN
Mar. 17, 2008	1:43 AM	LEO	Aug. 28, 2008	3:26 AM	LEO	Feb. 8, 2009	4:48 AM	LEO
Mar. 19, 2008	9:14 AM	VIR	Aug. 30, 2008	6:51 AM	VIR	Feb. 10, 2009	6:24 AM	VIR
Mar. 21, 2008	4:37 PM	LIB	Sep. 1, 2008	12:55 PM	LIB	Feb. 12, 2009	8:00 AM	LIB
Mar. 24, 2008	4:00 AM	SCO	Sep. 3, 2008	8:18 PM	SCO	Feb. 14, 2009	4:37 PM	SCO
Mar. 26, 2008	5:27 PM	SAG	Sep. 6, 2008	8:00 AM	SAG	Feb. 17, 2009	2:00 AM	SAG

Date	Time	Moon	Date	Time	Moon	Date	Time	Moon
Feb. 19, 2009	2:00 PM	CAP	Jul. 30, 2009	10:00 PM	SAG	Jan. 8, 2010	10:17 AM	SCO
Feb. 22, 2009	4:22 AM	AQU	Aug. 2, 2009	10:55 AM	CAP	Jan. 10, 2010	6:28 PM	SAG
Feb. 24, 2009	2:00 PM	PIS	Aug. 4, 2009	10:00 PM	AQU	Jan. 13, 2010	6:00 AM	CAP
Feb. 26, 2009	10:09 PM	ARI	Aug. 7, 2009	10:00 AM	PIS	Jan. 15, 2010	6:00 PM	AQU
Mar. 1, 2009	5:32 AM	TAU	Aug. 9, 2009	10:00 PM	ARI	Jan. 18, 2010	8:44 AM	PIS
Mar. 3, 2009	8:34 AM	GEM	Aug. 12, 2009	5:32 AM	TAU	Jan. 20, 2010	8:00 PM	ARI
Mar. 5, 2009	12:00 PM	CAN	Aug. 14, 2009	10:17 AM	GEM	Jan. 23, 2010	5:32 AM	TAU
Mar. 7, 2009	3:26 PM	LEO	Aug. 16, 2009	12:48 PM	CAN	Jan. 25, 2010	12:55 PM	GEM
Mar. 9, 2009	5:09 PM	VIR	Aug. 18, 2009	2:24 PM	LEO	Jan. 27, 2010	3:26 PM	CAN
Mar. 11, 2009	5:36 PM	LIB	Aug. 20, 2009	2:24 PM	VIR	Jan. 29, 2010	2:24 PM	LEO
Mar. 14, 2009	1:51 AM	SCO	Aug. 22, 2009	5:09 PM	LIB	Jan. 31, 2010	2:24 PM	VIR
Mar. 16, 2009	9:14 AM	SAG	Aug. 24, 2009	6:51 PM	SCO	Feb. 2, 2010	2:24 PM	LIB
Mar. 18, 2009	10:00 PM	CAP	Aug. 27, 2009	3:42 AM	SAG	Feb. 4, 2010	5:09 PM	SCO
Mar. 21, 2009	1:05 PM	AQU	Aug. 29, 2009	4:00 PM	CAP	Feb. 7, 2010	2:00 AM	SAG
Mar. 23, 2009	8:18 PM	PIS	Sep. 1, 2009	4:00 AM	AQU	Feb. 9, 2010	12:00 PM	CAP
Mar. 26, 2009	5:32 AM	ARI	Sep. 3, 2009	7:38 PM	PIS	Feb. 11, 2010	12:00 AM	AQU
Mar. 28, 2009	10:17 AM	TAU	Sep. 6, 2009	4:00 AM	ARI	Feb. 14, 2010	3:16 PM	PIS
Mar. 30, 2009	1:43 PM	GEM	Sep. 8, 2009	11:05 AM	TAU	Feb. 17, 2010	2:00 AM	ARI
Apr. 1, 2009	5:09 PM	CAN	Sep. 10, 2009	6:28 PM	GEM	Feb. 19, 2010	11:05 AM	TAU
Apr. 3, 2009	8:34 PM	LEO	Sep. 12, 2009	8:34 PM	CAN	Feb. 21, 2010	8:18 PM	GEM
Apr. 5, 2009	12:00 AM	VIR	Sep. 14, 2009	12:00 AM	LEO	Feb. 23, 2010	12:00 AM	CAN
Apr. 8, 2009	3:26 AM	LIB	Sep. 16, 2009	12:00 AM	VIR	Feb. 26, 2010	1:36 AM	LEO
Apr. 10, 2009	11:05 AM	SCO	Sep. 19, 2009	1:36 AM	LIB	Feb. 28, 2010	1:36 AM	VIR
Apr. 12, 2009	6:28 PM	SAG	Sep. 21, 2009	5:09 AM	SCO	Mar. 2, 2010	1:36 AM	LIB
Apr. 15, 2009	6:00 AM	CAP	Sep. 23, 2009	12:55 PM	SAG	Mar. 4, 2010	3:26 AM	SCO
Apr. 17, 2009	9:49 PM	AQU	Sep. 25, 2009	12:00 AM	CAP	Mar. 6, 2010	9:14 AM	SAG
Apr. 20, 2009	8:00 AM	PIS	Sep. 28, 2009	12:00 PM	AQU	Mar. 8, 2010	4:37 PM	CAP
Apr. 22, 2009	2:46 PM	ARI	Sep. 30, 2009	12:00 AM	PIS	Mar. 11, 2010	6:00 AM	AQU
Apr. 24, 2009	6:51 PM	TAU	Oct. 3, 2009	9:14 AM	ARI	Mar. 13, 2010	8:00 PM	PIS
Apr. 26, 2009	10:17 PM	GEM	Oct. 5, 2009	6:28 PM	TAU	Mar. 16, 2010	8:00 AM	ARI
Apr. 28, 2009	10:24 PM	CAN	Oct. 7, 2009	12:00 AM	GEM	Mar. 18, 2010	4:37 PM	TAU
May. 1, 2009	1:43 AM	LEO	Oct. 10, 2009	3:42 AM	CAN	Mar. 21, 2010	1:51 AM	GEM
May. 3, 2009	5:09 AM	VIR	Oct. 12, 2009	4:48 AM	LEO	Mar. 23, 2010	6:51 AM	CAN
May. 5, 2009	11:05 AM	LIB	Oct. 14, 2009	8:34 AM	VIR	Mar. 25, 2010	10:17 AM	LEO
May. 7, 2009	6:28 PM	SCO	Oct. 16, 2009	12:00 PM	LIB	Mar. 27, 2010	11:12 AM	VIR
May. 10, 2009	1:51 AM	SAG	Oct. 18, 2009	3:26 PM	SCO	Mar. 29, 2010	1:43 PM	LIB
May. 12, 2009	2:00 PM	CAP	Oct. 20, 2009	10:09 PM	SAG	Mar. 31, 2010	12:48 PM	SCO
May. 15, 2009	4:22 AM	AQU	Oct. 23, 2009	8:00 AM	CAP	Apr. 2, 2010	5:09 PM	SAG
May. 17, 2009	4:00 PM	PIS	Oct. 25, 2009	8:00 AM	AQU	Apr. 5, 2010	1:51 AM	CAP
May. 19, 2009	12:00 AM	ARI	Oct. 28, 2009	8:00 AM	PIS	Apr. 7, 2010	2:00 PM	AQU
May. 22, 2009	5:09 AM	TAU	Oct. 30, 2009	8:00 AM	ARI	Apr. 10, 2010	2:00 AM	PIS
May. 24, 2009	8:34 AM	GEM	Nov. 2, 2009	1:51 AM	TAU	Apr. 12, 2010	2:00 AM	ARI
May. 26, 2009	8:00 AM	CAN	Nov. 4, 2009	5:09 AM	GEM	Apr. 17, 2010	7:23 AM	GEM
May. 28, 2009	8:00 AM	LEO	Nov. 6, 2009	8:34 AM	CAN	Apr. 19, 2010	12:00 PM	CAN
May. 30, 2009	12:00 PM	VIR	Nov. 8, 2009	12:00 PM	LEO	Apr. 21, 2010	6:28 PM	LEO
Jun. 1, 2009	3:26 PM	LIB	Nov. 10, 2009	1:43 PM	VIR	Apr. 23, 2010	5:36 PM	VIR
Jun. 3, 2009	12:00 AM	SCO	Nov. 12, 2009	5:09 PM	LIB	Apr. 25, 2010	10:17 PM	LIB
Jun. 6, 2009	10:00 AM	SAG	Nov. 14, 2009	10:17 PM	SCO	Apr. 27, 2010	12:00 AM	SCO
Jun. 8, 2009	6:28 PM	CAP	Nov. 17, 2009	5:32 AM	SAG	Apr. 30, 2010	3:26 AM	SAG
Jun. 11, 2009	10:00 AM	AQU	Nov. 19, 2009	2:46 PM	CAP	May. 2, 2010	11:05 AM	CAP
Jun. 13, 2009	10:00 PM	PIS	Nov. 22, 2009	4:00 AM	AQU	May. 4, 2010	10:00 PM	AQU
Jun. 16, 2009	10:00 AM	ARI	Nov. 24, 2009	4:00 PM	PIS	May. 7, 2010	10:00 AM	PIS
Jun. 18, 2009	4:37 PM	TAU	Nov. 27, 2009	3:42 AM	ARI	May. 9, 2010	10:00 PM	ARI
Jun. 20, 2009	6:51 PM	GEM	Nov. 29, 2009	11:05 AM	TAU	May. 12, 2010	7:23 AM	TAU
Jun. 22, 2009	5:36 PM	CAN	Dec. 1, 2009	3:26 PM	GEM	May. 14, 2010	2:46 PM	GEM
Jun. 24, 2009	5:36 PM	LEO	Dec. 3, 2009	4:00 PM	CAN	May. 16, 2010	8:18 PM	CAN
Jun. 26, 2009	5:36 PM	VIR	Dec. 5, 2009	5:36 PM	LEO	May. 18, 2010	10:17 PM	LEO
Jun. 28, 2009	10:17 PM	LIB	Dec. 7, 2009	8:34 PM	VIR	May. 23, 2010	3:26 AM	LIB
Jul. 1, 2009	5:32 AM	SCO	Dec. 9, 2009	12:00 AM	LIB	May. 25, 2010	6:51 AM	SCO
Jul. 3, 2009	4:00 PM	SAG	Dec. 12, 2009	5:32 AM	SCO	May. 27, 2010	12:55 PM	SAG
Jul. 6, 2009	4:22 AM	CAP	Dec. 14, 2009	12:55 PM	SAG	May. 29, 2010	6:28 PM	CAP
Jul. 8, 2009	4:00 PM	AQU	Dec. 16, 2009	12:00 AM	CAP	Jun. 1, 2010	6:00 AM	AQU
Jul. 11, 2009	4:00 AM	PIS	Dec. 19, 2009	12:00 PM	AQU	Jun. 3, 2010	6:00 PM	PIS
Jul. 13, 2009	4:00 PM	ARI	Dec. 21, 2009	12:00 AM	PIS	Jun. 6, 2010	6:00 AM	ARI
Jul. 15, 2009	12:00 AM	TAU	Dec. 24, 2009	12:00 AM	ARI	Jun. 8, 2010	6:00 PM	TAU
Jul. 18, 2009	3:26 AM	GEM	Dec. 26, 2009	12:00 AM	TAU	Jun. 10, 2010	12:00 AM	GEM
Jul. 20, 2009	4:48 AM	CAN	Dec. 29, 2009	1:43 AM	GEM	Jun. 13, 2010	3:26 AM	CAN
Jul. 22, 2009	4:48 AM	LEO	Dec. 31, 2009	3:12 AM	CAN	Jun. 15, 2010	5:09 AM	LEO
Jul. 24, 2009	4:48 AM	VIR	Jan. 2, 2010	3:12 AM	LEO	Jun. 17, 2010	6:51 AM	VIR
Jul. 26, 2009	6:51 AM	LIB	Jan. 4, 2010	3:12 AM	VIR	Jun. 19, 2010	8:00 AM	LIB
Jul. 28, 2009	10:17 AM	SCO	Jan. 6, 2010	4:48 AM	LIB	Jun. 21, 2010	12:00 PM	SCO

Date	Time	Moon	Date	Time	Moon	Date	Time	Moon
Jun. 23, 2010	5:09 PM	SAG	Dec. 6, 2010	10:17 PM	CAP	May. 22, 2011	3:42 AM	AQU
Jun. 26, 2010	4:00 PM	CAP	Dec. 9, 2010	7:23 AM	AQU	May. 24, 2011	2:00 PM	PIS
Jun. 28, 2010	2:00 PM	AQU	Dec. 11, 2010	8:00 PM	PIS	May. 27, 2011	2:00 AM	ARI
Jul. 1, 2010	2:00 AM	PIS	Dec. 14, 2010	8:00 AM	ARI	May. 29, 2011	2:00 PM	TAU
Jul. 3, 2010	2:00 AM	ARI	Dec. 16, 2010	8:00 PM	TAU	Jun. 3, 2011	9:14 AM	CAN
Jul. 6, 2010	2:00 AM	TAU	Dec. 19, 2010	3:42 AM	GEM	Jun. 5, 2011	4:37 PM	LEO
Jul. 8, 2010	9:14 AM	GEM	Dec. 21, 2010	11:05 AM	CAN	Jun. 7, 2011	10:09 PM	VIR
Jul. 10, 2010	12:00 PM	CAN	Dec. 23, 2010	1:43 PM	LEO	Jun. 9, 2011	12:00 AM	LIB
Jul. 12, 2010	12:48 PM	LEO	Dec. 25, 2010	5:09 PM	VIR	Jun. 12, 2011	1:43 AM	SCO
Jul. 14, 2010	2:24 PM	VIR	Dec. 27, 2010	6:51 PM	LIB	Jun. 14, 2011	3:26 AM	SAG
Jul. 16, 2010	2:24 PM	LIB	Dec. 29, 2010	10:17 PM	SCO	Jun. 16, 2011	6:51 AM	CAP
Jul. 18, 2010	6:51 PM	SCO	Jan. 1, 2011	1:43 AM	SAG	Jun. 18, 2011	12:55 PM	AQU
Jul. 23, 2010	9:14 AM	CAP	Jan. 3, 2011	9:14 AM	CAP	Jun. 20, 2011	8:18 PM	PIS
Jul. 25, 2010	6:28 PM	AQU	Jan. 5, 2011	4:37 PM	AQU	Jun. 23, 2011	10:00 AM	ARI
Jul. 28, 2010	8:00 AM	PIS	Jan. 8, 2011	4:00 AM	PIS	Jun. 25, 2011	10:00 PM	TAU
Jul. 30, 2010	10:00 PM	ARI	Jan. 10, 2011	4:00 PM	ARI	Jun. 28, 2011	10:00 AM	GEM
Aug. 2, 2010	10:00 AM	TAU	Jan. 13, 2011	4:00 AM	TAU	Jun. 30, 2011	4:37 PM	CAN
Aug. 4, 2010	8:00 PM	GEM	Jan. 15, 2011	4:00 PM	GEM	Jul. 2, 2011	12:00 AM	LEO
Aug. 6, 2010	10:17 PM	CAN	Jan. 17, 2011	10:09 PM	CAN	Jul. 5, 2011	1:43 AM	VIR
Aug. 10, 2010	12:00 AM	VIR	Jan. 19, 2011	12:00 AM	LEO	Jul. 7, 2011	5:09 AM	LIB
Aug. 12, 2010	12:00 AM	LIB	Jan. 23, 2011	12:00 AM	LIB	Jul. 9, 2011	6:24 AM	SCO
Aug. 15, 2010	1:43 AM	SCO	Jan. 26, 2011	3:26 AM	SCO	Jul. 11, 2011	10:17 AM	SAG
Aug. 17, 2010	7:23 AM	SAG	Jan. 28, 2011	6:51 AM	SAG	Jul. 13, 2011	4:37 PM	CAP
Aug. 19, 2010	2:46 PM	CAP	Jan. 30, 2011	2:46 PM	CAP	Jul. 15, 2011	10:09 PM	AQU
Aug. 22, 2010	2:00 AM	AQU	Feb. 4, 2011	12:00 PM	PIS	Jul. 18, 2011	5:32 AM	PIS
Aug. 24, 2010	5:27 PM	PIS	Feb. 6, 2011	12:00 AM	ARI	Jul. 20, 2011	6:00 AM	ARI
Aug. 27, 2010	4:00 AM	ARI	Feb. 9, 2011	12:00 PM	TAU	Jul. 23, 2011	6:00 AM	TAU
Aug. 29, 2010	4:00 PM	TAU	Feb. 11, 2011	12:00 AM	GEM	Jul. 25, 2011	6:00 PM	GEM
Sep. 1, 2010	2:00 AM	GEM	Feb. 14, 2011	7:23 AM	CAN	Jul. 28, 2011	1:51 AM	CAN
Sep. 3, 2010	6:51 AM	CAN	Feb. 16, 2011	10:17 AM	LEO	Jul. 30, 2011	6:51 AM	LEO
Sep. 5, 2010	9:36 AM	LEO	Feb. 18, 2011	11:12 AM	VIR	Aug. 1, 2011	10:17 AM	VIR
Sep. 7, 2010	11:12 AM	VIR	Feb. 20, 2011	9:36 AM	LIB	Aug. 3, 2011	12:00 PM	LIB
Sep. 9, 2010	9:00 AM	LIB	Feb. 22, 2011	9:36 AM	SCO	Aug. 5, 2011	1:43 AM	SCO
Sep. 11, 2010	9:36 AM	SCO	Feb. 24, 2011	1:43 PM	SAG	Aug. 7, 2011	3:26 AM	SAG
Sep. 13, 2010	1:43 AM	SAG	Feb. 26, 2011	8:18 PM	CAP	Aug. 9, 2011	8:34 AM	CAP
Sep. 15, 2010	8:18 PM	CAP	Mar. 1, 2011	5:32 AM	AQU	Aug. 12, 2011	6:00 AM	AQU
Sep. 18, 2010	8:00 AM	AQU	Mar. 3, 2011	6:00 PM	PIS	Aug. 14, 2011	12:55 PM	PIS
Sep. 20, 2010	8:00 PM	PIS	Mar. 6, 2011	6:00 AM	ARI	Aug. 17, 2011	2:00 AM	ARI
Sep. 23, 2010	10:00 AM	ARI	Mar. 8, 2011	6:00 PM	TAU	Aug. 19, 2011	2:00 PM	TAU
Sep. 25, 2010	10:00 PM	TAU	Mar. 11, 2011	6:00 AM	GEM	Aug. 22, 2011	2:00 AM	GEM
Sep. 28, 2010	8:00 AM	GEM	Mar. 13, 2011	2:46 PM	CAN	Aug. 24, 2011	11:05 AM	CAN
Sep. 30, 2010	2:46 PM	CAN	Mar. 15, 2011	10:09 PM	LEO	Aug. 26, 2011	6:28 PM	LEO
Oct. 2, 2010	6:51 PM	LEO	Mar. 17, 2011	8:48 PM	VIR	Aug. 28, 2011	8:34 PM	VIR
Oct. 4, 2010	10:17 PM	VIR	Mar. 19, 2011	7:30 PM	LIB	Aug. 30, 2011	7:12 PM	LIB
Oct. 6, 2010	8:48 PM	LIB	Mar. 21, 2011	8:48 PM	SCO	Sep. 1, 2011	7:12 PM	SCO
Oct. 8, 2010	8:48 PM	SCO	Mar. 23, 2011	8:48 PM	SAG	Sep. 3, 2011	10:17 PM	SAG
Oct. 10, 2010	8:48 PM	SAG	Mar. 26, 2011	3:42 AM	CAP	Sep. 6, 2011	3:42 AM	CAP
Oct. 13, 2010	5:32 AM	CAP	Mar. 28, 2011	11:05 AM	AQU	Sep. 8, 2011	11:05 AM	AQU
Oct. 15, 2010	4:00 AM	AQU	Mar. 30, 2011	12:00 AM	PIS	Sep. 10, 2011	10:00 PM	PIS
Oct. 18, 2010	4:00 AM	PIS	Apr. 2, 2011	12:00 PM	ARI	Sep. 13, 2011	8:00 AM	ARI
Oct. 20, 2010	4:00 AM	ARI	Apr. 4, 2011	12:00 AM	TAU	Sep. 15, 2011	8:00 PM	TAU
Oct. 23, 2010	4:00 AM	TAU	Apr. 7, 2011	12:00 PM	GEM	Sep. 18, 2011	10:55 AM	GEM
Oct. 25, 2010	2:00 PM	GEM	Apr. 9, 2011	12:00 AM	CAN	Sep. 20, 2011	6:28 PM	CAN
Oct. 27, 2010	8:18 PM	CAN	Apr. 12, 2011	5:32 AM	LEO	Sep. 23, 2011	3:42 AM	LEO
Oct. 30, 2010	1:43 AM	LEO	Apr. 14, 2011	8:34 AM	VIR	Sep. 25, 2011	4:48 AM	VIR
Nov. 1, 2010	5:09 PM	VIR	Apr. 16, 2011	8:00 AM	LIB	Sep. 27, 2011	6:24 AM	LIB
Nov. 3, 2010	6:51 AM	LIB	Apr. 18, 2011	8:00 AM	SCO	Sep. 29, 2011	4:48 AM	SCO
Nov. 5, 2010	6:24 PM	SCO	Apr. 20, 2011	8:34 AM	SAG	Oct. 1, 2011	4:48 AM	SAG
Nov. 7, 2010	8:00 AM	SAG	Apr. 22, 2011	10:17 AM	CAP	Oct. 3, 2011	8:34 AM	CAP
Nov. 9, 2010	1:43 PM	CAP	Apr. 24, 2011	6:28 PM	AQU	Oct. 5, 2011	4:37 PM	AQU
Nov. 11, 2010	10:09 PM	AQU	Apr. 27, 2011	6:00 AM	PIS	Oct. 8, 2011	2:00 AM	PIS
Nov. 14, 2010	12:00 PM	PIS	Apr. 29, 2011	6:00 PM	ARI	Oct. 10, 2011	2:00 PM	ARI
Nov. 16, 2010	12:00 AM	ARI	May. 2, 2011	6:00 AM	TAU	Oct. 13, 2011	2:00 AM	TAU
Nov. 19, 2010	12:00 PM	TAU	May. 4, 2011	6:00 PM	GEM	Oct. 15, 2011	5:27 PM	GEM
Nov. 21, 2010	10:00 PM	GEM	May. 7, 2011	3:42 AM	CAN	Oct. 18, 2011	1:51 AM	CAN
Nov. 24, 2010	1:43 AM	CAN	May. 9, 2011	11:05 AM	LEO	Oct. 20, 2011	11:05 AM	LEO
Nov. 26, 2010	6:51 AM	LEO	May. 11, 2011	4:37 PM	VIR	Oct. 22, 2011	3:26 AM	VIR
Nov. 28, 2010	10:17 AM	VIR	May. 13, 2011	4:00 PM	LIB	Oct. 24, 2011	4:00 PM	LIB
Nov. 30, 2010	1:43 PM	LIB	May. 15, 2011	5:36 PM	SCO	Oct. 26, 2011	4:00 PM	SCO
Dec. 2, 2010	2:24 PM	SCO	May. 17, 2011	5:36 PM	SAG	Oct. 28, 2011	4:00 PM	SAG
Dec. 4, 2010	6:51 PM	SAG	May. 19, 2011	7:12 PM	CAP	Oct. 30, 2011	4:00 PM	CAP

Date	Time	Moon	Date	Time	Moon	Date	Time	Moon
Nov. 1, 2011	12:00 AM	AQU	Apr. 11, 2012	6:51 PM	CAP	Sep. 20, 2012	4:00 PM	SAG
Nov. 4, 2011	7:23 AM	PIS	Apr. 13, 2012	12:00 AM	AQU	Sep. 22, 2012	8:34 PM	CAP
Nov. 6, 2011	8:00 PM	ARI	Apr. 16, 2012	5:32 AM	PIS	Sep. 24, 2012	12:00 AM	AQU
Nov. 9, 2011	8:00 AM	TAU	Apr. 18, 2012	6:00 PM	ARI	Sep. 27, 2012	5:09 AM	PIS
Nov. 11, 2011	12:00 AM	GEM	Apr. 21, 2012	6:33 AM	TAU	Sep. 29, 2012	4:00 PM	ARI
Nov. 14, 2011	8:00 AM	CAN	Apr. 23, 2012	6:00 PM	GEM	Oct. 1, 2012	10:09 PM	TAU
Nov. 16, 2011	4:37 PM	LEO	Apr. 26, 2012	6:00 AM	CAN	Oct. 4, 2012	12:00 PM	GEM
Nov. 18, 2011	12:00 AM	VIR	Apr. 28, 2012	6:00 PM	LEO	Oct. 7, 2012	2:00 AM	CAN
Nov. 21, 2011	1:36 AM	LIB	Apr. 30, 2012	12:00 AM	VIR	Oct. 9, 2012	2:00 PM	LEO
Nov. 23, 2011	3:12 AM	SCO	May. 3, 2012	3:26 AM	LIB	Oct. 11, 2012	8:18 PM	VIR
Nov. 25, 2011	3:12 AM	SAG	May. 5, 2012	3:12 AM	SCO	Oct. 13, 2012	12:00 AM	LIB
Nov. 27, 2011	3:12 AM	CAP	May. 7, 2012	3:12 AM	SAG	Oct. 16, 2012	1:43 AM	SCO
Nov. 29, 2011	6:51 AM	AQU	May. 9, 2012	3:26 AM	CAP	Oct. 18, 2012	1:36 AM	SAG
Dec. 1, 2011	2:46 PM	PIS	May. 11, 2012	5:09 AM	AQU	Oct. 20, 2012	3:26 AM	CAP
Dec. 4, 2011	2:00 AM	ARI	May. 13, 2012	12:55 PM	PIS	Oct. 22, 2012	5:09 AM	AQU
Dec. 6, 2011	4:00 PM	TAU	May. 15, 2012	12:00 AM	ARI	Oct. 24, 2012	12:55 PM	PIS
Dec. 9, 2011	4:00 AM	GEM	May. 18, 2012	10:00 AM	TAU	Oct. 26, 2012	10:00 PM	ARI
Dec. 11, 2011	12:55 PM	CAN	May. 20, 2012	12:00 AM	GEM	Oct. 29, 2012	8:00 AM	TAU
Dec. 13, 2011	10:09 PM	LEO	May. 23, 2012	12:00 PM	CAN	Oct. 31, 2012	8:00 PM	GEM
Dec. 16, 2011	5:32 AM	VIR	May. 25, 2012	12:00 AM	LEO	Nov. 3, 2012	8:00 AM	CAN
Dec. 18, 2011	8:34 AM	LIB	May. 28, 2012	7:23 AM	VIR	Nov. 5, 2012	8:00 PM	LEO
Dec. 20, 2011	12:00 PM	SCO	May. 30, 2012	12:00 PM	LIB	Nov. 8, 2012	5:32 AM	VIR
Dec. 22, 2011	1:43 PM	SAG	Jun. 1, 2012	12:48 PM	SCO	Nov. 10, 2012	10:17 AM	LIB
Dec. 24, 2011	3:26 PM	CAP	Jun. 3, 2012	12:48 PM	SAG	Nov. 12, 2012	11:12 AM	SCO
Dec. 26, 2011	5:09 PM	AQU	Jun. 5, 2012	12:48 PM	CAP	Nov. 14, 2012	10:30 AM	SAG
Dec. 28, 2011	10:17 PM	PIS	Jun. 7, 2012	3:26 PM	AQU	Nov. 16, 2012	11:12 AM	CAP
Dec. 31, 2011	9:14 AM	ARI	Jun. 9, 2012	6:51 PM	PIS	Nov. 18, 2012	1:43 PM	AQU
Jan. 2, 2012	10:00 PM	TAU	Jun. 12, 2012	6:00 AM	ARI	Nov. 20, 2012	5:09 PM	PIS
Jan. 5, 2012	12:00 PM	GEM	Jun. 14, 2012	6:00 PM	TAU	Nov. 23, 2012	1:51 AM	ARI
Jan. 7, 2012	12:00 AM	CAN	Jun. 17, 2012	6:00 AM	GEM	Nov. 25, 2012	2:00 PM	TAU
Jan. 10, 2012	5:32 AM	LEO	Jun. 19, 2012	6:00 PM	CAN	Nov. 28, 2012	2:00 AM	GEM
Jan. 12, 2012	10:17 AM	VIR	Jun. 22, 2012	3:42 AM	LEO	Nov. 30, 2012	2:00 PM	CAN
Jan. 14, 2012	1:43 PM	LIB	Jun. 24, 2012	12:55 PM	VIR	Dec. 3, 2012	1:51 AM	LEO
Jan. 16, 2012	5:09 PM	SCO	Jun. 26, 2012	5:09 PM	LIB	Dec. 5, 2012	2:00 PM	VIR
Jan. 18, 2012	8:34 PM	SAG	Jun. 28, 2012	10:17 PM	SCO	Dec. 7, 2012	8:18 PM	LIB
Jan. 20, 2012	12:00 AM	CAP	Jun. 30, 2012	12:00 AM	SAG	Dec. 11, 2012	10:24 PM	SAG
Jan. 23, 2012	3:26 AM	AQU	Jul. 4, 2012	12:00 AM	CAP	Dec. 13, 2012	10:24 PM	CAP
Jan. 25, 2012	8:34 AM	PIS	Jul. 5, 2012	1:43 AM	AQU	Dec. 15, 2012	10:24 PM	AQU
Jan. 27, 2012	6:28 PM	ARI	Jul. 7, 2012	5:09 AM	PIS	Dec. 18, 2012	1:43 AM	PIS
Jan. 30, 2012	8:00 AM	TAU	Jul. 9, 2012	12:55 PM	ARI	Dec. 20, 2012	9:14 AM	ARI
Feb. 1, 2012	8:00 PM	GEM	Jul. 11, 2012	12:00 AM	TAU	Dec. 22, 2012	8:00 PM	TAU
Feb. 4, 2012	8:00 AM	CAN	Jul. 14, 2012	3:16 PM	GEM	Dec. 25, 2012	8:00 AM	GEM
Feb. 6, 2012	2:46 PM	LEO	Jul. 17, 2012	2:00 AM	CAN	Dec. 27, 2012	8:00 PM	CAN
Feb. 8, 2012	6:51 PM	VIR	Jul. 19, 2012	12:00 PM	LEO	Dec. 30, 2012	7:23 AM	LEO
Feb. 10, 2012	7:12 PM	LIB	Jul. 21, 2012	6:28 PM	VIR	Jan. 1, 2013	8:00 PM	VIR
Feb. 12, 2012	12:00 AM	SCO	Jul. 23, 2012	10:17 PM	LIB	Jan. 4, 2013	1:51 AM	LIB
Feb. 15, 2012	1:43 AM	SAG	Jul. 26, 2012	3:26 AM	SCO	Jan. 6, 2013	6:51 AM	SCO
Feb. 17, 2012	5:09 AM	CAP	Jul. 28, 2012	6:51 AM	SAG	Jan. 8, 2013	10:17 AM	SAG
Feb. 19, 2012	10:17 AM	AQU	Jul. 30, 2012	8:34 AM	CAP	Jan. 10, 2013	9:36 AM	CAP
Feb. 21, 2012	6:28 PM	PIS	Aug. 1, 2012	9:36 AM	AQU	Jan. 12, 2013	9:36 AM	AQU
Feb. 24, 2012	4:00 AM	ARI	Aug. 3, 2012	1:43 PM	PIS	Jan. 14, 2013	12:00 PM	PIS
Feb. 26, 2012	4:00 PM	TAU	Aug. 5, 2012	10:09 PM	ARI	Jan. 16, 2013	3:26 PM	ARI
Feb. 29, 2012	4:00 AM	GEM	Aug. 8, 2012	8:00 AM	TAU	Jan. 19, 2013	1:51 AM	TAU
Mar. 2, 2012	4:00 PM	CAN	Aug. 10, 2012	8:00 PM	GEM	Jan. 21, 2013	2:00 PM	GEM
Mar. 4, 2012	12:00 AM	LEO	Aug. 13, 2012	10:00 AM	CAN	Jan. 24, 2013	4:00 AM	CAN
Mar. 7, 2012	5:09 AM	VIR	Aug. 15, 2012	6:28 PM	LEO	Jan. 26, 2013	4:00 PM	LEO
Mar. 9, 2012	4:48 AM	LIB	Aug. 18, 2012	1:51 AM	VIR	Jan. 28, 2013	12:00 AM	VIR
Mar. 11, 2012	6:24 AM	SCO	Aug. 20, 2012	5:09 AM	LIB	Jan. 31, 2013	7:23 AM	LIB
Mar. 13, 2012	8:34 AM	SAG	Aug. 22, 2012	8:34 AM	SCO	Feb. 2, 2013	12:00 PM	SCO
Mar. 15, 2012	10:17 AM	CAP	Aug. 24, 2012	12:00 PM	SAG	Feb. 4, 2013	5:09 PM	SAG
Mar. 17, 2012	3:26 PM	AQU	Aug. 26, 2012	3:26 PM	CAP	Feb. 6, 2013	5:36 PM	CAP
Mar. 20, 2012	2:00 AM	PIS	Aug. 28, 2012	6:51 PM	AQU	Feb. 8, 2013	7:12 PM	AQU
Mar. 22, 2012	12:00 PM	ARI	Aug. 30, 2012	10:17 PM	PIS	Feb. 10, 2013	8:48 PM	PIS
Mar. 24, 2012	10:00 PM	TAU	Sep. 2, 2012	8:00 AM	ARI	Feb. 13, 2013	3:42 AM	ARI
Mar. 27, 2012	12:00 PM	GEM	Sep. 4, 2012	2:46 PM	TAU	Feb. 15, 2013	12:00 PM	TAU
Mar. 29, 2012	12:00 AM	CAN	Sep. 7, 2012	6:33 AM	GEM	Feb. 17, 2013	10:00 PM	GEM
Apr. 1, 2012	9:14 AM	LEO	Sep. 9, 2012	6:00 PM	CAN	Feb. 20, 2013	12:00 PM	CAN
Apr. 3, 2012	4:37 PM	VIR	Sep. 12, 2012	3:42 AM	LEO	Feb. 22, 2013	12:00 AM	LEO
Apr. 5, 2012	4:00 PM	LIB	Sep. 14, 2012	11:05 AM	VIR	Feb. 25, 2013	7:23 AM	VIR
Apr. 7, 2012	4:00 PM	SCO	Sep. 16, 2012	1:43 PM	LIB	Feb. 27, 2013	2:46 PM	LIB
Apr. 9, 2012	4:00 PM	SAG	Sep. 18, 2012	2:24 PM	SCO	Mar. 1, 2013	8:18 PM	SCO

Date	Time	Moon	Date	Time	Moon	Date	Time	Moon
Mar. 3, 2013	10:17 PM	SAG	Aug. 12, 2013	10:09 PM	SCO	Jan. 23, 2014	10:09 PM	SCO
Mar. 6, 2013	1:43 AM	CAP	Aug. 15, 2013	1:43 AM	SAG	Jan. 26, 2014	3:26 AM	SAG
Mar. 8, 2013	3:26 AM	AQU	Aug. 17, 2013	5:09 AM	CAP	Jan. 28, 2014	6:51 AM	CAP
Mar. 10, 2013	6:51 AM	PIS	Aug. 19, 2013	4:48 AM	AQU	Jan. 30, 2014	4:30 AM	AQU
Mar. 12, 2013	12:55 PM	ARI	Aug. 21, 2013	4:48 AM	PIS	Feb. 1, 2014	4:48 AM	PIS
Mar. 14, 2013	8:18 PM	TAU	Aug. 23, 2013	8:34 AM	ARI	Feb. 3, 2014	4:48 AM	ARI
Mar. 17, 2013	8:00 AM	GEM	Aug. 25, 2013	2:46 PM	TAU	Feb. 5, 2014	11:05 AM	TAU
Mar. 19, 2013	8:00 PM	CAN	Aug. 27, 2013	10:09 PM	GEM	Feb. 7, 2014	6:28 PM	GEM
Mar. 22, 2013	8:00 AM	LEO	Aug. 30, 2013	12:00 PM	CAN	Feb. 10, 2014	8:00 AM	CAN
Mar. 24, 2013	4:37 PM	VIR	Sep. 2, 2013	2:11 AM	LEO	Feb. 12, 2014	8:00 PM	LEO
Mar. 26, 2013	12:00 AM	LIB	Sep. 4, 2013	12:00 PM	VIR	Feb. 15, 2014	8:00 AM	VIR
Mar. 29, 2013	1:43 AM	SCO	Sep. 6, 2013	8:18 PM	LIB	Feb. 17, 2014	8:00 PM	LIB
Mar. 31, 2013	3:12 AM	SAG	Sep. 9, 2013	1:43 AM	SCO	Feb. 20, 2014	3:42 AM	SCO
Apr. 2, 2013	6:51 AM	CAP	Sep. 11, 2013	6:51 AM	SAG	Feb. 22, 2014	11:05 AM	SAG
Apr. 4, 2013	10:17 AM	AQU	Sep. 13, 2013	10:17 AM	CAP	Feb. 24, 2014	3:26 PM	CAP
Apr. 6, 2013	1:43 PM	PIS	Sep. 15, 2013	1:43 PM	AQU	Feb. 26, 2014	5:09 PM	AQU
Apr. 8, 2013	8:18 PM	ARI	Sep. 17, 2013	3:26 PM	PIS	Feb. 28, 2014	4:00 PM	PIS
Apr. 11, 2013	3:42 AM	TAU	Sep. 19, 2013	4:00 PM	ARI	Mar. 2, 2014	4:00 PM	ARI
Apr. 13, 2013	4:00 PM	GEM	Sep. 21, 2013	12:00 AM	TAU	Mar. 4, 2014	5:36 PM	TAU
Apr. 16, 2013	4:00 AM	CAN	Sep. 24, 2013	7:23 AM	GEM	Mar. 7, 2014	3:42 AM	GEM
Apr. 18, 2013	4:00 PM	LEO	Sep. 26, 2013	8:00 PM	CAN	Mar. 9, 2014	2:00 PM	CAN
Apr. 21, 2013	1:51 AM	VIR	Sep. 29, 2013	8:00 AM	LEO	Mar. 12, 2014	4:22 AM	LEO
Apr. 23, 2013	9:14 AM	LIB	Oct. 1, 2013	8:00 PM	VIR	Mar. 14, 2014	4:00 PM	VIR
Apr. 25, 2013	12:00 PM	SCO	Oct. 4, 2013	3:42 AM	LIB	Mar. 17, 2014	2:00 AM	LIB
Apr. 27, 2013	1:43 PM	SAG	Oct. 6, 2013	8:34 AM	SCO	Mar. 19, 2014	9:14 AM	SCO
Apr. 29, 2013	12:48 PM	CAP	Oct. 8, 2013	1:43 PM	SAG	Mar. 21, 2014	4:37 PM	SAG
May. 1, 2013	3:26 PM	AQU	Oct. 10, 2013	5:09 PM	CAP	Mar. 23, 2014	8:34 PM	CAP
May. 3, 2013	6:51 PM	PIS	Oct. 12, 2013	6:51 PM	AQU	Mar. 25, 2014	12:00 AM	AQU
May. 6, 2013	1:51 AM	ARI	Oct. 14, 2013	10:17 PM	PIS	Mar. 28, 2014	1:43 AM	PIS
May. 8, 2013	12:00 PM	TAU	Oct. 17, 2013	1:43 AM	ARI	Mar. 30, 2014	3:26 AM	ARI
May. 10, 2013	10:00 PM	GEM	Oct. 19, 2013	9:14 AM	TAU	Apr. 1, 2014	7:23 AM	TAU
May. 13, 2013	10:00 AM	CAN	Oct. 21, 2013	4:37 PM	GEM	Apr. 3, 2014	12:55 PM	GEM
May. 15, 2013	12:00 AM	LEO	Oct. 24, 2013	4:00 AM	CAN	Apr. 5, 2014	12:00 AM	CAN
May. 18, 2013	9:14 AM	VIR	Oct. 26, 2013	7:38 PM	LEO	Apr. 8, 2014	10:00 AM	LEO
May. 20, 2013	6:28 PM	LIB	Oct. 29, 2013	3:42 AM	VIR	Apr. 13, 2014	10:00 AM	LIB
May. 22, 2013	10:17 PM	SCO	Oct. 31, 2013	12:55 PM	LIB	Apr. 15, 2014	4:37 PM	SCO
May. 24, 2013	10:24 PM	SAG	Nov. 2, 2013	8:18 PM	SCO	Apr. 17, 2014	12:00 AM	SAG
May. 26, 2013	10:24 PM	CAP	Nov. 4, 2013	10:17 PM	SAG	Apr. 20, 2014	1:43 AM	CAP
May. 28, 2013	10:24 PM	AQU	Nov. 6, 2013	12:00 AM	CAP	Apr. 22, 2014	5:09 AM	AQU
May. 31, 2013	1:43 AM	PIS	Nov. 11, 2013	3:26 AM	PIS	Apr. 24, 2014	8:34 AM	PIS
Jun. 2, 2013	7:23 AM	ARI	Nov. 13, 2013	9:14 AM	ARI	Apr. 26, 2014	10:17 AM	ARI
Jun. 4, 2013	6:00 PM	TAU	Nov. 15, 2013	2:46 PM	TAU	Apr. 28, 2014	4:37 PM	TAU
Jun. 7, 2013	4:00 AM	GEM	Nov. 18, 2013	2:00 AM	GEM	Apr. 30, 2014	10:09 PM	GEM
Jun. 9, 2013	7:38 PM	CAN	Nov. 20, 2013	12:00 PM	CAN	May. 3, 2014	8:00 AM	CAN
Jun. 12, 2013	6:00 AM	LEO	Nov. 22, 2013	12:00 AM	LEO	May. 5, 2014	6:00 PM	LEO
Jun. 14, 2013	6:00 PM	VIR	Nov. 25, 2013	2:00 PM	VIR	May. 8, 2014	8:00 AM	VIR
Jun. 17, 2013	1:51 AM	LIB	Nov. 27, 2013	10:09 PM	LIB	May. 10, 2014	4:37 PM	LIB
Jun. 19, 2013	6:51 AM	SCO	Nov. 30, 2013	5:32 AM	SCO	May. 13, 2014	1:51 AM	SCO
Jun. 21, 2013	10:17 AM	SAG	Dec. 2, 2013	6:24 AM	SAG	May. 15, 2014	6:51 AM	SAG
Jun. 23, 2013	9:36 AM	CAP	Dec. 4, 2013	8:00 AM	CAP	May. 17, 2014	8:00 AM	CAP
Jun. 25, 2013	8:00 AM	AQU	Dec. 6, 2013	8:00 AM	AQU	May. 19, 2014	12:00 PM	AQU
Jun. 27, 2013	10:17 AM	PIS	Dec. 8, 2013	10:17 AM	PIS	May. 21, 2014	1:43 PM	PIS
Jun. 29, 2013	2:46 PM	ARI	Dec. 10, 2013	1:43 PM	ARI	May. 23, 2014	5:09 PM	ARI
Jul. 1, 2013	10:09 PM	TAU	Dec. 12, 2013	8:18 PM	TAU	May. 25, 2014	8:34 PM	TAU
Jul. 4, 2013	10:00 AM	GEM	Dec. 15, 2013	8:00 AM	GEM	May. 28, 2014	5:32 AM	GEM
Jul. 6, 2013	10:00 PM	CAN	Dec. 17, 2013	8:00 PM	CAN	May. 30, 2014	4:00 PM	CAN
Jul. 9, 2013	12:00 PM	LEO	Dec. 20, 2013	8:00 AM	LEO	Jun. 2, 2014	2:00 AM	LEO
Jul. 11, 2013	12:00 AM	VIR	Dec. 22, 2013	8:00 PM	VIR	Jun. 4, 2014	5:27 PM	VIR
Jul. 14, 2013	10:00 AM	LIB	Dec. 25, 2013	8:00 AM	LIB	Jun. 7, 2014	4:00 AM	LIB
Jul. 16, 2013	4:37 PM	SCO	Dec. 27, 2013	2:46 PM	SCO	Jun. 9, 2014	11:05 AM	SCO
Jul. 18, 2013	6:51 PM	SAG	Dec. 29, 2013	6:51 PM	SAG	Jun. 11, 2014	3:26 PM	SAG
Jul. 20, 2013	7:12 PM	CAP	Dec. 31, 2013	7:12 PM	CAP	Jun. 13, 2014	6:51 PM	CAP
Jul. 22, 2013	7:12 PM	AQU	Jan. 2, 2014	4:30 PM	AQU	Jun. 15, 2014	5:36 PM	AQU
Jul. 24, 2013	7:12 PM	PIS	Jan. 4, 2014	5:36 PM	PIS	Jun. 17, 2014	8:34 PM	PIS
Jul. 26, 2013	10:17 PM	ARI	Jan. 6, 2014	8:34 AM	ARI	Jun. 19, 2014	10:17 PM	ARI
Jul. 29, 2013	5:32 AM	TAU	Jan. 9, 2014	3:42 AM	TAU	Jun. 22, 2014	3:42 AM	TAU
Jul. 31, 2013	2:46 PM	GEM	Jan. 11, 2014	2:00 PM	GEM	Jun. 24, 2014	11:05 AM	GEM
Aug. 3, 2013	6:00 AM	CAN	Jan. 14, 2014	2:00 AM	CAN	Jun. 26, 2014	8:18 PM	CAN
Aug. 5, 2013	6:00 PM	LEO	Jan. 16, 2014	2:00 PM	LEO	Jun. 29, 2014	10:00 AM	LEO
Aug. 8, 2013	6:00 AM	VIR	Jan. 19, 2014	2:00 AM	VIR	Jul. 1, 2014	10:00 PM	VIR
Aug. 10, 2013	12:55 PM	LIB	Jan. 21, 2014	2:00 PM	LIB	Jul. 4, 2014	10:00 AM	LIB

Date	Time	Moon	Date	Time	Moon	Date	Time	Moon
Jul. 6, 2014	10:00 PM	SCO	Dec. 19, 2014	12:00 AM	SAG	Jun. 8, 2015	8:34 AM	PIS
Jul. 9, 2014	1:43 AM	SAG	Dec. 22, 2014	1:36 AM	CAP	Jun. 10, 2015	12:00 PM	ARI
Jul. 11, 2014	5:09 AM	CAP	Dec. 24, 2014	3:12 AM	AQU	Jun. 12, 2015	3:26 PM	TAU
Jul. 13, 2014	3:00 AM	AQU	Dec. 26, 2014	4:48 AM	PIS	Jun. 14, 2015	6:51 PM	GEM
Jul. 15, 2014	3:12 AM	PIS	Dec. 28, 2014	6:24 AM	ARI	Jun. 16, 2015	10:17 PM	CAN
Jul. 17, 2014	5:09 AM	ARI	Dec. 30, 2014	12:55 PM	TAU	Jun. 19, 2015	7:23 AM	LEO
Jul. 19, 2014	8:34 AM	TAU	Jan. 1, 2015	6:28 PM	GEM	Jun. 21, 2015	6:00 PM	VIR
Jul. 21, 2014	4:37 PM	GEM	Jan. 4, 2015	1:51 AM	CAN	Jun. 24, 2015	6:00 AM	LIB
Jul. 24, 2014	4:00 AM	CAN	Jan. 6, 2015	11:05 AM	LEO	Jun. 26, 2015	9:49 PM	SCO
Jul. 26, 2014	4:00 PM	LEO	Jan. 8, 2015	12:00 AM	VIR	Jun. 29, 2015	3:42 AM	SAG
Jul. 29, 2014	4:00 AM	VIR	Jan. 11, 2015	12:00 PM	LIB	Jul. 1, 2015	11:05 AM	CAP
Jul. 31, 2014	7:38 PM	LIB	Jan. 16, 2015	9:14 AM	SAG	Jul. 3, 2015	1:43 PM	AQU
Aug. 3, 2014	4:00 AM	SCO	Jan. 18, 2015	1:43 PM	CAP	Jul. 5, 2015	2:24 PM	PIS
Aug. 5, 2014	11:05 AM	SAG	Jan. 20, 2015	3:26 PM	AQU	Jul. 7, 2015	4:00 PM	ARI
Aug. 7, 2014	3:26 PM	CAP	Jan. 22, 2015	2:24 PM	PIS	Jul. 9, 2015	8:34 PM	TAU
Aug. 9, 2014	2:24 PM	AQU	Jan. 24, 2015	2:24 PM	ARI	Jul. 12, 2015	1:51 AM	GEM
Aug. 11, 2014	2:24 PM	PIS	Jan. 26, 2015	5:09 PM	TAU	Jul. 14, 2015	7:23 AM	CAN
Aug. 13, 2014	12:48 PM	ARI	Jan. 28, 2015	12:00 AM	GEM	Jul. 16, 2015	2:46 PM	LEO
Aug. 15, 2014	5:09 PM	TAU	Jan. 31, 2015	7:23 AM	CAN	Jul. 19, 2015	2:00 AM	VIR
Aug. 17, 2014	12:00 AM	GEM	Feb. 2, 2015	4:37 PM	LEO	Jul. 21, 2015	2:00 PM	LIB
Aug. 20, 2014	10:00 AM	CAN	Feb. 5, 2015	6:00 AM	VIR	Jul. 24, 2015	4:22 AM	SCO
Aug. 22, 2014	10:00 PM	LEO	Feb. 7, 2015	8:00 PM	LIB	Jul. 26, 2015	2:00 PM	SAG
Aug. 25, 2014	10:00 AM	VIR	Feb. 10, 2015	8:00 AM	SCO	Jul. 28, 2015	8:18 PM	CAP
Aug. 27, 2014	10:00 PM	LIB	Feb. 12, 2015	4:37 PM	SAG	Jul. 30, 2015	8:48 PM	AQU
Aug. 30, 2014	10:00 AM	SCO	Feb. 14, 2015	10:17 PM	CAP	Aug. 1, 2015	10:24 PM	PIS
Sep. 1, 2014	6:28 PM	SAG	Feb. 17, 2015	1:43 AM	AQU	Aug. 3, 2015	12:00 AM	ARI
Sep. 3, 2014	10:17 PM	CAP	Feb. 20, 2015	12:00 AM	ARI	Aug. 6, 2015	1:36 AM	TAU
Sep. 9, 2014	12:00 AM	ARI	Feb. 23, 2015	1:43 AM	TAU	Aug. 8, 2015	7:23 AM	GEM
Sep. 12, 2014	1:36 AM	TAU	Feb. 25, 2015	5:09 AM	GEM	Aug. 10, 2015	12:55 PM	CAN
Sep. 14, 2014	7:23 AM	GEM	Feb. 27, 2015	12:55 PM	CAN	Aug. 12, 2015	8:18 PM	LEO
Sep. 16, 2014	2:46 PM	CAN	Mar. 1, 2015	10:09 PM	LEO	Aug. 15, 2015	7:23 AM	VIR
Sep. 19, 2014	4:00 AM	LEO	Mar. 4, 2015	12:00 PM	VIR	Aug. 17, 2015	12:00 AM	LIB
Sep. 21, 2014	4:00 PM	VIR	Mar. 7, 2015	2:00 AM	LIB	Aug. 20, 2015	10:00 AM	SCO
Sep. 24, 2014	6:00 AM	LIB	Mar. 9, 2015	2:00 PM	SCO	Aug. 22, 2015	10:00 PM	SAG
Sep. 26, 2014	4:00 PM	SCO	Mar. 14, 2015	7:23 AM	CAP	Aug. 25, 2015	5:32 AM	CAP
Sep. 28, 2014	12:00 AM	SAG	Mar. 16, 2015	12:00 PM	AQU	Aug. 27, 2015	8:34 AM	AQU
Oct. 1, 2014	5:09 AM	CAP	Mar. 18, 2015	11:12 AM	PIS	Aug. 29, 2015	9:36 AM	PIS
Oct. 3, 2014	8:34 AM	AQU	Mar. 20, 2015	11:12 AM	ARI	Aug. 31, 2015	9:36 AM	ARI
Oct. 5, 2014	9:36 AM	PIS	Mar. 22, 2015	11:12 AM	TAU	Sep. 2, 2015	9:36 AM	TAU
Oct. 7, 2014	11:12 AM	ARI	Mar. 24, 2015	1:43 PM	GEM	Sep. 4, 2015	12:00 PM	GEM
Oct. 9, 2014	1:43 PM	TAU	Mar. 26, 2015	8:18 PM	CAN	Sep. 6, 2015	5:09 PM	CAN
Oct. 11, 2014	3:26 PM	GEM	Mar. 29, 2015	5:32 AM	LEO	Sep. 9, 2015	4:00 AM	LEO
Oct. 13, 2014	12:00 AM	CAN	Mar. 31, 2015	6:00 PM	VIR	Sep. 11, 2015	12:55 PM	VIR
Oct. 16, 2014	12:00 PM	LEO	Apr. 3, 2015	8:00 AM	LIB	Sep. 14, 2015	4:00 AM	LIB
Oct. 18, 2014	12:00 AM	VIR	Apr. 5, 2015	8:00 PM	SCO	Sep. 16, 2015	4:00 PM	SCO
Oct. 21, 2014	12:00 PM	LIB	Apr. 8, 2015	5:32 AM	SAG	Sep. 19, 2015	4:00 AM	SAG
Oct. 23, 2014	12:00 AM	SCO	Apr. 10, 2015	4:00 PM	CAP	Sep. 21, 2015	12:55 PM	CAP
Oct. 26, 2014	5:32 AM	SAG	Apr. 12, 2015	8:18 PM	AQU	Sep. 23, 2015	8:18 PM	AQU
Oct. 28, 2014	10:17 AM	CAP	Apr. 14, 2015	10:17 PM	PIS	Sep. 25, 2015	10:17 PM	PIS
Oct. 30, 2014	3:26 PM	AQU	Apr. 16, 2015	8:48 PM	ARI	Sep. 27, 2015	8:48 PM	ARI
Nov. 1, 2014	4:00 PM	PIS	Apr. 18, 2015	10:24 PM	TAU	Sep. 29, 2015	6:00 PM	TAU
Nov. 3, 2014	8:34 PM	ARI	Apr. 20, 2015	10:24 PM	GEM	Oct. 1, 2015	10:17 PM	GEM
Nov. 5, 2014	10:17 PM	TAU	Apr. 23, 2015	5:32 AM	CAN	Oct. 4, 2015	1:51 AM	CAN
Nov. 8, 2014	1:43 AM	GEM	Apr. 25, 2015	12:55 PM	LEO	Oct. 6, 2015	9:14 AM	LEO
Nov. 10, 2014	9:14 AM	CAN	Apr. 28, 2015	2:00 AM	VIR	Oct. 8, 2015	6:28 PM	VIR
Nov. 12, 2014	8:00 PM	LEO	Apr. 30, 2015	2:00 PM	LIB	Oct. 11, 2015	10:00 AM	LIB
Nov. 15, 2014	8:00 AM	VIR	May. 3, 2015	1:51 AM	SCO	Oct. 13, 2015	10:00 PM	SCO
Nov. 17, 2014	8:00 PM	LIB	May. 5, 2015	11:05 AM	SAG	Oct. 16, 2015	10:00 AM	SAG
Nov. 20, 2014	5:32 AM	SCO	May. 7, 2015	8:18 PM	CAP	Oct. 18, 2015	6:28 PM	CAP
Nov. 22, 2014	12:00 PM	SAG	May. 12, 2015	3:26 PM	PIS	Oct. 21, 2015	1:43 AM	AQU
Nov. 24, 2014	5:09 PM	CAP	May. 14, 2015	6:51 AM	ARI	Oct. 23, 2015	6:51 AM	PIS
Nov. 26, 2014	8:34 PM	AQU	May. 16, 2015	8:34 AM	TAU	Oct. 25, 2015	6:24 AM	ARI
Nov. 28, 2014	12:00 AM	PIS	May. 18, 2015	10:17 AM	GEM	Oct. 27, 2015	6:24 AM	TAU
Dec. 1, 2014	1:43 AM	ARI	May. 20, 2015	1:43 PM	CAN	Oct. 29, 2015	6:24 AM	GEM
Dec. 3, 2014	7:23 AM	TAU	May. 22, 2015	10:09 PM	LEO	Oct. 31, 2015	10:17 AM	CAN
Dec. 5, 2014	10:17 AM	GEM	May. 25, 2015	10:00 AM	VIR	Nov. 2, 2015	4:37 PM	LEO
Dec. 7, 2014	6:28 PM	CAN	May. 27, 2015	10:00 PM	LIB	Nov. 5, 2015	4:00 AM	VIR
Dec. 10, 2014	3:42 AM	LEO	May. 30, 2015	10:00 AM	SCO	Nov. 7, 2015	4:00 PM	LIB
Dec. 12, 2014	4:00 PM	VIR	Jun. 1, 2015	6:28 PM	SAG	Nov. 10, 2015	6:33 AM	SCO
Dec. 15, 2014	6:33 AM	LIB	Jun. 4, 2015	1:51 AM	CAP	Nov. 12, 2015	2:46 PM	SAG
Dec. 17, 2014	2:46 PM	SCO	Jun. 6, 2015	5:09 AM	AQU	Nov. 15, 2015	2:00 AM	CAP

185

Date	Time	Moon	Date	Time	Moon	Date	Time	Moon
Nov. 17, 2015	9:14 AM	AQU	May. 3, 2016	6:51 PM	ARI	Oct. 14, 2016	5:09 PM	ARI
Nov. 19, 2015	2:46 PM	PIS	May. 5, 2016	5:36 PM	TAU	Oct. 16, 2016	4:00 PM	TAU
Nov. 21, 2015	5:09 PM	ARI	May. 7, 2016	5:36 PM	GEM	Oct. 18, 2016	4:00 PM	GEM
Nov. 23, 2015	6:51 PM	TAU	May. 9, 2016	5:36 PM	CAN	Oct. 20, 2016	4:00 PM	CAN
Nov. 25, 2015	5:36 PM	GEM	May. 11, 2016	10:17 PM	LEO	Oct. 22, 2016	10:09 PM	LEO
Nov. 27, 2015	8:34 PM	CAN	May. 14, 2016	8:00 AM	VIR	Oct. 25, 2016	3:42 AM	VIR
Nov. 30, 2015	1:51 AM	LEO	May. 16, 2016	6:00 PM	LIB	Oct. 27, 2016	4:00 PM	LIB
Dec. 2, 2015	12:00 PM	VIR	May. 19, 2016	8:00 AM	SCO	Oct. 30, 2016	4:22 AM	SCO
Dec. 4, 2015	12:00 AM	LIB	May. 21, 2016	8:00 PM	SAG	Nov. 1, 2016	4:00 PM	SAG
Dec. 7, 2015	12:00 PM	SCO	May. 24, 2016	5:32 AM	CAP	Nov. 4, 2016	4:00 AM	CAP
Dec. 9, 2015	12:00 AM	SAG	May. 26, 2016	2:46 PM	AQU	Nov. 6, 2016	4:00 PM	AQU
Dec. 12, 2015	7:23 AM	CAP	May. 28, 2016	10:09 PM	PIS	Nov. 8, 2016	10:09 PM	PIS
Dec. 14, 2015	2:46 PM	AQU	May. 31, 2016	1:43 AM	ARI	Nov. 11, 2016	3:26 AM	ARI
Dec. 16, 2015	8:18 PM	PIS	Jun. 2, 2016	3:12 AM	TAU	Nov. 13, 2016	3:12 AM	TAU
Dec. 18, 2015	10:17 PM	ARI	Jun. 4, 2016	3:12 AM	GEM	Nov. 15, 2016	1:30 AM	GEM
Dec. 21, 2015	1:43 AM	TAU	Jun. 6, 2016	5:09 AM	CAN	Nov. 17, 2016	1:36 AM	CAN
Dec. 23, 2015	3:26 AM	GEM	Jun. 8, 2016	6:51 AM	LEO	Nov. 19, 2016	3:26 AM	LEO
Dec. 25, 2015	6:51 AM	CAN	Jun. 10, 2016	2:46 PM	VIR	Nov. 21, 2016	11:05 AM	VIR
Dec. 27, 2015	10:17 AM	LEO	Jun. 13, 2016	2:00 AM	LIB	Nov. 23, 2016	10:00 PM	LIB
Dec. 29, 2015	6:28 PM	VIR	Jun. 15, 2016	2:00 PM	SCO	Nov. 26, 2016	8:00 AM	SCO
Jan. 1, 2016	8:00 AM	LIB	Jun. 18, 2016	2:00 AM	SAG	Nov. 28, 2016	10:00 PM	SAG
Jan. 3, 2016	8:00 PM	SCO	Jun. 20, 2016	2:00 PM	CAP	Dec. 1, 2016	10:00 AM	CAP
Jan. 6, 2016	8:00 AM	SAG	Jun. 22, 2016	8:18 PM	AQU	Dec. 3, 2016	10:00 PM	AQU
Jan. 8, 2016	4:37 PM	CAP	Jun. 25, 2016	3:42 AM	PIS	Dec. 6, 2016	5:32 AM	PIS
Jan. 10, 2016	8:34 PM	AQU	Jun. 27, 2016	9:14 AM	ARI	Dec. 8, 2016	10:17 AM	ARI
Jan. 15, 2016	3:26 AM	ARI	Jun. 29, 2016	12:00 PM	TAU	Dec. 10, 2016	12:48 PM	TAU
Jan. 17, 2016	6:51 AM	TAU	Jul. 1, 2016	1:43 PM	GEM	Dec. 12, 2016	2:24 PM	GEM
Jan. 19, 2016	10:17 AM	GEM	Jul. 3, 2016	3:26 PM	CAN	Dec. 14, 2016	12:48 PM	CAN
Jan. 21, 2016	1:43 PM	CAN	Jul. 5, 2016	5:09 PM	LEO	Dec. 16, 2016	12:48 PM	LEO
Jan. 23, 2016	6:51 PM	LEO	Jul. 7, 2016	12:00 AM	VIR	Dec. 18, 2016	5:09 PM	VIR
Jan. 26, 2016	3:42 AM	VIR	Jul. 10, 2016	10:00 AM	LIB	Dec. 21, 2016	4:00 AM	LIB
Jan. 28, 2016	4:00 PM	LIB	Jul. 12, 2016	10:00 PM	SCO	Dec. 23, 2016	4:00 PM	SCO
Jan. 31, 2016	4:00 AM	SCO	Jul. 15, 2016	10:00 AM	SAG	Dec. 26, 2016	4:00 AM	SAG
Feb. 2, 2016	6:00 PM	SAG	Jul. 17, 2016	10:00 PM	CAP	Dec. 28, 2016	4:00 PM	CAP
Feb. 5, 2016	1:51 AM	CAP	Jul. 20, 2016	3:42 AM	AQU	Dec. 31, 2016	1:51 AM	AQU
Feb. 7, 2016	6:51 AM	AQU	Jul. 22, 2016	8:34 AM	PIS	Jan. 2, 2017	11:05 AM	PIS
Feb. 9, 2016	10:17 AM	PIS	Jul. 24, 2016	1:43 PM	ARI	Jan. 4, 2017	6:28 PM	ARI
Feb. 11, 2016	12:00 PM	ARI	Jul. 26, 2016	5:09 PM	TAU	Jan. 6, 2017	8:34 PM	TAU
Feb. 13, 2016	11:12 AM	TAU	Jul. 28, 2016	5:36 PM	GEM	Jan. 8, 2017	12:00 AM	GEM
Feb. 15, 2016	3:26 PM	GEM	Jul. 30, 2016	10:17 PM	CAN	Jan. 12, 2017	12:00 AM	CAN
Feb. 17, 2016	6:51 PM	CAN	Aug. 2, 2016	1:43 AM	LEO	Jan. 13, 2017	1:43 AM	LEO
Feb. 20, 2016	3:42 AM	LEO	Aug. 4, 2016	9:14 AM	VIR	Jan. 15, 2017	5:32 AM	VIR
Feb. 22, 2016	11:05 AM	VIR	Aug. 6, 2016	4:37 PM	LIB	Jan. 17, 2017	11:05 AM	LIB
Feb. 24, 2016	12:00 AM	LIB	Aug. 9, 2016	6:00 AM	SCO	Jan. 19, 2017	12:00 AM	SCO
Feb. 27, 2016	12:00 PM	SCO	Aug. 11, 2016	6:00 PM	SAG	Jan. 22, 2017	12:00 PM	SAG
Feb. 29, 2016	12:00 AM	SAG	Aug. 14, 2016	6:00 AM	CAP	Jan. 24, 2017	12:00 AM	CAP
Mar. 3, 2016	12:00 PM	CAP	Aug. 16, 2016	12:55 PM	AQU	Jan. 27, 2017	9:14 AM	AQU
Mar. 5, 2016	6:28 PM	AQU	Aug. 18, 2016	5:09 PM	PIS	Jan. 29, 2017	4:37 PM	PIS
Mar. 7, 2016	8:34 PM	PIS	Aug. 20, 2016	8:34 PM	ARI	Jan. 31, 2017	12:00 AM	ARI
Mar. 9, 2016	8:48 PM	ARI	Aug. 22, 2016	8:48 PM	TAU	Feb. 3, 2017	3:42 AM	TAU
Mar. 11, 2016	8:48 PM	TAU	Aug. 27, 2016	3:26 AM	CAN	Feb. 5, 2017	4:48 AM	GEM
Mar. 13, 2016	8:48 PM	GEM	Aug. 29, 2016	8:34 AM	LEO	Feb. 7, 2017	8:34 AM	CAN
Mar. 16, 2016	1:43 AM	CAN	Aug. 31, 2016	4:37 PM	VIR	Feb. 9, 2017	10:17 AM	LEO
Mar. 18, 2016	9:14 AM	LEO	Sep. 3, 2016	2:00 AM	LIB	Feb. 11, 2017	1:43 PM	VIR
Mar. 20, 2016	8:00 PM	VIR	Sep. 5, 2016	2:00 PM	SCO	Feb. 13, 2017	10:09 PM	LIB
Mar. 23, 2016	6:00 AM	LIB	Sep. 8, 2016	2:00 AM	SAG	Feb. 16, 2017	8:00 AM	SCO
Mar. 25, 2016	6:00 PM	SCO	Sep. 10, 2016	2:00 PM	CAP	Feb. 18, 2017	8:00 PM	SAG
Mar. 28, 2016	8:00 AM	SAG	Sep. 12, 2016	10:09 PM	AQU	Feb. 21, 2017	8:00 AM	CAP
Mar. 30, 2016	8:00 PM	CAP	Sep. 15, 2016	3:26 AM	PIS	Feb. 23, 2017	8:00 PM	AQU
Apr. 2, 2016	1:43 AM	AQU	Sep. 17, 2016	4:48 AM	ARI	Feb. 26, 2017	1:51 AM	PIS
Apr. 4, 2016	6:51 AM	PIS	Sep. 19, 2016	6:51 AM	TAU	Feb. 28, 2017	5:09 AM	ARI
Apr. 6, 2016	8:00 AM	ARI	Sep. 21, 2016	6:24 AM	GEM	Mar. 2, 2017	8:34 AM	TAU
Apr. 8, 2016	6:00 AM	TAU	Sep. 23, 2016	8:00 AM	CAN	Mar. 4, 2017	12:00 PM	GEM
Apr. 10, 2016	6:24 AM	GEM	Sep. 25, 2016	1:43 PM	LEO	Mar. 6, 2017	1:43 PM	CAN
Apr. 12, 2016	8:00 AM	CAN	Sep. 27, 2016	10:09 PM	VIR	Mar. 8, 2017	5:09 PM	LEO
Apr. 14, 2016	2:46 PM	LEO	Sep. 30, 2016	10:00 AM	LIB	Mar. 10, 2017	12:00 AM	VIR
Apr. 19, 2016	12:00 PM	LIB	Oct. 2, 2016	8:00 PM	SCO	Mar. 13, 2017	5:32 AM	LIB
Apr. 22, 2016	2:11 AM	SCO	Oct. 5, 2016	10:00 AM	SAG	Mar. 15, 2017	2:46 PM	SCO
Apr. 24, 2016	2:00 PM	SAG	Oct. 7, 2016	10:00 PM	CAP	Mar. 18, 2017	4:00 AM	SAG
Apr. 29, 2016	9:14 AM	AQU	Oct. 10, 2016	7:23 AM	AQU	Mar. 20, 2017	4:00 PM	CAP
May. 1, 2016	4:37 PM	PIS	Oct. 12, 2016	2:46 PM	PIS	Mar. 23, 2017	4:00 AM	AQU

Date	Time	Moon	Date	Time	Moon	Date	Time	Moon
Mar. 25, 2017	11:05 AM	P I S	Sep. 5, 2017	5:32 AM	P I S	Feb. 18, 2018	12:55 PM	A R I
Mar. 27, 2017	3:26 PM	A R I	Sep. 7, 2017	12:55 PM	A R I	Feb. 20, 2018	8:18 PM	T A U
Mar. 29, 2017	4:00 PM	T A U	Sep. 9, 2017	5:09 PM	T A U	Feb. 23, 2018	1:51 AM	G E M
Mar. 31, 2017	6:51 PM	G E M	Sep. 11, 2017	8:34 PM	G E M	Feb. 25, 2018	3:12 AM	C A N
Apr. 2, 2017	8:34 PM	C A N	Sep. 13, 2017	12:00 AM	C A N	Feb. 27, 2018	4:48 AM	L E O
Apr. 4, 2017	10:17 PM	L E O	Sep. 16, 2017	1:43 AM	L E O	Mar. 1, 2018	6:24 AM	V I R
Apr. 7, 2017	5:32 AM	V I R	Sep. 18, 2017	5:09 AM	V I R	Mar. 3, 2018	8:00 AM	L I B
Apr. 9, 2017	12:55 PM	L I B	Sep. 20, 2017	10:17 AM	L I B	Mar. 5, 2018	2:46 PM	S C O
Apr. 11, 2017	10:09 PM	S C O	Sep. 22, 2017	6:28 PM	S C O	Mar. 7, 2018	10:09 PM	S A G
Apr. 14, 2017	12:00 PM	S A G	Sep. 25, 2017	6:00 AM	S A G	Mar. 10, 2018	10:00 AM	C A P
Apr. 16, 2017	12:00 AM	C A P	Sep. 27, 2017	6:00 PM	C A P	Mar. 12, 2018	12:00 AM	A Q U
Apr. 19, 2017	12:00 PM	A Q U	Sep. 30, 2017	6:00 AM	A Q U	Mar. 15, 2018	12:00 PM	P I S
Apr. 21, 2017	8:18 PM	P I S	Oct. 2, 2017	2:46 PM	P I S	Mar. 17, 2018	10:00 PM	A R I
Apr. 24, 2017	1:43 AM	A R I	Oct. 4, 2017	10:09 PM	A R I	Mar. 20, 2018	1:43 AM	T A U
Apr. 26, 2017	3:26 AM	T A U	Oct. 9, 2017	3:26 AM	G E M	Mar. 22, 2018	7:23 AM	G E M
Apr. 28, 2017	3:12 AM	G E M	Oct. 11, 2017	5:09 AM	C A N	Mar. 24, 2018	10:17 AM	C A N
Apr. 30, 2017	3:26 AM	C A N	Oct. 13, 2017	6:51 AM	L E O	Mar. 26, 2018	11:12 AM	L E O
May. 2, 2017	5:09 AM	L E O	Oct. 15, 2017	12:00 PM	V I R	Mar. 28, 2018	3:26 PM	V I R
May. 4, 2017	11:05 AM	V I R	Oct. 17, 2017	6:28 PM	L I B	Mar. 30, 2018	6:51 PM	L I B
May. 6, 2017	6:28 PM	L I B	Oct. 20, 2017	1:51 AM	S C O	Apr. 1, 2018	10:17 PM	S C O
May. 9, 2017	6:00 AM	S C O	Oct. 22, 2017	2:00 PM	S A G	Apr. 4, 2018	7:23 AM	S A G
May. 11, 2017	6:00 PM	S A G	Oct. 25, 2017	2:11 AM	C A P	Apr. 6, 2018	8:00 PM	C A P
May. 14, 2017	6:00 AM	C A P	Oct. 27, 2017	2:00 PM	A Q U	Apr. 9, 2018	8:00 AM	A Q U
May. 16, 2017	6:00 PM	A Q U	Nov. 1, 2017	6:51 AM	A R I	Apr. 11, 2018	8:00 PM	P I S
May. 19, 2017	6:00 AM	P I S	Nov. 3, 2017	9:36 AM	T A U	Apr. 14, 2018	3:42 AM	A R I
May. 21, 2017	10:17 AM	A R I	Nov. 5, 2017	11:12 AM	G E M	Apr. 16, 2018	11:05 AM	T A U
May. 23, 2017	1:43 PM	T A U	Nov. 7, 2017	11:12 AM	C A N	Apr. 18, 2018	1:43 PM	G E M
May. 25, 2017	12:48 PM	G E M	Nov. 9, 2017	1:43 PM	L E O	Apr. 20, 2018	3:26 PM	C A N
May. 27, 2017	12:48 PM	C A N	Nov. 11, 2017	5:09 PM	V I R	Apr. 22, 2018	6:51 PM	L E O
May. 29, 2017	12:48 PM	L E O	Nov. 13, 2017	12:00 AM	L I B	Apr. 24, 2018	8:34 PM	V I R
May. 31, 2017	5:09 PM	V I R	Nov. 16, 2017	10:00 AM	S C O	Apr. 27, 2018	1:43 AM	L I B
Jun. 3, 2017	2:00 AM	L I B	Nov. 18, 2017	8:00 PM	S A G	Apr. 29, 2018	6:51 AM	S C O
Jun. 5, 2017	12:00 PM	S C O	Nov. 21, 2017	8:00 AM	C A P	May. 1, 2018	6:00 PM	S A G
Jun. 7, 2017	12:00 AM	S A G	Nov. 23, 2017	8:00 PM	A Q U	May. 4, 2018	4:00 AM	C A P
Jun. 10, 2017	12:00 PM	C A P	Nov. 26, 2017	10:00 AM	P I S	May. 6, 2018	4:00 PM	A Q U
Jun. 12, 2017	12:00 AM	A Q U	Nov. 28, 2017	8:00 PM	A R I	May. 9, 2018	4:00 AM	P I S
Jun. 15, 2017	12:00 PM	P I S	Nov. 30, 2017	12:00 AM	T A U	May. 11, 2018	12:55 PM	A R I
Jun. 17, 2017	6:28 PM	A R I	Dec. 2, 2017	12:00 AM	G E M	May. 13, 2018	8:18 PM	T A U
Jun. 19, 2017	10:17 PM	T A U	Dec. 4, 2017	10:24 PM	C A N	May. 15, 2018	10:17 PM	G E M
Jun. 23, 2017	12:00 AM	C A N	Dec. 6, 2017	8:48 PM	L E O	May. 17, 2018	10:24 PM	C A N
Jun. 25, 2017	10:24 PM	L E O	Dec. 8, 2017	12:00 AM	V I R	May. 22, 2018	3:26 AM	V I R
Jun. 28, 2017	1:43 AM	V I R	Dec. 11, 2017	5:32 AM	L I B	May. 24, 2018	6:51 AM	L I B
Jun. 30, 2017	7:23 AM	L I B	Dec. 13, 2017	4:00 PM	S C O	May. 26, 2018	2:46 PM	S C O
Jul. 2, 2017	4:37 PM	S C O	Dec. 16, 2017	2:00 AM	S A G	May. 28, 2018	10:09 PM	S A G
Jul. 5, 2017	6:00 AM	S A G	Dec. 18, 2017	2:00 PM	C A P	May. 31, 2018	10:00 AM	C A P
Jul. 7, 2017	6:00 PM	C A P	Dec. 21, 2017	4:00 AM	A Q U	Jun. 2, 2018	10:00 PM	A Q U
Jul. 10, 2017	6:00 AM	A Q U	Dec. 23, 2017	4:00 PM	P I S	Jun. 5, 2018	12:00 PM	P I S
Jul. 12, 2017	6:00 PM	P I S	Dec. 26, 2017	2:00 AM	A R I	Jun. 7, 2018	12:00 AM	A R I
Jul. 14, 2017	12:00 AM	A R I	Dec. 28, 2017	6:51 AM	T A U	Jun. 10, 2018	5:32 AM	T A U
Jul. 17, 2017	5:09 AM	T A U	Dec. 30, 2017	10:17 AM	G E M	Jun. 12, 2018	8:34 AM	G E M
Jul. 19, 2017	8:34 AM	G E M	Jan. 1, 2018	9:36 AM	C A N	Jun. 14, 2018	8:00 AM	C A N
Jul. 21, 2017	10:17 AM	C A N	Jan. 3, 2018	8:00 AM	L E O	Jun. 16, 2018	8:00 AM	L E O
Jul. 23, 2017	9:36 AM	L E O	Jan. 5, 2018	8:00 AM	V I R	Jun. 18, 2018	10:17 AM	V I R
Jul. 25, 2017	12:00 PM	V I R	Jan. 7, 2018	12:00 PM	L I B	Jun. 20, 2018	2:46 PM	L I B
Jul. 27, 2017	3:26 PM	L I B	Jan. 9, 2018	8:18 PM	S C O	Jun. 22, 2018	8:18 PM	S C O
Jul. 30, 2017	2:00 AM	S C O	Jan. 12, 2018	8:00 AM	S A G	Jun. 25, 2018	6:00 AM	S A G
Aug. 1, 2017	11:05 AM	S A G	Jan. 14, 2018	8:00 PM	C A P	Jun. 27, 2018	2:46 PM	C A P
Aug. 4, 2017	2:00 AM	C A P	Jan. 17, 2018	10:00 AM	A Q U	Jun. 30, 2018	6:00 AM	A Q U
Aug. 6, 2017	2:00 PM	A Q U	Jan. 19, 2018	10:00 PM	P I S	Jul. 2, 2018	6:00 PM	P I S
Aug. 8, 2017	12:00 AM	P I S	Jan. 22, 2018	8:00 AM	A R I	Jul. 5, 2018	6:00 AM	A R I
Aug. 11, 2017	5:09 AM	A R I	Jan. 24, 2018	2:46 PM	T A U	Jul. 7, 2018	4:00 PM	T A U
Aug. 13, 2017	12:55 PM	T A U	Jan. 26, 2018	6:51 PM	G E M	Jul. 9, 2018	8:18 PM	G E M
Aug. 15, 2017	3:26 PM	G E M	Jan. 28, 2018	7:12 PM	C A N	Jul. 11, 2018	8:34 PM	C A N
Aug. 17, 2017	4:00 PM	C A N	Jan. 30, 2018	7:12 PM	L E O	Jul. 13, 2018	7:12 PM	L E O
Aug. 19, 2017	5:36 PM	L E O	Feb. 1, 2018	7:12 PM	V I R	Jul. 15, 2018	5:36 PM	V I R
Aug. 21, 2017	10:17 PM	V I R	Feb. 3, 2018	8:48 PM	L I B	Jul. 17, 2018	7:12 PM	L I B
Aug. 24, 2017	1:43 AM	L I B	Feb. 6, 2018	5:32 AM	S C O	Jul. 20, 2018	1:51 AM	S C O
Aug. 26, 2017	9:14 AM	S C O	Feb. 8, 2018	4:00 PM	S A G	Jul. 22, 2018	12:00 PM	S A G
Aug. 28, 2017	6:28 PM	S A G	Feb. 11, 2018	4:22 AM	C A P	Jul. 24, 2018	10:00 PM	C A P
Aug. 31, 2017	10:55 AM	C A P	Feb. 13, 2018	4:00 PM	A Q U	Jul. 27, 2018	12:00 PM	A Q U
Sep. 2, 2017	10:00 PM	A Q U	Feb. 16, 2018	4:00 AM	P I S	Jul. 29, 2018	12:00 AM	P I S

187

Date	Time	Moon	Date	Time	Moon	Date	Time	Moon
Aug. 1, 2018	12:00 PM	A R I	Jan. 14, 2019	6:28 PM	T A U	Jun. 25, 2019	4:00 AM	A R I
Aug. 3, 2018	8:18 PM	T A U	Jan. 17, 2019	1:43 AM	G E M	Jun. 27, 2019	4:00 PM	T A U
Aug. 6, 2018	1:43 AM	G E M	Jan. 19, 2019	5:09 AM	C A N	Jun. 29, 2019	10:09 PM	G E M
Aug. 8, 2018	5:09 AM	C A N	Jan. 21, 2019	4:48 AM	L E O	Jul. 2, 2019	1:43 AM	C A N
Aug. 10, 2018	4:48 AM	L E O	Jan. 23, 2019	4:48 AM	V I R	Jul. 4, 2019	5:09 AM	L E O
Aug. 12, 2018	4:48 AM	V I R	Jan. 25, 2019	4:48 AM	L I B	Jul. 6, 2019	4:48 AM	V I R
Aug. 14, 2018	4:48 AM	L I B	Jan. 27, 2019	8:34 AM	S C O	Jul. 8, 2019	6:24 AM	L I B
Aug. 16, 2018	11:05 AM	S C O	Jan. 29, 2019	2:46 PM	S A G	Jul. 10, 2019	10:17 AM	S C O
Aug. 18, 2018	4:37 PM	S A G	Feb. 1, 2019	2:00 AM	C A P	Jul. 12, 2019	4:37 PM	S A G
Aug. 21, 2018	6:00 AM	C A P	Feb. 3, 2019	2:00 PM	A Q U	Jul. 14, 2019	12:00 AM	C A P
Aug. 23, 2018	6:00 AM	A Q U	Feb. 6, 2019	4:22 AM	P I S	Jul. 17, 2019	9:14 AM	A Q U
Aug. 26, 2018	6:00 AM	P I S	Feb. 8, 2019	4:00 PM	A R I	Jul. 19, 2019	10:00 PM	P I S
Aug. 28, 2018	6:00 PM	A R I	Feb. 11, 2019	1:51 AM	T A U	Jul. 22, 2019	10:00 AM	A R I
Aug. 31, 2018	1:51 AM	T A U	Feb. 13, 2019	11:05 AM	G E M	Jul. 24, 2019	12:00 AM	T A U
Sep. 2, 2018	9:14 AM	G E M	Feb. 15, 2019	4:37 PM	C A N	Jul. 27, 2019	7:23 AM	G E M
Sep. 4, 2018	2:46 PM	C A N	Feb. 17, 2019	4:00 PM	L E O	Jul. 29, 2019	12:00 PM	C A N
Sep. 6, 2018	3:26 PM	L E O	Feb. 19, 2019	4:00 PM	V I R	Jul. 31, 2019	3:26 PM	L E O
Sep. 8, 2018	2:24 PM	V I R	Feb. 21, 2019	1:30 PM	L I B	Aug. 2, 2019	2:24 PM	V I R
Sep. 10, 2018	4:00 PM	L I B	Feb. 23, 2019	4:00 PM	S C O	Aug. 4, 2019	2:24 PM	L I B
Sep. 12, 2018	6:51 PM	S C O	Feb. 25, 2019	8:34 PM	S A G	Aug. 6, 2019	5:09 PM	S C O
Sep. 15, 2018	1:51 AM	S A G	Feb. 28, 2019	8:00 AM	C A P	Aug. 8, 2019	8:34 PM	S A G
Sep. 17, 2018	12:00 PM	C A P	Mar. 2, 2019	8:00 PM	A Q U	Aug. 11, 2019	5:32 AM	C A P
Sep. 19, 2018	12:00 AM	A Q U	Mar. 5, 2019	10:55 AM	P I S	Aug. 13, 2019	2:46 PM	A Q U
Sep. 22, 2018	2:00 PM	P I S	Mar. 7, 2019	10:00 PM	A R I	Aug. 16, 2019	4:00 PM	P I S
Sep. 24, 2018	10:09 PM	A R I	Mar. 10, 2019	7:23 AM	T A U	Aug. 18, 2019	6:00 PM	A R I
Sep. 27, 2018	7:23 AM	T A U	Mar. 12, 2019	4:37 PM	G E M	Aug. 21, 2019	6:00 AM	T A U
Sep. 29, 2018	2:46 PM	G E M	Mar. 14, 2019	12:00 AM	C A N	Aug. 23, 2019	2:46 PM	G E M
Oct. 1, 2018	6:51 PM	C A N	Mar. 17, 2019	1:43 AM	L E O	Aug. 25, 2019	10:09 PM	C A N
Oct. 3, 2018	10:17 PM	L E O	Mar. 19, 2019	3:26 AM	V I R	Aug. 31, 2019	12:00 AM	L I B
Oct. 8, 2018	1:36 AM	L I B	Mar. 21, 2019	1:30 AM	L I B	Sep. 2, 2019	12:00 AM	S C O
Oct. 10, 2018	5:09 AM	S C O	Mar. 23, 2019	3:12 AM	S C O	Sep. 5, 2019	3:26 AM	S A G
Oct. 12, 2018	11:05 AM	S A G	Mar. 25, 2019	6:51 AM	S A G	Sep. 7, 2019	11:05 AM	C A P
Oct. 14, 2018	6:28 PM	C A P	Mar. 27, 2019	2:46 PM	C A P	Sep. 9, 2019	8:18 PM	A Q U
Oct. 17, 2018	8:00 AM	A Q U	Mar. 30, 2019	2:00 AM	A Q U	Sep. 12, 2019	10:00 AM	P I S
Oct. 19, 2018	12:00 AM	P I S	Apr. 1, 2019	4:00 PM	P I S	Sep. 14, 2019	12:00 AM	A R I
Oct. 22, 2018	7:23 AM	A R I	Apr. 4, 2019	4:00 AM	A R I	Sep. 17, 2019	12:00 PM	T A U
Oct. 24, 2018	6:00 AM	T A U	Apr. 6, 2019	12:55 PM	T A U	Sep. 19, 2019	8:18 PM	G E M
Oct. 26, 2018	10:09 PM	G E M	Apr. 8, 2019	10:09 PM	G E M	Sep. 22, 2019	5:32 AM	C A N
Oct. 28, 2018	12:00 AM	C A N	Apr. 11, 2019	3:26 AM	C A N	Sep. 24, 2019	10:17 AM	L E O
Oct. 31, 2018	3:26 AM	L E O	Apr. 13, 2019	8:34 AM	L E O	Sep. 26, 2019	11:12 AM	V I R
Nov. 2, 2018	6:51 AM	V I R	Apr. 15, 2019	12:00 PM	V I R	Sep. 28, 2019	11:12 AM	L I B
Nov. 4, 2018	10:17 AM	L I B	Apr. 17, 2019	11:12 AM	L I B	Sep. 30, 2019	11:12 AM	S C O
Nov. 6, 2018	1:43 AM	S C O	Apr. 19, 2019	12:48 PM	S C O	Oct. 2, 2019	11:12 AM	S A G
Nov. 8, 2018	8:18 PM	S A G	Apr. 21, 2019	5:09 PM	S A G	Oct. 4, 2019	6:28 PM	C A P
Nov. 11, 2018	6:00 AM	C A P	Apr. 23, 2019	12:00 AM	C A P	Oct. 7, 2019	3:42 AM	A Q U
Nov. 13, 2018	4:00 PM	A Q U	Apr. 26, 2019	10:00 AM	A Q U	Oct. 9, 2019	4:00 PM	P I S
Nov. 16, 2018	6:00 AM	P I S	Apr. 28, 2019	10:00 PM	P I S	Oct. 12, 2019	6:00 AM	A R I
Nov. 18, 2018	6:00 PM	A R I	May. 1, 2019	12:00 PM	A R I	Oct. 14, 2019	6:00 PM	T A U
Nov. 23, 2018	5:09 AM	G E M	May. 3, 2019	8:18 PM	T A U	Oct. 17, 2019	4:00 AM	G E M
Nov. 25, 2018	6:24 AM	C A N	May. 6, 2019	5:32 AM	G E M	Oct. 19, 2019	11:05 AM	C A N
Nov. 27, 2018	10:17 AM	L E O	May. 8, 2019	11:05 AM	C A N	Oct. 21, 2019	6:28 PM	L E O
Nov. 29, 2018	12:00 PM	V I R	May. 10, 2019	1:43 PM	L E O	Oct. 23, 2019	8:34 PM	V I R
Dec. 1, 2018	3:26 PM	L I B	May. 12, 2019	5:09 PM	V I R	Oct. 25, 2019	8:48 PM	L I B
Dec. 3, 2018	10:09 PM	S C O	May. 14, 2019	8:34 PM	L I B	Oct. 27, 2019	8:48 PM	S C O
Dec. 6, 2018	3:42 AM	S A G	May. 16, 2019	10:17 PM	S C O	Oct. 29, 2019	12:00 AM	S A G
Dec. 8, 2018	2:00 PM	C A P	May. 19, 2019	1:43 AM	S A G	Nov. 1, 2019	3:42 AM	C A P
Dec. 10, 2018	12:00 AM	A Q U	May. 21, 2019	9:14 AM	C A P	Nov. 3, 2019	11:05 AM	A Q U
Dec. 13, 2018	2:00 PM	P I S	May. 23, 2019	8:00 PM	A Q U	Nov. 5, 2019	12:00 AM	P I S
Dec. 16, 2018	2:00 AM	A R I	May. 26, 2019	8:44 AM	P I S	Nov. 8, 2019	12:00 PM	A R I
Dec. 18, 2018	12:00 PM	T A U	May. 28, 2019	8:00 PM	A R I	Nov. 10, 2019	12:00 AM	T A U
Dec. 20, 2018	3:26 PM	G E M	May. 31, 2019	5:32 AM	T A U	Nov. 13, 2019	9:14 AM	G E M
Dec. 22, 2018	6:51 PM	C A N	Jun. 2, 2019	12:55 PM	G E M	Nov. 15, 2019	4:37 PM	C A N
Dec. 24, 2018	5:36 AM	L E O	Jun. 4, 2019	5:09 PM	C A N	Nov. 17, 2019	12:00 AM	L E O
Dec. 26, 2018	5:36 AM	V I R	Jun. 6, 2019	8:34 PM	L E O	Nov. 20, 2019	3:26 AM	V I R
Dec. 28, 2018	7:12 PM	L I B	Jun. 8, 2019	8:48 PM	V I R	Nov. 22, 2019	5:09 AM	L I B
Dec. 31, 2018	1:43 AM	S C O	Jun. 11, 2019	1:43 AM	L I B	Nov. 24, 2019	6:24 AM	S C O
Jan. 2, 2019	9:14 AM	S A G	Jun. 13, 2019	5:09 AM	S C O	Nov. 26, 2019	8:00 AM	S A G
Jan. 4, 2019	6:28 PM	C A P	Jun. 15, 2019	11:05 AM	S A G	Nov. 28, 2019	2:46 PM	C A P
Jan. 7, 2019	8:00 AM	A Q U	Jun. 17, 2019	4:37 PM	C A P	Nov. 30, 2019	8:18 PM	A Q U
Jan. 9, 2019	8:00 PM	P I S	Jun. 20, 2019	4:00 AM	A Q U	Dec. 3, 2019	8:00 AM	P I S
Jan. 12, 2019	10:00 AM	A R I	Jun. 22, 2019	2:00 PM	P I S	Dec. 5, 2019	8:00 PM	A R I

188

Date	Time	Moon	Date	Time	Moon	Date	Time	Moon
Dec. 8, 2019	8:00 AM	TAU	May. 22, 2020	12:55 PM	GEM	Nov. 4, 2020	12:00 AM	CAN
Dec. 10, 2019	4:37 PM	GEM	May. 27, 2020	7:23 AM	LEO	Nov. 7, 2020	7:23 AM	LEO
Dec. 15, 2019	5:09 AM	LEO	May. 29, 2020	12:00 PM	VIR	Nov. 9, 2020	2:46 PM	VIR
Dec. 17, 2019	8:34 AM	VIR	May. 31, 2020	3:26 PM	LIB	Nov. 11, 2020	5:09 PM	LIB
Dec. 19, 2019	9:36 AM	LIB	Jun. 2, 2020	4:00 PM	SCO	Nov. 13, 2020	5:36 PM	SCO
Dec. 21, 2019	1:43 PM	SCO	Jun. 4, 2020	5:36 PM	SAG	Nov. 15, 2020	3:00 PM	SAG
Dec. 23, 2019	5:09 PM	SAG	Jun. 6, 2020	8:34 PM	CAP	Nov. 17, 2020	6:51 PM	CAP
Dec. 25, 2019	12:00 AM	CAP	Jun. 9, 2020	1:51 AM	AQU	Nov. 19, 2020	8:34 PM	AQU
Dec. 28, 2019	5:32 AM	AQU	Jun. 11, 2020	9:14 AM	PIS	Nov. 22, 2020	6:00 AM	PIS
Dec. 30, 2019	2:46 PM	PIS	Jun. 13, 2020	10:00 PM	ARI	Nov. 24, 2020	4:00 PM	ARI
Jan. 2, 2020	4:00 AM	ARI	Jun. 16, 2020	10:00 AM	TAU	Nov. 27, 2020	4:00 AM	TAU
Jan. 4, 2020	6:00 PM	TAU	Jun. 18, 2020	10:00 PM	GEM	Nov. 29, 2020	6:00 PM	GEM
Jan. 7, 2020	4:00 AM	GEM	Jun. 21, 2020	8:00 AM	CAN	Dec. 2, 2020	3:42 AM	CAN
Jan. 9, 2020	8:34 AM	CAN	Jun. 23, 2020	2:46 PM	LEO	Dec. 4, 2020	12:55 PM	LEO
Jan. 11, 2020	1:43 PM	LEO	Jun. 25, 2020	5:09 PM	VIR	Dec. 6, 2020	6:51 PM	VIR
Jan. 13, 2020	2:24 PM	VIR	Jun. 27, 2020	8:34 PM	LIB	Dec. 9, 2020	1:51 AM	LIB
Jan. 15, 2020	4:00 PM	LIB	Jun. 29, 2020	12:00 AM	SCO	Dec. 11, 2020	3:26 AM	SCO
Jan. 17, 2020	5:36 PM	SCO	Jul. 2, 2020	1:36 AM	SAG	Dec. 13, 2020	3:12 AM	SAG
Jan. 19, 2020	10:17 PM	SAG	Jul. 4, 2020	5:09 AM	CAP	Dec. 15, 2020	5:09 AM	CAP
Jan. 22, 2020	5:32 AM	CAP	Jul. 6, 2020	10:17 AM	AQU	Dec. 17, 2020	6:51 AM	AQU
Jan. 24, 2020	4:00 PM	AQU	Jul. 8, 2020	6:28 PM	PIS	Dec. 19, 2020	12:00 PM	PIS
Jan. 29, 2020	12:00 PM	ARI	Jul. 11, 2020	6:00 AM	ARI	Dec. 21, 2020	12:00 AM	ARI
Feb. 1, 2020	2:00 AM	TAU	Jul. 13, 2020	6:00 PM	TAU	Dec. 24, 2020	12:00 PM	TAU
Feb. 3, 2020	11:05 AM	GEM	Jul. 16, 2020	6:00 AM	GEM	Dec. 26, 2020	12:00 AM	GEM
Feb. 5, 2020	8:18 PM	CAN	Jul. 18, 2020	2:46 PM	CAN	Dec. 29, 2020	12:00 PM	CAN
Feb. 7, 2020	12:00 AM	LEO	Jul. 20, 2020	10:09 PM	LEO	Dec. 31, 2020	10:00 PM	LEO
Feb. 9, 2020	12:00 AM	VIR	Jul. 22, 2020	12:00 AM	VIR	Jan. 3, 2021	1:43 AM	VIR
Feb. 11, 2020	12:00 AM	LIB	Jul. 25, 2020	3:26 AM	LIB	Jan. 5, 2021	6:51 AM	LIB
Feb. 14, 2020	1:43 AM	SCO	Jul. 27, 2020	5:09 AM	SCO	Jan. 7, 2021	10:17 AM	SCO
Feb. 16, 2020	5:09 AM	SAG	Jul. 29, 2020	8:34 AM	SAG	Jan. 9, 2021	11:12 AM	SAG
Feb. 18, 2020	11:05 AM	CAP	Jul. 31, 2020	12:00 PM	CAP	Jan. 11, 2021	3:26 PM	CAP
Feb. 20, 2020	10:00 PM	AQU	Aug. 2, 2020	5:09 PM	AQU	Jan. 13, 2021	5:09 PM	AQU
Feb. 23, 2020	8:00 AM	PIS	Aug. 5, 2020	4:00 AM	PIS	Jan. 15, 2021	12:00 AM	PIS
Feb. 25, 2020	8:00 PM	ARI	Aug. 7, 2020	2:00 PM	ARI	Jan. 18, 2021	7:23 AM	ARI
Feb. 28, 2020	8:00 AM	TAU	Aug. 10, 2020	2:00 AM	TAU	Jan. 20, 2021	8:00 PM	TAU
Mar. 1, 2020	8:00 PM	GEM	Aug. 12, 2020	2:00 PM	GEM	Jan. 23, 2021	8:00 AM	GEM
Mar. 4, 2020	5:32 AM	CAN	Aug. 17, 2020	7:23 AM	LEO	Jan. 25, 2021	8:00 PM	CAN
Mar. 6, 2020	10:17 AM	LEO	Aug. 19, 2020	10:17 AM	VIR	Jan. 28, 2021	3:42 AM	LEO
Mar. 8, 2020	11:12 AM	VIR	Aug. 21, 2020	9:36 AM	LIB	Jan. 30, 2021	8:34 AM	VIR
Mar. 10, 2020	11:12 AM	LIB	Aug. 23, 2020	12:00 PM	SCO	Feb. 1, 2021	12:00 PM	LIB
Mar. 12, 2020	9:00 AM	SCO	Aug. 25, 2020	1:43 PM	SAG	Feb. 3, 2021	3:26 PM	SCO
Mar. 14, 2020	11:12 AM	SAG	Aug. 27, 2020	5:09 PM	CAP	Feb. 5, 2021	6:51 PM	SAG
Mar. 16, 2020	6:28 PM	CAP	Aug. 30, 2020	1:51 AM	AQU	Feb. 7, 2021	10:17 PM	CAP
Mar. 19, 2020	1:51 AM	AQU	Sep. 1, 2020	9:14 AM	PIS	Feb. 10, 2021	1:43 AM	AQU
Mar. 21, 2020	2:00 PM	PIS	Sep. 3, 2020	10:00 PM	ARI	Feb. 12, 2021	9:14 AM	PIS
Mar. 24, 2020	2:00 AM	ARI	Sep. 6, 2020	10:00 AM	TAU	Feb. 14, 2021	4:37 PM	ARI
Mar. 26, 2020	2:00 PM	TAU	Sep. 8, 2020	10:00 PM	GEM	Feb. 17, 2021	4:00 AM	TAU
Mar. 29, 2020	2:00 AM	GEM	Sep. 11, 2020	10:00 AM	CAN	Feb. 19, 2021	4:00 PM	GEM
Mar. 31, 2020	2:00 PM	CAN	Sep. 13, 2020	4:37 PM	LEO	Feb. 22, 2021	3:42 AM	CAN
Apr. 2, 2020	8:18 PM	LEO	Sep. 15, 2020	8:34 PM	VIR	Feb. 24, 2021	12:55 PM	LEO
Apr. 4, 2020	10:17 PM	VIR	Sep. 17, 2020	7:12 AM	LIB	Feb. 26, 2021	5:09 PM	VIR
Apr. 6, 2020	10:24 PM	LIB	Sep. 19, 2020	7:12 AM	SCO	Feb. 28, 2021	8:34 PM	LIB
Apr. 8, 2020	7:30 PM	SCO	Sep. 21, 2020	7:12 AM	SAG	Mar. 2, 2021	8:48 PM	SCO
Apr. 10, 2020	8:48 PM	SAG	Sep. 23, 2020	12:00 AM	CAP	Mar. 4, 2021	12:00 AM	SAG
Apr. 13, 2020	1:51 AM	CAP	Sep. 26, 2020	7:23 AM	AQU	Mar. 7, 2021	3:26 AM	CAP
Apr. 15, 2020	10:00 AM	AQU	Sep. 28, 2020	6:00 PM	PIS	Mar. 9, 2021	9:14 AM	AQU
Apr. 17, 2020	8:00 PM	PIS	Oct. 1, 2020	4:00 AM	ARI	Mar. 11, 2021	1:43 PM	PIS
Apr. 20, 2020	8:00 AM	ARI	Oct. 3, 2020	4:00 PM	TAU	Mar. 13, 2021	12:00 AM	ARI
Apr. 22, 2020	8:00 PM	TAU	Oct. 6, 2020	6:33 AM	GEM	Mar. 16, 2021	12:00 PM	TAU
Apr. 25, 2020	8:00 AM	GEM	Oct. 8, 2020	6:00 PM	CAN	Mar. 18, 2021	12:00 AM	GEM
Apr. 27, 2020	8:00 PM	CAN	Oct. 11, 2020	1:51 AM	LEO	Mar. 21, 2021	2:00 PM	CAN
Apr. 30, 2020	1:51 AM	LEO	Oct. 13, 2020	5:09 AM	VIR	Mar. 23, 2021	10:09 PM	LEO
May. 2, 2020	6:51 AM	VIR	Oct. 15, 2020	6:24 AM	LIB	Mar. 26, 2021	5:32 AM	VIR
May. 4, 2020	8:00 AM	LIB	Oct. 17, 2020	6:24 AM	SCO	Mar. 28, 2021	6:51 AM	LIB
May. 6, 2020	8:00 AM	SCO	Oct. 19, 2020	4:48 AM	SAG	Mar. 30, 2021	6:24 AM	SCO
May. 8, 2020	8:00 AM	SAG	Oct. 21, 2020	6:24 AM	CAP	Apr. 1, 2021	6:24 AM	SAG
May. 10, 2020	10:17 AM	CAP	Oct. 23, 2020	12:00 PM	AQU	Apr. 3, 2021	8:00 AM	CAP
May. 12, 2020	4:37 PM	AQU	Oct. 25, 2020	12:00 AM	PIS	Apr. 5, 2021	2:46 PM	AQU
May. 15, 2020	2:00 AM	PIS	Oct. 28, 2020	10:00 AM	ARI	Apr. 7, 2021	8:18 PM	PIS
May. 17, 2020	2:00 PM	ARI	Oct. 30, 2020	10:00 PM	TAU	Apr. 10, 2021	8:00 AM	ARI
May. 20, 2020	4:00 AM	TAU	Nov. 2, 2020	10:00 AM	GEM	Apr. 12, 2021	6:00 PM	TAU

Date	Time	Moon	Date	Time	Moon	Date	Time	Moon
Apr. 15, 2021	8:00 AM	GEM	Sep. 23, 2021	2:00 PM	TAU	Mar. 11, 2022	8:00 AM	CAN
Apr. 17, 2021	8:00 PM	CAN	Sep. 26, 2021	2:00 AM	GEM	Mar. 13, 2022	8:00 PM	LEO
Apr. 20, 2021	8:00 AM	LEO	Sep. 28, 2021	2:00 PM	CAN	Mar. 16, 2022	5:32 AM	VIR
Apr. 22, 2021	2:46 PM	VIR	Oct. 1, 2021	2:00 AM	LEO	Mar. 18, 2022	12:55 PM	LIB
Apr. 24, 2021	5:09 PM	LIB	Oct. 3, 2021	9:14 AM	VIR	Mar. 20, 2022	6:28 PM	SCO
Apr. 26, 2021	5:36 PM	SCO	Oct. 5, 2021	1:43 PM	LIB	Mar. 22, 2022	8:34 PM	SAG
Apr. 28, 2021	3:00 PM	SAG	Oct. 7, 2021	2:24 PM	SCO	Mar. 24, 2022	8:48 PM	CAP
Apr. 30, 2021	4:00 PM	CAP	Oct. 9, 2021	4:00 PM	SAG	Mar. 27, 2022	1:43 AM	AQU
May. 2, 2021	8:34 PM	AQU	Oct. 11, 2021	6:51 PM	CAP	Mar. 29, 2022	5:09 AM	PIS
May. 5, 2021	3:42 AM	PIS	Oct. 13, 2021	7:12 PM	AQU	Mar. 31, 2022	11:05 AM	ARI
May. 7, 2021	2:00 PM	ARI	Oct. 16, 2021	3:42 AM	PIS	Apr. 2, 2022	3:26 PM	TAU
May. 9, 2021	12:00 AM	TAU	Oct. 18, 2021	11:05 AM	ARI	Apr. 5, 2022	4:00 AM	GEM
May. 12, 2021	2:00 PM	GEM	Oct. 20, 2021	10:00 PM	TAU	Apr. 7, 2022	4:00 PM	CAN
May. 15, 2021	2:00 AM	CAN	Oct. 23, 2021	8:00 AM	GEM	Apr. 10, 2022	6:33 AM	LEO
May. 17, 2021	2:00 PM	LEO	Oct. 25, 2021	10:00 PM	CAN	Apr. 12, 2022	4:00 PM	VIR
May. 19, 2021	10:09 PM	VIR	Oct. 28, 2021	10:00 AM	LEO	Apr. 14, 2022	10:09 PM	LIB
May. 22, 2021	1:43 AM	LIB	Oct. 30, 2021	6:28 PM	VIR	Apr. 17, 2022	1:43 AM	SCO
May. 24, 2021	3:12 AM	SCO	Nov. 4, 2021	1:36 AM	SCO	Apr. 19, 2022	3:26 AM	SAG
May. 26, 2021	3:12 AM	SAG	Nov. 6, 2021	1:36 AM	SAG	Apr. 21, 2022	5:09 AM	CAP
May. 28, 2021	3:12 AM	CAP	Nov. 8, 2021	1:36 AM	CAP	Apr. 23, 2022	6:51 AM	AQU
May. 30, 2021	5:09 AM	AQU	Nov. 10, 2021	3:12 AM	AQU	Apr. 25, 2022	10:17 AM	PIS
Jun. 1, 2021	11:05 AM	PIS	Nov. 12, 2021	9:14 AM	PIS	Apr. 27, 2022	3:26 PM	ARI
Jun. 3, 2021	8:00 PM	ARI	Nov. 14, 2021	4:37 PM	ARI	Apr. 30, 2022	2:00 AM	TAU
Jun. 6, 2021	6:00 AM	TAU	Nov. 17, 2021	4:00 AM	TAU	May. 2, 2022	12:00 PM	GEM
Jun. 8, 2021	8:00 PM	GEM	Nov. 19, 2021	4:00 PM	GEM	May. 4, 2022	12:00 AM	CAN
Jun. 11, 2021	8:00 AM	CAN	Nov. 22, 2021	4:00 AM	CAN	May. 7, 2022	12:00 PM	LEO
Jun. 13, 2021	8:00 PM	LEO	Nov. 24, 2021	7:38 PM	LEO	May. 9, 2022	12:00 AM	VIR
Jun. 16, 2021	3:42 AM	VIR	Nov. 27, 2021	4:00 AM	VIR	May. 12, 2022	7:23 AM	LIB
Jun. 18, 2021	11:05 AM	LIB	Nov. 29, 2021	11:05 AM	LIB	May. 14, 2022	12:00 PM	SCO
Jun. 20, 2021	1:43 PM	SCO	Dec. 1, 2021	1:43 PM	SCO	May. 16, 2022	1:43 PM	SAG
Jun. 22, 2021	3:26 PM	SAG	Dec. 3, 2021	12:48 PM	SAG	May. 18, 2022	12:48 PM	CAP
Jun. 24, 2021	2:24 PM	CAP	Dec. 5, 2021	12:48 PM	CAP	May. 20, 2022	12:48 PM	AQU
Jun. 26, 2021	2:24 PM	AQU	Dec. 7, 2021	12:48 PM	AQU	May. 22, 2022	5:09 PM	PIS
Jun. 28, 2021	6:51 PM	PIS	Dec. 9, 2021	3:26 PM	PIS	May. 24, 2022	8:34 PM	ARI
Jul. 1, 2021	1:51 AM	ARI	Dec. 11, 2021	10:09 PM	ARI	May. 27, 2022	8:00 AM	TAU
Jul. 3, 2021	2:00 PM	TAU	Dec. 14, 2021	10:00 AM	TAU	May. 29, 2022	6:00 PM	GEM
Jul. 6, 2021	2:00 AM	GEM	Dec. 16, 2021	10:00 PM	GEM	Jun. 1, 2022	6:00 AM	CAN
Jul. 8, 2021	2:00 PM	CAN	Dec. 19, 2021	10:00 AM	CAN	Jun. 3, 2022	8:00 PM	LEO
Jul. 11, 2021	2:00 AM	LEO	Dec. 21, 2021	10:00 PM	LEO	Jun. 6, 2022	8:00 AM	VIR
Jul. 13, 2021	9:14 AM	VIR	Dec. 24, 2021	10:00 AM	VIR	Jun. 8, 2022	6:00 PM	LIB
Jul. 15, 2021	4:37 PM	LIB	Dec. 26, 2021	4:37 PM	LIB	Jun. 10, 2022	8:34 PM	SCO
Jul. 17, 2021	6:51 PM	SCO	Dec. 28, 2021	12:00 AM	SCO	Jun. 12, 2022	10:24 PM	SAG
Jul. 19, 2021	10:17 PM	SAG	Jan. 1, 2022	12:00 AM	CAP	Jun. 14, 2022	12:00 AM	CAP
Jul. 21, 2021	10:24 PM	CAP	Jan. 3, 2022	12:00 AM	AQU	Jun. 16, 2022	10:24 PM	AQU
Jul. 24, 2021	1:43 AM	AQU	Jan. 6, 2022	1:43 AM	PIS	Jun. 18, 2022	10:24 PM	PIS
Jul. 26, 2021	5:32 AM	PIS	Jan. 8, 2022	5:09 AM	ARI	Jun. 21, 2022	5:32 AM	ARI
Jul. 28, 2021	11:05 AM	ARI	Jan. 10, 2022	2:46 PM	TAU	Jun. 23, 2022	2:00 PM	TAU
Jul. 30, 2021	10:00 PM	TAU	Jan. 13, 2022	4:00 AM	GEM	Jun. 25, 2022	12:00 AM	GEM
Aug. 2, 2021	10:00 AM	GEM	Jan. 15, 2022	4:00 PM	CAN	Jun. 28, 2022	12:00 PM	CAN
Aug. 4, 2021	10:00 PM	CAN	Jan. 18, 2022	6:00 AM	LEO	Jul. 1, 2022	2:00 AM	LEO
Aug. 7, 2021	7:23 AM	LEO	Jan. 20, 2022	4:00 PM	VIR	Jul. 3, 2022	2:00 PM	VIR
Aug. 9, 2021	4:37 PM	VIR	Jan. 22, 2022	10:09 PM	LIB	Jul. 5, 2022	10:09 PM	LIB
Aug. 11, 2021	10:09 PM	LIB	Jan. 25, 2022	5:32 AM	SCO	Jul. 8, 2022	5:09 AM	SCO
Aug. 14, 2021	1:51 AM	SCO	Jan. 27, 2022	8:34 AM	SAG	Jul. 10, 2022	10:17 AM	SAG
Aug. 16, 2021	3:26 AM	SAG	Jan. 29, 2022	9:36 AM	CAP	Jul. 12, 2022	9:36 AM	CAP
Aug. 18, 2021	6:51 AM	CAP	Jan. 31, 2022	12:00 PM	AQU	Jul. 14, 2022	9:36 AM	AQU
Aug. 20, 2021	10:17 AM	AQU	Feb. 2, 2022	11:12 AM	PIS	Jul. 16, 2022	9:36 AM	PIS
Aug. 22, 2021	1:43 PM	PIS	Feb. 4, 2022	3:26 PM	ARI	Jul. 18, 2022	12:00 PM	ARI
Aug. 24, 2021	8:18 AM	ARI	Feb. 9, 2022	12:00 PM	GEM	Jul. 20, 2022	6:28 PM	TAU
Aug. 27, 2021	6:00 AM	TAU	Feb. 11, 2022	12:00 AM	CAN	Jul. 23, 2022	6:00 AM	GEM
Aug. 29, 2021	6:00 PM	GEM	Feb. 14, 2022	12:00 PM	LEO	Jul. 25, 2022	6:00 PM	CAN
Sep. 1, 2021	6:00 AM	CAN	Feb. 16, 2022	8:18 PM	VIR	Jul. 28, 2022	8:00 AM	LEO
Sep. 3, 2021	6:00 PM	LEO	Feb. 19, 2022	5:32 AM	LIB	Jul. 30, 2022	8:00 PM	VIR
Sep. 5, 2021	12:00 AM	VIR	Feb. 21, 2022	11:05 AM	SCO	Aug. 2, 2022	6:00 AM	LIB
Sep. 8, 2021	3:26 AM	LIB	Feb. 23, 2022	1:43 PM	SAG	Aug. 4, 2022	12:55 PM	SCO
Sep. 10, 2021	6:51 AM	SCO	Feb. 25, 2022	5:09 PM	CAP	Aug. 6, 2022	5:09 PM	SAG
Sep. 12, 2021	10:17 AM	SAG	Feb. 27, 2022	8:34 PM	AQU	Aug. 8, 2022	8:34 PM	CAP
Sep. 14, 2021	12:00 PM	CAP	Mar. 1, 2022	10:17 PM	PIS	Aug. 10, 2022	7:12 PM	AQU
Sep. 16, 2021	3:26 AM	AQU	Mar. 4, 2022	1:43 AM	ARI	Aug. 12, 2022	7:12 PM	PIS
Sep. 18, 2021	8:34 PM	PIS	Mar. 6, 2022	9:14 AM	TAU	Aug. 14, 2022	10:17 PM	ARI
Sep. 21, 2021	3:42 AM	ARI	Mar. 8, 2022	8:00 PM	GEM	Aug. 17, 2022	3:42 AM	TAU

Date	Time	Moon	Date	Time	Moon	Date	Time	Moon
Aug. 19, 2022	2:00 PM	GEM	Feb. 1, 2023	10:00 PM	CAN	Jul. 13, 2023	7:23 AM	GEM
Aug. 22, 2022	2:00 AM	CAN	Feb. 4, 2023	10:00 AM	LEO	Jul. 15, 2023	4:37 PM	CAN
Aug. 24, 2022	2:00 PM	LEO	Feb. 6, 2023	10:00 PM	VIR	Jul. 18, 2023	6:00 AM	LEO
Aug. 27, 2022	2:00 AM	VIR	Feb. 9, 2023	10:00 AM	LIB	Jul. 20, 2023	6:00 PM	VIR
Aug. 29, 2022	12:00 PM	LIB	Feb. 11, 2023	6:28 PM	SCO	Jul. 23, 2023	6:00 AM	LIB
Aug. 31, 2022	6:28 PM	SCO	Feb. 14, 2023	1:43 AM	SAG	Jul. 25, 2023	6:00 PM	SCO
Sep. 2, 2022	10:17 PM	SAG	Feb. 16, 2023	6:51 AM	CAP	Jul. 28, 2023	1:51 AM	SAG
Sep. 5, 2022	3:26 AM	CAP	Feb. 18, 2023	6:24 AM	AQU	Jul. 30, 2023	5:09 AM	CAP
Sep. 7, 2022	5:09 AM	AQU	Feb. 20, 2023	6:24 AM	PIS	Aug. 1, 2023	4:48 AM	AQU
Sep. 9, 2022	4:48 AM	PIS	Feb. 22, 2023	6:24 AM	ARI	Aug. 3, 2023	3:00 AM	PIS
Sep. 11, 2022	6:24 AM	ARI	Feb. 24, 2023	8:34 AM	TAU	Aug. 5, 2023	5:09 AM	ARI
Sep. 13, 2022	12:00 PM	TAU	Feb. 26, 2023	4:37 PM	GEM	Aug. 7, 2023	6:51 AM	TAU
Sep. 15, 2022	8:18 PM	GEM	Mar. 1, 2023	4:00 AM	CAN	Aug. 9, 2023	2:46 PM	GEM
Sep. 18, 2022	8:00 AM	CAN	Mar. 3, 2023	4:00 PM	LEO	Aug. 11, 2023	10:09 PM	CAN
Sep. 20, 2022	10:00 PM	LEO	Mar. 6, 2023	4:00 AM	VIR	Aug. 14, 2023	12:00 PM	LEO
Sep. 23, 2022	10:00 AM	VIR	Mar. 8, 2023	4:00 PM	LIB	Aug. 16, 2023	12:00 AM	VIR
Sep. 25, 2022	4:37 PM	LIB	Mar. 11, 2023	2:00 AM	SCO	Aug. 19, 2023	12:00 PM	LIB
Sep. 27, 2022	10:17 PM	SCO	Mar. 13, 2023	9:14 AM	SAG	Aug. 21, 2023	12:00 AM	SCO
Sep. 30, 2022	5:09 AM	SAG	Mar. 15, 2023	2:46 PM	CAP	Aug. 24, 2023	9:14 AM	SAG
Oct. 2, 2022	8:34 AM	CAP	Mar. 17, 2023	2:24 PM	AQU	Aug. 26, 2023	1:43 PM	CAP
Oct. 4, 2022	12:00 PM	AQU	Mar. 19, 2023	4:00 PM	PIS	Aug. 28, 2023	5:09 PM	AQU
Oct. 6, 2022	1:43 PM	PIS	Mar. 21, 2023	4:00 PM	ARI	Aug. 30, 2023	1:30 PM	PIS
Oct. 8, 2022	5:09 PM	ARI	Mar. 23, 2023	5:36 PM	TAU	Sep. 1, 2023	2:24 PM	ARI
Oct. 10, 2022	8:34 PM	TAU	Mar. 26, 2023	1:51 AM	GEM	Sep. 3, 2023	2:24 PM	TAU
Oct. 13, 2022	5:32 AM	GEM	Mar. 28, 2023	12:00 PM	CAN	Sep. 5, 2023	10:09 PM	GEM
Oct. 15, 2022	6:00 PM	CAN	Mar. 30, 2023	12:00 AM	LEO	Sep. 8, 2023	5:32 AM	CAN
Oct. 18, 2022	6:00 AM	LEO	Apr. 2, 2023	12:00 PM	VIR	Sep. 10, 2023	6:00 PM	LEO
Oct. 20, 2022	6:00 PM	VIR	Apr. 4, 2023	12:00 AM	LIB	Sep. 13, 2023	6:00 AM	VIR
Oct. 23, 2022	1:51 AM	LIB	Apr. 7, 2023	7:23 AM	SCO	Sep. 15, 2023	6:00 PM	LIB
Oct. 25, 2022	9:14 AM	SCO	Apr. 9, 2023	2:46 PM	SAG	Sep. 18, 2023	6:00 AM	SCO
Oct. 27, 2022	12:00 PM	SAG	Apr. 11, 2023	8:18 PM	CAP	Sep. 20, 2023	2:46 PM	SAG
Oct. 29, 2022	12:48 PM	CAP	Apr. 13, 2023	10:17 PM	AQU	Sep. 22, 2023	10:09 PM	CAP
Oct. 31, 2022	5:09 PM	AQU	Apr. 15, 2023	10:24 PM	PIS	Sep. 24, 2023	12:00 AM	AQU
Nov. 2, 2022	5:36 PM	PIS	Apr. 18, 2023	1:36 AM	ARI	Sep. 27, 2023	1:36 AM	PIS
Nov. 7, 2022	5:09 AM	TAU	Apr. 20, 2023	5:09 AM	TAU	Sep. 29, 2023	1:36 AM	ARI
Nov. 9, 2022	4:00 PM	GEM	Apr. 22, 2023	11:05 AM	GEM	Oct. 1, 2023	1:36 AM	TAU
Nov. 12, 2022	2:00 AM	CAN	Apr. 24, 2023	6:28 PM	CAN	Oct. 3, 2023	5:09 AM	GEM
Nov. 14, 2022	2:00 PM	LEO	Apr. 27, 2023	8:00 AM	LEO	Oct. 5, 2023	12:55 PM	CAN
Nov. 17, 2022	2:00 AM	VIR	Apr. 29, 2023	8:00 PM	VIR	Oct. 7, 2023	10:09 PM	LEO
Nov. 19, 2022	11:05 AM	LIB	May. 2, 2023	8:00 AM	LIB	Oct. 10, 2023	12:00 PM	VIR
Nov. 21, 2022	6:28 PM	SCO	May. 4, 2023	2:46 PM	SCO	Oct. 13, 2023	2:00 AM	LIB
Nov. 23, 2022	10:17 PM	SAG	May. 6, 2023	10:09 PM	SAG	Oct. 15, 2023	11:05 AM	SCO
Nov. 25, 2022	12:00 AM	CAP	May. 8, 2023	12:00 AM	CAP	Oct. 17, 2023	8:18 PM	SAG
Nov. 27, 2022	10:24 PM	AQU	May. 11, 2023	3:26 AM	AQU	Oct. 20, 2023	3:42 AM	CAP
Nov. 30, 2022	1:43 AM	PIS	May. 13, 2023	5:09 AM	PIS	Oct. 22, 2023	6:51 AM	AQU
Dec. 2, 2022	5:09 AM	ARI	May. 15, 2023	8:34 AM	ARI	Oct. 24, 2023	10:17 AM	PIS
Dec. 4, 2022	12:55 PM	TAU	May. 17, 2023	2:46 PM	TAU	Oct. 26, 2023	12:00 PM	ARI
Dec. 6, 2022	8:18 PM	GEM	May. 19, 2023	8:18 PM	GEM	Oct. 28, 2023	1:43 PM	TAU
Dec. 9, 2022	7:23 AM	CAN	May. 22, 2023	3:42 AM	CAN	Oct. 30, 2023	3:26 PM	GEM
Dec. 11, 2022	8:00 PM	LEO	May. 24, 2023	4:00 PM	LEO	Nov. 1, 2023	10:09 PM	CAN
Dec. 14, 2022	10:00 AM	VIR	May. 27, 2023	4:00 AM	VIR	Nov. 4, 2023	7:23 AM	LEO
Dec. 16, 2022	10:00 PM	LIB	May. 29, 2023	4:00 PM	LIB	Nov. 6, 2023	8:00 PM	VIR
Dec. 19, 2022	3:26 AM	SCO	May. 31, 2023	12:00 AM	SCO	Nov. 9, 2023	10:00 AM	LIB
Dec. 21, 2022	8:34 AM	SAG	Jun. 3, 2023	5:09 AM	SAG	Nov. 11, 2023	6:28 PM	SCO
Dec. 23, 2022	8:00 AM	CAP	Jun. 5, 2023	8:34 AM	CAP	Nov. 14, 2023	3:42 AM	SAG
Dec. 25, 2022	8:00 AM	AQU	Jun. 7, 2023	10:17 AM	AQU	Nov. 16, 2023	9:14 AM	CAP
Dec. 27, 2022	8:00 AM	PIS	Jun. 9, 2023	12:00 PM	PIS	Nov. 18, 2023	12:00 PM	AQU
Dec. 29, 2022	12:00 PM	ARI	Jun. 11, 2023	1:43 PM	ARI	Nov. 20, 2023	3:26 PM	PIS
Dec. 31, 2022	6:28 PM	TAU	Jun. 13, 2023	8:18 PM	TAU	Nov. 22, 2023	6:51 PM	ARI
Jan. 3, 2023	4:00 AM	GEM	Jun. 16, 2023	1:51 AM	GEM	Nov. 24, 2023	7:12 PM	TAU
Jan. 5, 2023	4:00 PM	CAN	Jun. 18, 2023	11:05 AM	CAN	Nov. 27, 2023	1:43 AM	GEM
Jan. 8, 2023	4:00 AM	LEO	Jun. 20, 2023	12:00 AM	LEO	Nov. 29, 2023	7:23 AM	CAN
Jan. 10, 2023	4:00 PM	VIR	Jun. 23, 2023	12:00 PM	VIR	Dec. 1, 2023	6:00 PM	LEO
Jan. 13, 2023	4:00 AM	LIB	Jun. 25, 2023	12:00 AM	LIB	Dec. 4, 2023	4:00 AM	VIR
Jan. 15, 2023	12:55 PM	SCO	Jun. 28, 2023	9:14 AM	SCO	Dec. 6, 2023	6:00 PM	LIB
Jan. 17, 2023	8:18 PM	SAG	Jun. 30, 2023	4:37 PM	SAG	Dec. 9, 2023	3:42 AM	SCO
Jan. 19, 2023	7:12 PM	CAP	Jul. 2, 2023	6:51 PM	CAP	Dec. 11, 2023	12:55 PM	SAG
Jan. 21, 2023	6:00 PM	AQU	Jul. 4, 2023	5:36 PM	AQU	Dec. 13, 2023	6:28 PM	CAP
Jan. 23, 2023	7:12 PM	PIS	Jul. 6, 2023	5:36 PM	PIS	Dec. 15, 2023	5:36 PM	AQU
Jan. 25, 2023	7:12 PM	ARI	Jul. 8, 2023	7:12 PM	ARI	Dec. 17, 2023	7:12 PM	PIS
Jan. 30, 2023	10:00 AM	GEM	Jul. 10, 2023	12:00 AM	TAU	Dec. 19, 2023	12:00 AM	ARI

Date	Time	Moon	Date	Time	Moon	Date	Time	Moon
Dec. 22, 2023	3:26 AM	TAU	Jun. 3, 2024	6:51 AM	TAU	Nov. 18, 2024	10:17 AM	CAN
Dec. 24, 2023	8:34 AM	GEM	Jun. 5, 2024	10:17 AM	GEM	Nov. 20, 2024	1:43 PM	LEO
Dec. 26, 2023	4:37 PM	CAN	Jun. 7, 2024	1:43 PM	CAN	Nov. 22, 2024	10:09 PM	VIR
Dec. 29, 2023	2:00 AM	LEO	Jun. 9, 2024	8:18 PM	LEO	Nov. 25, 2024	12:00 PM	LIB
Dec. 31, 2023	12:00 PM	VIR	Jun. 12, 2024	5:32 AM	VIR	Nov. 28, 2024	2:00 AM	SCO
Jan. 3, 2024	2:00 AM	LIB	Jun. 14, 2024	6:00 PM	LIB	Nov. 30, 2024	2:00 PM	SAG
Jan. 5, 2024	2:00 PM	SCO	Jun. 17, 2024	8:00 AM	SCO	Dec. 2, 2024	12:00 AM	CAP
Jan. 7, 2024	10:09 PM	SAG	Jun. 19, 2024	4:37 PM	SAG	Dec. 5, 2024	5:32 AM	AQU
Jan. 10, 2024	1:43 AM	CAP	Jun. 21, 2024	10:17 PM	CAP	Dec. 7, 2024	10:17 AM	PIS
Jan. 12, 2024	3:12 AM	AQU	Jun. 24, 2024	3:26 AM	AQU	Dec. 9, 2024	1:43 PM	ARI
Jan. 14, 2024	4:48 AM	PIS	Jun. 26, 2024	6:51 AM	PIS	Dec. 11, 2024	5:09 PM	TAU
Jan. 16, 2024	4:48 AM	ARI	Jun. 28, 2024	10:17 AM	ARI	Dec. 13, 2024	5:36 PM	GEM
Jan. 18, 2024	8:34 AM	TAU	Jun. 30, 2024	1:43 PM	TAU	Dec. 15, 2024	8:34 PM	CAN
Jan. 20, 2024	1:43 PM	GEM	Jul. 2, 2024	5:09 PM	GEM	Dec. 17, 2024	12:00 AM	LEO
Jan. 22, 2024	10:09 PM	CAN	Jul. 4, 2024	8:34 PM	CAN	Dec. 20, 2024	7:23 AM	VIR
Jan. 25, 2024	7:23 AM	LEO	Jul. 7, 2024	5:32 AM	LEO	Dec. 22, 2024	8:00 PM	LIB
Jan. 27, 2024	8:00 PM	VIR	Jul. 9, 2024	4:00 PM	VIR	Dec. 25, 2024	10:55 AM	SCO
Jan. 30, 2024	8:00 AM	LIB	Jul. 12, 2024	4:22 AM	LIB	Dec. 27, 2024	10:00 PM	SAG
Feb. 1, 2024	10:00 PM	SCO	Jul. 14, 2024	4:00 PM	SCO	Dec. 30, 2024	5:32 AM	CAP
Feb. 4, 2024	7:23 AM	SAG	Jul. 17, 2024	1:51 AM	SAG	Jan. 1, 2025	12:55 PM	AQU
Feb. 6, 2024	2:46 PM	CAP	Jul. 19, 2024	9:14 AM	CAP	Jan. 3, 2025	3:26 PM	PIS
Feb. 8, 2024	2:24 PM	AQU	Jul. 21, 2024	12:00 PM	AQU	Jan. 5, 2025	8:34 PM	ARI
Feb. 10, 2024	2:24 PM	PIS	Jul. 23, 2024	3:26 PM	PIS	Jan. 7, 2025	12:00 AM	TAU
Feb. 12, 2024	2:24 PM	ARI	Jul. 25, 2024	2:24 PM	ARI	Jan. 10, 2025	1:43 AM	GEM
Feb. 14, 2024	2:24 PM	TAU	Jul. 27, 2024	6:51 PM	TAU	Jan. 12, 2025	5:09 AM	CAN
Feb. 16, 2024	10:09 PM	GEM	Jul. 29, 2024	10:17 PM	GEM	Jan. 14, 2025	11:05 AM	LEO
Feb. 19, 2024	3:42 AM	CAN	Aug. 1, 2024	3:26 AM	CAN	Jan. 16, 2025	4:37 PM	VIR
Feb. 21, 2024	12:55 PM	LEO	Aug. 3, 2024	11:05 AM	LEO	Jan. 19, 2025	4:00 AM	LIB
Feb. 24, 2024	2:00 AM	VIR	Aug. 5, 2024	8:18 PM	VIR	Jan. 21, 2025	7:38 PM	SCO
Feb. 26, 2024	5:27 PM	LIB	Aug. 8, 2024	10:00 AM	LIB	Jan. 24, 2025	6:00 AM	SAG
Feb. 29, 2024	4:00 AM	SCO	Aug. 13, 2024	12:00 PM	SAG	Jan. 26, 2025	4:00 PM	CAP
Mar. 2, 2024	4:00 PM	SAG	Aug. 15, 2024	6:28 PM	CAP	Jan. 28, 2025	10:09 PM	AQU
Mar. 4, 2024	10:09 PM	CAP	Aug. 17, 2024	10:17 PM	AQU	Jan. 30, 2025	12:00 AM	PIS
Mar. 7, 2024	1:43 AM	AQU	Aug. 21, 2024	12:00 AM	ARI	Feb. 2, 2025	1:36 AM	ARI
Mar. 9, 2024	1:36 AM	PIS	Aug. 24, 2024	1:43 AM	TAU	Feb. 4, 2025	5:09 AM	TAU
Mar. 11, 2024	1:36 AM	ARI	Aug. 26, 2024	3:26 AM	GEM	Feb. 6, 2025	6:51 AM	GEM
Mar. 13, 2024	1:36 AM	TAU	Aug. 28, 2024	8:34 AM	CAN	Feb. 8, 2025	12:00 PM	CAN
Mar. 15, 2024	3:26 AM	GEM	Aug. 30, 2024	8:00 PM	LEO	Feb. 10, 2025	6:28 PM	LEO
Mar. 17, 2024	11:05 AM	CAN	Sep. 2, 2024	3:42 AM	VIR	Feb. 13, 2025	1:51 AM	VIR
Mar. 19, 2024	6:28 PM	LEO	Sep. 4, 2024	4:00 PM	LIB	Feb. 15, 2025	11:05 AM	LIB
Mar. 22, 2024	8:00 AM	VIR	Sep. 7, 2024	6:00 AM	SCO	Feb. 18, 2025	2:11 AM	SCO
Mar. 24, 2024	12:00 AM	LIB	Sep. 9, 2024	6:00 PM	SAG	Feb. 20, 2025	2:00 PM	SAG
Mar. 27, 2024	10:00 AM	SCO	Sep. 12, 2024	3:42 AM	CAP	Feb. 25, 2025	7:23 AM	AQU
Mar. 29, 2024	10:00 PM	SAG	Sep. 14, 2024	8:34 AM	AQU	Feb. 27, 2025	10:17 PM	PIS
Apr. 1, 2024	5:32 AM	CAP	Sep. 16, 2024	9:36 AM	PIS	Mar. 1, 2025	12:00 PM	ARI
Apr. 3, 2024	11:05 AM	AQU	Sep. 18, 2024	9:00 AM	ARI	Mar. 3, 2025	11:12 AM	TAU
Apr. 5, 2024	11:12 AM	PIS	Sep. 20, 2024	9:36 AM	TAU	Mar. 5, 2025	1:43 PM	GEM
Apr. 7, 2024	12:48 PM	ARI	Sep. 22, 2024	12:00 PM	GEM	Mar. 7, 2025	5:09 PM	CAN
Apr. 9, 2024	12:48 PM	TAU	Sep. 24, 2024	3:26 PM	CAN	Mar. 9, 2025	12:00 AM	LEO
Apr. 11, 2024	12:48 PM	GEM	Sep. 29, 2024	9:14 AM	VIR	Mar. 12, 2025	10:00 AM	VIR
Apr. 13, 2024	5:09 PM	CAN	Oct. 1, 2024	10:00 PM	LIB	Mar. 14, 2025	8:00 PM	LIB
Apr. 16, 2024	4:00 AM	LEO	Oct. 4, 2024	12:00 PM	SCO	Mar. 17, 2025	8:00 AM	SCO
Apr. 18, 2024	4:00 PM	VIR	Oct. 6, 2024	12:00 AM	SAG	Mar. 19, 2025	12:00 AM	SAG
Apr. 21, 2024	4:00 AM	LIB	Oct. 9, 2024	12:00 PM	CAP	Mar. 22, 2025	7:23 AM	CAP
Apr. 23, 2024	4:00 PM	SCO	Oct. 11, 2024	6:28 PM	AQU	Mar. 24, 2025	4:37 PM	AQU
Apr. 26, 2024	1:51 AM	SAG	Oct. 13, 2024	8:34 PM	PIS	Mar. 26, 2025	8:34 PM	PIS
Apr. 28, 2024	11:05 AM	CAP	Oct. 15, 2024	8:48 PM	ARI	Mar. 28, 2025	8:48 PM	ARI
Apr. 30, 2024	3:26 PM	AQU	Oct. 17, 2024	8:48 PM	TAU	Mar. 30, 2025	8:48 PM	TAU
May. 2, 2024	8:34 PM	PIS	Oct. 19, 2024	8:48 PM	GEM	Apr. 1, 2025	8:48 PM	GEM
May. 4, 2024	10:17 PM	ARI	Oct. 21, 2024	12:00 AM	CAN	Apr. 3, 2025	12:00 AM	CAN
May. 6, 2024	12:00 AM	TAU	Oct. 24, 2024	5:32 AM	LEO	Apr. 6, 2025	5:32 AM	LEO
May. 11, 2024	3:26 AM	CAN	Oct. 26, 2024	2:46 PM	VIR	Apr. 8, 2025	4:00 PM	VIR
May. 13, 2024	11:05 AM	LEO	Oct. 29, 2024	6:00 AM	LIB	Apr. 11, 2025	2:00 AM	LIB
May. 15, 2024	8:18 PM	VIR	Oct. 31, 2024	6:00 PM	SCO	Apr. 13, 2025	2:00 PM	SCO
May. 18, 2024	1:05 PM	LIB	Nov. 3, 2024	6:00 AM	SAG	Apr. 16, 2025	4:00 AM	SAG
May. 20, 2024	12:00 AM	SCO	Nov. 5, 2024	6:00 PM	CAP	Apr. 18, 2025	4:00 PM	CAP
May. 23, 2024	10:00 AM	SAG	Nov. 7, 2024	12:00 AM	AQU	Apr. 23, 2025	5:09 AM	PIS
May. 25, 2024	4:37 PM	CAP	Nov. 10, 2024	5:09 PM	PIS	Apr. 25, 2025	8:34 AM	ARI
May. 27, 2024	8:34 PM	AQU	Nov. 12, 2024	6:24 AM	ARI	Apr. 27, 2025	8:00 AM	TAU
May. 30, 2024	1:43 PM	PIS	Nov. 14, 2024	8:00 AM	TAU	Apr. 29, 2025	8:00 AM	GEM
Jun. 1, 2024	5:09 AM	ARI	Nov. 16, 2024	8:00 AM	GEM	May. 1, 2025	8:00 AM	CAN

Date	Time	Moon	Date	Time	Moon	Date	Time	Moon
May. 3, 2025	12:00 PM	LEO	Jul. 29, 2025	5:32 AM	LIB	Oct. 16, 2025	6:28 PM	VIR
May. 5, 2025	8:18 PM	VIR	Jul. 31, 2025	6:00 PM	SCO	Oct. 19, 2025	6:00 AM	LIB
May. 8, 2025	8:00 AM	LIB	Aug. 3, 2025	8:44 AM	SAG	Oct. 21, 2025	4:00 PM	SCO
May. 10, 2025	8:00 PM	SCO	Aug. 5, 2025	6:00 PM	CAP	Oct. 24, 2025	6:33 AM	SAG
May. 13, 2025	10:00 AM	SAG	Aug. 8, 2025	1:51 AM	AQU	Oct. 26, 2025	6:00 PM	CAP
May. 15, 2025	10:00 PM	CAP	Aug. 10, 2025	6:51 AM	PIS	Oct. 29, 2025	6:00 AM	AQU
May. 18, 2025	5:32 AM	AQU	Aug. 12, 2025	12:00 PM	ARI	Oct. 31, 2025	12:55 PM	PIS
May. 20, 2025	12:00 PM	PIS	Aug. 14, 2025	12:48 PM	TAU	Nov. 2, 2025	5:09 PM	ARI
May. 22, 2025	5:09 PM	ARI	Aug. 16, 2025	5:09 PM	GEM	Nov. 4, 2025	6:51 PM	TAU
May. 24, 2025	5:36 PM	TAU	Aug. 18, 2025	8:34 PM	CAN	Nov. 6, 2025	3:00 PM	GEM
May. 26, 2025	4:30 PM	GEM	Aug. 20, 2025	12:00 AM	LEO	Nov. 8, 2025	4:00 PM	CAN
May. 28, 2025	5:36 PM	CAN	Aug. 23, 2025	5:09 AM	VIR	Nov. 10, 2025	6:51 PM	LEO
May. 30, 2025	7:12 PM	LEO	Aug. 25, 2025	2:46 PM	LIB	Nov. 12, 2025	10:17 PM	VIR
Jun. 2, 2025	3:42 AM	VIR	Aug. 28, 2025	2:00 AM	SCO	Nov. 15, 2025	9:14 AM	LIB
Jun. 4, 2025	12:55 PM	LIB	Aug. 30, 2025	2:00 PM	SAG	Nov. 17, 2025	10:00 PM	SCO
Jun. 7, 2025	4:22 AM	SCO	Sep. 2, 2025	1:51 AM	CAP	Nov. 20, 2025	12:00 PM	SAG
Jun. 9, 2025	4:00 PM	SAG	Sep. 4, 2025	11:05 AM	AQU	Nov. 22, 2025	12:00 AM	CAP
Jun. 12, 2025	1:51 AM	CAP	Sep. 6, 2025	6:28 PM	PIS	Nov. 25, 2025	12:00 PM	AQU
Jun. 14, 2025	11:05 AM	AQU	Sep. 8, 2025	8:34 PM	ARI	Nov. 27, 2025	10:00 PM	PIS
Jun. 16, 2025	8:18 PM	PIS	Sep. 10, 2025	10:17 PM	TAU	Nov. 30, 2025	1:43 AM	ARI
Jun. 21, 2025	3:26 AM	TAU	Sep. 12, 2025	12:00 AM	GEM	Dec. 2, 2025	3:12 AM	TAU
Jun. 23, 2025	3:12 AM	GEM	Sep. 15, 2025	1:43 AM	CAN	Dec. 4, 2025	3:00 AM	GEM
Jun. 25, 2025	4:48 AM	CAN	Sep. 17, 2025	5:09 AM	LEO	Dec. 6, 2025	3:12 AM	CAN
Jun. 27, 2025	6:51 AM	LEO	Sep. 19, 2025	12:55 PM	VIR	Dec. 8, 2025	3:12 AM	LEO
Jun. 29, 2025	12:55 PM	VIR	Sep. 21, 2025	12:00 AM	LIB	Dec. 10, 2025	9:14 AM	VIR
Jul. 1, 2025	8:18 PM	LIB	Sep. 24, 2025	10:00 AM	SCO	Dec. 12, 2025	6:00 PM	LIB
Jul. 4, 2025	10:00 AM	SCO	Sep. 26, 2025	10:00 PM	SAG	Dec. 15, 2025	4:00 AM	SCO
Jul. 9, 2025	10:00 AM	CAP	Sep. 29, 2025	10:00 AM	CAP	Dec. 17, 2025	6:00 PM	SAG
Jul. 11, 2025	6:28 PM	AQU	Oct. 1, 2025	10:00 PM	AQU	Dec. 20, 2025	6:00 AM	CAP
Jul. 16, 2025	5:09 AM	ARI	Oct. 4, 2025	3:42 AM	PIS	Dec. 22, 2025	6:00 PM	AQU
Jul. 18, 2025	8:34 AM	TAU	Oct. 6, 2025	4:48 AM	ARI	Dec. 25, 2025	1:51 AM	PIS
Jul. 20, 2025	12:00 PM	GEM	Oct. 8, 2025	6:24 AM	TAU	Dec. 27, 2025	9:14 AM	ARI
Jul. 22, 2025	1:43 PM	CAN	Oct. 10, 2025	6:24 AM	GEM	Dec. 29, 2025	2:46 PM	TAU
Jul. 24, 2025	2:24 PM	LEO	Oct. 12, 2025	6:24 AM	CAN	Dec. 31, 2025	3:26 PM	GEM
Jul. 26, 2025	8:34 PM	VIR	Oct. 14, 2025	12:55 PM	LEO			

Venus

Date	Venus	Date	Venus	Date	Venus	Date	Venus
Jan. 1, 1920	SCO	Mar. 13, 1922	ARI	Oct. 7, 1924	VIR	Feb. 26, 1927	ARI
Jan. 4, 1920	SAG	Apr. 6, 1922	TAU	Nov. 2, 1924	LIB	Mar. 22, 1927	TAU
Jan. 29, 1920	CAP	May. 1, 1922	GEM	Nov. 27, 1924	SCO	Apr. 16, 1927	GEM
Feb. 23, 1920	AQU	May. 25, 1922	CAN	Dec. 21, 1924	SAG	May. 12, 1927	CAN
Mar. 18, 1920	PIS	Jun. 19, 1922	LEO	Jan. 14, 1925	CAP	Jun. 8, 1927	LEO
Apr. 12, 1920	ARI	Jul. 15, 1922	VIR	Feb. 7, 1925	AQU	Jul. 7, 1927	VIR
May. 6, 1920	TAU	Aug. 10, 1922	LIB	Mar. 4, 1925	PIS	Nov. 9, 1927	LIB
May. 31, 1920	GEM	Sep. 7, 1922	SCO	Mar. 28, 1925	ARI	Dec. 8, 1927	SCO
Jun. 24, 1920	CAN	Oct. 10, 1922	SAG	Apr. 21, 1925	TAU	Jan. 4, 1928	SAG
Jul. 18, 1920	LEO	Nov. 28, 1922	SCO	May. 15, 1925	GEM	Jan. 29, 1928	CAP
Aug. 12, 1920	VIR	Jan. 2, 1923	SAG	Jun. 9, 1925	CAN	Feb. 22, 1928	AQU
Sep. 5, 1920	LIB	Feb. 6, 1923	CAP	Jul. 3, 1925	LEO	Mar. 18, 1928	PIS
Sep. 29, 1920	SCO	Mar. 6, 1923	AQU	Jul. 28, 1925	VIR	Apr. 11, 1928	ARI
Oct. 24, 1920	SAG	Apr. 1, 1923	PIS	Aug. 22, 1925	LIB	May. 6, 1928	TAU
Nov. 17, 1920	CAP	Apr. 26, 1923	ARI	Sep. 16, 1925	SCO	May. 30, 1928	GEM
Dec. 12, 1920	AQU	May. 21, 1923	TAU	Oct. 11, 1925	SAG	Jun. 23, 1928	CAN
Jan. 6, 1921	PIS	Jun. 15, 1923	GEM	Nov. 6, 1925	CAP	Jul. 18, 1928	LEO
Feb. 2, 1921	ARI	Jul. 10, 1923	CAN	Dec. 5, 1925	AQU	Aug. 11, 1928	VIR
Mar. 7, 1921	TAU	Aug. 3, 1923	LEO	Apr. 6, 1926	PIS	Sep. 4, 1928	LIB
Apr. 25, 1921	ARI	Aug. 27, 1923	VIR	May. 6, 1926	ARI	Sep. 29, 1928	SCO
Jun. 2, 1921	TAU	Sep. 21, 1923	LIB	Jun. 2, 1926	TAU	Oct. 23, 1928	SAG
Jul. 8, 1921	GEM	Oct. 15, 1923	SCO	Jun. 28, 1926	GEM	Nov. 17, 1928	CAP
Aug. 5, 1921	CAN	Nov. 8, 1923	SAG	Jul. 24, 1926	CAN	Dec. 12, 1928	AQU
Aug. 31, 1921	LEO	Dec. 2, 1923	CAP	Aug. 18, 1926	LEO	Jan. 6, 1929	PIS
Sep. 26, 1921	VIR	Dec. 26, 1923	AQU	Sep. 11, 1926	VIR	Feb. 2, 1929	ARI
Oct. 20, 1921	LIB	Jan. 19, 1924	PIS	Oct. 5, 1926	LIB	Mar. 8, 1929	TAU
Nov. 13, 1921	SCO	Feb. 13, 1924	ARI	Oct. 29, 1926	SCO	Apr. 20, 1929	ARI
Dec. 7, 1921	SAG	Mar. 9, 1924	TAU	Nov. 22, 1926	SAG	Jun. 3, 1929	TAU
Dec. 31, 1921	CAP	Apr. 5, 1924	GEM	Dec. 16, 1926	CAP	Jul. 8, 1929	GEM
Jan. 24, 1922	AQU	May. 6, 1924	CAN	Jan. 9, 1927	AQU	Aug. 5, 1929	CAN
Feb. 17, 1922	PIS	Sep. 8, 1924	LEO	Feb. 2, 1927	PIS	Aug. 31, 1929	LEO

Date	Venus	Date	Venus	Date	Venus	Date	Venus
Sep. 25, 1929	V I R	Feb. 26, 1935	A R I	Sep. 8, 1940	L E O	Apr. 5, 1946	T A U
Oct. 20, 1929	L I B	Mar. 22, 1935	T A U	Oct. 6, 1940	V I R	Apr. 29, 1946	G E M
Nov. 13, 1929	S C O	Apr. 16, 1935	G E M	Nov. 1, 1940	L I B	May. 24, 1946	C A N
Dec. 7, 1929	S A G	May. 11, 1935	C A N	Nov. 26, 1940	S C O	Jun. 18, 1946	L E O
Dec. 31, 1929	C A P	Jun. 7, 1935	L E O	Dec. 20, 1940	S A G	Jul. 13, 1946	V I R
Jan. 24, 1930	A Q U	Jul. 7, 1935	V I R	Jan. 13, 1941	C A P	Aug. 9, 1946	L I B
Feb. 16, 1930	P I S	Nov. 9, 1935	L I B	Feb. 6, 1941	A Q U	Sep. 7, 1946	S C O
Mar. 12, 1930	A R I	Dec. 8, 1935	S C O	Mar. 2, 1941	P I S	Oct. 16, 1946	S A G
Apr. 6, 1930	T A U	Jan. 3, 1936	S A G	Mar. 27, 1941	A R I	Nov. 8, 1946	S C O
Apr. 30, 1930	G E M	Jan. 28, 1936	C A P	Apr. 20, 1941	T A U	Jan. 5, 1947	S A G
May. 25, 1930	C A N	Feb. 22, 1936	A Q U	May. 14, 1941	G E M	Feb. 6, 1947	C A P
Jun. 19, 1930	L E O	Mar. 17, 1936	P I S	Jun. 7, 1941	C A N	Mar. 5, 1947	A Q U
Jul. 14, 1930	V I R	Apr. 11, 1936	A R I	Jul. 2, 1941	L E O	Mar. 30, 1947	P I S
Aug. 10, 1930	L I B	May. 5, 1936	T A U	Jul. 27, 1941	V I R	Apr. 25, 1947	A R I
Sep. 7, 1930	S C O	May. 29, 1936	G E M	Aug. 21, 1941	L I B	May. 20, 1947	T A U
Oct. 12, 1930	S A G	Jun. 23, 1936	C A N	Sep. 15, 1941	S C O	Jun. 13, 1947	G E M
Nov. 22, 1930	S C O	Jul. 17, 1936	L E O	Oct. 10, 1941	S A G	Jul. 8, 1947	C A N
Jan. 3, 1931	S A G	Aug. 11, 1936	V I R	Nov. 6, 1941	C A P	Aug. 2, 1947	L E O
Feb. 6, 1931	C A P	Sep. 4, 1936	L I B	Dec. 5, 1941	A Q U	Aug. 26, 1947	V I R
Mar. 5, 1931	A Q U	Sep. 28, 1936	S C O	Apr. 6, 1942	P I S	Sep. 19, 1947	L I B
Mar. 31, 1931	P I S	Oct. 23, 1936	S A G	May. 6, 1942	A R I	Oct. 13, 1947	S C O
Apr. 26, 1931	A R I	Nov. 16, 1936	C A P	Jun. 2, 1942	T A U	Nov. 6, 1947	S A G
May. 21, 1931	T A U	Dec. 11, 1936	A Q U	Jun. 27, 1942	G E M	Nov. 30, 1947	C A P
Jun. 14, 1931	G E M	Jan. 6, 1937	P I S	Jul. 23, 1942	C A N	Dec. 24, 1947	A Q U
Jul. 9, 1931	C A N	Feb. 2, 1937	A R I	Aug. 17, 1942	L E O	Jan. 18, 1948	P I S
Aug. 3, 1931	L E O	Mar. 9, 1937	T A U	Sep. 10, 1942	V I R	Feb. 11, 1948	A R I
Aug. 27, 1931	V I R	Apr. 14, 1937	A R I	Oct. 4, 1942	L I B	Mar. 8, 1948	T A U
Sep. 20, 1931	L I B	Jun. 14, 1937	T A U	Oct. 28, 1942	S C O	Apr. 4, 1948	G E M
Oct. 14, 1931	S C O	Jul. 7, 1937	G E M	Nov. 21, 1942	S A G	May. 7, 1948	C A N
Nov. 7, 1931	S A G	Aug. 4, 1937	C A N	Dec. 15, 1942	C A P	Jun. 29, 1948	G E M
Dec. 1, 1931	C A P	Aug. 31, 1937	L E O	Jan. 8, 1943	A Q U	Aug. 3, 1948	C A N
Dec. 25, 1931	A Q U	Sep. 25, 1937	V I R	Feb. 1, 1943	P I S	Sep. 8, 1948	L E O
Jan. 19, 1932	P I S	Oct. 19, 1937	L I B	Feb. 25, 1943	A R I	Oct. 6, 1948	V I R
Feb. 12, 1932	A R I	Nov. 12, 1937	S C O	Mar. 21, 1943	T A U	Nov. 1, 1948	L I B
Mar. 9, 1932	T A U	Dec. 6, 1937	S A G	Apr. 15, 1943	G E M	Nov. 26, 1948	S C O
Apr. 5, 1932	G E M	Dec. 30, 1937	C A P	May. 11, 1943	C A N	Dec. 20, 1948	S A G
May. 6, 1932	C A N	Jan. 23, 1938	A Q U	Jun. 7, 1943	L E O	Jan. 13, 1949	C A P
Jul. 13, 1932	G E M	Feb. 16, 1938	P I S	Jul. 7, 1943	V I R	Feb. 6, 1949	A Q U
Jul. 28, 1932	C A N	Mar. 12, 1938	A R I	Nov. 9, 1943	L I B	Mar. 2, 1949	P I S
Sep. 8, 1932	L E O	Apr. 5, 1938	T A U	Dec. 8, 1943	S C O	Mar. 26, 1949	A R I
Oct. 7, 1932	V I R	Apr. 29, 1938	G E M	Jan. 3, 1944	S A G	Apr. 19, 1949	T A U
Nov. 2, 1932	L I B	May. 24, 1938	C A N	Jan. 28, 1944	C A P	May. 14, 1949	G E M
Nov. 27, 1932	S C O	Jun. 18, 1938	L E O	Feb. 21, 1944	A Q U	Jun. 7, 1949	C A N
Dec. 21, 1932	S A G	Jul. 14, 1938	V I R	Mar. 17, 1944	P I S	Jul. 1, 1949	L E O
Jan. 14, 1933	C A P	Aug. 9, 1938	L I B	Apr. 10, 1944	A R I	Jul. 26, 1949	V I R
Feb. 7, 1933	A Q U	Sep. 7, 1938	S C O	May. 4, 1944	T A U	Aug. 20, 1949	L I B
Mar. 3, 1933	P I S	Oct. 13, 1938	S A G	May. 29, 1944	G E M	Sep. 14, 1949	S C O
Mar. 27, 1933	A R I	Nov. 15, 1938	S C O	Jun. 22, 1944	C A N	Oct. 10, 1949	S A G
Apr. 20, 1933	T A U	Jan. 4, 1939	S A G	Jul. 17, 1944	L E O	Nov. 6, 1949	C A P
May. 15, 1933	G E M	Feb. 6, 1939	C A P	Aug. 10, 1944	V I R	Dec. 6, 1949	A Q U
Jun. 8, 1933	C A N	Mar. 5, 1939	A Q U	Sep. 3, 1944	L I B	Apr. 6, 1950	P I S
Jul. 3, 1933	L E O	Mar. 31, 1939	P I S	Sep. 28, 1944	S C O	May. 5, 1950	A R I
Jul. 27, 1933	V I R	Apr. 25, 1939	A R I	Oct. 22, 1944	S A G	Jun. 1, 1950	T A U
Aug. 21, 1933	L I B	May. 20, 1939	T A U	Nov. 16, 1944	C A P	Jun. 27, 1950	G E M
Sep. 15, 1933	S C O	Jun. 14, 1939	G E M	Dec. 11, 1944	A Q U	Jul. 22, 1950	C A N
Oct. 11, 1933	S A G	Jul. 9, 1939	C A N	Jan. 5, 1945	P I S	Aug. 16, 1950	L E O
Nov. 6, 1933	C A P	Aug. 2, 1939	L E O	Feb. 2, 1945	A R I	Sep. 10, 1950	V I R
Dec. 5, 1933	A Q U	Aug. 26, 1939	V I R	Mar. 11, 1945	T A U	Oct. 4, 1950	L I B
Apr. 6, 1934	P I S	Sep. 20, 1939	L I B	Apr. 7, 1945	A R I	Oct. 28, 1950	S C O
May. 6, 1934	A R I	Oct. 14, 1939	S C O	Jun. 4, 1945	T A U	Nov. 21, 1950	S A G
Jun. 2, 1934	T A U	Nov. 7, 1939	S A G	Jul. 7, 1945	G E M	Dec. 14, 1950	C A P
Jun. 28, 1934	G E M	Dec. 1, 1939	C A P	Aug. 4, 1945	C A N	Jan. 7, 1951	A Q U
Jul. 23, 1934	C A N	Dec. 25, 1939	A Q U	Aug. 30, 1945	L E O	Jan. 31, 1951	P I S
Aug. 17, 1934	L E O	Jan. 1, 1940	A Q U	Sep. 24, 1945	V I R	Feb. 24, 1951	A R I
Sep. 11, 1934	V I R	Jan. 18, 1940	P I S	Oct. 19, 1945	L I B	Mar. 21, 1951	T A U
Oct. 5, 1934	L I B	Feb. 12, 1940	A R I	Nov. 12, 1945	S C O	Apr. 15, 1951	G E M
Oct. 29, 1934	S C O	Mar. 8, 1940	T A U	Dec. 6, 1945	S A G	May. 7, 1951	C A N
Nov. 22, 1934	S A G	Apr. 4, 1940	G E M	Dec. 30, 1945	C A P	Jun. 7, 1951	L E O
Dec. 16, 1934	C A P	May. 6, 1940	C A N	Jan. 22, 1946	A Q U	Jul. 8, 1951	V I R
Jan. 8, 1935	A Q U	Jul. 5, 1940	G E M	Feb. 15, 1946	P I S	Nov. 9, 1951	L I B
Feb. 1, 1935	P I S	Aug. 1, 1940	C A N	Mar. 11, 1946	A R I	Dec. 8, 1951	S C O

Date	Venus	Date	Venus	Date	Venus	Date	Venus
Jan. 2, 1952	SAG	Apr. 19, 1957	TAU	Mar. 4, 1963	AQU	Jun. 21, 1968	CAN
Jan. 27, 1952	CAP	May. 13, 1957	GEM	Mar. 30, 1963	PIS	Jul. 15, 1968	LEO
Feb. 21, 1952	AQU	Jun. 6, 1957	CAN	Apr. 24, 1963	ARI	Aug. 8, 1968	VIR
Mar. 16, 1952	PIS	Jul. 1, 1957	LEO	May. 19, 1963	TAU	Sep. 2, 1968	LIB
Apr. 9, 1952	ARI	Jul. 26, 1957	VIR	Jun. 12, 1963	GEM	Sep. 26, 1968	SCO
May. 4, 1952	TAU	Aug. 20, 1957	LIB	Jul. 7, 1963	CAN	Oct. 21, 1968	SAG
May. 28, 1952	GEM	Sep. 14, 1957	SCO	Jul. 31, 1963	LEO	Nov. 14, 1968	CAP
Jun. 22, 1952	CAN	Oct. 10, 1957	SAG	Aug. 25, 1963	VIR	Dec. 9, 1968	AQU
Jul. 16, 1952	LEO	Nov. 5, 1957	CAP	Sep. 18, 1963	LIB	Jan. 4, 1969	PIS
Aug. 9, 1952	VIR	Dec. 6, 1957	AQU	Oct. 12, 1963	SCO	Feb. 2, 1969	ARI
Sep. 3, 1952	LIB	Apr. 6, 1958	PIS	Nov. 5, 1963	SAG	Jun. 6, 1969	TAU
Sep. 27, 1952	SCO	May. 5, 1958	ARI	Nov. 29, 1963	CAP	Jul. 6, 1969	GEM
Oct. 22, 1952	SAG	Jun. 1, 1958	TAU	Dec. 23, 1963	AQU	Aug. 3, 1969	CAN
Nov. 15, 1952	CAP	Jun. 26, 1958	GEM	Jan. 17, 1964	PIS	Aug. 29, 1969	LEO
Dec. 10, 1952	AQU	Jul. 22, 1958	CAN	Feb. 10, 1964	ARI	Sep. 23, 1969	VIR
Jan. 5, 1953	PIS	Aug. 16, 1958	LEO	Mar. 7, 1964	TAU	Oct. 17, 1969	LIB
Feb. 2, 1953	ARI	Sep. 9, 1958	VIR	Apr. 4, 1964	GEM	Nov. 10, 1969	SCO
Mar. 14, 1953	TAU	Oct. 3, 1958	LIB	May. 9, 1964	CAN	Dec. 4, 1969	SAG
Mar. 31, 1953	ARI	Oct. 27, 1958	SCO	Jun. 17, 1964	GEM	Dec. 28, 1969	CAP
Jun. 5, 1953	TAU	Nov. 20, 1958	SAG	Aug. 5, 1964	CAN	Jan. 21, 1970	AQU
Jul. 7, 1953	GEM	Dec. 14, 1958	CAP	Sep. 8, 1964	LEO	Feb. 14, 1970	PIS
Aug. 4, 1953	CAN	Jan. 7, 1959	AQU	Oct. 5, 1964	VIR	Mar. 10, 1970	ARI
Aug. 30, 1953	LEO	Jan. 31, 1959	PIS	Oct. 31, 1964	LIB	Apr. 3, 1970	TAU
Sep. 24, 1953	VIR	Feb. 24, 1959	ARI	Nov. 25, 1964	SCO	Apr. 27, 1970	GEM
Oct. 18, 1953	LIB	Mar. 20, 1959	TAU	Dec. 19, 1964	SAG	May. 22, 1970	CAN
Nov. 11, 1953	SCO	Apr. 14, 1959	GEM	Jan. 12, 1965	CAP	Jun. 16, 1970	LEO
Dec. 5, 1953	SAG	May. 10, 1959	CAN	Feb. 5, 1965	AQU	Jul. 12, 1970	VIR
Dec. 29, 1953	CAP	Jun. 6, 1959	LEO	Mar. 1, 1965	PIS	Aug. 8, 1970	LIB
Jan. 22, 1954	AQU	Jul. 8, 1959	VIR	Mar. 25, 1965	ARI	Sep. 7, 1970	SCO
Feb. 15, 1954	PIS	Sep. 20, 1959	LEO	Apr. 18, 1965	TAU	Jan. 7, 1971	SAG
Mar. 11, 1954	ARI	Sep. 25, 1959	VIR	May. 12, 1965	GEM	Feb. 5, 1971	CAP
Apr. 4, 1954	TAU	Nov. 9, 1959	LIB	Jun. 6, 1965	CAN	Mar. 4, 1971	AQU
Apr. 28, 1954	GEM	Dec. 7, 1959	SCO	Jun. 30, 1965	LEO	Mar. 29, 1971	PIS
May. 23, 1954	CAN	Jan. 2, 1960	SAG	Jul. 25, 1965	VIR	Apr. 23, 1971	ARI
Jun. 17, 1954	LEO	Jan. 27, 1960	CAP	Aug. 19, 1965	LIB	May. 18, 1971	TAU
Jul. 13, 1954	VIR	Feb. 20, 1960	AQU	Sep. 13, 1965	SCO	Jun. 12, 1971	GEM
Aug. 9, 1954	LIB	Mar. 16, 1960	PIS	Oct. 9, 1965	SAG	Jul. 6, 1971	CAN
Sep. 6, 1954	SCO	Apr. 9, 1960	ARI	Nov. 5, 1965	CAP	Jul. 31, 1971	LEO
Oct. 23, 1954	SAG	May. 3, 1960	TAU	Dec. 7, 1965	AQU	Aug. 24, 1971	VIR
Oct. 27, 1954	SCO	May. 28, 1960	GEM	Feb. 6, 1966	CAP	Sep. 17, 1971	LIB
Jan. 6, 1955	SAG	Jun. 21, 1960	CAN	Feb. 25, 1966	AQU	Oct. 11, 1971	SCO
Feb. 6, 1955	CAP	Jul. 16, 1960	LEO	Apr. 6, 1966	PIS	Nov. 5, 1971	SAG
Mar. 4, 1955	AQU	Aug. 9, 1960	VIR	May. 5, 1966	ARI	Nov. 29, 1971	CAP
Mar. 30, 1955	PIS	Sep. 2, 1960	LIB	May. 31, 1966	TAU	Dec. 23, 1971	AQU
Apr. 24, 1955	ARI	Sep. 27, 1960	SCO	Jun. 26, 1966	GEM	Jan. 16, 1972	PIS
May. 19, 1955	TAU	Oct. 21, 1960	SAG	Jul. 21, 1966	CAN	Feb. 10, 1972	ARI
Jun. 13, 1955	GEM	Nov. 15, 1960	CAP	Aug. 15, 1966	LEO	Mar. 7, 1972	TAU
Jul. 8, 1955	CAN	Dec. 10, 1960	AQU	Sep. 8, 1966	VIR	Apr. 3, 1972	GEM
Aug. 1, 1955	LEO	Jan. 5, 1961	PIS	Oct. 3, 1966	LIB	May. 10, 1972	CAN
Aug. 25, 1955	VIR	Feb. 2, 1961	ARI	Oct. 27, 1966	SCO	Jun. 11, 1972	GEM
Sep. 18, 1955	LIB	Jun. 5, 1961	TAU	Nov. 20, 1966	SAG	Aug. 6, 1972	CAN
Oct. 13, 1955	SCO	Jul. 7, 1961	GEM	Dec. 13, 1966	CAP	Sep. 7, 1972	LEO
Nov. 6, 1955	SAG	Aug. 3, 1961	CAN	Jan. 6, 1967	AQU	Oct. 5, 1972	VIR
Nov. 30, 1955	CAP	Aug. 29, 1961	LEO	Jan. 30, 1967	PIS	Oct. 30, 1972	LIB
Dec. 24, 1955	AQU	Sep. 23, 1961	VIR	Feb. 23, 1967	ARI	Nov. 24, 1972	SCO
Jan. 17, 1956	PIS	Oct. 18, 1961	LIB	Mar. 20, 1967	TAU	Dec. 18, 1972	SAG
Feb. 11, 1956	ARI	Nov. 11, 1961	SCO	Apr. 14, 1967	GEM	Jan. 11, 1973	CAP
Mar. 7, 1956	TAU	Dec. 5, 1961	SAG	May. 10, 1967	CAN	Feb. 4, 1973	AQU
Apr. 4, 1956	GEM	Dec. 29, 1961	CAP	Jun. 6, 1967	LEO	Feb. 28, 1973	PIS
May. 8, 1956	CAN	Jan. 21, 1962	AQU	Jul. 8, 1967	VIR	Mar. 24, 1973	ARI
Jun. 23, 1956	GEM	Feb. 14, 1962	PIS	Sep. 9, 1967	LEO	Apr. 18, 1973	TAU
Aug. 4, 1956	CAN	Mar. 10, 1962	ARI	Oct. 1, 1967	VIR	May. 12, 1973	GEM
Sep. 8, 1956	LEO	Apr. 3, 1962	TAU	Nov. 9, 1967	LIB	Jun. 5, 1973	CAN
Oct. 6, 1956	VIR	Apr. 28, 1962	GEM	Dec. 7, 1967	SCO	Jun. 30, 1973	LEO
Oct. 31, 1956	LIB	May. 23, 1962	CAN	Jan. 1, 1968	SAG	Jul. 25, 1973	VIR
Nov. 25, 1956	SCO	Jun. 17, 1962	LEO	Jan. 26, 1968	CAP	Aug. 19, 1973	LIB
Dec. 19, 1956	SAG	Jul. 12, 1962	VIR	Feb. 20, 1968	AQU	Sep. 13, 1973	SCO
Jan. 12, 1957	CAP	Aug. 8, 1962	LIB	Mar. 15, 1968	PIS	Oct. 9, 1973	SAG
Feb. 5, 1957	AQU	Sep. 7, 1962	SCO	Apr. 8, 1968	ARI	Nov. 5, 1973	CAP
Mar. 1, 1957	PIS	Jan. 6, 1963	SAG	May. 3, 1968	TAU	Dec. 7, 1973	AQU
Mar. 25, 1957	ARI	Feb. 5, 1963	CAP	May. 27, 1968	GEM	Jan. 29, 1974	CAP

Date	Venus	Date	Venus	Date	Venus	Date	Venus
Feb. 28, 1974	A Q U	Oct. 11, 1979	S C O	Feb. 2, 1985	A R I	Oct. 25, 1990	S C O
Apr. 6, 1974	P I S	Nov. 4, 1979	S A G	Jun. 6, 1985	T A U	Nov. 18, 1990	S A G
May. 4, 1974	A R I	Nov. 28, 1979	C A P	Jul. 6, 1985	G E M	Dec. 12, 1990	C A P
May. 31, 1974	T A U	Dec. 22, 1979	A Q U	Aug. 2, 1985	C A N	Jan. 5, 1991	A Q U
Jun. 25, 1974	G E M	Jan. 16, 1980	P I S	Aug. 28, 1985	L E O	Jan. 29, 1991	P I S
Jul. 21, 1974	C A N	Feb. 9, 1980	A R I	Sep. 22, 1985	V I R	Feb. 22, 1991	A R I
Aug. 14, 1974	L E O	Mar. 6, 1980	T A U	Oct. 16, 1985	L I B	Mar. 18, 1991	T A U
Sep. 8, 1974	V I R	Apr. 3, 1980	G E M	Nov. 9, 1985	S C O	Apr. 13, 1991	G E M
Oct. 2, 1974	L I B	May. 12, 1980	C A N	Dec. 3, 1985	S A G	May. 9, 1991	C A N
Oct. 26, 1974	S C O	Jun. 5, 1980	G E M	Dec. 27, 1985	C A P	Jun. 6, 1991	L E O
Nov. 19, 1974	S A G	Aug. 6, 1980	C A N	Jan. 20, 1986	A Q U	Jul. 11, 1991	V I R
Dec. 13, 1974	C A P	Sep. 7, 1980	L E O	Feb. 13, 1986	P I S	Aug. 21, 1991	L E O
Jan. 6, 1975	A Q U	Oct. 4, 1980	V I R	Mar. 9, 1986	A R I	Oct. 6, 1991	V I R
Jan. 30, 1975	P I S	Oct. 30, 1980	L I B	Apr. 2, 1986	T A U	Nov. 9, 1991	L I B
Feb. 23, 1975	A R I	Nov. 24, 1980	S C O	Apr. 26, 1986	G E M	Dec. 6, 1991	S C O
Mar. 19, 1975	T A U	Dec. 18, 1980	S A G	May. 21, 1986	C A N	Dec. 31, 1991	S A G
Apr. 13, 1975	G E M	Jan. 11, 1981	C A P	Jun. 15, 1986	L E O	Jan. 25, 1992	C A P
May. 9, 1975	C A N	Feb. 4, 1981	A Q U	Jul. 11, 1986	V I R	Feb. 18, 1992	A Q U
Jun. 6, 1975	L E O	Feb. 28, 1981	P I S	Aug. 7, 1986	L I B	Mar. 13, 1992	P I S
Jul. 9, 1975	V I R	Mar. 24, 1981	A R I	Sep. 7, 1986	S C O	Apr. 7, 1992	A R I
Sep. 2, 1975	L E O	Apr. 17, 1981	T A U	Jan. 7, 1987	S A G	May. 1, 1992	T A U
Oct. 4, 1975	V I R	May. 11, 1981	G E M	Feb. 5, 1987	C A P	May. 26, 1992	G E M
Nov. 9, 1975	L I B	Jun. 5, 1981	C A N	Mar. 3, 1987	A Q U	Jun. 19, 1992	C A N
Dec. 7, 1975	S C O	Jun. 29, 1981	L E O	Mar. 28, 1987	P I S	Jul. 13, 1992	L E O
Jan. 1, 1976	S A G	Jul. 24, 1981	V I R	Apr. 22, 1987	A R I	Aug. 7, 1992	V I R
Jan. 26, 1976	C A P	Aug. 18, 1981	L I B	May. 17, 1987	T A U	Aug. 31, 1992	L I B
Feb. 19, 1976	A Q U	Sep. 12, 1981	S C O	Jun. 11, 1987	G E M	Sep. 25, 1992	S C O
Mar. 15, 1976	P I S	Oct. 9, 1981	S A G	Jul. 5, 1987	C A N	Oct. 19, 1992	S A G
Apr. 8, 1976	A R I	Nov. 5, 1981	C A P	Jul. 30, 1987	L E O	Nov. 13, 1992	C A P
May. 2, 1976	T A U	Dec. 8, 1981	A Q U	Aug. 23, 1987	V I R	Dec. 8, 1992	A Q U
May. 27, 1976	G E M	Jan. 23, 1982	C A P	Sep. 16, 1987	L I B	Jan. 3, 1993	P I S
Jun. 20, 1976	C A N	Mar. 2, 1982	A Q U	Oct. 10, 1987	S C O	Feb. 2, 1993	A R I
Jul. 14, 1976	L E O	Apr. 6, 1982	P I S	Nov. 3, 1987	S A G	Jun. 6, 1993	T A U
Aug. 8, 1976	V I R	May. 4, 1982	A R I	Nov. 28, 1987	C A P	Jul. 6, 1993	G E M
Sep. 1, 1976	L I B	May. 30, 1982	T A U	Dec. 22, 1987	A Q U	Aug. 1, 1993	C A N
Sep. 26, 1976	S C O	Jun. 25, 1982	G E M	Jan. 15, 1988	P I S	Aug. 27, 1993	L E O
Oct. 20, 1976	S A G	Jul. 20, 1982	C A N	Feb. 9, 1988	A R I	Sep. 21, 1993	V I R
Nov. 14, 1976	C A P	Aug. 14, 1982	L E O	Mar. 6, 1988	T A U	Oct. 16, 1993	L I B
Dec. 9, 1976	A Q U	Sep. 7, 1982	V I R	Apr. 3, 1988	G E M	Nov. 9, 1993	S C O
Jan. 4, 1977	P I S	Oct. 2, 1982	L I B	May. 17, 1988	C A N	Dec. 2, 1993	S A G
Feb. 2, 1977	A R I	Oct. 26, 1982	S C O	May. 27, 1988	G E M	Dec. 26, 1993	C A P
Jun. 6, 1977	T A U	Nov. 18, 1982	S A G	Aug. 6, 1988	C A N	Jan. 19, 1994	A Q U
Jul. 6, 1977	G E M	Dec. 12, 1982	C A P	Sep. 7, 1988	L E O	Feb. 12, 1994	P I S
Aug. 2, 1977	C A N	Jan. 5, 1983	A Q U	Oct. 4, 1988	V I R	Mar. 8, 1994	A R I
Aug. 28, 1977	L E O	Jan. 29, 1983	P I S	Oct. 29, 1988	L I B	Apr. 1, 1994	T A U
Sep. 22, 1977	V I R	Feb. 22, 1983	A R I	Nov. 23, 1988	S C O	Apr. 26, 1994	G E M
Oct. 17, 1977	L I B	Mar. 19, 1983	T A U	Dec. 17, 1988	S A G	May. 21, 1994	C A N
Nov. 10, 1977	S C O	Apr. 13, 1983	G E M	Jan. 10, 1989	C A P	Jun. 15, 1994	L E O
Dec. 4, 1977	S A G	May. 9, 1983	C A N	Feb. 3, 1989	A Q U	Jul. 11, 1994	V I R
Dec. 27, 1977	C A P	Jun. 6, 1983	L E O	Feb. 27, 1989	P I S	Aug. 7, 1994	L I B
Jan. 20, 1978	A Q U	Jul. 10, 1983	V I R	Mar. 23, 1989	A R I	Sep. 7, 1994	S C O
Feb. 13, 1978	P I S	Aug. 27, 1983	L E O	Apr. 16, 1989	T A U	Jan. 7, 1995	S A G
Mar. 9, 1978	A R I	Oct. 5, 1983	V I R	May. 11, 1989	G E M	Feb. 4, 1995	C A P
Apr. 2, 1978	T A U	Nov. 9, 1983	L I B	Jun. 4, 1989	C A N	Mar. 2, 1995	A Q U
Apr. 27, 1978	G E M	Dec. 6, 1983	S C O	Jun. 29, 1989	L E O	Mar. 28, 1995	P I S
May. 22, 1978	C A N	Jan. 1, 1984	S A G	Jul. 24, 1989	V I R	Apr. 22, 1995	A R I
Jun. 16, 1978	L E O	Jan. 25, 1984	C A P	Aug. 18, 1989	L I B	May. 16, 1995	T A U
Jul. 12, 1978	V I R	Feb. 19, 1984	A Q U	Sep. 12, 1989	S C O	Jun. 10, 1995	G E M
Aug. 8, 1978	L I B	Mar. 14, 1984	P I S	Oct. 8, 1989	S A G	Jul. 5, 1995	C A N
Sep. 7, 1978	S C O	Apr. 7, 1984	A R I	Nov. 5, 1989	C A P	Jul. 29, 1995	L E O
Jan. 7, 1979	S A G	May. 2, 1984	T A U	Dec. 10, 1989	A Q U	Aug. 23, 1995	V I R
Feb. 5, 1979	C A P	May. 26, 1984	G E M	Jan. 16, 1990	C A P	Sep. 16, 1995	L I B
Mar. 3, 1979	A Q U	Jun. 20, 1984	C A N	Mar. 3, 1990	A Q U	Oct. 10, 1995	S C O
Mar. 29, 1979	P I S	Jul. 14, 1984	L E O	Apr. 6, 1990	P I S	Nov. 3, 1995	S A G
Apr. 23, 1979	A R I	Aug. 7, 1984	V I R	May. 4, 1990	A R I	Nov. 27, 1995	C A P
May. 18, 1979	T A U	Sep. 1, 1984	L I B	May. 30, 1990	T A U	Dec. 21, 1995	A Q U
Jun. 11, 1979	G E M	Sep. 25, 1984	S C O	Jun. 25, 1990	G E M	Jan. 15, 1996	P I S
Jul. 6, 1979	C A N	Oct. 20, 1984	S A G	Jul. 20, 1990	C A N	Feb. 9, 1996	A R I
Jul. 30, 1979	L E O	Nov. 13, 1984	C A P	Aug. 13, 1990	L E O	Mar. 6, 1996	T A U
Aug. 24, 1979	V I R	Dec. 9, 1984	A Q U	Sep. 7, 1990	V I R	Apr. 3, 1996	G E M
Sep. 17, 1979	L I B	Jan. 4, 1985	P I S	Oct. 1, 1990	L I B	Aug. 7, 1996	C A N

Date	Venus	Date	Venus	Date	Venus	Date	Venus
Sep. 7, 1996	LEO	Feb. 12, 2002	PIS	Nov. 8, 2007	LIB	Apr. 15, 2013	TAU
Oct. 4, 1996	VIR	Mar. 8, 2002	ARI	Dec. 5, 2007	SCO	May. 9, 2013	GEM
Oct. 29, 1996	LIB	Apr. 1, 2002	TAU	Dec. 30, 2007	SAG	Jun. 3, 2013	CAN
Nov. 23, 1996	SCO	Apr. 25, 2002	GEM	Jan. 24, 2008	CAP	Jun. 27, 2013	LEO
Dec. 17, 1996	SAG	May. 20, 2002	CAN	Feb. 17, 2008	AQU	Jul. 22, 2013	VIR
Jan. 10, 1997	CAP	Jun. 14, 2002	LEO	Mar. 12, 2008	PIS	Aug. 16, 2013	LIB
Feb. 3, 1997	AQU	Jul. 10, 2002	VIR	Apr. 6, 2008	ARI	Sep. 11, 2013	SCO
Feb. 27, 1997	PIS	Aug. 7, 2002	LIB	Apr. 30, 2008	TAU	Oct. 7, 2013	SAG
Mar. 23, 1997	ARI	Sep. 8, 2002	SCO	May. 24, 2008	GEM	Nov. 5, 2013	CAP
Apr. 16, 1997	TAU	Jan. 7, 2003	SAG	Jun. 18, 2008	CAN	Mar. 5, 2014	AQU
May. 10, 1997	GEM	Feb. 4, 2003	CAP	Jul. 12, 2008	LEO	Apr. 5, 2014	PIS
Jun. 4, 1997	CAN	Mar. 2, 2003	AQU	Aug. 6, 2008	VIR	May. 3, 2014	ARI
Jun. 28, 1997	LEO	Mar. 27, 2003	PIS	Aug. 30, 2008	LIB	May. 29, 2014	TAU
Jul. 23, 1997	VIR	Apr. 21, 2003	ARI	Sep. 24, 2008	SCO	Jun. 23, 2014	GEM
Aug. 17, 1997	LIB	May. 16, 2003	TAU	Oct. 18, 2008	SAG	Jul. 18, 2014	CAN
Sep. 12, 1997	SCO	Jun. 10, 2003	GEM	Nov. 12, 2008	CAP	Aug. 12, 2014	LEO
Oct. 8, 1997	SAG	Jul. 4, 2003	CAN	Dec. 7, 2008	AQU	Sep. 5, 2014	VIR
Nov. 5, 1997	CAP	Jul. 29, 2003	LEO	Jan. 3, 2009	PIS	Sep. 29, 2014	LIB
Dec. 12, 1997	AQU	Aug. 22, 2003	VIR	Feb. 3, 2009	ARI	Oct. 23, 2014	SCO
Jan. 9, 1998	CAP	Sep. 15, 2003	LIB	Apr. 11, 2009	PIS	Nov. 16, 2014	SAG
Mar. 4, 1998	AQU	Oct. 9, 2003	SCO	Apr. 24, 2009	ARI	Dec. 10, 2014	CAP
Apr. 6, 1998	PIS	Nov. 2, 2003	SAG	Jun. 6, 2009	TAU	Jan. 3, 2015	AQU
May. 3, 1998	ARI	Nov. 27, 2003	CAP	Jul. 5, 2009	GEM	Jan. 27, 2015	PIS
May. 29, 1998	TAU	Dec. 21, 2003	AQU	Aug. 1, 2009	CAN	Feb. 20, 2015	ARI
Jun. 24, 1998	GEM	Jan. 14, 2004	PIS	Aug. 26, 2009	LEO	Mar. 17, 2015	TAU
Jul. 19, 1998	CAN	Feb. 8, 2004	ARI	Sep. 20, 2009	VIR	Apr. 11, 2015	GEM
Aug. 13, 1998	LEO	Mar. 5, 2004	TAU	Oct. 14, 2009	LIB	May. 7, 2015	CAN
Sep. 6, 1998	VIR	Apr. 3, 2004	GEM	Nov. 8, 2009	SCO	Jun. 5, 2015	LEO
Sep. 30, 1998	LIB	Aug. 7, 2004	CAN	Dec. 1, 2009	SAG	Jul. 18, 2015	VIR
Oct. 24, 1998	SCO	Sep. 6, 2004	LEO	Dec. 25, 2009	CAP	Jul. 31, 2015	LEO
Nov. 17, 1998	SAG	Oct. 3, 2004	VIR	Jan. 18, 2010	AQU	Oct. 8, 2015	VIR
Dec. 11, 1998	CAP	Oct. 29, 2004	LIB	Feb. 11, 2010	PIS	Nov. 8, 2015	LIB
Jan. 4, 1999	AQU	Nov. 22, 2004	SCO	Mar. 7, 2010	ARI	Dec. 5, 2015	SCO
Jan. 28, 1999	PIS	Dec. 16, 2004	SAG	Mar. 31, 2010	TAU	Dec. 30, 2015	SAG
Feb. 21, 1999	ARI	Jan. 9, 2005	CAP	Apr. 25, 2010	GEM	Jan. 23, 2016	CAP
Mar. 18, 1999	TAU	Feb. 2, 2005	AQU	May. 20, 2010	CAN	Feb. 17, 2016	AQU
Apr. 12, 1999	GEM	Feb. 26, 2005	PIS	Jun. 14, 2010	LEO	Mar. 12, 2016	PIS
May. 8, 1999	CAN	Mar. 22, 2005	ARI	Jul. 10, 2010	VIR	Apr. 5, 2016	ARI
Jun. 5, 1999	LEO	Apr. 15, 2005	TAU	Aug. 7, 2010	LIB	Apr. 30, 2016	TAU
Jul. 12, 1999	VIR	May. 10, 2005	GEM	Sep. 8, 2010	SCO	May. 24, 2016	GEM
Aug. 15, 1999	LEO	Jun. 3, 2005	CAN	Nov. 8, 2010	LIB	Jun. 17, 2016	CAN
Oct. 7, 1999	VIR	Jun. 28, 2005	LEO	Nov. 30, 2010	SCO	Jul. 12, 2016	LEO
Nov. 9, 1999	LIB	Jul. 23, 2005	VIR	Jan. 7, 2011	SAG	Aug. 5, 2016	VIR
Dec. 5, 1999	SCO	Aug. 17, 2005	LIB	Feb. 4, 2011	CAP	Aug. 30, 2016	LIB
Dec. 31, 1999	SAG	Sep. 11, 2005	SCO	Mar. 2, 2011	AQU	Sep. 23, 2016	SCO
Jan. 24, 2000	CAP	Oct. 8, 2005	SAG	Mar. 27, 2011	PIS	Oct. 18, 2016	SAG
Feb. 18, 2000	AQU	Nov. 5, 2005	CAP	Apr. 21, 2011	ARI	Nov. 12, 2016	CAP
Mar. 13, 2000	PIS	Dec. 15, 2005	AQU	May. 15, 2011	TAU	Dec. 7, 2016	AQU
Apr. 6, 2000	ARI	Jan. 1, 2006	CAP	Jun. 9, 2011	GEM	Jan. 3, 2017	PIS
May. 1, 2000	TAU	Mar. 5, 2006	AQU	Jul. 4, 2011	CAN	Feb. 3, 2017	ARI
May. 25, 2000	GEM	Apr. 6, 2006	PIS	Jul. 28, 2011	LEO	Apr. 3, 2017	PIS
Jun. 18, 2000	CAN	May. 3, 2006	ARI	Aug. 21, 2011	VIR	Apr. 28, 2017	ARI
Jul. 13, 2000	LEO	May. 29, 2006	TAU	Sep. 15, 2011	LIB	Jun. 6, 2017	TAU
Aug. 6, 2000	VIR	Jun. 24, 2006	GEM	Oct. 9, 2011	SCO	Jul. 5, 2017	GEM
Aug. 31, 2000	LIB	Jul. 19, 2006	CAN	Nov. 2, 2011	SAG	Jul. 31, 2017	CAN
Sep. 24, 2000	SCO	Aug. 12, 2006	LEO	Nov. 26, 2011	CAP	Aug. 26, 2017	LEO
Oct. 19, 2000	SAG	Sep. 6, 2006	VIR	Dec. 20, 2011	AQU	Sep. 20, 2017	VIR
Nov. 13, 2000	CAP	Sep. 30, 2006	LIB	Jan. 14, 2012	PIS	Oct. 14, 2017	LIB
Dec. 8, 2000	AQU	Oct. 24, 2006	SCO	Feb. 8, 2012	ARI	Nov. 7, 2017	SCO
Jan. 3, 2001	PIS	Nov. 17, 2006	SAG	Mar. 5, 2012	TAU	Dec. 1, 2017	SAG
Feb. 2, 2001	ARI	Dec. 11, 2006	CAP	Apr. 3, 2012	GEM	Dec. 25, 2017	CAP
Jun. 6, 2001	TAU	Jan. 4, 2007	AQU	Aug. 7, 2012	CAN	Jan. 18, 2018	AQU
Jul. 5, 2001	GEM	Jan. 28, 2007	PIS	Sep. 6, 2012	LEO	Feb. 10, 2018	PIS
Aug. 1, 2001	CAN	Feb. 21, 2007	ARI	Oct. 3, 2012	VIR	Mar. 6, 2018	ARI
Aug. 27, 2001	LEO	Mar. 17, 2007	TAU	Oct. 28, 2012	LIB	Mar. 31, 2018	TAU
Sep. 21, 2001	VIR	Apr. 12, 2007	GEM	Nov. 22, 2012	SCO	Apr. 24, 2018	GEM
Oct. 15, 2001	LIB	May. 8, 2007	CAN	Dec. 16, 2012	SAG	May. 19, 2018	CAN
Nov. 8, 2001	SCO	Jun. 5, 2007	LEO	Jan. 9, 2013	CAP	Jun. 13, 2018	LEO
Dec. 2, 2001	SAG	Jul. 14, 2007	VIR	Feb. 2, 2013	AQU	Jul. 10, 2018	VIR
Dec. 26, 2001	CAP	Aug. 9, 2007	LEO	Feb. 26, 2013	PIS	Aug. 6, 2018	LIB
Jan. 19, 2002	AQU	Oct. 8, 2007	VIR	Mar. 22, 2013	ARI	Sep. 9, 2018	SCO

Date	Venus	Date	Venus	Date	Venus	Date	Venus
Oct. 31, 2018	L I B	Oct. 2, 2020	V I R	Aug. 11, 2022	L E O	Jun. 17, 2024	C A N
Dec. 2, 2018	S C O	Oct. 28, 2020	L I B	Sep. 5, 2022	V I R	Jul. 11, 2024	L E O
Jan. 7, 2019	S A G	Nov. 21, 2020	S C O	Sep. 29, 2022	L I B	Aug. 5, 2024	V I R
Feb. 3, 2019	C A P	Dec. 15, 2020	S A G	Oct. 23, 2022	S C O	Aug. 29, 2024	L I B
Mar. 1, 2019	A Q U	Jan. 8, 2021	C A P	Nov. 16, 2022	S A G	Sep. 23, 2024	S C O
Mar. 26, 2019	P I S	Feb. 1, 2021	A Q U	Dec. 10, 2022	C A P	Oct. 17, 2024	S A G
Apr. 20, 2019	A R I	Feb. 25, 2021	P I S	Jan. 3, 2023	A Q U	Nov. 11, 2024	C A P
May. 15, 2019	T A U	Mar. 21, 2021	A R I	Jan. 27, 2023	P I S	Dec. 7, 2024	A Q U
Jun. 9, 2019	G E M	Apr. 14, 2021	T A U	Feb. 20, 2023	A R I	Jan. 3, 2025	P I S
Jul. 3, 2019	C A N	May. 9, 2021	G E M	Mar. 16, 2023	T A U	Feb. 4, 2025	A R I
Jul. 28, 2019	L E O	Jun. 2, 2021	C A N	Apr. 11, 2023	G E M	Mar. 27, 2025	P I S
Aug. 21, 2019	V I R	Jun. 27, 2021	L E O	May. 7, 2023	C A N	Apr. 30, 2025	A R I
Sep. 14, 2019	L I B	Jul. 22, 2021	V I R	Jun. 5, 2023	L E O	Jun. 6, 2025	T A U
Oct. 8, 2019	S C O	Aug. 16, 2021	L I B	Oct. 9, 2023	V I R	Jul. 4, 2025	G E M
Nov. 1, 2019	S A G	Sep. 10, 2021	S C O	Nov. 8, 2023	L I B	Jul. 31, 2025	C A N
Nov. 26, 2019	C A P	Oct. 7, 2021	S A G	Dec. 4, 2023	S C O	Aug. 25, 2025	L E O
Dec. 20, 2019	A Q U	Nov. 5, 2021	C A P	Dec. 29, 2023	S A G	Sep. 19, 2025	V I R
Jan. 13, 2020	P I S	Mar. 6, 2022	A Q U	Jan. 23, 2024	C A P	Oct. 13, 2025	L I B
Feb. 7, 2020	A R I	Apr. 5, 2022	P I S	Feb. 16, 2024	A Q U	Nov. 6, 2025	S C O
Mar. 5, 2020	T A U	May. 2, 2022	A R I	Mar. 11, 2024	P I S	Nov. 30, 2025	S A G
Apr. 3, 2020	G E M	May. 28, 2022	T A U	Apr. 5, 2024	A R I	Dec. 24, 2025	C A P
Aug. 7, 2020	C A N	Jun. 23, 2022	G E M	Apr. 29, 2024	T A U		
Sep. 6, 2020	L E O	Jul. 18, 2022	C A N	May. 23, 2024	G E M		

Printed in the United States
36976LVS00007B/55-81